ADVANCED ACCOUNTING

HARCOURT BRACE COLLEGE OUTLINE SERIES

ADVANCED ACCOUNTING

Raymond R. Poteau, MBA, CPA

Dean of the School of Business Administration and
Associate Professor of Accounting
Philadelphia College Textiles and Science

The Dryden Press
Harcourt Brace College Publishers

Fort Worth Philadelphia San Diego New York Orlando Austin San Antonio
Toronto Montreal London Sydney Tokyo

ISBN: 0-15-601510-2

Library of Congress Catalog Card Number: 94-69821

Printed in the United States of America

4 5 6 7 8 9 0 1 2 3 066 9 8 7 6 5 4 3 2 1

The Dryden Press
Harcourt Brace CollegePublishers

PREFACE

The purpose of this book is to present a course in advanced accounting theory in the clear, concise format of an outline. Although comprehensive enough to be used by itself for independent study, this outline is specifically designed to be used as a supplement to college courses and textbooks on the subject. Even though the sequence of topics in this outline may differ from your text, you can easily locate the material you want.

Alternatively, the book could be used as the primary text in an accelerated advanced accounting course. Supplemented by readings of original authoritative pronouncements of generally accepted accounting principles of the Financial Accounting Standards Board, the American Institute of Certified Public Accountants, or the Governmental Accounting Standards Board, the book could provide an excellent vehicle for more complex coverage of a wide range of advanced accounting applications in a relatively short time. In this way, students would be exposed to both the original theory and its applications.

Advanced accounting courses typically look closely at partnership accounting, consolidation accounting theory, including the cost and equity methods of carrying investments, foreign currency transactions, and foreign currency translation or remeasurement of financial statements. This book provides numerous straightforward examples and problems to illustrate various accounting standards and concepts.

Regular features at the end of each chapter are specially designed to supplement your course work in advanced accounting:

- RAISE YOUR GRADES. This feature consists of a checkmarked list of open-ended thought questions to help you assimilate the material you have just studied. By inviting you to compare concepts, interpret ideas, explain concepts, and examine the whys and wherefores of chapter material, these questions help to prepare you for class discussions, quizzes, and tests.
- SUMMARY. This feature consists of a brief restatement of the main ideas in each chapter, including definitions of key terms. Because it it presented in the efficient form of a numbered list, you can use it to refresh your memory quickly before an exam.
- RAPID REVIEW. Like the summary, this feature is designed to provide you with a quick review of the principles presented in the body of each chapter. Consisting primarily of short problems, multiple-choice, and short-answer questions, it allows you to test your retention and reinforce your learning at the same time. Should you have trouble answering any of these questions, you can locate and review the relevant sections of the outline by following the cross references provided.
- SOLVED PROBLEMS. Each chapter of this outline concludes with a set of problems and their step-by-step solutions. Undoubtedly the most valuable feature of the outline, these problems allow you to apply your knowledge of advanced accounting to the solution of both numerical and essay-type questions. Along with three examinations, they also give you ample exposure to the kinds of questions that you are likely to encounter on a typical college exam. To make the most of these problems, try writing your own solutions first. Then compare your answers to the detailed solutions provided in the book.

Of course, there are other features of this outline that you will find very helpful. One is the format itself, which serves both as a clear guide to important ideas and as a convenient structure upon which to organize your knowledge. A second is the step-by-step approach to applying various accounting methods. The text lists these steps and illustrates them with straightforward examples. You should be able to solve complex problems by carefully following the steps described in the text.

CONTENTS

1 THE PARTNERSHIP BUSINESS FORM AND ITS GENERAL ACCOUNTING

THIS CHAPTER IS ABOUT

- ☑ **Partnership Characteristics**
- ☑ **General Accounting for Partnership Operations**
- ☑ **Partnership Profit or Loss Distribution**
- ☑ **Admission of a New Partner: Buying Directly from Original Partners**
- ☑ **Admission of a New Partner: Investing in a Partnership**
- ☑ **Retirement of Partners**

1-1. Partnership Characteristics

The Uniform Partnership Act, which has been adopted by most states, defines a partnership as "an association of two or more persons to carry on, as co-owners, a business for profit." The term "persons" may mean individuals, other partnerships, or corporations.

This association should include an oral or (ideally) a written **partnership agreement** specifying the partnership's fiscal year, place of business, profit- and loss-sharing arrangements, investment and withdrawal procedures, and partners' responsibilities. The Uniform Partnership Act regulates formation, operation, and liquidation of partnerships to the extent that these areas are not addressed by the partnership agreement. For example, if the partnership agreement is silent regarding profit and loss distribution, profits or losses would be shared equally by the partners by law.

Partnerships pay no federal income tax, but are required to file an information return (Form 1065) showing the partnership's income or loss, and separate schedules (Schedules K or K-1) showing distribution of that profit or loss to the individual partners. The individual partners are then taxed personally on their share of the partnership's profit or loss.

Other major characteristics of partnerships include:

1. **Ease of formation**. A partnership is easily formed by written or oral agreement.
2. **Limited life.** Technically, the partnership ends whenever a change in partners occurs or whenever the partnership's purpose has been achieved. However, from a practical standpoint, a change in the mix of partners may have no real effect on public perception, so that the partnership will continue functioning normally.
3. **Unlimited liability.** In a general partnership, each partner has unlimited liability for partnership debt. If partnership assets are inadequate to pay creditors, creditors may move against the personal assets of the individual partners. (In a limited partnership, allowed in some states, the "limited partners" are personally liable only to the extent of their investment in the partnership. However, even limited partnerships will have one or more "general partners," who have unlimited liability for the partnership's debt.)

4. **Mutual agency**. Each partner acts as an agent for the partnership and, therefore, the partnership is bound by contracts or agreements made by a partner in the normal course of partnership business operations.
5. **Co-ownership of partnership property**. On investing in a partnership, a partner's personal rights to the assets cease and the property becomes jointly owned by all partners.

1-2. General Accounting for Partnership Operations

The general accounting for a partnership is in most respects the same as the general accounting for any form of business. Assets still equal liabilities plus equity. Assets and expenses still have normal debit balances and liabilities, equities, and revenues still have normal credit balances. Transactions take place throughout the fiscal year that must be recorded according to the usual accounting process. At the end of the fiscal year, the books must be adjusted and closed, and the financial statements must be prepared.

However, there are some significant differences in the closing process for a partnership. First, the equity section of the balance sheet for a partnership consists of an individual capital account for each partner, rather than retained earnings and capital stock (as in a corporate balance sheet). When the books are closed in the corporate setting, net income (loss) is closed to retained earnings. But when the books are closed in the partnership setting, net income (loss) is closed to the individual partner's capital accounts.

Next, the question naturally arises, how much of the income or loss does each individual partner recognize? The answer to this question will be addressed in Section 1-3; it is generally a function of the partnership agreement (or the Uniform Partnership Act, if the partnership agreement is silent). Finally, just as shareholders' dividends are charged to retained earnings in the corporate setting, an individual partner's withdrawal account balance is charged against that partner's capital account.

1-3. Partnership Profit or Loss Distribution

An infinite number of arrangements for profit or loss distribution may be devised for a partnership, but no matter how creatively conceived the arrangement, some fundamental accounting treatments will always be required. Partners' capital accounts will increase if there is a gain, or will decrease if there is a loss, for the partnership on the year. Some of the ways in which profits or losses might be distributed are:

- equally
- in a specified ratio
- based on partners' beginning capital
- based on partners' average capital
- based on partners' ending capital
- based on salary, interest, or bonus to selected partners first

note: The following examples 1-1 through 1-7 relate to the information contained in the balance sheet at the top of p. 3.

XYZ Partnership
Trial Balance
As of 12/31/X8

Account	Debits	Credits
Cash	$ 200,000	
Accounts receivable	200,000	
Inventory	400,000	
Equipment	500,000	
Accumulated depreciation		$ 150,000
Accounts payable		100,000
Loan payable (10%) – Partner X		30,000
X – Capital		120,000
Y – Capital		100,000
Z – Capital		160,000
X – Draw	30,000	
Y – Draw	20,000	
Z – Draw	30,000	
Sales		850,000
Cost of goods sold	107,000	
Operating expenses	20,000	
Interest expense on loan to Partner X	3,000	
	$ 1,510,000	$ 1,510,000

From this trial balance, the net income is:

Sales	$ 850,000	
Cost of goods sold	107,000	
Gross profit	$ 743,000	
Operating expenses	20,000	
Income from operations	$ 723,000	
Interest expense*	3,000	
Net income	$ 720,000	(closed to Income Summary)

* As will be demonstrated shortly, interest on a partner's capital balance is not interest expense but rather a form of profit distribution. However, interest expense on loans to partners is treated as a financial expense to the partnership, in the same way that interest expense on borrowing from any financial institution is treated. Conversely, interest income on accounts receivable from partners is financial income. If a partnership is in liquidation, which will be demonstrated in Chapter 2, it will be evident that partners' receivables and payables will simply be offset against their capital balances, because external creditors have the only meaningful claim.

A. The simplest form of distributing a partnership's profits or losses is to divide them equally among all the partners.

If the partnership has no agreement, or if the agreement does not specify how profits or losses are to be distributed, the Uniform Partnership Act specifies that profits or losses are to be distributed equally.

To divide the year's profit or loss for a partnership equally, simply divide the amount of the profit or loss by the total number of partners. Then credit the proper amount to the capital accounts of the partners.

EXAMPLE 1-1: The partnership agreement of the XYZ partnership is silent regarding the sharing of profit or loss. What portion of the $720,000 profit for the year should each partner receive?

Under the Uniform Partnership Act, this situation results in an equal distribution of the profit among the partners. First, determine each partner's share of the profit:

Partner	Income Share	
X	33.3%	$ 240,000
Y	33.3%	240,000
Z	33.3%	240,000
	100.0%	
Net income		$ 720,000

Then distribute the profit to each partner's capital account:

Income Summary	$720,000	
X — Capital		$ 240,000
Y — Capital		240,000
Z — Capital		240,000

Finally, close the partners' withdrawal accounts for the year to their respective capital accounts:

X — Capital	$ 30,000	
Y — Capital	20,000	
Z — Capital	30,000	
X — Draw		$ 30,000
Y — Draw		20,000
Z — Draw		30,000

The ending balances for the capital accounts on 12/31/X8 are:

X — Capital	$ 330,000	(120,000 + 240,000 − 30,000)
Y — Capital	320,000	(100,000 + 240,000 − 20,000)
Z — Capital	370,000	(160,000 + 240,000 − 30,000)

B. Profits or losses may be distributed according to a prearranged ratio.

A partnership agreement may specify a distribution of profits and losses in some manner other than an equal division, according to ratios or percentages that all the partners have already agreed upon.

To make such a distribution, simply multiply the amount of the profit or loss by the specified ratio, and distribute the proper amount to each partner's capital account.

EXAMPLE 1-2: The partnership agreement for the XYZ Partnership specifies that profits or losses should be distributed in a ratio of 5:3:2 to X, Y, and Z, respectively. What portion of the $720,000 profit should each partner receive?

First, determine each partner's share of the $720,000 profit according to the ratio:

Partner	Income Share	
X	50%	$ 360,000
Y	30%	216,000
Z	20%	144,000
	100%	
Net income		$ 720,000

Then distribute the profit to each partner's capital account:

Income Summary	$720,000	
X — Capital		$ 360,000
Y — Capital		216,000
Z — Capital		144,000

Finally, close the partners' withdrawal accounts for the year to their respective capital accounts:

X — Capital	$ 30,000	
Y — Capital	20,000	
Z — Capital	30,000	
X — Draw		$ 30,000
Y — Draw		20,000
Z — Draw		30,000

The ending balances for the capital accounts on 12/31/X8 are:

X — Capital	$ 450,000	(120,000 + 360,000 – 30,000)
Y — Capital	296,000	(100,000 + 216,000 – 20,000)
Z — Capital	274,000	(160,000 + 144,000 – 30,000)

C. Profits or losses may be distributed according to a partner's capital position.

Because capital is crucial to the success of a business, a partnership agreement may specify that profits or losses should be distributed according to the capital in each partner's account at a certain point in the partnership's fiscal year. Under such an agreement, the percentage of profit each partner is entitled to receive may change from year to year.

To determine the rates of distribution of profit at the close of the year, calculate the relative percentages of the partner's capital accounts at the point specified by the partnership agreement.

In Examples 1-3 through 1-5, consider the following information regarding the partners' capital accounts, in addition to the information given on page 3:

	Partner		
	X	Y	Z
1/1/X8 Capital Balance	$ 60,000	$ 60,000	$ 110,000
4/1/X8 Investment (Draw)	(30,000)	40,000	50,000
9/1/X8 Investment (Draw)	60,000	(20,000)	(30,000)
12/31/X8 Capital Balance (before profit or loss distribution but after draw)	$ 90,000	$ 80,000	$ 130,000

1. *Distributions based on beginning capital.* To make a distribution of profits or losses based on each partner's beginning capital balance, first determine the balances in each partner's capital account at the beginning of the partnership's fiscal year. Next, determine what percentage of the partnership's total capital on that date is represented by each partner's account. Finally, apply those percentages to the year's net profits, and distribute the proper amount to each partner's capital account.

EXAMPLE 1-3: The partnership agreement for the XYZ Partnership specifies that distributions of profits and losses should be based on the partners' beginning capital balances. What portion of the $720,000 profit should each partner receive?

First, determine the beginning balances in each partner's capital account on 1/1/X8 (the beginning of the fiscal year), and what percentage of the partnership's total capital on that date each balance represented:

Partner	1/1/X8 Capital Balance	Income Share
X	$ 60,000	26.1%
Y	60,000	26.1%
Z	110,000	47.8%
	$ 230,000	100.0%

Next, apply those percentages to the year's net profit:

Partner X	$ 720,000 × 26.1%	=	$187,920
Partner Y	720,000 × 26.1%	=	187,920
Partner Z	720,000 × 47.8%	=	344,160

Then distribute the appropriate amount of profit to each partner's capital account:

Income Summary	$ 720,000	
X — Capital		$ 187,920
Y — Capital		187,920
Z — Capital		344,160

Finally, close the partners' withdrawal accounts for the year to their respective capital accounts:

X — Capital	$ 30,000	
Y — Capital	20,000	
Z — Capital	30,000	
X — Draw		$ 30,000
Y — Draw		20,000
Z — Draw		30,000

The ending balances for the capital accounts on 12/31/X8 are:

X — Capital	$ 277,920	(120,000 + 187,920 − 30,000)
Y — Capital	267,920	(100,000 + 187,920 − 20,000)
Z — Capital	474,160	(160,000 + 344,160 − 30,000)

2. *Distributions based on average capital.* To make a distribution of profits based on each partner's average capital, first determine the average balances in each partner's capital account during the course of the partnership's fiscal year. Next, determine what percentage of the partnership's total capital is represented by each partner's average. Finally, apply those percentages to the year's net profits.

EXAMPLE 1-4: The partnership agreement of the XYZ Partnership specifies that profits and losses should be distributed according to each partner's average capital balance. What portion of the $720,000 profit should each partner receive?

First, determine the average balance in each partner's capital account over the last 12 months. Do this by taking the actual balances the partner maintained and multiplying them by the number of months each balance was maintained. When these balances are added together and divided by 12, they yield the average capital balance for that partner for the year.

Partnership Distribution by Average Capital Balance

		PARTNER X		PARTNER Y		PARTNER Z	
	No. of Months	Actual Balance	No. of Months × Actual Balance	Actual Balance	No. of Months × Actual Balance	Actual Balance	No. of Mos. × Actual Balance
1/1–4/1	3	$ 60,000	$ 180,000	$ 60,000	$ 180,000	$110,000	$ 330,000
4/1–9/1	5	30,000	150,000	100,000	500,000	160,000	800,000
9/1–12/31	4	90,000	360,000	80,000	320,000	130,000	520,000
	12		$ 690,000		$ 1,000,000		$ 1,650,000
Divide by			12 months		12 months		12 months
Average capital balance			$ 57, 500		$ 83,333		$ 137,500

Next, determine what percentage of the partnership's total capital is represented by each partner's average:

Partner	Average Capital Balance	Income Share
X	$ 57,500	20.7%
Y	83,333	29.9%
Z	137,500	49.4%
	$ 278,333	100.0%

Next, apply those percentages to the year's net profit:

Partner X	$ 720,000 × 20.7%	=	$149,040
Partner Y	720,000 × 29.9%	=	215,280
Partner Z	720,000 × 49.4%	=	355,680

Then distribute the appropriate amount of profit to each partner's capital account:

	Debit	Credit
Income Summary	$ 720,000	
X — Capital		$ 149,040
Y — Capital		215,280
Z — Capital		355,680

Finally, close the partners' withdrawal accounts for the year to their respective capital accounts:

	Debit	Credit
X — Capital	$ 30,000	
Y — Capital	20,000	
Z — Capital	30,000	
X — Draw		$ 30,000
Y — Draw		20,000
Z — Draw		30,000

The ending balances for the capital accounts on 12/31/X8 are:

X — Capital	$ 239,040	(120,000 + 149,040 − 30,000)
Y — Capital	295,280	(100,000 + 215,280 − 20,000)
Z — Capital	485,680	(160,000 + 355,680 − 30,000)

3. *Distributions based on ending capital.* To make a distribution of profits or losses based on each partner's ending capital, first determine the balances in each partner's capital account at the end of the partnership's fiscal year. Next, determine what percentage of the partnership's total capital is represented by each partner's account. Finally, apply those percentages to the year's net profit.

EXAMPLE 1-5: The partnership agreement of the XYZ Partnership specifies that profits and losses should be distributed according to each partner's ending capital balance. What portion of the $720,000 profit should each partner receive?

First, determine the ending balances in each partner's capital account, and what percentage of the partnership's total capital each balance represents:

Partner	12/31/X8 Capital Balance	Income Share
X	$ 90,000	30.0%
Y	80,000	26.7%
Z	130,000	43.3%
	$ 300,000	100.0%

Next, apply those percentages to the year's net profit:

Partner X	$ 720,000 × 30.0%	=	$ 216,000
Partner Y	720,000 × 26.7%	=	192,240
Partner Z	720,000 × 43.3%	=	311,760

Then distribute the appropriate amount of profit to each partner's capital account:

	Debit	Credit
Income Summary	$ 720,000	
X — Capital		$ 216,000
Y — Capital		192,240
Z — Capital		311,760

Finally, close the partners' withdrawal accounts for the year to their respective capital accounts:

	Debit	Credit
X — Capital	$ 30,000	
Y — Capital	20,000	
Z — Capital	30,000	
X — Draw		$ 30,000
Y — Draw		20,000
Z — Draw		30,000

The ending balances for the capital accounts on 12/31/X8 are:

X — Capital	$ 306,000	(120,000 + 216,000 – 30,000)
Y — Capital	272,240	(100,000 + 192,240 – 20,000)
Z — Capital	441,760	(160,000 + 311,760 – 30,000)

D. Distribute salaries, interest, and bonuses to partners before profit or loss.

Under the Uniform Partnership Act, salary, interest, or bonuses, if any, must be distributed to partners first, before any distribution of profit or loss, unless the partnership agreement specifies otherwise. After the salaries, interest payments, or bonuses are distributed from net income, the remaining income or loss (if any) is distributed to the partners according to one of the distribution methods describe above.

Note that salaries to partners are not considered an operating expense of the business, but rather a distribution of its profits. (Salaries to employees are considered operating expenses.) Likewise, the interest expense on a partner's capital balance should not be considered when determining the partnership's net income, but should instead be viewed as a disbursement out of net income.

Finally, a bonus to a partner is not considered an expense of the partnership's operations, but rather a method of allocating income from operations to partners. Note the distinction, however, between interest on partners' capital accounts balances and interest on loans payable to partners; unlike interest on capital balances, interest on a debt owed to a partner is an expense of the partnership used in the determination of a partnership's net income.

EXAMPLE 1-6: The partnership agreement of the XYZ Partnership specifies that Partner X is entitled to a salary of $100,000, that Partner Y is entitled to a bonus of 10% of the partnership's net income, and that Partner Z is entitled to interest at 8% on Z's average capital balance. The agreement also states that X, Y, and Z share profits and losses in a ratio of 5:3:2, respectively. What portion of the profit should each partner receive?

First, distribute the salaries, bonuses, and interest as specified by the partnership agreement:

		Partner		
		X = 50%	Y = 30%	Z = 20%
Average Capital Balances (From Example 1-4)		$ 57,500	$ 83,333	$137,500
Partnership Income	$720,000			
Salary to Partner X	$100,000	$100,000		
Interest to Partner Z @ 8% of Average Capital Balance	11,000			$ 11,000
Bonus to Partner Y @ 10% of Partnership Income	72,000		72,000	

Then distribute the remainder of the net income according to the profit- or loss-sharing ratio:

		Partner		
		X = 50%	Y = 30%	Z = 20%
Remaining partnership income distributed in profit and loss ratio	537,000	268,500	161,100	107,400
Total Partnership Income	$720,000	$368,500	$233,100	$118,400

The journal entries to close the accounts at the year-end are:

	Debit	Credit
Income Summary	720,000	
X – Capital		368,500
Y – Capital		233,100
Z – Capital		118,400
To distribute profits.		
X – Capital	30,000	
Y – Capital	20,000	
Z – Capital	30,000	
X – Draw		30,000
Y – Draw		20,000
Z – Draw		30,000
To close partners' withdrawal accounts.		

The ending balances for the partners are:

X – Capital:	$458,500	(120,000 + 368,500 – 30,000)
Y – Capital:	$313,100	(100,000 + 233,100 – 20,000)
Z – Capital:	$248,400	(160,000 + 118,400 – 30,000)

In Example 1-6, adequate partnership income existed to provide distribution of salary, interest, and bonus, as well as to provide a profit remainder for distribution in the profit and loss ratio. But under the Uniform Partnership Act, partners' salaries, interest, and bonuses would always be distributed first (unless the partnership agreement specified otherwise), even if such distribution results in the development of a net loss for the partnership.

EXAMPLE 1-7: The partnership agreement of the XYZ Partnership specifies that Partner X is entitled to a $400,000 salary, that Partner Y is entitled to a bonus of 380,000, and that Partner Z is entitled to interest of $20,000. The agreement also states that X, Y, and Z share profits and losses in a ration of 5:3:2, respectively. What portion of the profit (or loss) should each partner receive?

First, distribute the salaries, bonuses, and interest as specified by the partnership agreement:

		Partner		
		X = 50%	Y = 30%	Z = 20%
Partnership Income	$720,000			
Salary to Partner X	$400,000	$400,000		
Bonus to Partner Y	380,000		$380,000	
Interest to Partner Z	20,000			$ 20,000

Then distribute the resulting loss according to the profit and loss sharing ratio:

		Partner		
		X = 50%	Y = 30%	Z = 20%
Remaining partnership loss distributed in profit and loss ratio	<80,000>	<40,000>	<24,000>	<16,000>
Total Partnership Income	$720,000	$360,000	$356,000	$ 4,000

The journal entries to close the accounts at year-end are:

Income Summary	720,000	
X – Capital		360,000
Y – Capital		356,000
Z – Capital		4,000
To distribute profits.		

X – Capital	30,000	
Y – Capital	20,000	
Z – Capital	30,000	
X – Draw		30,000
Y – Draw		20,000
Z – Draw		30,000
To close partners' withdrawal accounts.		

The ending account balances for the partners are:

X – Capital:	$450,000	(120,000 + 360,000 – 30,000)
Y – Capital:	$436,000	(100,000 + 356,000 – 20,000)
Z – Capital:	$134,000	(160,000 + 4,000 – 30,000)

The need to apply the Uniform Partnership Act in Example 1-7 could be removed by a specific statement in the partnership agreement. The agreement could, for example, specify that salary, bonus, and interest are to be distributed to Partners X, Y, and Z in that order, but *only to the extent available.*

Because only $720,000 in partnership income exists, the first $400,000 would go to Partner X as salary and the next $320,000 would go to Partner Y as a bonus. Partner Z would receive no distribution in this case, but would not be forced to absorb a loss.

1-4. Admission of a New Partner—Buying Directly from Original Partners

In theory, whenever a new partner is admitted to the partnership, the old partnership is dissolved and a new one is established. But from a practical standpoint, outsiders may perceive little or no change in the nature or activities of the partnership. A new partnership agreement is advisable, however, to specify the new profit or loss distribution arrangement and to ensure smooth partnership operations after the change in partners. The accountant's task is to determine how the admission of the new partner affects the accounts of the original partnership, and to establish correct capital account balances for all the partners after the admission has taken place.

A most fundamental point, which must be determined immediately upon admission of a new partner, is who the new partner is paying for his or her interest in the partnership: is the new partner paying one or more of the original partners directly, or is the new partner investing in (contributing to) the partnership entity itself? The difference is significant. If the new partner pays the original partners directly, the flows of cash or other assets take place outside the partnership. On the other hand, if the new partner invests in the partnership, the flows of cash or other assets take place within the partnership entity itself. This section examines payment from the new partner directly to the original partners. The following section examines investment of the new partner in the partnership itself.

Some of the ways in which a new partner may be admitted—with no cash paid to the partnership itself—include situations in which the new partner purchases an interest in the partnership directly from:

- one of the original partners
- the original partners at book value
- the original partners at a price above book value using the goodwill method
- the original partners at a price above book value using the bonus method
- the original partners at a price below book value using the goodwill method
- the original partners at a price below book value using the bonus method

In Examples 1-8 through 1-13, assume the following information regarding the original partnership equity for Partners A, B, and C, before admission of new Partner D. Also, assume that the partnership's net assets have fair values that equal book values, unless otherwise indicated.

12/31/X8	Partnership Equity	Profit & Loss
A – Capital	$100,000	33 1/3%
B – Capital	25,000	33 1/3%
C – Capital	75,000	33 1/3%
Total Equity	$200,000	100%

A. Buying an interest directly from one original partner.

When a new partner pays cash to an original partner for an interest in the partnership, the payment is made outside of the partnership entity. As long as the other original partners agree to admit the new partner, the only adjustment necessary to the partnership's books is to record the new partner's interest (that is, to establish that partner's capital account), and to adjust the original partner's capital balance accordingly. The total amount of the partnership's capital and assets remains the same.

It could be argued that the amount of consideration the new partner pays directly to the original partner is irrelevant to the partnership's accounting for the change of partners, because this transfer of cash takes place outside the partnership entity. Only the transfer of equity, from the original partner (or partners) to the new partner, is of concern.

EXAMPLE 1-8: D purchases B's interest in the ABC Partnership and pays $25,000 directly to B. In this case, the only entry necessary on the books of the partnership is one to close B's capital account and establish D's.

B – Capital	25,000	
D – Capital		25,000

To record D as a partner and removal of B's partnership interest.

B. Buying an interest directly from all the original partners.

A new partner may be admitted into a partnership by buying a percentage of the partnership's total capital. To do this, the new partner buys the agreed-upon percentage of each original partner's capital account. Again, such payments are made directly from the new partner to the original partners, outside the partnership itself. If the payments are equal to book value of the percentage of the partnership the new partnership is acquiring, the only entries necessary on the books of the partnership are those to record the decrease in the capital accounts of the original partners, and the establishment of the new partner's capital account.

EXAMPLE 1-9: D buys a 20% interest in the ABC Partnership, and pays $40,000 directly to the original partners. (Because 20% of the partnership's existing capital of $200,000 is $40,000, this payment is at book value.) In this case, the only entry necessary on the partnership's books is one that decreases the original partners' capital accounts by 20% and establishes the capital account for D.

A – Capital	(20% × 100,000)	20,000	
B – Capital	(20% × 25,000)	5,000	
C – Capital	(20% × 75,000)	15,000	
D – Capital			40,000

C. Buying an interest at a price above book value.

A new partner may sometimes agree, because of the future prospects of the business, to buy an interest in a partnership for more than book value. That is, the new partner agrees to pay more for his or her share than the capital accounts of the original partners say the share is worth. In this situation, the new partner may be admitted using either the implied-value-of-the-business approach (the *goodwill* method), or the book-value-of-the business approach (the *bonus* method).

1. *The goodwill method.* Under the goodwill method of admitting a new partner, the true value of the business is implied by the price the new partner is willing to pay. That is, if the new partner is willing to pay more than book value, then the business is implied to be worth more than book value. Assuming the book and fair values of the partnership are equal, the difference between the book value of the partnership and its implied value is considered goodwill, an intangible, unrecorded asset created by the original partners. At the point the new partner is admitted, this intangible asset is recorded in the capital accounts according to the profit distribution requirements of the original partnership agreement.

To admit a new partner using the goodwill method when the price of the interest is greater than book value, determine the implied value of the business from the sale price, then make the entries in the partnership's books to record the goodwill against the original partners' capital balances and to record admission of the new partner. Remember that all cash transactions take place outside the partnership; the only changes on the partnership's books relate to the partners' capital account balances and the recording of goodwill.

EXAMPLE 1-10: D buys a 20% interest in the ABC Partnership for $61,000. Because the partnership uses the goodwill method to admit new partners, the implied value of the business must first be determined, then the entries necessary to record the admission of D may be made.

The implied value of the business is determined by the price the new partner pays the original partners for the capital interest received. If D pays $61,000 for a 20% interest, the implied value of the business is $305,000:

$$20\%\ \text{Implied Value} = \$61{,}000$$
$$\text{Implied Value} = \$61{,}000 \div 0.20$$
$$\text{Implied Value} = \$305{,}000$$

Because the implied value of the business is $305,000, while its book (and fair) value is only $200,000, goodwill of $105,000 is implied in the purchase price D is willing to pay. The entries in the journal of the partnership to distribute the goodwill, and to admit D under the goodwill method, are:

	Debit	Credit
Goodwill	105,000	
A – Capital		35,000
B – Capital		35,000
C – Capital		35,000
To distribute goodwill.		

	Debit	Credit
A – Capital	27,000	
B – Capital	12,000	
C – Capital	22,000	
D – Capital		61,000
To record admission of D and reduction of Partners A, B, and C capital accounts by 20%.		

After the admission of the new partner, capital balances for all partners are:

	Partner				Total
	A	B	C	D	
Beginning Balance	$100,000	$25,000	$ 75,000	—	$200,000
Goodwill recognition before admission of Partner D	35,000	35,000	35,000	—	105,000
Subtotal	135,000	60,000	110,000		305,000
Admission of D by sale of 20% interest by each partner	(27,000)	(12,000)	(22,000)	$61,000	
Capital Balances after admission of D	$108,000	$48,000	$88,000	$61,000	$305,000

Note that after D is admitted, D's capital account balance of $61,000 is exactly 20% of the new partnership's total capital of $305,000.

2. *The bonus method.* Under the bonus method of admitting a new partner, the implied value of the business is ignored and the new partner is admitted on the basis of the book value of the partnership. The difference between the book value of the interest purchased and price the new partner actually pays for it is considered a bonus, which the new partner pays directly to the original partners outside the partnership. Therefore the total equity of the partnership does not change. The only entries on the partnership's books relate to the partners' capital account balances.

EXAMPLE 1-11: D buys a 20% interest in the ABC Partnership for $61,000. The partnership uses the bonus method to record the admittance of the new partner, so the implied value of the business based on D's payment is ignored, and D is admitted on the basis of book values. The entry on the partnership's books to record the admittance of D is:

A – Capital	20,000	
B – Capital	5,000	
C – Capital	15,000	
D – Capital		40,000

Bear in mind that although D really paid $61,000 for a 20% capital interest valued at $40,000, the payment was made directly to the partners, not to the partnership entity itself. The original partners receive the additional $21,000 as "bonuses." After the admission of the new partner, capital balances for all partners are:

	Partner				Total
	A	B	C	D	
Beginning Balance	$100,000	$25,000	$ 75,000	—	$200,000
Admission of D by sale of 20% interest	(20,000)	(5,000)	(15,000)	$40,000	
Capital Balance after admission of D	$ 80,000	$20,000	$60,000	$40,000	$200,000

Note that although D's capital balance is only $40,000 (instead of $61,000 as it is under the goodwill method), this $40,000 still represents a 20% interest in the total partnership equity of $200,000.

D. Buying an interest at a price below book value.

The members of a partnership may sometimes agree, in order to attract a desirable partner or necessary capital, to sell an interest in their partnership for less than its book value. That is, the new partner is asked to pay less for his or her interest than the capital accounts of the original partners say that interest is worth. Under these circumstances, the new partner may be admitted using the goodwill method or the bonus method.

1. *The goodwill method.* Under the goodwill method, the implied value of the business is based on the price the new partner is willing to pay for an interest. If the new partner is willing only to pay a price below book value, then the business is implied to be worth less than book value. Assuming book and fair values of the partnership are equal, the difference between the book value of the partnership and the lower implied value is *negative* goodwill.

   To admit a new partner using the goodwill method when the price of the interest is below its book value, determine the implied value of the business from the sale price, then make the entries in the partnership's books to record negative goodwill against the original partners' capital balances and to record admission of the new partner. Remember that all cash transactions take place outside the partnership; the only changes on the partnership's books relate to the partners' capital account balances and the recording of negative goodwill.

EXAMPLE 1-12: D buys a 20% interest in the ABC Partnership for $34,000. Because the partnership uses the goodwill method to admit new partners, the implied value of the business must first be determined, then the entries necessary to record the admission of D may be made.

The implied value of the business is determined by the price the new partner pays the original partners for the capital interest received. If D pays $34,000 for a 20% interest, the implied value of the business is $170,000:

20% Implied Value = $34,000
Implied Value = $34,000 ÷ 0.20
Implied Value = $170,000

Because the implied value of the business is $170,000 while its book (and fair) value is $200,000, negative goodwill of $30,000 is implied in the purchase price D is willing to pay. The entries in the journal of the partnership to distribute the negative goodwill, and to admit D under the goodwill method, are:

A – Capital	10,000	
B – Capital	10,000	
C – Capital	10,000	
Assets		30,000
To record negative goodwill.		

A – Capital	18,000	
B – Capital	3,000	
C – Capital	13,000	
D – Capital		34,000
To record admission of Partner D.		

After the admission of the new partner, capital balances for all partners are:

	Partner				Total
	A	B	C	D	
Beginning Balance	$100,000	$25,000	$ 75,000	—	$200,000
Net asset overstatement before admission of Partner D	(10,000)	(10,000)	(10,000)	—	(30,000)
Subtotal	90,000	15,000	65,000		170,000
Admission of D by sale of 20% interest by each partner	(18,000)	(3,000)	(13,000)	$34,000	—
Capital Balances after admission of Partner D	$ 72,000	$12,000	$52,000	$34,000	$170,000

Note that after D is admitted, D's capital account balance of $34,000 is exactly 20% of the new partnership's total capital of $170,000.

2. *The bonus method.* If the bonus method is used to admit the new partner, the implied value of the business is ignored and the new partner is admitted on the basis of book values. The difference between the book value of the interest purchased and the price the new partner actually pays for it is considered a bonus to the new partner, and is in effect a discount on the price the new partner would have paid at book value.

Remember that all cash transactions take place outside the partnership. The total equity of the partnership does not change. The only entries on the partnership's books relate to the partners' capital account balances.

EXAMPLE 1-13: D buys a 20% interest in the ABC Partnership from the owners for $34,000. The partnership uses the bonus method to record the admittance of the new partner, so the implied value of the business based on D's payment is ignored, and D is admitted on the basis of book values. The entry on the partnership's books to record the admittance of D is:

A – Capital	20,000	
B – Capital	5,000	
C – Capital	15,000	
D – Capital		40,000

Bear in mind that although D really paid $34,000 for a 20% capital interest valued at $40,000, the payment was made directly to the partners, not to the partnership entity itself. The new partner receives the additional $6,000 as a "bonus," or discount on the purchase price. After the admission of the new partner, capital balances for all partners are:

	Partner				Total
	A	B	C	D	
Beginning Balance	$100,000	$25,000	$75,000	—	$200,000
Admission of D by sale of 20% interest by each partner	(20,000)	(5,000)	(15,000)	$40,000	—
Capital Balances after admission of D	$ 80,000	$20,000	$60,000	$40,000	$200,000

Note that although D's capital balance is $40,000 (instead of 34,000 as under the goodwill method), this $40,000 represents a 20% interest in the total partnership equity of $200,000.

1-5. Admission of a New Partner—Investing in a Partnership

An incoming partner may acquire an interest by investing in (or making a contribution to) a partnership entity directly. In such a case, exchanges of assets take place within the partnership entity; no assets are exchanged between the partners.

Some of the ways in which a new partner may be admitted—with cash invested in or contributed to the partnership (that is, no cash is paid directly to individual partners)—include situations in which the new partner invests:

- at exactly book value
- at a price above book value using the goodwill method
- at a price above book value using the bonus method
- at a price below book value using the goodwill method
- at a price below book value using the bonus method

In Examples 1-14 through 1-18, assume the following information regarding the original partnership equity for Partners A, B, and C before the admission of Partner D. Also, assume that the partnership's net assets have fair values equal to their book values unless otherwise stated.

12/31/X8	Partnership Equity	Profit & Loss
A – Capital	$100,000	33 1/3%
B – Capital	25,000	33 1/3%
C – Capital	75,000	33 1/3%
Total Equity	$200,000	100%

A. Investing in a partnership at exactly book value.

When a new partner contributes assets in exchange for a percentage of an existing partnership, those assets become property of the partnership entity, not the individual partners. The accounting problem in this case is to determine how much the new partner should pay for that percentage.

If the new partner is to be admitted at book value (that is, if no goodwill or bonus exists), the accountant needs to determine the new required total capital of the partnership after admission of the new partner. To do this, subtract the new partner's percentage from 100 percent. This gives the original partners' new percentage of ownership. Next, divide the original partners' current capital by their new percentage; this will give the new required total capital. Finally, subtract the current total capital from the new required total capital; this will show how much the new partner must contribute to acquire his or her share.

EXAMPLE 1-14: D invests in the ABC Partnership in return for a 20% interest by contributing assets directly to the partnership. The partnership must first determine the new required total capital of the ABCD Partnership, then how much D must pay for a 20% share.

If D's interest will be 20%, then the existing partners' interest must be 80% of the new required total capital after admitting D. That is:

Existing Partners' Capital	=	80% (New Required Total Capital)
$200,000	=	80% (New Required Total Capital)
$\frac{\$200{,}000}{.8}$	=	(New Required Total Capital)
$250,000	=	(New Required Total Capital)

New Required Total Capital	$250,000
Less: Existing Capital	200,000
Partner D investment required	$ 50,000

The entry to admit D is:

Cash	50,000	
D – Capital		50,000

After admission of D, the partners' capital balances are:

Partner A	$100,000	
Partner B	25,000	
Partner C	75,000	
Partner D	50,000	20% as required
Total	$250,000	

B. Investing in a partnership at a price above book value.

A new partner may sometimes agree, because of the future prospects of the business, to invest in a share of a partnership for more than book value. That is, the new partner agrees to contribute more for his or her share than the capital accounts of the original partners say it is worth. In such a case, the new partner may be admitted using the implied-value-of-the-business approach (the goodwill method) or the book-value-of-the-business approach (the bonus method).

1. *The goodwill method.* Under the goodwill method, the true value of the business is implied by the amount the new partner is willing to invest in return for his or her share. That is, if the new partner is willing to pay more than book value, then the business is implied to be worth more than book value. Assuming book and fair values are equal, the difference between the book value and the implied value is considered goodwill created by the original partners. At the point the new partner is admitted the goodwill is recorded in the asset accounts of the partnership, and is also recorded in the capital accounts of the original partners.

To admit a new partner using the goodwill method when his or her investment is greater than the book value of the share of the partnership received, determine the implied value of the business from the amount of the investment. Then make the necessary entries in the partnership's books, adding the goodwill to the original partners' capital accounts and admitting the new partner.

Remember that exchanges of assets take place within the partnership, not directly between the partners themselves.

EXAMPLE 1-15: D invests $62,000 in return for a 20% interest in the ABC Partnership. Because the partnership uses the goodwill method to admit new partners, the implied value of the business must first be determined, then the entries necessary to record the goodwill and the admission of D may be made.

If Partner D is willing to invest $62,000 for a 20% interest in the business, then the implied value of the partnership must be $310,000:

$$20\% \quad \text{Implied Value} = \$\,62{,}000$$

$$\text{Implied Value} = \frac{\$\,62{,}000}{20\%}$$

$$\text{Implied Value} = \$310{,}000$$

Because the implied value of the business is $310,000, while its book value is only $262,000 (the original $200,000 *plus* Partner D's $62,000), goodwill of $48,000 is implied in the purchase price, which is distributed to the original partners' capital accounts according to their original profit-and-loss ratio. The journal entries to admit D under the goodwill method are:

	Debit	Credit
Goodwill	48,000	
A – Capital		16,000
B – Capital		16,000
C – Capital		16,000
To record goodwill.		

	Debit	Credit
Cash	62,000	
D – Capital		62,000
To admit D.		

After the admission of the new partner, capital balances for all partners are:

	Partner				Total
	A	B	C	D	
Beginning Balance	$100,000	$25,000	$ 75,000	—	$200,000
Goodwill recognition before admission of Partner D	16,000	16,000	16,000		48,000
Admission of D upon receipt of cash of $62,000 by partnership				$62,000	$ 62,000
Capital Balances after admission of D	$116,000	$41,000	$91,000	$62,000	$310,000

Note that after D is admitted, D's capital account balance of $62,000 is exactly 20% of the partnership's total capital of $310,000.

2. *The bonus method.* When the bonus method is used the implied value of the business is ignored. Instead, the new required total capital is based on the original book value, plus the new partner's investment. The difference between the book value of the new partner's share and the assets actually contributed for it is considered a bonus, and is added to the capital accounts of the original partners according to their original profit-and-loss ratio.

EXAMPLE 1-16: D invests $62,000 for a 20% interest in the ABC Partnership. The partnership uses the bonus method to record the admittance of the new partner, so the implied value of the business based on D's payment is ignored, and D is admitted on the basis of book values.

The new required capital is based on the original book value (of $200,000), plus the new partner's investment (of $62,000), or $262,000. The difference between D's investment ($62,000) and the book value of the share received (20% of $262,000, or $52,400) is a bonus ($62,000 – $52,400 = $9,600), distributed to the capital accounts of the original partners according to their original profit-and-loss ratio. The journal entry to admit D under the bonus method is:

	Debit	Credit
Cash	62,000	
A – Capital		3,200
B – Capital		3,200
C – Capital		3,200
D – Capital		52,400*

*Based on: 20% of $262,000.

After the admission of the new partner, capital balances for all partners are:

	Partner				Total
	A	B	C	D	
Beginning Balance	$100,000	$25,000	$75,000	—	$200,000
Entry (partial) to admit Partner D	3,200	3,200	3,200	$52,400	62,000
Capital Balances after admission of D	$103,200	$28,200	$78,200	$52,400	$262,000

Note that after D is admitted, D's capital account balance of $52,400 is exactly 20% of the partnership's total capital of $262,000.

C. Investing in a partnership at a price below book value.

The members of a partnership may sometimes agree, in order to attract a desirable partner or necessary capital, to offer a share in their business in return for an investment that is less than the share's book value. That is, the new partner is asked to contribute less for his or her share than the capital accounts of the original partners say it is worth. Under these circumstances, the new partner may be admitted using the goodwill method or the bonus method.

1. *The goodwill method.* Under the goodwill method, the implied value of the business is based on the amount the new partner is willing to invest for a specified percentage of interest. If the new partner is willing to invest an amount below the book value of the new partner's interest, then the business is implied to be worth less than book value. Assuming book value and fair value are equal, the difference between the book value and the lower implied value is considered negative goodwill.

To admit a new partner using the goodwill method when his or her investment is less than the book value of the share of the partnership received, determine the implied value of the business from the amount of the investment. Then make the necessary entries in the partnership's books, subtracting the negative goodwill from the original partners' capital accounts and admitting the new partner.

Remember that exchanges of assets take place within the partnership, not directly between the partners themselves.

EXAMPLE 1-17: D is willing to invest $47,000 in the ABC Partnership in return for a 20% interest. Because the partnership uses the goodwill method to admit new partners, the implied value of the business must first be determined, then the entries necessary to record the negative goodwill and the admission of D may be made.

If Partner D is willing to invest $47,000 for a 20% interest in the business, then the implied value of the partnership must be $235,000:

$$20\% \text{ Implied Value} = \$\,47{,}000$$

$$\text{Implied Value} = \frac{\$\,47{,}000}{20\%}$$

$$\text{Implied Value} = \$235{,}000$$

Because the implied value of the business is $235,000, while its book value is $247,000 (the original $200,000 *plus* Partner D's $47,000), negative goodwill of $12,000 is implied in the purchase price which is subtracted from the original partners' capital accounts according to their original profit-and-loss ratio. The journal entries to admit D under the goodwill method are:

	Debit	Credit
A – Capital	4,000	
B – Capital	4,000	
C – Capital	4,000	
Assets		12,000
To record negative goodwill.		
Cash	47,000	
D – Capital		47,000
To record admission of D.		

After the admission of the new partner, capital balances for all partners are:

	Partner				Total
	A	B	C	D	
Beginning Balance	$100,000	$25,000	$75,000	—	$200,000
Net asset overstatement before admission of Partner D	(4,000)	(4,000)	(4,000)		(12,000)
Subtotal	$ 96,000	$21,000	$71,000		$188,000
Admission of D upon receipt of cash of $47,000 by partnership				$47,000	$ 47,000
Capital Balances after admission of D	$ 96,000	$21,000	$71,000	$47,000	$235,000

Note that after D is admitted, D's capital account balance of $47,000 is exactly 20% of the partnership's total capital of $235,000.

2. *The bonus method.* If the bonus method is used to admit the new partner, the implied value of the business is ignored and the new partner is admitted on the basis of book values. The difference

between the amount of the investment and the book value of the share received in return is considered a bonus.

To admit a new partner using the bonus method, determine the book value of the new partnership. Then make the necessary entry in the partnership's books, charging cash for the investment received, crediting the new partner's capital account for his or her percentage of interest in the total book value, and charging any difference against the original partners' capital accounts in their original profit-and-loss ratio.

Remember that exchanges of assets take place within the partnership, not directly between the partners themselves.

EXAMPLE 1-18: D is willing to invest $47,000 in the ABC Partnership in return for a 20 percent share. The partnership uses the bonus method to record the admittance of the new partner, so the implied value of the business based on D's payment is ignored, and D is admitted on the basis of book values.

The new required capital is based on the original book value (of $200,000), plus the new partner's investment (of $47,000), or $247,000. The difference between D's investment ($47,000) and the book value of the share received (20% of $247,000, or $49,400) is a bonus ($49,400 – $47,000 = $2,400), charged to the capital accounts of the original partners according to their original profit-and-loss ratio. The journal entry to admit D under the bonus method is:

Cash	47,000	
A – Capital	800	
B – Capital	800	
C – Capital	800	
D – Capital		49,400*
*Based on:	20% of $247,000	

After the admission of the new partner, capital balances for all partners are:

	Partner				Total
	A	B	C	D	
Beginning Balance	$100,000	$25,000	$ 75,000	—	$200,000
Entry (partial) to admit Partner D	(800)	(800)	(800)	49,400	47,000
Capital Balances after admission of D	$ 99,200	$24,200	$74,200	$49,400	$247,000

Note that after D is admitted, D's capital account balance of $49,400 is exactly 20% of the partnership's total capital of $247,000.

D. Special circumstances when admitting a new partner.

Some other issues may develop when a new partner is admitted to a partnership. For example, goodwill or a bonus may be attributable to the new partner, the new partner may contribute assets other than cash, or assets may be revalued before admission of a new partner.

1. *Goodwill or bonus attributable to a new partner.* Goodwill or a bonus could conceivably be attributable to the new partner rather than to existing partners. For example, a new partner may invest at the book value in the partnership but be given a capital interest in excess of the book value in consideration of special expertise or access to special markets.

To admit a new partner under such circumstances, an entry is necessary to indicate what the extra amount in the new partner's capital account is attributable to: goodwill or bonus.

EXAMPLE 1-19: D invests $15,000 in the ABC Partnership but is given a $20,000 capital interest.

Under the goodwill method, a goodwill account is established to record the difference between D's cash contribution and her new capital account:

Cash	15,000	
Goodwill	5,000	
D – Capital		20,000

Under the bonus method, the $5,000 difference is charged against the original partners' capital accounts, according to their original profit-and-loss ratio:

Cash	15,000	
*Original Partners' Capital	5,000	
D – Capital		20,000

*Charged to original partners in the profit-and-loss ratio.

2. *A new partner contributes assets other than cash.* New partners may contribute assets other than cash to a partnership. When this occurs, the new partner's capital account should be credited for the assets' fair value as of the date the asset is invested in the partnership. The assets' historical cost, tax-assessed value, and federal tax basis to the new partner are not in themselves relevant to the financial accounting for the partnership.

EXAMPLE 1-20: On 12/31/X8, the ABC Partnership admitted Partner D, who invested the following net assets in the partnership:

	Fair Value	Book Value
Land	$100,000	$ 40,000
Building (net)	500,000	400,000
Equipment (net)	30,000	20,000
Mortgage payable	(130,000)	(130,000)
Net assets	$500,000	$330,000

The original partners have determined that the fair value of the assets invested by Partner D will exactly equal the book value of the interest in the partnership D receives (that is, there will be no goodwill or bonus).

Record the assets (and liabilities) contributed by D in their appropriate accounts, at their fair values on the date they are contributed:

Land	100,000	
Building	500,000	
Equipment	30,000	
Mortgage payable		130,000
D – Capital		500,000

Notice that book values or original costs are not relevant to the partnership's financial accounting, although they may be quite relevant to an individual partner's personal federal income tax.

3. *Revaluation of assets before admission of a new partner.* Sometimes before the admission of a new partner the original partners may deem it necessary to raise the value of some assets from their book values to their fair values. This is done to protect the original partners; they are the ones entitled to any fair value increases on assets they acquired before the admission of the new partner. Admission of a new partner at a price based on book values instead of fair values would permit the new partner to make unfair profits on the sale of any of those original assets.

To find the proper price at which to admit a new partner when assets should be revalued, first determine the fair value of all assets. Then subtract the liabilities. The remainder is the amount on which the price of the new partner's share should be based.

EXAMPLE 1-21: The following information is available regarding the R & B Partnership on 12/31/X7:

Balance Sheet
R & B Partnership as of 12/31/X7

Assets	Book Value	Fair Value
Current assets:		
Cash	$ 200,000	$ 200,000
Accounts receivable (net)	400,000	400,000
Inventory	300,000	500,000
Prepaid insurance	100,000	100,000
Total current assets	$1,000,000	$1,200,000
Property, plant and equipment:		
Land	300,000	400,000
Equipment (net)	100,000	200,000
Building (net)	400,000	800,000
Total property, plant and equipment	800,000	1,400,000
Total assets	$1,800,000	$2,600,000
Liabilities		
Current liabilities:		
Accounts payable	400,000	400,000
Long-term debt:		
Mortgage note payable	600,000	600,000
Equity:		
R. Capital	500,000	
B. Capital	300,000	
Total liabilities and equity	$1,800,000	

M wants to purchase 20% capital interest from the original partners directly, with no goodwill or bonus. R and B should revalue the partnership's assets from book values to fair values before determining how much M should pay for the 20% interest in the partnership.

As shown on the balance sheet, revaluation of the assets increases the value of the partnership by $800,000. A journal entry is made to increase the appropriate asset account balances and the capital accounts of the original partners, R and B, as follows:

Inventory	200,000	
Land	100,000	
Equipment (net)	100,000	
Building (net)	400,000	
R – Capital (50%)		400,000
B – Capital (50%)		400,000

If M paid 20% of the partnership's net asset book value of $800,000, then M would pay only $160,000. M would then be able to share in the profits of any sale of the assets at fair value. These assets may have been purchased years ago by the original partners, long before any contribution by M.

Based on fair values, however, M should pay 20% of $1,600,000 (assets of $2,600,000 at fair values less liabilities of $1,000,000), or $320,000. The journal entry to admit M decreases the capital accounts of R and B by 20%, after they have been increased by asset revaluation as follows:

R – Capital (20% × 900,000)	180,000*	
B – Capital (20% × 700,000)	140,000*	
M – Capital		320,000

*See schedule below.

Ending capital balances are now:

	R	B	M	Total
Beginning Capital	$500,000	$300,000		$ 800,000
Entry to revalue assets prior to M admission	400,000	400,000		800,000
Subtotal	900,000	700,000		1,600,000
Entry to admit Partner M	(180,000)	(140,000)	320,000	
Capital Balances after admission of Partner M	$720,000	$560,000	$320,000	$1,600,000

Note that after M is admitted, M's capital account balance of $320,000 is exactly 20% of the partnership's total capital of $160,000.

1-6. Retirement of Partners

Generally, a retiring partner is entitled to be paid the balance in his or her capital account at the date of retirement. However, the partnership agreement may specify a formula for distribution to retiring partners. For example, a retiring partner may be entitled to his or her capital balance plus some portion of revenue, or the partnership agreement may require revaluation of assets as of the partner's retirement date. Most important from an accounting viewpoint, however, is that the retirement of a partner's capital account may result in goodwill or a bonus.

The following information, to be used in Examples 1-22 and 1-23, is taken from the trial balance of a partnership on 12/31/X8:

Partner	Capital Balance	Profit and Loss Ratio
Smith	$ 60,000	50%
Jones	40,000	30%
Williams	50,000	20%
Total capital	$150,000	100%

Jones plans to retire from the partnership. The partnership agreement states that assets should be revalued as of the withdrawal date, before any distribution is made. After revaluation it is determined that certain property, plant, and equipment has a fair value that is $40,000 more than its book value.

EXAMPLE 1-22: Jones retires from the partnership. The partnership uses the bonus method to retire Jones' capital account.

Under this approach, Jones is paid $52,000 based on the following calculation:

Capital balance	$40,000
Plus: 30% of raise of assets to fair value of $40,000	12,000
Total Paid	$52,000

Under the bonus method of retirement, entries are not actually made to raise the assets to their fair values; any difference that develops through revaluation of assets during a retirement is charged entirely to the remaining partners in their profit-and-loss ratio. In this case, Smith is charged for 5/7 of the $12,000 bonus, or $8,571, while Williams is charged for 2/7, or $3,429. The journal to retire Jones under the bonus method is:

Jones Capital	40,000	
Smith Capital	8,571	
Williams Capital	3,429	
Cash		52,000

EXAMPLE 1-22: Jones retires from the partnership. The partnership uses the goodwill method to retire Jones' capital account.

Under this method, Jones is still paid $52,000, as calculated in Example 1-22. However, under the goodwill method, assets (including goodwill, if any) are first brought to fair value on the partnership's books. The journal entry to revalue the assets is:

Property, Plant, & Equipment	40,000	
Smith – Capital		20,000
Jones – Capital		12,000
Williams – Capital		8,000

Then the retiring partner may be paid. The journal entry to record the retirement of Jones is:

Jones – Capital (40,000 + 12,000)	52,000	
Cash		52,000

RAISE YOUR GRADES

Can you explain . . . ?

- ☑ the partnership business form (definition)
- ☑ the five major characteristics of a partnership
- ☑ general accounting principles for a partnership as compared to the sole proprietorship or corporate form
- ☑ the partnership agreement contents
- ☑ the methods of profit and loss distribution
- ☑ the goodwill method of admitting a new partner to a partnership when the new partner purchases an interest directly from the original partners
- ☑ the bonus method of admitting a new partner to a partnership when the new partner purchases an interest directly from the original partners
- ☑ the goodwill method of admitting a new partner to a partnership when the new partner invests in or contributes to the partnership itself
- ☑ the bonus method of admitting a new partner to a partnership when the new partner invests in or contributes to the partnership itself
- ☑ how to retire a partner

SUMMARY

1. A partnership is an "association of two or more persons to carry on as co-owners a business for profit."
2. The Uniform Partnership Act and the partnership agreement (which may be oral but should ideally be written) govern formation, operation, and liquidation of partnerships.
3. Five major characteristics of partnerships include ease of formation, limited life, unlimited liability, mutual agency, and co-ownership of partnership property.
4. Partnerships pay no federal tax; however, partnership income or loss passes through to the individual partners who do have federal tax responsibility.
5. Partnership accounting is similar to that of any business form as far as accounting for normal operations is concerned except that the equity of the partnership is lodged in individual partner capital and draw accounts (not in retained earnings or stock accounts).
6. The partnership agreement should specify the method of distribution of profit and loss and an infinite number of possibilities exist. A few of the more common distribution plans illustrated include equal distribution, distribution based on beginning, average, or ending capital balances, distribution based on specified ratios, and distributions which consider salary, interest on capital balances, or bonus to one or more partners.
7. If a partnership agreement is silent regarding profit and loss distribution, then profits and losses must be shared equally in accordance with the Uniform Partnership Act.
8. A new partner may be admitted to a partnership in two ways. The new partner may pay existing partners directly for a partnership interest or the new partner may invest in (or contribute to) the partnership itself for a partnership interest.
9. When the goodwill method is used to admit a new partner, the implied value of the business is determined and compared with book value. Generally, goodwill is created to the credit of the original partners and then the new partner is admitted. On the other hand, goodwill may sometimes be attributable to the new partner upon his or her admission.
10. When the bonus method is used to admit a new partner, the implied value of the business is ignored and the new partner is credited for his or her capital interest in the partnership's net assets at book value.
11. New partners may contribute assets other than cash into the partnership. The contributing partner's capital account balance should be credited in consideration of the contributed assets' fair value, on the date contributed. The asset's tax basis, assessed value, original cost, or book value to the contributing partner are not relevant to determining the new partner's capital account balance on the partnership's books. These amounts may, of course, be relevant to the individual partner in terms of personal taxation.
12. A partnership may find it necessary to revalue assets before admission of a new partner.
13. Retiring partners are generally entitled to the balance in their capital accounts at the date of retirement. However, the partnership agreement may specify that the capital balance be adjusted by revaluation of assets or debts, by a percentage of prospective revenue, or for other reasons.
14. The retirement of a partner may result in the use of either the bonus method or goodwill method when the planned payment to retire a partner initially differs from the partner's capital account balance.

RAPID REVIEW

True or False

1. If the partnership agreement is silent about the method of sharing profit and loss, partners share profit and loss based on their average capital balance during the period.
2. A partnership agreement must be written to be legal.
3. The liability of a partnership is limited in the sense that if profits are inadequate (or losses too frequent) to permit payment of creditors, the partnership could declare bankruptcy and pay creditors only to the extent partnership assets were available.

4. Partnerships pay federal income tax at a relatively high rate compared to corporate tax rates.
5. The major difference between partnership and corporate accounting lies in the accounting treatment of assets and liabilities.
6. Assets other than cash contributed to a partnership by a partner as an investment should be valued at their fair market value when contributed.
7. When a new partner invests in (or contributes to) a partnership an amount which gives the new partner a 20% capital interest in the partnership, goodwill may never result.
8 Under the bonus method, goodwill is not recorded upon admission of a new partner.
9. It may be appropriate for a partnership to adjust its net assets to fair value prior to admission of a new partner.
10. Loans payable to (or receivable from) individual partners on the partnership's books should be netted against the respective partner's capital account in the partnership's formal financial statements.

Answers:

1. *False* In this situation the Uniform Partnership Act specifies profit and loss be shared equally no matter what the average capital balances of each partner are.
2. *False* A partnership agreement may be written or oral. However, it is advisable that the agreement be in writing.
3. *False* Partnerships have unlimited liability and therefore the partners are also personally liable for the debts of the partnership.
4. *False* Partnerships do not pay federal income tax. They must, however, file an information tax return showing profit or loss.
5. *False* The major difference lies in the treatment of equity. A partnership has no retained earnings, capital stock, or dividend accounts. Instead, it has individual partner's accounts for capital and withdrawal.
6. *True* Tax-assessed values, original cost to the contributing partner or tax basis to the contributing partner are not in themselves relevant.
7. *False* Goodwill may result. For example, an investment of, say, $70,000 for a 20% interest in a partnership by a new partner in a situation where the total capital of the original partners was, say, $250,000 before admission of the new partner would under the goodwill method, result in goodwill of $30,000 as follows:

Implied Value of Business	$\frac{\$70,000}{.2}$	=	$350,000
Book Value ($250,000 + $70,000)		=	320,000
Goodwill		=	$ 30,000

(It is, of course, possible that a portion of this $30,000 is attributable to asset fair values in excess of book values, if any.)

8. *True* Under the bonus method, the implied value of the business is ignored and, therefore, goodwill is not recorded. Any difference between the amount a new partner pays in cash (either to individual partners or the partnership) for a partnership interest and the credit to the new partner's capital account is bonus. (See Examples 1-11, 1-13, 1-16, and 1-18.)
9. *True* (See Example 1-21.)
10. *False* Loans payable to (or receivable from) partners should be shown as such on the partnership's balance sheet and not netted against partners' capital balances. These payables and receivables actually result in financial accounting interest expense or interest income respectively to the partnership. (However, loans payable to (or receivable from) partners may be offset against partners' capital balances when the partnership is in the process of liquidation as will be demonstrated in the next chapter.)

SOLVED PROBLEMS

PROBLEM 1-1: The partnership of Washington, Lincoln, and Jefferson had net income of $300,000. The average capital balances of Washington, Lincoln, and Jefferson were $500,000, $200,000 and $300,000 respectively. How should partnership profit of $300,000 be distributed?

Answer: Equally. Each partner is credited for one-third of $300,000 or $100,000 in income. The capital balances (beginning, average, or ending) are not the basis for distribution of profit unless a partnership agreement specifically states that this is the case. The problem does not specifically state this is the case. Therefore, under the Uniform Partnership Act, profits and losses are shared equally.

PROBLEM 1-2: On 1/1/X1, Davis and Williams began a partnership. Davis contributed $100,000 in cash and Williams contributed land. The land originally cost Williams $120,000. On 1/3/X1, the land was sold by the partnership for a total selling price of $300,000. Record the journal entry which the partnership should have made on 1/1/X1 to form the partnership and on 1/3/X1 to record the land sale.

Answer: The point here is that non-cash assets contributed to the partnership should be recorded at fair market value when contributed.

Date	Account	Debit	Credit
1/1/X1	Cash	100,000	
	Land	300,000	
	Davis – Capital		100,000
	Williams – Capital		300,000
	To record partnership formation.		
1/3/X1	Cash	300,000	
	Land		300,000
	To record sale of land.		

PROBLEM 1-3: During the past year, Robin and Marion had the following activity in their capital accounts:

		Robin	Marion
Jan. 1	Capital Balance	$100,000	$60,000
April 1	Investment	20,000	
July 1	Investment		40,000
Sept. 1	Withdrawal	(30,000)	
Dec. 31	Withdrawal		(10,000)

Partnership income for the current year was $50,500. Robin and Marion share profits and losses in the ratio of 60% and 40% respectively after each partner is credited for 10% interest on average capital balances. Prepare a schedule showing the distribution of the partnership profit.

Answer: First, average capital balances must be determined for the purpose of calculating interest.

Robin

3 months × $100,000 =	$300,000
5 months × 120,000 =	600,000
4 months × 90,000 =	360,000
12 months	$1,260,000
	÷ 12 mos.
Average Capital Balance	$ 105,000

Marion

6 months × $ 60,000 =	$360,000
6 months × 100,000 =	600,000
12 months	$960,000
	÷ 12 mos.
Average Capital Balance	$ 80,000

		Partner	
		Robin (60%)	Marion (40%)
Partnership Income	$ 50,500		
Interest on average capital balances @ 10%	18,500	$10,500	$ 8,000
Balance in profit and loss ratio	32,000	19,200	12,800
Distribution	$ 50,500	$29,700	$20,800

PROBLEM 1-4: Assume the same facts as in Problem 1-3 except that partnership income for the current year was $30,000, Marion is entitled to a salary of $10,000 by partnership agreement, and Robin is entitled to a bonus of $8,000. Prepare a schedule showing the distribution of partnership profit.

Answer:

		Partner	
		Robin (60%)	Marion (40%)
Partnership Income	$ 30,000		
Interest on average capital balances @ 10%	18,500	$10,500	$ 8,000
Salary	10,000		10,000
Bonus	8,000	8,000	
Balance in profit and loss ratio	(6,500)	(3,900)	(2,600)
Distribution	$ 30,000	$14,600	$15,400

PROBLEM 1-5: Andrews, Sanford and Harris formed a partnership on January 1, 19X1 with the following cash investments:

Andrews	$ 50,000
Sanford	$100,000
Harris	$160,000

The partnership agreement specified the following profit distribution:

	Salary	Interest on Average Capital Balance	Excess over Salary and Interest
Andrews	$10,000	10%	30%
Sanford	8,000	10%	30%
Harris	6,000	10%	40%

Partnership net income for the year ended December 31, 19X1 was $80,000. Andrews invested an additional $40,000 on July 1, 19X1. Harris withdrew $25,000 on October 1, 19X1. Sanford withdrew $3,000 at the end of each month.

Prepare:

(*a*) a profit distribution schedule
(*b*) a journal entry to distribute profit
(*c*) a schedule showing December 31, 19X1 capital balances for each of the partners.

Answer:

(*a*)

		Partner		
		Andrews	Sanford	Harris
Partnership Income	$ 80,000			
Salary	24,000	$10,000	$ 8,000	$ 6,000
Interest (See Sched. 1)	30,725	7,000	8,350	15,375
Balance in profit and loss ratio	25,275	7,583	7,583	10,109
Distribution	$ 80,000	$24,583	$23,933	$31,484

Schedule 1
Partners' Average Capital Balances and Interest Determination

Andrews:

6 months × $50,000 =	$300,000			
6 months × $90,000 =	540,000			
12 months	$840,000			
	÷ 12 mo.			
Average Capital Balance	$70,000	×	10% =	$7,000 Interest

Sanford:

The balance began at $100,000 and was reduced $3,000 per month by draw. The average balance is based on ($100,000 + 97,000 + 94,000 + 91,000 + 88,000 + 85,000 + 82,000 + 79,000 + 76,000 + 73,000 + 70,000 + 67,000) divided by 12 months. That is $1,002,000 divided by 12 months for an Average Capital Balance of $83,500 × 10% = $8,350 Interest.

Harris:

9 months × $160,000 =	$1,440,000			
3 months × $135,000 =	405,000			
12 months	$1,845,000			
	÷ 12 mo.			
Average Capital Balance	$ 153,750	×	10% =	$15,375 Interest

(*b*)

Income Summary	80,000	
Andrews—Capital		24,583
Sanford—Capital		23,933
Harris—Capital		31,484
To record profit distribution.		

(*c*)

	Partner		
	Andrews	Sanford	Harris
1/1/X1 Capital Balance	$ 50,000	$100,000	$160,000
Add: Profit Distribution	24,583	23,933	31,484
Additional Investment	40,000	—	—
Deduct: Withdrawals	—	(36,000)*	(25,000)
12/31/X1 Capital Balance	$114,583	$ 87,933	$166,484

*12 months × $3,000/mo.

PROBLEM 1-6: Fred wants to purchase directly from the partners of the partnership of Larry, Bob, and Ray a 25% capital and profit and loss interest. The three partners each agree to sell 25% of their respective capital and profit and loss interests in exchange for a payment of $20,000 to each partner (that is, a total payment of $60,000 from Fred). Immediately before the admission of the new partner (Fred) the following situation existed:

	Capital Balances	Profit and Loss Ratios
Larry	$ 75,000	40%
Bob	$ 75,000	20%
Ray	$ 50,000	40%
	$200,000	

The partnership's net asset fair values and book values are equal. Assuming the partnership admits Fred using the goodwill method, prepare the journal entries to admit Fred and determine the partners' capital balances after admission of Fred.

Answer:

$60,000	=	25% Implied Value
$60,000/.25	=	Implied Value
$240,000	=	Implied Value

Implied Value of Business	240,000
Less: Fair Value of Business Net Assets (Book Value)	200,000
Goodwill	40,000

The entries to admit Fred under the goodwill method are:

Goodwill	40,000	
Larry – Capital		16,000
Bob – Capital		8,000
Ray – Capital		16,000

To record goodwill in the profit and loss ratio before admission of Fred.

Larry – Capital	22,750	
Bob – Capital	20,750	
Ray – Capital	16,500	
Fred – Capital		60,000

To record admission of Fred to the partnership (see schedule below for further explanation of charges to capital accounts of Larry, Bob, and Ray).

Schedule of Capital Balances After Admission of Fred

	Total Balance	Partner			
		Larry	Bob	Ray	Fred
Before Fred's admission	$200,000	$75,000	$75,000	$50,000	—
To record goodwill	40,000	16,000	8,000	16,000	
Subtotal	240,000	91,000	83,000	66,000	
To record sale of 25% interest to Fred	—	(22,750)	(20,750)	(16,500)	60,000
After Fred's admission	$240,000	$68,250	$62,250	$49,500	$60,000

Note that Fred's interest is 25% ($60,000 of $240,000).

PROBLEM 1-7: Assume the same facts as those shown in Problem 1-6 except that the bonus method is used. Prepare the journal entry to admit Fred and determine the partners' capital balances after admission of Fred.

Answer: Under the bonus method the implied value of the business is not used in developing the journal entry to admit Fred. The entry to admit Fred under the bonus method is:

Larry – Capital	18,750	
Bob – Capital	18,750	
Ray – Capital	12,500	
Fred – Capital		50,000
To admit Fred with a 25% interest.		

Schedule of Capital Balances After Admission of Fred

	Total Balance	Partner			
		Larry	Bob	Ray	Fred
Before Fred's admission	$200,000	$75,000	$75,000	$50,000	—
To record admission of Fred	—	(18,750)	(18,750)	(12,500)	$50,000
After Fred's admission	$200,000	$56,250	$56,250	$37,500	$50,000

Note that Fred's interest is 25% ($50,000 of $200,000).

PROBLEM 1-8: Mary wishes to purchase a 20% interest in the capital and profits and losses of the partnership of Moe, Larry, and Curley by investing $70,000 in the partnership. Immediately before the admission of Mary, the following capital balances and profit and loss rations existed:

	Capital Balances	Profit and Loss Ratios
Moe	$ 60,000	30%
Larry	$100,000	20%
Curley	$ 40,000	50%
	$200,000	

The partnership's net asset fair values and book values are equal. Not being financial stooges, the partnership of Moe, Larry, and Curley has developed goodwill in the marketplace. The partnership agrees to admit Mary and chooses to use the goodwill method of recording Mary's admission. Prepare the journal entries to admit Mary and a schedule of the partners' capital balances after admission.

Answer:

$$\$70{,}000 = 20\%\ \text{Implied Value}$$

$$\frac{70{,}000}{.2} = \text{Implied Value}$$

$$\$350{,}000 = \text{Implied Value}$$

Implied Value of Business	$350,000
Less: Fair Value of Business Net Assets (which includes the $70,000 Investment of Mary) after Mary's admission	270,000
Goodwill	$ 80,000

The entries to admit Mary under the goodwill method are:

	Debit	Credit
Goodwill	80,000	
Moe – Capital		24,000
Larry – Capital		16,000
Curley – Capital		40,000

To record goodwill in the profit and loss ratio before admission of Mary.

	Debit	Credit
Cash	70,000	
Mary – Capital		70,000

To record admission of Mary to the partnership.

Schedule of Capital Balances After Admission of Mary

		Partner			
	Total Balance	Moe	Larry	Curley	Mary
Before Mary's admission	$200,000	$60,000	$100,000	$40,000	—
To record goodwill	80,000	24,000	16,000	40,000	—
Subtotal	$280,000	$84,000	$116,000	$80,000	—
To record sale of 20% interest to Mary	70,000	--	--	--	70,000
After Mary's admission	$350,000	$84,000	$116,000	$80,000	$70,000

Note that Mary's interest is 20% ($70,000 of $350,000).

PROBLEM 1-9: Assume the same facts as those shown in Problem 1-8 except that the bonus method is used. Prepare the journal entry to admit Mary and a schedule of the partners' capital balances after Mary's admission.

Answer: Under the bonus method, the implied value of the business is not used in developing the entry to admit Mary. The entry to admit Mary under the bonus method is:

Cash	70,000	
Moe – Capital		4,800
Larry – Capital		3,200
Curley – Capital		8,000
Mary – Capital		54,000

To admit Mary with a 20% interest.

Schedule of Capital Balances After Admission of Mary

	Total Balance	Moe	Larry	Curley	Mary
		Partner			
Before Mary's admission	$200,000	$60,000	$100,000	$40,000	
To record admission of Mary	70,000	4,800	3,200	8,000	$54,000
After Mary's admission	$270,000	$64,800	$103,200	$48,000	$54,000

Note that Mary's interest is 20% ($54,000 of $270,000).

PROBLEM 1-10: The fair value of the net assets of the Irene, Joseph, and Vera partnership exceed the book value of the assets by $45,000 on 12/31/X1. The entire difference is attributable to land purchased by the partnership several years ago. The balance sheet of the partnership at 12/31/X1 shows the following:

Assets		Liabilities and Capital	
Cash	$ 60,000	Accounts payable	$ 20,000
Accounts receivable (net)	110,000	Loan payable—Vera	10,000
Land	80,000	Irene—Capital	50,000
		Joseph—Capital	90,000
		Vera—Capital	80,000
Total assets	$250,000	Total liabilities and capital	$250,000

Vera plans to retire and the partnership will, before Vera's retirement, formally recognize the appreciation in the value of the land in the accounts. The partnership shares profits and losses equally. The partnership pays Vera $120,000 to both retire Vera from the business and honor the loan payable. No goodwill is recorded upon retirement of Vera. Prepare all journal entries necessary to retire Vera.

Answer:

Land	45,000	
Irene – Capital		15,000
Joseph – Capital		15,000
Vera – Capital		15,000

To recognize appreciation in land in the profit and loss ratio before retirement of Vera.

Vera – Capital	95,000	
Loan payable – Vera	10,000	
Irene – Capital	7,500	
Joseph – Capital	7,500	
Cash		120,000

To retire Vera and honor all outstanding debt to Vera.

PROBLEM 1-11: Assume the same facts as those described in Problem 1-10 except that goodwill, if any, is recognized upon retirement of Vera. Prepare all journal entries necessary to retire Vera.

Answer:

	Debit	Credit
Land	45,000	
Irene – Capital		15,000
Joseph – Capital		15,000
Vera – Capital		15,000

To recognize appreciation in land in the profit and loss ratio before retirement of Vera.

	Debit	Credit
Goodwill	45,000	
Irene – Capital		15,000
Joseph – Capital		15,000
Vera – Capital		15,000

To record goodwill before retirement of Vera based on the following:

Total paid to Vera on retirement	$120,000
Less: Portion applicable to debt	10,000
Portion applicable to capital balance	110,000
Less: Capital balance before recognition of goodwill ($80,000 + $15,000)	95,000
Goodwill applicable to Vera	15,000
Divide: Vera's profit and loss ratio	33 1/3%
Total Goodwill	$ 45,000

	Debit	Credit
Vera – Capital	110,000	
Loan payable – Vera	10,000	
Cash		120,000

To retire Vera and honor all outstanding debt to Vera.

PARTNERSHIP LIQUIDATION

THIS CHAPTER IS ABOUT

☑ **Partnership Liquidation Procedures**
☑ **Lump Sum Liquidations**
☑ **Installment Liquidation**

2-1. Partnership Liquidation Procedures

The process of winding down the activities of a partnership, selling partnership assets, and paying off creditors and partners is known as **liquidation**. When a partnership liquidates, it sells its noncash assets and distributes available cash from liquidation to the partnership's creditors and partners. The specific order of cash distribution according to the Uniform Partnership Act (UPA) is:

1. Debts to creditors other than partners
2. Debts to partners
3. Partners' capital
4. Partners' profit

The last two categories (3 and 4) may simply be viewed as one category representing the partners' capital balances.

A special legal doctrine called **setoff** exists to avoid inequities in the liquidation process. Setoff essentially stipulates that loans receivable from partners and loans payable to partners may simply be treated as a part of the partners' capital balances, by adding or deducting the proper loan amount to each partner's capital account before the profits or losses from the sale of noncash assets of the partnership are distributed (according to the percentages stipulated in the partnership agreement).

EXAMPLE 2-1: Partners A and B decide to liquidate their business. At the date of liquidation, the partners have capital balances of $50,000 and $40,000, respectively. The partnership balance sheet also shows loans receivable from Partner A of $10,000, and loans payable to Partner B of $15,000.

According to the doctrine of setoff, Partner A's capital balance should be $40,000 ($50,000 balance less $10,000 loans due), because this represents A's true investment in the partnership at the time of liquidation. Partner B's capital balance should be $55,000 ($40,000 balance plus $15,000 loans owed).

The reason for the setoff doctrine is clear if we consider what would happen if the liquidation of the partnership resulted in a loss. If Partner B were to be paid the loan payable of $15,000 before any distribution to Partner A, and then the partnership sustained a loss of $100,000 on the sale of noncash assets in the liquidation process, then a portion of the loss would have to be distributed to both partners. If Partners A and B share profits and losses equally, then Partner B's capital balance after liquidation would be a debit balance (deficit) of $10,000 ($40,000 original balance less $50,000 loss). Partner A would have to absorb this deficit if Partner B was not personally able to contribute $10,000. If, however, the loan payable to Partner B is more equitably treated as an offset against Partner B's capital account, Partner B's capital account would not be a deficit but rather a credit balance of $5,000 ($40,000 original credit plus $15,000 loan payable credit less $50,000 loss debit).

2-2. Lump Sum Liquidation

In a **lump sum liquidation,** all the noncash assets of the partnership are sold at one time and all available cash is distributed in accordance with the UPA. Lump sum liquidation may result in:

- A sale of noncash assets at a gain
- A sale of noncash assets at a loss with no deficiencies in partners' capital accounts
- A sale of noncash assets at a loss with deficiencies in some or all partners' capital accounts

Examples 2-2 through 2-4 are based on the following trial balance at 12/31/X8, just before the lump sum partnership liquidation:

Account	Debit	Credit
Cash	$100,000	
Noncash assets	200,000	
Loan receivable—Partner A	40,000	
Accounts payable		$220,000
Loan payable—Partner C		20,000
A—Capital (30%)*		60,000
B—Capital (30%)*		10,000
C—Capital (40%)*		30,000
	$340,000	$340,000

*Profit-and-loss ratios

A. Sale of noncash assets at a gain.

To record the liquidation of a partnership when the noncash assets are sold at a gain, observe the following procedure:

1. Set off any outstanding loans to or from partners against their respective capital accounts.
2. Record the sale of the noncash assets, and apply the gain to the partners' capital accounts according to their profit-and-loss ratios.
3. Pay all the outside creditors.
4. Distributed the remaining cash to the partners to close their capital accounts.

EXAMPLE 2-2: The A, B, and C Partnership decides to liquidate, and sells all its noncash assets, which had a book value of $200,000, for $250,000, which results in a $50,000 gain.

To account for the lump sum liquidation of the ABC Partnership, set off the partners' loans receivable and payable against their respective capital accounts.

	Debit	Credit
Loan payable—Partner C	20,000	
A—Capital	40,000	
C—Capital		20,000
Loan receivable—Partner A		40,000
To record setoff of partners' loans.		

Next, record the sale of the noncash assets and apply the $50,000 gain to the partners' capital accounts according to the profit-and-loss ratios.

	Debit	Credit
Cash	250,000	
Noncash assets		200,000
A—Capital (30%)		15,000
B—Capital (30%)		15,000
C—Capital (40%)		20,000
To record sale of noncash assets.		

Next, record the payment of all the outside creditors.

Accounts payable	220,000	
Cash		220,000
To record payments of outside creditors.		

Finally, distribute the remaining cash to the partners to close their capital accounts.

A—Capital	35,000	
B—Capital	25,000	
C—Capital	70,000	
Cash		130,000
To record payments to partners.		

Exhibit 2-A is a Statement of Partnership Liquidation, showing the distribution of cash during the liquidation process.

Exhibit 2-A
A, B, and C Partnership
Statement of Partnership Liquidation December 31, 19X8

	Assets			Liabilities		Partners' Capital		
	Cash	Noncash	Receivable Partner A	Accounts Payable	Payable Partner C	A(30%)	B(30%)	C(40%)
Balances before liquidation	$100,000	$200,000	$40,000	$220,000	$20,000	$60,000	$10,000	$30,000
Setoff of partners' loans against capital balances			(40,000)		(20,000)	(40,000)		20,000
SUBTOTAL	100,000	200,000	0	220,000	0	20,000	10,000	50,000
Sale of assets and allocation of gain or loss	250,000	(200,000)				15,000	15,000	20,000
SUBTOTAL	350,000	0	0	220,000	0	35,000	25,000	70,000
Pay outside creditors	(220,000)			(220,000)				
SUBTOTAL	130,000	0	0	0	0	35,000	25,000	70,000
Pay partners	(130,000)					(35,000)	(25,000)	(70,000)
Balances after liquidation	$0	$0	$0	$0	$0	$0	$0	$0

B. Sale of noncash assets at a loss with no deficiencies in partners' capital accounts.

The procedure used to record the liquidation of a partnership when the noncash assets are sold at a loss, but none of the partners' capital accounts are deficient, is essentially the same as when the noncash assets are sold at a gain.

1. Set off any loans to or from partners against their capital accounts.
2. Record the sale of the noncash assets, and apply the loss to the partner's capital accounts according to their profit-and-loss ratios.
3. Pay all the outside creditors.
4. Distribute the remaining cash to the partners to close their capital accounts.

EXAMPLE 2-3: The A, B, and C Partnership decides to liquidate, and sells all its noncash assets, which had a book value of $200,000, for $170,000 which results in a $30,000 loss.

The journal entries to record this liquidation follow the same form as those shown in Example 2-2, with the following exception. The entry to record the sale of the noncash assets must show the loss of $30,000 applied to the partners' capital accounts in the profit-and-loss ratio, resulting in a decrease in the balances of those accounts.

Cash	170,000	
A—Capital	9,000	
B—Capital	9,000	
C—Capital	12,000	
Noncash assets		200,000
To record sale of noncash assets.		

Exhibit 2-B is a Statement of Partnership Liquidation, showing the distribution of cash during the liquidation process.

Exhibit 2-B
A, B, and C Partnership
Statement of Partnership Liquidation December 31, 19X8

	Assets			Liabilities		Partners' Capital		
	Cash	Noncash	Receivable Partner A	Accounts Payable	Payable Partner C	A(30%)	B(30%)	C(40%)
Balances before liquidation	$100,000	$200,000	$40,000	$220,000	$20,000	$60,000	$10,000	$30,000
Setoff of partners loans against capital balances			(40,000)		(20,000)	(40,000)		20,000
SUBTOTAL	100,000	200,000	0	220,000	0	20,000	10,000	50,000
Sale of assets and allocation of gain or loss*	170,000	(200,000)				(9,000)	(9,000)	(12,000)
SUBTOTAL	270,000	0	0	220,000	0	11,000	1,000	38,000
Pay outside creditors	(220,000)			(220,000)				
SUBTOTAL	50,000	0	0	0	0	11,000	1,000	38,000
Pay partners *	(50,000)					(11,000)	(1,000)	(38,000)
Balances after liquidation	$0	$0	$0	$0	$0	$0	$0	$0

* Results in journal entry.

C. Sale of noncash assets at a loss with deficiencies in some or all partners' capital accounts.

An extra step is necessary in the accounting process if one (or more) of the partners' capital accounts becomes deficient as a result of the loss taken on the sale of noncash assets during liquidation.

The procedure begins as usual. First, set off any outstanding loans to or from partners against their capital accounts. Next, record the sale of the noncash assets and allocate the loss to the partners' capital accounts according to their profit-and-loss ratios. It is at this point that you will observe the deficiency. Continue the regular process and pay all outside creditors. Before the remaining cash may be distributed, however, the debit balance in the deficient partner's account must be allocated to the accounts of the remaining partners, according to their remaining profit-and-loss ratios. (If possible, the deficient partner should contribute personal funds to the partnership, thereby eliminating the deficiency and the need for its allocation to the other partners.) Now distribute the remaining cash to the remaining partners.

EXAMPLE 2-4: The A, B, and C Partnership decides to liquidate, and sells all its noncash assets, which had a book value of $200,000, for $162,000, which results in a $38,000 loss.

The procedure to record this liquidation is the same as that followed in Example 2-3, except that distribution of the loss to the partners' capital accounts results in a deficit of $1,400 for Partner B ($10,000 original balance less 30% of $38,000, or $11,400, equals a deficit of $1,400). After paying outside creditors, B's deficit must be distributed among the remaining two partners before the final distribution of cash can be made. It is important to remember that the allocation of the $1,400 deficiency in Partner B's capital account must be based on the remaining profit-and-loss ratios of Partners A and C. Therefore, Partner A is charged 3/7 of $1,400, or $600, and Partner C is charged 4/7 of $1,400, or $800. Partners A and C now have claims of $600 and $800, respectively, against Partner B. In fact, if Partner B is solvent, he or she should contribute $1,400 cash to the partnership during the liquidation process, thereby eliminating the deficiency and the need for its allocation to Partners A and C.

The journal entry to record the allocation of B's deficit is:

A—Capital	600	
C—Capital	800	
B—Capital		1,400
To eliminate B's capital deficit.		

Exhibit 2-C is a Statement of Partnership Liquidation, showing the distribution of cash during the liquidation process.

Exhibit 2-C
A, B, and C Partnership
Statement of Partnership Liquidation December 31, 19X8

	Assets			Liabilities		Partners' Capital		
	Cash	Noncash	Receivable Partner A	Accounts Payable	Payable Partner C	A(30%)	B(30%)	C(40%)
Balances before liquidation	$100,000	$200,000	$40,000	$220,000	$20,000	$60,000	$10,000	$30,000
Setoff of partners' loans against capital balances*			(40,000)		(20,000)	(40,000)		20,000
SUBTOTAL	100,000	200,000	0	220,000	0	20,000	10,000	50,000
Sale of assets and allocation of gain or loss*	162,000	(200,000)				(11,400)	(11,400)	(15,200)
SUBTOTAL	262,000	0	0	220,000	0	8,600	(1,400)	34,800
Pay outside creditors*	(220,000)			(220,000)				
SUBTOTAL	42,000	0	0	0	0	8,600	(1,400)	34,800
Allocate deficiency*						(600)	1,400	(800)
SUBTOTAL	42,000	0	0	0	0	8,000	0	34,000
Pay partners*	(42,000)					(8,000)		(34,000)
Balances after liquidation	$0	$0	$0	$0	$0	$0	$0	$0

* Results in journal entry.

2-3. Installment Liquidation

In an installment liquidation, the noncash assets are not sold at one time. Rather, they are sold in stages. This presents an accounting problem in terms of distribution of cash as it becomes available; there is a lack of certainty regarding the ultimate cash receipts from the sales of noncash assets. After outside creditors are paid, distribution to partners after each installment sale of assets must be made carefully in an effort to avoid overpaying a partner to the point where that partner's remaining capital account balance would be too low to sustain an appropriate portion of potential loss on future installment sales of assets. To avoid this potential problem, only the "strongest" partner(s) should be paid first. The strongest partners are those with the greatest ability to sustain loss on installment sales. Therefore, the installment liquidation process must proceed as follows:

1. Rank partners in terms of their ability to sustain loss.
2. Prepare a maximum potential loss schedule
3. Prepare a cash distribution plan
4. As installment sales of assets take place, distribute cash to partners according to the cash distribution plan.

In Examples 2-5 through 2-8, refer to the following trial balance of the A, B, and C Partnership at 12/31/X8, just before its installment liquidation:

Account	Debit	Credit
Cash	100,000	
Noncash assets	200,000	
Loan receivable—Partner A	40,000	
Accounts payable		220,000
Loan payable—Partner C		20,000
A—Capital (30%)*		60,000
B—Capital (30%)*		10,000
C—Capital (40%)*		30,000
	340,000	340,000

*Profit and loss ratios.

A. Rank partners in terms of their ability to sustain loss.

To rank partners according to their ability to sustain loss, first adjust their capital accounts by setting off any outstanding loans to or from the partners. Next, determine each partner's maximum sustainable loss by dividing that partner's adjusted capital balance by his or her profit-and-loss ratio. Finally, rank the partners according to the amount of their maximum sustainable losses, from greatest to least.

EXAMPLE 2-5: To rank the partners of the A, B, and C Partnership in terms of the loss each is capable of sustaining during the installment liquidation of the partnership, first set off the loans to and from the partners to give their adjusted capital balances.

Partner	Balance	Loan		Adjusted Balance
A	$60,000	–$40,000	=	$20,000
B	10,000	0		10,000
C	30,000	+ 20,000	=	50,000

Next, determine the maximum sustainable loss for each partner by dividing his or her adjusted balance by the appropriate profit-and-loss ratio.

Partner	Adjusted Balance		Ratio		Sustainable Loss
A	$20,000	÷	30%	=	$ 66,667
B	10,000	÷	30%	=	33,333
C	50,000	÷	40%	=	125,000

Finally, rank the partners according to their sustainable losses, from greatest to least:

Partner	Sustainable Loss	Rank
A	$ 66,667	2
B	33,333	3
C	125,000	1

B. Prepare a maximum potential loss schedule.

A schedule must now be prepared that shows the greatest losses that the partnership can sustain on the sale of its noncash assets before each partner's capital account is depleted.

To prepare such a schedule, list the partners from weakest to strongest. Then enter the amount of loss that would be necessary to eliminate the weakest partner, and subtract the appropriate amounts from each partner's capital account (according to the profit-and-loss ratios). Repeat these steps with the next weakest partners. Note, however, that the amount needed to eliminate the next weakest partner will not be the same as the amount used to rank that partner earlier; this is because the weakest partner has been eliminated, and losses must now be sustained by only the remaining partners. Repeat the process until the amount of loss necessary to eliminate each remaining partner is entered in the schedule.

EXAMPLE 2-6: To prepare a maximum possible loss schedule for the A, B, and C Partnership, first rank the partners from weakest to strongest, and show their preliquidation capital balances (including any setoff):

		Capital Balance		
Partner/Rank	Maximum Loss to Eliminate	A (30%)	B (30%)	C (40%)
12/31/X8 Balance		$20,000	$10,000	$50,000
B/3				
A/2				
C/1				

Now enter the amount of total loss necessary to eliminate Partner B, and subtract the appropriate amounts from each partner's capital account:

		Capital Balance		
Partner/Rank	Maximum Loss to Eliminate	A (30%)	B (30%)	C (40%)
12/31/X8 Balance		$20,000	$10,000	$50,000
B/3	$33,333	(10,000)	(10,000)	(13,333)
		10,000	-0-	36,667
A/2				
C/1				

Repeat this step to eliminate Partner A. Note that the loss necessary to eliminate Partner A is not the same as the sustainable loss for Partner A in Example 2-5. This is because the loss to eliminate Partner A must now assume that Partner B is gone; therefore any remaining loss must be sustained solely by Partners A and C. Partner A now has a capital balance of $10,000, and will be charged 3/7 of any further loss. The maximum loss to eliminate Partner A is therefore $23,333 ($10,000 ÷ 3/7).

		Capital Balance		
Partner/Rank	Maximum Loss to Eliminate	A (30%)	B (30%)	C (40%)
12/31/X8 Balance		$20,000	$10,000	$50,000
B/3	$33,333	(10,000)	(10,000)	(13,333)
		10,000	-0-	36,667
A/2	23,000	(10,000)		(13,333)
		-0-		23,334
C/1				

Repeat this step to eliminate Partner C. The completed schedule looks like this:

Partner/Rank	Maximum Loss to Eliminate	Capital Balance A (30%)	B (30%)	C (40%)
12/31/X8 Balance		$20,000	$10,000	$50,000
B/3	$33,333	(10,000)	(10,000)	(13,333)
		10,000	-0-	36,667
A/2	23,000	(10,000)		(13,333)
		-0-		23,334
C/1	23,334			(23,334)
				-0-

C. Prepare a cash distribution plan.

A cash distribution plan must now be prepared to show how the proceeds from each installment of the sale of the partnership's noncash assets should be distributed to the partners. This plan is basically a reversal of the information developed in the maximum possible loss schedule, which is reasonable, because any sale of noncash assets negates some of the possible loss the partners can sustain before their capital balances are eliminated.

To prepare a cash distribution plan, list the amounts needed to eliminate each partner (found in the maximum possible loss schedule) in reverse order. These amounts are now considered amounts to be distributed to the partners as the cash becomes available from the installment sale of the noncash assets. Indicate also the portion of each amount each partner is entitled to receive (also a reversal of the information in the maximum possible loss schedule). Any amounts in addition to those accounted for in the cash distribution plan (i.e., gains realized on the sale of noncash assets) should be distributed to the partners according to the profit-and-loss ratio.

EXAMPLE 2-7: To prepare a cash distribution plan for the liquidation of the A, B, and C Partnership, first list the amounts necessary to eliminate each partner (from the maximum possible loss schedule) in reverse order. These are now the amounts to be paid out to the partners as cash become available from the sale of noncash assets. Next, indicate which portion of each amount each partner is entitled to. The completed schedule looks like this:

Cash Distribution Plan

		Partner A	B	C
First	$23,334			$23,334
Next	$23,333	$10,000		$13,333
Next	$33,333	$10,000	$10,000	$13,333

Any additional amounts are distributed in the profit-and-loss ratio.

D. Applying the cash distribution plan.

As installment sales of noncash assets take place, distribute the cash to partners in accordance with the cash distribution plan. Remember, should the cash received from later installments exceed the amounts listed in the plan (in other words, if the noncash assets are sold at a gain), those amounts should be distributed in the regular profit-and-loss ratio.

EXAMPLE 2-8: The noncash assets of the A, B, and C Partnership were sold in two installments:

Date of Sale	Selling Price	Noncash Asset Book Value
1/15/X9	$150,334	$170,334
4/15/X9	11,666	29,666
Totals	$162,000	$200,000

To account for the installment liquidation of the A, B, and C Partnership, first set off the loans payable to and receivable from partners against their capital accounts.

Loan payable—C	20,000	
A—Capital	40,000	
C—Capital		20,000
Loan receivable—A		40,000

Now the first installment sale takes place. It results in a loss of $20,000 ($150,334 selling price less the $170,334 book value). The loss is distributed to the partners according to their profit-and-loss ratios.

Cash	150,334	
A—Capital	6,000	
B—Capital	6,000	
C—Capital	8,000	
Noncash assets		170,334

Now the outside creditors are paid.

Accounts payable	220,000	
Cash		220,000

The remainder of the cash ($30,334) is now distributed to the partners according to the previously prepared cash distribution plan (Schedule I). Note that Partner B is not entitled to any distribution at this point.

Schedule I - Installment 1 to Partners per Plan (1/15/X9)

	Total	A	B	C
First	$23,334	–	–	$23,334
Next (3/7:4/7)	7,000	$ 3,000	–	4,000
Installment 1	$30,334	$ 3,000	–	$27,334

A—Capital	3,000	
C—Capital	27,334	
Cash		30,334

The second installment of the sale of noncash assets now takes place. It too results in a loss, this time of $18,000 ($11,666 selling price less the $29,666 book value). The second loss is distributed to the partners.

Cash	11,666	
A—Capital	5,400	
B—Capital	5,400	
C—Capital	7,200	
Noncash Assets		29,666

At this point the distribution of the loss results in a deficit of $1,400 for Partner B. This deficit must be allocated to the capital accounts of the other two partners, based on their remaining profit-and-loss ratios. Partner A, therefore, is charged 3/7 of $1,400, or $600. Partner C is charged 4/7 of $1,400, or $800. Of course, if Partner B is capable he or she should contribute $1,400 to the partnership, thereby eliminating the deficit and the need for its allocation to Partners A and C.

A—Capital	600	
B—Capital	800	
B—Capital		1,400

Finally, the remaining cash may be distributed to Partners A and C according to the cash distribution plan (Schedule II).

Schedule II - Installment 2 to Partners per Plan (4/15/X9)	Total	A	B	C
Next (3/7:4/7)	$11,666	$ 5,000	–	$ 6,666

	Debit	Credit
A—Capital	5,000	
C—Capital	6,666	
Cash		11,666

Exhibit 2-D is a Statement of Partnership Liquidation, showing the distribution of cash during the liquidation process.

Exhibit 2-D
A, B, and C Partnership
Statement of Partnership Liquidation
December 31, 19X8 through April 15, 19X9

	Assets			Liabilities		Partners' Capital		
	Cash	Noncash	Receivable Partner A	Accounts Payable	Payable Partner C	A(30%)	B(30%)	C(40%)
Balances before liquidation	$100,000	$200,000	$40,000	$220,000	$20,000	$60,000	$10,000	$30,000
Setoff of partners' loans against capital balances *			(40,000)		(20,000)	(40,000)		20,000
SUBTOTAL	100,000	200,000	0	220,000	0	20,000	10,000	50,000
Sale of assets and allocation of gain or loss 1/15/X9 *	150,334	(170,334)				(6,000)	(6,000)	(8,000)
SUBTOTAL	250,334	29,666	0	220,000	0	14,000	4,000	42,000
Pay outside creditors *	(220,000)			(220,000)				
SUBTOTAL	30,334	29,666	0	0	0	14,000	4,000	42,000
Instmt 1 to partners (see Schedule I) *	(30,334)					(3,000)		(27,334)
SUBTOTAL	0	29,666	0	0	0	11,000	4,000	14,666
Sale of assets and allocation of gain or loss 4/15/X9 *	11,666	(29,666)				(5,400)	(5,400)	(7,200)
SUBTOTAL	11,666	0	0	0	0	5,600	(1,400)	7,466
Allocation of Ptnr B's deficiency (3/7:4/7) *						(600)	1,400	(800)
SUBTOTAL	11,666	0	0	0	0	5,000	0	6,666
Instmt 2 to partners (see Schedule II) *	(11,666)					(5,000)		(6,666)
Balances after liquidation	$0	$0	$0	$0	$0	$0	$0	$0

* Results in journal entry.

E. Retaining cash for special reasons.

During the course of an installment liquidation, additional expenses, such as legal or accounting fees, may occur. These outlays may be charged to partners' capital accounts in the profit-and-loss ratio. Also, if these outlays are expected, distribution of cash to partners should be reduced and cash retained to meet these obligations as they arise.

EXAMPLE 2-9: The liquidation of the A, B, and C Partnership takes place as described in Example 2-8, except that the partners are informed that $3,500 in legal and accounting fees will become due on March 10, 19X9.

In this case the partners must be sure to retain enough cash to pay the obligation when it comes due. Although the cash balance is $30,334 just before the first installment to the partners on January 15, 19X9, only $26,834 is actually paid ($30,334 less $3,500 retained). The cash is distributed to Partners A and C on that date according to the cash distribution plan (Schedule I).

Schedule I - Installment 1

	Total	A	B	C
First	$23,334	–	–	$23,334
Next (3/7:4/7)	3,500	$ 1,500	–	2,000
	$26,834	$ 1,500	$0	$25,334

When the $3,500 is paid to creditors on March 10, 19X9, it is charged against the partners' capital accounts according to the profit-and-loss ratios.

A—Capital	1,050	
B—Capital	1,050	
C—Capital	1,400	
Cash		3,500

After this charge, B's capital account balance is $2,950 credit (original $10,000 less $6,000 offset less $1,050 loss). After the distribution of the loss on the second installment, B has a deficit of $2,450 ($2,950 less $5,400 loss). The allocation of this deficit is based on the remaining profit-and-loss ratios of Partners A and C. Therefore, Partner A is charged 3/7 of $2,450, or $1,050. Partner C is charged 4/7 of $2,450, or $1,400.

A—Capital	1,050	
C—Capital	1,400	
B—Capital		2,450

After the second installment sale on April 15, 19X9, the remaining cash is distributed to Partners A and C according to the cash distribution plan (Schedule II).

Schedule II - Installment 2

	Total	A	B	C
Next (3/7:4/7)	$11,666	$5,000	$0	$6,666

Exhibit 2-E is a Statement of Partnership Liquidation, showing the distribution of cash during the entire liquidation process.

Exhibit 2-E
A, B, and C Partnership
Statement of Partnership Liquidation
December 31, 19X8 through April 15, 19X9

	Assets			Liabilities		Partners' Capital		
	Cash	Noncash	Receivable Partner A	Accounts Payable	Payable Partner C	A(30%)	B(30%)	C(40%)
Balances before liquidation	$100,000	$200,000	$40,000	$220,000	$20,000	$60,000	$10,000	$30,000
Setoff of partners' loans against capital balances *			(40,000)		(20,000)	(40,000)		20,000
SUBTOTAL	100,000	200,000	0	220,000	0	20,000	10,000	50,000
Sale of assets and allocation of gain or loss 1/15/X9 *	150,334	(170,334)				(6,000)	(6,000)	(8,000)
SUBTOTAL	250,334	29,666	0	220,000	0	14,000	4,000	42,000
Pay outside creditors *	(220,000)			(220,000)				
SUBTOTAL	30,334	29,666	0	0	0	14,000	4,000	42,000
Instmt 1 to partners (see Schedule I) *	(26,834)					(1,500)		(25,334)
SUBTOTAL	3,500	29,666	0	0	0	12,500	4,000	16,666
Pay accounting and legal fees 3/10/X9 *	(3,500)					(1,050)	(1,050)	(1,400)
SUBTOTAL	0	29,666	0	0	0	11,450	2,950	15,266
Sale of assets and allocation of gain or loss 4/15/X9 *	11,666	(29,666)				(5,400)	(5,400)	(7,200)
SUBTOTAL	11,666	0	0	0	0	6,050	(2,450)	8,066
Allocation of Ptnr B's deficiency (3/7:4/7) *						(1,050)	2,450	(1,400)
SUBTOTAL	11,666	0	0	0	0	5,000	0	6,666
Instmt 2 to partners (see Schedule II) *	(11,666)					(5,000)		(6,666)
Balances after liquidation	$0	$0	$0	$0	$0	$0	$0	$0

* Results in journal entry.

note: The allocation of the $2,450 deficiency in Partner B's capital is based on the remaining profit and loss ratios of Partners A and C. Therefore, Partner A is charged 3/7 of $2,450 or $1,050 and Partner C is charged 4/7 of $2,450 or $1,400. Partners A and C have claims of $1,050 and $1,400 against Partner B. In fact, if Partner B is solvent, Partner B should contribute $2,450 cash to the partnership during the liquidation process, thereby eliminating the deficiency and the need for its allocation to Partners A and C.

RAISE YOUR GRADES

Can you explain . . . ?

☑ the order of cash distribution under the Uniform Partnership Act in a partnership liquidation

- ☑ the treatment of loans receivable from (or payable to) partners carried on the partnership's books in a liquidation process
- ☑ the lump sum liquidation process when noncash assets are sold at a gain, at a loss with no partner's capital balance becoming deficient, or at a loss with a partner's capital balance becoming deficient
- ☑ the installment liquidation process
- ☑ the need for a maximum possible loss schedule in an installment liquidation, and how this schedule is developed
- ☑ the need for a cash distribution plan as cash becomes available in an installment liquidation, and how this plan is developed

SUMMARY

1. The Uniform Partnership Act determines the order of cash distribution in liquidation essentially to be debts to outside creditors first and amounts due to partners (debt and equity) second.
2. The legal doctrine of setoff results in treating partners' loans as a part of capital in the liquidation process.
3. A lump sum liquidation involves the sale of noncash assets at one time, and immediate distribution of available cash to partners based on capital balances.
4. Gains and losses on asset sales are credited or charged to partners' capital account balances in the profit-and-loss ratio.
5. If the charge of a loss to a partner results in a capital account deficiency (debit balance), that partner should, if possible, contribute cash to the partnership to eliminate the deficiency.
6. If a partner is unable to contribute cash to remove a capital balance deficiency, this deficiency will be closed against *remaining* partners' capital balances in their *remaining* profit-and-loss ratios.
7. An installment liquidation involves the sale of noncash assets in installments rather than all at once.
8. Because a lack of certainty regarding the ultimate cash receipts on installment sales exists, a cash distribution plan must be developed to avoid overpayment (or inequitable payment) to any partner on an installment basis.
9. In its development, the cash distribution plan must involve ranking partners in terms of their ability to sustain loss, and recognition of the fact that partners most capable of sustaining loss are entitled to the earliest cash distributions.
10. Any cash outlays that result in an expense in the liquidation process are charged to partners' capital accounts in the profit-and-loss ratio.

RAPID REVIEW

1. The process of winding down partnership activities (selling partnership assets and paying creditors and partners the proceeds) is known as __________.
2. In a partnership liquidation the first party that should be paid cash as it becomes available is:
   (*a*) the "weakest" partner (that is, the partner least able to sustain losses on installment sales of assets).
   (*b*) the "strongest" partner (that is, the partner best able to sustain losses on installment sales of assets).
   (*c*) the partnership's creditors.
   (*d*) creditors of individual partners.

3. To avoid inequities during the liquidation process, partners' loan balances are treated as part of partners' capital balances. This procedure is referred to as the legal doctrine of __________.

4. In a partnership liquidation, gain or loss on noncash asset sales is credited or charged to partners' capital balances
   (*a*) on the basis of average capital balances of the partners for the year preceding the liquidation, according to the Uniform Partnership Act.
   (*b*) on the basis of year-end capital balances of the partners for the year, according to the Uniform Partnership Act.
   (*c*) on the basis of the profit-and-loss ratio of the partnership agreement, or if an agreement does not exist, equally according to the Uniform Partnership Act.
   (*d*) on the basis of the court's determination.

5. If a loss on the sale of assets occurs during a partnership installment liquidation, and this loss causes a partner's capital balance to be deficient (debit balance), then
   (*a*) the deficiency must be charged to the remaining partners in their remaining profit-and-loss ratios.
   (*b*) the deficient partner should contribute cash to the partnership to remove the deficiency and any need for its allocation to other partners.
   (*c*) the partnership need not take any action since the deficiency may be overcome in later installment sales at a gain.
   (*d*) the deficiency should be charged against remaining partners based on their capital balances at the time the deficiency on the asset sale occurs.

6. In an installment liquidation, the following events occur:
   W. A maximum possible loss schedule is prepared.
   X. Partners are ranked in terms of their ability to sustain loss during the liquidation.
   Y. A cash distribution plan is developed.
   Z. As cash becomes available it is distributed to the partnership's creditors and partners.

   Which of the following answer choices best lists these events in a chronological order?
   (*a*) WXYZ
   (*b*) ZYXW
   (*c*) XWYZ
   (*d*) YWXZ

7. The Tom, Jerry and Bill partnership had the following condensed balance sheet on February 20, 19X6:

Cash	$ 40,000	Liabilities (non-partner)	$ 70,000
Other assets	140,000	Tom—Capital (50%)*	50,000
		Jerry—Capital (30%)*	50,000
		Bill—Capital (20%)*	10,000
Total assets	$180,000	Total liabilities and capital	$180,000

*Profit and loss ratios

The partnership liquidated and sold its assets for $80,000. What journal entry is necessary to record the sale?

8. Based on the facts of Question 7, what journal entry is necessary to record the payment of amounts due to the partnership's creditors?

9. Based on the facts of Question 7, what journal entry is necessary to allocate the deficiency in Bill's capital account which has resulted from the sale of other assets at a loss?

10. Based on the facts of Question 7, what journal entry is necessary to distribute available cash to partners Tom and Jerry (after payment is made to creditors and partner Bill's capital deficiency is removed)?

Answers:

1. Liquidation.

2. (*c*) Partnership creditors must be paid first under the Uniform Partnership Act before any payment to partners.

3. Setoff.

4. (*c*) Gains and losses on asset sales are distributed in the profit-and-loss ratio of the partnership agreement. When the partnership agreement is silent regarding profits and losses, the Uniform Partnership Act states profits and losses are shared equally.

5. (*b*) Although answer choice "a" may be tempting, the ideal choice is "b" because this answer has the deficient partner contributing cash to the partnership to honor the deficiency. Even if a deficient partner's capital balance is charged against remaining partners' capital balances, remaining partners would still have a right to recover any charge made for the deficiency from the deficient partner.

6. (*c*) Note that this was the chronological order followed in Examples 2-5, 2-6, 2-7 and 2-8.

7.

Cash	80,000	
Tom—Capital	30,000	
Jerry—Capital	18,000	
Bill—Capital	12,000	
Other assets		140,000

To record sale of other assets and allocate the $60,000 loss in the profit and loss ratio.

8.

Liabilities	70,000	
Cash		70,000

To record payment of creditors.

Fred—Capital		15,000

To record receipt from partner to remove capital deficiency.

Mary—Capital	55,000	
Jane—Capital	65,000	
Cash		120,000

To record payment to partners in liquidation of partnership.

9. Note that Bill's capital balance is now deficient by $2,000 ($10,000 original balance less $12,000 loss charge).

Tom—Capital (5/8)	1,250	
Jerry—Capital (3/8)	750	
Bill—Capital		2,000

To record removal of Bill's deficiency.

10.

Tom—Capital	18,750	
Jerry—Capital	31,250	
Cash		50,000

To record distribution of available cash to partners.

SOLVED PROBLEMS

PROBLEM 2-1. The partnership of Fred, Mary, and Jane had the following condensed balance sheet on 6/30/X4:

Cash	$ 40,000
Noncash assets	300,000
Total assets	$340,000

Liabilities	$ 35,000
Fred—Capital	45,000
Mary—Capital	135,000
Jane—Capital	125,000
Total liabilities and capital	$340,000

Fred, Mary, and Jane share profits and losses in the ratio of 30%, 40%, 30% respectively. On 6/30/X4, the partners agreed to liquidate the partnership because they received an offer of $330,000 for the noncash assets. What journal entries are necessary to record the partnership liquidation, assuming the sale of the noncash assets?

Answer:

	Debit	Credit
Cash	330,000	
Noncash assets		300,000
Fred—Capital (30%)		9,000
Mary—Capital (40%)		12,000
Jane—Capital (30%)		9,000
To record sale of noncash assets.		
Liabilities	35,000	
Cash		35,000
To record payment of creditors.		
Fred—Capital	54,000	
Mary—Capital	147,000	
Jane—Capital	134,000	
Cash		335,000
To record payments to partners in liquidation of partnership.		

PROBLEM 2-2. Using the facts of Problem 2-1, assume that the partnership of Fred, Mary, and Jane received an offer of only $100,000 on 6/30/X4 for its noncash assets. Because the partnership had experienced continued losses in recent years, the partners decided to sell the business and avoid further loss. What journal entries are necessary to record the partnership liquidation, assuming Fred is personally insolvent?

Answer:

	Debit	Credit
Cash	100,000	
Fred—Capital (30%)	60,000	
Mary—Capital (40%)	80,000	
Jane—Capital (30%)	60,000	
Noncash assets		300,000
To record sale of noncash assets.		
Liabilities	35,000	
Cash		35,000
To record payment of creditors.		
Mary—Capital (40%)	8,571	
Jane—Capital (30%)	6,429	
Fred—Capital		15,000
To allocate Fred's capital deficiency against Mary and Jane capital.		
Mary—Capital	46,429	
Jane—Capital	58,571	
Cash		105,000
To record payment to partners in liquidation of partnership.		

PROBLEM 2-3. Using the facts of Problem 2-2, assume that Fred is personally solvent and will contribute cash to compensate the partnership for any capital deficiency that might develop in the liquidation process. What journal entries are necessary to record the partnership liquidation under these assumptions?

Answer:

	Debit	Credit
Cash	100,000	
Fred—Capital (30%)	60,000	
Mary—Capital (40%)	80,000	
Jane—Capital (30%)	60,000	
Noncash assets		300,000
To record sale of noncash assets.		
Liabilities	35,000	
Cash		35,000
To record payment of creditors.		
Cash	15,000	
Fred—Capital		15,000
To record receipt from partner to remove capital deficiency.		
Mary—Capital	55,000	
Jane—Capital	65,000	
Cash		120,000
To record payment to partners in liquidation of partnership.		

PROBLEM 2-4. The partnership of A, B, and C had the following balance sheet just before they decided to liquidate the business on 9/30/X7:

Assets	
Cash	$100,000
Loan receivable—Partner A	25,000
Noncash assets	360,000
Total assets	$485,000

Liabilities and Capital	
Accounts payable (outsiders)	$175,000
Loan payable—Partner C	45,000
A—Capital (50%)*	65,000
B—Capital (30%)*	150,000
C—Capital (20%)*	50,000
	$485,000

*Profit-and-loss sharing ratios.

Prepare a maximum possible loss schedule and a cash distribution plan in contemplation of liquidation.

Answer: First, rank the partners according to their ability to sustain loss.

	Adjusted Capital*		Profit and Loss Ratio		Sustainable Loss	Rank
Partner A	$ 40,000	÷	50%	=	$ 80,000	3
Partner B	$150,000	÷	30%	=	$500,000	1
Partner C	$ 95,000	÷	20%	=	$475,000	2

*Capital balance plus loans payable minus loans receivable.

Next, use this information to prepare the maximum possible loss schedule:

Maximum Possible Loss Schedule

	Partner Rank	Maximum Loss to Eliminate	Capital Balances (9/30/X7) A (50%)	B (30%)	C (20%)
9/30/X7 Bal.			$ 40,000	$150,000	$95,000
	A/3	$ 80,000	(40,000)	(24,000)	(16,000)
			0	126,000	79,000
	C/2	$197,500*		(118,500)	(79,000)
				7,500	0
	B/1	$ 7,500		(7,500)	
				0	

*Note that the loss to eliminate C is based on the assumption that any loss sustained after the elimination of A must be shared by B and C alone in a ratio of 3/5 and 2/5 respectively. Therefore:

$$2/5\ (\text{Loss}) = 79{,}000$$
$$(\text{Loss}) = 79{,}000 \times 5/2$$
$$(\text{Loss}) = 197{,}500$$

Finally, use the information developed in the maximum possible loss schedule to develop the cash distribution plan:

Cash Distribution Plan

		Partner A	B	C
First	$ 7,500		$ 7,500	
Next	$197,500		$118,500	$ 79,000
Next	$ 80,000	$ 40,000	$ 24,000	$ 16,000

Any additional amounts are distributed in the profit-and-loss ratio.

PROBLEM 2-5. Using the facts of Problem 2-4, assume that the A, B, and C partnership liquidates as follows:

Date of Sale	Selling Price	Noncash Asset Book Value
10/27/X7	$170,000	$160,000
12/15/X7	90,000	200,000
Totals	$260,000	$360,000

Also assume that Partner A is not personally solvent. Prepare a Statement of Partnership Liquidation for the A, B, and C Partnership.

Answer:

A, B, and C Partnerships
Statement of Partnership Liquidation
September 30, 19X7 through December 15, 19X7

	Assets			Liabilities		Partners' Capital		
	Cash	Noncash	Receivable Partner A	Accounts Payable	Payable Partner C	A(30%)	B(30%)	C(40%)
Balances before liquidation	$100,000	$360,000	$25,000	$175,000	$45,000	$65,000	$150,000	$50,000
Setoff of partners' loans against capital balances *			(25,000)		(45,000)	(25,000)		45,000
SUBTOTAL	100,000	360,000	0	175,000	0	40,000	150,000	95,000
Sale of assets and allocation of gain or loss 10/27/X7 *	170,000	(160,000)				5,000	3,000	2,000
SUBTOTAL	270,000	200,000	0	175,000	0	45,000	153,000	97,000
Pay outside creditors *	(175,000)			(175,000)				
SUBTOTAL	95,000	200,000	0	0	0	45,000	153,000	97,000
Instmt 1 to partners (see Schedule I) *	(95,000)						(60,000)	(35,000)
SUBTOTAL	0	200,000	0	0	0	45,000	93,000	62,000
Sale of assets and allocation of gain or loss 12/15/X7 *	90,000	(200,000)				(55,000)	(33,000)	(22,000)
SUBTOTAL	90,000	0	0	0	0	(10,000)	60,000	40,000
Allocation of Ptnr A's deficiency (3/5:2/5) *						10,000	(6,000)	(4,000)
SUBTOTAL	90,000	0	0	0	0	0	54,000	36,000
Instmt 2 to partners (see Schedule II) *	(90,000)						(54,000)	(36,000)
Balances after liquidation	$0	$0	$0	$0	$0	$0	$0	$0

* Results in journal entry

***note*:** The allocation of the $10,000 deficiency in Partner A's capital is based on the remaining profit-and-loss ratios of Partners B and C.

Schedule I - Installment 1 to Partners per Plan

	Total	A	B	C
First	$ 7,500	—	$ 7,500	—
Next (3/5:2/5)	87,500	—	52,500	$ 35,000
Installment 1	$ 95,000	—	$ 60,000	$ 35,000

Schedule II - Installment 2 to Partners per Plan

	Total	A	B	C
Next (3/5:2/5)	$90,000	—	$54,000	$ 36,000

PROBLEM 2-6. Prepare a partnership liquidation for the A, B, and C Partnership using the facts of Problem 2-5, except now assume the following constraining factors:

- After the first installment sale, the partnership estimates it will sustain $10,000 in liquidation expenses. For this reason, the partnership does not distribute the full $95,000 available to partners, but instead retains $10,000.

- At the time the second installment payment is made (12/15X7), the partnership actually sustains and pays $7,500 in liquidation expenses.

Answer: The liquidation schedule used in answer to Problem 2-5 may now be used again with only minor adjustments. The first installment will involve distribution to partners of $85,000 ($95,000 available less retention of $10,000 in anticipated liquidation expenses). Schedule I will now appear as follows:

Schedule I - Installment 1 to Partners per Plan

	Total	A	B	C
First	$ 7,500	—	$ 7,500	—
Next (3/5:2/5)	77,500	—	46,500	$ 31,000
Installment 1	$ 85,000	—	$ 54,000	$ 31,000

The second installment will involve distribution to partners of $92,500 ($10,000 cash balance after Installment 1, plus $90,000 proceeds on 12/15/X7 sale of noncash assets, less $7,500 in liquidation expenses).

Schedule II - Installment 2 to Partners per Plan

	Total	A	B	C
Next (3/5:2/5)	$92,500	—	$55,500	$ 37,000

A, B, and C Partnership
Statement of Partnership Liquidation
September 30, 19X7 through December 15, 19X7

	Assets			Liabilities		Partners' Capital		
	Cash	Noncash	Receivable Partner A	Accounts Payable	Payable Partner C	A(50%)	B(30%)	C(20%)
Balances before liquidation	$100,000	$360,000	$25,000	$175,000	$45,000	$65,000	$150,000	$50,000
Setoff of partners' loans against capital balances *			(25,000)		(45,000)	(25,000)		45,000
SUBTOTAL	100,000	360,000	0	175,000	0	40,000	150,000	95,000
Sale of assets and allocation of gain or loss 10/27/X7*	170,000	(160,000)				5,000	3,000	2,000
SUBTOTAL	270,000	200,000	0	175,000	0	45,000	153,000	97,000
Pay outside creditors*	(175,000)			(175,000)				
SUBTOTAL	95,000	200,000	0	0	0	45,000	153,000	97,000
Instmt 1 to partners (see Schedule I)*	(85,000)						(54,000)	(31,000)
SUBTOTAL	10,000	200,000	0	0	0	45,000	99,000	66,000
Sale of assets and allocation of loss 12/15/X7*	90,000	(200,000)				(55,000)	(33,000)	(22,000)
Pay liquidation expenses *	(7,500)					(3,750)	(2,250)	(1,500)
SUBTOTAL	92,500	0	0	0	0	(13,750)	63,750	42,500
Allocation of Ptnr A deficiency (3/5:2/5)*						13,750	(8,250)	(5,500)
SUBTOTAL	92,500	0	0	0	0	0	55,500	37,000
Instmt 2 to partners (see Schedule II) *	(92,500)						(55,500)	(37,000)
Balances after liquidation	$0	$0	$0	$0	$0	$0	$0	$0

* Results in journal entry.

***note*:** The allocation of the $13,750 deficiency in Partner A's capital is based on the remaining profit-and-loss ratios of Partners B and C.

PROBLEM 2-7. What journal entries are necessary to record the liquidation of the A, B, C Partnership of Problem 2-6?

Answer:

Account	Debit	Credit
Loan payable—Partner C	45,000	
Partner A—Capital	25,000	
Partner C—Capital		45,000
Loan receivable—Partner A		25,000
To record setoff of partners' loan balances.		
Cash	170,000	
Noncash assets		160,000
Partner A—Capital (50%)		5,000
Partner B—Capital (30%)		3,000
Partner C—Capital (20%)		2,000
To record 10/27/X7 noncash asset sale.		
Accounts payable	175,000	
Cash		175,000
To record payment of partnership debt.		
Partner B—Capital	54,000	
Partner C—Capital	31,000	
Cash		85,000
To record first installment payment to partners.		
Cash	90,000	
Partner A—Capital (50%)	55,000	
Partner B—Capital (30%)	33,000	
Partner C—Capital (20%)	22,000	
Noncash assets		200,000
To record 12/15/X7 sale of noncash assets.		
Partner A—Capital (50%)	3,750	
Partner B—Capital (30%)	2,250	
Partner C—Capital (20%)	1,500	
Cash		7,500
To record payment of liquidation expenses.		
Partner B—Capital	8,250	
Partner C—Capital	5,500	
Partner A—Capital		13,750
To record allocation of deficiency in Partner A's capital to partners B and C in their remaining profit-and-loss ratios.		
Partner B—Capital	55,500	
Partner C—Capital	37,000	
Cash		92,500
To record second installment payment to partners.		

3 HOME AND BRANCH OFFICE ACCOUNTING

THIS CHAPTER IS ABOUT

☑ **Characteristics of Branch Operations**
☑ **General Accounting for Home and Branch Offices**

3-1. Characteristics of Branch Operations

When an existing business sees an opportunity to expand the current market, or to create a new market, for its goods or services, it may establish a branch office to concentrate on that new market. The branch office may be located across town or on the other side of the country, wherever the new market is perceived to be. The main activity of a branch office is thus to increase sales for the business as a whole. Although not a separate legal entity, the branch office usually functions as a fairly autonomous unit, and maintains the accounts related to its sales, inventory, receivables, payables, and expenses. The branch may, however, leave certain activities common to the entire company (for instance, production or payroll) to the home office.

Another organizational form that may be used to capture the new market is the **agency**. An agency is a separate office that provides samples of the company's products, or descriptions of the company's services, for the purpose of developing sales orders for the company. Unlike the true branch office, however, the agency usually does not approve or fill the orders it generates; this remains a centrally controlled function of the home office.

In practice, of course, the degree of independence or control maintained by the home office over the branch office or agency is a matter of the company's management policy, and may result in many hybrid forms of branch operation: agencies that maintain their own accounts receivable, branches that must have approved by the home office's credit department, and so on. In this chapter the word branch will also refer to an agency or one of the hybrid forms, as appropriate.

Whatever its exact organizational from, a branch office's operations may be accounted for separately either because it is more convenient to keep separate (decentralized) record (because the branch operates at some distance from the home office), or because a determination of the branch's profit or loss is desired, or both.

A. Branch accounting uses control accounts.

Home and branch accounting is essentially an application of the controlling account principle, where one **control account** represents the combination of several **subsidiary records**. In this case the subsidiary records are those accounts maintained independently by the branch office.

When establishing a branch office the home office must create a special control account called **Branch Control** (or Investment in Branch, or something similar). Likewise, the branch office must create a special control account called **Home Office Control** (or something similar). As the home office transfers cash or other assets to the branch office, the home office must charge its Branch Control account for the resources transferred. The branch office in return should credit its Home Office Control account for the resources received. If the home office pays any branch office expenses, the home office should reduce its expenses by charging its Branch Control account. Likewise, the branch office would charge its expenses and credit its Home Office Control account.

In short, at any point in time, the Branch Office Control account and the Home Office Control account should have equal balances (generally a debit balance in the Branch Control account because this account represents the home office's investment in the branch, and a credit balance in the Home Office Control account because this account represents the branch office's equity).

At the end of the year or any other accounting period, the branch office's profit or loss is closed to its Home Office Control account, because a branch office has no separate retained earnings of its own. The home office then treats the branch office's operational net income (or loss) as an increase (or decrease) in its Branch Control account.

The unique aspects of branch accounting involve the transfer of assets from one office to another. It is important to note that the control accounts do not record actual assets or equity, but merely the transfers made between the offices. In fact, when combined financial statements are prepared to show the home and branch offices considered together, the control accounts are eliminated during the combining process.

B. Combined financial statements require eliminating entries.

At the end of a given accounting period standard financial statements must be prepared that show the performance of the **combined business entity** (the home and branch offices). A single figure showing the branch's net income or loss is generally not adequate for a thorough analysis of the company's performance. Therefore, combined financial statements are prepared to show the entire range of branch office as well as home office operations. These combined statements, however, do not include the control accounts for each office. In order to prevent net assets from being counted twice, the Home Office Control and Branch Office Control accounts are removed by the use of **eliminating entries** during the preparation of combined financial statements. Eliminating entries are made only in the working papers used to prepare the financial statements for the combined business entity; they are never made on the separate books of either the home or branch office.

To make the eliminations of home and branch control accounts,working papers are prepared with columns for the home office, the branch office, the eliminations, and the combined totals:

Account	Home office		Branch office		Eliminations		Combined	
Name	Dr.	Cr.	Dr.	Cr.	Dr.	Cr.	Dr.	Cr.

For every intracompany transfer of assets recorded in the columns of the home or branch office, make the appropriate entry in the eliminations column to eliminate that amount from the combined column. It is customary to add a note explaining why the elimination was made:

Account	Home office		Branch office		Eliminations		Combined	
Name	Dr.	Cr.	Dr.	Cr.	Dr.	Cr.	Dr.	Cr.
Cash	100,000		5,000				105,000	
Branch Control	10,000					10,000[1]		
Home Control				10,000	10,000[1]			
Receivables	20,000		10,000				30,000	
Etc.								

[1]To eliminate Branch Control and Home Control accounts.

3-2. General Accounting for Home and Branch Offices

The bulk of day-to-day accounting in either the home or branch office is the same as it is for any individual business entity. As implied above, the unique aspect of accounting in home and branch offices is the intracompany transfer of assets from one branch to another. This may mean, in addition to the transfer of cash, the shipment of goods for use or sale from the home office to the branch office. In such a case the home office may charge the branch office a transfer price that is either at cost or above cost.

The accounting for such transfers of goods from the home office will vary depending on whether the company as a whole uses the periodic inventory system or the perpetual inventory system to account for such material.

Under the periodic inventory method, the Inventory account balance is determined by a physical count at the end of the accounting period. Intracompany sales are recorded in the home office's books in an account called Shipments to Branch Office, and in the branch's books as Shipments from Home Office. Like the control accounts, these shipment accounts must be eliminated at the end of the accounting period. No entries are made in the Inventory account at the time of shipment. The periodic system works best for companies with large numbers of relatively inexpensive merchandise, like grocery stores.

On the other hand, when using the perpetual inventory system the cost of each item in the inventory is deducted from the Inventory account and debited to the Cost of Goods Sold account as the item is sold, resulting in an up-to-the-minute, or perpetual Inventory account balance. No shipment or purchase accounts are used to record the intracompany inventory transfers. The perpetual system works best with relatively expensive items, such as cars or refrigerators, the cost of which can be easily determined.

In Examples 3-1 through 3-6, assume that the Raven Company established a branch office operation on January 1, 19X1. During the year 19X1, the following transactions took place:

1. The home office transferred $12,000 to the branch office for branch operations.
2. The home office shipped inventory costing $40,000 to the branch office.
3. The branch office purchased additional inventory at a cost of $7,000 from outside vendors on account.
4. The branch office had total sales during the year of $150,000, and all sales were credit sales.
5. The branch collected $140,000 on its sales.
6. The branch drew a check for $20,000 to buy equipment.
7. The branch paid outside vendors $6,000 on account.
8. The home office paid $11,000 in operating expenses (selling, general, and administrative) for the branch office.
9. The branch recorded depreciation expense of $2,000 on the equipment it purchased.
10. The branch office remitted $80,000 to the home office.
11. The branch office closed its books at the end of year 19X1.

note: The December 31, 19X1 physical inventory for Raven Company is $15,000 for the branch office and $30,000 for the home office.

A. Intracompany transfers at cost (periodic inventory system).

When a home office ships goods to its branch, the home office charges its Branch Office Control account for the shipment. If the home office charges the branch at its cost for the goods, there is no "profit" for the home office, and the transfer is simply recorded on the books of each office in the appropriate shipment account, which is eliminated during the preparation of the combined financial statements at the end of the accounting period.

EXAMPLE 3-1: The Raven Company home office charged the branch office at cost for the shipments of inventory it made (see entry 2 above). The Raven Company uses the periodic inventory system.

The journal entries for the year 19X1, for both the home and branch offices, make use of the control accounts, but are otherwise the same as those for any business.

Home Office Books

	Account	Debit	Credit
(1)	Branch office control	12,000	
	Cash		12,000
(2)	Branch office control	40,000	
	Shipments to branch office		40,000
(8)	Branch office control	11,000	
	Operating expenses		11,000
(10)	Cash	80,000	
	Branch office control		80,000
(11)	Branch office control	105,000	
	Branch income		105,000

(Branch Income and Shipments to branch office accounts are closed to retained earnings.)

Branch Office Books

	Account	Debit	Credit
(1)	Cash	12,000	
	Home Office Control		12,000
(2)	Shipments from home office	40,000	
	Home office control		40,000
(3)	Purchases	7,000	
	Accounts payable		7,000
(4)	Accounts receivable	150,000	
	Sales		150,000
(5)	Cash	140,000	
	Accounts receivable		140,000
(6)	Property, plant and equipment	20,000	
	Cash		20,000
(7)	Accounts payable	6,000	
	Cash		6,000
(8)	Operating expenses	11,000	
	Home office control		11,000
(9)	Operating expenses	2,000	
	Accum. deprec.		2,000
(10)	Home office control	80,000	
	Cash		80,000
(11)	Inventory	15,000	
	Sales	150,000	
	Shipments from home office		40,000
	Purchases		7,000
	Operating expenses		13,000
	Home office control		105,000

Note that the balance in the Branch Office Control account ($88,000 debit) equals the balance in the Home Office Control account ($88,000 credit). On December 31, 19X1, Raven Company prepares basic financial statements. To facilitate preparation of these statements a worksheet is used which includes a column for entries to eliminate the Home Office and Branch Office Control accounts, as well as any other intracompany accounts. Remember that these eliminating entries are made only on the worksheet; they are not made on the books of the home or branch office.

Exhibit 3-A shows the eliminating worksheet for Raven Company on December 31, 19X1, before the branch's books are closed for the year. Note that because of this the Branch Office Control account balance and the Home Office control account balance differ in this preclosing trial balance. After the branch office closes its $105,000 net income to the Home Office Control account, the Home Office Control account debit balance of $17,000 will become a credit balance of $88,000. The home office is presumed to have already recognized the branch income of $105,000, as shown in the trial balance.

Exhibit 3-A
12/31/X1 Trial Balances (Preclosing)

Account	Home Office Debit	Home Office Credit	Branch Office Debit	Branch Office Credit	Eliminations Debit	Eliminations Credit	Income Statement Dr.(Cr.)	Retained Earnings Dr.(Cr.)	Balance Sheet Dr.(Cr.)
Cash	100,000		46,000						146,000
Accounts receiv.	70,000		10,000						80,000
Inventory (1/1)	40,000		0				40,000		
Property, plant, & equip.	300,000		20,000						320,000
Accum. deprec.		100,000		2,000					(102,000)
Branch off. control	88,000					88,000[1]			0
Accounts payable		50,000		1,000					(51,000)
Home off. control			17,000			17,000[1]			0
Common stock		160,000							(160,000)
Retained earnings (1/1)		83,000						(83,000)	
Sales		200,000		150,000			(350,000)		
Purchases	100,000		7,000				107,000		
Operating exp.	40,000		13,000				53,000		
Shipments from home office			40,000			40,000[2]	0		
Shipments to branch office		40,000			40,000[2]		0		
Branch income		105,000			105,000[1]		0		
Totals	$738,000	738,000	153,000	153,000	145,000	145,000			
Inventory (12/31) (see entry #11)	30,000		15,000				(45,000)		45,000
Net income							(195,000)	(195,000)	
Retained earnings (12/31)								(278,000)	(278,000)
Total.									0

[1] To eliminate Home Office Control and Branch Office Control accounts and intracompany income.
[2] To eliminate shipments from home office to branch office.

B. Intracompany transfers above cost (periodic inventory system).

When the home office ships goods to the branch office at a cost above what it paid for them, the home office clearly makes a profit on that shipment. That profit, however, cannot be realized by the company as a whole until the goods are sold by the branch. The intracompany profit is therefore considered **deferred**. When such an intracompany transfer above cost is debited to the Branch control account, the actual cost of the goods transferred is credited to the Shipments to Branch account, and the difference is credited to a Deferred Profit account. The percentage of the profit should be determined and noted.

At the end of the accounting period the physical inventory will yield the Inventory account balance for the branch office. The percentage of the deferred profit is then applied to that Inventory account balance, revealing how much of the original deferred profit still remains in the branch's unsold inventory. That remaining deferred profit, subtracted from the original deferred profit, gives the realized profit on the intracompany transfer above cost. That amount should then be debited to the home office's Deferred Profit account, and credited to its Branch Income account.

The deferred profit, both the realized portion and the remaining portion in the unsold branch inventory, must also be eliminated when combined financial statements are prepared, because the true profit really comes from, and is counted as part of, the branch's sales.

EXAMPLE 3-2: The home office of Raven Company shipped merchandise costing $40,000 to its branch office, but billed the branch $50,000 for this shipment. The Raven Company uses the periodic inventory system.

To find the amount of the deferred profit, simply subtract the actual cost of the merchandise from the price at which it was billed:

$$\$50,000 - \$40,000 = \$10,000$$

Then determine the percentage of profit as usual:

$$\$10,000 \div \$50,000 = 20\% \text{ profit on sale}$$

The journal entries to record this transfer are:

Home Office Books			Branch Office Books		
(2) Branch office control	50,000		(2) Shipments from home office	50,000	
Shipments to branch office		40,000	Home office control		50,000
Deferred profit		10,000			

At the end of the year a physical count of the branch's inventory places its cost at $15,000. But if all this inventory came from the home office, we know that the true cost of the inventory is $12,000, and that $3,000 represents the deferred profit:

$$\$15,000 \times 20\% \text{ profit percentage} = \$3,000 \text{ deferred profit}$$

The home office's original deferred profit, less the deferred profit remaining in the branch's ending inventory, yields the home office's realized profit, which is reflected in the Branch Income account:

$$\$10,000 - \$3,000 = \$7,000 \text{ realized profit}$$

The journal entries to record these end-of-year determinations are:

Home Office Books			Branch Office Books		
(11) Branch office control	95,000		(11) Inventory	15,000	
Branch income		95,000	Sales	150,000	
			Shipments from home office		50,000
Deferred profit	7,000				
Branch income		7,000	Purchases		7,000
			Operating expenses		13,000
			Home office control		95,000

Exhibit 3-B shows the eliminating worksheet for Raven Company on December 31, 19X1, before the branch's books are closed for the year. Note that because of this the Branch Office Control account balance and the Home Office control account balance differ in this preclosing trail balance. After the branch office closes its $95,000 net income to the Home Office Control account, the Home Office Control account debit balance of $7,000 will become a credit balance of $88,000. The home office is presumed to have already recognized the branch income of $102,000 ($95,000 plus $7,000 from deferred profit), as shown in the trial balance.

Exhibit 3-B
12/31/X1 Trial Balances (Preclosing)

	Home Office		Branch Office		Eliminations		Income Statement	Retained Earnings	Balance Sheet
Account Name	Debit	Credit	Debit	Credit	Debit	Credit	Dr.(Cr.)	Dr.(Cr.)	Dr.(Cr.)
Cash	100,000		46,000						146,000
Accts receiv.	70,000		10,000						80,000
Inventory (1/1)	40,000		0				40,000		
Property, plant, & equipment	300,000		20,000						320,000
Accum. deprec.		100,000		2,000					(102,000)
Branch office control	88,000					88,000[1]			0
Accounts payable		50,000		1,000					(51,000)
Home office control			7,000			7,000[1]			0
Common stock		160,000							(160,000)
Retained earnings (1/1)		83,000						(83,000)	
Sales		200,000		150,000			(350,000)		
Purchases	100,000		7,000				107,000		
Operating expenses	40,000		13,000				53,000		
Shipments from home office			50,000			50,000[2]	0		
Shipments to branch office		40,000			40,000[2]			0	
Branch income		102,000			102,000[1]				
Deferred profit.		3,000			10,000[2]	7,000[1]			0
Totals	738,000	738,000	153,000	153,000	152,000	152,000			
Inventory (12/31) (see entry #11)	30,000		12,000				(42,000)		42,000
Net income							(192,000)	(192,000)	
Retained earnings (12/31)								(275,000)	(275,000)
Total									0

[1]To eliminate Home Office Control and Branch Office Control accounts and intracompany income, including deferred gross profit included in the home office account "Branch income."
[2]To eliminate shipments from home office to branch office, including deferred profits.

C. Deferred profits in beginning inventory (periodic inventory system).

Deferred profits that remain in inventory at the end of one accounting period are, of course, lodged in the beginning inventory for the next accounting period. When that inventory is sold in the new accounting period, the home office may realize the remaining deferred profit in that inventory.

EXAMPLE 3-3: What will happen next year (19X2) relative to the profits remaining in the year-end 12/31/X1 branch office inventory? These profits will, of course, become profits lodged in 1/1/X2 beginning inventory. In order to see how these beginning inventory profits are accounted for, refer to the information from Example 3-2. For the sake of simplicity, assume that during the year 19X2 the only activity for Raven Company was:

Home Office Entries			Branch Office Entries		
			(1) Accounts receivable	20,000	
			Sales		20,000
			Sold all of the beginning inventory.		
			(2) Operating expenses	2,000	
			Accum. depreciation		2,000
			To record depreciation of equipment.		
			(3) Sales	20,000	
			Operating expenses		2,000
			Inventory (1/1)		15,000
			Home Office control		3,000
			To close branch office books at 12/31/X2.		
(4) Branch office control	3,000				
Branch Income		3,000			
(5) Deferred profit	3,000				
Branch Income		3,000			
(The deferred profit relates to inventory which has been sold and may now be recognized. Recall that this deferred profit 20% of $15,000 in year-end 12/31/X1 inventory.)					
(Branch income of $6,000 is closed to retained earnings.)					

Excluding entry (3), ending account balances in the home and branch office records which will require worksheet elimination at the end of year X2 are:

Home Office Books

Branch office control

	Debit	Credit
12/31/X1 Balance	88,000	
Entry #4, Year X2	3,000	
12/31/X2	91,000	

Branch income

	Debit	Credit
Entry #4, Year X2		3,000
Entry #5, Year X2		3,000
12/31/X2 Balance		6,000 (before closing)

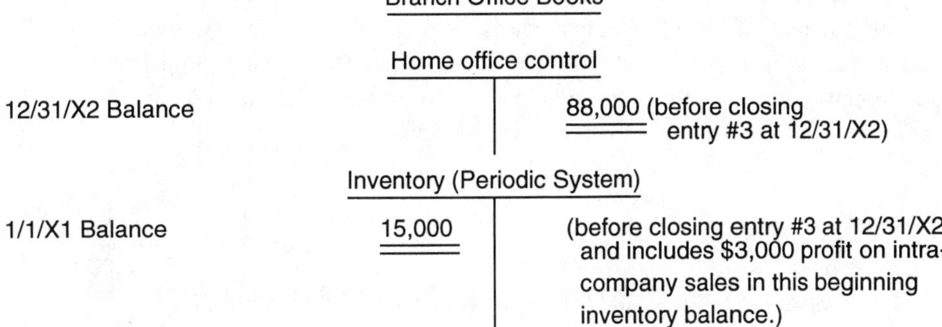

Branch Office Books

Home office control

	Debit	Credit
12/31/X2 Balance		88,000 (before closing entry #3 at 12/31/X2)

Inventory (Periodic System)

	Debit	Credit
1/1/X1 Balance	15,000	(before closing entry #3 at 12/31/X2 and includes $3,000 profit on intra-company sales in this beginning inventory balance.)

The 12/31/X2 worksheet elimination entry required based on these account balances is:

Branch office income	6,000	
Home office control	88,000	
Inventory (1/1)		3,000
Branch office control		91,000

A partial worksheet at 12/31/X2 showing relevant account balances and the elimination entry just described follows.

12/31/X1 Selected Trial Balance Accounts (Preclosing)

	Home Office		Branch Office		Eliminations		Combined Totals
Account Name	Debit	Credit	Debit	Credit	Debit	Credit	Dr.(Cr.)
Branch office control	91,000					91,000	0
Branch income		6,000			6,000		0
Home office control				88,000	88,000		0
Inventory (1/1)			15,000			3,000	12,000*

* Note that beginning inventory, which will become a part of cost of goods sold, is correctly shown in the combined total column for Raven Company at cost at 12/31/X2.

D. Intracompany transfers at cost (perpetual inventory system).

Recall that under the periodic inventory system the balance of the Inventory account is based on a physical count at the end of the accounting period. Under the perpetual inventory system, however, the Inventory account balance changes with every purchase or sale of merchandise. As a result, there is no need for a Purchases account; as merchandise is purchased its cost is charged directly to Inventory. Each sale (or shipment) of merchandise requires two entries: one to reduce the Inventory account and charge the Cost of Goods Sold account, and a second to record the sale and increase the Cash or Accounts Receivable account.

When an intracompany sale takes place at cost and the firm uses the perpetual inventory system, the home office debits its Branch Office Control account and credits its Inventory account for the amount of the goods transferred. The branch office then debits its Inventory account and credits its Home Office Control account for the same amount. As each branch office sale is made, Cash or Accounts Receivable is debited and Sales credited, as usual. But, in addition, Cost of Goods Sold is debited and Inventory is credited at the appropriate cost. No eliminations are necessary at the end of the accounting period to remove the effects of this type of transfer at cost. (Of course, the Control accounts must still be eliminated.)

EXAMPLE 3-4: The Raven Company home office charged the branch office at cost ($40,000) for shipments of inventory it made. The Raven Company uses the perpetual inventory system.

Under the perpetual inventory system, the charges for the intracompany purchases taking place at cost are made directly to the Inventory accounts (as shown in entry 2 below), as are any purchases of merchandise from outside vendors (as shown in entry 3 below).

Home Office Books			Branch Office Books		
(1) Branch office control	12,000		(1) Cash	12,000	
Cash		12,000	Home office control		12,000
(2) Branch office control	40,000		(2) Inventory	40,000	
Inventory		40,000	Home office control		40,000
			(3) Inventory	7,000	
			Accounts payable		7,000

Each sale then requires two entries: one to record the sale and another to adjust the Inventory and Cost of Goods Sold accounts. In entry 4 below, the cost of goods sold for the year 19X1 ($32,000) is determined and recorded ($40,000 from entry 2 plus $7,000 from entry 3 less the ending inventory of $15,000 taken from the perpetual records and usually verified by a year-end count).

Branch Office Books		
(4) Accounts receivable	150,000	
Sales		150,000
Cost of goods sold	32,000	
Inventory		32,000

In the final entries, then, the Cost of Goods Sold, rather than Shipments from Home Office or Purchases, is credited against the year's sales, giving the net profit on sales (shown in Home Office Control).

Home Office Books			Branch Office Books		
(11) Branch office control	105,000		(11) Sales	150,000	
Branch income		105,000	Cost of goods sold		32,000
(Branch income is closed to retained earnings.)			Operating expenses		13,000
			Home office control		105,000

Exhibit 3-D shows the eliminating worksheet for Raven Company on December 31, 19X1, before the branch's books are closed for the year. Note that because of this the Branch Office Control account balance and the Home Office control account balance differ in this preclosing trail balance. After the branch office closes its $105,000 net income to the Home Office Control account. The Home Office Control account debit balance of $17,000 will become a credit balance of $88,000. The home office is presumed to have already recognized the branch income of $105,000, as shown in the trial balance. The home office's cost of goods sold includes:

1/1/X1	Inventory	$ 40,000
Plus:	Purchases	100,000
Less:	Shipments to branch office	(40,000)
	12/31/X1 Inventory	(30,000)
		$ 70,000

Exhibit 3-D
12/31/X1 Trial Balances (Preclosing)

	Home Office		Branch Office		Eliminations		Income Statement	Retained Earnings	Balance Sheet
Account Name	Debit	Credit	Debit	Credit	Debit	Credit	Dr.(Cr.)	Dr.(Cr.)	Dr.(Cr.)
Cash	100,000		46,000						146,000
Accts receiv.	70,000		10,000						80,000
Inventory (12/31)	30,000		15,000						45,000
Property, plant, & equipment	300,000		20,000						320,000
Accum. deprec.		100,000		2,000					(102,000)
Branch office control	88,000					88,000*			0
Accounts payable		50,000		1,000					(51,000)
Home office control			17,000			17,000*			0
Common stock		160,000							(160,000)
Retained earnings (1/1)		83,000						(83,000)	
Sales		200,000		150,000			(350,000)		
Cost of goods sold	70,000		32,000				102,000		
Operating expenses	40,000		13,000				53,000		
Branch income		105,000			105,000*				
Totals	698,000	698,000	153,000	153,000	105,000	105,000			
				Net income			(195,000)	(195,000)	
				Retained earnings (12/31)				(278,000)	(278,000)
				Total					0

* To eliminate Home Office Control and Branch Office Control accounts and intracompany income.

E. Intracompany sales above cost (perpetual inventory system).

If an intracompany sale is made above cost in a company using the perpetual inventory system, the general accounting procedure is a combination of those demonstrated in Examples 3-2 and 3-4.

First use Inventory and Cost of Goods Sold accounts, rather than Purchases and Shipment accounts, and make two entries for each sale (see Example 3-4). Then, use a Deferred Profit account to record the home office's profit on the sale (see Example 3-2.).

EXAMPLE 3-5: The home office of the Raven Company shipped merchandise costing $40,000 to its branch office, but billed the branch $50,000 for the shipment. The Raven Company uses the perpetual inventory system.

As it was in Example 3-2, the deferred profit for the home office is $10,000, representing a 20 percent profit on the sale. The journal entries for this transfer, when using the perpetual inventory system, show the use of Inventory rather than Shipment accounts. Purchases from outside vendors are also charged to inventory (as shown in entry 3 below).

Home Office Books			Branch Office Books		
(2) Branch office control	50,000		(2) Inventory	50,000	
Inventory		40,000	Home office control		50,000
Deferred profit		10,000	(3) Inventory	7,000	
			Accounts payable		7,000

Two entries are necessary to record the branch office's sales. First, Accounts Receivable is debited, and Sales is credited. Next, Cost of Goods is increased and the Inventory is decreased. The cost of the goods sold for the year 19X1 ($42,000) is determined and recorded ($50,000 from entry 2 plus $7,000 from entry 3 less the ending inventory of $15,000, which is taken from the perpetual records and usually verified by a year-end count).

Branch Office Books		
(4) Accounts receivable	150,000	
Sales		150,000
Cost of goods sold	42,000	
Inventory		42,000

In the year-end entries, the branch office's Cost of Goods Sold, rather than Shipments from Home Office or Purchases, is credited against the year's sales (along with operating expenses), giving the net income (reported in the Home Office Control account) without the need for a physical inventory. Also, the home office's original deferred profit ($10,000) less the deferred profit left in branch's ending inventory ($3,000) yields the home office's realized profit ($7,000), which is reported as a part of the Branch Income account.

Home Office Books			Branch Office Books		
(11) Branch office control	95,000		(11) Sales	150,000	
Branch income		95,000	Cost of goods sold		42,000
			Operating expenses		13,000
Deferred profit	7,000		Home office control		95,000
Branch income		7,000			

Exhibit 3-E shows the eliminating worksheet for Raven Company on December 31, 19X1, before the branch's books are closed for the year. Note that because of this the Branch Office Control account balance and the Home Office control account balance differ in this preclosing trail balance. After the branch office closes its $95,000 net income to the Home Office Control account, the Home Office Control account debit balance of $7,000 will become a credit balance of $88,000. The home office is presumed to have already recognized the branch income of $102,000 ($95,000 net income plus $7,000 realized profit on intracompany sales), as shown in the trial balance. The home office's cost of goods sold includes:

1/1/X1	Inventory	$ 40,000
Plus:	Purchases	100,000
Less:	Shipments to branch office	(40,000)
	12/31/X1 Inventory	(30,000)
		$ 70,000

Exhibit 3-E
12/31/X1 Trial Balances (Preclosing)

	Home Office		Branch Office		Eliminations		Income Statement	Retained Earnings	Balance Sheet
Account Name	Debit	Credit	Debit	Credit	Debit	Credit	Dr.(Cr.)	Dr.(Cr.)	Dr.(Cr.)
Cash	100,000		46,000						146,000
Accts receiv.	70,000		10,000						80,000
Inventory (12/31)	30,000		15,000			3,000[2]			42,000
Property, plant, & equipment	300,000		20,000						320,000
Accum. deprec.		100,000		2,000					(102,000)
Branch office control	88,000					88,000[1]			0
Accounts payable		50,000		1,000					(51,000)
Home office control			7,000			7,000[1]			0
Common stock		160,000							(160,000)
Retained earnings (1/1)		83,000						(83,000)	
Sales		200,000		150,000			(350,000)		
Cost of goods sold	70,000		42,000			7,000[2]	105,000		
Operating expenses	40,000		13,000				53,000		
Branch1 income		102,000			102,000[1]		0		
Deferred profit		3,000			10,000	7,000[1]			0
Totals	698,000	698,000	153,000	153,000	112,000	112,000			
				Net income			(192,000)	(192,000)	
				Retained earnings (12/31)				(275,000)	(275,000)
				Total					0

[1]To eliminate Home Office Control and Branch Office Control accounts and intracompany income.
[2]To eliminate original $10,000 deferred profit against Cost of Goods Sold and ending inventory.

F. Deferred profits in beginning inventory (perpetual inventory system).

Deferred profits that remain in inventory at the end of one accounting period are, of course, lodged in the beginning inventory for the next accounting period.

EXAMPLE 3-6: What will happen next year (19X2) relative to the profits remaining in the year-end 12/31/X1 branch inventory (when a perpetual inventory system is used)? These profits will, of course, become profits lodged in 1/1/X2 beginning inventory. In order to see how these beginning inventory profits are accounted for, refer to the information in the previous Example 3-5. Suppose for the sake of simplicity that during year 19X2 the only branch and home office activity was:

Home Office Entries			Branch Office Entries		
			(1) Accounts receivable	20,000	
			Sales		20,000
			Cost of goods sold	15,000	
			Inventory		15,000
			Sold all of the beginning inventory.		
			(2) Operating expenses	2,000	
			Accum. depreciation		2,000
			To record depreciation of equipment.		
			(3) Sales	20,000	
			Cost of goods sold		15,000
			Operating expenses		2,000
			Home Office control		3,000
			To close branch office books at 12/31/X2.		
(4) Branch office control	3,000				
Branch Income		3,000			
(5) Deferred profit	3,000				
Branch Income		3,000			
(The deferred profit now relates to inventory which has been sold and may now be recognized.)					
(Branch income of $6,000 is closed to retained earnings.)					

Excluding entry #3, ending account balances in the home and branch office records which will require worksheet elimination at the end of year X2 are:

Home Office Books

Branch office control

	Debit	Credit
12/31/X1 Balance	88,000	
Entry #4, Year X2	3,000	
12/31/X2	91,000	

Branch income

	Debit	Credit
Entry #4, Year X2		3,000
Entry #5, Year X2		3,000
12/31/X2 Balance		6,000 (before closing)

Branch Office Books

Home office control

	Debit	Credit
12/31/X1 Balance		88,000 (before closing

The 12/31/X2 *worksheet elimination entry* required based on these account balances is:

Branch office income	6,000	
Home office control	88,000	
Cost of goods sold		3,000
Branch office control		91,000

A partial worksheet at 12/31/X2 showing relevant account balances and the elimination entry just described follows.

Exhibit 3-F
12/31/X1 Selected Trial Balance Accounts (Preclosing)

Account Name	Home Office Debit	Home Office Credit	Branch Office Debit	Branch Office Credit	Eliminations Debit	Eliminations Credit	Combined Totals Dr.(Cr.)
Branch office control	91,000					91,000	0
Branch income		6,000			6,000		0
Home office control				88,000	88,000		0
Cost of goods sold			15,000			3,000	12,000

* Note that cost of goods sold by the branch office is correctly shown in the combined total column for Raven Company at cost at 12/31/X2.

G. Interbranch transactions.

A company may have a home office and more than one branch office, and consequently transfers of the types discussed in this chapter may take place between the branches. These **interbranch transfers** should be recorded as such on the books of each branch involved, using Interbranch Receivable, Interbranch Payable, Shipments to Branch, and Shipments from Branch accounts.

All interbranch transfers must be eliminated when the combined financial statements for the entire company are prepared as follows:

EXAMPLE 3-7: Branch Y transfers inventory costing $3,000 to Branch Z on 12/31/X1. The company uses the periodic inventory system.

Record the interbranch transfer on the books of both branches involved using the appropriate accounts.

Branch Y Books			Branch Z Books		
Interbranch receivable—Z	3,000		Shipments from branch Y	3,000	
Shipments to branch Z		3,000	Interbranch payable—Y		3,000

On the worksheet to prepare combined financial statements for the whole company, make the entries to eliminate the shipment of inventory and the amounts receivable and payable. Note that when Branch Z pays Branch Y for the shipment (sometime during the year 19X2) the balance of the Receivable and Payable accounts will change, and the dollar amount of the interbranch eliminations will consequently change at the end of that accounting period.

12/31/X1 Worksheet Elimination Entries		
Shipments to branch Z	3,000	
Shipments from branch Y		3,000
Interbranch payable—Y	3,000	
Interbranch receivable—Z		3,000

RAISE YOUR GRADES

Can you explain . . . ?

- ☑ the function of a branch office operation
- ☑ the function of an agency operation
- ☑ the purpose of accounts such as Branch Office Control (Investment in Branch) and Home Office Control

- ☑ the reason for elimination of the Home Office Control and Branch Office Control accounts when preparing combined corporate financial statements
- ☑ general accounting for branch operations which use periodic inventory systems and buy goods at cost from the home office
- ☑ general accounting for branch operations which use periodic inventory systems and buy goods above cost from the home office
- ☑ general accounting for branch operations which use perpetual inventory systems and buy goods at cost from the home office
- ☑ general accounting for branch operations which use perpetual inventory systems and buy goods above cost from the home office
- ☑ general accounting for interbranch transfers of goods

SUMMARY

1. Branch office operations expand a business's ability to attract new markets by providing products or services at locations other than the home office.
2. Agency operations are offices that provide samples of products or services for the purpose of the generation of sales to be filled by the home office.
3. Separate (decentralized) accounting records are often necessary to account for branch operations for the purpose of measuring branch profitability and because branches may operate at some distance from the home office.
4. The home office establishes an account on its books called Branch Office Control (Branch Office or Investment in Branch) which shows the home office's investment in branch office operations at any balance sheet date.
5. The branch office establishes an account on its books called Home Office Control (Home Office) which represents the equity position of the branch office at any balance sheet date.
6. The Home Office Control and Branch Office Control accounts should have equal balances or, at least, have reconcilable differences at any point.
7. The Home Office Control and Branch Office Control accounts should be eliminated at the time a worksheet is prepared for the purpose of combining home and branch operations into a single set of financial statements showing the performance of the whole company.
8. If a periodic inventory system is used, an eliminating worksheet entry is also needed each period to eliminate the Shipments from the Home Office account on branch books against the Shipments to Branch account on home office books.
9. If a perpetual inventory system is used, no Shipment accounts will exist, because all inventory movement results in entries against the Inventory account.
10. If the home office transfers inventory to the branch office at a price above home office cost, the home office must establish a Deferred Profit account at the time of transfer because no real (outside) sale has occurred. (As the branch office sells this inventory to outsiders, the home office's Deferred Profit account is charged and its Branch Income account is credited.)
11. The home office's Deferred Profit account must also be eliminated when combined financial statements are prepared.
12. Interbranch transactions may also occur, and must also be eliminated when combined statements are prepared.

RAPID REVIEW

1. Which of the following accounts must be eliminated when combining home and branch office records?
   (*a*) Mortgage Payable
   (*b*) Common Stock
   (*c*) Shipments to Branch Office
   (*d*) Cash
2. Which of the following accounts represents the investment of the home office in branch operations?
   (*a*) Branch Office Control
   (*b*) Home Office Control
   (*c*) Branch Income
   (*d*) Retained Earnings and Common Stock
3. If the home office is able to transfer inventory to a branch office at a price above the home office cost, the home office generates a profit on the sale which, in turn, enhances the company's overall profits.
   (*a*) True
   (*b*) False
4. A branch office closes its Revenues and Expenses at year end to:
   (*a*) Retained Earnings
   (*b*) Branch Office Control
   (*c*) Home Office Control
   (*d*) Inventory
5. Which of the following accounts represents the equity of a branch office?
   (*a*) Branch Office Control
   (*b*) Home Office Control
   (*c*) Branch Income
   (*d*) Retained Earnings and Common Stock
6. A home office billed a branch office $60,000 for inventory, which represents a 20% markup on cost. The deferred profit the home office must record on the transfer is $__________.
7. Using the facts from item 6 and assuming that at year-end only $15,000 remains in ending inventory at the branch office from these intercompany sales, deferred profit which must be removed from the ending inventory when preparing combined financial statements is $__________.
8. A home office billed a branch office $60,000 for inventory, which represents a 20% gross profit on sales. The deferred profit the home office must record on the transfer is $__________.
9. The accounts Shipment to Branch and Shipments from Home Office exist in which of the following situations:
   (*a*) periodic inventory system in use
   (*b*) perpetual inventory system in use
   (*c*) may exist when either periodic or perpetual system in use
10. An outlying location which takes sales orders for the home office which ultimately approves and fills the orders is known as a(an) __________.

Answers

1. (*c*) (See Example 3-1.)
2. (*a*) (See Examples 3-1 through 3-6.)
3. (*b*) False. The "profit" generated on the transfer is not a real profit because no outside sale has actually occurred. It is merely a deferred profit, which will be eliminated when combined financial statements are prepared.
4. (*c*) (See Examples 3-1 and 3-4.)
5. (*b*) (See Examples 3-1 through 3-6.)

6. $10,000. 120% Cost = $60,000
Cost = $60,000/120%
Cost = $50,000
Profit on sale = $10,000 ($60,000 – $50,000)

7. $ 2,500. 120% Cost = $15,000
Cost = $15,000/120%
Cost = $12,500
Profit in ending inventory = $2,500 ($15,000 – $12,500)

8. $12,000. 20% × Selling Price
= 20% × $60,000 = $12,000 profit on sale

9. (*a*) (See Examples 3-1, 3-2, 3-4, and 3-5.)

10. agency.

SOLVED PROBLEMS

PROBLEM 3-1. On January 2, 19X7, the Davis Company opened the Crispy Branch and shipped inventory to Crispy charging $200,000. Eighty percent of this inventory was sold by the branch during 19X7, for $250,000. Crispy's operating expenses for 19X7 were $40,000. Based on this information, determine the following:

(*a*) net income according to branch books assuming the home office inventory transfer was at cost.

(*b*) net income according to branch books assuming the home office inventory transfer includes gross profit of 10% on sales.

(*c*) journal entries required to record branch income on home office books, assuming gross profit of 10% on sales.

Answer:

(*a*)

Sales	$250,000
Cost of goods sold (80% × $200,000)	160,000
Gross profit	90,000
Operating expenses	40,000
Net income	$ 50,000

(*b*) The answer is still $50,000 net income *according to branch books*. If the question asked for net income from branch operations included in the Davis Company's combined income statement then the answer would differ because, on a corporate basis, cost of goods sold is actually below $160,000 (see answer to part C).

(*c*)

Branch office control	50,000	
Branch income		50,000
Deferred profit	16,000	
Branch income		16,000

10% × Cost of goods sold
= 10% × $160,000
= $16,000 gross profit included in cost of goods sold by branch.

Note that the branch income is actually $66,000 ($50,000 + $16,000). From the David Company viewpoint, the branch income is seen as follows:

Sales	$250,000
Cost of goods sold*	144,000
Gross profit	106,000
Operating expenses	40,000
Net income	$ 66,000

*Branch cost of goods sold	$160,000
Less: Profit included in this cost of goods sold at 10%	16,000
Actual cost of goods sold	$144,000

PROBLEM 3-2. The following information is available regarding the transfer of inventory from the home office to the branch office:

- Transfer price $ 60,000
- Cost to home office $ 50,000

(*a*) Prepare journal entries to record the transfer on home office and branch books assuming a periodic inventory system is used.
(*b*) Prepare journal entries to record the transfer on home office and branch books assuming a perpetual inventory system is used.

Answer:

	Home Office Books			Branch Office Books		
(*a*)	Branch office control	60,000		Shipments from home office	60,000	
	Shipments to branch office		50,000	Home office control		60,000
	Deferred profit		10,000			
(*b*)	Branch office control	60,000		Inventory	60,000	
	Inventory		50,000	Home office control		60,000
	Deferred profit		10,000			

Note that in any event the balance in the branch office control and home office control accounts remain equal.

PROBLEM 3-3. On July 1, 19X5, the Henley Company opened the Ajax branch office and the following transactions took place during fiscal year ending June 30, 19X6:

(*a*) The home office sent $45,000 in cash to Ajax.
(*b*) The home office shipped inventory to Ajax and billed $60,000, which equals home office cost.
(*c*) Ajax purchased $15,000 of inventory from outside vendors on account.
(*d*) Credit sales of Ajax for the period were $130,000.
(*e*) Ajax collected $100,000 on account during the year.
(*f*) Ajax incurred and paid operating expenses of $27,000 (this excludes depreciation).
(*g*) Henley Company paid $6,000 in operating expenses for Ajax.
(*h*) Ajax paid $11,000 for inventory purchased on account.
(*i*) Ajax remitted $52,000 to Henley during the year.
(*j*) Ajax purchased equipment for $10,000 cash.
(*k*) The depreciation charge on Ajax's equipment for the year was $2,500.
(*l*) Ajax's ending inventory on 6/30/X6 was $8,000, all of which was purchased from the home office.

Prepare all necessary journal entries (including branch office closing entry) to record these transactions on both home office and branch office books. Henley and Ajax use a periodic inventory system.

Answer:

Home Office Books

		Debit	Credit
(*a*)	Branch office control	45,000	
	Cash		45,000
(*b*)	Branch office control	60,000	
	Shipments to branch office		60,000
(*g*)	Branch office control	6,000	
	Operating expenses		6,000
(*i*)	Cash	52,000	
	Branch office control		52,000
(*l*)	Branch office control	27,500	
	Branch income		27,500

(Branch Income and Shipments to Branch are closed to Retained Earnings.)

Branch Office Books

		Debit	Credit
(*a*)	Cash	45,000	
	Home office control		45,000
(*b*)	Shipments from home office	60,000	
	Home office control		60,000
(*c*)	Purchases	15,000	
	Accounts payable		15,000
(*d*)	Accts. Receivable	130,000	
	Sales		130,000
(*e*)	Cash	100,000	
	Accts. Receivable		100,000
(*f*)	Operating expenses	27,000	
	Cash		27,000
(*g*)	Operating expenses	6,000	
	Home office control		6,000
(*h*)	Accts. Payable	11,000	
	Cash		11,000
(*i*)	Home office control	52,000	
	Cash		52,000
(*j*)	Property, plant, and equipment	10,000	
	Cash		10,000
(*k*)	Operating expenses	2,500	
	Accum. deprec.		2,500
(*l*)	Inventory	8,000	
	Sales	130,000	
	Purchases		15,000
	Operating expenses		35,500
	Shipments from home office		60,000
	Home office control		27,500

PROBLEM 3-4. Based on the information provided in Problem 3-3, prepare all necessary journal entries (including the branch office closing entry) to record the transactions on both home and branch books, assuming Henley and Ajax use a perpetual inventory system.

Answer:

Home Office Books			Branch Office Books		
(*a*) Branch office control	45,000		(*a*) Cash	45,000	
Cash		45,000	Home office control		45,000
(*b*) Branch office control	60,000		(*b*) Inventory	60,000	
Inventory		60,000	Home office control		60,000
			(*c*) Inventory	15,000	
			Accounts payable		15,000
			(*d*) Accts. Receivable	130,000	
			Sales		130,000
			Cost of goods sold	67,000	
			Inventory		67,000

Note:

7/2/X5 Inventory	$ 0
Purchases:	
Outside	15,000
From home office	60,000
Available for sale	75,000
Less: 6/30/X6 Inventory	8,000
Cost of goods sold	$67,000

Home Office Books			Branch Office Books		
			(*e*) Cash	100,000	
			Accts. Receivable		100,000
			(*f*) Operating expenses	27,000	
			Cash		27,000
(*g*) Branch office control	6,000		(*g*) Operating expenses	6,000	
Operating expenses		6,000	Home office control		6,000
			(*h*) Accts. Payable	11,000	
			Cash		11,000
(*i*) Cash	52,000		(*i*) Home office control	52,000	
Branch office control		52,000	Cash		52,000
			(*j*) Property, plant, and equipment	10,000	
			Cash		10,000
			(*k*) Operating expenses	2,500	
			Accum. deprec.		2,500
(*l*) Branch office control	27,500		(*l*) Sales	130,000	
Branch income		27,500	Cost of goods sold		67,000
			Operating expenses		35,500
			Home office control		27,500

(Branch Income is closed to retained earnings.)

PROBLEM 3-5. You are presented with the following June 30, 19X6 preclosing trial balance for Henley Company (home office) and its Ajax branch office. This trial balance assumes all the information included in Problem 3-3 (that is, the company uses a periodic inventory system). Complete this worksheet, including the columns for elimination entries, income statement, retained earnings, and balance sheet.

6/30/X6 Trial Balances (Preclosing)

	Home Office		Branch Office		Eliminations		Income Statement	Retained Earnings	Balance Sheet
Account Name	Debit	Credit	Debit	Credit	Debit	Credit	Dr.(Cr.)	Dr.(Cr.)	Dr.(Cr.)
Cash	57,000		45,000						
Accts receiv.	92,000		30,000						
Inventory 7/1/X5	50,000		0						
Property, plant, & equipment	350,000		10,000						
Accum. deprec.		50,000		2,500					
Branch office control	86,500								
Accounts payable		42,000		4,000					
Home office control				59,000					
Common stock		125,000							
Retained earnings (7/1/X5)		271,000							
Sales		225,000		130,000					
Purchases	120,000		15,000						
Operating expenses	45,000		35,500						
Shipments from home office			60,000						
Shipments to branch office		60,000							
Branch income		27,500							
Totals	800,500	800,500	195,500	195,500					
Inventory as of 6/30/X6	60,000		8,000						
Net income									
Retained earnings (6/30/X6)									
Total									

note: The Branch Office Control account balance and the Home Office Control account balance differ in this preclosing trial balance. This is so because the books have not been closed by the branch office. Note that the Home Office Control account credit balance of $59,000 will become a credit balance of $86,500 after the branch office closes its $27,500 net income to the Home Office Control account. The home office is presumed to have already recognized the branch income of $27,500 as shown on the trial balance.

Answer:

6/30/X6 Trial Balances (Preclosing)

	Home Office		Branch Office		Eliminations		Income Statement	Retained Earnings	Balance Sheet
Account Name	Debit	Credit	Debit	Credit	Debit	Credit	Dr.(Cr.)	Dr.(Cr.)	Dr.(Cr.)
Cash	57,000		45,000						102,000
Accts receiv.	92,000		30,000						122,000
Inventory 7/1/X5	50,000		0				50,000		
Property, plant, & equipment	350,000		10,000						360,000
Accum. deprec.		50,000		2,500					(52,500)
Branch office control	86,500					86,500[1]			0
Accounts payable		42,000		4,000					(46,000)
Home office control				59,000	59,000[1]				0
Common stock		125,000							(125,000)
Retained earnings (7/1/X5)		271,000						(271,000)	
Sales		225,000		130,000			(355,000)		
Purchases	120,000		15,000				135,000		
Operating expenses	45,000		35,500				80,500		
Shipments from home office			60,000			60,000[2]	0		
Shipments to branch office		60,000			60,000[2]		0		
Branch income		27,500			27,500[1]		0		
Totals	800,500	800,500	195,500	195,500	146,500	146,500			
Inventory as of 6/30/X6	60,000		8,000				(68,000)		68,000
Net income							(157,500)	(157,500)	
Retained earnings (6/30/X6)								(428,500)	(428,500)
Total									0

note: The Branch Office Control account balance and the Home Office Control account balance differ in this preclosing trial balance. This is so because the books have not been closed by the branch office. Note that the Home Office Control account credit balance of $59,000 will become a credit balance of $86,500 after the branch office closes its $27,500 net income to the Home Office Control account. The home office is presumed to have already recognized the branch income of $27,500 as shown on the trial balance.

[1]To eliminate Home Office Control and Branch Office Control accounts and intracompany income.
[2]To eliminate shipments from home office to branch office.

PROBLEM 3-6. Refer again to the transaction information of Problem 3-3 included in items *a* through *l*, except for item *b*, which should now read:

(*b*) The home office shipped inventory to Ajax and billed $60,000, which included a gross profit on the selling price of 15%.

Prepare all necessary journal entries (including branch office closing entry) to record these transactions on both home office and branch office books. Henley and Ajax use a perpetual inventory system. Also, prepare the home office entry to recognize the earned portion of deferred profit.

Answer:

Home Office Books	Dr.	Cr.	Branch Office Books	Dr.	Cr.
(*a*) Branch office control	45,000		(*a*) Cash	45,000	
Cash		45,000	Home office control		45,000
(*b*) Branch office control	60,000		(*b*) Inventory	60,000	
Inventory		51,000	Home office control		60,000
Deferred profit		9,000			
(15% × $60,000 = $9,000)					
			(*c*) Inventory	15,000	
			Accounts payable		15,000
			(*d*) Accts. Receivable	130,000	
			Sales		130,000
			Cost of goods sold	67,000	
			Inventory		67,000

Note:

7/1/X5 Inventory	$ 0
Purchases:	
Outside	15,000
From home office	60,000
Available for sale	75,000
Less: 6/30/X6 Inventory	8,000
Cost of goods sold	$67,000

Home Office Books	Dr.	Cr.	Branch Office Books	Dr.	Cr.
			(*e*) Cash	100,000	
			Accts. Receivable		100,000
			(*f*) Operating expenses	27,000	
			Cash		27,000
(*g*) Branch office control	6,000		(*g*) Operating expenses	6,000	
Operating expenses		6,000	Home office control		6,000
			(*h*) Accts. Payable	11,000	
			Cash		11,000
(*i*) Cash	52,000		(*i*) Home office control	52,000	
Branch office control		52,000	Cash		52,000
			(*j*) Property, plant, and equipment	10,000	
			Cash		10,000
			(*k*) Operating expenses	2,500	
			Accum. deprec.		2,500
(*l*) Branch office control	27,500		(*l*) Sales	130,000	
Branch income		27,500	Cost of goods sold		67,000
Deferred profit	7,800		Operating expenses		35,500
Branch income		7,800	Home office control		27,500

note: The balance in deferred profit should now be 15% of $8,000 in branch ending inventory or $1,200.
The adjusted entry is for $7,800 ($9,000 less $1,200).
(Branch income is closed to retained earnings.)

PROBLEM 3-7. You are presented with the following June 30, 19X6 preclosing trial balance for Henley Company (home office) and its Ajax branch office. This trial balance assumes the journal entries prepared during the fiscal year ending June 30, 19X6 by the home and branch offices were those described in the answer to Problem 3-6, except that the branch office has not yet made closing entry *l*. Complete the worksheet including columns for elimination entries, income statement, retained earnings, and balance sheet.

6/30/X6 Trial Balances (Preclosing)

	Home Office		Branch Office		Eliminations		Income Statement	Retained Earnings	Balance Sheet
Account Name	Debit	Credit	Debit	Credit	Debit	Credit	Dr.(Cr.)	Dr.(Cr.)	Dr.(Cr.)
Cash	57,000		45,000						
Accts receiv.	92,000		30,000						
Inventory (6/30/X6)	60,000		8,000						
Property, plant, & equipment	350,000		10,000						
Accum. deprec.		50,000		2,500					
Branch office control	86,500								
Accounts payable		42,000		4,000					
Home office control				59,000					
Common stock		125,000							
Retained earnings (7/1/X5)		271,000							
Sales		225,000		130,000					
Cost of goods sold	59,000		67,000						
Operating expenses	45,000		35,500						
Branch income		35,300							
Deferred profit		1,200							
Totals	749,500	749,500	195,500	195,500					
Net income									
Retained earnings (6/30/X6)									
Total									

notes:

(a) The Branch Office Control account balance and the Home Office Control account balance differ in this preclosing trial balance. This is so because the books have not been closed by the branch office. Note that the Home Office Control account credit balance of $59,000 will become a credit balance of $86,500 after the branch office closes its $27,500 net income to the Home Office Control account. The home office is presumed to have already recognized the branch income of $35,300 as shown on the trial balance.

(b) Home office cost of goods sold includes:

7/1/X5	Inventory (given)	$50,000	
Plus:	Purchases (given)	120,000	
Less:	Shipments to branch office	(51,000)	See entry "b".
	6/30/X6 Inventory (given)	(60,000)	
	Cost of goods sold	$59,000	

6/30/X6 Trial Balances (Preclosing)

	Home Office		Branch Office		Eliminations		Income Statement	Retained Earnings	Balance Sheet
Account Name	Debit	Credit	Debit	Credit	Debit	Credit	Dr.(Cr.)	Dr.(Cr.)	Dr.(Cr.)
Cash	57,000		45,000						102,000
Accts receiv.	92,000		30,000						122,000
Inventory (6/30/X6)	60,000		8,000			1,200[1]			66,800
Property, plant, & equipment	350,000		10,000						360,000
Accum. deprec.		50,000		2,500					(52,500)
Branch office control	86,500					86,500[1]			0
Accounts payable		42,000		4,000					(46,000)
Home office control				59,000	59,000[1]				0
Common stock		125,000							(125,000)
Retained earnings (7/1/X5)		271,000						(271,000)	
Sales		225,000		130,000			(355,000)		
Cost of goods sold	59,000		67,000			7,800[2]	118,200		
Operating expenses	45,000		35,500				80,500		
Branch income		35,300			35,300[1]		0		
Deferred profit		1,200			9,000[2]	7,800[1]			0
Totals	749,500	749,500	195,500	195,500	103,000	103,000			
				Net income			(156,300)	(156,300)	
				Retained earnings (6/30/X6)				(427,300)	(427,300)
				Total					0

notes:

(a) The Branch Office Control account balance and the Home Office Control account balance differ in this preclosing trial balance. This is so because the books have not been closed by the branch office. Note that the Home Office Control account credit balance of $59,000 will become a credit balance of $86,500 after the branch office closes its $27,500 net income to the Home Office Control account. The home office is presumed to have already recognized the branch income of $35,300 as shown on the trial balance.

(b) Home office cost of goods sold includes:

7/1/X5	Inventory (given)	$50,000
Plus:	Purchases (given)	120,000
Less:	Shipments to branch office	(51,000) See entry "b".
	6/30/X6 Inventory (given)	(60,000)
	Cost of goods sold	$59,000

[1]To eliminate Home Office Control and Branch Office Control accounts and intracompany income.
[2]To eliminate original $9,000 deferred profit against cost of goods sold and ending inventory.

PROBLEM 3-8. Farmer Company has two branch offices (branches "L" and "M"). Branch L shipped merchandise to branch M on 6/30/X3 which cost $11,000.

(*a*) Prepare the 6/30/X3 entries on the books of branches L and M to record the transfer.
(*b*) Prepare the 6/30X3 worksheet elimination entries needed by Farmer Company.

Answer:

(*a*)

Branch L Books			Branch M Books		
Interbranch receivable	11,000		Shipments from branch L	11,000	
Shipments to branch M		11,000	Interbranch payable		11,000

(*b*)

6/30X3 Worksheet Elimination Entries

Shipments to branch M	11,000	
Shipments from branch L		11,000
Interbranch payable	11,000	
Interbranch receivable		11,000

PROBLEM 3-9. As of the 12/31/X6 balance sheet date, home and branch office control account balances were not in agreement as follows:

Home Office Books — Branch Office Books

Thousands (000) omitted

Branch office control (Home Office Books)

Debit		Credit	
1/1/ Balance	90	6/30 Receipt from branch	40
4/10 Shipped to branch	30		
12/31 Shipped to branch	20		
12/31 Branch salary expense	10		
12/31 Balance	110		

Home office control (Branch Office Books)

Debit		Credit	
		1/1/ Balance	90
		4/10 Shipped from home	30
6/30 Paid home office	40		
12/31/ Paid home office	30		
		12/31 Balance	50

(*a*) Reconcile the branch and home office control accounts.
(*b*) Prepare adjusting entries for the home and branch offices.

Answer:

(*a*)

Branch office control at 12/31/X6	$110,000
Less: Cash receipt in transit	30,000
Adjusted branch office control at 12/31/X6	$ 80,000
Home office control at 12/31/X6	$ 50,000
Add: Shipments in transit	20,000
Operating expense paid at home office	10,000
Adjusted home office control at 12/31/X6	$ 80,000

(*b*)

Home Office Books			Branch Office Books		
Cash (in transit)	30,000		Shipment from home office (in transit)	20,000	
Branch office control		30,000	Home office control		20,000
			Operating expenses	10,000	
			Home office control		10,000

EXAMINATION I (CHAPTERS 1 THROUGH 3)

Problem 1: Problem 1 consists of the following 10 true and false questions.

1. When a new partner is admitted to a partnership by contributing land, the land should be recorded at fair market value by the partnership, but the new partner's capital account should be credited for the new partner's original cost or tax basis.
2. Partners must share profits and losses equally if the partnership agreement is silent regarding profit-and-loss sharing, even if the partners' average capital invested in the partnership is vastly different.
3. If a partner buys a 20% capital and profit-and-loss interest in a partnership by paying existing partners a total of $100,000 when the book and fair value of partnership net assets is $460,000, goodwill is implied.
4. A general partner's liability is limited to the partner's investment in the partnership.
5. If a partner buys a 20% capital and profit-and-loss interest in a partnership by investing $100,000 in the partnership when the book and fair value of partnership net assets is $460,000 before the new partner's investment, goodwill is implied.
6. Under the bonus method, goodwill will not be recorded upon admission of the new partner.
7. In a partnership liquidation, the legal doctrine of setoff exists to avoid inequities as available cash is distributed to partners.
8. When a noncash asset sale in a partnership installment liquidation results in gain (or loss), a credit (or charge) is made against partners' capital balances on the basis of year-end capital balances in accordance with the Uniform Partnership Act.
9. When a combined worksheet is prepared for home and branch offices of a company, an eliminating entry must be prepared to eliminate Branch Office Control, Branch Income, Branch Sales, Home Office Control, Deferred Profit, and Shipments accounts.
10. The accounts Shipments to Branch Office and Shipments from Home Office do not exist when a perpetual inventory system is used.

Problem 2: The Tom and Jerry partnership had net income for the year of $40,000. Tom and Jerry share profit and loss in the ratio of 30% and 70% respectively. Sales revenues generated by the partnership during the year were $100,000. Tom is entitled to a salary for the large amount of time he puts into the operation of the business of $25,000. During the past year, Tom and Jerry had the following activity in their capital accounts:

		Tom	Jerry
Jan. 1	Capital balance	$ 90,000	$150,000
April 1	Investment		20,000
June 1	Withdrawal	(15,000)	
Sept. 1	Withdrawal	(18,750)	
Oct. 1	Withdrawal		(20,000)
Dec. 31	Investment	30,000	
Dec. 31	Capital balance	$ 86,250	$150,000

The partnership agreement specifies that the partners are entitled to interest at 8% on average capital balances, and that Jerry is entitled to a bonus of 5% of sales revenue for his special marketing efforts. Prepare a schedule showing the distribution of partnership profit.

Problem 3: Ralph, Norton, and Trixie have the following capital balances and profit-and-loss ratios on 12/31/X8:

	Capital Balances	Profit-and-Loss Ratios
Ralph	$ 60,000	30%
Norton	90,000	40%
Trixie	40,000	30%
	$190,000	

On 1/1/X9 Alice wants to purchase a 20% interest in capital and profit-and-loss of the partnership by paying the partners directly $49,000 in total. The partnership's net asset book and fair values are equal. Assuming the partnership admits Alice using the goodwill method, prepare the journal entries necessary to admit Alice and determine the partners' capital balances after the admission of Alice.

Problem 4: Assume the same facts as described in Problem 3, except that Alice contributes to (invests the cash in) the partnership rather than paying partners directly. Prepare journal entries to admit Alice and determine the partners' capital balances after admission of Alice.

Problem 5: Again, use the facts of Problem 3, except that Alice's $49,000 is invested in the partnership rather than being paid to the partners directly, and that the bonus method rather than the goodwill method is used to record the admission of Alice. Prepare journal entries to admit Alice and determine the partners' capital balances after Alice is admitted.

Problem 6: Barney, Fred, and Wilma, who share profits and losses in the ratio of 1:7:2, decided to liquidate the partnership on August 1, 19X6. On that date, the partnership trial balance was as follows:

	Debit	Credit
Cash	$ 45,000	$
Noncash assets	255,000	
Loan receivable—Barney	25,000	
Accounts payable (outside creditors)		30,000
Loan payable—Wilma		25,000
Barney—Capital		155,000
Fred—Capital		45,000
Wilma—Capital		70,000
Totals	$325,000	$325,000

The noncash assets were sold for $185,000. Also, liquidation expenses were incurred and paid of another $8,000. Prepare a statement of partnership liquidation assuming Fred and Wilma are insolvent.

Problem 7: Once again, the partnership of Barney, Fred, and Wilma decides to liquidate on August 1, 19X6. However, this time the liquidation must take place in installments since all of the noncash assets are not immediately marketable. The August 1, 19X6 trial balance and profit-and-loss ratios of Problem 6 still apply. The new information is as follows:

(*a*)

Date of Sale	Selling Price	Noncash Asset Book Value
9/15/X6	$100,000	$ 90,000
11/19/X6	85,000	165,000
Totals	$185,000	$255,000

(*b*) After the first installment sale of assets on 9/15/X6, the partnership did not distribute all of the available cash to partners. In anticipation of liquidation expenses, the partnership retained $10,000 in cash.

(*c*) At the time of the second installment sale of assets (11/19/X6), the partnership incurred and paid $8,000 in liquidation expenses.

Prepare a maximum possible loss schedule, cash distribution plan, and a statement of partnership liquidation.

Problem 8: During the first year in which the Adler Company had branch operations, among the many transactions between the home and branch offices were the following:

Home Office Books

Branch office control	80,000	
Shipments to branch office		72,000
Deferred profit		8,000
Branch office control	40,000	
Branch income		40,000
Deferred profit	7,000	
Branch income		7,000

A 10% gross profit on selling price is charged by the home office. Therefore, 10% of the branch ending inventory of $10,000 (or $1,000) should remain at year-end in deferred gross profit.

Branch Office Books

Shipments from home office	80,000	
Home office control		80,000

(All branch inventory is purchased from home office.)

Sales	125,000	
Inventory (12/31)	10,000	
Shipments from home office		80,000
Operating expenses		15,000
Home office control		40,000

This is a closing entry not included in the following preclosing trial balance.

As a result of all home and branch office transactions for the year, the preclosing trial balance which follows was developed. Note that the balance in deferred profit is carried by the home office appropriately at $1,000 credit. Note also that the branch office ending inventory is shown on the worksheet at original cost to the company of $9,000 ($10,000 per branch records less deferred profit in ending inventory of $1,000). Complete the elimination entry, income statement, retained earnings, and balance sheet columns of the worksheet.

12/31/X1 Trial Balances (Preclosing)

	Home Office		Branch Office		Eliminations		Income Statement	Retained Earnings	Balance Sheet
Account	Debit	Credit	Debit	Credit	Debit	Credit	Dr.(Cr.)	Dr.(Cr.)	Dr.(Cr.)
Cash	240,000		93,000						
Accounts receiv.	20,000		38,000						
Inventory (1/1)	60,000		0						
Property, plant, & equip.	180,000		26,000						
Accum. deprec.		80,000		2,000					
Branch off. control	160,000								
Accounts payable		65,000		5,000					
Home off. control				120,000					
Common stock		155,000							
Retained earnings (1/1)		125,000							
Sales		300,000		125,000					
Purchases	150,000		0						
Operating expenses	35,000		15,000						
Shipments from home office			80,000						
Shipments to branch office		72,000							
Branch income		47,000							
Deferred profit		1,000							
Totals	$845,000	845,000	252,000	252,000					
Inventory (12/31)—at original cost	30,000		9,000						
Net income									
Retained earnings (12/31)									
Total.									

Note: The Branch Office Control account balance and the Home Office Control account balance differ in this preclosing trial balance. This is so because the books have not been closed by the branch office. Note that the Home Office Control account credit balance of $120,000 will become a credit balance of $160,000 after the branch office closes its $40,000 net income to the Home Office Control account. The home office is presumed to have already recognized the branch income of $47,000 as shown on the trial balance.

ANSWERS

Problem 1:

1. *False*
2. *True*
3. *True* ($100,000 ÷ 20% = $500,000 implied value. $500,000 less net assets of $460,000 = $40,000 goodwill.)

4. *False*
5. *False* ($100,000 ÷ 20% = $500,000 implied value. $500,000 less net assets of $560,000 = $60,000 "negative" goodwill.)
6. *True*
7. *True*
8. *False*
9. *False* (Branch outside sales are not eliminated.)
10. *True*

Problem 2: Average capital must first be determined for the purpose of determining interest at 8% to the partners.

Tom		Jerry	
5 months × $90,000 =	$450,000	3 months × $150,000 =	$ 450,000
3 months × $75,000 =	225,000	6 months × $170,000 =	1,020,000
4 months × $56,250 =	225,000	3 months × $150,000 =	450,000
12 months	$900,000	12 months	$1,920,000
	÷ 12 mo.		÷ 12 mo.
Average capital balance	$ 75,000		$ 160,000

		Partner	
		Tom 30%	Jerry 70%
Partnership income	$ 40,000		
• Interest at 8% on average capital balances	$ 18,800	$ 6,000	$ 12,800
• Salary	25,000	25,000	
• Bonus	5,000		5,000
• Balance in profit-and-loss ratio	(8,800)	(2,640)	(6,160)
Distribution	$ 40,000	$ 28,360	$ 11,640

Problem 3:

$ 49,000 = 20% Implied Value
$245,000 = Implied Value

Implied Value of Business	$245,000
Less: Fair and book value of net assets	190,000
Goodwill	$ 55,000

The entries to admit Alice under the goodwill method are:

Goodwill	55,000	
Ralph—Capital		16,500
Norton—Capital		22,000
Trixie—Capital		16,500
To record goodwill in the profit-and-loss ratio before admitting Alice.		

Ralph—Capital	15,300	
Norton—Capital	22,400	
Trixie—Capital	11,300	
Alice—Capital		49,000
To record admission of Alice.		

Capital Balances after Admission of Alice

	Capital before admission of Alice		Goodwill distribution		Interest sold to Alice (20%)		Capital after admission of Alice
Ralph	$ 60,000	+	$ 16,500	–	$ 15,300	=	$ 61,200
Norton	90,000	+	22,000	–	22,400	=	89,600
Trixie	40,000	+	16,500	–	11,300	=	45,200
Alice	—			+	49,000	=	49,000
	$190,000	+	$ 55,000		—		$245,000

Problem 4:

Implied Value of Business ($49,000 ÷ .2)	$245,000
Less: Fair and book value of net assets including Alice's investment ($190,000 + $49,000)	239,000
Goodwill	$ 6,000

Goodwill	6,000	
Ralph—Capital		1,800
Norton—Capital		2,400
Trixie—Capital		1,800
To record goodwill in the profit-and-loss ratio.		
Cash	49,000	
Alice—Capital		49,000
To record Alice's investment.		

Capital Balances after Admission of Alice

	Capital before admission of Alice		Goodwill distribution		Interest sold to Alice (20%)		Capital after admission of Alice
Ralph	$ 60,000	+	$ 1,800			=	$ 61,800
Norton	90,000	+	2,400			=	92,400
Trixie	40,000	+	1,800			=	41,800
Alice	—			+	$ 49,000	=	49,000
	$190,000	+	$ 6,000		$ 49,000		$245,000

Problem 5:

Cash	49,000	
Ralph—Capital		360
Norton—Capital		480
Trixie—Capital		360
Alice—Capital		47,800
To record admission of Alice.		

Capital Balances after Admission of Alice

	Capital before admission of Alice		Bonus distribution		Interest sold to Alice		Capital after admission of Alice
Ralph	$ 60,000	+	$ 360			=	$ 60,360
Norton	90,000	+	480			=	90,480
Trixie	40,000	+	360			=	40,360
Alice	—			+	$ 47,800	=	47,800
	$190,000	+	$ 1,200		$ 47,800		$239,000

Problem 6:

Barney, Fred, and Wilma Partnership
Statement of Partnership Liquidation
August 1, 19X6

	Assets			Liabilities		Partners' Capital		
	Cash	Noncash	Receivable Barney	Accounts Payable	Payable Wilma	Barney (10%)	Fred (70%)	Wilma (20%)
Balances before liquidation	$ 45,000	$255,000	$25,000	$ 30,000	$25,000	$155,000	$45,000	$70,000
Setoff of partners' loans against capital balances*			(25,000)		(25,000)	(25,000)		25,000
SUBTOTAL	45,000	255,000	0	30,000	0	130,000	45,000	95,000
Sale of assets and allocation of gain or loss*	185,000	(255,000)				(7,000)	(49,000)	(14,000)
Pay liquidation expenses*	(8,000)					(800)	(5,600)	(1,600)
SUBTOTAL	222,000	0	0	30,000	0	122,200	(9,600)	79,400
Pay outside creditors*	(30,000)			(30,000)				
SUBTOTAL	192,000	0	0	0	0	122,200	(9,600)	79,400
Allocate deficiency (see note below)*						(3,200)	9,600	(6,400)
SUBTOTAL	192,000	0	0	0	0	119,000	0	73,000
Pay partners*	(192,000)					(119,000)		(73,000)
Balances after liquidation	$0	$0	$0	$0	$0	$0	$0	$0

*Results in journal entry.
Note: The allocation of the $9,600 deficiency in Fred's capital is based on the remaining profit and loss ratios of Barney and Wilma. Therefore, Barney is charged 1/3 of $9,600 or $3,200, and Wilma is charged 2/3 of $9,600 or $6,400. Barney and Wilma now have claims against Fred. In fact, if Fred were solvent, Fred should contribute the $9,600 cash deficiency to the partnership during the liquidation process thereby eliminating the deficiency and the need for its allocation to Barney and Wilma.

Problem 7:

	Adjusted Capital*	Profit-and-Loss Ratio	Sustainable Loss	Rank
Barney	$130,000	10%	$1,300,000	1
Fred	$ 45,000	70%	$ 64,286	3
Wilma	$ 95,000	20%	$ 475,000	2

*Capital balances plus loans payable minus loans receivable (setoff).

Maximum Possible Loss Schedule

	Partner Rank	Maximum Loss to Eliminate	Barney 10%	Fred 70%	Wilma 20%
			Capital Balances		
8/1/X6 Balances			$130,000	$45,000	$95,000
	3 (Fred)	$ 64,286	(6,429)	(45,000)	(12,857)
			123,571	- 0 -	82,143
	2 (Wilma)	$123,214*	(41,071)		(82,143)
			82,500		- 0 -
	1 (Barney)	$ 82,500	(82,500)		
			- 0 -		

*Note that the loss to eliminate Wilma is based on the assumption that once Fred has been eliminated, any remaining loss must be charged to Barney and Wilma in their remaining profit-and-loss ratios of 1/3 and 2/3 respectively. Therefore:

2/3 Loss = $82,143
Loss = $82,143 × 3/2 = $123,214

Cash Distribution Plan

		Partner		
		Barney	Fred	Wilma
First	$ 82,500	$82,500		
Next	$123,214	$41,071 (1/3)		$82,143 (2/3)
Next	$ 64,286	$ 6,429 (10%)	$45,000 (70%)	$12,857 (20%)

Problem 7:

Barney, Fred, and Wilma Partnership
Statement of Partnership Liquidation
August 1, 19X6 through November 19, 19X6

	Assets			Liabilities		Partners' Capital		
	Cash	Noncash	Receivable Barney	Accounts Payable	Payable Wilma	Barney (10%)	Fred (70%)	Wilma (20%)
Balances before liquidation	$ 45,000	$255,000	$25,000	$ 30,000	$25,000	$155,000	$45,000	$70,000
Setoff of partners' loans against capital balances*			(25,000)		(25,000)	(25,000)		25,000
SUBTOTAL	45,000	255,000	0	30,000	0	130,000	45,000	95,000
Sale of assets and allocation of gain or loss 9/15/X6*	100,000	(90,000)				1,000	7,000	2,000
SUBTOTAL	145,000	165,000	0	30,000	0	131,000	52,000	97,000
Pay outside creditors*	(30,000)			(30,000)				
SUBTOTAL	115,000	165,000	0	0	0	131,000	52,000	97,000
Installment #1 to partners (see Schedule I)*	(105,000)					(90,000)		(15,000)
SUBTOTAL	10,000	165,000	0	0	0	41,000	52,000	82,000
Sale of assets and allocation of gain or loss —11/19/X6*	85,000	(165,000)				(8,000)\,	(56,000)	(16,000)
Pay liquidation expenses*	(8,000)					(800)	(5,600)	(1,600)
SUBTOTAL	87,000	0	0	0	0	32,200	(9,600)	64,400
Allocation of Fred's deficiency (1/3:2/3)*						(3,200)	9,600	(6,400)
SUBTOTAL	87,000	0	0	0	0	29,000	0	58,000
Installment #2 to partners (see Schedule II)*	(87,000)					(29,000)		(58,000)
Balances after liquidation	$0	$0	$0	$0	$0	$0	$0	$0

*Results in journal entry.

Schedule I – Installment #1 to Partners Per Plan

	Total	Barney	Fred	Wilma
First	$ 82,000	$ 82,500	—	—
Next (1/3:2/3)	22,500	7,500	—	$ 15,000
Installment #1	$105,000	$ 90,000	—	$ 15,000

Schedule II – Installment #2 to Partners Per Plan

	Total	Barney	Fred	Wilma
Next (1/3:2/3)	$ 87,000	$ 29,000	—	$ 58,000

Problem 8:

12/31/X1 Trial Balances (Preclosing)

	Home Office		Branch Office		Eliminations		Income Statement	Retained Earnings	Balance Sheet
Account	Debit	Credit	Debit	Credit	Debit	Credit	Dr.(Cr.)	Dr.(Cr.)	Dr.(Cr.)
Cash	240,000		93,000						333,000
Accounts receiv.	20,000		38,000						58,000
Inventory (1/1)	60,000		0				60,000		
Property, plant, & equip.	180,000		26,000						206,000
Accum. deprec.		80,000		2,000					(82,000)
Branch off. control	160,000					160,000[1]			0
Accounts payable		65,000		5,000					(70,000)
Home off. control				120,000	120,000[1]				0
Common stock		155,000							(155,000)
Retained earnings (1/1)		125,000						(125,000)	
Sales		300,000		125,000			(425,000)		
Purchases	150,000		0				150,000		
Operating expenses	35,000		15,000				50,000		
Shipments from home office			80,000			80,000[1]	0		
Shipments to branch office		72,000			72,000[2]		0		
Branch income		47,000			47,000[1]				
Deferred profit		1,000			8,000[2]	7,000[1]			0
Totals	$845,000	845,000	252,000	252,000	247,000	247,000			
Inventory (12/31)—at original cost	30,000		9,000				(39,000)		39,000
Net income							(204,000)	(204,000)	
Retained earnings (12/31)								(329,000)	(329,000)
Total.									0

Note: The Branch Office Control account balance and the Home Office Control account balance differ in this pre-closing trial balance. This is so because the books have not been closed by the branch office. Note that the Home Office Control account credit balance of $120,000 will become a credit balance of $160,000 after the branch office closes its $40,000 net income to the Home Office Control account. The home office is presumed to have already recognized the branch income of $47,000 as shown on the trial balance.

[1]To eliminate Home Office Control and Branch Office Control accounts and intracompany income, including deferred profit in the home office account "branch income."

[2]To eliminate shipments from home office to branch office, including deferred profit.

BUSINESS COMBINATIONS AND THE CONSOLIDATED BALANCE SHEET

THIS CHAPTER IS ABOUT

☑ **Business Combination Theory**
☑ **The Consolidated Balance Sheet**
☑ **Acquisition of 100 Percent of a Subsidiary**
☑ **Acquisition of Less Than 100 Percent of a Subsidiary**
☑ **Revaluation of a Subsidiary's Debt**

4-1. Business Combination Theory

Business combinations occur when two separate business are brought together under common ownership and treated as one economic entity. When one company buys more than 50% of the stock of another company, a parent-subsidiary relationship is generally established and the parent company is in control. This will result in the need for consolidated financial statements. The two approaches to accounting for business combinations are the *purchase method* and *pooling of interests method*. As will be seen in this and later chapters, these two methods may yield widely diverse results when used to combine businesses and report income and financial position. In general, the purchase method results in lower net income for the combined business than does the pooling of interests method. However, companies may not simply choose one method or the other because of the method's impact on income or financial position. Accounting Principles Board Opinion No. 16, "Accounting for Business Combinations" (APB-16) provides guidelines regarding situations in which the pooling of interests method may be used; the purchase method must be used in all others.

A. The pooling of interests method.

The fundamental idea underlying the pooling of interests method is that no actual purchase and sale of a business takes place; rather, the two (or more) companies involved are considered to combine their ownership interests and managerial abilities to form one economic entity, even though one of the companies does exercise control over the other(s). When the pooling of interests method applies to a business combination, net assets of the combining companies are carried at book (historical) values, and goodwill may not result from the combination. The separate income statements of the combining companies are simply combined and shown as income of one economic entity. Even if the combination is not effected until the end of the year, the income of all companies that are party to the pooling will be merged for the full year, because a continuity of ownership interest is presumed to have existed for the full year. However, continuity of ownership interest is not the only criterion that must be met in order to account for a business combination as a pooling of interests. APB-16 lists 12 criteria which must all be met if the combination is to be accounted for as a pooling of interests. These criteria and the pooling of interests method will be addressed in detail in Chapter 11.

B. The purchase method.

The fundamental idea underlying the purchase method is that a purchase and sale of a business takes place. In a purchase, the net assets of the acquired company are essentially carried at their cost to the acquiring company. This cost may, for example, exceed the acquired company's book value, resulting in greater depreciation charges than under the pooling of interests method. Furthermore, if the acquiring company's cost exceeds the fair value of net assets acquired, goodwill results from the business combination. This leads to goodwill amortization expense under the purchase method which would not exist under the pooling of interests method. Under the purchase method, asset revaluation and the potential development of goodwill may result in lower net income through greater depreciation and goodwill amortization expense than under the pooling of interests method. The purchase method as it applies to acquisitions will be addressed in this chapter and in Chapters 6 and 7. The pooling of interests method will be addressed in Chapter 11.

C. Incidental costs in business combinations.

In addition to the actual purchase price of a business, there are other costs incidental to business combinations. The accounting treatment of these costs depends upon whether the business combination is considered a purchase or pooling of interests:

Type of Cost	Purchase Method Treatment
1. Direct costs of acquisition.	1. Part of cost of acquired company (charge investment).
2. Costs of registering equity securities.	2. Reduction of fair value of securities issued (charge additional paid in capital).
3. Indirect and general expenses related to acquisition.	3. Deducted as incurred in determining net income (charge expense).

Type of Cost	Pooling Method Treatment
1. Direct costs of acquisition.	
2. Costs of registering equity securities.	Deducted as incurred in determining net income (charge expense).
3. Indirect and general expenses related to acquisition.	

4-2. The Consolidated Balance Sheet

Because both the parent company and subsidiary company continue as legal entities after an acquisition, each may issue standard financial statements relating to its own operations. An accurate analysis of the combined business entity (the parent *and* subsidiary companies taken together), however, requires the use of consolidated financial statements, which treat the affiliated companies as a single business enterprise (one economic entity).

On the date of the actual investment by the parent company in the subsidiary company, it is customary to prepare a *consolidated balance sheet* (a summary of the assets and liabilities of the parent and subsidiary companies without regard to their separate legal status) to provide a "starting point" against which to judge future performance.

Under the purchase method for accounting for business combinations, only the balance sheets of the affiliated companies may be consolidated on the acquisition date; their income statements may not be consolidated at this point because the purchase method allows the parent company to report its subsidiary's operations only after the acquisition date.

The remainder of this chapter is concerned with the preparation of a consolidated balance sheet on the date of acquisition using the purchase method of business combinations.

In the working papers used to prepare the consolidated balance sheet all intercompany investments, account balances, or operating transactions must be eliminated (as were the intracompany accounts between home and branch offices in Chapter 3), in order to avoid counting those assets or liabilities twice.

To prepare the consolidated balance sheet for a newly combined business entity, prepare a worksheet with columns that show the balance sheets of the parent and subsidiary companies as of the acquisition date. Add columns to eliminate the parent company's investment against the subsidiary company's equity accounts, as well as any other intercompany account balances or operating expenses. As with *intra*company eliminations, these *inter*company eliminations are made *only* in the working papers; they are not made in the books of the parent or subsidiary. Finally, add a fifth column showing the combined assets and liabilities of both companies, after eliminations. This final column represents the consolidated balance sheet for the new combined business entity on its acquisition date:

Parent Company and Subsidiary Company
Consolidating Worksheet
XX/XX/XX

BALANCE SHEET	Parent Dr. (Cr.)	Subsidiary Dr. (Cr.)	Eliminations Dr.	 (Cr.)	Consolidated Dr. (Cr.)

4-3. Acquisition of 100 Percent of a Subsidiary

The simplest type of acquisition, from the accountant's point of view, is one in which the acquiring company buys 100 percent of the common stock of the acquired company (or 100 percent of the ownership interest, if the company to be acquired is a proprietorship or partnership). In such a case, the price paid by the acquiring company may be equal to, greater than, or less than the book value and the fair value of the acquired company. Each of these possibilities requires slightly different accounting procedures.

A. The subsidiary's cost equals its fair value and book value.

This is the simplest form of business acquisition. Because the cost for the subsidiary equals its book value and its fair value, no goodwill results from the purchase, and the subsidiary's net assets do not have to be revalued during the preparation of consolidated financial statements. All that is necessary to produce the consolidated balance sheet is to eliminate the parent's investment against the subsidiary's equity in the worksheet.

EXAMPLE 4-1: On 1/1/X1, Parent Company (P Co.) purchased 100% of Subsidiary Company (S Co.) common stock for $100,000. Immediately after the purchase, the balance sheets of P Co. and S Co. were:

	P Co.	S Co.
Cash	$ 70,000	$ 30,000
Accounts receivable (net)	80,000	50,000
Inventory	90,000	25,000
Land	50,000	20,000
Equipment (net)	60,000	35,000
Investment in S Co.	100,000	—
Total Assets	$450,000	$160,000
Accounts payable	$ 40,000	$ 30,000
Notes payable	60,000	30,000
Common stock	100,000	50,000
Additional paid-in capital	130,000	40,000
Retained earnings	120,000	10,000
Total liabilities and equity	$450,000	$160,000

S Co.'s book values equal its fair values. To prepare a consolidated balance sheet, use a worksheet to show P Co. and S Co. as one economic entity.

Set up the worksheet with columns to show the balance sheets of P Co. and S Co., columns to make the necessary eliminations, and a final column that will show the balances for the affiliated group "P Co. and its subsidiary S Co."

Because S Co.'s book values equal its fair values, the only elimination necessary on the worksheet is the investment by P Co. ($100,000) against the various equity accounts of S Co.: common stock ($50,000), additional paid-in capital ($40,000), and retained earnings (10,000). The elimination entry for the worksheet is:

S Co. Common Stock	50,000	
S Co. Additional paid-in capital	40,000	
S Co. Retained earnings	10,000	
Investment in S Co.		100,000

The final worksheet showing the eliminations and the consolidated balance sheet of the combined business entity on the acquisition date is:

P Co. and S Co.
Consolidating Worksheet
1/01/X1

	P Co.	S Co.	Eliminations		Consolidated
BALANCE SHEET	Dr. (Cr.)	Dr. (Cr.)	Dr.	(Cr.)	Dr. (Cr.)
Cash	70,000	30,000			100,000
Accounts receiv. (net)	80,000	50,000			130,000
Inventory	90,000	25,000			115,000
Land	50,000	20,000			70,000
Equipment (net)	60,000	35,000			95,000
Investment in S Co.	100,000			[1](100,000)	0
Accounts payable	(40,000)	(30,000)			(70,000)
Notes payable	(60,000)	(30,000)			(90,000)
Common stock:					
P Co.	(100,000)				(100,000)
S Co.		(50,000)	[1]50,000		0
Additional paid-in					
capital: P Co.	(130,000)				(130,000)
S Co.		(40,000)	[1]40,000		0
Retained earnings:					
P Co.	(120,000)				(120,000)
S Co.		(10,000)	[1]10,000		0
Totals	0	0	100,000	(100,000)	0

[1]To eliminate investment in S Co. against S Co. equity.

B. The subsidiary's cost exceeds its fair value or book value.

If the cost paid by the acquiring company is greater than the fair value of the acquired company's net assets, then *goodwill* is implied in the sale and must be accounted for in the consolidated balance sheet.

In addition, the fair value of the acquired company's net assets will in many cases be greater (or less) than their book values. In such a case, a worksheet adjustment will be necessary to raise (or lower) these assets to their fair values (assuming the acquiring company paid at least fair value for them).

This revaluation of assets is achieved while making the eliminations on the worksheet to prepare the consolidated balance sheet. After all the acquired company's book values are adjusted to their fair values, and all its equity accounts are eliminated, any remaining investment by the acquiring company may be debited to goodwill. The goodwill will be amortized against consolidated net income over its expected useful life (which may not exceed 40 years).

EXAMPLE 4-2: On 1/1/X1, P Co. purchased 100% of S Co. common stock for $130,000. Immediately after the purchase, the balance sheets of P Co. and S Co. were:

		S Co.	
BALANCE SHEET	P Co.	Book Values	Fair Values
Cash	$ 40,000	$ 30,000	$ 30,000
Accounts receivable (net)	80,000	50,000	50,000
Inventory	90,000	25,000	20,000
Land	50,000	20,000	35,000
Equipment (net)	60,000	35,000	45,000
Investment in S Co.	130,000		
Total Assets	$450,000	$160,000	
Accounts payable	$ 40,000	$ 30,000	$ 30,000
Notes payable	60,000	30,000	30,000
Common stock:			
P. Co.	100,000		
S. Co.		50,000	
Additional paid-in capital: P. Co.	130,000		
S. Co.		40,000	
Retained earnings:			
P. Co.	120,000		
S. Co.		10,000	
Total Liabilities and Equity	$ 450,000	$160,000	
S Co. Fair Value			$120,000

To prepare a consolidated balance sheet, use a worksheet to show P Co. and S Co. as one economic entity.

Note the differences between the book values and fair values for certain of S Co.'s assets; both Land and Equipment have appreciated in value while Inventory has declined in value from historical cost or book values. P Co. is assumed to have paid the fair values for S Co.'s assets, and this must be reflected in the consolidated balance sheet. This is achieved by debiting or crediting the appropriate portions of P Co.'s investment against the assets to be revalued when making the eliminations on the worksheet, thereby raising or lowering S Co.'s asset valuations overall. After all book values are adjusted to fair values, and all S Co.'s equity accounts have been eliminated, the remaining investment by P Co. is debited to goodwill. In this case the elimination entry is:

	Debit	Credit
S Co. Common Stock	50,000	
S Co. Additional paid-in capital	40,000	
S Co. Retained earnings	10,000	
Land	15,000	
Equipment	10,000	
Goodwill	10,000	
Inventory		5,000
Investment in S Co.		130,000

Note that the worksheet elimination entry allocates P Co.'s $130,000 investment three ways:

1. $100,000 S Co. book value ($160,000 assets less $60,000 debt).
2. $ 20,000 Raise assets to fair value on the worksheet.
3. $ 10,000 Record goodwill implicit in the purchase price.

The $10,000 goodwill portion can readily be determined as follows:

Price paid for investment		$130,000
Fair value of S Co.	$120,000	
Interest in S Co.	× 100%	
Fair value received		120,000
Goodwill		10,000

The final worksheet showing the eliminations and the consolidated balance sheet of the combined business entity on the acquisition date is:

P Co. and S Co.
Consolidating Worksheet
1/01/X1

BALANCE SHEET	P Co. Dr. (Cr.)	S Co. Dr. (Cr.)	Eliminations Dr.	Eliminations (Cr.)	Consolidated Dr. (Cr.)
Cash	40,000	30,000			70,000
Accounts receiv. (net)	80,000	50,000			130,000
Inventory	90,000	25,000		[1](5,000)	110,000
Land	50,000	20,000	[1]15,000		85,000
Equipment (net)	60,000	35,000	[1]10,000		105,000
Investment in S Co.	130,000			[1](130,000)	0
Goodwill			[1]10,000		10,000
Accounts payable	(40,000)	(30,000)			(70,000)
Notes payable	(60,000)	(30,000)			(90,000)
Common stock:					
P Co.	(100,000)				(100,000)
S Co.		(50,000)	[1]50,000		0
Additional paid-in capital: P Co.	(130,000)				(130,000)
S Co.		(40,000)	[1]40,000		0
Retained earnings:					
P Co.	(120,000)				(120,000)
S Co.		(10,000)	[1]10,000		0
Totals	0	0	135,000	(135,000)	0

[1]To eliminate investment in S Co. against S Co. equity and adjust S Co. assets to fair value.

C. The subsidiary's cost is less than its fair value.

When the cost paid by the acquiring company is less than the fair value of the acquired company's net assets, the resulting purchase is termed a *bargain purchase*. A bargain purchase must be accounted for in the consolidated balance sheet.

The difference between the purchase price and the fair value of the acquired company is called the *bargain purchase amount*. This amount must be allocated against the book values of the subsidiary's noncurrent assets (except for long-term marketable securities). A percentage of the bargain purchase amount is deducted from each noncurrent asset, according to the percentage which that separate asset represents to the total noncurrent assets. These deductions are made during the elimination process.

EXAMPLE 4-3: On 1/1/X1, P Co. paid $90,000 for 100% of the common stock of S Co. The book and fair values of S Co.'s net assets were $100,000. Immediately after the acquisition, the balance sheets of P Co. and S Co. were:

BALANCE SHEET	P Co.	S. Co.
Cash	$ 80,000	$ 30,000
Accounts Receivable	80,000	50,000
Inventory	90,000	25,000
Land	50,000	20,000
Equipment	60,000	35,000
Investment in S Co.	90,000	
Total Assets	$450,000	$160,000
Accounts Payable	$ 40,000	$ 30,000
Notes Payable	60,000	30,000
Common Stock:		
P Co.	100,000	
S Co.		50,000
Additional paid-in capital:		
P Co.	130,000	
S Co.		40,000
Retained earnings:		
P Co.	120,000	
S Co.		10,000
Total Liabilities and Equity	$450,000	$160,000

Prepare a consolidated balance sheet using a worksheet to account for the bargain purchase amount and show P Co. and S Co. as one economic entity.

The bargain purchase amount is determined from the fair value of S Co. less the actual purchase price:

$100,000 fair value – $90,000 purchase price = $10,000 bargain purchase amount

This $10,000 must now be deducted from the book values of S Co.'s noncurrent assets, which are Land and Equipment. Combined, these two assets have book values of $55,000, of which Land represents 36 percent ($20,000 ÷ $55,000) and Equipment 64 percent ($35,000 ÷ $55,000). The bargain purchase price is allocated to these accounts according to these same percentages:

	Fair (and book) value	% to total	Allocation of bargain
Land	$20,000	36%	$ 3,600
Equipment	35,000	64%	6,400
	$55,000	100%	$10,000

The complete worksheet elimination entry is therefore:

	Debit	Credit
S Co. Common Stock	50,000	
S Co. Additional paid-in capital	40,000	
S Co. Retained earnings	10,000	
Land		3,600
Equipment		6,400
Investment		90,000

The final worksheet, showing the eliminations and the allocation of the bargain purchase amount, and the consolidated balance sheet for the combined business entity on the acquisition date, is:

P Co. and S Co.
Consolidating Worksheet
1/01/X1

BALANCE SHEET	P Co. Dr. (Cr.)	S Co. Dr. (Cr.)	Eliminations Dr.	Eliminations (Cr.)	Consolidated Dr. (Cr.)
Cash	80,000	30,000			110,000
Accounts receiv. (net)	80,000	50,000			130,000
Inventory	90,000	25,000			115,000
Land	50,000	20,000		[1](3,600)	66,400
Equipment (net)	60,000	35,000		[1](6,400)	88,600
Investment in S Co.	90,000			[1](90,000)	0
Accounts payable	(40,000)	(30,000)			(70,000)
Notes payable	(60,000)	(30,000)			(90,000)
Common stock:					
P Co.	(100,000)				(100,000)
S Co.		(50,000)	[1]50,000		0
Additional paid-in capital: P Co.	(130,000)				(130,000)
S Co.		(40,000)	[1]40,000		0
Retained earnings:					
P Co.	(120,000)				(120,000)
S Co.		(10,000)	[1]10,000		0
Totals	0	0	100,000	(100,000)	0

[1]To eliminate investment in S Co. against S Co. equity and allocate bargain purchase amount.

If there is a bargain purchase, but the acquired company does not have enough noncurrent assets to allow for complete removal of the bargain purchase amount, then a Deferred Credit account is established in the consolidated balance sheet. This credit will be amortized to consolidated income over the expected period of benefit resulting from the purchase (which may not exceed 40 years).

EXAMPLE 4-4: On 1/1/X1, P Co. paid $90,000 for 100% of the common stock of S Co. The book and fair values of S Co.'s net assets were $100,000, but its noncurrent assets were valued at only $5,000. How would the $10,000 bargain purchase amount be accounted for in the worksheet used to prepare a consolidated balance sheet for the combined business entity?

The first $5,000 of the bargain purchase amount should go toward eliminating the noncurrent asset accounts of S Co. There is no need to calculate the apportionment of this amount as there was in Example 4-3; whatever their balances, the noncurrent assets are completely eliminated.

The remaining $5,000 of the bargain purchase amount should be credited to a Deferred Credit account in the consolidated balance sheet (which will be amortized over the next few years).

The worksheet elimination entry (assuming S Co. had the same balances shown in Example 4-3 for Common Stock, Additional Paid-in Capital, and Retained Earnings) would be:

	Dr.	Cr.
S Co. Common Stock	50,000	
S Co. Additional paid-in capital	40,000	
S Co. Retained earnings	10,000	
Noncurrent assets		5,000
Investment in S Co.		90,000
Deferred credit		5,000

In the examples in this section on bargain purchases, the book values and the fair values of the acquired company have so far been equal. If the book values and fair values of the acquired company's assets are *not* equal, then the bargain purchase amount must be apportioned among the noncurrent assets according to their *fair* values. The determination of the correct apportionment involves three steps:

1. Determine the portion of the purchase price paid by the acquiring company that is assignable to noncurrent assets. To find this amount, subtract the bargain purchase amount from the combined *book* value of the noncurrent assets.
2. Allocate a portion of this amount to each noncurrent asset according to the percentage each asset represents of the combined *fair* value of all noncurrent assets.
3. Determine the adjustment necessary to the *book* values of the noncurrent assets to yield the amounts assigned to each asset according to *fair* values, as determined in Steps 1 and 2.

The amounts determined in Step 3 above should equal the bargain purchase amount, and also indicate the eliminations necessary on the worksheet.

EXAMPLE 4-5: On 1/1/X1, P Co. paid $90,000 for 100% of the common stock of S Co., which has a book value of $100,000. The book and fair values of s Co.'s net assets are equal, except as follows:

	Book Value	Fair Value
Land	$20,000	$24,000
Equipment	35,000	26,000
	$55,000	$50,000

How would the $10,000 bargain purchase amount be accounted for in the worksheet used to prepare a consolidated balance sheet for the combined business entity?

The bargain purchase amount must be apportioned among the noncurrent assets (as in Example 4–4) according to their fair values. To do this, follow the three steps outlined above.

First, find the amount of the purchase price that is assignable to noncurrent assets by subtracting the bargain purchase amount from the book values of the noncurrent assets:

$55,000 book value – $10,000 bargain purchase amount = $45,000 of purchase price assignable to noncurrent assets

Second, allocate a portion of the $45,000 to each noncurrent asset according to the percentage each asset represents of the fair value of all the noncurrent assets:

	Fair Value				Percentage of Fair Value
Land	$24,000	÷	50,000	=	48
Equipment	26,000	÷	50,000	=	52
	$50,000				100

	Percentage of Assignable Value				Amount Assigned to Each Asset
Land	48%	×	45,000	=	$21,600
Equipment	52%	×	45,000	=	23,400
	100%				$45,000

Finally, make the adjustment necessary to bring the book values of the noncurrent assets to match the amounts assigned to each according to *fair* values:

	Book Value	Assignable Value Allocation	Difference Dr. (Cr.)
Land	$20,000	$21,600	$ 1,600
Equipment	35,000	23,400	(11,600)
	$55,000	$45,000	$10,000

The amounts of these differences equal the bargain purchase amount ($10,000), and also indicate the eliminations necessary on the worksheet used to prepare the consolidated balance sheet. The worksheet elimination entry is:

S Co. Common Stock	50,000	
S Co. Additional paid-in capital	40,000	
S Co. Retained earnings	10,000	
Land	1,600	
Equipment		11,600
Investment		90,000

4-4. Acquisition of Less Than 100 Percent of a Subsidiary

One of the advantages of a business combination accomplished through the purchase of a subsidiary's common stock is that it is not necessary to buy all of the subsidiary's stock to gain control. An interest of greater than 50% in the voting stock assures control, and generally results in the need to prepare consolidated financial statements showing the separate legal entities as one economic entity.

When a company acquires less than a 100 percent interest in the equity of another company, the remaining equity is termed the minority interest. (This minority interest may or may not be considered part of the combined business entity; see the next section, "Parent Company Versus Entity Theories.") Special accounts are established for the minority interest, and these must be shown on the consolidated balance sheet. These minority interest accounts are shown on the consolidating worksheets which follow by placing the letter *M* after their balances (e.g., $10,000M).

A. The subsidiary's cost equals its fair value and book value.

When a company buys less than a 100 percent interest in another company, and the acquired company's fair values and book values are equal, the acquiring company's investment is simply eliminated against the acquired company's equity accounts *according to the percentage of ownership held by the acquiring company.* The remaining equity of the acquired company is now considered minority interest, and clearly marked accounts are established for it in the consolidating worksheet balance sheet columns of the newly combined business entity.

EXAMPLE 4-6: On 1/1/X1, P Co. paid $80,000 for 80% of the common stock of S Co. Immediately after the purchase the balance sheets of P Co. and S Co. were:

BALANCE SHEETS	P Co.	S Co.
Cash	$ 90,000	$ 30,000
Accounts receivable	80,000	50,000
Inventory	90,000	25,000
Land	50,000	20,000
Equipment	60,000	35,000
Investment in S Co.	80,000	
Total Assets	$450,000	$160,000
Accounts payable	$ 40,000	$ 30,000
Notes payable	60,000	30,000
Common stock:		
P. Co.	100,000	
S. Co.		50,000
Additional paid-in		
capital: P. Co.	130,000	
S. Co.		40,000

Retained earnings:		
P. Co.	120,000	
S. Co.		10,000
Total Liabilities and Equity	$ 450,000	$160,000

The book values of S Co. equal its fair values. Prepare a consolidated balance sheet using a worksheet to show P Co. and S Co. as one economic entity.

Because P Co. bought an 80 percent interest, its investment ($80,000) must be eliminated against only *80 percent* of S Co.'s equity account balances. In this case the elimination entry is:

S Co. Common Stock	40,000 (50,000 × 80%)	
S Co. Additional paid-in capital	32,000 (40,000 × 80%)	
S Co. Retained earnings	8,000 (10,000 × 80%)	
Investment in S Co.		80,000

The remaining S Co. equity is the minority interest, and must be labeled as such in the consolidating worksheet balance sheet columns. The worksheet showing the eliminations and consolidated balance sheet with minority interest is:

P Co. and S Co.
Consolidating Worksheet
1/01/X1

	P Co.	S Co.	Eliminations		Consolidated
BALANCE SHEET	Dr. (Cr.)	Dr. (Cr.)	Dr.	(Cr.)	Dr. (Cr.)
Cash	90,000	30,000			120,000
Accounts receiv. (net)	80,000	50,000			130,000
Inventory	90,000	25,000			115,000
Land	50,000	20,000			70,000
Equipment (net)	60,000	35,000			95,000
Investment in S Co.	80,000			[1](80,000)	0
Accounts payable	(40,000)	(30,000)			(70,000)
Notes payable	(60,000)	(30,000)			(90,000)
Common stock:					
P Co.	(100,000)				(100,000)
S Co.		(50,000)	[1]40,000		(10,000)M
Additional paid-in capital: P Co.	(130,000)				(130,000)
S Co.		(40,000)	[1]32,000		(8,000)M
Retained earnings:					
P Co.	(120,000)				(120,000)
S Co.		(10,000)	[1]8,000		(2,000)M
Totals	0	0	80,000	(80,000)	0
		Total minority interest			($20,000)

M = Minority interest
[1]To eliminate investment in S Co. against S Co. equity.

B. Minority interest: Parent company theory versus entity theory.

If a parent company's cost to acquire a company exceeds the fair value of the acquired company's net assets, goodwill results. In addition, if the acquired company's fair value exceeds its book value, a worksheet adjustment is necessary to raise net assets as carried by the acquired company to fair value. When minority interest also exists, a question arises regarding the amount of goodwill and the amount by which net assets should be adjusted to fair value. That is, if an 80% owned subsidiary's book value of land is $20,000 and fair value of land is $35,000, should the land's book value be adjusted upward by $15,000 or by $12,000 (80% of $15,000)? Two theories of accounting for this situation exist: the parent company theory, and the entity theory.

Under the parent company theory, the reporting entity does not change; the parent company remains the reporting entity. Minority interest is not a part of equity, and the subsidiary's net assets should be revalued only to the extent of the parent's interest in the subsidiary. Under the parent company theory, the land revaluation worksheet adjustment for the example in the last paragraph would be for $12,000 (80% of $15,000). Also, minority interest will normally appear on the formal consolidated balance sheet between debt and stockholders' equity.

Under the entity theory, the reporting entity does change. A new reporting entity exists, with two types of ownership interest: a controlling interest and a minority interest. Subsidiary net assets should be revalued to full fair value to reflect total ownership interest. Under the entity theory, the land revaluation would be for the full $15,000, but $3,000 of this amount (20%) would represent minority interest. Also, minority interest will appear on the formal consolidated balance sheet as a part of stockholders' equity.

There is also a third theory, the combination entity–parent company theory. This is a hybrid approach wherein the subsidiary's net assets are revalued in a way similar to that used under the entity theory (to full fair value), but consolidated goodwill is determined in a way similar to that used under the parent company theory (only to the extent it is *purchased* by the parent company).

Both the parent company and entity theories are acceptable under generally accepted accounting principles. The remainder of this book uses the parent company theory unless stated otherwise.

EXAMPLE 4–7: A parent company paid $500,000 for an 80 percent interest in a subsidiary with net assets the fair value of which was $600,000. Determine the goodwill in this transaction, using first the parent company theory and then the entity theory.

Parent company theory: Under this theory, the parent company is only entitled to the goodwill it created through the purchase of the subsidiary:

Price paid by P Co.		$500,000
Fair value of S Co. net assets	$600,000	
Interest purchased by P Co.	× 80%	
Fair value received by P Co.		480,000
Goodwill		$ 20,000

Goodwill would also be determined the same way under the combination parent company–entity theory.

Entity theory: Under this theory, the combined business entity of the parent company and the subsidiary is entitled to report all the goodwill resulting from the purchase, both the controlling interest and the minority interest, as long as the minority interest is clearly labeled as such:

Goodwill from P Co. purchase (above)	$20,000
P Company's interest in total goodwill	÷ 80%
Goodwill	$25,000*

*20% (or ($5,000) of this goodwill is minority interest.

C. The subsidiary's cost exceeds its fair value or book value and minority interest exists.

If a company acquires less than 100 percent of another company but pays more than fair value for the percentage of ownership it receives, then goodwill is implied in the purchase and must be accounted for in the consolidated balance sheet. In addition, if the acquired company's fair values exceed book values for its net assets, worksheet adjustments will be necessary to raise these assets to their fair values in the consolidated balance sheet.

The procedures to account for goodwill (using the parent company theory), and to revalue assets, are the same as those demonstrated in Example 4-2, except that all eliminating entries, and entries for goodwill and asset revaluation, must reflect the acquiring company's percentage of ownership.

EXAMPLE 4-8: On 1/1/X1, P Co. paid $130,000 for 80 percent of the common stock of S Co. Immediately after the purchase, the balance sheets of P Co. and S Co. were:

		S Co.	
BALANCE SHEET	P Co.	Book Values	Fair Values
Cash	$ 40,000	$ 30,000	$ 30,000
Accounts receivable (net)	80,000	50,000	50,000
Inventory	90,000	25,000	20,000
Land	50,000	20,000	35,000
Equipment	60,000	35,000	45,000
Investment in S Co.	130,000		
Total Assets	$450,000	$160,000	
Accounts payable	$ 40,000	$ 30,000	$ 30,000
Notes payable	60,000	30,000	30,000
Common stock:			
P. Co.	100,000		
S. Co.		50,000	
Additional paid-in capital: P. Co.	130,000		
S. Co.		40,000	
Retained earnings:			
P. Co.	120,000		
S. Co.		10,000	
Total Liabilities and Equity	$450,000	$160,000	
S Co. Fair Value			$120,000

Prepare a consolidated balance sheet using a worksheet to show P. Co. and S Co. as one economic entity.

Note the differences between the book values and fair values for certain of S Co.'s assets; both Land and Equipment have appreciated while Inventory has declined in value from historical cost or book values. Because P Co. bought an 80 percent interest in S Co., it is assumed that P Co. paid 80 percent of the *fair* values for S Co.'s assets. This must be reflected in the consolidated balance sheet. This revaluation of S Co.'s assets is achieved in the elimination process by debiting or crediting the appropriate assets for P Co.'s 80% interest in these assets. After all the book values have been adjusted to an appropriate fair value for S Co.'s assets, and 80 percent of S Co.'s equity accounts have been eliminated, any remaining investment by P Co. may be debited to goodwill. In this case the elimination entry is:

S Co. Common stock (80% × $50,000)	40,000	
S Co. Additional paid-in capital (80% × $40,000)	32,000	
S Co. Retained earnings (80% × $10,000)	8,000	
Land (80% × $15,000)	12,000	
Equipment (80% × $10,000)	8,000	
Goodwill	34,000	
Inventory (80% × $5,000)		4,000
Investment in S Co.		130,000

Note that the worksheet elimination entry allocates P Co.'s $130,000 investment three ways:

1. $80,000 80% interest in S Co. book value of $100,000.
2. $16,000 Revalue net assets to 80% interest in fair value in excess of book value (80% of $20,000).
3. $34,000 Record goodwill for excess purchase price over fair value of net assets.

The $34,000 goodwill portion can readily be determined as follows:

Price paid for investment		$130,000
Fair value of S Co.	$120,000	
Interest in S Co.	× 80%	
Fair value received		96,000
Goodwill		$ 34,000

The final worksheet showing the eliminations and the consolidated balance sheet of the combined business entity on the acquisition date is:

P Co. and S Co.
Consolidating Worksheet
1/01/X1

	P Co.	S Co.	Eliminations		Consolidated
BALANCE SHEET	Dr. (Cr.)	Dr. (Cr.)	Dr.	(Cr.)	Dr. (Cr.)
Cash	40,000	30,000			70,000
Accounts receiv. (net)	80,000	50,000			130,000
Inventory	90,000	25,000		[1](4,000)	111,000
Land	50,000	20,000	[1]12,000		82,000
Equipment (net)	60,000	35,000	[1]8,000		103,000
Investment in S Co.	130,000			[1](130,000)	0
Goodwill			[1]34,000		34,000
Accounts payable	(40,000)	(30,000)			(70,000)
Notes payable	(60,000)	(30,000)			(90,000)
Common stock:					
P Co.	(100,000)				(100,000)
S Co.		(50,000)	[1]40,000		(10,000)M
Additional paid-in capital: P Co.	(130,000)				(130,000)
S Co.		(40,000)	[1]32,000		(8,000)M
Retained earnings:					
P Co.	(120,000)				(120,000)
S Co.		(10,000)	[1]8,000		(2,000)M
Totals	0	0	134,000	(134,000)	0
		Total minority interest			($20,000)

M = Minority interest
[1]To eliminate investment in S Co. against S Co. equity and adjust S Co. assets to fair value.

4-5. Revaluation of a Subsidiary's Debt

The illustrations thus far assumed that fair and book values of a subsidiary's debt were the same. However, if debt is long-term, its interest rate is fixed, and the acquisition date interest rate differs from the fixed rate, the debt will have to be revalued for consolidation purposes. (The acquisition date interest rate is the parent company's borrowing rate on the date the parent acquires its interest in the subsidiary.) The process of debt revaluation involves these steps:

1. Determine the present discounted value (fair value) of the subsidiary's long-term debt principal and interest payments at the parent's borrowing rate on the date the parent acquires the subsidiary.
2. Compute the difference between the debt's fair value as determined in step 1 with the debt's book value as shown on the subsidiary's books.
3. Adjust the debt's book value in the elimination process for the difference developed in step 2.

EXAMPLE 4-9: On 1/1/X1, P Co. purchases all of S Co.'s common stock. On this date, S Co. is carrying at face value an 8% note payable for $100,000 maturing on 12/31/X3 (in 3 years). The acquisition date interest rate is 10%. The present discounted value of $1 paid in 3 years at 10% is $.751. The present discounted value of an ordinary annuity of $1 for 3 years at 10% is $2.487. Therefore, the present discounted value of the debt is:

— Present value of $100,000 principal due in 3 years at 10% = $100,000 × .751 =	$ 75,100
— Present value of $8,000 interest at end of each of 3 years at 10% = $8,000 × 2.487 =	19,896
Debt fair value	$ 94,996
Debt book value	100,000
Required worksheet adjustment	$ 5,004

A portion of the elimination entry will result in a worksheet presentation as follows:

	P Co. Dr. (Cr.)	S Co. Dr. (Cr.)	Eliminations Dr. (Cr.)	Consolidated Totals
Note payable		(100,000)	5,004	(94,996)

The remainder of the worksheet elimination entry will, of course, result in removal of S Co. equity against the Investment in S Co. account and in revaluation of other accounts as described earlier.

EXAMPLE 4-10: On 1/1/X1, P Co. acquired all of S Co.'s common stock for $1,005,004. On this date, S Co.'s book and fair values were as follows:

	Book Value	Fair Value
Assets	$1,100,000	$1,100,000
Long-term debt	(100,000)	(94,996)*
Common stock	(400,000)	
Retained earnings	(600,000)	
	$ 0	$1,005,004

*See Example 4-9 computation of $94,996.

In this case, the required worksheet elimination entry on 1/1/X1 is:

S Co. Common stock	400,000	
S Co. Retained earnings	600,000	
Long-term debt	5,004	
Investment in S Co.		1,005,004

RAISE YOUR GRADES

Can you explain . . . ?

- ☑ why consolidated financial statements are needed in reporting on a parent company and its subsidiaries
- ☑ the purchase method of accounting for business combinations
- ☑ the pooling of interests method of accounting for business combinations
- ☑ the consolidation process under the purchase method when the parent's cost for a 100% interest in a subsidiary equals the subsidiary's net asset's fair and book values
- ☑ the consolidation process under the purchase method when the parent's cost for a 100% interest in a subsidiary exceeds the subsidiary's net asset's fair values and the subsidiary's fair values exceed book values

- ☑ the consolidation process when the parent's cost for a 100% interest in a subsidiary is below the subsidiary's net asset's fair values (bargain purchase)
- ☑ the effect of a minority interest on the consolidation process under the parent company theory
- ☑ the effect of a minority interest on the consolidation process under the entity theory
- ☑ revaluation of a subsidiary's debt

SUMMARY

1. Consolidated financial statements, which show the two (or more) separate legal entities as one economic entity, should generally be prepared when one company gains control of another company.
2. Greater than 50% ownership indicates control.
3. Two approaches exist in accounting for business combinations: the purchase method and the pooling of interests method.
4. The pooling of interests method fundamentally represents a merger of ownership interests and managerial abilities of two or more companies, not a purchase/sale arrangement.
5. Under the pooling of interests method, net assets of the combined companies are added at book value, not fair value, and goodwill does not develop as a function of a pooling (see Chapter 11).
6. The purchase method fundamentally represents a purchase/sale arrangement wherein the ownership interests of one party (subsidiary) are purchased by (not merged with) another party (parent).
7. Under the purchase method, the acquiring company adjusts the acquired company's net assets to fair value to the extent the acquiring company's cost represents fair value. Any excess paid over fair value by the acquiring company for the acquired company's net assets represents goodwill.
8. In the consolidation process, if a parent company owns all of the stock of a subsidiary company, before adding the assets and debt of the two companies so that they may be reported as one economic entity, a worksheet elimination entry is necessary to remove the parent's interest in the subsidiary's equity against the parent's investment in a subsidiary account.
9. The elimination of a parent's interest in a subsidiary equity against the Investment in Subsidiary account is a simple process if the investment cost equals the subsidiary's fair value and book value.
10. If the investment cost exceeds a subsidiary's net assets at fair value, goodwill will result, and must be shown in the consolidated financial statements as an intangible asset to be amortized against consolidated net income over its expected useful life (not to exceed 40 years).
11. If an acquired company's net asset fair values and book values differ, revaluation of these net assets is necessary on the consolidating worksheet.
12. If the investment cost is below a subsidiary's net assets at fair value, noncurrent assets of the subsidiary (excluding long-term marketable securities) must first be reduced in the consolidation process. If the excess fair value over cost is still not removed, the remainder must be treated as a deferred credit during consolidation. This deferred credit, if any, will be amortized to consolidated net income over the years of expected benefit (not to exceed 40 years).

RAPID REVIEW

1. Henley Corporation purchased all of the outstanding stock of Lock Company for $4,000,000. Henley also paid finder's fees and fees to attorneys of $100,000 to accomplish the business combination. Indirect and general expenses related to the acquisition were another $60,000. The charge to the account "Investment in Lock Company" on Henley's books should be
   (*a*) $4,000,000.
   (*b*) $4,100,000.
   (*c*) $4,060,000.
   (*d*) $4,160,000.

2. Consolidated financial statements are prepared because
(*a*) the companies involved are one legal entity although separate entities in substance.
(*b*) the companies involved are separate legal entities although one entity in substance.
(*c*) the companies are one entity in form and substance.
(*d*) the companies are separate entities in form and substance.

Questions 3 through 6 are based on the following information:

Lion Company purchased 80% of the common stock of Antler Company for $350,000. Just before the purchase, the balance sheets of Lion and Antler were as follows:

		Antler Co.	
(Amounts shown in thousands)	Lion Co.	Book Value	Fair Value
Cash	$ 800	$ 200	$ 200
Accounts receivable	100	50	50
Equipment (net)	400	100	120
Land	500	90	100
Total Assets	$1,800	$ 440	
Accounts payable	$ 300	$ 40	$ 40
Mortgage payable	400	100	90
Common stock	400	200	
Retained earnings	700	100	
Total Liabilities and equity	$1,800	$ 440	

3. Goodwill resulting from the purchase under the parent company theory is
(*a*) $50,000
(*b*) $10,000
(*c*) $78,000
(*d*) $97,500

4. The consolidated balance sheet for Lion Company and Subsidiary Antler Company will show Land on the acquisition date, using the parent company theory, at
(*a*) $600,000
(*b*) $590,000
(*c*) $500,000
(*d*) $598,000

5. The consolidated balance sheet for Lion Company and Subsidiary Antler Company will show Land on the acquisition date, using the entity theory, at
(*a*) $600,000
(*b*) $590,000
(*c*) $500,000
(*d*) $598,000

6. Goodwill resulting from the purchase under the entity theory is
(*a*) $50,000
(*b*) $10,000
(*c*) $78,000
(*d*) $97,500

7. Registration fees associated with the issue of stock to effect a business combination should be charged to additional paid-in capital and not charged to expense in determining consolidated net income in the year such fees are incurred for a

	Pooling of Interests	Purchase
(*a*)	No	Yes
(*b*)	No	No
(*c*)	Yes	No
(*d*)	Yes	Yes

8. If a parent company owns 90% of the stock of its subsidiary, the portion of the subsidiary's assets and liabilities that will appear on the consolidated balance sheet is
(*a*) 100%
(*b*) 90%

9. Under the parent company theory, minority interest will normally appear in the balance sheet
(*a*) as a part of stockholders' equity
(*b*) between liabilities and stockholders' equity
(*c*) as debt

10. Under the entity theory, minority interest will normally appear in the balance sheet
(*a*) as a part of stockholders' equity
(*b*) between liabilities and stockholders' equity
(*c*) as debt

Answers:

1. (*b*) The investment account charge should be for $4,100,000, to include the $4,000,000 purchase price plus $100,000 in direct costs of acquisition. However, the $60,000 in indirect and general expenses should not be included as part of the investment cost, but expensed as incurred.

2. (*b*) The purpose of preparing consolidated financial statements is to show two or more separate legal entities as, in substance, one economic entity.

3. (*c*)

Price paid		$350,000
Fair value of net assets	$340,000	
Lion's interest	× 80%	
Fair value received		272,000
Goodwill		$ 78,000

4. (*d*)

Lion's land account (book value)	$500,000
Antler's land account (book value)	90,000
Lion's interest in revaluation of Antler's land account to fair value (80% × $10,000)	8,000
Land (Consolidated)	$598,000

5. (*a*)

Lion's land account (book value)	$500,000
Antler's land account (book value)	100,000
Land (Consolidated)	$600,000

note: $2,000 of the $10,000 land revaluation (which will bring the land from a book value of $90,000 to a fair of $100,000) represents a credit to minority interest.

6. (*d*) Note that goodwill in answer to question 3 under the parent company theory was $78,000 when the parent company holds an 80% interest. Therefore:

$78,000	=	80% Entity Goodwill
$78,000/.8	=	Entity Goodwill
$97,500	=	Entity Goodwill

7. (*a*) (See page 97, Section 4-1.C of this chapter.)

8. (*a*) Even though a parent owns only a portion of a subsidiary, all of the subsidiary's assets are shown on the consolidated balance sheet. However, in this case, 10% (100% – 90%) of the net assets (equity) will be labeled as minority interest.

9. (*b*) (See section 4B.)

10. (*a*) (See section 4B.)

SOLVED PROBLEMS

(Unless otherwise indicated, all problems should be solved using the parent company theory).

PROBLEM 4-1: On October 15, 19X5, Penelope Corporation purchased 100% of Sarah Company for $1,800,000. On this date, Sarah Company's net assets had a fair value of $1,900,000, but its noncurrent assets had a book value totaling only $80,000 because most of its property, plant, and equipment was leased, and the leases were appropriately acounted for as operating leases. Also, on October 15, 19X5, Sarah Company had book balances in common stock, additional paid-in capital, and retained earnings of $1,000,000, $400,000, and $450,000 respectively. Prepare the October 15, 19X5 worksheet elimination entry.

Answer:

Sarah Co. – Common stock	1,000,000	
Sarah Co. – Additional paid-in capital	400,000	
Sarah Co. – Retained earnings	450,000	
Noncurrent Assets*		50,000
Investment in Sarah Co.		1,800,000

**Allocation to various noncurrent assets would be based on their fair values (see Example 4-3).*

PROBLEM 4-2: Using the information in Problem 4-1, except that Sarah Company's retained earnings on October 15, 19X5 were $550,000, prepare the October 15, 19X5 worksheet elimination entry:

Answer:

Sarah Co. – Common stock	1,000,000	
Sarah Co. – Additional paid-in capital	400,000	
Sarah Co. – Retained earnings	550,000	
Noncurrent Assets*		80,000
Deferred credit		70,000
Investment in Sarah Co.		1,800,000

**Note the noncurrent assets have a total book value of $80,000 and may be reduced by no more than this. The excess, if any, represents a deferred credit from consolidation which will be amortized to consolidated income over its expected life (not to exceed 40 years).*

PROBLEM 4-3: Parnell Company purchased for $500,000 all of the voting stock of Small Company on July 1, 19X3. Immediately after the purchase, balance sheet information for both companies was as follows:

	Parnell Co.	Small Co.
Cash	$ 150,000	$100,000
Accounts receivable (net)	180,000	210,000
Inventories	120,000	78,000
Land	200,000	100,000
Building	600,000	350,000
Accumulated Depreciation	(200,000)	(138,000)
Investment – Small Co.	500,000	—
Total Assets	$1,550,000	$700,000
Accounts payable	$ 50,000	$ 70,000
Long-term debt	150,000	130,000
Common stock	300,000	100,000
Additional paid-in capital:	150,000	50,000
Retained earning:	900,000	350,000
Total Liabilities and Equity	$1,550,000	$700,000

Prepare the consolidated elimination working papers as of July 1, 19X3. Assume the book value of Small Company's net assets equals the fair value.

Answer:

Parnell Company and Small Company
Consolidating Worksheet
7/01/X3

BALANCE SHEET	Parnell Co. Dr. (Cr.)	Small Co. Dr. (Cr.)	Eliminations Dr.	Eliminations (Cr.)	Consolidated Dr. (Cr.)
Cash	150,000	100,000			250,000
Accounts receiv. (net)	180,000	210,000			390,000
Inventory	120,000	78,000			198,000
Land	200,000	100,000			300,000
Building	600,000	350,000			950,000
Accum. depr.	(200,000)	(138,000)			(338,000)
Investment in Small Co.	500,000			[1](500,000)	0
Accounts payable	(50,000)	(70,000)			(120,000))
Long-term debt	(150,000)	(130,000)			(280,000)
Common stock:					
Parnell Co.	(300,000)				(300,000)
Small Co.		(100,000)	[1]100,000		0
Additional paid-in capital: Parnell Co.	(150,000)				(150,000)
Small Co.		(50,000)	[1]50,000		0
Retained earnings:					
Parnell Co.	(900,000)				(900,000)
Small Co.		(350,000)	[1]350,000		0
Totals	0	0	500,000	(500,000)	0

[1]To eliminate investment in Small Co. against its equity.

PROBLEM 4-4: On June 15, 19X3, Peach Company purchased all of the voting stock of Shadow Corporation for $180,000. After the purchase, balance sheet information for both companies was as follows:

	Peach Co.	Shadow Corp. Book Values	Shadow Corp. Fair Values
Cash	$ 30,000	$ 2,000	$ 2,000
Accounts receivable (net)	70,000	16,000	16,000
Inventories	120,000	12,000	26,000
Land	50,000	30,000	50,000
Building (net)	145,000	64,000	64,000
Patent	5,000	1,000	35,000
Investment – Shadow Corp.	180,000	—	
Total Assets	$600,000	$125,000	
Accounts payable	$ 42,000	$ 5,000	$ 5,000
Long-term debt	140,000	30,000	25,000
Common stock	200,000	—	
Common stock	—	53,000	
Additional paid-in capital:	75,000	12,000	
Retained earning:	143,000	25,000	
Total Liabilities and Equity	$600,000	$125,000	

Prepare the consolidated elimination working papers as of June 15, 19X3.

Answer: Note that goodwill may be seen as follows:

Price paid by Peach Co.		$180,000
Fair value of Shadow Corp.	$163,000*	
Interest purchased by Peach Co.	× 100%	
Fair value received		163,000
Goodwill		$ 17,000

**Fair value of Shadow Corp. equals fair value of its assets less the fair value of its liabilities.*

Peach Company and Shadow Corporation
Consolidating Worksheet
6/15/X3

BALANCE SHEET	Peach Co. Dr. (Cr.)	Shadow Corp. Dr. (Cr.)	Eliminations Dr.	Eliminations (Cr.)	Consolidated Dr. (Cr.)
Cash	30,000	2,000			32,000
Accounts receiv. (net)	70,000	16,000			86,000
Inventory	120,000	12,000	[1]14,000		146,000
Land	50,000	30,000	[1]20,000		100,000
Building (net)	145,000	64,000			209,000
Patent	5,000	1,000	[1]34,000		40,000
Investmt in Shadow Corp.	180,000			[1](180,000)	0
Goodwill			[1]17,000		17,000
Accounts payable	(42,000)	(5,000)			(47,000)
Long-term debt	(140,000)	(30,000)			(170,000)
Discount on long-term debt			[1]5,000		5,000

Common stock:					
Peach Co.	(200,000)				(200,000)
Shadow Corp.		(53,000)	[1]53,000		0
Additional paid-in capital:					
Peach Co.	(75,000)				(75,000)
Shadow Corp.		(12,000)	[1]12,000		0
Retained earnings:					
Peach Co.	(143,000)				(143,000)
Shadow Corp.		(25,000)	[1]25,000		0
Totals	0	0	180,000	(180,000)	0

[1]To eliminate investment in Shadow Corp. against its equity and adjust Shadow Corp. assets to fair value.

PROBLEM 4-5: Immediately before an April 1, 19X7 purchase by P Co. of 80% of the stock of S Co., the balance sheets of the two companies were as follows:

		S Co.	
BALANCE SHEET	P Co.	Book Values	Fair Values
Cash	$ 350,000	$ 65,000	$ 65,000
Accounts receivable (net)	120,000	45,000	45,000
Notes receivable)	35,000	26,000	20,000
Inventory	80,000	24,000	15,000
Land	60,000	30,000	40,000
Building (net)	300,000	275,000	350,000
Equipment (net)	70,000	25,000	35,000
Patent	45,000	25,000	10,000
Goodwill	50,000	20,000	
Total Assets	$1,110,000	$535,000	
Accounts payable	$ 50,000	$ 25,000	$ 25,000
Notes payable	100,000	45,000	45,000
Mortgage payable	210,000	100,000	90,000
Common stock:			
P. Co.	400,000		
S. Co.		150,000	
Additional paid-in			
capital: P. Co.	200,000		
S. Co.		100,000	
Retained earnings:			
P. Co.	150,000		
S. Co.		115,000	
Total liabilities and equity	$1,110,000	$535,000	
S Co. Fair Value			$420,000

P Co. purchased its 80% interest in S Co. in the following manner:

- Issued common stock, 20,000 shares, $10 par per share. The fair market value per share on 4/1/X7 is $15.
- Paid $265,000 in cash.
- Paid $5,000 in securities registration fees associated with the 20,000 shares of stock which were issued.
- Paid $5,000 in direct costs associated with the purchase.

1. Prepare the journal entries on the books of P Co. to record the purchase of S Co., including any entries necessary to record direct costs and registration fees.

2. Prepare a consolidating worksheet on 4/1/X7 immediately after the purchase.

Answer:

Investment in S Co.	570,000	
Cash.		270,000
Common stock (20,000 @ $10 par)		200,000
Additional paid-in capital (20,000 @ $5)		100,000

To record P Co. investment in S Co. (The cash outlay includes the $265,000 purchase price plus direct costs of $5,000.)

Additional paid-in capital	5,000	
Cash		5,000

To record payment of registration fees.

Note that P Co. account balances have been adjusted on the worksheet to reflect the answers shown above. The worksheet elimination entry is as follows:

	Dr.	Cr.
S Co. Common stock	120,000	
S Co. Additional paid-in capital.	80,000	
S Co. Retained earnings.	92,000	
Notes receivable		4,800
Inventory		7,200
Land	8,000	
Building (net)	60,000	
Equipment (net)	8,000	
Patent		12,000
Goodwill (S Co.)		16,000
Goodwill (from consolidation).	234,000	
Mortgage payable.	8,000	
Investment in S Co.		570,000
Totals	610,000	610,000

This entry eliminates P Company's 80% interest in S Company and removes S Company's goodwill of $16,000 while recording the $234,000 in goodwill which has been confirmed in the purchase price as follows:

Price paid by P Co. for 80% interest		
Common stock issued (at fair value).	$300,000	
Cash payment	270,000	$570,000
Fair value received (80% of $420,000)		336,000
Goodwill (from consolidation) . .		$234,000

P Co. and S Co.
Consolidating Worksheet
4/01/X7

BALANCE SHEET	P Co. Dr. (Cr.)	S Co. Dr. (Cr.)	Eliminations Dr.	Eliminations (Cr.)	Consolidated Dr. (Cr.)
Cash	75,000	65,000			140,000
Accounts receiv. (net)	120,000	45,000			165,000
Notes receivable	35,000	26,000		[1](4,800)	56,200
Inventory	80,000	24,000		[1](7,200)	96,800
Land	60,000	30,000	[1]8,000		98,000
Building (net)	300,000	275,000	[1]60,000		635,000
Equipment (net)	70,000	25,000	[1]8,000		103,000
Investment in S Co.	570,000			[1](570,000)	0
Patent	45,000	25,000		[1](12,000)	58,000
Goodwill	50,000	20,000	[1]234,000	[1](16,000)	288,000
Accounts payable	(50,000)	(25,000)			(75,000)
Notes payable	(100,000)	(45,000)			(145,000)
Mortgage payable	(210,000)	(100,000)	[1]8,000		(302,000)
Common stock:					
P Co.	(600,000)				(600,000)
S Co.		(150,000)	[1]120,000		(30,000)M
Additional paid-in capital: P Co.	(295,000)				(295,000)
S Co.		(100,000)	[1]80,000		(20,000)M
Retained earnings:					
P Co.	(150,000)				(150,000)
S Co.		(115,000)	[1]92,000		(23,000)M
Totals	0	0	610,000	(610,000)	0
		Total minority interest			($73,000)

M = Minority interest
[1]To eliminate investment in S Co. against S Co. equity and adjust S Co. net assets to fair value.

PROBLEM 4-6: On November 1, 19X2, Pluto Company acquired a controlling interest in Saturn Company. On November 1, 19X2, Saturn Company's stockholders' equity section of its balance sheet included the following items:

Common stock, 10,000 shares authorized, $10 par, 8000 shares issued and outstanding	$ 80,000
Additional paid-in capital	270,000
Retained earnings - unappropriated	300,000
Retained earnings - appropriated for plant expansion	100,000
Total stockholders' equity	$750,000

Also on November 1, 19X2, Saturn Company's net asset book and fair values were equal except for the following two items:

	Book Value	Fair Value
Inventory	$20,000	$15,000
Land	30,000	45,000
Totals	$50,000	$60,000

Land is Saturn company's only noncurrent asset. Prepare the worksheet elimination entry for the acquisition by Pluto of a controlling interest in Saturn on November 1, 19X2 under each of the following situations:

(*a*) Purchased 100% of Saturn's common stock for $770,000
(*b*) Purchased 100% of Saturn's common stock for $700,000
(*c*) Purchased 80% of Saturn's common stock for $650,000
(*d*) Purchased 80% of Saturn's common stock for $560,000

Answer:

(*a*)

	Debit	Credit
Saturn Co. – Common Stock	80,000	
Saturn Co. – Additional paid-in capital	270,000	
Saturn Co. – Unappropriated retained earnings	300,000	
Saturn Co. – Appropriated retained earnings	100,000	
Land	15,000	
Goodwill	10,000	
Inventory		5,000
Investment in Saturn Co.		770,000

(*b*)

	Debit	Credit
Saturn Co. – Common Stock	80,000	
Saturn Co. – Additional paid-in capital	270,000	
Saturn Co. – Unappropriated retained earnings	300,000	
Saturn Co. – Appropriated retained earnings	100,000	
Inventory		5,000
Investment in Saturn Co.		700,000
Land (limited to 100% of book value)		30,000
Deferred credit		15,000

(*c*)

	Debit	Credit
Saturn Co. – Common Stock	64,000	
Saturn Co. – Additional paid-in capital	216,000	
Saturn Co. – Unappropriated retained earnings	240,000	
Saturn Co. – Appropriated retained earnings	80,000	
Land (80% × $5,000)	12,000	
Goodwill	42,000	
Inventory (80% × $5000)		4,000
Investment in Saturn Co.		650,000

(*d*) Recall: Land is the only noncurrent asset.

	Debit	Credit
Saturn Co. – Common Stock	64,000	
Saturn Co. – Additional paid-in capital	216,000	
Saturn Co. – Unappropriated retained earnings	240,000	
Saturn Co. – Appropriated retained earnings	80,000	
Land (limited to 80% of book value)		24,000
Inventory (80% × $5000)		4,000
Deferred credit		12,000
Investment in Saturn Co.		560,000

5 THE EQUITY AND COST METHODS OF CARRYING INVESTMENTS

THIS CHAPTER IS ABOUT

☑ **Using the Cost or Equity Method to Carry an Investment**
☑ **Carrying Investments under the Cost Method**
☑ **Carrying Investments under the Equity Method**
☑ **Carrying Investments in Subsidiaries**

5-1. Using the Cost or Equity Method to Carry an Investment

After one company makes a long-term investment in another (regardless of whether that company acquires a controlling interest), it must apply one of two possible methods of accounting for that investment during the period of time that has elapsed since the purchase date. The two possible accounting approaches to long-term investments are the *cost method* and the *equity method.*

A. The cost method.

Under the cost method, the investor company carries its investment in the investee company at historical cost. The investor's purchase price for its interest in the investee will generally remain on its books unchanged by the future performance of the investee. The investor company does not record the investee's profits or losses on its own books (except in special circumstances discussed in Section 5-2), and only recognizes income from the investment when the investee pays cash dividends on its stock.

B. The equity method.

Under the equity method, the investor company adjusts the historical cost of its investment to reflect the investee's performance after the acquisition date. The investor company's purchase price, entered on its books on the acquisition date, will change with the future performance of the investee.

Using this method, the investor company *does* record its share of the investee's profits and losses on its own books, in addition to cash dividends paid on the investee's stock. The result of such adjustments is that at any given time the equity interest the investor holds in the investee should represent the balance in the investment account.

C. Applicability of the cost and equity methods.

A company will use either the cost or equity method to account for its investment in the common stock of other companies depending largely on its level of ownership interest. If its ownership interest is less than 20%, it will generally use the cost method. If its ownership interest is between 20% and 50%, it will generally use the equity method. If its ownership interest level is greater than 50%, it may use either method, depending on its goals in terms of financial reporting.

When the investor owns over 50% interest in the investee, the advantage of using the equity method is that the investor's separate (unconsolidated) financial statements will better depict the investor's equity interest in the net assets of the investee over time. If separate financial statements are prepared, the additional cost of the accounting required to use the equity method may therefore be worth the benefit. Under the cost method, the changes in the investor's equity interest in the investee are not included in the investor's separate financial statements and, therefore, the separate statements of the investor company represent a less-than-complete picture of its involvement with the investee.

Exhibit 5-A illustrates the applicability of these methods at various levels of ownership interest, and the reasoning behind such applications.

Exhibit 5-A

Level of ownership interest (%)	General presumption	Appropriate accounting method
Below 20	Significant influence over investee does not exist.	Cost (using lower of aggregate cost or market for reporting purposes).*
20 to 50	Significant influence over investee does exist.	Equity.
Over 50	Significant influence and control over investee both exist.	Consolidated financial statements (may use either cost or equity method).**

*The rules of FASB Statement 115, "Accounting for Certain Investments in Debt and Equity Securities," generally apply when the cost method is used. The specifics of FASB Statement 115 are not relevant to the use of the cost method as it relates to controlling interests of over 50% in another company. Consequently, these specifics are not addressed, but application of the cost method to long-term investments is addressed.

**Control (over 50% interest) may exist in some situations that do not permit preparation of consolidated financial statements. For example, the parent company's position of control may be expected to be for a short time. In these situations, the equity method of accounting for the investment in the "unconsolidated subsidiary" must be used.

5-2. Carrying Investments under the Cost Method

Under the cost method, the investor company records and carries the investment in another company at the historical cost, even after the date of the investment. Generally, the investor company does not record the investee's profits or losses, or changes in the value of its equity in the investee, on its books. Under the cost method, the investor records income from cash dividends in a Dividend Income account, thus leaving the investment's purchase price untouched.

EXAMPLE 5-1: On July, 19X6, Brace Company purchased 10% of the Cannon Company's common stock for $1,000,000. Cannon Company had total net income for the fiscal year ended June 30, 19X7, of $1,200,000. Cannon Company declared and paid dividends on June 1, 19X7, totaling $700,000. Brace Company would record these events as follows under the cost method:

7/1/X6	Investment in Cannon Company	1,000,000	
	Cash		1,000,000
6/1/X7	Cash (10% × $700,000)	70,000	
	Dividend income		70,000

There are, however, two situations under the cost method in which the investor company may adjust the historical purchase price of its investment. The first is when clear evidence exists that the original investment cost has been permanently impaired, and can no longer be supported, as a result of the investee's performance after the acquisition date. In this case, the investment account is credited and a realized loss is charged. The second case in which the historical cost may be adjusted is when the investor receives a *liquidating dividend* from the investee. A liquidating dividend is paid from the investee's preacquisition earnings, and represents a return of investment to the investor company. The investor *does* record a liquidating dividend as a reduction in its investment account, even under the cost method.

EXAMPLE 5-2: Using the facts from Example 5-1, except that Cannon Company had a total net income of only $500,000 for the fiscal year ended June 30, 19X7, Brace Company would record these events as follows under the cost method:

7/1/X6	Investment in Cannon Company	1,000,000	
	Cash		1,000,000
6/1/X7	Cash (10% × $700,000)	70,000	
	Dividend income (limited to 10% of postacquisition earnings of $500,000)		50,000
	Investment in Cannon Co. (liquidating dividend)		20,000

5-3. Carrying Investments under the Equity Method

Under the equity method, the investor company records the historical cost of its investment on the purchase date, but thereafter records the performance of the investee as adjustments to its investment account. The investment account is periodically increased (or decreased) by the investor's share of the investee's profits (or losses). In addition, cash dividends received are recorded as a decrease in the investment account balance (not as dividend income).

If the investee's fair values equal its book values, no goodwill results from the investment. If, however, the investor's cost exceeds its share of the investee's fair value, goodwill does result, and must be amortized against the investee's income as recorded by the investor. Further, if the investee's book value and fair value differ, additional amortization or depreciation charges may be necessary.

A. Investor company's cost equals investor's share of investee's fair and book values.

Under the equity method, when the investor's cost equals the investor's share of investee's fair and book values, the investor company records the gains (or losses) of the investee after the purchase date as increases (or decreases) in its investment account, and as investment income (or loss).

If the investee pays a dividend, the investor credits its share of the dividend to its investment account, and debits the same amount to cash.

EXAMPLE 5-3: On July 1, 19X6, Brace Company purchased 30% of the Cannon Company common stock for $3,000,000. For the fiscal year ended June 30, 19X7, Cannon Company had a total net income of $1,200,000, and declared and paid dividends on June 1, 19X7, totalling $700,000. Brace Company would record these events as follows under the equity method:

7/1/X6	Investment in Cannon Company	3,000,000	
	Cash		3,000,000
6/1/X7	Cash (30% × $700,000)	210,000	
	Investment in Cannon Company		210,000
6/30/X7	Investment in Cannon Company	360,000	
	Investment income (30% × $1,200,000)		360,000

The Investment account balance at June 30, 19X7, is now $3,150,000 ($3,000,000 plus $360,000 less $210,000).

B. Investor company's cost exceeds investor's share of investee's fair and book values.

If the investor's cost exceeds the investment's fair value, then goodwill exists and is amortized by crediting the investment account and debiting the account Amortization of Cost in Excess of Book Value.

Goodwill is determined as demonstrated in Chapter 4 (Example 4-2), and is amortized over its useful life (which may not exceed 40 years).

EXAMPLE 5-4: On July 1, 19X6, Brace Company purchased a 30% interest in the common stock of Cannon Company for $3,000,000. The fair value of Cannon Company's net assets on July 1, 19X6, which equaled book value, was $9,500,000. Cannon Company had total net income of $1,200,000 for the fiscal year ended June 30, 19X7, and on June 1, 19X7 declared and paid dividends of $700,000. Brace Company would record these events as follows under the equity method:

Date	Account	Debit	Credit
7/1/X6	Investment in Cannon Company	3,000,000	
	Cash		3,000,000
6/1/X7	Cash (30% × $700,000)	210,000	
	Investment in Cannon Company		210,000
6/30/X7	Investment in Cannon Company	360,000	
	Investment income (30% × $1,200,000)		360,000

Brace Company would calculate the goodwill (on the date of the purchase) and its goodwill amortization expense (on 6/30/X7) in the following manner:

Investment cost	$3,000,000
Fair value received (30% × $9,500,000)	2,850,000
Goodwill	$ 150,000
Useful life	÷ 40 yrs
Goodwill amortization	$ 3,750

The amortization expense decreases the investment account, thereby decreasing Brace Company's equity interest in Cannon Company.

Date	Account	Debit	Credit
6/30/X7	Amortization of cost in excess of book value	3,750	
	Investment in Cannon Co		3,750

As a result of these entries, the June 30, 19X7 Investment account balance (Brace Company's equity) is $3,146,250 ($3,000,000 plus $360,000 less $210,000 less $3,750). Investment income is $356,250 ($360,000 less $3,750).

C. Investee's fair values and book values differ.

If, in addition to the investor's cost exceeding the investment's fair value, the investee's fair values and book values also differ, then additional (or reduced) amortization, or depreciation charges (or credits) to investment income, may be necessary in order to make the investment account accurately reflect the value of the investor's equity in the investee.

EXAMPLE 5-5: Use the facts of Example 5-4, with one change: the book value and fair value of Cannon Company's net assets are $9,000,000 and $9,500,000, respectively. The difference results from the following items on Cannon Company's books at July 1, 19X6:

	Book value	Fair value	Difference
Inventory	$ 150,000	$ 200,000*	$ 50,000
Equipment (net)	400,000	600,000**	200,000
Land	600,000	850,000	250,000
	$1,150,000	$1,650,000	$ 500,000

*Completely sold by December 1, 19X6.
**10-year remaining life, straight-line depreciation, no salvage value.

The $3,000,000 purchase price for a 30% interest may now be analyzed as follows:

Price paid by Brace Company for 30% interest	$3,000,000
Book value of underlying net assets received (30% × $9,000,000)	(2,700,000)
Excess cost over book value	300,000
Portion of excess attributable to:	
Inventory (30% × $50,000)	(15,000)
Equipment (30% × $200,000)	(60,000)
Land (30% × $250,000)	(75,000)
Goodwill	$ 150,000

Goodwill in this case may also be calculated as shown below:

Investment cost	$3,000,000
Fair value received (30% × $9,500,000)	(2,850,000)
Goodwill	$ 150,000

Brace Company would record these events as follows under the equity method during fiscal year ended June 30, 19X7:

7/1/X6	Investment in Cannon Company	3,000,000	
	Cash		3,000,000
6/1/X7	Cash (30% × $700,000)	210,000	
	Investment in Cannon Company		210,000
6/30/X7	Investment in Cannon Company	360,000	
	Investment income (30% × $1,200,000)		360,000

The amortization expense is determined as follows:

Goodwill ($150 ÷ 40 years)	$ 3,750
Inventory (completely sold)	15,000
Equipment ($60,000 ÷ 10 years)	6,000
	$24,750

The amortization expense decreases the investment account, thereby decreasing the Brace Company's equity interest in Cannon Company:

6/30/X7	Amortization of cost in excess of book value	24,750	
	Investment in Cannon Company		24,750

The investment account balance at June 30, 19X7, is $3,125,250 ($3,000,000 plus $360,000 less $210,000 less $24,750). Investment income is $335,250.

Note that the amortization entry will change in future years:

	Fiscal Year Ending June 30		
	Two years after purchase (19X8)	Eleven years after purchase (19X17)	Forty-one years after purchase (19X47)
Inventory (sold in X6)	$ 0	$ 0	$ 0
Equipment (10 yr. life)	6,000	0	0
Goodwill (40 yr. life)	3,750	3,750	0
Debit amortization account and credit investment account	$ 9,750	$ 3,750	$ 0

5-4. Carrying Investments in Subsidiaries

Until this point we have been considering the differences between the cost and equity methods of carrying long-term investments in general (regardless of the level of ownership interest acquired). We now consider the two methods as they apply specifically to parent-subsidiary affiliations.

When two companies enter a parent-subsidiary relationship, with the parent clearly exercising control over the subsidiary, the combined business entity almost always prepares consolidated financial statements. There are, however, a few situations in which the subsidiary does not prepare consolidated financial statements with its parent (such as lack of long-term control or ownership interest by the parent). Such a subsidiary is considered an *unconsolidated subsidiary.*

A. Accounting for unconsolidated subsidiaries.

When a parent company's subsidiary is unconsolidated, the parent *must* use the equity method to account for its investment in that subsidiary. Because there will be no consolidated financial statements prepared, the equity method is used to show the parent's equity interest in the subsidiary.

EXAMPLE 5-6: On July 1, 19X1, P Co. purchased 100% of S Co. common stock for $2,000,000. On July 1, 19X1, S Co.'s financial position was as follows (in condensed form):

Assets	
Assets (various)	$3,000,000
Liabilities and Stockholders' Equity	
Liabilities (various)	$1,200,000
Common stock ($10 par)	1,000,000
Retained earnings	800,000
	$3,000,000

On July 1, 19X1, the net assets of S Co. had book values equaling fair values, except for the following items:

	Book value	Fair value	Difference
Inventory	$100,000	$125,000	$25,000*
Equipment	200,000	250,000	50,000**
Land	300,000	375,000	75,000
	$600,000	$750,000	$150,000

*All sold as of 11/1/X1.
**5-year life remaining, straight-line depreciation, no salvage.

Both P Co. and S Co. have fiscal years ending on December 31. For the fiscal year ended December 31, 19X1, S Co. generated net income and declared and paid dividends as follows:

Six months ended	Net income	Dividends declared and paid
6/30/X1	$120,000	$140,000
12/31/X1	140,000	100,000
	$260,000	$240,000

Assume that consolidated financial statements for P Co. and S Co. are not feasible, and that P Co. must carry its investment under the equity method. No worksheet elimination entries will be made to eliminate the Investment in S Co. account carried by P Co. The entries P Co. will actually make on its books follow. Note that since P Co. purchased its interest on July 1, 19X1, S Co. net income and dividends for only the last six months of the fiscal year are recognized by P Co.

7/1/X1	Investment in S Co.	2,000,000	
	Cash		2,000,000
12/31/X1	Investment in S Co.	140,000	
	Subsidiary income		140,000
12/31/X1	Cash	100,000	
	Investment in S Co.		100,000

The amount of amortization necessary to bring the Investment in S Co. account to reflect the value of P Co.'s interest in S Co. on 12/31/89 is calculated in the following way:

Investment cost		$2,000,000
Book value of underlying net assets received ($3,000,000 assets less $1,200,000 debt)	$1,800,000	
Ownership level	× 100%	1,800,000
Excess cost over book value		200,000
Portion of excess attributable to:		
Inventory (100% × $25,000)		(25,000)
Equipment (100% × $50,000)		(50,000)
Land (100% × $75,000)		(75,000)
Goodwill		$ 50,000

The X1 year amortization charge is based on:

Inventory (all sold as of 11/1/X1)	$ 25,000
Depreciation ($50,000 ÷ 5-year life × 1/2 year)	5,000
Goodwill ($50,000 ÷ 40-year × 1/2 year)	625
Year X1 amortization	$ 30,625

The amortization is recorded as follows:

12/31/X1	Amortization of cost in excess of book value	30,625	
	Investment in S Co.		30,625

The December 31, 19X1 Investment in S Co. account balance is $2,009,375 ($2,000,000 plus $140,000 less $100,000 less $30,625). The subsidiary income is $109,375 ($140,000 less $30,625).

B. Accounting for consolidated subsidiaries.

A parent company may use either the cost method or the equity method to account for its investment in a subsidiary that it intends to include in its consolidated financial statements. Regardless of the method used, however, the financial statements for the combined business entity must yield the same results. This means that the eliminations on the working papers used to prepare the consolidated financial statements must vary according to the method used. (The consolidation process after the acquisition date, including eliminations, is the subject of Chapters 6 and 7.) It is crucial, therefore, to be aware of the carrying method used by the parent, and the difference such methods can make in the parent's balance sheet, before consolidation.

EXAMPLE 5-7: Using the information provided in Example 5-6, we will now assume that consolidation between P Co. and S Co. is appropriate. Under the cost method, P Co. would have made the following entries during year X1 to account for its investment in S Co.:

Investment in S Co.	2,000,000	
Cash		2,000,000
Cash	100,000	
Dividend income		100,000

Under the equity method, P Co. would have made the entries already shown in Example 5-6. Note that the different account balances under the two methods are:

	Balances at 12/31/X1	
	Cost	Equity
Investment in S Co.	$2,000,000	$2,009,375
Dividend Income	$ 100,000	
Subsidiary Income		$ 109,375

The worksheet elimination process must eliminate different account balances under the cost and equity methods in order to provide accurate consolidated financial statements.

RAISE YOUR GRADES

Can you explain . . . ?

- ☑ the situations requiring the use of the equity method
- ☑ the situations requiring the use of the cost method
- ☑ general accounting procedures under the equity method when the investment cost equals book and fair value
- ☑ general accounting procedures under the equity method when the investment cost exceeds fair value
- ☑ general accounting procedures under the equity method when the investee's net asset fair and book values differ.
- ☑ why the equity method must be used by a parent company in accounting for an investment in an unconsolidated subsidiary
- ☑ why the cost or equity method may be used in accounting for a consolidated subsidiary

SUMMARY

1. The methods of accounting for long-term investments in common stock are the cost method and the equity method.
2. The cost method should generally be used when less than 20% interest in an investee company exists, since this is indicative of a lack of significant influence.
3. The equity method should be used when a 20% to 50% interest in an investee company exists, since this is indicative of significant influence.
4. If over 50% interest is held, a parent-subsidiary relationship exists, and consolidated financial statements are generally prepared, and the Investment account balance and any other intercompany items are eliminated. Therefore, the parent may carry the investment by means of either the cost or equity methods.
5. If, as a result of extenuating circumstances, a subsidiary is unconsolidated, the parent company must use the equity method to carry its investment in that subsidiary.

6. The cost method involves recording the original investment at cost and recording dividends received as dividend income.
7. Under the cost method, the investment is originally recorded and continues to be carried at cost unless a liquidating dividend is received, or a decline in the investment's market value considered to be other than temporary occurs.
8. Under the cost method, liquidating dividends would not be recorded as dividend income, but rather as a return of investment.
9. The equity method involves recording the original investment at cost and recognizing the investor's pro-rata share of the investee's net income (or loss) as an increase (or decrease) in the Investment account balance. Dividends declared and paid to the investor are then treated as a return of investment (decrease Investment account balance).
10. Under the equity method, if the investment cost exceeds the investor's share of the underlying fair value of the investee's net assets, goodwill exists as a part of the investment cost, and must be amortized as a reduction against Investment Income and the Investment account balances over the period of estimated future benefit (not to exceed 40 years).
11. Under the equity method, if the fair and book values of the investee's net assets differ, this difference must also be amortized over the period of estimated future benefit to the Investment Income and the Investment account balances.

RAPID REVIEW

1. Under the equity method, the investor accounts for dividends received from the investee as
   (*a*) dividend income, unless paid from the investee's preacquisition retained earnings.
   (*b*) a credit to the Investment account balance.
   (*c*) dividend income.
   (*d*) a deferred credit.
2. Under the cost method, the investor accounts for dividends received from the investee as
   (*a*) dividend income, unless paid from the investee'spreacquisition retained earnings.
   (*b*) a credit to the Investment account balance.
   (*c*) dividend income.
   (*d*) a deferred credit.
3. Stephens Corporation purchased an 80% interest in Christine Company. The purchase price exceeded the underlying fair value of the net assets acquired. The fair value of Christine's net assets equals the book value. Consolidation of the two companies is not feasible and the equity method is used by Stephens Corporation. In Stephens' financial statements, this difference should be
   (*a*) ignored, because it represents an intangible asset(goodwill) which may have an indeterminate life.
   (*b*) charged to an account called goodwill amortization over its expected useful life not to exceed 40 years.
   (*c*) charged against Investment Income in the year of acquisition.
   (*d*) charged against Investment Income and the Investment account balance over its expected useful life not to exceed 40 years.
4. Raymond Company purchased a 90% interest in the Vera Company. Therefore, because control exists,
   (*a*) in all circumstances, consolidated financial statements must be prepared.
   (*b*) consolidated financial states are not appropriate.
   (*c*) Raymond's investment in Vera must be carried at equity if Vera is viewed as an unconsolidated subsidiary because of lack of long term control.
   (*d*) the cost method of accounting for the investment should be used.

5. Frederick Company invested in Melba Company and would most likely use the equity method of accounting for the investment in which of the following situations?
   (*a*) Purchased 3,000 of Melba's 100,000 shares of common stock outstanding.
   (*b*) Purchased 40,000 of Melba's 100,000 shares of common stock outstanding.
   (*c*) Purchased 80,000 of Melba's 100,000 shares of common stock outstanding.
   (*d*) Purchased all of Melba's common stock outstanding.
6. On January 1, 19X1, A Co., whose fiscal year-end is December 31, purchased a 40% interest in B Co. for $500,000. On this date, B Co. had net assets with a book and fair value of $1,000,000. During 19X1, B Co. generated $150,000 in net income and declared and paid cash dividends of $120,000. Goodwill, if any, implicit in the purchase price is $______.
7. Based on the information provided in Question 6, the maximum amount of investment income that A Co. should report for 19X1 from its investment in B Co. is $______.
8. On January 1, 19X1, X Co. purchased an 80% interest in Y Company for $1,600,000 when the fair value of Y Company's net assets was $1,900,000 and the book value of Y Company's net assets was $1,800,000. The entire difference between book and fair value was attributable to a piece of equipment with a 10-year remaining life and no expected salvage value. Goodwill, if any, implicit in the purchase price is $______.
9. In addition to the information provided in Question 8, assume the net income of Y Company during 19X1 was $200,000, and Y Company paid and declared dividends of $100,000. Assuming X Company carries the investment in Y Company at equity, the December 31, 19X1 Investment account balance is $______.
10. Using the facts provided in Questions 8 and 9, the maximum amount of net income which X Company should report for 19X1 from its investment in Y Company is $______.
11. Use the facts provided in Questions 8 and 9, but assume that X Company carries its investment in Y Company at cost. In this case, the December 31, 19X1 Investment account balance is $______, and the income from the investment would be reported for 19X1 at $______.

Answers

1. (*b*) (See Example 5-3.)
2. (*a*) (See Examples 5-1 and 5-2.)
3. (*d*) (See Example 5-6.)
4. (*c*) (See Example 5-6 and Exhibit 5-1.)
5. (*b*) (See Exhibit 5-1.)

6. $100,000.

Price paid for 40% interest		$ 500,000
Less: Fair value received (40% × $1,000,000)		400,000
Goodwill		$ 100,000

7. $ 57,500.

40% × B Co. net income of $150,000	=	$ 60,000
Less: Goodwill amortization ($100,000 ÷ 40 years)	=	2,500
		$ 57,500

8. $ 80,000.

Price paid for 80% interest	$1,600,000
Book value received (80% × $1,800,000)	1,440,000
Cost in excess of book value	$ 160,000
Portion of excess attributable to equipment (80% × $100,000)	80,000
Goodwill	$ 80,000

or

Investment cost	$1,600,000
Less: Fair value received (80% × $1,900,000)	1,520,000
Goodwill	$ 80,000

9. $1,670,000.

1/01/X1 Investment cost	$1,600,000
80% of Y Co. net income of $200,000	160,000
Goodwill amortization ($80,000 ÷ 40 years)	(2,000)
Excess equipment depreciation ($80,000 ÷ 10 years)	(8,000)
Dividends (80% of $100,000)	(80,000)
	$1,670,000

10. $150,000. From previous answer, $160,000 less $2,000 goodwill amortization less $8,000 excess depreciation.

11. $1,600,000 and $80,000. If the investment is carried at cost, the investment balance would in this case remain unchanged at $1,600,000. The only income reported from the investment would be the dividends of $80,000.

SOLVED PROBLEMS

PROBLEM 5-1. L Company purchased a 15% interest in the issued and outstanding stock of M Company on January 1, 19X1, for $100,000. M Company generated net income and paid dividends as follows for the next two years:

	M Co.	
Year	Net income	Dividends declared and paid
X1	$130,000	$120,000
X2	$120,000	$140,000

Prepare the journal entries L Company would have made relative to its investment in M Company during 19X1 and 19X2.

Answer: The entries are based on the cost method because a 15% interest would not generally represent significant influence. Under the cost method, L Company would normally record dividends from M Company as dividend income. However, in this case, the year X2 dividend results in part in a distribution of preacquisition earnings and is therefore treated in part as a reduction in the investment's carrying value.

	19X1	
Investment in M Co.	100,000	
Cash		100,000
Cash (15% × $120,000)	18,000	
Dividend income		18,000
	19X2	
Cash (15% × $140,000)	21,000	
Dividend income (15% × $130,000)		19,500
Investment in M Co. (15% × $10,000)		1,500

Note that the total dividend income for 19X1 and 19X2 of $37,500 represents 15% of postacquisition net income of M Company of $250,000.

PROBLEM 5-2. Silver Company purchased 40% of the issued and outstanding common stock of Gold Company on July 2, 19X6, for $600,000. On July 1, 19X6, Gold Company's net assets at fair and book values totalled $1,400,000. Gold Company had net income and paid dividends during 19X6 as follows:

	Gold Company	
Six months ended	Net Income	Dividends declared and paid
6/30/X6	$120,000	$ 80,000
12/31/X6	$140,000	$100,000

Prepare the journal entries for 19X6 made by Silver Company relative to the investment.

Answer:

	Debit	Credit
Investment in Gold Company	600,000	
Cash		600,000
To record investment in Gold Company.		
Investment in Gold Company	56,000	
Investment income		56,000
To record investment income. (Use only last 6 months of year. Since acquisition date was 7/1/X6, use 40% × $140,000).		
Amortization of cost in excess of book value	500*	
Investment in Gold Company		500
To record goodwill amortization.		

*Investment cost	$600,000
Fair value received (40% × $1,400,000)	560,000
Goodwill	$ 40,000
Useful life	÷ 40 years
Goodwill amortization (full year)	$ 1,000
	× 1/2 year
Goodwill amortization (half year)	$ 500

	Debit	Credit
Cash (40% × $100,000)	40,000	
Investment in Gold Company		40,000
To record receipt of dividends since acquisition.		

PROBLEM 5-3. P Co. purchased 90% of S Co. stock on January 1, 19X1, for $5,400,000. On this date, S Co. had net assets at book value of $5,700,000, and the net asset book value equaled fair value except for the following items:

	Book Value	Fair Value	Difference
Inventory*	$ 120,000	$ 115,000	($ 5,000)
Building (net)**	900,000	1,015,000	115,000)
Land	320,000	340,000	20,000
	$1,340,000	$1,470,000	$130,000

*This inventory was completely sold by June 6, 19X1.

**The building had an estimated remaining useful life of 20 years on 1/01/X1, and is being depreciated on a straight-line basis with no assumed salvage value.

During 19X1, S Co. generated net income of $1,254,000 and declared and paid dividends of $800,000.

(*a*) Prepare all journal entries made by P Co. relative to the investment in S Co. during 19X1, assuming P Co. carries the investment at equity.

(*b*) Determine the December 31, 19X1 investment account balance under the equity method.
(*c*) Determine the amount of income from the investment recorded by P Co. under the equity method.
(*d*) Determine the amount of amortization of cost in excess of book value for year ending December 31, 19X2, if any.

Answer:

(*a*) In order to record all necessary journal entries on P Company's books, the $5,400,000 purchase price for a 90% interest should first be analyzed as follows:

Price paid by P Co. for 90% interest	$5,400,000
Book value of underlying net assets received (90% of $5,700,000)	(5,130,000
Excess cost over book value	270,000
Portion of excess attributable to:	
Inventory (90% of ($5,000))	4,500
Building (net) (90% of $115,000)	(103,500)
Land (90% of $20,000)	(18,000)
Goodwill*	$ 153,000

*Proof of Goodwill:

Price paid by P Co. for 90% interest	$5,400,000
Fair value received: 90% of S Co. fair value of $5,830,000 ($5,700,000 plus $130,000)	5,247,000
Goodwill	$ 153,000

Investment in S Co.	5,400,000	
Cash		5,400,000
To record investment in S Co.		
Investment in S Co. (90% × $1,254,000)	1,128,600	
Investment income		1,128,600
To record P Co. share of S Co. income.		
Amortization of cost in excess of book value	4,500*	
Investment in S Co.		4,500
To record amortization of cost in excess of book value.		

*Goodwill ($153,000 ÷ 40 years)	$3,825
Inventory (completely sold)	(4,500)
Building ($103,500 ÷ 20 years)	5,175
	$4,500

Investment in S Co, which will not be eliminated in a worksheet consolidation process. (Note, however, that in situations where P Co. and S Co. consolidated financial statements are prepared, P Co. does have the option of using either the cost or equity methods since the Investment account will simply be eliminated in the consolidation process.)

(*a*) Cash (90% × $800,000)	720,000	
Investment in S Co.		720,000
To record receipt of dividends.		

(*b*) 1/01/X1	Investment cost		$5,400,000
19X1	Investment income	$1,128,600	
	Less: Amortization	(4,500)	1,124,100
91X1	Dividends received		(720,000)
12/31/X1	Investment account balance		$5,804,100

(*c*) $1,124,100 (see answer item "b" above).

(*d*) The amortization of cost in excess of book value for the year ending 12/31/X2 will be higher since inventory is no longer considered:

Goodwill ($153,000 ÷ 40 years)	$3,825
Building ($103,500 ÷ 20 years)	5,175
Year 19X2 amortization	$9,000

PROBLEM 5-4. Assume all of the same facts as those provided in Problem 5-3 except that P Co. carries the investment in S Co. at cost rather than equity.

(*a*) Prepare all journal entries made by P Co. relative to the investment in S Co. during 19X1.
(*b*) Determine the December 31, 19X1 investment account balance under the cost method.
(*c*) Determine the amount of income from the investment recorded by P Co. under the cost method.

Answer:

(*a*)

	Debit	Credit
Investment in S Co.	5,400,000	
Cash		5,400,000
To record investment in S Co.		
Cash (90% × $800,000)	720,000	
Dividend income		720,000

(*b*) 12/31/X1 investment account balance is the same as the 1/01/X1 balance under the cost method, or $5,400,000.

(*c*) P Co. income from the investment under the cost method would simply be the dividends of $720,000.

PROBLEM 5-5. Under generally accepted accounting principles, if control is temporary or does not rest with the majority owner, the subsidiary is not consolidated. Suppose P Company's 90% investment in S Company described in Problem 5-3 represents such a situation. Does P Company have the option of using either the equity method (as shown in Solution 5-4) or the cost method (as shown in Answer 5-5) of accounting for the investment?

Answer: No, P Co. does not have an option, and must use the equity method. This is so because consolidated financial statements will not be feasible. S Co. will have to be carried at equity as an unconsolidated subsidiary by P Co. The financial statements prepared for P Co. will include the account Investment in S Co., which will not be eliminated in a worksheet consolidation process. (Note, however, that in situations where P Co. and S Co. consolidated financial statements are prepared, P Co. does have the option of using either the cost or equity methods since the Investment account will simply be eliminated in the consolidation process.)

6 POSTACQUISITION CONSOLIDATED FINANCIAL STATEMENTS (EQUITY METHOD)

THIS CHAPTER IS ABOUT

☑ **Preparing Consolidated Financial Statements After Acquisition Date**
☑ **Consolidated Financial Statements for a Wholly Owned Subsidiary**
☑ **Consolidated Financial Statements for a Partially Owned Subsidiary**

6-1. Preparing Consolidated Financial Statements After the Acquisition Date

On the date a parent company acquires a subsidiary, the newly combined business entity's consolidated balance sheet establishes a "starting point" against which the new entity will measure its performance in the future (see Chapter 4). Under the purchase method, the affiliated companies prepare only the consolidated balance sheet at that point, because the subsidiary's operations before the acquisition are considered not to affect the parent company's other financial statements (income statement and retained earnings statement). After the acquisition date, however, the combined business entity will need to produce a full set of consolidated financial statements, which is combined from the separately produced financial statements of the affiliated companies.

In this chapter we consider the full set of consolidated financial statements. All the discussions and examples in this chapter assume the use of the purchase method of business combinations (see Chapter 11 for the pooling of interests method), and the equity method of carrying investments (see Chapter 7 for the cost method).

note: If the fundamental differences between the cost and equity methods of accounting for investments are not understood, be sure to study Chapter 5 before going further.

A. The statement of consolidated income.

The consolidated income statement shows the consolidated net income of the parent and subsidiary, which is defined as the combination of their revenues, expenses, gains, and losses, after (1) elimination of any account balances that may result from transactions between the affiliated companies, and (2) deduction of any minority ownership interest in the subsidiary.

B. The consolidated statement of retained earnings.

The consolidated statement of retained earnings shows the parent company's retained earnings at the beginning of the accounting period, increased by the consolidated net income carried over from the consolidated income statement, and decreased by any dividend declared by the parent company.

C. The consolidated balance sheet.

The consolidated balance sheet shows the combination of the parent's and subsidiary's assets, liabilities, and equity, including the consolidated retained earnings carried forward. Entries made on the worksheet used to prepare the consolidated balance sheet will eliminate the parent's investment in the subsidiary against its interest in the subsidiary's equity, net assets, and goodwill. Such entries may also include possible amortization of differences between book values and fair values of the subsidiary's net assets, and elimination of any intercompany investment income. Any minority ownership interest must be clearly labeled as such in the consolidated balance sheet; minority interest usually appears between liabilities and equity.

D. Worksheet used to prepare consolidated financial statements.

Consolidated financial statements are prepared using a worksheet (similar to that used to prepare the consolidated balance sheet in Chapter 4). The independently prepared trial balances of the parent and subsidiary are shown in the first two columns. The next two columns include eliminating entries. The fifth, sixth, and seventh columns show the consolidated income, retained earnings, and balance sheet respectively.

					Consolidated		
	P Co.	S Co.	Eliminations		Income	Retained Earnings	Balance Sheet
Account	Dr. (Cr.)	Dr. (Cr)	Dr.	Cr.	Dr. (Cr.)	Dr. (Cr.)	Dr.(Cr.)
Cash							
Accounts Receivable							
Etc.							

After entering the parent and subsidiary trial balances in the appropriate columns, entries are made to eliminate intercompany account balances, and to adjust and amortize goodwill and net assets. After making the eliminations, a consolidated income statement, retained earnings statement and balance sheet are prepared by carrying the adjust balances to the appropriate columns.

6-2. Consolidated Financial Statements for Wholly Owned Subsidiaries

A. The subsidiary's cost equals its fair and book values.

This is the simplest form of business combination, and consequently the preparation of consolidated financial statements is also the simplest we will examine in this chapter. If the subsidiary's cost equals its fair values and book values, no goodwill results from the acquisition, and the subsidiary's assets require no revaluation during the preparation of consolidated financial statements.

The only worksheet entries necessary are those to eliminate the parent's Investment in Subsidiary account against the subsidiary's equity accounts and any dividends the subsidiary has declared.

EXAMPLE 6-1: On 1/01/X1, P Co. purchased 100% of S Co. common stock for $100,000. S Co.'s net asset fair values equaled their book values. S Co. equity included common stock, additional paid-in capital, and retained earnings of $50,000,0 $40,000, and $10,000 respectively. P Co. carries its investment in S Co. under the equity method. The independent trial balances for P Co. and S Co. are given in the first two columns of the worksheet shown in Exhibit 6-A.

First, note that the Investment in S Co. account one year after acquisition now includes the following items in its balance, all of which must be eliminated in the consolidation process;

1/01/X1 Investment in S Co.	$100,000
P Co. 100% interest in S Co. net income of $40,000	40,000
P Co. 100% interest in S Co. dividends declared of $20,000	(20,000)
12/31/X1 Investment in S Co.	$120,000

For this reason, the entry to eliminate the Investment account balance must include Investment Income of $40,000 and S Co. Dividends Declared of $20,000. Also, if any portion of the S Co. dividends declared during 19X1 had not been paid by 12/31/X1, an additional worksheet elimination entry would be necessary to account for the remainder still to be paid:

Dividends payable (by S Co.)	$X	
Dividends receivable (by P Co.)		$X

After the eliminations are properly made, the consolidated financial statements are prepared by carrying the account balances to the proper worksheet column.

Exhibit 6-A
P Co. & 100% Owned Subsidiary S Co.
Consolidating Worksheet for the Year Ended 12/31/X1

					CONSOLIDATED Dr. (Cr.)		
	P Co.	S Co.	Eliminations		Income	Retained	Balance
Account Name	Dr. (Cr.)	Dr. (Cr.)	Dr.	(Cr.)	Statement	Earnings	Sheet
Cash	124,000	37,000					161,000
Accounts receivable (net)	126,000	43,000					169,000
Inventory	107,000	36,000					143,000
Land	50,000	20,000					70,000
Equipment	120,000	100,000					220,000
Accum. depr. —equip.	(80,000)	(70,000)					(150,000)
Building	400,000	200,000					600,000
Accum. depr. —bldg.	(305,000)	(155,000)					(460,000)
Investment in S Co.	120,000			(120,000)[1]			0
Liabilities	(72,000)	(91,000)					(163,000)
Common stock:							
P Co.	(100,000)						(100,000)
S Co.		(50,000)	50,000[1]				0
Additional paid-in capital: P Co.	(130,000)						(130,000)
S Co.		(40,000)	40,000[1]				0
Retained earnings:							
P Co.	(220,000)					(220,000)	
S Co.		(10,000)	10,000[1]				0
Dividends declared:							
P Co.	50,000					50,000	
S Co.		20,000		(20,000)[1]			0
Sales	(850,000)	(400,000)			(1,250,000)		
Investment income	(40,000)		40,000[1]		0		
Cost of goods sold	300,000	260,000			560,000		
Depreciation expense	25,000	10,000			35,000		
Operating expenses	375,000	90,000			465,000		
Totals	0	0	140,000	(140,000)			
Consolidated net income					(190,000)	(190,000)	
Consolidated retained earnings						(360,000)	(360,000)
					Total		0

[1] To eliminate Investment in S Co. against S Co. equity, investment income, and dividends declared.

B. Subsidiary's cost, book value, and fair value differ.

It is quite likely that during business combinations the parent's investment cost will differ from the fair values and book values of the subsidiary's net assets. Chapter 4 demonstrated how, if this is the case, the goodwill and/or asset accounts are revalued in the consolidating worksheet used to prepare a consolidated balance sheet on the acquisition date. Chapter 5 showed how these differences may have to be amortized against the parent's Investment Income account when using the equity method of carrying investments. When preparing complete consolidated financial statements after the acquisition date, (assuming the investment cost, fair values, and/or book values differ) both asset revaluation and amortization may be necessary. Both processes require worksheet elimination entries.

The first worksheet entry eliminates the parent's investment against the subsidiary's equity accounts and the investment income generated for the parent company. Also included in this elimination entry are entries to revalue assets as necessary, to account for any goodwill, to account for the amortization resulting from carrying the investment for the current accounting period, and to account for any dividends declared by the subsidiary.

If the subsidiary's book values and fair values do not equal the parent's cost, a second elimination entry will be necessary at the end of the accounting period. This second elimination is necessary to account for amortization and depreciation of revalued assets and goodwill.

EXAMPLE 6-2: On 1/01/X1, P Co. purchased 100% of S Co. common stock for $130,000, when S Co. common stock, additional paid-in capital, and retained earnings were $50,000, $40,000, and $10,000 respectively. On this date S Co.'s net asset fair values and book values were equal except as follows:

Account	Book Values	Fair Values	Difference
Inventory	$ 25,000	$ 22,000*	($ 3,000)
Land	20,000	22,000	2,000
Equipment (net)	35,000	56,000**	21,000
	$ 80,000	$100,000	$20,000

*Completely sold by 6/10/X1.
**Life remaining on 1/01/X1 was 7 years, and the asset is depreciated on a straight-line basis with no salvage value. (Original cost of $100,000 less accumulated depreciation as of 1/01/X1 of $65,000 equals $35,000 book value.)

S Co.'s net income for 19X1 totalled $40,000 and dividends declared and paid totalled $20,000. P Co.'s $130,000 investment can be analyzed as follows:

Investment cost		$130,000
Book value of underlying net assets acquired	$100,000	
Ownership level	× 100%	(100,000)
Excess cost over book value		30,000
Portion of excess attributable to:		
Inventory (100% × ($3,000))		3,000
Land (100% × $2,000)		(2,000)
Equipment (100% × $21,000)		(21,000)
Goodwill		10,000

During year 19X1, the equity method would require amortization against investment income on P Co. books of:

Inventory (completely sold during 19X1))	($3,000)
Equipment ($21,000 excess ÷ 7 years)	3,000
Goodwill ($10,000 ÷ 40 years)	250
19X1 Amortization	$ 250

As of 12/31/X1, the Invest in S Co. account is carried on P Co. books as follows:

1/01/X1 Investment cost	$130,000
100% of S Co. net income of $40,000	40,000
19X1 amortization of cost in excess of book value	(250)
100% of S Co. dividends of $20,000	(20,000)
12/31/X1 Investment in S Co.	$149,750

The first worksheet elimination entry of 12/31/X1 must eliminate the Investment in S Co. account one year after the acquisition, against any intercompany income (including amortization) and dividends:

S Co. Common stock	50,000	
S Co. Additional paid-in capital	40,000	
S Co. Retained earnings (1/01/X1)	10,000	
Investment income ($40,000 - $250)	39,750	
Land	2,000	
Equipment	21,000	
Goodwill	10,000	
Inventory		3,000
Investment in S Co.		149,750
Dividends declared		20,000

If this is the entry to eliminate the investment account at 12/31/X1, *one year after acquisition*, then certain net asset adjustments that resulted from the 1/01/X1 acquisition will now require one full year of amortization or depreciation on the worksheet. In this case, the assets equipment, goodwill, and inventory created by virtue of the first worksheet elimination entry on 12/31/X1 will result in the need for a second 12/31/X1 elimination entry. The second elimination of 12/31/X1 simply represents adjustments to the Inventory, Equipment, and Goodwill accounts created on the worksheet in the first elimination entry of 12/31/X1.

Inventory (entirely sold)	3,000	
Depreciation expense	3,000	
Goodwill amortization	250	
Cost of goods sold		3,000
Accum. depreciation—Equip.		3,000
Goodwill		250

Exhibit 6-B shows a trial balance for P Co. and S Co. on 12/31/X1, one year after the original acquisition, and also includes columns for the worksheet elimination entries just described and for consolidated financial statements.

Exhibit 6-B
P Co. & 100% Owned Subsidiary S Co.
Consolidating Worksheet for the Year Ended 12/31/X1

					CONSOLIDATED Dr. (Cr.)		
	P Co.	S Co.	Eliminations		Income	Retained	Balance
Account Name	Dr. (Cr.)	Dr. (Cr.)	Dr.	(Cr.)	Statement	Earnings	Sheet
Cash	94,000	37,000					131,000
Accounts receivable (net)	126,000	43,000					169,000
Inventory	107,000	36,000	3,000[2]	(3,000)[1]			143,000
Land	50,000	20,000	2,000[1]				72,000
Equipment	120,000	100,000	21,000[1]				241,000
Accum. depr. —equip.	(80,000)	(70,000)		(3,000)[2]			(153,000)
Building	400,000	200,000					600,000
Accum. depr. —bldg.	(305,000)	(155,000)					(460,000)
Investment in S Co.	149,750			(149,750)[1]			0
Goodwill			10,000[1]	(250)[2]			9,750
Liabilities	(72,000)	(91,000)					(163,000)
Common stock:							
P Co.	(100,000)						(100,000)
S Co.		(50,000)	50,000[1]				0
Additional paid-in capital: P Co.	(130,000)						(130,000)
S Co.		(40,000)	40,000[1]				0
Retained earnings:							
P Co.	(220,000)					(220,000)	
S Co.		(10,000)	10,000[1]				0
Dividends declared:							
P Co.	50,000					50,000	
S Co.		20,000		(20,000)[1]			0
Sales	(850,000)	(400,000)			(1,250,000)		
Investment income	(39,750)		39,750[1]		0		
Goodwill amortization			250[2]		250		
Cost of goods sold	300,000	260,000		(3,000)[2]	557,000		
Depreciation expense	25,000	10,000	3,000[2]		38,000		
Operating expenses	375,000	90,000			465,000		
Totals	0	0	179,000	(179,000)			
	Consolidated net income				(189,750)	(189,750)	
	Consolidated retained earnings					(359,750)	(359,750)
					Total		0

[1]To eliminate Investment in S Co. against S Co. equity, investment income, and dividends
[2]To amortize adjusted S Co. asset valuations and goodwill.

C. Consolidated financial statements two years after the acquisition.

At the end of two years (or any other kind of accounting period) after the acquisition, the combined business entity will again need to prepare consolidated financial statements.

These consolidated financial statements are prepared in the same way as those for the first year, except that depreciation of revalued assets and amortization of goodwill that took place during the first year must be carried over to the financial statements of the second year.

EXAMPLE 6-3: Refer to the information provided in Example 6-2, and also assume that S Co. net income for the year ended 12/31/X2 is $50,000, and that S Co. dividends of $30,000 were declared and paid during year 19X2. A logical question now is, under the equity method, what worksheet elimination entries are needed two years from acquisition?

P. Co.'s Investment in S Co. account balance on 12/31/X2 will now be:

12/31/X1 Investment in S Co.	$149,750
100% of S Co. net income of $50,000 for 19X2	50,000
19X2 amortization of cost in excess of book value*	(3,250)
100% of S Co. dividends of $30,000 for 19X2	(30,000)
12/31/X2 Investment in S Co.	$166,500

*19X2 Amortization:

Inventory	$ 0	(fully amortized in 19X1)
Equipment	3,000	($21,000 ÷ 7 years)
Goodwill	250	($10,000 ÷ 40 years)
	$3,250	

The 12/31/X2 worksheet eliminations are:

1. S Co. Common stock	50,000	
S Co. Additional paid-in capital	40,000	
S Co. Retained earnings (1/01/X2)	30,000**	
Investment income ($50,000 – $3,250)	46,750	
Land	2,000	
Equipment	21,000	
Goodwill ($10,000 less 19X1 amortization of $250)	9,750	
Accum. depreciation—equipment		3,000
Investment in S Co.		166,500
Dividends declared		30,000

*1/01/X1 S Co. Retained earnings	$10,000
S Co. 19X1 income	40,000
S Co. 19X1 dividends	(20,000)
1/01/X2 S Co. Retained earnings	$30,000

2. Depreciation expense	3,000	
Goodwill amortization	250	
Accum. depreciation—equipment		3,000
Goodwill		250

Note that entry 1 shows Land increased by the full $2,000 to the fair value of the acquisition date, because land is not a depreciable asset. Equipment, on the other hand, is increased by a net $18,000 only, because the original 1/01/X1 increase of $21,000 must be reduced by the accumulated depreciation for year 19X1 of $3,000. Similarly, Goodwill is increased by only $9,750 ($10,000 less $250). Note also that worksheet amortization and depreciation continues in entry 2, but now Inventory is excluded from the amortization entry, because all inventory of the original 1/01/X1 acquisition was sold during 19X1.

D. Bargain purchases.

Recall that in Chapter 4 you learned that a bargain purchase results in the need to create a Deferred Credit account on the consolidating worksheet when the bargain purchase amount cannot be allocated to the noncurrent assets of the subsidiary. If a Deferred Credit account is created, amortize it to Consolidated Net Income over the length of its expected benefit, which may not exceed 40 years. In addition to the eliminating entries discussed in the previous sections of this chapter, be sure to eliminate amortization of the Deferred Credit account at the end of the accounting period.

Because the purchase price is a bargain, from a consolidated perspective some assets cost the parent company less than the book value shown on the subsidiary's books. To the extent any of these assets are amortized or depreciated by the subsidiary, consolidated amortization or depreciation may be reduced.

EXAMPLE 6-4: On 1/01/X1, P Co. paid $95,000 for 100% of S Co.'s common stock. On this date, S Co.'s equity consisted of common stock, additional paid-in capital, and retained earnings of $50,000, $40,000, and $10,000, respectively. All of S Co.'s fair values equal its book values, except Inventory, which had a book value of $3,000 above fair value.

Such a bargain price results in the following elimination entry on the consolidating worksheet on the acquisition date:

S Co. Common stock	50,000	
S Co. Additional paid-in capital	40,000	
S Co. Retained earnings	10,000	
Investment in S Co.		95,000
Inventory		3,000
Noncurrent assets		2,000

On 12/31/X1, make the same worksheet elimination entry, keeping in mind that the balance in P Co.'s Investment account has changed by virtue of the recognition of investment income and S Co.'s dividends. Therefore, the year-end entry must also include the elimination of this investment income and the dividends against the Investment account balance.

In addition to the usual elimination entry, an eliminating entry to record the year's amortization is needed. In this case, assume the $2,000 Deferred Credit balance is to be allocated as follows:

$700 to seven-year life Equipment
800 to ten-year life Building
500 to Land

The 12/31/X1 worksheet amortization entry is:

Inventory	3,000	
Accum. depreciation—equipment ($700 ÷ 7 years)	100	
Accum. depreciation—building ($800 ÷ 10 years)	80	
Depreciation expense		180
Cost of goods sold		3,000

6-3. Consolidated Financial Statements for Partially Owned Subsidiaries

The process of preparing consolidated financial statements for a partially owned subsidiary is essentially the same as that followed for wholly owned subsidiaries. The basic difference is that the parent eliminates its investment account against only a portion of the subsidiary's equity (according to its level of ownership). The remaining equity of the subsidiary represents the minority interest, which must be clearly labeled and shown on the consolidated financial statements.

A. Subsidiary's cost equals its fair and book values.

When the parent's investment cost equals the subsidiary's underlying net asset fair values and book values, no goodwill is created, and none of the subsidiary's net assets need to be revalued. The parent's investment account is eliminated against the parent's percentage of the subsidiary's equity, and the remaining equity is shown as minority interest.

EXAMPLE 6-5: On 1/01/X1, P Co. purchased 80% of S Co.'s common stock for $80,000. S Co.'s net asset fair and book values were equal. On 1/01/X1, S Co. had common stock, additional paid-in capital, and retained earnings of $50,000, $40,000, and $10,000, respectively.

During 19X1, S Co. had net income of $40,000 and declared and paid dividends of $20,000. The Investment in S Co. account, one year after acquisition, includes the following items in its balance:

1/01/X1 Investment in S Co.	$80,000
P Co. 80% interest in S Co net income of $40,000	32,000
P Co. 80% interest in S Co. dividends declared of $20,000	(16,000)
12/31/X1 Investment in S Co.	$96,000

The worksheet elimination entry of 12/31/X1 must now eliminate both the investment income of $32,000 and the dividends declared of $16,000 held on an intercompany basis. Exhibit 6-C which follows shows trial balance columns for P Co. and S Co. on 12/31/X1, one year after the acquisition, and includes columns for intercompany eliminations and for consolidated financial statements. Note that Exhibit 6-C includes an item called "minority interest" as a way to reduce *combined* net income to yield *consolidated* net income. Note also that the consolidated balance sheet of Exhibit 6-C includes a series of items marked "M" that represents minority interest in subsidiary equity. This minority interest will generally appear between liabilities and stockholders' equity on the consolidated balance sheet (under the parent company theory).

Exhibit 6-C
P Co. & 80% Owned Subsidiary S Co.
Consolidating Worksheet for the Year Ended 12/31/X1

Investment cost = Fair value
and Fair value = Book value

					CONSOLIDATED Dr. (Cr.)		
Account Name	P Co. Dr. (Cr.)	S Co. Dr. (Cr.)	Eliminations Dr.	Eliminations Cr.	Income Statement	Retained Earnings	Balance Sheet
Cash	140,000	37,000					177,000
Accounts receivable (net)	126,000	43,000					169,000
Inventory	107,000	36,000					143,000
Land	50,000	20,000					70,000
Equipment	120,000	100,000					220,000
Accum. depr. —equip.	(80,000)	(70,000)					(150,000)
Building	400,000	200,000					600,000
Accum. depr. —bldg.	(305,000)	(155,000)					(460,000)
Investment in S Co.	96,000			96,000[1]			0
Liabilities	(72,000)	(91,000)					(163,000)
Common stock:							
P Co.	(100,000)						(100,000)
S Co.		(50,000)	40,000[1]				(10,000)M
Additional paid-in capital: P Co.	(130,000)						(130,000)
S Co.		(40,000)	32,000[1]				(8,000)M
Retained earnings:							
P Co.	(220,000)					(220,000)	
S Co.		(10,000)	8,000[1]				(2,000)M
Dividends declared:							
P Co.	50,000					50,000	
S Co.		20,000		16,000[1]			4,000M
Sales	(850,000)	(400,000)			(1,250,000)		
Investment income	(32,000)		32,000[1]		0		
Cost of goods sold	300,000	260,000			560,000		
Depreciation expense	25,000	10,000			35,000		
Operating expenses	375,000	90,000			465,000		
Totals	0	0	112,000	112,000			
	Combined net income				(190,000)		
	*Minority interest				8,000		(8,000)M
	Consolidated net income				(182,000)	(182,000)	
	Consolidated retained earnings					(352,000)	(352,000)
					Total		0
	Total minority interest (sum of items marked "M")						(24,000)M

M = Minority interest
*20% of S Co. net income of $40,000 = $8,000.

[1]To eliminate Investment in S Co. against investment income and 80% of S Co. equity and dividends declared.
note: 1/01/X1 S Co. equity of $100,000 plus 19X1 S Co. net income of $40,000 less 19X1 S Co. dividends of $20,000 equals 12/31/X1 S Co. equity of $120,000. Minority interest of 20% × $120,000 yields $24,000.

B. Subsidiary's cost, book value, and fair value differ.

Section 6-2B and Example 6-2 demonstrated the procedure for preparing consolidated financial statements for a business combination when the parent's investment cost and the subsidiary's net assets' fair values and book values differ. If, in addition, the parent company owns less than 100% of the subsidiary, then the revaluations of the subsidiary's net assets that may occur on the acquisition date may only be recognized to the extent of the parent's interest in the subsidiary. At the end of the accounting period, any revaluations must be amortized on the consolidating worksheet.

EXAMPLE 6-6: On 1/01/X1, P Co. purchased 80% of S Co.'s common stock for $106,000. S Co.'s common stock, additional paid-in capital, and retained earnings were $50,000, $40,000, and $10,000, respectively. On this date, S Co. net asset fair and book values were equal except:

Account	Book Values	Fair Values	Difference
Inventory	$ 25,000	$ 22,000*	($ 3,000)
Land	20,000	22,000	2,000
Equipment (net)	35,000	56,000**	21,000
	$ 80,000	$100,000	$20,000

*Completely sold by 6/10/X1.
**Life remaining on 1/01/X1 was 7 years, and the asset is depreciated on a straight-line basis with no salvage value. (Original cost of $100,000 less accumulated depreciation as of 1/01/X1 of $65,000 equals $35,000 book value.)

S Co. net income for 19X1 totalled $40,000, and dividends declared and paid totalled $20,000. The $106,000 investment cost can be analyzed as follows:

Investment cost		$106,000
Book value of underlying net assets acquired	$100,000	
Ownership level	× 80%	(80,000)
Excess cost over book value		26,000
Portion of excess attributable to:		
Inventory (80% × ($3,000))		2,400
Land (80% × $2,000)		(1,600)
Equipment (80% × $21,000)		(16,800)
Goodwill		10,000

During year 19X1, the equity method requires amortization against investment income on P Co.'s books of:

Inventory (completely sold during 19X1))	($2,400)
Equipment ($16,800 excess ÷ 7 years)	2,400
Goodwill ($10,000 ÷ 40 years)	250
19X1 Amortization	$ 250

As of 12/31/X1, the Investment in S Co. account is carried on P Co. books as follows:

1/01/X1 Investment cost	$106,000
80% of S Co. net income of $40,000	32,000
19X1 amortization of cost in excess of book value	(250)
80% of S Co. dividends of $20,000	(16,000)
12/31/X1 Investment in S Co.	$121,750

The 12/31/X1 worksheet elimination entries are:

		Debit	Credit
1.	S Co. Common stock	40,000	
	S Co. Additional paid-in capital	32,000	
	S Co. Retained earnings	8,000	
	Investment income	31,750	
	Land	1,600	
	Equipment	16,800	
	Goodwill	10,000	
	Inventory		2,400
	Investment in S Co.		121,750
	Dividends declared		16,000

To eliminate Investment in S Co. against investment income and 80% of S Co. Equity and dividends declared, and to adjust S Co. assets to fair value and record goodwill.

		Debit	Credit
2.	Inventory (entirely sold)	2,400	
	Depreciation expense	2,400	
	Goodwill amortization	250	
	Cost of goods sold		2,400
	Accum. depreciation—equipment		2,400
	Goodwill		250

To amortize adjusted S Co. asset valuations and goodwill (developed in worksheet entry 1).

Exhibit 6-D shows a trial balance for P Co. and S Co. on 12/31/X1, one year after the original acquisition, and also includes columns for the worksheet elimination entries just described and for consolidated financial statements. (Note that when the parent company carries its investment in the subsidiary using the equity method, the parent's net income and the consolidated income are the same.)

Exhibit 6-D
P Co. & 80% Owned Subsidiary S Co.
Consolidating Worksheet for the Year Ended 12/31/X1

			Eliminations		CONSOLIDATED Dr. (Cr.)		
Account Name	P Co. Dr. (Cr.)	S Co. Dr. (Cr.)	Dr.	(Cr.)	Income Statement	Retained Earnings	Balance Sheet
Cash	114,000	37,000					151,000
Accounts receivable (net)	126,000	43,000					169,000
Inventory	107,000	36,000	2,400[2]	(2,400)[1]			143,000
Land	50,000	20,000	1,600[1]				71,600
Equipment	120,000	100,000	16,800[1]				236,800
Accum. depr. —equip.	(80,000)	(70,000)		(2,400)[2]			(152,400)
Building	400,000	200,000					600,000
Accum. depr. —bldg.	(305,000)	(155,000)					(460,000)
Investment in S Co.	121,750			(121,750)[1]			0
Goodwill			10,000[1]	(250)[2]			9,750
Liabilities	(72,000)	(91,000)					(163,000)
Common stock:							
P Co.	(100,000)						(100,000)
S Co.		(50,000)	40,000[1]				(10,000)M
Additional paid-in capital: P Co.	(130,000)						(130,000)
S Co.		(40,000)	32,000[1]				(8,000)M
Retained earnings:							
P Co.	(220,000)					(220,000)	
S Co.		(10,000)	8,000[1]				(2,000)M
Dividends declared:							
P Co.	50,000					50,000	
S Co.		20,000		(16,000)[1]			4,000M
Sales	(850,000)	(400,000)			(1,250,000)		
Investment income	(31,750)		31,750[1]		0		
Goodwill amortization			250[2]		250		
Cost of goods sold	300,000	260,000		(2,400)[2]	557,600		
Depreciation expense	25,000	10,000	2,400[2]		37,400		
Operating expenses	375,000	90,000			465,000		
Totals	0	0	145,200	(145,200)			
	Combined net income				(189,750)		
	*Minority interest				8,000		(8,000)M
	Consolidated net income				(181,750)	(181,750)	
	Consolidated retained earnings					(351,750)	(351,750)
					Total		0
	Total minority interest (sum of items marked "M")						(24,000)M

M = Minority interest
*20% of S Co. net income of $40,000 = $8,000.

[1]To eliminate Investment in S Co. against investment income and 80% of S Co. equity and dividends declared and to adjust S Co. assets to fair value.

note: 1/01/X1 S Co. equity of $100,000 plus 19X1 S Co. net income of $40,000 less 19X1 S Co. dividends of $20,000 equals 12/31/X1 S Co. equity of $120,000. Minority interest of 20% × $120,000 yields $24,000.

[2]To amortize adjusted S Co. asset valuations and goodwill.

C. Consolidated financial statements two years after the acquisition.

At the end of two years after the acquisition, the combined business entity will again need to prepare consolidated financial statements.

These consolidated financial statements are prepared the same way as those for the first year (see Examples 6-5 and 6-6), but carry over the depreciation of any revalued assets, and the amortization of any goodwill, to the statements of the second year. Also, minority interest is shown clearly on the consolidated financial statements.

EXAMPLE 6-7: Refer to the information provided in Example 6-6, and also assume that S Co.'s net income for the year ended 12/31/X2 is $50,000 and that dividends of $30,000 were declared and paid during 19X2. A logical question now is, under the equity method, what worksheet elimination entries are needed two years from acquisition?

P. Co.'s Investment in S Co account balance on 12/31/X2 will be:

12/31/X1 Investment in S Co.	$121,750
80% of S Co. net income of $50,000 for 19X2	40,000
19X2 amortization of cost in excess of book value*	(2,650)
80% of S Co. dividends of $30,000 for 19X2	(24,000)
12/31/X1 Investment in S Co.	$135,100

*19X2 Amortization:

Inventory	$ 0	(fully amortized in 19X1)
Equipment	2,400	($16,800 ÷ 7 years)
Goodwill	250	($10,000 ÷ 40 years)
	$ 2,650	

The 12/31/X2 worksheet elimination entries are:

1. S Co. Common stock	40,000	
S Co. Additional paid-in capital	32,000	
S Co. Retained earnings	24,000**	
Investment income ($40,000 - $2,650)	37,350	
Land	1,600	
Equipment	16,800	
Goodwill ($10,000 less 19X1 amortization of $250)	9,750	
Accum. depreciation—equipment		2,400
Investment in S Co.		135,100
Dividends declared		24,000

To eliminate Investment in S Co. against investment income and 80% of S Co. equity and dividends declared, and to adjust S Co. net assets and record goodwill.

S Co. Retained earnings 1/01/X1	$10,000
S Co. 19X1 net income	40,000
S Co. 19X1 dividends	(20,000)
S Co. Retained earnings 12/31/X1	30,000
P Co. Ownership interest	× 80%
S Co. Retained earnings 1/1/X2	$24,000

2. Depreciation expense	2,400	
Goodwill amortization	250	
Accum. depreciation—equipment		2,400
Goodwill		250

To record amortization of adjusted S Co. net assets and goodwill (as recorded in entry 1).

Appendix. Alternate Worksheet Format

Some accountants perform the mechanics of consolidation using a two-tiered worksheet which consolidates the income statement and balance sheet in order. This format is demonstrated on Exhibit 6-E, which presents the same information as that used to develop Exhibit 6-D of Example 6-6. An extra elimination entry, number 3, appears on Exhibit 6-E to record minority interest in S Co.'s net income:

		Dr.	Cr.
3.	Minority interest—income statement	8,000	
	Minority interest—S Co. retained earnings		8,000
	(20% of S Co. net income of $40,000)		

Exhibit 6-E
P Co. & 80% Owned Subsidiary S Co.
Consolidating Worksheet for the Year Ended 12/31/X1

	P Co. Dr. (Cr.)	S Co. Dr. (Cr.)	Eliminations Dr.	Eliminations (Cr.)	CONSOLIDATED Dr. (Cr.)
INCOME STATEMENT					
Sales	(850,000)	(400,000)			(1,250,000)
Investment income	(31,750)		31,750[1]		0
Subtotal	(881,750)	(400,000)	31,750		(1,250,000)
Goodwill amortization			250[2]		250
Cost of goods sold	300,000	260,000		(2,400)[2]	557,600
Depreciation expense	25,000	10,000	2,400[2]		37,400
Operating expenses	375,000	90,000			465,000
Subtotal	700,000	360,000	2,650	(2,400)	1,060,250
Income before minority interest	(181,750)	(40,000)	34,400	(2,400)	(189,750)
Minority interest			8,000[3]		8,000
Net income	(181,750)	(40,000)	42,400	(2,400)	(181,750)
BALANCE SHEET					
Cash	114,000	37,000			151,000
Accounts rec. (net)	126,000	43,000			169,000
Inventory	107,000	36,000	2,400[2]	(2,400)[1]	143,000
Land	50,000	20,000	1,600[1]		71,600
Equipment	120,000	100,000	16,800[1]		236,800
Accum. depr.—equip.	(80,000)	(70,000)		(2,400)[1]	(152,400)
Building	400,000	200,000			600,000
Accum. depr.—building	(305,000)	(155,000)			(460,000)
Investment in S Co.	121,750			(121,750)[1]	0
Goodwill			10,000[1]	(250)[2]	9,750
Total assets	653,750	211,000	30,800	(126,800)	768,750
Liabilities	(72,000)	(91,000)			(163,000)
Common stock: P Co.	(100,000)				(100,000)
S Co.		(50,000)	40,000[1]		(10,000)[M]
Additional paid-in capital: P Co.	(130,000)				(130,000)
S Co.		(40,000)	32,000[1]		(8,000)[M]
Retained earnings: P Co.					
1/01/X1 Balance	(220,000)				(220,000)
+ 19X1 Net income	(181,750)				(181,750)
– 19X1 Dividends	50,000				50,000
12/31/19X1 Balance	(351,750)				(351,750)
Retained earnings: S Co.					
1/01/X1 Balance		(10,000)	8,000[1]		(2,000)
+ 19X1 Net income		(40,000)	42,400	(2,400)	0
				(8,000)[3]	(8,000)
– 19X1 Dividends		20,000		(16,000)[1]	4,000
12/31/19X1 Balance		(30,000)	50,400	(26,400)	(6,000)[M]
Total liabilities and equity	(653,750)	(211,000)	122,400	(26,400)	(768,750)
Minority interest (sum of items marked "M")					(24,000)

M = Minority interest
[1] To eliminate Investment in S Co. against investment income and 80% of S Co. equity and dividends declared and to adjust S Co. assets to fair value.
note: 1/01/X1 S Co. equity of $100,000 plus 19X1 S Co. net income of $40,000 less 19X1 S Co. dividends of $20,000 equals 12/31/X1 S Co. equity of $120,000. Minority interest of 20% × $120,000 yields $24,000.
[2] To amortize adjusted S Co. asset valuations and goodwill.
[3] To record minority interest in S Co. net income (20% × $40,000).

RAISE YOUR GRADES

Can you explain . . . ?

- ☑ the journal entries actually made by a parent company to carry an investment in a subsidiary when investment cost equals fair and book values of underlying net assets acquired
- ☑ the worksheet entries required to eliminate an investment in a subsidiary after the original acquisition date when investment cost equals fair and book values of underlying net assets acquired (whether minority interest exists or not)
- ☑ the journal entries actually made by a parent company to carry an investment in a subsidiary assuming investment cost, fair value of underlying subsidiary net assets, and book value of underlying subsidiary net assets differ
- ☑ the worksheet entries required to eliminate an investment in a subsidiary on dates after the original acquisition date assuming investment cost, fair value of underlying subsidiary net assets, and book value of underlying subsidiary net assets differ (whether minority interest exists or not)
- ☑ the consolidated financial statement treatment (on the income statement and balance sheet) of a minority interest

SUMMARY

1. When a parent company carries its investment in a subsidiary using the equity method, parent company's income is the same as the consolidated income.
2. Under the equity method, the investment in a subsidiary at any point in time consists of the original investment cost, plus (minus) the parent's share of the subsidiary's net income (loss), minus amortization of investment cost in excess of underlying subsidiary net assets at book value, plus amortization of underlying subsidiary net assets at book value in excess of investment cost, minus the parent's share of the subsidiary's dividend declarations.
3. The journal entries actually made on the books of a parent company which carries its investment in a subsidiary under the equity method are:

Investment in subsidiary	$X	
Cash, liabilities incurred, etc.		$X
To record investment cost.		

Cash (or Dividends receivable)	$X	
Investment in subsidiary		$X
To record parent's share of subsidiary dividend declarations.		

Amortization of excess cost over book value	$X	
Investment in subsidiary		$X
To record amortization of excess investment cover over book value of subsidiary net assets. (Entry is reversed if book value exceeds investment cost.)		

Investment in subsidiary	$X	
Investment income		$X

To record parent's share of subsidiary net income. (Entry is reversed if subsidiary sustains a net loss.)

note: Investment income is reduced by amortization of excess investment cost over book value or increased by amortization of excess book value over investment cost.

4. When a complete set of consolidated financial statements is prepared on dates after the original acquisition date, the worksheet elimination process is more complex than on the acquisition data. The worksheet entries not only eliminate the investment in the subsidiary against the parent's share of subsidiary stockholders' equity, net assets, and goodwill, but also may reflect amortization of differences between original investment cost, book value, and fair value of the subsidiary's net assets, and eliminate any intercompany investment income
5. If the investment cost exceeds the fair value of the underlying subsidiary net assets acquired, goodwill is created which must be recorded in the elimination process and, subsequently, amortized against consolidated net income over the future periods benefited (not to exceed 40 years).
6. If the fair value and book value of underlying subsidiary net assets differ, this difference must be recorded in the elimination process. Subsequently, to the extent the item recorded (equipment, patent, building) is depreciable or amortizable, the worksheet elimination process must include such depreciation and amortization.
7. If a minority interest exists, the combined net income of a parent and its subsidiary must (under the parent company theory) be reduced by the minority shareholders' interest to yield consolidated net income.
8. Minority interest normally appears (under the parent company theory) between liabilities and stockholders' equity on the consolidated balance sheet.

RAPID REVIEW

1. *True* or *False*: A parent company's net income is the same as consolidated net income when the parent carries its investment in a subsidiary under the equity method.
2. On January 1, 19X1, Pepper Company purchased all of Salt Company's stock for $1,000,000. Salt Company's net assets at book and fair value totalled $1,000,000 on that date. During the year 19X1, Salt Company had net income of $200,000 and paid dividends of $150,000. Under the equity method, the Investment in Salt Company account balance on Pepper's books at December 31, 19X1, is $_____.
3. Based on the information in Question 2, the worksheet elimination entry of December 31, 19X1, must eliminate the Investment in Salt Company account balance of $_______, investment income of $_______, subsidiary equity of $_______, and subsidiary dividend declarations of $_______.
4. Assume the same facts as those in Question 2, except that Pepper's purchase gave Pepper a 75% (rather than 100%) interest in Salt Company. The Investment in Salt Company account balance on Pepper's books at December 31, 19X1, under the equity method is $_______.
5. Based on the facts provided in Question 4, a 12/31/X1 worksheet elimination entry will result in charges to Salt Company equity of $_______, investment income of $_______, and goodwill of $_______, and in credits to Investment in Salt Company of $_______, and Salt Company dividends declared of $_______. An additional worksheet elimination entry will be required charging goodwill amortization for $_______ and crediting goodwill for $_______.
6. Based on the facts provided in Question 4, and the additional assumption that during 19X2 Salt Company generated net income of $230,000 and declared and paid dividends of $190,000, the Investment in Salt Company account balance at December 31, 19X2, is $_______.
7. Prepare the December 31, 19X2, worksheet elimination entries required based on your answer to Question 6.
8. *True or False:* The worksheet elimination entries prepared in your answer to Question 7 would be no different if Salt Company's net asset fair values and book values differed on the original 1/01/X1 acquisition date as long as the investment cost exceeded fair value by the same amount ($250,000).

Answers:

1. True. (By reviewing Exhibits 6-A through 6-E in this chapter, you will see that the parent company net income, taken alone, will equal consolidated net income when the investment is carried under the equity method.)

2. $1,050,000.

Original investment cost	$1,000,000
Plus: 100% of Salt net income of $200,000	200,000
Less: 100% of Salt dividends declared of $150,000	(150,000)
12/31/X1 Investment in Salt Co.	$1,050,000

3.

Investment in Salt Company	=	$1,050,000
Investment income (100% of $200,000)	=	$ 200,000
Subsidiary equity—common stock, additional paid-in capital capital, and retained earnings (100% of $1,000,000)	=	$1,000,000
Subsidiary dividend declarations	=	$ 150,000

note: The 12/31/X1 elimination entry is:

Salt Company (various equity accounts)	1,000,000	
Investment income	200,000	
Salt Company dividends declared		150,000
Investment in Salt Company		1,050,000

4. $1,031,250.

Investment cost on 1/01/X1	$1,000,000
Book value (and fair value) of underlying net asset of Salt Company acquired (75% × $1,000,000)	750,000
Goodwill	$ 250,000

Note that the entire excess cost over underlying net asset book value is goodwill in this case, because fair value equals book value.

Investment cost on 1/01/X1	$1,000,000
Plus: 75% of Salt Company net income of $200,000	150,000
Less: 75% of Salt Company dividends of $150,000	(112,500)
Goodwill amortization of $250,000 ÷ 40 years	(6,250)
12/31/X1 Investment in Salt Company	$1,031,250

5. The 12/31/X1 elimination entry under these circumstances would be:

Salt Company equity (various accounts including common stock, additional paid-in capital and retained earnings (75% × $1,000,000)	750,000	
Investment income ($150,000 – $6,250) (see answer to Question 4)	143,750	
Goodwill (see answer to Question 4)	250,000	
Investment in Salt Company		1,031,250
Salt Company dividends declared (75% × $150,000)		112,500
Goodwill amortization	6,250	
Goodwill ($250,000 ÷ 40 years)		6,250

6. $1,055,000.

12/31/X1 Investment in Salt Company account balance (from answer to Question 4)	$1,031,250
Plus: 75% of Salt Company net income of $230,000	172,500
Less: 75% of Salt Company dividends of $190,000	(142,500)
Goodwill amortization of $250,000 ÷ 40 years	(6,250)
12/31/X2 Investment in Salt Company	$1,055,000

7. (*a*)

Salt Company equity (75% × $1,050,000*)	787,500	
Investment income ($172,500 – $6,250)	166,250	
Goodwill ($250,000 less 19X1 $6,250 amortization)	243,750	
Investment in Salt Company		1,055,000
Salt Company dividends declared (75% × $190,000)		142,500

*1/01/X1 Salt Co. equity	$1,000,000
19X1 Salt Co. net income	200,000
19X1 Salt Co. dividends	(150,000)
12/31/X1 Salt Co. equity	$1,050,000

To eliminate investment account balance at 12/31/X2 against investment income and Pepper's share of Salt's equity and dividends, and to adjust goodwill.

(*b*)

Goodwill amortization	6,250	
Goodwill		6,250

To record 19X2 goodwill amortization.

8. False. The entries would not be the same. Salt Co.'s asset valuations would require worksheet adjustment and amortization also.

SOLVED PROBLEMS

PROBLEM 6-1. Berlin Company acquired 100% of the common stock of Brussels Company on July 1, 19X6, paying $50,000 in cash, and issuing 10,000 shares of $6 par nonparticipating and noncumulative preferred stock for $70,000. In addition, Berlin Company paid $10,000 in direct costs associated with the purchase and incurred and paid $5,000 in registration fees on the preferred stock issue. Prepare all journal entries which Berlin Company recorded on July 1, 19X6, to acquire the Brussels Company.

Answer:

Investment in Brussels Company	130,000	
Cash ($50,000 + direct costs $10,000)		60,000
Preferred stock (10,000 @ $6 par)		60,000
Additional paid-in capital—preferred stock (10,000 @ $1)		10,000

To record Investment in Brussels Company. (Recall from Chapter 4 that direct costs are considered to be part of the investment cost in a purchase type business combination.)

Additional paid-in capital—preferred stock	5,000	
Cash		5,000

To record registration fees. (Recall from Chapter 4 that registration fees are considered a reduction in the issue price of stock issued to effect a purchase type business combination.)

PROBLEM 6-2. This problem is a continuation of Problem 6-1. Berlin Company uses the equity method of carrying its Investment in Brussels Company, and on December 31, 19X6, the trial balances of Berlin and Brussels were as shown on the "Schedule I—Consolidating Worksheet." Assume that on July 1, 19X6, Brussels Company had net asset fair and book values which were equal. Also, assume that Schedule I shows revenues, expenses, and dividend declarations of Brussels Company for only the last six months of 19X6, while Berlin Company's revenues, expenses, and dividend declaration represent all 12 months of 19X6. Complete consolidating worksheet (Schedule I).

Schedule I
Berlin Co. and 100% Owned Subsidiary Brussels Co.
Consolidating Worksheet For the Year Ended 12/31/X6

Account Name	Berlin Co. Dr. (Cr.)	Brussels Co. Dr. (Cr.)	Eliminations Dr.	Eliminations (Cr.)	CONSOLIDATED Dr. (Cr.) Income Statement	Retained Earnings	Balance Sheet
Cash	100,000	15,000					
Accounts receivable (net)	175,000	75,000					
Inventory	65,000	80,000					
Land	70,000	20,000					
Equipment	150,000	70,000					
Accum. depr. —equip.	(70,000)	(50,000)					
Building	800,000	350,000					
Accum. depr. —bldg.	(300,000)	(250,000)					
Investment in Brussels	145,000						
Liabilities	(645,000)	(165,000)					
Common stock:							
Berlin	(150,000)						
Brussels		(50,000)					
Additional paid-in capital—common:							
Berlin	(100,000)						
Brussels		(20,000)					
Preferred stock: Berlin	(60,000)						
Additional paid-in capital—preferred:							
Berlin	(5,000)						
Retained earnings:							
Berlin	(130,000)						
Brussels		(60,000)					
Dividends declared:							
Berlin	30,000						
Brussels		10,000					
Sales	(700,000)	(300,000)					
Investment income	(25,000)						
Cost of goods sold	375,000	200,000					
Depreciation expense	100,000	30,000					
Operating expenses	175,000	45,000					
Totals	0	0					
Consolidated net income							
Consolidated retained earnings							
Total							

***Answer*:**

Schedule I
Berlin Co. and 100% Owned Subsidiary Brussels Co.
Consolidating Worksheet for the Year Ended 12/31/X6

Account Name	Berlin Co. Dr. (Cr.)	Brussels Co. Dr. (Cr.)	Eliminations Dr.	Eliminations (Cr.)	CONSOLIDATED Dr. (Cr.) Income Statement	Retained Earnings	Balance Sheet
Cash	100,000	15,000					115,000
Accounts receivable (net)	175,000	75,000					250,000
Inventory	65,000	80,000					145,000
Land	70,000	20,000					90,000
Equipment	150,000	70,000					220,000
Accum. depr.—equip.	(70,000)	(50,000)					(120,000)
Building	800,000	350,000					1,150,000
Accum. depr.—bldg.	(300,000)	(250,000)					(550,000)
Investment in Brussels.	145,000			(145,000)[1]			0
Liabilities	(645,000)	(165,000)					(810,000)
Common stock:							
Berlin.	(150,000)						(150,000)
Brussels		(50,000)	50,000[1]				0
Additional paid-in capital—common:							
Berlin	(100,000)						(100,000)
Brussels		(20,000)	20,000[1]				0
Preferred stock:							
Berlin	(60,000)						(60,000)
Additional paid-in capital —preferred:							
Berlin	(5,000)						(5,000)
Retained earnings:							
Berlin	(130,000)					(130,000)	
Brussels		(60,000)	60,000[1]				0
Dividends declared:							
Berlin	30,000					30,000	
Brussels		10,000		(10,000)[1]			0
Sales	(700,000)	(300,000)			(1,000,000)		
Investment income	(25,000)		25,000[1]		0		
Cost of goods sold	375,000	200,000			575,000		
Depreciation expense	100,000	30,000			130,000		
Operating expenses	175,000	45,000			220,000		
Totals	0	0	155,000	(155,000)			
Consolidated net income					(75,000)	(75,000)	
Consolidated retained earnings						(175,000)	(175,000)
Total							0

[1]To eliminate Investment in Brussels Co. against Brussels Co. equity, investment income, and dividends declared.

Note that the December 31, 19X1, Investment in Brussels account balance is determined as follows:

July 1, 19X6 Investment cost	$130,000
Brussels Company net income for 6 months ended 12/31/X6 (100% × $25,000)	25,000
Brussels Company dividends declared and paid during 6 months ended 12/31/X6 (100% × $10,000)	(10,000)
December 31, 19X6 Investment in Brussels	$145,000

PROBLEM 6-3: Assume the same facts as those provided in Problem 6-2, except that Berlin Company paid a total of $170,000 (that is, $70,000 for preferred stock, plus $10,000 for direct costs, plus $90,000 cash) for a 100% interest in Brussels Company common stock, and that on the July 1, 19X6, purchase date, Brussels Company had net asset fair values which equaled book values, except:

	Book Values	Fair Values	Difference
Land	$ 20,000	$ 21,000	$ 1,000
Equipment (net)	20,000	44,000*	24,000
Inventory	80,000	77,000**	(3,000)
	$120,000	$142,000	$22,000

*3-year life remaining as of 7/01/X6, straight line, no salvage.
**Completely sold by 11/18/X6.

Based on this new information, complete the Schedule II consolidating worksheet.

Schedule II
Berlin Co. and 100% Owned Subsidiary Brussels Co.
Consolidating Worksheet For the Year Ended 12/31/X6

Account Name	Berlin Co. Dr. (Cr.)	Brussels Co. Dr. (Cr.)	Eliminations Dr.	Eliminations (Cr.)	CONSOLIDATED Dr. (Cr.) Income Statement	Retained Earnings	Balance Sheet
Cash	60,000	15,000					
Accounts receivable (net)	175,000	75,000					
Inventory	65,000	80,000					
Land	70,000	20,000					
Equipment	150,000	70,000					
Accum. depr.—equip.	(70,000)	(50,000)					
Building	800,000	350,000					
Accum. depr.—bldg.	(300,000)	(250,000)					
Investment in Brussels.	183,775						
Goodwill							
Liabilities	(645,000)	(165,000)					
Common stock:							
Berlin	(150,000)						
Brussels		(50,000)					
Additional paid-in capital—common:							
Berlin	(100,000)						
Brussels		(20,000)					
Preferred stock:							
Berlin	(60,000)						
Additional paid-in capital—preferred:							
Berlin	(5,000)						
Retained earnings:							
Berlin	(130,000)						
Brussels		(60,000)					
Dividends declared:							
Berlin	30,000						
Brussels		10,000					
Sales	(700,000)	(300,000)					
Investment income	(23,775)						
Cost of goods sold	375,000	200,000					
Depreciation expense	100,000	30,000					
Operating expenses	175,000	45,000					
Totals	0	0					
Consolidated net income							
Consolidated retained earnings							
Total							

Answer: Note that the 7/01/X6 original investment cost of $170,000 represents these items:

7/01/X6 Investment cost		$170,000
Book value of underlying net assets acquired (7/01/X6 equity)	$130,000	
Ownership level	× 100%	(130,000)
Excess cost over book value		40,000
Portion of excess attributable to:		
Inventory (100% × ($3,000))		3,000
Land (100% × $1,000)		(1,000)
Equipment (100% × $24,000)		(24,000)
Goodwill		$ 18,000

For the last six months of 19X6, the equity method requires amortization against investment income on Berlin's books:

Inventory (completely sold by 11/18/X6)	($3,000)
Equipment ($24,000 ÷ 3 years) × 1/2 year	4,000
Goodwill ($18,000 ÷ 40 years) × 1/2 year	225
19X6 Amortization	$1,225

As of 12/31/X6, the Investment in Brussels account is carried on Berlin's books as follows, as shown on Schedule II:

7/01/X6 Investment cost	$170,000
Brussels Company net income for 6 months ended 12/31/X6 (100% × $25,000)	*25,000
19X6 Amortization of cost in excess of book value	*(1,225)
Brussels Company dividends declared and paid during 6 months ended 12/31/X6 (100% × $10,000)	(10,000)
12/31/X6 Investment in Brussels	$183,775

*Investment income = $25,000 – $1,225 = $23,775.

Schedule II
Berlin Co. and 100% Owned Subsidiary Brussels Co.
Consolidating Worksheet For the Year Ended 12/31/X6

Account Name	Berlin Co. Dr. (Cr.)	Brussels Co. Dr. (Cr.)	Eliminations Dr.	Eliminations (Cr.)	CONSOLIDATED Dr. (Cr.) Income Statement	Retained Earnings	Balance Sheet
Cash	60,000	15,000					75,000
Accounts receivable (net)	175,000	75,000					250,000
Inventory	65,000	80,000	3,000[2]	(3,000)[1]			145,000
Land	70,000	20,000	1,000[1]				91,000
Equipment	150,000	70,000	24,000[1]				244,000
Accum. depr.—equip.	(70,000)	(50,000)		(4,000)[2]			(124,000)
Building	800,000	350,000					1,150,000
Accum. depr.—bldg.	(300,000)	(250,000)					(550,000)
Investment in Brussels	183,775			(183,775)[1]			0
Goodwill			18,000[1]	(225)[2]			17,775
Liabilities	(645,000)	(165,000)					(810,000)
Common stock:							
Berlin	(150,000)						(150,000)
Brussels		(50,000)	50,000[1]				0
Additional paid-in capital—common:							
Berlin	(100,000)						(100,000)
Brussels		(20,000)	20,000[1]				0
Preferred stock:							
Berlin	(60,000)						(60,000)
Additional paid-in capital—preferred:							
Berlin	(5,000)						(5,000)
Retained earnings:							
Berlin	(130,000)					(130,000)	
Brussels		(60,000)	60,000[1]				0
Dividends declared:							
Berlin	30,000					30,000	
Brussels		10,000		(10,000)[1]			0
Sales	(700,000)	(300,000)			(1,000,000)		
Investment income	(23,775)		23,775[1]		0		
Goodwill amortization			225[2]		225		
Cost of goods sold	375,000	200,000		(3,000)[2]	572,000		
Depreciation expense	100,000	30,000	4,000[2]		134,000		
Operating expenses	175,000	45,000			220,000		
Totals	0	0	204,000	(204,000)			
Consolidated net income					(73,775)	(73,775)	
Consolidated retained earnings						(173,775)	(173,775)
Total							0

[1]To eliminate Investment in Brussels Co. against Brussels Co. equity, investment income, and dividends declared.

[2]To amortize Brussels Co. adjusted net asset valuations and goodwill.

PROBLEM 6-4: Based on the information provided in the answer to Problem 6-3, and assuming that Brussels Company generated net income of $60,000 and declared and paid dividends of $50,000 during 19X7, determine the following:

(*a*) the amount of 19X7 amortization of cost in excess of book value.
(*b*) the Investment in Brussels account balance on December 31, 19X7.
(*c*) the consolidating worksheet elimination entries required on December 31, 19X7.

Answer:

(*a*) A full year's amortization applies in 19X7:

Equipment (depreciation) ($24,000 ÷ 3 yrs.)	$ 8,000
Goodwill (amortization) ($18,000 ÷ 40 yrs.)	450
Inventory (completely sold in prior year 19X6)	0
19X7 Amortization	$8,450

(*b*)

12/31X6 Investment in Brussels (see Schedule II, Problem 6-3)	$183,775
Brussels Company net income for 19X7	60,000
19X7 Amortization of cost in excess of book value	(8,450)
Brussels Company dividends declared and paid for 19X7	(50,000)
12/31/X7 Investment in Brussels	$185,325

(*c*) 1.

	Debit	Credit
Brussels Co.—Common Stock	50,000	
Brussels Co.—Additional paid-in capital	20,000	
Brussels Co.—Retained earnings (12/31/X6)	75,000*	
Investment income	51,550	
Land	1,000	
Equipment	24,000	
Goodwill ($18,000 less 19X6 amortization $225)	17,775	
Accum. depreciation—equipment		4,000
Investment in Brussels		185,325
Brussels Co.—Dividends declared		50,000

*Brussels Co. retained earnings (7/01/X6)	$60,000
Brussels Co.net income for 6 months ended 12/31/X6	25,000
Brussels Co. dividends declared and paid during 6 months ended 12/31/X6	(10,000)
Brussels Co. retained earnings (12/31/X6)	$75,000

To eliminate Investment in Brussels against investment income and Brussels' equity and dividend declarations, and to revalue Brussels' net assets.

2.

	Debit	Credit
Depreciation expense	8,000	
Goodwill amortization	450	
Accum. depreciation—equipment		8,000
Goodwill		450

To amortize goodwill and Brussels' adjust net asset valuations.

PROBLEM 6-5: On January 1, 19X4, Bear Co. paid $450,000 for 90% of Cub Co. common stock in a business combination appropriately accounted for as a purchase. Bear Co. carries its Investment in Cub Co. account using the equity method. On January 1, 19X4, Cub Company's net asset book values and fair values were equal, except:

	Book Values	Fair Values	Difference
Inventory	$ 50,000	$ 56,000*	$ 6,000
Land	200,000	210,000	10,000
Building (net)	800,000	1,000,000**	200,000
	$1,050,000	$1,266,000	$216,000

*Completely sold during 19X4.
**As of 1/01/X4, 20-year life remains, straight-line depreciation and no salvage value used.

Based on the information above and on the 12/31/X4 trial balance columns for Bear Co. and Cub Co. provided on Schedule III, complete the consolidation worksheet (Schedule III).

Schedule III
Bear Co. and 90% Owned Subsidiary Cub Co.
Consolidating Worksheet for the Year Ended 12/31/X4

					CONSOLIDATED Dr. (Cr.)		
Account Name	Bear Co. Dr. (Cr.)	Cub Co. Dr. (Cr.)	Eliminations Dr.	Eliminations (Cr.)	Income Statement	Retained Earnings	Balance Sheet
Cash	50,000	20,000					
Accounts receivable (net)	30,000	20,000					
Inventory	50,000	30,000					
Land	50,000	20,000					
Equipment	500,000	200,000					
Accum. depr.—equip.	(250,000)	(160,000)					
Building	2,000,000	1,000,000					
Accum. depr.—bldg.	(800,000)	(240,000)					
Investment in Cub Co.	470,160						
Liabilities	(990,000)	(630,000)					
Common stock:							
Bear Co.	(200,000)						
Cub Co.		(90,000)					
Additional paid-in capital—common:							
Bear Co.	(400,000)						
Cub Co.		(60,000)					
Retained earnings:							
Bear Co.	(280,000)						
Cub Co.		(70,000)					
Dividends declared:							
Bear Co.	20,000						
Cub Co.		10,000					
Sales	(850,000)	(300,000)					
Investment income	(29,160)						
Cost of goods sold	400,000	160,000					
Depreciation expense	75,000	50,000					
Operating expenses	154,000	40,000					
Totals	0	0					
	Combined net income						
	Minority interest						
	Consolidated net income						
	Consolidated retained earnings						
					Total		
	Total minority interest						

Answer:

Note that the 1/01/X4 original investment cost of $450,000 represents the following items:

1/01/X4 Investment cost		$450,000
Book value of underlying net assets acquired(1/01/X4 equity)	$220,000	
Ownership level	× 90%	(198,000)
Excess cost over book value		252,000
Portion of excess attributable to:		
Inventory (90% × $6,000)		(5,400)
Land (90% × $10,000)		(9,000)
Building (90% × $200,000)		(180,000)
Goodwill		$ 57,600

The equity method amortization against investment income for 19X4 on Bear's books is:

Inventory (all sold during 19X4)	$ 5,400
Building ($180,000 ÷ 20 years)	9,000
Goodwill ($57,600 ÷ 40 years)	1,440
	$ 15,840

Investment income consists of:

90% Cub Co. net income of $50,000	$ 45,000
Less: 19X4 Amortization	(15,840)
Investment income	$ 29,160

As of 12/31/X4, the Investment in Cub Co. account consists of the following items:

1/01/X4 Investment cost	$450,000
90% of Cub Co. net income for 19X4 of $50,000	45,000
19X4 Amortization of cost in excess of book value	(15,840)
90% of Cub Co. 19X4 dividends declared and paid of $10,000	(9,000)
12/31/X4 Investment in Cub Co.	$470,160

Schedule III
Bear Co. and 90% Owned Subsidiary Cub Co.
Consolidating Worksheet for the Year Ended 12/31/X4

Account Name	Bear Co. Dr. (Cr.)	Cub Co. Dr. (Cr.)	Eliminations Dr.	Eliminations (Cr.)	CONSOLIDATED Dr. (Cr.) Income Statement	Retained Earnings	Balance Sheet
Cash	50,000	20,000					70,000
Accounts receivable (net)	30,000	20,000					50,000
Inventory	50,000	30,000	5,400[1]	(5,400)[2]			80,000
Land	50,000	20,000	9,000[1]				79,000
Equipment	500,000	200,000					700,000
Accum. depr. —equip.	(250,000)	(160,000)					(410,000)
Building	2,000,000	1,000,000	180,000[1]				3,180,000
Accum. depr. —bldg.	(800,000)	(240,000)		(9,000)[2]			(1,049,000)
Investment in Cub Co.	470,160			(470,160)[1]			0
Goodwill			57,600[1]	(1,440)[1]			56,160
Liabilities	(990,000)	(630,000)					(1,620,000)
Common stock:							
Bear Co.	(200,000)						(200,000)
Cub Co.		(90,000)	81,000[1]				(9,000)M
Additional paid-in capital—common:							
Bear Co.	(400,000)						(400,000)
Cub Co.		(60,000)	54,000[1]				(6,000)M
Retained earnings:							
Bear Co.	(280,000)					(280,000)	
Cub Co.		(70,000)	63,000[1]				(7,000)M
Dividends declared:							
Bear Co.	20,000					20,000	
Cub Co.		10,000		(9,000)[2]			1,000 M
Sales	(850,000)	(300,000)			(1,150,000)		
Investment income	(29,160)		29,160[1]		0		
Goodwill amortization			1,440[2]		1,440		
Cost of goods sold	400,000	160,000	5,400[2]		565,400		
Depreciation expense	75,000	50,000	9,000[2]		134,000		
Operating expenses	154,000	40,000			194,000		
Totals	0	0	495,000	(495,000)			
	Combined net income				(255,160)		
	*Minority interest				5,000		(5,000)M
	Consolidated net income				(250,160)	(250,160)	
	Consolidated retained earnings					(510,160)	(510,160)
					Total		0
	Total minority interest						(26,000)M

M = Minority interest
*10% of Cub Co. net income of $50,000 = $5,000.
[1]To eliminate Investment in Cub Co. against investment income and 90% of Cub Co. equity and dividends declared and to adjust Cub Co. assets to fair value.
[2]To amortize adjusted S Co. asset valuations and goodwill.

PROBLEM 6-6: Based on the information provided in Problem 6-5, and assuming that Cub Co. generated net income of $60,000 and declared and paid dividends of $40,000 during 19X5, determine the following:

(*a*) the amount of 19X5 amortization of cost in excess of book value.
(*b*) the Investment in Cub Co. account balance on December 31, 19X5.
(*c*) the consolidating worksheet elimination entries required on December 31, 19X5.

Answer:

(*a*)

Inventory (completely sold in prior year 19X4)	$ 0
Building ($180,000 ÷ 20 years)	9,000
Goodwill ($57,600 ÷ 40 years)	1,440
19X5 Amortization	$ 10,440

(*b*)

12/31/X4 Investment in Cub Co. (see Schedule III, Problem 6-5)	$470,160
90% of Cub Co. 19X5 net income of $60,000	54,000
19X5 Amortization of cost in excess of book value	(10,440)
90% of Cub Co. 19X5 dividends declared and paid of $40,000	(36,000)
12/31/X5 Investment in Cub Co.	$477,720

(*c*)

1. Cub Co. Common stock (90%)	81,000	
Cub Co. Additional paid-in capital (90%)	54,000	
Cub Co. Retained earnings (12/31/X4) (90%)	99,000*	
Investment income ($54,000 – $10,440)	43,560	
Land	9,000	
Building	180,000	
Goodwill ($57,600 – $1440 amort. 19X4)	56,160	
Accum depreciation—building		9,000
Investment in Cub Co.		477,720
Cub Co.—Dividends declared		36,000

*Cub Co.—Retained earnings 1/01/X4	$ 70,000
Cub Co.—19X4 net income	50,000
Cub Co.—19X4 dividends	(10,000)
Cub Co.—Retained earnings 12/31/X4	$110,000

To eliminate Investment in Cub Co. against investment income and 90% of Cub Co. equity and dividend declarations, and to revalue Cub Co. net assets.

2. Goodwill amortization	1,440	
Depreciation expense	9,000	
Accum. depr.—building		9,000
Goodwill		1,440

To amortize goodwill and Cub Co.'s adjusted net asset valuations.

7 BUSINESS COMBINATIONS ACCOUNTED FOR AS PURCHASES (COST METHOD)

THIS CHAPTER IS ABOUT

- ☑ **Consolidated Financial Statement Preparation After the Acquisition Date When the Cost Method Is Used**
- ☑ **Consolidation of a Wholly Owned Subsidiary When Cost, Fair Value, and Book Value Are Equal**
- ☑ **Consolidation of a Wholly Owned Subsidiary When Cost, Fair Value, and Book Value Differ**
- ☑ **Consolidation of a Partially Owned Subsidiary When Cost, Fair Value, and Book Value Are Equal**
- ☑ **Consolidation of a Partially Owned Subsidiary When Cost, Fair Value, and Book Value Differ**

note to the reader: If the fundamental differences between the cost and equity methods are not understood, be sure to study Chapter 5 which provides a brief review of these approaches before going further.

7-1. Consolidated Financial Statement Preparation After the Acquisition Date When the Cost Method Is Used

Discussion will once again emphasize the preparation of consolidated financial statements on dates after the original acquisition date, however, the assumption of this chapter is that the parent company carries its investment in the subsidiary using the cost method. Also, all examples and problems of this chapter assume that each business combination in question is appropriately accounted for as a purchase rather than a pooling of interests.

7-2. Consolidation of a Wholly Owned Subsidiary When Cost, Fair Value, and Book Value Are Equal

This is again a business combination of the simplest form since the underlying assumption is that the price paid by the acquiring company equals the net asset book and fair values of the acquired company. No goodwill results, and none of the acquired company's net assets require revaluation in the preparation of consolidated financial statements.

At the end of the first year after the business combination, entries are made on the consolidating worksheet to eliminate the parent's Investment in Subsidiary account against subsidiary equity accounts, and, if necessary, to eliminate any dividends declared by the subsidiary (paid and payable to the parent).

However, at the end of all years other than the first year after the combination, an initial worksheet entry will be required to update the Investment in Subsidiary account balance to a beginning of the year equity method position before the consolidation process can proceed. This will be necessary because the investment account balance will be representative of the acquisition date cost but the subsidiary retained earnings (at the beginning of any year after the year of acquisition) will be representative of a date other than the acquisition date. That is, subsidiary net income (or loss) and subsidiary dividend declarations of prior years will have been closed to subsidiary retained earnings. Without an initial worksheet entry to update the investment account balance in all years subsequent to the year of the parent's original investment, an acquisition date investment account balance would be eliminated against a post-acquisition date retained earnings balance. Therefore, in summary, the following two worksheet elimination entries should be contemplated each year:

1. in all years except the first year after the combination, an entry to update the investment account balance (carried at original cost) to a beginning of the year position as if the investment had been carried using the equity method.

note: The consolidating worksheet entry to recognize an *increase* in the subsidiary's retained earnings under the cost method is:

Investment in Subsidiary	X	
Retained Earnings – Parent		X

The consolidating worksheet entry to recognize a *decrease* in the subsidiary's retained earnings is:

Retained Earnings – Parent	X	
Investment in Subsidiary		X

2. an entry to eliminate the parent's Investment in Subsidiary account against subsidiary equity accounts and, if necessary, to eliminate any dividends declared by the subsidiary.

EXAMPLE 7-1: P Co. purchased 100 percent of S Co.'s common stock on 1/1/X1, for $100,000 when S Co.'s net asset fair values equaled book values and S Co. equity included common stock, additional paid-in capital, and retained earnings of $50,000, $40,000 and $10,000 respectively. P Co. carries its investment in S Co. under the cost method. Exhibit 7-A which follows shows trial balance columns for P Co. and S Co. on 12/31/X1, one year after original acquisition, and includes columns for intercompany eliminations and for consolidated financial statements.

Exhibit 7-A
P Co. and 100% Owned Subsidiary S Co.
Consolidating Worksheet
For the Year Ended 12/31/X1

Investment cost = Fair value
and Fair value = Book value

Account name	P Co. Dr. (Cr.)	S Co. Dr. (Cr.)	Eliminations Dr.	Eliminations (Cr.)	CONSOLIDATED Dr. (Cr.) Income Statement	Retained Earnings	Balance Sheet
Cash	124,000	37,000					161,000
Accounts receiv. (net)	126,000	43,000					169,000
Inventory	107,000	36,000					143,000
Land	50,000	20,000					70,000
Equipment	120,000	100,000					220,000
Accum. depr. – equip.	(80,000)	(70,000)					(150,000)
Building	400,000	200,000					600,000
Accum. depr. – bldg.	(305,000)	(155,000)					(460,000)
Investment in S Co.	100,000			[2](100,000)			0
Liabilities	(72,000)	(91,000)					(163,000)
Common stock:							
P Co.	(100,000)						(100,000)
S Co.		(50,000)	[2]50,000				0
Additional paid-in capital: P Co.	(130,000)						(130,000)
S Co.		(40,000)	[2]40,000				0
Retained earnings:							
P Co.	(220,000)					(220,000)	
S Co.		(10,000)	[2]10,000				0
Dividends declared:							
P Co.	50,000					50,000	
S Co.		20,000		[2](20,000)			0
Sales	(850,000)	(400,000)			(1,250,000)		
Dividend income	(20,000)		[2]20,000		0		
Cost of goods sold	300,000	260,000			560,000		
Depreciation expense	25,000	10,000			35,000		
Operating expenses	375,000	90,000			465,000		
Totals	0	0	120,000	(120,000)			
Consolidated net income					(190,000)	(190,000)	
Consolidated retained earnings						(360,000)	(360,000)
Total							0

[1]To update Investment in S Co. to a beginning of the year balance at equity. Note: No entry needed in the first investment year since the beginning investment account balance is the original investment cost under both equity and cost approaches.
[2]To eliminate Investment in S Co. against S Co. equity, dividend income, and dividends declared.

note: The "Investment in S Co." account one year after acquisition in Exhibit 7-A on 12/31/X1 is still the original cost of $100,000 of 1/1/X1. Since the books of P Co. and S Co. are open, the S Co. stockholder's equity accounts (particularly S Co. retained earnings) also represent 1/1/X1 balances. Therefore, Exhibit 7-A worksheet entry #2 eliminates the 1/1/X1 Investment in S Co. against the 1/1/X1 S Co. equity as follows:

	Dr.	Cr.
S Co. Common stock	50,000	
S Co. Additional paid-in capital	40,000	
S Co. Retained earnings (1/1/X1)	10,000	
Dividend Income	20,000	
Investment in S Co.		100,000
S Co. Dividends declared		20,000

However, in later years, the Investment in S Co. account will continue to be carried under the cost method at the original 1/1/X1 cost of $100,000. At the end of year 19X1, S Co. retained earnings will be:

S Co. 1/1/X1 retained earnings	$10,000
S Co. 19X1 net income	40,000
S Co. 19X1 dividends	(20,000)
S Co. 12/31/X1 retained earnings	$30,000

Therefore, at the end of year 19X2, the Investment in S Co. must be updated using a worksheet elimination entry to reflect changes in S Co. retained earnings before proceeding through the elimination process as follows:

Investment in S Co.	20,000	
P Co. – Retained earnings		20,000

To update Investment in S Co. to 1/1/X2 position for 12/31/X2 consolidation purposes. (100% × S Co. retained earnings increase of $20,000)

At the end of year 19X2, assuming S Co. 19X2 dividends declared and paid of $30,000, the worksheet entry to eliminate the Investment in S Co. becomes:

S Co. – Common stock	50,000	
S Co. – Additional paid-in capital	40,000	
S Co. – Retained earnings (1/1/X2)	30,000	
Dividend Income	30,000	
Investment in S Co.		120,000
S Co. Dividends declared		30,000

Exhibit 7-A shows no entry #1 to update the Investment in S Co. since S Co. retained earnings and the Investment in S Co. account are both shown with balances as of 1/1/X1. One final and important note regarding Exhibit 7-A is in order. Note that the columns headed consolidated income statement, retained earnings, and balance sheet yield precisely the same results as shown in Exhibit 6-A of the previous chapter (Chapter 6). The economic situations described in developing these exhibits were the same in both Chapters 6 and 7. Only the method used by P Co. to carry the Investment in S Co. (cost vs. equity) differed. No matter what method the parent company happens to use to carry its investment in a subsidiary, the end result of the consolidation process must be the same.

7-3. Consolidation of a Wholly Owned Subsidiary When Cost, Fair Value, and Book Value Differ

A. If the cost, fair value, and book value of an investment differ, such differences must be recorded and amortized.

In a business combination it is quite likely that the investment cost and subsidiary net asset fair values and book values will differ. Chapter 4 demonstrated that if investment cost, fair value of net assets acquired, or book value of net assets acquired differ, goodwill and/or asset account adjustments are required in the consolidation worksheet on the acquisition date. In Chapter 5, it was shown that on dates after acquisition, under the cost method of carrying investments, no amortization of differences between investment cost, fair values, and book values occurs. That is, under the cost method the parent company continues to carry the investment at original cost. The worksheet elimination process must contemplate not only subsidiary net asset revaluations, but also subsequent amortization that may result from these revaluations using the procedures extensively discussed in previous chapters.

EXAMPLE 7-2: P Co. purchased 100% of S Co. common stock on 1/1/X1 for $130,000 when S Co. common stock, additional paid-in capital, and retained earnings were $50,000, $40,000 and $10,000 respectively. On this date, S Co. net asset fair and book values were equal except as follows:

Account	Book Values	Fair Values	Difference
Inventory	$25,000	$ 22,000*	($ 3,000)
Land	20,000	22,000	2,000
Equipment (net)	35,000	56,000**	21,000
	$80,000	$100,000	$20,000

*Completely sold by 6/10/X1.
**Life remaining on 1/1/X1 was 7 years, and the asset is depreciated on a straight-line basis with no salvage value. (Original cost of $100,000 less accumulated depreciation as of 1/1/X1 of $65,000 equals $35,000 book value.)

S. Co net income for 19X1 totalled $40,000 and dividends declared and paid totalled $20,000. The $130,000 investment cost can be analyzed as follows:

Investment cost		$130,000
Book value of underlying net assets acquired	$100,000	
Ownership level	× 100%	(100,000)
Excess cost over book value		30,000
Portion of excess attributable to:		
Inventory (100% × ($3,000))		3,000
Land (100% × $2,000)		(2,000)
Equipment (100% × $21,000)		(21,000)
Goodwill		$ 10,000

During year 19X1, the cost method would result in no amortization against investment income or the investment account on P Co.'s books, however, consolidating worksheet amortization is needed as follows for 19X1:

Inventory (completely sold during 19X1)	($3,000)
Equipment ($21,000 excess ÷ 7 years)	3,000
Goodwill ($10,000 ÷ 40 years)	250
19X1 Amortization	$ 250

As of 12/31/X1, the "Investment in S Co." account is carried on P Co. books at the original 1/1/X1 investment cost of $130,000 under the cost method. At 12/31/X1, the worksheet elimination entries when the cost method of carrying investments is used must now be as follows:

1) To update the Investment in S Co. to a beginning of the year (1/1/X1) position at equity (as described earlier, no entry needed in the first investment year since the beginning investment account balance is the original investment cost under both equity and cost approaches).

2) To eliminate Investment in S Co. against S Co. equity, dividend income, and dividends declared, and to adjust S Co. net assets and record goodwill.

	Debit	Credit
S Co. Common stock	50,000	
S Co. Additional paid-in capital	40,000	
S Co. Retained earnings	10,000	
Land	2,000	
Equipment	21,000	
Goodwill	10,000	
Dividend income	20,000	
Inventory		3,000
Investment in S Co.		130,000
S Co. Dividends declared		20,000

3) To amortize adjusted S Co. asset valuations and goodwill.

	Dr.	Cr.
Inventory (entirely sold)	3,000	
Depreciation expense	3,000	
Goodwill amortization	250	
Cost of goods sold		3,000
Accumulated depreciation – equipment		3,000
Goodwill		250

Each item included in elimination entry #3 of 12/31/X1 simply represents adjustments to inventory, equipment, and goodwill accounts created on the worksheet in elimination entry #2. Exhibit 7-B which follows shows a trial balance for P Co. and S Co. on 12/31/X1, one year after original acquisition, and also included columns for the worksheet elimination entries just described and for conslidated financial statements.

Exhibit 7-B
P Co. and 100% Owned Subsidiary S Co.
Consolidating Worksheet
For the Year Ended 12/31/X1

Investment cost exceeds Fair value which exceeds Book value

					CONSOLIDATED Dr. (Cr.)		
Account name	P Co. Dr. (Cr.)	S Co. Dr. (Cr.)	Eliminations Dr.	Eliminations (Cr.)	Income Statement	Retained Earnings	Balance Sheet
Cash	94,000	37,000					131,000
Accounts receiv. (net)	126,000	43,000					169,000
Inventory	107,000	36,000	[3]3,000	[2](3,000)			143,000
Land	50,000	20,000	[2]2,000				72,000
Equipment	120,000	100,000	[2]21,000				241,000
Accum. depr. – equip.	(80,000)	(70,000)		[3](3,000)			(153,000)
Building	400,000	200,000					600,000
Accum. depr. – bldg.	(305,000)	(155,000)					(460,000)
Investment in S Co.	130,000			[2](130,000)			0
Goodwill			[2]10,000	[3](250)			9,750
Liabilities	(72,000)	(91,000)					(163,000)
Common stock:							
P Co.	(100,000)						(100,000)
S Co.		(50,000)	[2]50,000				0
Additional paid-in capital: P Co.	(130,000)						(130,000)
S Co.		(40,000)	[2]40,000				0
Retained earnings:							
P Co.	(220,000)					(220,000)	
S Co.		(10,000)	[2]10,000				0
Dividends declared:							
P Co.	50,000					50,000	
S Co.		20,000		[2](20,000)			0
Sales	(850,000)	(400,000)			(1,250,000)		
Dividend income	(20,000)		[2]20,000		0		
Goodwill amortization			[3]250		250		
Cost of goods sold	300,000	260,000		[3](3,000)	557,000		
Depreciation expense	25,000	10,000	[3]3,000		38,000		
Operating expenses	375,000	90,000			465,000		
Totals	0	0	159,250	(159,250)			
Consolidated net income					(189,750)	(189,750)	
Consolidated retained earnings						(359,750)	(359,750)
Total							0

[1]To update Investment in S Co. to a beginning of the year balance at equity.
note: No entry needed in the first investment year since the beginning investment account balance is the original investment cost under both equity and cost approaches.

[2]To eliminate Investment in S Co. against S Co. equity, dividend income, and dividends declared and to adjust S Co net assets and record goodwill.

[3]To amortize adjusted S Co. asset valuations and goodwill.

One final and important note regarding Exhibit 7-B is in order. Note that the columns headed consolidated income statement, retained earnings, and balance sheet yield precisely the same results as shown in Exhibit 6–B of the previous chapter (Chapter 6). The economic situations described in developing Exhibit B were the same in both Chapters 6 and 7. Only the method used by P Co. to carry the Investment in S Co. (cost vs. equity) differed. No matter what method the parent company happens to use to carry its investment in a subsidiary, the end result of the consolidation process must be the same.

B. Two years after the acquisition, consider accumulated depreciation and amortization while making the adjusting entries.

Recall that after a year or more of combined operation, the combined economic entity that carries its investment in the subsidiary under the cost method must make an adjusting entry on the consolidating worksheet to update the Investment in Subsidiary account to reflect the subsidiary's performance from the previous year (see Section 7-2).

After a year or more, any account that had been revalued on the original acquisition date as a result of differences between cost, fair value, and book value is adjusted by the original amount of difference. Also, however, accumulated depreciation and/or amortization for previous years must be considered as well as depreciation and amortization from the current year in the consolidation process.

EXAMPLE 7-3: Refer to the information provided in example 7–2 and also assume that S Co. net income for the year ended 12/31/X2 is $50,000, and that S Co. dividends of $30,000 were declared and paid during 19X2. On 12/31/X2, the "Investment in S Co." account balance would still be the 1/1/X1 original cost of $130,000. However, S Co. retained earnings on the 12/31/X2 trial balance (assuming the books are not closed by S Co.) would be the pre-closing 1/1/X2 S Co. retained earnings of $30,000 (1/1/X1 Balance $10,000 plus $40,000 income less $20,000 dividends). The 1/1/X1 "Investment in S Co." balance cannot be eliminated against the 1/1/X2 S Co. retained earnings balance. A 12/31/X2 worksheet entry is needed to update the investment account to a 1/1/X2 position as if the investment had been carried at equity. If the investment had been carried at equity, the 1/1/X2 Investment in S Co. would be as follows:

1/1/X1 Investment in S Co.	$130,000
100% of S Co. 19X1 net income of $40,000	40,000
19X1 Amortization of cost in excess of book value (as determined in Example 7–2)	(250)
100% of S. Co. 19X1 dividends of $20,000	(20,000)
1/1/X2 Investment in S. Co. (at equity)	149,750
1/1/X2 Investment in S. Co. (at cost)	(130,000)
Investment in S Co. adjustment required	$ 19,750

Therefore, the 12/31/X2 worksheet elimination entries would be as follows:

		Dr.	Cr.
1)	Investment in S Co.	19,750	
	P Co. Retained earnings		19,750
	To update investment account to a 1/1/X2 position at equity.		
2)	S Co. Common stock	50,000	
	S Co. Additional paid-in capital	40,000	
	S Co. Retained earnings	30,000	
	Land	2,000	
	Equipment	21,000	
	Goodwill ($10,000 less 19X1 amortization of $250.)	9,750	
	Dividend income (19X2)	30,000	
	Accum. depreciation – equipment (19X1)		3,000
	Investment in S Co.		149,750
	S Co. Dividends declared (19X2)		30,000

To eliminate Investment in S Co. against S Co. equity, dividend income, and dividends declared, and to adjust S Co. net assets and record goodwill.

3)	Depreciation expense	3,000	
	Goodwill amortization	250	
	Accum. depreciation – equipment (19X1)		3,000
	Goodwill		250
	To amortize adjusted S Co. asset valuations and goodwill.		

Note that entry (2) shows land increased by the full $2,000 to the fair value of the acquisition date since land is not a depreciable asset. Equipment, on the other hand, is increased by a net $18,000 only because the original 1/1/X1 increase of $21,000 must be reduced by the accumulated depreciation for 19X1 of $3,000. Similarly, goodwill is increased by only $9,750 ($10,000 less $250). Note also that worksheet amortization and depreciation in entry (3) continues, but now inventory is excluded from the amortization entry since all inventory of the original 1/1/X1 acquisition was sold during 19X1.

7-4. Consolidation of a Partially Owned Subsidiary When Cost, Fair Value, and Book Value Are Equal

A. Consider the minority's interest in the subsidiary's income and equity.

This is again a fairly simple form of business combination since investment cost equals underlying subsidiary net asset fair and book values. Therefore, no goodwill or subsidiary net asset revaluations are necessary. However, one complexity does exist. The parent company owns less than 100% of the subsidiary. Therefore, the parent will eliminate against its investment in the subsidiary only its portion of subsidiary equity. Any remaining equity which results represents minority interest.

EXAMPLE 7-4: P Co. purchased 80% of the common stock of S Co. on 1/1/X1 for $80,000 when S Co. net asset fair and book values were equal. On 1/1/X1, S Co. had common stock, additional paid-in capital, and retained earnings of $50,000, $40,000, and $10,000 respectively .During 19X1, S Co. had a net income of $40,000, and declared and paid dividends of $20,000. The "Investment in S Co." account balance on 12/31/X1, one year after acquisition, remains at the 1/1/X1 original cost of $80,000 under the cost method.

Exhibit 7-C which follows shows trial balance columns for P Co. and S Co. on 12/31/X1, and also includes columns for intercompany eliminations and for consolidated financial statements. Note that the worksheet elimination entries of Exhibit 7-C still involve: 1) updating the investment account to a beginning of the period balance assuming application of the equity method, and 2) elimination of the Investment in S Co. against S Co. equity, dividend income and dividends declared. However, Exhibit 7-C also includes an item called "minority interest" as a reduction from combined net income to yield consolidated net income. Note too that Exhibit 7-C includes a series of items marked "M" which represents minority interest in subsidiary equity. This minority interest will generally appear between liabilities and stockholders' equity on the consolidated balance sheet (under the parent company theory).

Investment cost = Fair value
and Fair value = Book value

Exhibit 7-C
P Co. and 80% Owned Subsidiary S Co.
Consolidating Worksheet
For the Year Ended 12/31/X1

					CONSOLIDATED Dr. (Cr.)		
Account name	P Co. Dr. (Cr.)	S Co. Dr. (Cr.)	Eliminations Dr.	Eliminations (Cr.)	Income Statement	Retained Earnings	Balance Sheet
Cash	140,000	37,000					177,000
Accounts receiv. (net)	126,000	43,000					169,000
Inventory	107,000	36,000					143,000
Land	50,000	20,000					70,000
Equipment	120,000	100,000					220,000
Accum. depr. – equip.	(80,000)	(70,000)					(150,000)
Building	400,000	200,000					600,000
Accum. depr. – bldg.	(305,000)	(155,000)					(460,000)
Investment in S Co.	80,000			[2](80,000)			0
Liabilities	(72,000)	(91,000)					(163,000)
Common stock:							
P Co.	(100,000)						(100,000)
S Co.		(50,000)	[2]40,000				(10,000)M
Additional paid-in capital: P Co.	(130,000)						(130,000)
S Co.		(40,000)	[2]32,000				(8,000)M
Retained earnings:							
P Co.	(220,000)					(220,000)	
S Co.		(10,000)	[2]8,000				(2,000)M
Dividends declared:							
P Co.	50,000					50,000	
S Co.		20,000		[2](16,000)			4,000M
Sales	(850,000)	(400,000)			(1,250,000)		
Dividend income	(16,000)		[2]16,000		0		
Cost of goods sold	300,000	260,000			560,000		
Depreciation expense	25,000	10,000			35,000		
Operating expenses	375,000	90,000			465,000		
Totals	0	0	96,000	(96,000)			
Combined net income					(190,000)		
Minority interest					8,000		(8,000)M
Consolidated net income					(182,000)	(182,000)	
Consolidated retained earnings						(352,000)	(352,000)
Total							0
Total minority interest (sum of items marked "M")							(24,000)

M = minority interest
*20% of S Co. net income of $40,000 = $8,000.
[1]To update Investment in S Co. to a beginning of the year balance at equity. Note: No entry needed in the first investment year since the beginning investment account balance is the original investment cost under both equity and cost approaches.
Note: 1/1/X1 S Co. equity.of $100,000 plus 19X1 S Co. net income of $40,000 less 19X1 S Co. dividends of $20,000 equals 12/31/X1 S Co. equity of $120,000. Minority interest of 20% × $120,000 yields $24,000.
[2]To eliminate Investment in S Co. and dividend income against 80% of S Co. equity and dividend declarations.

One final note regarding Exhibit 7-C is in order. The consolidated columns headed income statement, retained earnings, and balance sheet yield precisely the same results as shown in Exhibit 6-C of the last chapter (Chapter 6). The economic situations described in developing these exhibits were the same in both Chapters 6 and 7. Only the method used by P Co. to carry the Investment in S Co. (cost vs. equity) differed. No matter what method the parent company happens to use to carry its investment in a subsidiary, the end result of the consolidation process must be the same.

B. Two years after acquisition, make an adjusting entry to record the subsidiary's previous performance.

The subsidiary will close its net income to retained earnings on its separate books, causing its retained earnings to increase or decrease, depending on its performance. But as previously demonstrated, under the cost method the parent's Investment in Subsidiary account does not change with the subsidiary's performance (as it does under the equity method). As a result, the Investment account can no longer be completely eliminated against the parent's portion of the subsidiary's equity accounts without adjustment. Therefore, an additional entry is needed on the consolidating worksheet, from the second year of the business combination on, to adjust the parent's Investment account balance so that it represents the same date as the subsidiary's "revalued" equity. See Section 7-2 for details.

7-5. Consolidation of a Partially Owned Subsidiary When Cost, Fair Value, and Book Value Differ

If the parent company's investment cost and the subsidiary's net asset fair and book values are not all the same, worksheet entries may be necessary to record goodwill and/or asset revaluations on the acquisition date.

A. The parent recognized goodwill and asset revaluation only equal to its ownership percentage.

If the parent company owns less than 100% of the subsidiary, under the parent company theory, asset revaluations which occur at acquisition may be recognized only to the extent of the parent's interest in the subsidiary. After acquisition, worksheet amortization of asset revaluations may be necessary.

EXAMPLE 7-5: P Co. purchased 80% of S Co. common stock on 1/1/X1 for $106,000 when S Co. common stock, additional paid-in capital, and retained earnings were $50,000, $40,000, and $10,000 respectively. On this date S Co. net asset fair and book values were equal except as follows:

Account	Book Values	Fair Values	Difference
Inventory	$25,000	$ 22,000*	($ 3,000)
Land	20,000	22,000	2,000
Equipment (net)	35,000	56,000**	21,000
	$80,000	$100,000	$20,000

*Completely sold by 6/10/X1.
**Life remaining on 1/1/X1 was 7 years, and the asset is depreciated on a straight-line basis with no salvage value. (Original cost of $100,000 less accumulated depreciation as of 1/1/X1 of $65,000 equals $35,000 book value.)

S. Co net income for 19X1 totalled $40,000 and dividends declared and paid totalled $20,000. The $106,000 investment cost can be analyzed as follows:

Investment cost		$106,000
Book value of underlying net assets acquired	$100,000	
Ownership level	× 80%	(80,000)
Excess cost over book value		26,000
Portion of excess attributable to:		
Inventory (80% × ($3,000))		2,400
Land (80% × $2,000)		(1,600)
Equipment (80% × $21,000)		(16,800)
Goodwill		$ 10,000

During 19X1, under the cost method there would be no amortization of the cost in excess of book value on P Co.'s books against investment income and the Investment in S Co. Nevertheless, 19X1 amortization has in fact occurred and would have been recorded under the equity method as follows:

Inventory (completely sold during 19X1)	$(2,400)
Equipment ($16,800 excess ÷ 7 years)	2,400
Goodwill ($10,000 ÷ 40 years)	250
19X1 Amortization	$ 250

As of 12/31/X1, the "Investment in S Co." account is carried at the original 1/1/X1 cost of $106,000 under the cost method. The 12/31/X1 worksheet elimination entries are as follows:

1) To update the Investment in S Co. to a beginning of the year (1/1/X1) position at equity (as described earlier, no entry needed in the first investment year since the beginning investment account balance is the original investment cost under both equity and cost approaches).

2) To eliminate Investment in S Co. and dividend income against 80% of S Co. equity and dividend declarations, and to adjust S Co. net assets and record goodwill.

S Co. Common stock	40,000	
S Co. Additional paid-in capital	32,000	
S Co. Retained earnings	8,000	
Dividend income	16,000	
Land	1,600	
Equipment	16,800	
Goodwill	10,000	
Inventory		2,400
Investment in S Co.		106,000
S Co. Dividends declared		16,000

3) To amortize adjusted S Co. net asset valuations and goodwill (developed in worksheet entry #2).

Inventory (entirely sold)	2,400	
Depreciation expense	2,400	
Goodwill amortization	250	
Cost of goods sold		2,400
Accum. depreciation – equipment		2,400
Goodwill		250

Exhibit 7-D which follows shows a trial balance for P Co. and S Co. on 12/31/X1, one year after the original acquisition, and also includes columns for the worksheet elimination entries just described and for consolidated financial statements. Note once again in Exhibit 7-D that minority interest in subsidiary net income reduces combined parent and subsidiary net income to yield consolidated net income under the parent company theory. Also, the consolidated balance sheet column of Exhibit 7-D has items marked "M" which represent minority interest which will generally appear on the consolidated balance sheet between debt and equity under the parent company theory.

Exhibit 7-D
P Co. and 80% Owned Subsidiary S Co.
Consolidating Worksheet
For the Year Ended 12/31/X1

Investment cost exceeds Fair value which exceeds Book value

					CONSOLIDATED Dr. (Cr.)		
	P Co.	S Co.	Eliminations		Income	Retained	Balance
Account name	Dr. (Cr.)	Dr. (Cr.)	Dr.	(Cr.)	Statement	Earnings	Sheet
Cash	114,000	37,000					151,000
Accounts receiv. (net)	126,000	43,000					169,000
Inventory	107,000	36,000	[3]2,400	[2](2,400)			143,000
Land	50,000	20,000	[2]1,600				71,600
Equipment	120,000	100,000	[2]16,800				236,800
Accum. depr. – equip.	(80,000)	(70,000)		[3](2,400)			(152,400)
Building	400,000	200,000					600,000
Accum. depr. – bldg.	(305,000)	(155,000)					(460,000)
Investment in S Co.	106,000			[2](106,000)			0
Goodwill			[2]10,000	([3]250)			9,750
Liabilities	(72,000)	(91,000)					(163,000)
Common stock:							
P Co.	(100,000)						(100,000)
S Co.		(50,000)	[2]40,000				(10,000)M
Additional paid-in capital: P Co.	(130,000)						(130,000)
S Co.		(40,000)	[2]32,000				(8,000)M
Retained earnings:							
P Co.	(220,000)					(220,000)	
S Co.		(10,000)	[2]8,000				(2,000)M
Dividends declared:							
P Co.	50,000					50,000	
S Co.		20,000		[2](16,000)			4,000M
Sales	(850,000)	(400,000)			(1,250,000)		
Dividend income	(16,000)		[2]16,000		0		
Goodwill amortization			[3]250		250		
Cost of goods sold	300,000	260,000		[3](2,400)	557,600		
Depreciation expense	25,000	10,000	[3]2,400		37,400		
Operating expenses	375,000	90,000			465,000		
Totals	0	0	129,450	(129,450)			
	Combined net income				(189,750)		
	Minority interest*				8,000		(8,000)M
	Consolidated net income				(181,750)	(181,750)	
	Consolidated retained earnings					(351,750)	(351,750)
				Total			0
	Total minority interest (sum of items marked "M")						(24,000)M

M = minority interest

*20% of S Co. net income of $40,000 = $8,000.

[1]To update Investment in S Co. to a beginning of the year balance at equity.

note: No entry needed in the first investment year since the beginning investment account balance is the original investment cost under both equity and cost approaches.

note: 1/1/X1 S Co. equity of $100,000 plus 19X1 S Co. net income of $40,000 less 19X1 S Co. dividends of $20,000 equals 12/31/X1 S Co. equity of $120,000. Minority interest of 20% × $120,000 yields $24,000.

[2]To eliminate Investment in S Co. and dividend income against 80% of S Co. equity and dividend declarations, and to adjust S Co. net assets, and record goodwill.

[3]To amortize adjusted S Co. net asset valuations and goodwill.

Again, if you compare Exhibit 7-D with Exhibit 6-D, you can see that the consolidated columns headed income statement, retained earnings, and balance sheet are the same. The economic situations described in developing these exhibits were the same. Only the method used by P Co. to carry the Investment in S Co. (cost vs. equity) differed. No matter what method the parent company happens to use to carry its investment in a subsidiary, the end result of the consolidation process must be the same.

B. Two or more years after the acquisition, consider the accumulated depreciation and amortization while making the adjusting entries.

Recall that after a year or more of combined operation, the combined economic entity that carries its investment in the subsidiary under the cost method must make an adjusting entry on the consolidating worksheet to update the Investment account to reflect the subsidiary's performance from the previous year (see Section 7-2).

After a year or more, any account that had been revalued on the original acquisition date as a result of differences between cost, fair value, and book value is adjusted by the original amount of difference. Also, however, accumulated depreciation and/or amortization for previous years must be considered as well as depreciation and amortization from the current year in the consolidation process.

EXAMPLE 7-6: Refer to the information provided in Example 7-5 and also assume that S Co. net income for the year ended 12/31/X2 is $50,000 and that dividends of $30,000 were declared and paid during 19X2. The "Investment in S Co." account balance on 12/31/X2 would still be the original acquisition cost of $106,000 under the cost method. The investment account should be adjusted so that it represents a 1/1/X2 balance as if the equity method had been used. In this way, the "Investment in S Co." account balance and S Co. Retained earnings would be depicted on a 12/31/X2 worksheet as of the same date (1/1/X2 assuming the books have not been closed). Under the equity method, the "Investment in S Co." account balance at 1/1/X2 may be determined as follows:

1/1/X1 Investment cost	$106,000
80% of S Co. net income of $40,000	32,000
19X1 Amortization of cost in excess of book value	(250)
80% of S. Co. dividends of $20,000	(16,000)
1/1/X2 Investment in S. Co. (at equity)	$121,750

The 12/31/X2 worksheet elimination would therefore be as follows:

		Debit	Credit
1)	Investment in S Co.	15,750	
	P Co. Retained earnings		15,750
	To update the investment account to a beginning of the year 19X2 balance at equity ($121,750 equity basis less $106,000 cost basis equals required adjustment of $15,750).		
2)	S Co. Common stock	40,000	
	S Co. Additional paid-in capital	32,000	
	S Co. Retained earnings (1/1/X2)*	24,000	
	Dividend income (80% × $30,000 for 19X2)	24,000	
	Land	1,600	
	Equipment	16,800	
	Goodwill ($10,000 less 19X1 amortization of $250.)	9,750	
	Investment in S Co.		121,750
	Dividends declared		24,000
	Accum. depreciation – equipment (19X1)		2,400
	To eliminate Investment in S Co. and dividend income against 80% of S Co. equity and dividend declarations, and to adjust S Co. net assets and record goodwill.		

*1/1/X1 S Co. retained earnings	$10,000
19X1 S Co. net income	40,000
19X1 S Co. dividends	(20,000)
1/1/X2 S. Co. retained earnings	$30,000)
Ownership level	× 80%
	$24,000

		Dr.	Cr.
3)	Depreciation expense	2,400	
	Goodwill amortization	250	
	Accum. depreciation – equipment		2,400
	P Co. Retained earnings		250

To record amortization of adjusted S Co. net assets and goodwill (recorded) in entry #2).

Appendix: An Alternate Consolidating Worksheet Format.

Some accountants perform the mechanics of consolidation using a two-tiered worksheet which consolidates, in descending order, the income statement and balance sheet. This format is demonstrated in Exhibit 7-E which follows. Exhibit 7-E presents the same information as that used to develop Exhibit 7-D of Example 7-5. Extra entries (#4 and #5) appear on Exhibit 7-E to record minority interest in S Co.'s net income and to adjust P Co.'s retained earnings to reflect the equity method as follows:

4)	Minority interest – income statement	8,000	
	Minority interest – S Co. Retained earnings		8,000
	(20% of S Co. net income of $40,000)		
5)	S Co. Retained earnings (net income)	15,750	
	P Co. Retained earnings (net income)		15,750

Equity method investment income	$31,750
Cost method dividend income	16,000
Required adjustment	$15,750

Same as exhibit D showing alternate format used by some accountants

Exhibit 7-E (Cost Method)
P Co. and 80% Owned Subsidiary S Co.
Consolidating Worksheet
For the Year Ended 12/31/X1

	P Co. Dr. (Cr.)	S Co. Dr. (Cr.)	Eliminations Dr.	Eliminations (Cr.)	CONSOLIDATED Dr. (Cr.)
INCOME STATEMENT					
Sales	(850,000)	(400,000)			(1,250,000)
Dividend income	(16,000)		[2]16,000		0
Subtotal	(866,000)	(400,000)	16,000	0	(1,250,000)
Goodwill amortization			[3]250		250
Cost of goods sold	300,000	260,000		[3](2,400)	557,600
Depreciation expense	25,000	10,000	[3]2,400		37,400
Operating expenses	375,000	90,000			465,000
Subtotal	700,000	360,000	2,650	(2,400)	1,060,250
Income before minority interest	(166,000)	(40,000)	18,650	(2,400)	(189,750)
Minority interest			[4]8,000		8,000
Net income	(166,000)	(40,000)	26,650	(2,400)	(181,750)
BALANCE SHEET					
Cash	114,000	37,000			151,000
Accounts receiv. (net)	126,000	43,000			169,000
Inventory	107,000	36,000	[3]2,400	[2](2,400)	143,000
Land	50,000	20,000	[2]1,600		71,600
Equipment	120,000	100,000	[2]16,800		236,800
Accum. depr. – equip.	(80,000)	(70,000)		[2](2,400)	(152,400)
Building	400,000	200,000			600,000
Accum. depr. – bldg.	(305,000)	(155,000)			(460,000)
Investment in S Co.	106,000			[2](106,000)	0
Goodwill			[2]10,000	[3](250)	9,750
Total assets	638,000	211,000	30,800	(111,050)	768,750
Liabilities	(72,000)	(91,000)			(163,000)
Common stock:					
P Co.	(100,000)				(100,000)
S Co.		(50,000)	[2]40,000		(10,000)M
Additional paid-in capital: P Co.	(130,000)				(130,000)
S Co.		(40,000)	[2]32,000		(8,000)M
Retained earnings – P Co.:					
1/1/X1 Balance	(220,000)				(220,000)
+ 19X1 Net income	(166,000)			[5](15,750)	(181,750)
– 19X1 Dividends	50,000				50,000
12/31/19X1 Balance	(336,000)			(15,750)	(351,750
Retained earnings – S Co.:					
1/1/X1 Balance		(10,000)	[2]8,000		(2,000)M
+ 19X1 Net income		(40,000)	26,650 [5]15,750	(2,400) [4](8,000)	(8,000)M
– 19X1 Dividends		20,000		[2](16,000)	4,000 M
12/31/19X1 Balance		(30,000)	50,400	(26,400)	(6,000)M
Total liabilities and equity	(638,000)	(211,000)	122,400	(26,400)	(768,750)
Minority interest (sum of items marked "M")					(24,000)

M = minority interest

[1]To update Investment in S Co. to a beginning of the year balance at equity. Note: No entry needed in the first investment year since the beginning investment account balance is the original investment cost under both equity and cost approaches.

note: 1/1/X1 S Co. equity.of $100,000 plus 19X1 S Co. net income of $40,000 less 19X1 S Co. dividends of $20,000 equals 12/31/X1 S Co. equity of $120,000. Minority interest of 20% × $120,000 yields $24,000.

[2]To eliminate Investment in S Co. and dividend income against 80% of S Co. equity and dividend declarations, and to adjust S Co. net assets, and record goodwill.

[3]To amortize adjusted S Co. net asset valuations and goodwill.

[4]To record minority interest in S Co. net income (20% × $40,000)

[5]To adjust P Co. retained earnings to reflect application of the equity method.

RAISE YOUR GRADES

Can you explain . . . ?

- ☑ the journal entries a parent company makes to record its investment in a subsidiary under the cost method
- ☑ the difference between *combined* and *consolidated* net income
- ☑ the eliminating entries needed on the consolidating worksheet under the cost method, at the end of the first year of combined operation, when the subsidiary is wholly owned and its cost, fair values, and book values are equal
- ☑ the additional adjusting entry needed on the consolidating worksheet under the cost method after two years of combined operation
- ☑ the additional adjusting entries needed on the consolidating worksheet under the cost method when the subsidiary is wholly owned but cost, fair values, and book values differ
- ☑ how to account for accumulated amortization and depreciation resulting from differences in cost, fair values, and book values two or more years after the acquisition
- ☑ how to account for a minority interest in a subsidiary under the cost method when cost, fair values, and book values are equal
- ☑ how to account for a minority interest in a subsidiary under the cost method when cost, fair values, and book values differ

SUMMARY

1. When a parent company carries its investment in a subsidiary using the cost method (unlike the situation wherein the investment is carried at equity), parent company income is not the same as consolidated net income.
2. Under the cost method, at any point in time the investment in a subsidiary consists solely of original cost. That is, no part of subsidiary dividends or income affects the investment balance, and the parent books no entries to amortize differences between investment cost and underlying book value of subsidiary net assets acquired.
3. The journal entries actually made on the books of a parent company which carries its investment in a subsidiary under the cost method are as follows:

Investment in subsidiary	$X	
Cash, liabilities incurred, etc.		$X
Cash (or Dividends receivable)	$X	
Dividend income		$X
To record parent's share of subsidiary dividend declarations.		

4. Worksheet elimination entries on dates after original acquisition are more complex than the eliminations on the acquisition date. To prepare a complete set of consolidated financial statements on dates after the original acquisition date, worksheet entries are needed no only to eliminate the investment in the subsidiary against the parent's share of subsidiary stockholders' equity, net assets, and goodwill, but also elimination entries are needed to reflect amortization of any differences between original investment cost, book value, and fair value of the subsidiary's net assets, and to eliminate any intercompany dividend income. And if the investment is carried at cost, an initial elimination entry

should be made to reflect the beginning of the year investment account balance as if the investment had been carried at equity.

5. If the investment cost exceeds the fair value of the underlying subsidiary net assets acquired, goodwill is created which must be recorded in the elimination process and, subsequently, amortized against consolidated net income over the future periods benefited (not to exceed 40 years).
6. If the fair value and book value of the underlying subsidiary net assets differ, this difference must be recorded in the elimination process. Subsequently, to the extent the item recorded (equipment, patent, building) is depreciable or amortizable, the worksheet elimination process must include such depreciation and amortization.
7. If a minority interest exists, the combined net income of a parent and its subsidiary must (under the parent company theory) be reduced by the minority shareholders' interest to yield consolidated net income.
8. Minority interest normally appears (under the parent company theory) between liabilities and stockholders' equity on the consolidated balance sheet.

RAPID REVIEW

1. A parent company's net income is the same as consolidated net income when the parent carries its investment in a subsidiary under the cost method.
   (*a*) true
   (*b*) false

2. On January 1, 19X1, Pepper Company purchased all of Salt Company's stock for $1,000,000 when Salt Company's net assets at book and fair value totalled $1,000,000. During the year 19X1, Salt Company had net income of $200,000 and declard and paid dividends of $150,000. Under the cost method, the Investment in Salt Company account balance on Pepper's books at December 31, 19X1 is $____________.

3. Based on the information in question 2, the worksheet elimination entry of December 31, 19X1 must eliminate an "Investment in Salt Company" account balance of $____________, dividend income of $____________, subsidiary equity of $____________, and subsidiary dividend declarations of $____________.

4. Assuming the same facts as those of question 2 except that Pepper's purchase gave Pepper a 75% (rather than 100%) interest in Salt Company, the Investment in Salt Company account balance on Pepper's books at December 31, 19X1 under the cost method is $____________.

5. Based on the facts provided in question 4, a 12/31/X1 worksheet elimination entry will result in charges to Salt Company equity of $____________, dividend income of $____________, and goodwill of $____________, and in credits to Investment in Salt Company of $____________, and Salt Company dividends declared of $____________. An additional worksheet elimination entry will be required charging goodwill amortization for $____________, and crediting goodwill for $____________.

6. Again, based on the facts provided in question #4 and the additional assumption that during 19X2 Salt Company generated net income of $230,000 and declared and paid dividends of $190,000, the Investment in Salt Company account balance at December 31, 19X2 is $____________.

7. Prepare the December 31, 19X2 worksheet elimination entries required based on your answer to question 6.

8. The worksheet elimination entries prepared in your answer to question 7 would be no different if Salt Company's net asset fair values and book values differed on the original 1/1/X1 acquisition date as long as the investment cost exceeded fair value by the same amount ($250,000).
   (*a*) true
   (*b*) false

Answers:

1. False. (By reviewing Exhibits 7-A through 7-E, it can be seen that the parent company net income will not always been the same as consolidated net income when the investment is carried at cost.)

2. $1,000,000. (Under the cost method, carry at original cost. For comparison, see answer to Rapid Review question 2, Chapter 6.)

3.

Investment in Salt Company	=	$1,000,000
Dividend income (100% of $150,000)	=	$ 150,000
Subsidiary equity – common stock, additional paid-in capital and retained earnings (100% of $1,000,000)	=	$1,000,000
Subsidiary dividend declarations	=	$ 150,000

note: The 12/31/X1 elimination entry is:

Salt Company (various equity accounts)	1,000,000	
Dividend income (100% of $150,000)	150,000	
Salt Company dividends declared		150,000
Investment in Salt Company		1,000,000

(For comparison, see answer to Rapid Review question 3, Chapter 6.)

4. $1,000,000. (Under the cost method, carry at original cost. For comparison, see answer to Rapid Review question 4, Chapter 6.)

5. The 12/31/X1 elimination entry under these circumstances would be as follows:

Salt Company equity (various accounts) (75% × $1,000,000)	750,000	
Dividend income (75% × $150,000)	112,500	
Goodwill*	250,000	
Investment in Salt Company		1,000,000
Salt Company dividends declared (75% × $150,000)		112,500

*Investment cost		$1,000,000
Fair value of subsidiary's net assets acquired on 1/1/X1	$1,000,000	
Ownership level	× 75%	(750,000)
Goodwill		$ 250,000

Goodwill amortization	6,250	
Goodwill		6,250
($250,000 divided by 40 years)		

(For comparison, see answer to Rapid Review question 5, Chapter 6.)

6. $1,000,000. (Under the cost method, carry at original cost. For comparison, see answer to Rapid Review question 6, Chapter 6.)

7. (1)

Investment in Salt Company	31,250	
Pepper Company Retained earnings		31,250

To adjust investment account to beginning of 19X2 (1/1/X2 equity position based on the following:

1/1/X1 investment cost	$1,000,000
Plus: 75% of Salt Company 19X1 income of $200,000	150,000
Less: 19X1 Goodwill amortization	(6,250)
75% of Salt Company 19X1 dividends of $150,000	(112,500)
12/31/X1 Investment account balance under the equity method	$1,031,250
12/31/X1 Investment account balance under the costmethod	(1,000,000)
12/31/X1 Worksheet adjustment	$ 31,250

Note: As a result of this worksheet entry, the investment account balance is now shown on the worksheet at $1,031,250 (original cost $1,000,000 plus $31,250 worksheet adjustment.)

		Debit	Credit
2)	Salt Company equiity (75% × $1,050,000*)	787,500	
	Dividend income (75% × $190,000)		142,500
	Goodwill ($250,000 less 19X1 amortization of $6,250)	243,750	
	Investment in Salt Company		1,031,250
	Salt Company dividends declared		142,500

*1/1/X1 Salt company equity of $1,000,000 plus 19X1 Salt Company net income of $200,000 less 19X1 Salt Company dividends of $150,000 equals 1/1/X2 Salt Company equity of $1,050,000.

To eliminate the investment account and dividend income against Pepper's share of Salt's equity and dividends, and to record adjusted goodwill.

		Debit	Credit
3)	Goodwill amortization	6,250	
	Goodwill		6,250

To record 19X2 goodwill amortization.

(For comparison, see answer to Rapid Review question 7, Chapter 6.)

8. False. The entries would not be the same. Salt Co's asset valuations would require worksheet adjustment and amortization also. (This more lengthy process is demonstrated in problems which follow.)

SOLVED PROBLEMS

PROBLEM 7-1: Gray Company acquired 75% of the capital stock of Crum Company on January 1, 19X1 and 90% of the capital stock of Slade Company on July 1, 19X1. The investment costs, subsidiary net asset fair values and subsidiary net asset book values were equal on the acquisition dates. The following schedule depicts selected retained earnings, income, and dividend information for the three companies (expressed in thousands):

	Gray	Crum	Slade
1/1/X1 Retained earnings	$200	$100	$50
19X1 Net income:			
First six months	20	10	4
Last six months	19	10	6
19X1 Dividends declared and paid:			
First six months	–	(6)	(4)
Last six months	(18)	(10)	–
12/31/X1 Retained earnings	$221	$104	$56

Gray Company uses the cost method of carrying its investments in Crum and Slade, and the business combinations are appropriately accounted for as purchases. Determine consolidated net income for 19X1 and the December 31, 19X1 consolidated retained earnings.

Answer: (Expressed in thousands)

Gray Company net income for all of 19X1 ($20 + $19)	$39
Less: Intercompany dividends included in Gray Company net income:	
Crum: (75% of $16 dividends for full year)	(12)
Slade: (90% of $0 dividends for last half of year)	(0)
Adjusted Gray Company net income	$27
Plus: Equity interest in subsidiary net income as follows:	
75% × Crum Income of $20 for full year 19X1	15
90% × Slade Income of $6 for last six months of 19X1	5.4
Consolidated net income for 19X1	$47.4

1/1/X1 Gray Company retained earnings	$200.0
Plus: Consolidated net income for 19X1	47.4
Less: Gray Company 19X1 dividends declared and paid	(18.0)
Consolidated retained earnings as of 12/31/X1	$229.4

PROBLEM 7-2: On July 1, 19X6, Berlin Company purchased 100% of the common stock of Brussels Company making the following entry to record the purchase:

Investment in Brussels Company	130,000	
Cash		65,000
Preferred stock (10,000 shares at $6 par)		60,000
Additional paid-in capital		5,000

Berlin Company carries its investment in Brussels using the cost method. On December 31, 19X6, the trial balances of Berlin and Brussels were as shown on the "Schedule I" which follows. Assume that on July 1, 19X6, Brussels Company had net asset fair and book values which were equal. Also, assume that Schedule I shows revenues, expenses, and dividend declarations of Brussels Company for only the last six months of 19X6, while Berlin Company's revenues, expenses, and dividend declarations represent all twelve months of 19X6. Complete consolidating worksheet (Schedule I) which follows. (Compare your Problem 7-2 Schedule I answer with your Problem 6-2 Schedule I answer in the previous chapter. Note that although in one case the investment is carried at equity, and in the other case the investment is carried at cost, the end results are the same.)

Schedule I Problem 7-2
Berlin Co. and 100% Owned Subsidiary Brussels Co.
Consolidating Worksheet
For the Year Ended 12/31/X6

Account name	Berlin Co. Dr. (Cr.)	Brussels Co. Dr. (Cr.)	Eliminations Dr.	Eliminations (Cr.)	CONSOLIDATED Dr. (Cr.) Income Statement	Retained Earnings	Balance Sheet
Cash	100,000	15,000					
Accounts receiv. (net)	175,000	75,000					
Inventory	65,000	80,000					
Land	70,000	20,000					
Equipment	150,000	70,000					
Accum. depr. – equip.	(70,000)	(50,000)					
Building	800,000	350,000					
Accum. depr. – bldg.	(300,000)	(250,000)					
Investment in Brussels	130,000						
Liabilities.	(645,000)	(165,000)					
Common stock:							
Berlin	(150,000)						
Brussels		(50,000)					
Additional paid-in capital							
– common: Berlin	(100,000)						
Brussels		(20,000)					
Preferred stock: Berlin	(60,000)						
Additional paid-in capital							
– preferred: Berlin	(5,000)						
Retained earnings:							
Berlin	(130,000)						
Brussels		(60,000)					
Dividends declared:							
Berlin	30,000						
Brussels		10,000					
Sales	(700,000)	(300,000)					
Dividend income	(10,000)						
Cost of goods sold.	375,000	200,000					
Depreciation expense.	100,000	30,000					
Operating expenses	175,000	45,000					
Totals	0	0					
Consolidated net income							
Consolidated retained earnings							
Total							

Schedule I Problem 7-2 Answer

Berlin Co. and 100% Owned Subsidiary Brussels Co.
Consolidating Worksheet
For the Year Ended 12/31/X6

Account name	Berlin Co. Dr. (Cr.)	Brussels Co. Dr. (Cr.)	Eliminations Dr.	Eliminations (Cr.)	CONSOLIDATED Dr. (Cr.) Income Statement	Retained Earnings	Balance Sheet
Cash	100,000	15,000					115,000
Accounts receiv. (net)	175,000	75,000					250,000
Inventory	65,000	80,000					145,000
Land	70,000	20,000					90,000
Equipment	150,000	70,000					220,000
Accum. depr. – equip.	(70,000)	(50,000)					(120,000)
Building	800,000	350,000					1,150,000
Accum. depr. – bldg.	(300,000)	(250,000)					(550,000)
Investment in Brussels	130,000			[2] (130,000)			0
Liabilities.	(645,000)	(165,000)					(810,000)
Common stock:							
Berlin	(150,000)						(150,000)
Brussels		(50,000)	[2] 50,000				0
Additional paid-in capital – common: Berlin	(100,000)						(100,000)
Brussels		(20,000)	[2] 20,000				0
Preferred stock: Berlin	(60,000)						(60,000)
Additional paid-in capital – preferred: Berlin	(5,000)						(5,000)
Retained earnings:							
Berlin	(130,000)					(130,000)	
Brussels		(60,000)	[2] 60,000				0
Dividends declared:							
Berlin	30,000					30,000	
Brussels		10,000		[2] (10,000)			0
Sales	(700,000)	(300,000)			(1,000,000)		
Dividend income	(10,000)		[2] 10,000		0		
Cost of goods sold.	375,000	200,000			575,000		
Depreciation expense.	100,000	30,000			130,000		
Operating expenses	175,000	45,000			220,000		
Totals	0	0	140,000	140,000			
	Consolidated net income				(75,000)	(75,000)	
	Consolidated retained earnings					(175,000)	(175,000)
				Total			0

[1] To update Investment in Brussels to a beginning of the year balance at equity. Note: No entry needed in the first investment year since the beginning investment account balance is the original investment cost under both equity and cost approaches.

[2] To eliminate Investment in Brussels against Brussels equity, dividend income, and dividends declared.

PROBLEM 7-3: Assume the same facts as those provided in problem 7-2 except that Berlin Company paid a total of $170,000 (rather than the $130,000 assumed in problem 7-2) for a 100% interest in Brussels Company common stock, and that on the July 1, 19X6 purchase date Brussels had net asset fair values which equaled book values except as follows:

	Book Values	Fair Values	Difference
Land	$ 20,000	$21,000	$ 1,000
Equipment (net)	20,000	44,000*	24,000
Inventory	80,000	$ 77,000**	(3,000)
	$120,000	$142,000	$22,000

*3-year life remaining as of 7/1/X6, straight line, no salvage.
**Completely sold by 11/18/X6.

Based on this new information, complete the Schedule II consolidating worksheet which follows. (Compare your Problem 7-3 Schedule II answer with your Problem 6-3 Schedule II answer in the previous chapter. Note that although in one case the investment is carried at equity, and in the other case the investment is carried at cost, the end results are the same.)

Schedule II Problem 7-3
Berlin Co. and 100% Owned Subsidiary Brussels Co.
Consolidating Worksheet
For the Year Ended 12/31/X6

Account name	Berlin Co. Dr. (Cr.)	Brussels Co. Dr. (Cr.)	Eliminations Dr.	Eliminations (Cr.)	CONSOLIDATED Dr. (Cr.) Income Statement	Retained Earnings	Balance Sheet
Cash	60,000	15,000					
Accounts receiv. (net)	175,000	75,000					
Inventory	65,000	80,000					
Land	70,000	20,000					
Equipment	150,000	70,000					
Accum. depr. – equip.	(70,000)	(50,000)					
Building	800,000	350,000					
Accum. depr. – bldg.	(300,000)	(250,000)					
Investment in Brussels	170,000						
Liabilities	(645,000)	(165,000)					
Common stock:							
Berlin	(150,000)						
Brussels		(50,000)					
Additional paid-in capital – common: Berlin	(100,000)						
Brussels		(20,000)					
Preferred stock: Berlin	(60,000)						
Additional paid-in capital – preferred: Berlin	(5,000)						
Retained earnings:							
Berlin	(130,000)						
Brussels		(60,000)					
Dividends declared:							
Berlin	30,000						
Brussels		10,000					
Sales	(700,000)	(300,000)					
Dividend income	(10,000)						
Cost of goods sold	375,000	200,000					
Depreciation expense	100,000	30,000					
Operating expenses	175,000	45,000					
Totals	0	0					
Consolidated net income							
Consolidated retained earnings							
Total							

Answer: Note that the 7/1/X6 original investment cost of $170,000 represents the following items:

7/1/X6 Investment cost		$170,000
Book value of underlying net assets acquired (7/1/X6 equity)	$130,000	
Ownership level	× 100%	(130,000)
Excess cost over book value		$ 40,000
Portion of excess attributable to:		
Inventory (100% × ($3,000))		$ 3,000
Land (100% × $1,000)		(1,000)
Equipment (100% × ($24,000))		(24,000)
Goodwill		$ 18,000

Under the cost method, no amortization of the excess cost over book value has taken place on Berlin Company's books. However, worksheet amortization is necessary for the last six months of 19X6 as follows:

Inventory (completely sold by 11/18/X6)	($3,000)
Equipment ($24,000 ÷ 3 years) × 1/2 year	4,000
Goodwill ($18,000 ÷ 40 years) × 1/2 year	225
19X6 Amortization	$1,225

As of 12/31/X6, the "Investment in Brussels" account is still carried at original 7/1/X6 cost of $170,000 under the cost method on Schedule II. The worksheet elimination shown on Schedule II which follows eliminates the $170,000 investment balance.

Schedule II Problem 7-3 Answer

Berlin Co. and 100% Owned Subsidiary Brussels Co.
Consolidating Worksheet
For the Year Ended 12/31/X6

Account name	Berlin Co. Dr. (Cr.)	Brussels Co. Dr. (Cr.)	Eliminations Dr.	Eliminations (Cr.)	CONSOLIDATED Dr. (Cr.) Income Statement	Retained Earnings	Balance Sheet
Cash	60,000	15,000					75,000
Accounts receiv. (net)	175,000	75,000					250,000
Inventory	65,000	80,000	[3]3,000	[2](3,000)			145,000
Land	70,000	20,000	[2]1,000				91,000
Equipment	150,000	70,000	[2]24,000				244,000
Accum. depr. – equip.	(70,000)	(50,000)		[3](4,000)			(124,000)
Building	800,000	350,000					1,150,000
Accum. depr. – bldg.	(300,000)	(250,000)					(550,000)
Investment in Brussels	170,000			[2](170,000)			0
Goodwill			[2]18,000	[3](225)			17,775
Liabilities	(645,000)	(165,000)					(810,000)
Common stock:							
Berlin	(150,000)						(150,000)
Brussels		(50,000)	[2]50,000				0
Additional paid-in capital – common: Berlin	(100,000)						(100,000)
Brussels		(20,000)	[2]20,000				0
Preferred stock: Berlin	(60,000)						(60,000)
Additional paid-in capital – preferred: Berlin	(5,000)						(5,000)
Retained earnings:							
Berlin	(130,000)					(130,000)	
Brussels		(60,000)	[2]60,000				0
Dividends declared:							
Berlin	30,000					30,000	
Brussels		10,000		[2](10,000)			0
Sales	(700,000)	(300,000)			(1,000,000)		
Dividend income	(10,000)		[2]10,000		0		
Goodwill amortization			[3]225		225		
Cost of goods sold	375,000	200,000		[3](3,,000)	572,000		
Depreciation expense	100,000	30,000	[3]4,000		134,000		
Operating expenses	175,000	45,000			220,000		
Totals	0	0	190,225	190,225			
	Consolidated net income				(73,775)	(73,775)	
	Consolidated retained earnings					(173,775)	(173,775)
				Total			0

[1]To update Investment in Brussels to a beginning of the year balance at equity.
note: No entry needed in the first investment year since the beginning investment account balance is the original investment cost under both equity and cost approaches.

[2]To eliminate Investment in Brussels against Brussels equity, dividend income, and dividends declared and to adjust Brussels net assets and record goodwill.

[3]To amortize adjusted Brussels Co. net asset valuations and goodwill.

PROBLEM 7-4: Based on the information provided in the answer to problem 7-3, and assuming that Brussels Company generated net income of $60,000 and declared and paid dividends of $50,000 during 19X7, determine the following:

(*a*) the amount of 19X7 amortization of cost in excess of book value.

(*b*) the "Investment in Brussels" account balance on December 31, 19X7.

(*c*) the consolidating worksheet elimination entries required on December 31, 19X7.

(Compare your Problem 7-4 answer under the cost method with your Problem 6-4 answer under the equity method.)

Answer:

(*a*) Under the cost method, no amortization will be recorded on Berlin Company's books. However, for worksheet elimination entry purposes, a full year's amortization applies in 19X7:

Equipment (depreciation) ($24,000 ÷ 3 years)	$8,000
Goodwill (amortization) ($18,000 ÷ 40 years)	450
Inventory (completely sold in prior year 19X6)	0
19X7 Amortization	$8,450

(*b*) Under the cost method, the 12/31/X7 Investment in Brussels account balance remains at the original 7/1/X6 cost of $170,000.

(*c*) (1)

Investment in Brussels	13,775	
Berlin Company retained earnings		13,775

To update Investment in Brussels to a beginning of the year balance at equity based on the following:

7/1/X6 Investment in Brussels	$170,000
80% Brussels Company net income for the six months ended 12/31/X6 (100% of $25,000 from Problem 7-3 Schedule II trial balance)	25,000
19X6 Amortization of cost in excess of book value as shown in answer to Problem 7-3	(1,225)
19X6 Brussels Company dividends for the last six months of 19X6 (100% of $10,000 from Problem 7-3 Schedule II trial balance)	(10,000)
1/1/X7 Investment in Brussels (at equity)	183,775
7/1/X6 Investment in Brussels (at cost)	170,000
Investment in Brussels adjustment required	$ 13,775

(2)

Brussels Company Common stock	50,000	
Brussels Company Additional paid-in capital	20,000	
Brussels Company Retained earnings (1/1/X7)*	75,000	
Land	1,000	
Equipment	24,000	
Goodwill ($18,000 less $225 19X1 amortization)	17,775	
Dividend income	50,000	
Investment in Brussels		183,775
Accum. depreciation – equipment (19X6)		4,000
Brussels Company Dividends declared (19X7)		50,000

*See Problem 7-3 Schedule II 7/1/X6 retained earnings of $60,000 plus net income of $25,000 less dividends $10,000 equals $75,000.

To eliminate Investment in Brussels Company against Brussels Company equity, dividend income, and dividends declared, and to adjust Brussels Company net assets and record goodwill.

(3) Goodwill amortization ($18,000 ÷ 40 years)	450	
Depreciation expense ($24,000 ÷ 3 years)	8,000	
Goodwill		450
Accum. depreciation – equipment		8,000
To amortize adjusted Brussels Company net assets and goodwill.		

PROBLEM 7-5: On January 1, 19X4, Bear Co. paid $450,000 for 90% of Cub Co. common stock in a business combination appropriately accounted for as a purchase. Bear Co. carries its "Investment in Cub Co." using the cost method. On January 19X4, Cub Co.'s net asset book and fair values were equal except as follows:

	Book Values	Fair Values	Difference
Inventory	$ 50,000	$ 56,000**	$ 6,000
Land	200,000	210,000	10,000
Building (net)	800,000	1,000,000**	200,000
	$1,050,000	$1,266,000	$216,000

*Completely sold during 19X4.
**As of 1/1/X4, 20-year life remains, straight-line depreciation and no salvage value used.

Based on the information provided in this question and on the 12/31/X4 trial balance columns for Bear Co. and Cub Co. provided on Schedule III which follows, complete the consolidating worksheet (Schedule III) which follows. (Compare your Problem 7-5 Schedule III answer with your Problem 6-5 Schedule III answer in the previous chapter. Note that although in one case the investment is carried at equity, and in the other case the investment is carried at cost, the end results are the same.)

Schedule III Problem 7-5
Bear Co. and 90% Owned Subsidiary Cub Co.
Consolidating Worksheet
For the Year Ended 12/31/X4

Account name	Bear Co. Dr. (Cr.)	Cub Co. Dr. (Cr.)	Eliminations Dr.	Eliminations (Cr.)	CONSOLIDATED Dr. (Cr.) Income Statement	Retained Earnings	Balance Sheet
Cash	50,000	20,000					
Accounts receiv. (net)	30,000	20,000					
Inventory	50,000	30,000					
Land	50,000	20,000					
Equipment	500,000	200,000					
Accum. depr. – equip.	(250,000)	(160,000)					
Building	2,000,000	1,000,000					
Accum. depr. – bldg.	(800,000)	(240,000)					
Investment in Cub Co.	450,000						
Liabilities	(990,000)	(630,000)					
Common stock:							
Bear Co.	(200,000)						
Cub Co.		(90,000)					
Additional paid-in capital – common: Bear Co.	(400,000)						
Cub Co.		(60,000)					
Retained earnings:							
Bear Co.	(280,000)						
Cub Co.		(70,000)					
Dividends declared:							
Bear Co.	20,000						
Cub Co.		10,000					
Sales	(850,000)	(300,000)					
Dividend income	(9,000)						
Cost of goods sold	400,000	160,000					
Depreciation expense	75,000	50,000					
Operating expenses	154,000	40,000					
Totals	0	0					
Combined net income							
Minority interest							
Consolidated net income							
Consolidated retained earnings							
Total							
Total minority interest (sum of items marked "M")							

Answer: Note that the 1/1/X4 original investment cost of $450,000 represents the following items:

7/1/X4 Investment cost		$450,000
Book value of underlying net assets acquired (1/1/X4 equity)	$220,000	
Ownership level	× 90%	(198,000)
Excess cost over book value		$252,000
Portion of excess attributable to:		
Inventory (90% × $6,000)		(5,400)
Land (90% × $10,000)		(9,000)
Building (90% × ($200,000))		(180,000)
Goodwill		$ 57,600

No amortization of the excess cost over book value will occur on the separate books of Bear Co. under the cost method. However, worksheet elimination columns (Schedule III answer) include 19X4 amortization as follows:

Inventory (all sold during 19X4)	$5,400
Building ($180,000 ÷ 20 years)	9,000
Goodwill ($57,600 ÷ 40 years)	1,440
	$15,840

The 12/31/X4 "Investment in Cub Co." under the cost method is simply the original 1/1/X4 cost of $450,000. Dividend income recognized by Bear Company as shown on the 12/31/X4 trial balance is 90% of total Cub Co. dividends of $10,000 (or $9,000 under the cost method).

Schedule III Problem 7-5 Answer

Bear Co. and 90% Owned Subsidiary Cub Co.
Consolidating Worksheet
For the Year Ended 12/31/X4

	Bear	Cub			CONSOLIDATED Dr. (Cr.)		
	Co.	Co.	Eliminations		Income	Retained	Balance
Account name	Dr. (Cr.)	Dr. (Cr.)	Dr.	(Cr.)	Statement	Earnings	Sheet
Cash	50,000	20,000					70,000
Accounts receiv. (net)	30,000	20,000					50,000
Inventory	50,000	30,000	[2]5,400	[3](5,400)			80,000
Land	50,000	20,000	[2]9,000				79,000
Equipment	500,000	200,000					700,000
Accum. depr. – equip.	(250,000)	(160,000)					(410,000)
Building	2,000,000	1,000,000	[2]180,000				3,180,000
Accum. depr. – bldg.	(800,000)	(240,000)		[3](9,000)			(1,049,000)
Investment in Cub Co.	450,000			[2](450,000)			0
Goodwill			[2]57,600	[3](1,440)			56,160
Liabilities	(990,000)	(630,000)					(1,620,000)
Common stock:							
Bear Co.	(200,000)						(200,000)
Cub Co.		(90,000)	[2]81,000				(9,000)M
Additional paid-in capital							
– common: Bear Co.	(400,000)						(400,000)
Cub Co.		(60,000)	[2]54,000				(6,000)M
Retained earnings:							
Bear Co.	(280,000)					(280,000)	
Cub Co.		(70,000)	[2]63,000				(7,000)M
Dividends declared:							
Bear Co.	20,000					20,000	
Cub Co.		10,000		[2](9,000)			1,000 M
Sales	(850,000)	(300,000)			(1,150,000)		
Dividend income	(9,000)		[2]9,000		0		
Goodwill amortization			[3]1,440		1,440		
Cost of goods sold	400,000	160,000	[3]5,400		565,400		
Depreciation expense	75,000	50,000	[3]9,000		134,000		
Operating expenses	154,000	40,000			194,000		
Totals	0	0	474,840	(474,840)			
	Combined net income				(255,160)		
	*Minority interest				5,000		(5,000)M
	Consolidated net income				(250,160)	(250,160)	
	Consolidated retained earnings					(510,160)	(510,160)
				Total			0
	Total minority interest (sum of items marked "M")						(26,000)

M = Minority interest
*10% of Cub Co. net income of $50,000 = $5,000.
[1]To update Investment in Cub Co. to a beginning of the year balance at equity.
note: No entry needed in the first investment year since the beginning investment account balance is the original investment cost under both equity and cost approaches.
[2]To eliminate Investment in Cub Co. and dividend income against 90% of Cub Co. equity and dividend declarations, and to adjust Cub Co. net assets and record goodwill.
[3]To amortize adjusted Cub Co. net asset valuations and goodwill.

PROBLEM 7-6: Based on the information provided in problem 7-5 and assuming that Cub Co. generated net income of $60,000 and declared and paid dividends of $40,000 during 19X5, determine the following:

(*a*) the amount of 19X5 amortization of cost in excess of book value.
(*b*) the "Investment in Cub Co." account balance on December 31, 19X5.
(*c*) the consolidating worksheet elimination entries required on December 31, 19X5.

(Compare your answer to Problem 7-6 on the cost basis with your answer to Problem 6-6 on the equity basis.)

Answer:

(*a*) No amortization of cost in excess of book value occurs on the separate books of Bear Co. under the cost method. However, worksheet amortization for 19X5 is needed as follows:

Inventory (completely sold in prior year 19X4	$ 0
Building ($180,000 ÷ 20 years)	9,000
Goodwill ($57,600 ÷ 40 years)	1,440
19X5 Amortization	$10,440

(*b*) Under the cost method, the balance in the "Investment in Cub Co." account at 12/31/X5 remains at the original 1/1/X4 cost of $450,000.

(*c*) (1)

	Debit	Credit
Investment in Cub Co.	20,160	
Bear Co. retained earnings		20,160

To update Investment in Cub Co. to a beginning of the year balance at equity based on the following:

1/1/X5 Investment in Cub Co. account balance at equity (see problem 6-5 answer for details)	$470,160
1/1/X5 Investment in Cub Co. account balance at cost	(450,000)
Investment in Cub Co. adjustment required	$ 20,160

(2)

	Debit	Credit
Cub Co. Common stock (90%)	81,000	
Cub Co. Additional paid-in capital (90%)	54,000	
Cub Co. Retained earnings (12/31/X4) (90%)	99,000	
Dividend income	36,000	
Land	9,000	
Building	180,000	
Goodwill ($57,600 less $1,440 amortization 19X4)	56,160	
Investment in Cub Co.		470,160
Accum. depreciation – building		9,000
Cub Co. Dividends declared		36,000

To eliminate Investment in Cub Co. and dividend income against 90% of Cub Co. equity and dividend declarations, and to adjust Cub Co. net assets and record goodwill. (Note: Cub Co. 12/31/X4 retained earnings are based on 1/1/X4 balance $70,000 plus 19X4 income of $50,000 less 19X4 dividends of $10,000, for a total of $110,000.)

(3)

	Debit	Credit
Depreciation expense	9,000	
Goodwill amortization	1,440	
Accum. depreciation – building		9,000
Goodwill		1,440

To amortize adjusted Cub Co. net asset valuations and goodwill (developed in previous worksheet entry #2).

CONSOLIDATED FINANCIAL STATEMENTS

THIS CHAPTER IS ABOUT

- ☑ **Intercompany Sales of Goods or Services**
- ☑ **Unrealized Profit in Ending Inventory**
- ☑ **Unrealized Profit in Beginning Inventory**
- ☑ **Minority Interest and Unrealized Profit**
- ☑ **Comprehensive Example**

8-1. Intercompany Sales of Goods or Services

Companies that are separate legal entities but which have been combined to form a single economic entity frequently provide one another with products and services. The sale and purchase of these goods and services are recorded as ordinary transactions on the books of each company involved.

Because these separate companies are viewed as a single economic entity, however, any "intercompany" sales and purchases of goods or services must be eliminated during the consolidation process. If they are not, the consolidated financial statements will be inflated by the amount of those transactions, as if the goods and services had been sold to or bought from outside sources. The process to eliminate intercompany sales of goods or services is in addition to the basic elimination processes, described in Chapters 4, 6, and 7, which eliminate the parent company's investment in the subsidiary against the subsidiary's equity.

A. Eliminate intercompany purchases and sales of inventory from the consolidated financial statements.

When the parent company sells inventory to its subsidiary, the transaction is referred to as a "downstream" sale. Conversely, when a subsidiary sells inventory to its parent, the transaction is referred to as an "upstream" sale. Although legally considered sales, the economic substance of these transactions is that no sale or purchase takes place from the viewpoint of a single economic entity which cannot buy and sell inventory to itself. Therefore intercompany sales and purchases must be fully eliminated during the preparation of consolidated financial statements. This is true regardless of the parent company's level of interest in the subsidiary company.

The company selling the inventory generates sales and receivables to be recorded, while the company buying the inventory generates purchases (cost of goods sold) and payables. Two entries are therefore necessary on the consolidating worksheet to eliminate intercompany sales and purchases of inventory. The first eliminates the amount of intercompany sales against the cost of those goods. The consolidating worksheet entry to eliminate intercompany sales and purchases of inventory is:

Sales	$X	
Cost of goods sold		$X

The second entry eliminates any intercompany amounts receivable or payable that may result from the sale and purchase of inventory. The consolidating worksheet entry to eliminate intercompany receivables and payables from sales and purchases of inventory is:

Payables $X	
Receivables	$X

EXAMPLE 8-1: During the year ended 12/31/X1, P Co. made a downstream sale of inventory to its subsidiary S Co. for $20,000. S Co. received the inventory and paid P Co. $17,500, leaving an amount receivable on the sale of $2,500. The following journal entries were made on the books of P Co. and S Co. during 19X1 to account for this transaction:

P Co.			S Co.		
Accounts receivable	20,000		Purchases (cost of goods sold)	20,000	
Sales		20,000	Accounts payable		20,000
Cash	17,500		Accounts payable	17,500	
Accounts receivable		17,500	Cash		17,500

In addition to entries to eliminate P Co.'s interest in S Co.'s equity, the following worksheet entries are made at 12/31/X1 to eliminate the effect of these intercompany transactions recorded on the separate books of P Co. and S Co.:

Accounts payable	2,500	
Accounts receivable		2,500

To eliminate intercompany receivables and payables resulting from inventory sales. ($20,000 billed less $17,500 collected)

Sales	20,000	
Cost of goods sold		20,000

To eliminate intercompany sales.

If the transactions recorded in Example 8-1 had resulted from an upstream rather than a downstream sale (i.e., P Co. buys the inventory from S Co.), the overstated payable and cost of goods sold amounts would appear on P Co. books while the overstated receivables and sales would appear on S Co. books; but the eliminating worksheet entries would be the same. Also, the eliminating worksheet entries are the same no matter what level of interest P Co. has in S Co.

B. Eliminate intercompany services performed from the consolidated financial statements.

In addition to selling inventory, one company in a combined economic entity may provide services for another company. As with intercompany purchases and sales of inventory, any intercompany transactions involving performance of intercompany services must be fully eliminated during the preparation of consolidated financial statements.

The company providing the service generates revenue and receivables, and the company receiving the service generates expenses and payables. Two entries are therefore necessary on the consolidating worksheet to eliminate the intercompany accounts created. The first eliminates revenues from services performed against expenses for services bought. The consolidating worksheet entry to eliminate intercompany service revenue and expense is:

Service revenue $X	
Service expense	$X

The second entry eliminates any amounts receivable or payable from one company to another in the same economic entity resulting from intercompany services rendered. The consolidating worksheet entry to eliminate intercompany receivables and payables from services performed is:

Payables $X	
Receivables	$X

EXAMPLE 8-2: P Co. has a contract to provide computer maintenance for its subsidiary S Co., for which it charges $5,000 a month. During the year 19X1 P Co. billed S Co. $60,000 for this service (12 months @ $5,000), and S Co. paid $55,000, leaving an amount receivable of $5,000. The following journal entries were made on the books of P Co. and S Co. during 19X1 to account for this transaction:

P Co.			S Co.		
Accounts receivable	60,000		Service expense	60,000	
Service revenue		60,000	Accounts payable		60,000
To record annual billing.					
Cash	55,500		Accounts payable	55,000	
Accounts receivable		55,000	Cash		55,000
To record cash receipts (payments) on service contract.					

On 12/31/X1 the combined economic entity of P Co. and S Co. prepares consolidated financial statements. In addition to entries to eliminate P Co.'s interest in S Co.'s equity, the following entries are made to eliminate the effect of these intercompany transactions recorded on the separate books of P Co. and S Co.:

Service revenue	60,000	
Service expense		60,000
To eliminate intercompany revenue and expense.		
Accounts payable	5,000	
Accounts receivable		5,000
To eliminate intercompany accounts payable and receivable from service contracts.		

If the transaction recorded in Example 8-2 had resulted from S Co. performing the service for P Co., the overstated payable and expense amounts would appear on P Co. books while the overstated receivable and sales amounts would appear on S Co. books; but the eliminating worksheet entries would be the same. Also, the eliminating worksheet entries are the same no matter what level of interest P Co. has in S Co.

C. Eliminate intercompany dividends from the consolidated financial statements.

One company may declare and pay dividends to another company in the same combined economic entity. Any intercompany transactions involving dividends must be fully eliminated during the preparation of consolidated financial statements.

When a subsidiary company declares a dividend, it debits Dividends Declared and credits Dividends Payable. Under the equity method, the parent company simultaneously debits dividends receivable and credits (decreases) its Investment in Subsidiary account by the portion of the dividend due to the parent. If the parent has not received all the dividends due by the end of the accounting period, then, of course, intercompany Dividends Receivable and Payable accounts remain on the books of P Co. and S Co. at year end. Therefore, at least one, and possibly two, entries are necessary on the consolidating worksheet to eliminate any intercompany dividends. The first eliminates the subsidiary company's dividends declared against the parent company's investment account. The consolidating worksheet entry to eliminate intercompany dividends declared is

Investment in Subsidiary Company	$X	
Dividends Declared		$X

(Of course, this entry is a part of a larger elimination entry explained in Chapters 5, 6, and 7.)

If all the dividends have not been paid by the end of the accounting period, then the second entry eliminates the dividends payable against the dividends receivable. The consolidating worksheet entry to eliminate intercompany dividends payable is:

Dividends Payable	$X	
Dividends Receivable		$X

8-2. Unrealized Profit in Ending Inventory

A company may sell inventory to its affiliate in a combined economic entity at a profit. The profit from such a sale is realized, or counted, at different times for the different accounting entities involved. The selling company, as a separate legal entity, may recognize its profit at the time of the sale. On the other hand, the profit generated on inventory sold to an affiliate is realized for the combined economic entity only when it is sold to an outside company by the affiliate. If that inventory is not resold by the affiliate company to an outside company, then the "profit" may not be recognized by the combined economic entity, and must be eliminated during the preparation of the consolidated financial statements. If this unrealized profit is not eliminated, the purchasing (affiliate) company's ending Inventory account on its balance sheet would be overstated from the point of view of the combined economic entity, and its Cost of Goods Sold account on its income statement would be understated.

A. Determine the amount of intercompany profit.

To accurately eliminate any unrealized profit in the purchasing company's ending inventory, the selling company's gross profit rate must be considered. The gross profit rate may be expressed either as a percentage of the cost of the inventory (e.g., a 25% markup on cost), or as a percentage of the selling price (e.g., a 25% gross profit on sales). Apply the appropriate seller's gross profit rate to the transfer price of the transaction to determine the amount of intercompany profit.

EXAMPLE 8-3: S Co. sold inventory to its parent company P Co. at a transfer price of $40,000. If S Co.'s gross profit rate is a 25% markup on cost (a percentage of the cost of the inventory) the gross profit on this sale is $8,000 determined as:

$$\begin{aligned} \$40{,}000 &= \text{cost of inventory} + \text{profit} \\ \$40{,}000 &= \text{cost of inventory} + 25\%\ (\text{cost of inventory}) \\ \$40{,}000 &= 125\%\ \text{cost of inventory} \\ \$40{,}000/1.25 &= \text{cost of inventory} \\ \$32{,}000 &= \text{cost of inventory} \\ \$40{,}000 - \$32{,}000 &= \$8{,}000\ \text{profit.} \end{aligned}$$

If S Co.'s gross profit rate is 25% of the transfer price (a percentage of the selling price), the profit on this sale is $10,000 determined as:

$$\begin{gathered} \text{profit} = 25\%\ \text{of}\ 40{,}000 \\ \text{profit: } \$10{,}000 \\ \text{cost of inventory: } \$30{,}000 \end{gathered}$$

B. Eliminate unrealized intercompany profit in ending inventory.

At the end of an accounting period all unrealized profit lodged in ending inventory must be eliminated in the consolidation process. The unrealized profit in ending inventory is eliminated in the consolidation process by reducing (crediting) inventory and increasing (debiting) cost of goods sold. The consolidating worksheet entry to eliminate unrealized profit in ending inventory is:

Cost of Goods Sold	$X	
Inventory		$X

This entry is made in addition to those needed to eliminate intercompany sales and purchases, and intercompany receivables and payables.

EXAMPLE 8-4: During 19X1, P Co. sold inventory to its subsidiary S Co. for $100,000. P Co. made a gross profit on sales of 20% on all these intercompany sales. At the end of 19X1, S Co. still owed P Co. $6,000 for these purchases, and its inventory included $40,000 in purchases from P Co. The 12/31/X1 consolidating worksheet entries needed to eliminate the effects of these sales are:

Sales	100,000	
Cost of goods sold		100,000
To eliminate intercompany sales.		

Accounts payable	6,000	
Accounts receivable		6,000
To eliminate intercompany accounts receivables and payables.		

These entries eliminate the sale, but not the profit. To do that, first determine the remaining profit in S Co.'s inventory:

$$\$40,000 \times 20\% = \$8,000$$

Then eliminate the profit on the consolidating worksheet:

Cost of goods sold	8,000	
Inventory		8,000
To eliminate profit in ending inventory (20% gross profit on sales times $40,000).		

This last entry removes the profit in the ending inventory, as well as the understatement of the cost of goods sold, on S Co.'s books.

If the transaction recorded in Example 8-3 had resulted from an upstream rather than a downstream sale (i.e., P Co. buys the inventory from S Co.), the eliminating worksheet entries would remain the same. However, the entry to eliminate the profit in the ending inventory would then represent the overstatement of ending inventory and the understatement of cost of goods sold on P Co.'s books.

8-3. Unrealized Profit in Beginning Inventory

Any unrealized profits in the ending inventory of a company are simply carried over and become unrealized profits in the beginning inventory of the next accounting period.

It is important to recognize, however, that the unrealized profit in beginning inventory results in an overstatement (from the combined-economic-entity point of view) of the purchasing company's Cost of Goods Sold account for the current period, because the unrealized profit lodged in inventory will "raise" the cost of the inventory sold from the purchasing company's perspective. Recall that the unrealized profit in beginning inventory also represents an understatement of prior period cost of goods sold and consequently in an overstatement of retained earnings as of the beginning of the current period. Therefore, unrealized profit in beginning inventory is eliminated against retained earnings. The consolidating worksheet entry to eliminate profit in beginning inventory is:

Retained Earnings	$X	
Cost of Goods Sold		$X

note: The charge to retained earnings will be a charge to either parent or subsidiary retained earnings depending on two factors:

(1) who the seller was (parent or subsidiary)
(2) whether or not any minority interest exists.

If the parent company made the intercompany sale at a profit, then regardless of the level of parent ownership interest in the subsidiary, the charge will be to the parent's retained earnings since no minority interest exists in the intercompany profit. Also, if a 100% owned subsidiary made the sale at a profit, the charge will be to the parent's retained earnings since once again no minority interest exists in intercompany profit. However, if a less than 100% owned subsidiary made the intercompany sale at a profit, then a portion of the charge will be to retained earnings of the subsidiary for the minority interest in the intercompany profit, and the rest of the charge will be to the parent's (consolidated) retained earnings. In Section 8-4, it will be shown that the determination of minority interest in combined net income will be affected by profits in beginning and ending inventory.

EXAMPLE 8-5: During 19X1, P Co. sold inventory to its subsidiary S Co. at a 20% gross profit. On 1/01/X2, S Co.'s inventory still included $40,000 in purchases from P Co. The following entry is necessary on the consolidating worksheet on 12/31/X2 to eliminate the unrealized profit in the beginning inventory:

$40,000 × 20% gross profit rate = $8,000 profit

Retained Earnings-P Co.	$8,000	
Cost of Goods Sold		$8,000

If the sale resulting in the eliminating entry in Example 8-5 had been an upstream sale (from S Co. to P Co.), the unrealized profit would still be eliminated against P Co.'s retained earnings assuming S Co. was a 100% owned subsidiary of P Co., because all of S Co.'s equity, including its retained earnings, will be eliminated against P Co.'s Investment in Subsidiary account during the consolidation process. But if a minority interest exists in S Co., then special consolidation procedures are required, as discussed in Section 8-4.

8-4. Minority Interest and Unrealized Profit

The methods of accounting for intercompany sales discussed so far in this chapter apply to all downstream sales, and to all upstream sales involving wholly-owned subsidiaries. Upstream sales involving less-than-wholly-owned subsidiaries, however, present special accounting problems because of the minority interest involved.

A. Determine and eliminate unrealized profit in ending inventory for a less-than-wholly-owned subsidiary.

The entries to eliminate an upstream sale and unrealized profit in ending inventory involving a minority interest are identical to those shown in the previous sections of this chapter. The complication arises, however, when preparing consolidated financial statement, since a percentage of the unrealized profit lodged in the ending inventory is attributable to the minority stockholders.

The minority stockholders' interest in the combined entity's net income for the period may be determined as follows in the event unrealized profit in ending inventory exists:

1. Find the minority's interest in the subsidiary's net income for the accounting period. (Minority interest % × subsidiary net income)
2. Find the minority's interest in the unrealized profit in the ending inventory. (Minority interest % × unrealized ending inventory profit)
3. Subtract the minority's portion of the unrealized profit in ending inventory (step 2) from its portion of the subsidiary's net income (step 1) to find the minority's portion of the combined net income.

Minority interest in subsidiary's net income:	$X
Less minority interest in unrealized profit in ending inventory:	(X)
Minority interest in combined net income:	$X

EXAMPLE 8-6: During 19X1, S Co., an 80%-owned subsidiary, sold inventory at a 20% gross profit on sales to its parent P Co. for $100,000. S Co. also had a net income of $20,000 for the year. At the end of the accounting period, inventory from these sales worth $40,000 remained on P Co.'s books. The unrealized profit in ending inventory on P Co.'s books is therefore $8,000 (or, 20% of $40,000). The entries on the consolidating worksheet to eliminate the intercompany sale and purchase, any payables or receivables, and the unrealized profit in ending inventory are the same as those shown in Examples 8-1, 8-3, and 8-4. Adjustments are needed, however, to account for S Co.'s minority stockholders' interest in the unrealized profit.

The minority stockholders' portion of S Co.'s net income is:

20% of $20,000 = $4,000

The minority stockholders' portion of the unrealized profit in ending inventory is:

20% of $8,000 = $1,600

The minority interest in the consolidated net income is:

$4,000 – 1,600 = $2,400

Assuming that the 12/31/X1 consolidating worksheet showed a combined net income of $90,000, P Co. 1/1/X1 retained earnings of $150,000, and P Co. 19X2 dividends of $40,000, the minority interest is subtracted from the combined net income on the income statement, giving consolidated net income for the period:

	Consolidated Income Dr. (Cr.)
Combined net income:	($90,000)
Minority interest:	2,400
Consolidated net income:	($87,600)

The consolidated balance sheet must also show a minority interest of $2,400.

These relationships are shown on the following partial 12/31/X1 consolidating worksheet for further clarification:

	Consolidated Dr. (Cr.)		
	Income Statement	Retained Earnings	Balance Sheet
Retained earnings—P Co. 1/1/X1		(150,000)	
Dividends declared—P Co.		40,000	
Revenues	(X)		
Expenses	X		
Combined net income	(90,000)		
*Minority interest	2,400		(2,400)M
Consolidated net income	(87,600)	(87,600)	
Consolidated retained earnings		(197,600)	(197,600)

M = Minority interest

*Minority interest in S Co. net income (20% × $20,000)	$4,000
Less: Minority interest in unrealized profit in ending inventory from S Co. sales to P. Co. (20% minority interest times $8,000 profit in ending inventory)	(1,600)
Minority interest (in combined 19X1 net income)	$2,400

B. Determine and eliminate unrealized profit in beginning inventory for a less-than-wholly-owned subsidiary.

If a less-than-wholly-owned subsidiary made an upstream sale at a profit in an earlier accounting period, and all or some of that profit remains unrealized in the buyer's inventory at the beginning of the current period, then a portion of the entry to eliminate that unrealized profit (the overstatement of the cost of goods sold) is applied against the retained earnings of the subsidiary as well as the parent.

To properly distribute the charge for beginning-inventory unrealized profit to the retained earnings of both the parent and subsidiary, apply the percentage of ownership to the amount of the profit. The consolidating worksheet entry to eliminate intercompany profit on beginning inventory for upstream sales involving less-than-wholly-owned subsidiaries is:

Retained Earnings—P Co.	$X*	
Retained Earnings—S Co.	$X**	
Cost of Goods Sold		$X

*Based on parent company's percentage interest in subsidiary company.
**Based on minority shareholder percentage interest in subsidiary company.

EXAMPLE 8-7: P Co. owns 80% of S Co. On 1/1/X2, P Co. has $8,000 of unrealized profit in its inventory as a result of purchases it made from S Co. during the year 19X1. On 12/31/X2, the beginning-inventory unrealized profit is eliminated during preparation of the consolidated financial statements by the following entry:

Retained Earnings—P Co. (80%)	$6,400	
Retained Earnings—S Co. (20%)	$1,600	
Cost of Goods Sold		$8,000

This entry correctly distributes the overvaluation of 1/1/X2 retained earnings among both majority and minority stockholders of S Co.

An additional consideration during the preparation of consolidated financial statements is the effect of unrealized profit in beginning inventory on the determination of the minority's interest in the consolidated net income since a percentage of the unrealized profit lodged in the beginning inventory is attributable to the minority shareholders.

The minority stockholders' interest in the combined entity's income for the period may be determined as follows in the event unrealized profit in beginning inventory exists:

1. Find the minority's interest in the subsidiary's net income for the accounting period. (Minority interest % × subsidiary net income)
2. Find the minority's interest in the unrealized profit in the beginning inventory. (Minority interest % × unrealized beginning inventory profit)
3. Combine these two amounts.

Minority interest in subsidiary's net income:	$X
Plus minority interest in unrealized profit in beginning inventory:	X
Minority interest in combined net income:	$X

EXAMPLE 8-8: On 1/1/X2, P Co. had $40,000 worth of inventory on its books resulting from purchases from its 80%-owned subsidiary S Co. S Co.'s gross profit rate is 20% on sales. Therefore, unrealized profit lodged in beginning inventory on P Co.'s books is $8,000 (20% × $40,000).

For the year ended 12/31/X2, S Co. had a net income on its separate books of $25,000. The minority shareholders' portion of the consolidated income is:

20% of 25,000:	$5,000
Plus the minority interest in the unrealized profit in beginning inventory (20% of $8,000):	1,600
Minority interest in combined net income:	$6,600

Assuming that the 12/31/X2 consolidating worksheet showed a combined net income of $110,000, P Co. 1/1/X2 retained earnings of $181,600 and P Co. 19X2 dividends of $31,600, the minority's interest is subtracted from the combined net income on the consolidated income statement, giving consolidated net income for the period:

	Consolidated Income Dr. (Cr.)
Combined Net Income:	(110,000)
Minority Interest:	6,600
Consolidated Net Income:	(103,400)

The consolidated balance sheet must also show a minority interest of $6,600.

These relationships are shown on the following partial 12/31/X2 consolidating worksheet for further clarification:

	Consolidated Dr. (Cr.)		
	Income Statement	Retained Earnings	Balance Sheet
Retained earnings—P Co. 1/1/X2		(181,600)	
Dividends declared—P Co.		31,600	
Revenues	(X)		
Expenses	X		
Combined net income	(110,000)		
*Minority interest	6,600		(6,600)M
Consolidated net income	(103,400)	(103,400)	
Consolidated retained earnings		(253,400)	(253,400)

M = Minority interest

*Minority interest in S Co. net income (20% × $25,000)	$5,000
Less: Minority interest in unrealized gross profit in beginning inventory from S Co. sales to P. Co. (20% minority interest times $8,000 profit in beginning inventory)	1,600
Minority interest (in combined 19X2 net income)	$6,600

(If intercompany profits also existed in ending inventory of 19X2, they would be deducted from S Co. net income in determining minority interest in combined net income as described earlier.)

8-5. A Comprehensive Example of Consolidation Involving Intercompany Sales

Example 8-9 below gives a comprehensive example of the consolidation process involving information discussed in this chapter and in Chapters 4 through 6.

EXAMPLE 8-9: On 1/1/X1, P Co. acquired an 80% interest in S Co. for $106,000. Trial balances of P Co. and S Co. on 12/31/X2 are shown in the first two columns of Exhibit 8-A.

P Co.'s original investment cost of $106,000 can be analyzed as follows:

Investment cost	$106,000
Book value of underlying net assets acquired ($100,000 × 80% interest)	(80,000)
Excess cost over book value	26,000
Portion of excess attributable to:	
Inventory (80% × ($3,000))	2,400
Land (80% × $2,000)	(1,600)
Equipment (80% × $21,000)	(16,800)
Goodwill	$ 10,000

P Co.'s Investment in S Co. account balance on 12/31/X2 as shown on Exhibit 8-A ($135,100) is based on the following application of the equity method:

1/1/X1 Investment cost	$106,000
80% of S Co. 19X1 net income of $40,000	32,000
19/X1 amortization of cost in excess of book value	(250)*
80% of S Co. 19X1 dividends of $20,000	(16,000)
12/31/X1 Investment in S Co.	121,750
80% of S Co. 19X2 net income of $50,000	40,000
19X2 amortization of cost in excess of book value	(2,650)
80% of S Co. 19X2 dividends of $30,000	(24,000)
12/31/X2 Investment in S Co.	$135,100

*Amortization of cost in excess of book value was:

	19X1	19X2
Inventory (completely sold during 19X1)	($2,400)	$ 0
Equipment (depreciation addition)	2,400	2,400
Goodwill (amortization addition)	250	250
Amortization	$ 250	$2,650

Based on this information, the first two elimination entries (as discussed in Chapters 4 through 7) are shown in the "Eliminations" columns of Exhibit 8-A as follows:

1. S Co. Common stock:	40,000	
S Co. Additional paid-in capital:	32,000	
S Co. Retained earnings:	24,000	
Investment income ($40,000 – $2,650)	37,350	
Land	1,600	
Equipment	16,800	
Goodwill ($10,000 – $250 amortization of 19X1)	9,750	
Accum. depreciation—prop. and equip.		2,400
Investment in S Co.		135,100
Dividends declared		24,000

To eliminate Investment in S Co. against investment income and 80% of S Co. equity and dividends declared, and to adjust S Co. net assets and record goodwill.

2. Depreciation expense	2,400	
Goodwill amortization	250	
Accum. depreciation - prop. and equip.		2,400
Goodwill		250

To record amortization of adjusted S Co. net assets and goodwill (recorded in entry 1).

In addition to these basic elimination entries, consolidating worksheet elimination entries 3, 4, 5, 6, and 7 were recorded as a result of the following information:

	P Co. to S Co.	S Co. to P Co.
Net sales (19X2)	$20,000	$30,000
Intercompany sales included in buying company's ending inventory	$ 5,000	$ 3,000
Intercompany sales included in buying company's beginning inventory	$ 4,000	$ 6,000

P Co. sells inventory at a gross profit on sales of 30%, and S Co. sells inventory at a gross profit on sales of 40%.

3.	Sales	50,000	
	Cost of goods sold		50,000
	To eliminate intercompany sales. ($20,000 plus $30,000).		

4.	Cost of goods sold	2,700	
	Inventory		2,700
	To eliminate profit in ending inventory.		

	S Co.	P Co.	Total
Ending inventory of:	$5,000	$3,000	
P Co. gross profit	× 30%		
S Co. gross profit		× 40%	
Intercompany profit	$1,500	$1,200	$2,700

5.	Retained earnings—P Co.	3,120	
	Retained earnings—S Co.	480	
	Cost of goods sold		3,600
	To eliminate profit in beginning inventory.		

	S Co.	P Co.	Total
Beginning inventory of:	$4,000	$6,000	
P Co. gross profit	× 30%		
S Co. gross profit		× 40%	
Intercompany profit	$1,200	$2,400	$3,600
Minority interest		× 20%	
Retained earnings—S Co.		$ 480	(480)
Retained earnings—P Co.			$3,120

6.	Service charge revenue	15,000	
	Service charge expense		15,000
	To eliminate intercompany service charges. (P Co. performed service for S Co. during 19X2 charging and collecting $15,000.)		

7.	Dividends payable	8,000	
	Dividends receivable		8,000
	To eliminate intercompany dividends payable and receivable. (S Co. declared dividends of $30,000 during 19X2 and had paid $20,000 by year end, resulting in $10,000 in dividends payable. P Co. will receive 80% (or $8,000) of the $10,000 payable.)		

Exhibit 8-A
P Co. and 80% Owned Subsidiary S Co.
Consolidating Worksheet for the Year Ended 12/31/X2

Investment cost exceeds Fair value which exceeds Book value

Account Name	P Co. Dr. (Cr.)	S Co. Dr. (Cr.)	Eliminations Dr.	Eliminations (Cr.)	CONSOLIDATED Dr. (Cr.) Income Statement	Retained Earnings	Balance Sheet
Other assets	325,000	100,000					425,000
Inventory	153,000	46,000		(2,700)[4]			196,300
Dividends receivable	8,000			(8,000)[7]			0
Land	50,000	20,000	1,600[1]				71,600
Property and equipment	520,000	300,000	16,800[1]				836,800
Accum. depr.	(410,000)	(235,000)		(2,400)[1] (2,400)[2]			(649,800)
Investment in S Co.	135,100			(135,100)[1]			0
Goodwill			9,750[1]	(250)[2]			9,500
Liabilities	(72,000)	(81,000)					(153,000)
Dividends payable		(10,000)	8,000[7]				(2,000)
Common stock:							
P Co.	(100,000)						(100,000)
S Co.		(50,000)	40,000[1]				(10,000)[M]
Additional paid-in capital: P Co.	(130,000)						(130,000)
S Co.		(40,000)	32,000[1]				(8,000)[M]
Retained earnings:							
P Co.	(351,750)		3,120[5]			(348,630)	
S Co.		(30,000)	24,000[1] 480[5]				(5,520)[M]
Dividends declared:							
P Co.	50,000					50,000	
S Co.		30,000		(24,000)[1]			6,000[M]
Sales	(850,000)	(410,000)	50,000[3]		(1,210,000)		
Investment income	(37,350)		37,350[1]		0		
Goodwill amortization			250[2]		250		
Cost of goods sold	370,000	245,000	2,700[4]	(50,000)[3] (3,600)[5]	564,100		
Depreciation expense	25,000	10,000	2,400[2]		37,400		
Operating expenses	330,000	90,000			420,000		
Service charge revenue	(15,000)		15,000[6]		0		
Service charge expense		15,000		(15,000)[6]	0		
Totals	0	0	243,450	(243,450)			
	Combined net income				(188,250)		
	Minority interest*				10,240		(10,240)[M]
	Consolidated net income				(178,010)	(178,010)	
	Consolidated retained earnings					(476,640)	(476,640)
					Total		0
	Total minority interest (sum of items marked "M")						(27,760)

M = Minority interest

* Minority interest in S Co. net income:

20% of S Co. net income of $50,000 ($410,000 revenue – $360,000 expense)	$10,000
Less: Minority interest in unrealized profit of $1,200 in ending inventory (20% of $1,200)	(240)
Plus: Minority interest in unrealized profit of $2,400 in beginning inventory (20% of $2,400)	480
Minority interest in S Co. net income	$10,240

[1] To eliminate Investment in S Co. against investment income and 80% of S Co. equity and dividends declared and to adjust S Co. assets to fair value.

note: 1/1/X2 S Co. equity of $120,000 plus 19X2 S Co. net income of $50,000 less 19X2 S Co. dividends of $30,000 equals 12/31/X2 S Co. equity of $140,000. Minority interest of 20% × $140,000 yields $28,000. $28,000 less minority interest in unrealized profit in ending inventory of $240 yields $27,760 year-end minority interest.

[2] To amortize adjusted S Co. asset valuations and goodwill.
[3] To eliminate intercompany sales.
[4] To eliminate profit in ending inventory.
[5] To eliminate profit in beginning inventory.
[6] To eliminate intercompany service charges.
[7] To eliminate intercompany dividends payable and receivable.

RAISE YOUR GRADES

Can you explain . . . ?

- ☑ "upstream" and "downstream" intercompany sales
- ☑ how to eliminate intercompany sales and purchases of inventory in the consolidation process
- ☑ how to eliminate intercompany service transactions in the consolidation process
- ☑ how to eliminate intercompany dividends in the consolidation process
- ☑ unrealized profit
- ☑ the two approaches to gross profit determination
- ☑ how to determine the amount of intercompany profit in inventory (beginning and ending)
- ☑ how to eliminate unrealized profit from ending inventory
- ☑ how to eliminate unrealized profit from beginning inventory
- ☑ how to determine and eliminate unrealized profit in ending inventory when a less-than-wholly-owned subsidiary sells goods to its parent company
- ☑ how to determine and eliminate unrealized profit in beginning inventory when a less-than-wholly-owned subsidiary sells goods to its parent company
- ☑ how to determine the effect of unrealized profit in beginning or ending inventory (resulting from an upstream sale) on minority interest in combined net income

SUMMARY

1. The consolidating worksheet entry to eliminate intercompany sales and purchases is:

Sales	$X	
Cost of goods sold		$X

2. The consolidating worksheet entry to eliminate intercompany receivables and payables (from dividends, inventory sales, sales of service, etc.) is:

Payables (various)	$X	
Receivables (various)		$X

3. The consolidating worksheet entry to eliminate profit in ending inventory on intercompany sales made by the parent or the subsidiary is:

Cost of goods sold	$X	
Inventory		$X

4. The consolidating worksheet elimination entry to eliminate profit in beginning inventory on intercompany sales made by a parent or by a 100% owned subsidiary is:

Retained earnings—parent	$X	
Cost of goods sold		$X

5. The consolidating worksheet elimination entry to eliminate profit in beginning inventory on intercompany sales made by a less than 100% owned subsidiary is:

Retained earnings – parent	$X	
Retained earnings – subsidiary	$X	
Cost of goods sold		$X

(The retained earnings account of the subsidiary is charged for the minority interest in any beginning inventory profit which resulted from upstream sales made by the less than 100% owned subsidiary to the parent.)

6. The effect of unrealized beginning and ending inventory profits on the determination of minority interest in combined net income may be viewed as follows:

Minority interest in subsidiary net income	$X
Less: Minority interest in unrealized profit in ending inventory resulting from upstream sales	(X)
Plus: Minority interest in unrealized profit in beginning inventory resulting from sales	X
Minority interest in combined net income	$X

7. The consolidating worksheet elimination entry to eliminate intercompany contract service revenue and expense is:

Contract service revenue	$X	
Contract service expense		$X

RAPID REVIEW

True or False

1. Intercompany sales of $500,000 are made by a subsidiary to a parent company. The subsidiary is 100% owned by the parent. The full $500,000 in intercompany sales should be eliminated.
2. Intercompany sales of $500,000 are made by an 80% owned subsidiary to a parent company. Only $400,000 (80% of $500,000) in intercompany sales should be eliminated.
3. Intercompany payables and receivables at the balance sheet date should be eliminated fully regardless of the level of minority interest and regardless of which party (parent or subsidiary) made the sale.
4. The consolidating worksheet entry to eliminate profits in ending inventory no matter which party originally sold the inventory and no matter what the level of minority interest is:

Cost of goods sold	$X	
Inventory		$X

5. Profits in ending inventory resulting from sales of a less than 100% owned subsidiary to a parent company will increase minority interest in combined net income.
6. The consolidating worksheet entry to eliminate profit in beginning inventory from intercompany sales made by a parent (downstream) will differ from the worksheet entry required if a 100% owned subsidiary made the sale to a parent (upstream).
7. The consolidating worksheet entry to eliminate profit in beginning inventory from intercompany sales made by a parent (downstream) will differ from the worksheet entry required if a less than 100% owned subsidiary made the sale to a parent (upstream).
8. Profits in beginning inventory resulting from sales of a less than 100% owned subsidiary to a parent company will decrease minority interest in combined net income.
9. The amount of intercompany profit eliminated is affected by the existence of minority interest.
10. Since the major objective of the consolidation process is to treat two or more legal entities as one economic entity, 100% of all intercompany transactions are eliminated, even if a minority exists. Minority interest in profit and loss may, however, affect the final determination of consolidated net income.

Answers:

1. *True*
2. *False* (Eliminate $500,000)
3. *True*
4. *True*
5. *False* (Decrease)
6. *False* (Entry is same)
7. *True*
8. *False* (Increase)
9. *False* (100% elimination even if minority interest exists)
10. *True*

SOLVED PROBLEMS

Problem 8-1: Big Company owns 100% of Small Company's common stock. During 19X4, Big Company made sales to Small Company of $800,000 and Small Company made sales to Big Company of $300,000. The gross profit on sales of Big Company and Small Company are 30% and 20% respectively. The following situation also existed at December 31, 19X4:

	Big Company	Small Company
Portion of January 1, 19X4 inventory resulting from intercompany purchases	$30,000	$50,000
Portion of December 31, 19X4 inventory resulting from intercompany purchases	$40,000	$60,000
Debt due to affiliate from intercompany sales as of December 31, 19X4	$24,000	$62,000
Dividends declared during 19X4	$90,000	$40,000
Dividends paid during 19X4	$90,000	$25,000

Prepare the December 31, 19X4 consolidating worksheet elimination entries necessary based on the facts provided.

Answer:

1. Sales	1,100,000		
Cost of goods sold		1,100,000	
To eliminate intercompany sales. (Big Co. $800,000 plus Small Co. $300,000)			
2. Retained earnings—Big Company	21,000		
Cost of goods sold		21,000	
To eliminate profit in beginning inventory.			
Beginning inventory of:			
Big Company	$30,000		
3. Cost of goods sold	26,000		
Inventory		26,000	
To eliminate profit in ending inventory.			
Ending inventory of:			
Big Company	$40,000		
Small Company		$60,000	
Gross profit on sales of:			
Big Company		30%	
Small Company	20%		
Profit in ending inventory	$ 8,000	$18,000	$26,000

4. Accounts payable	86,000	
Accounts receivable		86,000
To eliminate intercompany payables and receivables resulting from inventory sales		
5. Dividends payable	15,000	
Dividends receivable		15,000
To eliminate intercompany dividends payable and receivable. ($40,000 declared by Small Company less $25,000 paid.)		

note: Small Company's dividends declared will also be eliminated in the consolidation process against either the Investment in Small Co. account if the equity method is used (Chapter 6) or the Dividend Income account if the cost method is used (Chapter 7).

PROBLEM 8-2: Assume all the same facts as those used in Problem 8-1 except that Big Company owns 90% of Small Company. Prepare the December 31, 19X4 consolidating worksheet elimination entries necessary based on the facts provided.

Answer:

1. Sales	1,100,000	
Cost of goods sold		1,100,000
To eliminate intercompany sales. (Big Co. $800,000 plus Small Co. $300,000.)		
2. Retained earnings—Big Company	20,400	
Retained earnings—Small Company	600	
Cost of goods sold		21,000
To eliminate profit in beginning inventory.		

Beginning inventory of:			
Big Company	$30,000		
Small Company		$50,000	
Gross profit on sales of:			
Big Company		30%	
Small Company	20%		
Profit in ending inventory	$ 6,000	$15,000	$21,000
Minority interest @ 10% on sales from Small Co. to Big Co. (in Big Co.'s beginning inventory:	(600)		(600)
Controlling interest	$ 5,400	$15,000	$20,400

3. Cost of goods sold	26,000	
Inventory		26,000
To eliminate profit in ending inventory. (See Problem 8-1, entry 3 explanation.)		
4. Accounts payable	86,000	
Accounts receivable		86,000
To eliminate intercompany receivables and payables resulting from inventory sales.		
5. Dividends payable	13,500	
Dividends receivable		13,500
To eliminate intercompany dividends payable and receivable.		

Small Co. Dividends declared	$40,000
Small Co. Dividends paid	25,000
Dividends payable by Small Co.	15,000
Big Co. Interest	90%
Big Co. Dividends receivable	$13,500

(Also, see note in explanation to Problem 8-1, Entry 5.)

PROBLEM 8-3: Again, assume the same facts as those described in Problem 8-1 except that Big Company has a 90% interest in Small Company. Also assume that the income of Small Company for the fiscal year ended December 31, 19X4 is $400,000. Fill in items marked "a" through "f" on the following 12/31/X4 partial consolidating worksheet:

	Consolidated Dr. (Cr.)		
	Income Statement	Retained Earnings	Balance Sheet
Retained earnings—Big Co. (1/1/X4)		(5,000,000)	
Dividends declared—Big Co.		500,000	
Revenues	(X)		
Expenses	X		
Combined net income	(1,000,000)		
Minority interest	(*a*)		(*b*) (M)
Consolidated net income	(*c*)	(*d*)	
Consolidated retained earnings		(*e*)	(*f*)

Answer:

	Consolidated Dr. (Cr.)		
	Income Statement	Retained Earnings	Balance Sheet
Retained earnings—Big Co. (1/1/X4)		(5,000,000)	
Dividends declared—Big Co.		500,000	
Revenues	(X)		
Expenses	X		
Combined net income	(1,000,000)		
Minority interest*	39,800		(39,800)(M)
Consolidated net income	(960,200)	(960,200)	
Consolidated retained earnings		(5,460,200)	(5,460,200)

*10% of Small Co. 19X4 net income of $400,000	$40,000
Less: Minority interest in ending inventory profit (10% of $8,000)	(800)
Plus: Minority interest in beginning inventory profit (10% of $6,000)	600
Minority interest in combined net income	$39,800

PROBLEM 8-4: Monette Co. owns 85% of Banks Co. common stock. Sales from Monette Co. to Banks Co. were $500,000 and from Banks Co. to Monette Co. were $300,000 during 19X7. There were no intercompany receivables or payables at year end December 31, 19X7. There were no beginning inventory amounts on the books of Monette Co. or Banks Co. which were the result of intercompany sales. However, ending inventories resulting from intercompany sales were:

Ending inventory of:

Monette Co.	$45,000 (purchased from Banks Co.)
Banks Co.	$20,000 (purchased from Monette Co.)

Monette Co. charges a 25% markup on cost.
Banks Co. charges a 20% markup on cost.

Prepare December 31, 19X7 consolidating worksheet entries to eliminate intercompany sales and ending inventory profits.

Answer:

note: The expression "markup on cost" differs from the expression "gross profit on sales" in earlier problems.

		Dr.	Cr.
1.	Sales	800,000	
	Cost of goods sold		800,000

To eliminate intercompany sales. (Monette Co. sales of $500,000 plus Banks Co. sales of $300,000.)

2. Cost of goods sold 11,500
   Inventory 11,500
   To eliminate profit in ending inventory.

The profit is determined as follows:

a)	Monette Co. ending inventory		= 1.2 Banks Co. cost
		$45,000	= 1.2 Banks Co. cost
		$45,000/1.2	= Banks Co. cost
		$37,500	= Banks Co. cost
	$45,000 less	$37,500	= $7,500. Profit
b)	Banks Co. ending inventory		= 1.25 Monette Co. cost
		$20,000	= 1.25 Monette Co. cost
		$20,000/1.25	= Monette Co. cost
		$16,000	= Monette Co. cost
	$20,000 less	$16,000	= $4,000. Profit
c)	Total profit in ending inventory:		$7,500 + $4,000 = $11,500.

PROBLEM 8-5: A partially completed 12/31/X4 consolidating worksheet follows for Bear Co. and its 90% owned subsidiary Cub Co. Worksheet entries have already been provided to:

(1) eliminate Investment in Cub Co. against income and 90% of Cub Co. equity and dividends declared and to adjust Cub Co. assets to fair value, and
(2) amortize adjusted S Co. asset valuations and goodwill.

The following additional information regarding 19X4 activities is available:

- During 19X4, Bear Co. made sales of inventory to Cub Co. of $50,000 and Cub made sales of inventory to Bear of $30,000.
- Bear Co. charges a gross profit on its sales of 40% and Cub Co. charges a gross profit of 50% on its sales.
- There was no beginning or ending inventory on Cub Co.'s books which represented intercompany sales.
- There was $10,000 in beginning inventory on Bear Co.'s books which was the result of intercompany sales.
- There was $15,000 in ending inventory on Bear Co.'s books which was the result of intercompany sales.
- Bear Co. had collected $40,000 and Cub Co. had collected $15,000 on the 19X4 intercompany sales by year-end 12/31/X4.
- Cub Co. declared dividends of $10,000 during 19X4 and had paid $5,000 by year-end.

Based on the additional information provided, complete the worksheet (Schedule I):

Schedule I
Bear Co. and 90% Owned Subsidiary Cub Co.
Consolidating Worksheet for the Year Ended 12/31/X4

Account Name	Bear Co. Dr. (Cr.)	Cub Co. Dr. (Cr.)	Eliminations Dr.	Eliminations (Cr.)	CONSOLIDATED Dr. (Cr.) Income Statement	Retained Earnings	Balance Sheet
Cash	5,500	10,000					
Accounts receivable	70,000	30,000					
Inventory	50,000	30,000	5,400[1]	(5,400)[2]			
Dividends receivable	4,500						
Land	50,000	20,000	9,000[1]				
Property and equipment	2,500,000	1,200,000	180,000[1]				
Accum. depr.	(1,050,000)	(400,000)		(9,000)[2]			
Investment in Cub Co.	470,160			(470,160)[1]			
Goodwill			57,600[1]	(1,440)[2]			
Liabilities	(990,000)	(625,000)					
Dividends payable		(5,000)					
Common stock:							
Bear Co.	(200,000)						
Cub Co.		(90,000)	81,000[1]				
Additional paid-in capital—common:							
Bear Co.	(400,000)						
Cub Co.		(60,000)	54,000[1]				
Retained earnings:							
Bear Co.	(280,000)						
Cub Co.		(70,000)	63,000[1]				
Dividends declared:							
Bear Co.	20,000						
Cub Co.		10,000		(9,000)[1]			
Sales	(850,000)	(300,000)					
Investment income	(29,160)		29,160[1]				
Goodwill amortization			1,440[2]				
Cost of goods sold	400,000	160,000	5,400[2]				
Depreciation expense	75,000	50,000	9,000[2]				
Operating expenses	154,000	40,000					
Totals	0	0					
	Combined net income						
	Minority interest						
	Consolidated net income						
	Consolidated retained earnings						
					Total		
	Total minority interest						

[1]To eliminate Investment in Cub Co. against investment income and 90% of Cub Co equity and dividends declared and to adjust Cub Co. assets to fair value.

[2]To amortize adjusted Cub Co. asset valuations and goodwill.

Answer:

The following additional worksheet entries are necessary:

3. Sales 80,000
   Cost of goods sold 80,000
   To eliminate intercompany sales and purchases. ($50,000 Bear Co. to Cub Co. plus $30,000 Cub Co. to Bear Co.)

4. Retained earnings—Bear Co. 4,500
   Retained earnings—Cub Co. (10%) 500
   Cost of goods sold 5,000
   To eliminate intercompany profit in beginning inventory.

Ending inventory on Bear's books (buyer) from intercompany purchases	$10,000
Cub Co. gross profit	× 50%
Unrealized profit	$ 5,000
Minority interest	× 10%
Minority interest in unrealized beginning inventory profit	$ 500

5. Cost of goods sold 7,500
   Inventory 7,500
   To eliminate intercompany profit in ending inventory.
   (50% of ending inventory of $15,000 resulting from intercompany sales.)

6. Accounts payable (liabilities) 25,000
   Accounts receivable 25,000
   To eliminate intercompany receivables and payables from intercompany sales.

	Bear Co.	Cub Co.	Total
Intercompany sales	$50,000	$30,000	$80,000
Intercompany cash receipts on sales	(40,000)	(15,000)	(55,000)
Intercompany accounts receivable and payable at year-end	$10,000	$15,000	$25,000

7. Dividends payable 4,500
   Dividends receivable 4,500
   To eliminate intercompany dividends payable and receivable. (90% of Cub Co. dividends payable of $5,000.)

Schedule I
Bear Co. and 90% Owned Subsidiary Cub Co.
Consolidating Worksheet for the Year Ended 12/31/X4

Account Name	Bear Co. Dr. (Cr.)	Cub Co. Dr. (Cr.)	Eliminations Dr.	Eliminations (Cr.)	CONSOLIDATED Dr. (Cr.) Income Statement	Retained Earnings	Balance Sheet
Cash	5,500	10,000					15,500
Accounts receivable	70,000	30,000		(25,000)[6]			75,000
Inventory	50,000	30,000	5,400[1]	(5,400)[2] (7,500)[5]			72,500
Dividends receivable	4,500			(4,500)[7]			0
Land	50,000	20,000	9,000[1]				79,000
Property and equipment	2,500,000	1,200,000	180,000[1]				3,880,000
Accum. depr.	(1,050,000)	(400,000)		(9,000)[2]			(1,459,000)
Investment in Cub Co.	470,160			(470,160)[1]			0
Goodwill			57,600[1]	(1,440)[2]			56,160
Liabilities	(990,000)	(625,000)	25,000[6]				(1,590,000)
Dividends payable		(5,000)	4,500[7]				(500)
Common stock:							
Bear Co.	(200,000)						(200,000)
Cub Co.		(90,000)	81,000[1]				(9,000)M
Additional paid-in capital—common:							
Bear Co.	(400,000)						(400,000)
Cub Co.		(60,000)	54,000[1]				(6,000)M
Retained earnings:							
Bear Co.	(280,000)		4,500[4]			(275,500)	
Cub Co..		(70,000)	63,000[1] 500[4]				(6,500)M
Dividends declared:							
Bear Co.	20,000					20,000	
Cub Co.		10,000		(9,000)[1]			1,000M
Sales	(850,000)	(300,000)	80,000[3]		(1,070,000)		
Investment income	(29,160)		29,160[1]		0		
Goodwill amortization		1,440[2]		1,440			
Cost of goods sold	400,000	160,000	5,400[2] 7,500[5]	(80,000)[3] (5,000)[4]	487,900		
Depreciation expense	75,000	50,000	9,000[2]		134,000		
Operating expenses	154,000	40,000			194,000		
Totals	0	0	617,000	(617,000)			
Combined net income					(252,660)		
*Minority interest					4,750		(4,750)M
Consolidated net income					(247,910)	(247,910)	
Consolidated retained earnings						(503,410)	(503,410)
					Total		0
Total minority interest (sum of items marked "M")							(25,250)

M = Minority interest

* Minority interest in Cub Co. net income:

10% of Cub Co. net income of $50,000	$5,000
Less: Minority interest in unrealized profit of $7,500 in ending inventory (10% of $7,500)	(750)
Plus: Minority interest in unrealized profit of $5,000 in beginning inventory (10% of $5,000)	500
Minority interest in S Co. net income	$4,750

[1] To eliminate Investment in Cub Co. against investment income and 90% of Cub Co equity and dividends declared and to adjust Cub Co. assets to fair value.
[2] To amortize adjusted Cub Co. asset valuations and goodwill.
[3] To eliminate intercompany sales.
[4] To eliminate profit in beginning inventory.
[5] To eliminate profit in ending inventory.
[6] To eliminate intercompany accounts receivable and payable.
[7] To eliminate intercompany dividends payable and receivable.

INTERCOMPANY SALES OF LAND AND DEPRECIABLE ASSETS

THIS CHAPTER IS ABOUT

☑ **Intercompany Sales of Land**
☑ **Intercompany Sales of Depreciable Assets**

9-1. Intercompany Sales of Land.

Companies that are separate legal entities but which have been combined to form a single economic entity may sell land to one another. The sale and purchase of land, including any gain or loss, are recorded as ordinary transactions on the books of each company involved.

From the consolidated point of view, however, the transaction is not considered a sale as much as it is a transfer of assets; one company transfers one type of asset (cash) in return for another type (land). If there is no gain or loss on the sale, there is no need for eliminating entries during the consolidation process. But any gain or loss on the intercompany sale of land must be eliminated during the consolidation process, which in effect will change the sale into an even transfer of assets. If the gains or losses are not eliminated, the consolidated financial statements will be inaccurate by the amounts of those gains or losses. Only when the land is sold to a party outside the combined economic entity may the gain or loss be recognized in the consolidated financial statements.

The process to eliminate the gain or loss on intercompany sales of land is performed in addition to the basic elimination processes, described in Chapters 4, 6, and 7, which eliminate the parent company's investment in the subsidiary against the subsidiary's equity.

A. A parent company sells land to its subsidiary.

If the intercompany sale of land is from the parent company to a subsidiary (that is, a "downstream" sale), then the percentage of the parent's interest in the subsidiary is not important. The parent will eventually recognize all the gain or loss from the sale.

1. *Downstream sale of land in the current accounting year.* When a parent company sells land to a subsidiary it records the sale, including any gain or loss, on its books as it would if the sale had taken place to a party outside the combined entity:

Cash	$X	
Land		$X
Gain – Land Sale		$X

or

Cash	$X	
Loss – Land Sale	$X	
Land		$X

Likewise, the subsidiary records the purchase on its books as it would a purchase from a source outside the combined economic entity:

Land	$X	
Cash		$X

When consolidated financial statements are prepared, however, any gain or loss from the intercompany sale of land must be eliminated, and the consolidated Land account returned to its original cost.

The consolidating worksheet entry in the year of the sale to eliminate a gain from a downstream sale of land, and to return the consolidated Land account to its original value, is:

Gain – Land Sale	$X	
Land		$X

The consolidating worksheet entry in the year of the sale to eliminate a loss from a downstream sale, and to return the consolidated Land account to its original value, is:

Land	$X	
Loss – Land Sale		$X

EXAMPLE 9-1: During 19X1, P Co. sold land to its wholly-owned subsidiary S Co. for $100. P Co.'s original cost for the land was $90.

During 19X1, P Co. and S Co. recorded the sale and purchase of the land on their respective books as follows:

P Co. Books			S Co. Books		
Cash	100		Land	100	
Land		90	Cash		100
Gain-Land Sale		10			

On 12/31/X1, the combined economic entity of P Co. and S Co. prepares consolidated financial statements using the following entry on the consolidating worksheet to eliminate the gain on the sale and to return the consolidated Land account to its original value:

Gain – land sale	10	
Land		10
To eliminate intercompany gain on land sale.		

The following partial worksheet shows how the intercompany gain is eliminated and the Land account is restored to original cost:

P Co. & 100% Owned Subsidiary S Co.
(PARTIAL) Consolidating Worksheet
For the Year Ended 12/31/X1

					CONSOLIDATED Dr. (Cr.)		
Account name	P Co. Dr. (Cr.)	S Co. Dr. (Cr.)	Eliminations Dr.	Eliminations (Cr.)	Income Statement	Retained Earnings	Balance Sheet
Land		100		(10)			90
Gain – land sale	(10)		10		0		

2. *Downstream sale of land in subsequent years.* At the end of the year during which the downstream sale of land occurred, the parent company closes its gain or loss on the sale to its Retained Earnings account. During the consolidation process the following year, and for every subsequent year that the combined economic entity continues to hold the land, it must eliminate that gain or loss against the retained earnings, to return the Land account to its original value, and to avoid a misstatement of the consolidated retained earnings.

The consolidating worksheet entry to eliminate a gain on a downstream sale of land in the years after the year of the sale is:

Retained Earnings – Parent	$X	
Land		$X

In the years after the sale, the consolidating worksheet entry to eliminate a loss on a downstream sale of land, and to return the consolidated Land account to its original value, is:

Land	$X	
Retained Earnings – Parent		$X

EXAMPLE 9-2: During 19X1, P Co. sold land to its wholly-owned subsidiary S Co. for $100. P Co.'s original cost of the land was $90. At the end of 19X2, S Co. still held the land.

On 12/31/X2, the combined economic entity of P Co. and S Co. prepares consolidated financial statements using the following entry on the consolidating worksheet to eliminate the gain on the sale and to return the consolidated Land account to its original value:

Retained Earnings – P Co	10	
Land		10
To eliminate intercompany gain on land sale.		

3. *Subsequent sale of the land outside the combined economic entity.* If the subsidiary company eventually sells the land it originally bought from its parent company to a party outside the combined economic entity, it records the sale, including any gain or loss, on its books as it would any sale.

   From the consolidated point of view, however, the sale must be based on the original (or historic) cost of the land (that is, the original cost of the land to the combined economic entity). Therefore, the consolidated income statement must reflect the gain or loss on the outside sale based on the parent's original cost of the land, and not necessarily on whatever the subsidiary's carrying cost for it might have been.

   To determine the consolidated gain or loss on the outside sale, find the difference between the historic cost of the land and the subsidiary's selling price:

Subsidiary's Selling Price	$X
Original (Historical) Cost	$(X)
Consolidated Gain (Loss)	$X

Then compare the consolidated gain (or loss) on the sale to the gain or loss as recorded by the subsidiary. Determine the necessary adjustment by finding the difference between the consolidated gain (or loss) and the subsidiary's recorded gain (or loss). Then prepare a worksheet elimination entry which adjusts the gain or loss shown by the subsidiary to the true *consolidated* gain or loss. The elimination entry adjusts gain (or loss) through the parent's Retained Earnings account, because those earnings (or losses) will have been overstated (or understated) as a result of closing the parent's original gain (or loss) on the sale to the parent's retained earnings.

The consolidated worksheet entry to adjust the gain on an outside sale of land is:

Retained Earnings – Parent	$X	
Gain – Land Sale		$X

(This entry assumes a gain on the sale by the subsidiary to an outside party is increased. If the subsidiary had sold the property to an outside party at a loss, then this entry would reduce that loss. That is, the credit would be to the account "Loss - Land Sale" to the extent of any loss recorded on the sale by the subsidiary.)

The consolidating worksheet entry to adjust the loss on an outside sale of land is:

Loss – Land Sale	$X	
Retained Earnings - Parent		$X

(This entry assumes a loss on the sale by the subsidiary to an outside party is increased. If the subsidiary had sold the property to an outside party at a gain, then this entry would reduce that gain. That is, the debit would be to the account "Gain - Land Sale" to the extent of any gain recorded on the sale by the subsidiary.)

These adjusting entries have the effect of moving the recognition of the full gain or loss from the sale to the year of sale to an outside party, where it belongs from the consolidated perspective.

After the land has been sold to an outside party, no worksheet eliminating entries will be needed in subsequent years.

EXAMPLE 9-3: During 19X1, P Co. sold land to its wholly-owned subsidiary S Co. for $100. P Co.'s original cost of the land was $90. At the end of 19X2, S Co. still held the land. During 19X3, however, S Co. sold the land to an outside company for $115.

On the date of the sale, S Co. records the transaction, including the gain, on its books according to the price it paid for the land:

Cash	115	
Land		100
Gain – Land Sale		15
To record land sale.		

From a consolidated perspective, however, the land's historic cost is $90 (not $100), and the gain on the outside sale is $25 ($115 – $90 = $25). Therefore, when the combined economic entity of P Co. and S Co. prepares consolidated financial statements on 12/31/X3, an additional eliminating entry is necessary on the consolidating worksheet to adjust S Co.'s recorded gain ($15) to the consolidated gain ($25).

The necessary amount of the adjustment is $10 ($25 consolidated gain – $15 S Co. recorded gain = $10). This amount is added to the Gain from Land Sale account and eliminated against P Co.'s retained earnings as follows:

Retained earnings – P Co.	10	
Gain – Land Sale		10
To adjust gain on land sale.		

The following partial worksheet shows how the 19X3 gain is adjusted (assuming P Co. retained earnings of $400).

P Co. & 100% Owned Subsidiary S Co.
(PARTIAL) Consolidating Worksheet
For the Year Ended 12/31/X1

					CONSOLIDATED Dr. (Cr.)		
Account name	P Co. Dr. (Cr.)	S Co. Dr. (Cr.)	Eliminations Dr.	Eliminations (Cr.)	Income Statement	Retained Earnings	Balance Sheet
Gain – land sale		(15)		(10)	(25)		
Retained earnings – P	(400)		10			(390)	

Note that the 19X3 consolidated income statement appropriately shows a gain of $25. The charge of $10 to parent retained earnings on the worksheet merely has the effect of moving the gain recognition from 19X1 to 19X3 where it belongs from a consolidated perspective. Since the land has actually been sold to a company outside of the consolidated group during 19X3, no further worksheet elimination entries will be necessary in subsequent years.

B. A wholly owned subsidiary sells land to its parent.

If the intercompany sale of land is from the subsidiary company to its parent company (an "upstream" sale), then the percentage of the parent's ownership interest in the subsidiary becomes relevant. Only if the parent owns 100 percent of the subsidiary will it eventually realize all the gain or loss from an upstream sale; otherwise a portion of the gain or loss will be attributable to the minority interest in the subsidiary's net income (or loss). In this section we will focus on upstream sales of land by wholly owned subsidiaries. In the following section we will consider upstream intercompany land sales with a minority interest.

When a wholly owned subsidiary sells land to its parent it records the sale, including any loss or gain, on its books as it would if the sale had taken place outside the combined economic entity. Likewise, the parent records the purchase on its books as it would a purchase from a source outside the combined economic entity.

When the combined economic entity prepares its consolidated financial statements at the end of the accounting period during which the sale took place, however, it must eliminate any gain or loss from the sale, and return the consolidated Land account to its original cost.

The consolidating worksheet entries to eliminate a gain or loss from an upstream sale of land, and to return the consolidated Land account to its original value, are the same as those to eliminate the downstream sale, assuming that the subsidiary is wholly owned by the parent, because all the subsidiary's gain or loss is eventually attributable to the parent.

EXAMPLE 9-4: During 19X1, S Co., a wholly owned subsidiary of P Co., sold land to P Co. for $100. S Co.'s original cost of the land was $90.

During 19X1, S Co. and P Co. recorded the sale and purchase of the land on their respective books as follows:

P Co. Books		
Land	100	
Cash		100

S Co. Books		
Cash	100	
Land		90
Gain-Land Sale		10

On 12/31/X1, the combined economic entity of P Co. and S Co. prepares consolidated financial statements using the following entry on the consolidating worksheet to eliminate the gain on the sale and to return the consolidated Land account to its original value:

Gain – Land Sale	10	
Land		10

To eliminate intercompany gain on land sale.

Note that this eliminating entry is identical to the one needed for the downstream sale shown in Example 9-1. Because S Co. is wholly owned, all the gain or loss on the sale (regardless of the direction of the sale) belongs ultimately to P Co., and must be eliminated.

The following partial worksheet shows how the intercompany gain is eliminated and the Land account is restored to original cost:

P Co. & 100% Owned Subsidiary S Co.
(PARTIAL) Consolidating Worksheet
For the Year Ended 12/31/X1

					CONSOLIDATED Dr. (Cr.)		
Account name	P Co. Dr. (Cr.)	S Co. Dr. (Cr.)	Eliminations Dr.	Eliminations (Cr.)	Income Statement	Retained Earnings	Balance Sheet
Land	100			(10)			90
Gain – land sale		(10)	10		0		

At the end of the year during which the upstream sale of land took place, the subsidiary closes its gain or loss to its Retained Earnings account, which is eliminated in the consolidation process. The consolidation process (as described in Chapters 4 through 7) results in the inclusion of the parent's portion of the subsidiary's net income or loss in consolidated retained earnings. In the year after the land sale, and for every subsequent year that the combined economic entity continues to hold the land, the gain or loss must be eliminated against the parent's retained earnings during the consolidation process, to return the consolidated Land account to its original (historical) cost and to avoid misstatement of the consolidated retained earnings.

The consolidating worksheet entries to eliminate a gain or loss on an upstream sale of land in years subsequent to the year of the sale are the same as those shown in section 9–1.A.

EXAMPLE 9-5: During 19X1, S Co., a wholly owned subsidiary of P Co., sold land to P Co. for $100. S Co.'s original cost for the land was $90. At the end of 19X2, P Co. still owned the land.

On 12/31/X2, the combined economic entity of P Co. and S Co. prepares consolidated financial statements. At that time it must make the following entry on the consolidating worksheet, to eliminate the gain on the sale and to return the consolidated Land account to its original value:

Retained earnings – P Co.	10	
Land		10
To eliminate intercompany gain on land sale		

If the parent company eventually sells the land it originally bought from its wholly owned subsidiary to a party outside the combined economic entity, it records the sale, including any gain or loss, on its books based on its purchase price from the subsidiary (not on the basis of the land's original historical cost to the subsidiary).

The consolidated point of view, however, bases the sale on the original (or historical) cost of the land. Therefore, the consolidated income statement must reflect the gain or loss on the sale based on the subsidiary's original cost of the land, not on whatever the parent's carrying cost might have been.

To determine the consolidated gain or loss on the outside sale, find the difference between the historical cost of the land and the parent's selling price:

Parent's Selling Price	$ X
Original (Historical) Cost	$(X)
Consolidated Gain (Loss)	$ X

Then compare the consolidated gain (or loss) to the gain (or loss) recorded by the parent. Any difference between the two values will result in a consolidating worksheet elimination entry adjusting the gain or loss shown by the parent to reflect the true consolidated gain or loss. These elimination entries adjust the parent's retained earnings, which will have been overstated (or understated) as a result of the consolidation process by the parent's portion of the subsidiary's gains (or losses).

The consolidated worksheet entry to adjust the gain on an outside sale of land is:

Retained Earnings – Parent	$X	
Gain – Land Sale		$X

(This entry assumes a gain on the sale by the parent to an outside party is increased. If the parent had sold the property to an outside party at a loss, then this entry would reduce that loss. That is, the credit would be to the account "Loss - Land Sale" to the extent of any loss recorded on the sale by the parent.)

The consolidating worksheet entry to adjust the loss on an outside sale of land is:

Loss – Land Sale	$X	
Retained Earnings – Parent		$X

(This entry assumes a loss on the sale by the parent to an outside party is increased. If the parent had sold the property to an outside party at a gain, then this entry would reduce that gain. That is, the debit would be to the account "Gain - Land Sale" to the extent of any gain recorded on the sale by the parent.)

These adjusting entries have the effect of moving the recognition of the full gain or loss from the sale to the year of sale to an outside party, where it belongs from the consolidated perspective.

After the land has been sold to an outside party, no worksheet eliminating entries will be needed in subsequent years.

EXAMPLE 9-6: During 19X1, S Co., a wholly owned subsidiary of P Co., sold land to P Co. for $100. S Co.'s original cost of the land was $90. At the end of 19X2, P Co. still held the land. During 19X3, however, P Co. sold the land to an outside company for $115.

On the date of the sale, P Co. records the transaction, including the gain, on its books according to the price it paid for the land:

Cash	115	
Land		100
Gain – Land Sale		15

From a consolidated perspective, however, the land's historical cost is $90 (not $100), and the gain on the outside sale is $25 ($115 – $90 = $25). Therefore, when the combined economic entity of P Co. and S Co. prepares consolidated financial statements on 12/31/X3, an additional eliminating entry on the consolidating worksheet to adjust P Co.'s recorded gain ($15) to the *consolidated* gain ($25) is required.

The necessary amount of the adjustment is $10 ($25 consolidated gain – $15 P Co. recorded gain = $10). This amount is added to the Gain from Land Sale account and eliminated against P Co.'s retained earnings as follows:

Retained Earnings – P Co.	10	
Gain – Land Sale	10	

To adjust gain on land sale from $15 ($115 less $100) to $25.

C. A subsidiary with a minority interest sells land to its parent.

If a parent company owns less than 100 percent of its subsidiary, a portion of any gain or loss from an upstream sale of land will be attributable to the minority interest in the subsidiary.

When a subsidiary with a minority interest sells land to its parent it records the sale, including any gain or loss, on its books as it would if the sale had taken place to a party outside the combined economic entity. Likewise, the parent records the purchase on its books as it would a purchase from a source outside the combined economic entity.

When the combined economic entity prepares its consolidated financial statements, it must eliminate any gain or loss from the sale, and return the consolidated Land account to its original cost. It does this by making entries on the consolidating worksheet to eliminate the amount of the gain or loss against the Land account. The procedures necessary to do this in the year of sale are covered in detail in the earlier sections of this chapter.

A special problem arises, however, when determining the consolidated net income. The minority interest is entitled to a portion of the subsidiary's net income at the end of the accounting period. But because the subsidiary's net income includes the gain (or loss) on the land sale, the minority's portion of that gain (or loss) must be deducted from (or added to) the minority's share of subsidiary net income to avoid overstatement (or understatement) of minority interest.

To determine minority interest in the subsidiary's net income, first multiply the amount of the intercompany gain or loss by the minority's percentage of ownership:

Gain or Loss on Upstream Sale × Minority's Ownership % =
Minority's Portion of Gain or Loss

Next, determine the minority's interest in the subsidiary's net income:

Subsidiary Net Income × Minority's Ownership % =
Unadjusted Minority's Net Income

Then combine these two amounts as follows:

Unadjusted Minority's Net Income:	$ X
Minus (or Plus) Minority's Portion of Gain (or Loss:)	(X)
Minority's Adjusted Net Income:	$ X

Explain this adjustment in a note to consolidated financial statements, and clearly show the adjusted minority interest on the balance sheet.

EXAMPLE 9-7: During 19X1, S Co. sold land to P Co. for $100. S Co.'s original cost of the land was $90. Eighty percent of S Co. is owned by P Co.

During 19X1, P Co. and S Co. recorded the sale and purchase of land on their respective books as follows:

P Co. Books			S Co. Books		
Land	100		Cash	100	
Cash		100	Land		90
			Gain – Land Sale		10

On 12/31/X1 the combined economic entity of P. Co. and S Co. prepares consolidated financial statements. At that time the following entry is necessary on the consolidating worksheet to eliminate the gain on the sale and return the consolidated Land account to its original value:

Gain – Land Sale	10	
Land		10
To eliminate intercompany gain on land sale.		

Assume that for the year ended 12/31/X1, the combined economic entity had a combined net income of $1,000, and S Co. had a net income of $300. Because there is a 20% minority interest in S Co., the minority's interest in the subsidiary's net income must be determined and excluded from the combined net income of P Co. and S Co. in determining consolidated net income.

The minority's interest in the gain is $2:

$10 × 20% = $2

The unadjusted minority's interest in S Co.'s net income is $60:

$300 × 20% = $60

Therefore the minority's adjusted interest in S Co.'s net income is $58:

Unadjusted Minority's Net Income	$60
Minus: Minority's Portion of Gain	(2)
Minority's Adjusted Net Income	$58

The minority interest in the combined net income will be included in the determination of consolidated net income as shown on the following partial consolidating worksheet for the year ended 12/31/X1:

P Co. & 100% Owned Subsidiary S Co.
(PARTIAL) Consolidating Worksheet
For the Year Ended 12/31/X1

Account name	P Co. Dr. (Cr.)	S Co. Dr. (Cr.)	Eliminations Dr.	Eliminations Cr.	CONSOLIDATED Dr. (Cr.) Income Statement	Retained Earnings	Balance Sheet
Land	100			(10)			90
Gain – land sale		(10)	10		0		
Various Accounts	*****	*****	*****	*****	*****	*****	*****
Totals	*****	*****	*****	*****			
Combined net income					(1,000)		
Minority interest*					58		(58)M
Consolidated net income					(942)	(942)	
Consolidated retained earnings						*****	*****
Total							*****

M = Minority interest
* Minority interest in S Co. net income:

20 % of S Co. net income of $300	$60
Less: Minority interest in unrealized profit of $10 on land sale (20% × $10)	(2)
Minority interest in S Co. net income	$58

***note*:** The worksheet shows elimination of the full $10 gain on land sale and adjustment of the land balance to original (historical) cost of $90.

At the end of the year during which the upstream sale of land takes place, the subsidiary's entire gain or loss on the sale is closed to its Retained Earnings account, which is eliminated in the cosolidation process in the following year, and for every subsequent year that the combined economic entity continues to hold the land. Any gain or loss must also be eliminated during the consolidation process, to return the Land account to its original (historical) cost, and to avoid misstatement of the *consolidated* retained earnings and minority interest. When there is a minority interest in the subsidiary, the adjustment to the Land account is eliminated against both retained earnings and the minority interest, in proportions determined by the percentage of ownership.

The consolidating worksheet entry to eliminate a gain on an upstream sale of land in the years subsequent to the year of the sale, when there is a minority interest in the subsidiary, is:

Retained Earnings – Parent (P% × intercompany gain)	$X	
Minority Interest (M% × intercompany gain)	$X	
Land (reduced by intercompany gain)		$X

The consolidating worksheet entry to eliminate a loss on an upstream sale of land in the years subsequent to the year of the sale, when there is a minority interest in the subsidiary, is:

Land (increased by intercompany loss)	$X	
Retained Earnings – Parent (P% × intercompany loss)		$X
Minority Interest (M% × intercompany loss)		$X

EXAMPLE 9-8: During 19X1, S Co. sold land to P Co. for $100. S Co.'s original cost for the land was $90. Eighty percent of S Co. is owned by P Co.

P Co. continued to hold the land through all of 19X1 and 19X2. On 12/31/X2, the combined economic entity of P Co. and S Co. prepares consolidated financial statements. At that point the following entry is needed on the consolidating worksheet to return the consolidated Land account to its original value and to prevent an overstatement of both P Co.'s retained earnings and the minority interest:

Retained Earnings – P Co.(80%)	8	
Minority Interest (20%)	2	
Land		10
To eliminate intercompany gain on land sale.		

If the parent company eventually sells the land it originally bought from its subsidiary to a party outside the combined economic entity, it records the sale, including any gain or loss, on its books based on its purchase price from the subsidiary.

From the consolidated point of view, however, any gain or loss must be based on the combined economic entity's original (historical) cost of the land. To accomplish this, an eliminating entry may be needed on the consolidating worksheet adjusting gain or loss based on the land's original (historical) cost. (See section 9-1B on how to calculate this adjustment.) If the subsidiary has a minority interest, the elimination entry adjusts gain (or loss) through the parent's retained earnings and through minority interest in proportions determined by their respective percentages of ownership.

The consolidating worksheet entry to adjust the gain on an outside sale of land, when there is a minority interest in the subsidiary, is:

Retained Earnings – Parent (P%)	P% × $X	
Minority Interest (M%)	M% × $X	
Gain – Land Sale		$X
To adjust gain on land sale.		

(This entry assumes a gain on the sale by the parent to an outside party is increased. If the parent had sold the land to an outside party at a loss, then this entry would reduce that loss. That is, the credit would be to the account "Loss - Land Sale" to the extent of any loss recorded on the sale by the parent.)

The consolidating worksheet entry to adjust the loss on an outside sale of land, when there is a minority interest in the subsidiary, is:

Loss – Land Sale	$X	
Retained Earnings – Parent (P%)		P% × $X
Minority Interest (M%)		M% × $X
To adjust loss on land sale.		

(This entry assumes a loss on the sale by the parent to an outside party is increased. If the parent had sold the land to an outside party at a gain, then this entry would reduce that gain. That is, the debit would be to the account "Gain - Land Sale" to the extent of any gain recorded on the sale by the parent.)

EXAMPLE 9-9: During 19X1, S Co. sold land to P Co. for $100. S Co.'s original cost of the land was $90. P Co. owns 80 percent of S Co.

P Co. continued to hold the land through all of 19X1 and 19X2. During 19X3, however, P Co. sold the land to an outside company for $115. On the date of the sale P Co. makes the following entry on its books, showing its gain on the sale:

Cash	115	
Land		100
Gain – land sale		15
To record land sale.		

But because the combined economic entity's historical cost for the land is $90, the consolidated gain on the sale is $25 ($115 - $90 = $25).

On 12/31/X3 the combined economic entity of P Co. and S Co. prepares consolidated financial statements. At that point an entry is needed on the consolidating worksheet to adjust the gain on the sale to reflect the historical cost of the land, and to properly disclose P Co.'s retained earnings and the minority interest. To determine the amount of the adjustment necessary, P Co.'s gain of $15 on the sale is subtracted from the consolidated gain of $25 ($25 – $15 = $10). Further, because there is a minority interest in S Co., the $10 adjustment must be eliminated against P Co.'s retained earnings and the minority interest according to their respective percentages of ownership:

P Co.: 80% of $10 = $8
Minority: 20% of $10 = $2

Considering all this, the following entry is necessary on the consolidating worksheet:

Retained Earnings – P Co. (80%)	8	
Minority Interest (20%)	2	
Gain – Land sale		10
To adjust gain on land sale.		

Note that this entry increased the gain of $15 recorded by P Co. by $10. The full $25 consolidated gain will now be disclosed.

Assume that for the year ended 12/31/X3, the combined economic entity had a combined net income of $1,000, and S Co. had a net income of $300. Because there is a 20% minority interest in S Co., the minority's interest in the subsidiary's net income must be determined and excluded from the combined net income of P Co. and S Co. in determining consolidated net income.

The unadjusted minority's interest in S Co.'s net income is $60:

20% of $300 = $60

The minority's interest in the realized profit on the sale is $2; therefore the minority's adjusted net income is $62:

Unadjusted Minority's Net Income:	$60
Plus: Minority's Portion of Gain	2
Minority's Adjusted Net Income:	$62

The minority interest in the combined net income will be included in the determination of consolidated net income as shown on the following partial consolidating worksheet for the year ended 12/31/X3:

P Co. & 80% Owned Subsidiary S Co.
(PARTIAL) Consolidating Worksheet
For the Year Ended 12/31/X3

Account name	P Co. Dr. (Cr.)	S Co. Dr. (Cr.)	Eliminations Dr.	Eliminations (Cr.)	CONSOLIDATED Dr. (Cr.) Income Statement	CONSOLIDATED Dr. (Cr.) Retained Earnings	CONSOLIDATED Dr. (Cr.) Balance Sheet
Retained earnings – P	*****		8			*****	
Minority interest			2				2M
Gain – land sale	(15)			(10)	(25)		
Various Accounts	*****	*****	*****	*****	*****	*****	*****
Totals	*****	*****	*****	*****			
Combined net income					(1,000)		
Minority interest*					62		(62)M
Consolidated net income					(938)	(938)	
Consolidated retained earnings						*****	*****
Total							*****

M = Minority interest

* Minority interest in S Co. net income:

20 % of S Co. net income of $300	$60
Less: Minority interest in realized profit of $10 on land sale (20% × $10)	2
Minority interest in S Co. net income	$62

9-2. Intercompany Sales of Depreciable Assets.

Companies that are separate legal entities but which have combined to form a single economic entity may sell depreciable assets, such as equipment, buildings, and machinery, to one another. Each company involved records the sale or purchase of the depreciable assets, including any gain or loss, on its books on the basis of its purchase price, and not necessarily on the basis of original historical cost to the consolidated group.

The consolidated point of view, however, does not recognize sales between affiliates. Therefore, the elinimation process requires that all the effects of intercompany sales be nullified including removal of intercompany gain or loss, adjustment of assets to original historical cost, and adjustment of depreciation expense and accumulated depreciation to amounts which appropriately reflect original historical cost.

A. A parent sells depreciable assets to its subsidiary.

If the intercompany sale of assets is from a parent company to a subsidiary (a downstream sale), then the percentage of the parent's interest in the subsidiary will not be relevant in the intercompany sale's elimination process. In a downstream sale the parent eventually recognizes all the loss or gain.

1. *Downstream sale of depreciable assets in the current accounting year.* When a parent company sells a depreciable asset to a subsidiary, it records the sale, including the depreciation accumulated to that point, and any gain or loss, as it would if the sale had taken place outside the combined economic entity:

Cash	$X	
Accumulated Depreciation	$X	
Assets		$X
Gain – Assets Sale		$X

or

Cash	$X	
Accumulated Depreciation	$X	
Loss – Assets Sale	$X	
Assets		$X

Likewise, the subsidiary records the purchase as it would a purchase from a source outside the combined economic entity:

Assets	$X	
Cash		$X

At the end of the current accounting period, the subsidiary will also record the depreciation on its recently acquired equipment based on the price the subsidiary paid the parent for the asset (not necessarily based on original historical cost) as follows:

Depreciation Expense	$X	
Accumulated Depreciation		$X

When the combined economic entity prepares consolidated financial statements, however, it must return the assets to their historical cost, less any accumulated depreciation based on historical cost, by eliminating any loss or gain on the intercompany sale.

As of the date of intercompany sale, the asset account balance must be adjusted to its original historical cost, accumulated depreciation as recorded by the parent company must be reinstated, and any intercompany gain or loss on sale must be eliminated.

The intercompany sale date eliminating worksheet entry on the downstream sale of depreciable assets to return the consolidated assets account to its original historical cost, reinstate accumulated depreciation, and eliminate intercompany gain (or loss) on sale is as follows:

Assets*	$X	
Gain – Assets Sale**	$X	
Accumulated Depreciation		$X

*Credit to assets if subsidiary's purchase price from parent exceeds original historical cost.
**Credit to "Loss – Assets Sale" if intercompany sale had resulted in a loss rather than a gain.

Once this eliminating entry is made an additional problem arises. After the sale the subsidiary will record on its books further depreciation expenses based on its cost for the equipment. But from a consolidated viewpoint the depreciation expense should be based on the parent company's original historical cost, not the subsidiary's cost. Consequently, an additional entry will be necessary on the consolidating worksheet to adjust the depreciation expense for the year, and the accumulated depreciation to date. Depreciation based on the historical cost of the equipment versus depreciation based on the subsidiary's cost represents the required adjustment to depreciation expense and accumulated depreciation in the year of the intercompany sale.

The consolidating worksheet entry to eliminate excess depreciation expense in the year of the intercompany sale, and to return the Accumulated Depreciation account to its original historical cost, is:

Accumulated Depreciation	$X	
Depreciation Expense		$X

The consolidating worksheet entry to add necessary depreciation expense in the year of the intercompany sale, and to return the Accumulated Depreciation account to its original historical cost, is:

Depreciation Expense	$X	
Accumulated Depreciation		$X

EXAMPLE 9-10: On 1/1/X1, P Co. sold equipment to S Co. for $90. P Co.'s original cost of the equipment was $120, and it depreciates it on a straight-line basis. On the date of the sale the accumulated depreciation on the equipment was $40, with only two years of remaining life and no salvage value.

P Co. and S Co. recorded the sale and purchase of the equipment on their respective books as follows:

P Co. Books			S Co. Books		
1/1/X1 Cash	90		1/1/X1 Equipment	90	
Accum. depr. – equip.	40		Cash		90
Equipment		120	12/31/X1 Depr. expense	45	
Gain – equip. sale		10	Accum. depr. – equip.		45
			($90 divided by 2 year life)		

As a result of these entries, the carrying value of the equipment changes from $80 on P Co.'s books ($120 original cost – $40 accumulated depreciation = $80) to $90 on S Co.'s books, reflecting the gain of $10. The amount needed to return the Equipment account to its historical cost is $30 ($120 historic cost – $90 subsidiary's cost = $30).

On 12/31/X1, the combined economic entity of P Co. and S Co. prepares consolidated financial statements. At that point the following entry is necessary on the consolidating worksheet to eliminate the intercompany gain on the sale, to reinstate accumulated depreciation as of the intercompany sale date, and to return the Equipment account to its original historical cost:

Equipment ($120 – $90)	$30	
Gain – Equipment Sale	$10	
Accumulated Depreciation – Equipment		$40

Note that on 12/31/X1 S Co. takes a depreciation expense based on its purchase price for the equipment ($90 ÷ 2 years = $45). From the consolidated viewpoint, however, the depreciation expense for 19X1 should be based on the original carrying cost of the equipment on 1/1/X1, $80,yielding a consolidated depreciation expense for the year of $40 ($80 ÷ 2 years = $40). The excess recorded by S Co. ($5) must be eliminated during the consolidation process, as follows:

Accumulated Depreciation – Equipment	$5	
Depreciation Expense		$5

The following partial consolidating worksheet shows how the intercompany gain on the sale is eliminated, the equipment is restored to its original cost and carrying value, and the depreciation expense is properly adjusted:

P Co. & 100% Owned Subsidiary S Co.
(PARTIAL) Consolidating Worksheet
For the Year Ended 12/31/X1

Account name	P Co. Dr. (Cr.)	S Co. Dr. (Cr.)	Eliminations Dr.	Eliminations (Cr.)	CONSOLIDATED Dr. (Cr.) Income Statement	Retained Earnings	Balance Sheet
Equipment		90	30[1]				120
Accum. depr. – equip.		(45)	5[2]	(40)[1]			(80)
Gain – equip. sale	(10)		10[1]		0		
Depreciation expense		45		(5)[2]	40		

[1] To restore equipment to original cost and carry value and eliminate intercompany gain on sale.
[2] To eliminate excess depreciation recorded on S Co.'s separate books.

2. *Downstream sale of depreciable assets in subsequent years.* At the end of the year during which the downstream sale of depreciable assets occurs, the parent company's gain or loss is closed to its Retained Earnings account. During the consolidation process the following year, and for every year the combined economic entity continues to hold and use the assets, intercompany gain or loss included in the parent company's Retained Earnings must be eliminated, assets must be adjusted to original historical cost, and depreciation expense and accumulated depreciation must be adjusted to reflect original historical cost.

   The consolidating worksheet entry to eliminate a gain or loss on a downstream sale of depreciable assets in the year after the sale is:

Assets*	$X	
Retained Earnings – Parent**	$X	
Accumulated Depreciation		$X

*Credit to assets if subsidiary's purchase price from parent exceeds original historical cost.
**Credit to Retained Earnings – Parent if intercompany sale had resulted in a loss rather than a gain.

   During this second year the subsidiary will continue to depreciate the assets based on the price it paid the parent for the asset. Consequently, an additional entry on the consolidating worksheet is necessary to adjust the depreciation expense for the year to reflect historical costs, and to adjust the Accumulated Depreciation account. To determine the amount of this entry, see the previous section.

   The form of this additional entry is determined by the fact that this is the second year that the subsidiary has recorded the depreciation based on the subsidiary's purchase price from the parent; therefore, two years' worth of accumulated depreciation adjustments must be made on the consolidating worksheet. The current year's adjustment is made to the Depreciation Expense account; the previous year's adjustment is made to the parent's Retained Earnings account. The combined amount is eliminated against the Accumulated Depreciation account. The consolidating worksheet entry to eliminate *excess* depreciation expense in the second year, and to return the Accumulated Depreciation account to a balance based on historical cost is as follows:

Accumulated Depreciation	$X	
Depreciation Expense (current year)		$1/2X
Retained Earnings – Parent		$1/2X

The consolidating worksheet entry to add necessary depreciation expense in the second year, and to return the Accumulated Depreciation account to a balance based on historical cost is as follows:

Depreciation Expense (current year)	$1/2X	
Retained Earnings – Parent	$1/2X	
Accumulated Depreciation		$X

A similar adjusting entry will be made every year the subsidiary continues to hold and use the asset, until it is fully depreciated. In subsequent years, the current year's adjustment to the Depreciation Expense will be performed as shown, but the charge (or credit) to the parent's Retained Earnings account will be based on the cumulative prior year(s) depreciation expense adjustments. For instance, the consolidating worksheet entry to eliminate excess depreciation in the third year is:

Accumulated Depreciation (3 years)	$X	
Depreciation Expense (current year)		$1/3X
Retained Earnings – Parent (previous years)		$2/3X

note: The credit to the parent's Retained Earnings represents excessive depreciation for two prior years while the credit to depreciation expense represents excessive depreciation expense for the current year only.

EXAMPLE 9-11: On 1/1/X1, P Co. sold equipment to S Co. for $90. P Co.'s original cost for the equipment was $120, and it depreciates this equipment on a straight-line basis. On the date of the sale the accumulated depreciation on P Co.'s books was $40, with only two years of life left and no salvage value.

On 12/31/X2, the combined economic entity of P Co. and S Co. prepares consolidated financial statements. The following entry is necessary on the consolidating worksheet to eliminate the intercompany gain on the sale, and to return the Equipment account to its original value:

Equipment	30	
Retained earnings – P Co.	10	
Accumulated Depreciation – Equipment		40

To restore equipment to original cost or carry value and eliminate intercompany gain on sale.

note: The gain would have been closed to P Co. retained earnings at the end of 19X1, so the 19X2 elimination results in a charge to retained earnings rather than to gain on sale.

A second eliminating entry is necessary on this date to eliminate two years of excess depreciation recorded by S Co.

Accum. Depr. – Equipment (2 yrs. × $5)	10	
Depreciation expense (19X2)		5
Retained earnings – P Co. (19X1 depreciation)		5

To eliminate excess depreciation recorded on the books by S. Co.

The following partial consolidating worksheet shows how the intercompany gain on the sale is eliminated, the equipment is restored to its original cost and carrying value, and the depreciation is properly adjusted:

P Co. & 100% Owned Subsidiary S Co.
(PARTIAL) Consolidating Worksheet
For the Year Ended 12/31/X2

Account name	P Co. Dr. (Cr.)	S Co. Dr. (Cr.)	Eliminations Dr.	Eliminations (Cr.)	CONSOLIDATED Dr. (Cr.) Income Statement	CONSOLIDATED Dr. (Cr.) Retained Earnings	CONSOLIDATED Dr. (Cr.) Balance Sheet
Equipment		90	30[1]				120
Accum. depr. – equip.		(90)	10[2]	(40)[1]			(120)
Retained earnings – P	(400)*		10[1]	(5)[2]		(395)	
Depreciation expense		45		(5)[2]	40		

*Arbitrary balance
1 To restore equipment to original cost and carry value and eliminate intercompany gain on sale.
2 To eliminate excess depreciation recorded on S Co.'s separate books.

note: The 12/31/X2 partial worksheet shows that the equipment is now fully depreciated (cost $120 less accumulated depreciation $120), and that the consolidated depreciation expense for 19X2 is $40.

If the asset is on hand and in use after it has been fully depreciated, adjustments on the consolidating worksheet must continue. The entry to eliminate the gain or loss, and to return the asset to its historical cost and carrying value remains the same. The entry to adjust the depreciation expense results in a charge or a credit to the parent's Retained Earnings account. The entry to record previous years of excess depreciation is:

	Dr.	Cr.
Accumulated Depreciation	$X	
Retained earnings – Parent		$X

The entry to record previous years of additional depreciation is:

	Dr.	Cr.
Retained earnings – Parent	$X	
Accumulated Depreciation		$X

note: No further adjustments to depreciation expense are necessary since the asset has been fully depreciated.

EXAMPLE 9-12: Assume the same information as that given in Example 9-11. S Co. found that, although the equipment was fully depreciated at the end of 19X2, it was still able to be used during 19X3 and on hand at year end 12/31/X3.

On 12/31/X3, therefore, the combined economic entity must make the following entries on the consolidating worksheet, to eliminate the gain on the sale, return the equipment to its original cost, and to adjust the two previous years' worth of excess depreciation:

	Dr.	Cr.
Equipment	30	
Retained earnings – P Co.	10	
Accumulated Depreciation – Equipment		40

To restore equipment to original cost or carry value and eliminate intercompany gain on sale.

	Dr.	Cr.
Accumulated Depreciation – Equipment	10	
Retained earnings – P Co.		10

To eliminate excess depreciation recorded by S Co. during prior years (x1 and x2).

note: The above two entries can simply be combined into one entry.

	Dr.	Cr.
Equipment	30	
Accumulated Depreciation – Equipment		30

This single entry shows that the end result of the entire process is simply to record the equipment and accumulated depreciation at $120 ($90 S Co. intercompany purchase price plus $30 worksheet adjustment), the original cost to P Co.

B. A wholly owned subsidiary sells depreciable assets to its parent.

When a subsidiary sells depreciable assets to its parent company, each records the sale and purchase on its respective books as it would a transaction with a source outside the combined economic entity. But from the combined perspective, of course, no sale actually takes place, and entries during the consolidation process must eliminate any gain or loss, restore the asset sold to its original (historical) cost, and adjust depreciation expense and accumulated depreciation. If there is no minority interest in the subsidiary, then the consolidating worksheet entries to make these adjustments will be identical to those shown in Examples 9-10, 9-11, and 9-12, because all intercompany gain or loss will eventually become a part of the parent company's retained earnings. The only difference will be that the depreciable asset itself will be carried by the parent, and the intercompany gain or loss on the sale will be recorded by the subsidiary.

C. A subsidiary with depreciable assets sells depreciable assets to its parent.

If a parent company owns less than 100 percent of its subsidiary, a portion of any gain or loss from an upstream sale of depreciable assets will be attributable to the minority interest in the subsidiary. Furthermore, the minority will have an interest in any adjustment made to the consolidated depreciation expense during the accounting period.

When consolidated financial statements are prepared for the parent and its subsidiary with a minority interest at the end of the accounting period during which the sale took place, any gain or loss from the sale must be eliminated and the asset sold must be returned to original (historical) cost. Minority's interest in the unrealized profit or loss on the sale must be determined, as reflected in the minority's interest in the subsidiary's net income (the procedures for doing this are covered in Section 9-1C, and in Example 9-7).

In addition to eliminating the loss or gain, depreciation expenses and accumulated depreciation are adjusted to reflect depreciation based on the historical cost of the equipment (the procedures for doing this are covered in Section 9-2A).

Finally, the minority's interest in the subsidiary's net income is adjusted to show the minority's portion of the adjustment to the depreciation expense. This adjustment is determined as follows:

Total Adjustment to Depreciation Expense × Minority's Ownership % =
Minority's Portion of Depreciation Adjustment

Then combine that amount with the minority's portion of the subsidiary's net income *and* its portion of the gain or loss on the sale:

Minority's Unadjusted Net Income:	$ X
Minority's Portion of (Gain or) Loss:	(X)
Minority's Portion of Depreciation Adjustment	X*
Minority's Adjusted Net Income:	$ X

*This item is shown as an addition assuming excessive depreciation charges have been recorded on the parent's books. If, on the other hand, too little depreciation expense had been recorded, then this would be a deduction.

These adjustments and the corrected minority interest on the balance sheet are fully disclosed in the consolidated financial statements.

EXAMPLE 9-13: On 1/1/X1, S Co. sold equipment to its parent P Co. for $90. P Co. owns 80% of S Co. S Co.'s original cost of the equipment was $120, and it depreciates the equipment on a straight-line basis. On the date of the sale accumulated depreciation on S Co.'s books was $40, with two years of remaining life and no salvage value.

P Co. and S Co. recorded the purchase and sale of the equipment on their respective books as follows:

P Co. Books		
1/1/X1 Equipment	90	
Cash		90
12/31/X1 Depreciation exp.	45	
Accum. depr. – equip.		45
($90 divided by 2 year life)		

S Co. Books		
1/1/X1 Cash	90	
Accum. depr. – equip.	40	
Equipment		120
Gain - equip. sale		10

Note that as a result of these entries, the carrying value of the equipment changes from $80 on S Co.'s books to $90 on P Co.'s books, a gain of $10. The amount needed on the consolidating worksheet to return the Equipment account to its original historical cost is $30 ($120 original cost – $90). Further, the depreciation expense is overstated by $5 ($45 as recorded by P Co. versus the $40 that would have been recorded based on S Co.'s original carrying cost of $80 divided by 2 years). Therefore, when the combined economic entity prepares its consolidated financial statements on 12/31/X1, it must make the following entries:

Equipment ($120 – $90)	30	
Gain – equipment sale	10	
Accumulated Depreciation – Equipment		40
To restore equipment to original cost or carry value and eliminate intercompany gain on sale.		
Accumulated Depreciation – Equipment	5	
Depreciation Expense		5
To eliminate excess depreciation recorded on the books of P Co. ($45 P Co. depreciation less $40 consolidated depreciation).		

Assume that for the year ended 12/31/X1, the combined economic entity had a combined net income of $1,000, and S Co. had a net income of $300. Because there is a minority interest in S Co., it must adjust its net income, and thereby the consolidated net income, to show the minority's interest in the gain and its share of the adjustment to the depreciation expense.

The minority's interest in the intercompany gain is $2:

$10 × 20% = $2

Its interest in the adjustment for escessivee depreciation expense is $1:

$5 × 20% = $1

Its interest in S Co.'s net income is $60:

$300 × 20% = $60

Combining these figures yields the adjusted minority interest of $59 in S Co.'s income:

Minority's Unadjusted Net Income:	$60.00
Less: Minority's Portion of Intercompany Gain:	(2.00)
Plus: Minority's Portion of Excessive Depreciation	1.00
Minority's Adjusted Net Income:	$59.00

The minority interest in the combined net income and the effect of the consolidating elimination entries are shown on the following partial consolidated worksheet for the year ended 12/31/X1:

P Co. & 80% Owned Subsidiary S Co.
(PARTIAL) Consolidating Worksheet
For the Year Ended 12/31/X1

Account name	P Co. Dr. (Cr.)	S Co. Dr. (Cr.)	Eliminations Dr.	Eliminations Cr.	CONSOLIDATED Dr. (Cr.) Income Statement	Retained Earnings	Balance Sheet
Equipment	90		30[1]				120
Accum. depr. – equip.	(45)		5[2]	(40)[1]			(80)
Gain – equip. sale		(10)	10[1]		0		
Depreciation expense	45			(5)[2]	40		
Various Accounts	*****	*****	*****	*****	*****	*****	*****
Totals	*****	*****	*****	*****			
Combined net income					(1,000)		
Minority interest*					59		(59)[M]
Consolidated net income					(941)	(941)	
Consolidated retained earnings						*****	*****
Total							*****

M = Minority interest
* Minority interest in S Co. net income:

20 % of S Co. net income of $300	$60
Less: Minority interest in unrealized profit of $10 on land sale (20% × $10)	(2)
Plus: Minority interest in excess depreciation expense($5 × 20%)	1
Minority interest in S Co. net income	$59

1 To restore equipment to original cost and carry value and eliminate intercompany gain on sale.
2 To eliminate excess depreciation recorded on P Co.'s separate books.

At the end of the year during which the upstream sale of depreciable assets occurs, the subsidiary's gain or loss is closed to its Retained Earnings account, which is eliminated in the consolidation process. During the consolidation process the following year, and for every year the combined economic entity continues to hold and use the assets, intercompany gain or loss must be eliminated against the parent's retained earnings. Also, assets and related depreciation expense and accumulated depreciation are adjusted to amounts reflecting original historical cost. Adjustments to eliminate gain or loss or to restate depreciation expense and accumulated depreciation must properly consider minority interest.

The consolidating worksheet entry to eliminate a gain or loss in the second year after the sale is as follows:

	Dr.	Cr.
Assets*	$X	
Retained Earnings – Parent (%)**	$X	
Minority Interest (%)**	$X	
Accumulated Depreciation		$X

*Credit to assets if subsidiary's purchase price from the parent exceeds original historical cost.
**Credit these accounts if intercompany sale had resulted in a loss rather than a gain.

Also, depreciation expense for the year must be adjusted to match depreciation expense based on historical cost. Because this is the second year that the parent records its depreciation expense based on its purchase price from the subsidiary, two years' worth of adjustments are needed. The current year's adjustment is applied to the Depreciation Expense account. The previous year's adjustment is applied to the parent's Retained Earnings account and the minority interest, according to their respective percentages of ownership. The consolidating worksheet entry to eliminate excess depreciation expense in the second year, and to return the Accumulated Depreciation account to a historical cost basis is:

Accumulated Depreciation	$X	
Depreciation Expense (current year)		$1/2X
Retained Earnings – Parent (P%)		P% × $1/2X
Minority Interest (M%)		M% × $1/2X

The consolidating worksheet entry to add necessary depreciation expense in the second year, and to return the Accumulated Depreciation account to an historical cost basis is:

Depreciation Expense (current year)	$1/2X	
Retained Earnings – Parent (P%)	P% × $1/2X	
Minority Interest (M%)	M% × $1/2X	
Accumulated Depreciation		$X

The minority interest in the subsidiary's net income is adjusted to reflect its percentage of the current year's adjustment to depreciation expense, as previously shown. These adjustments are fully disclosed in the consolidated financial statements and footnotes.

EXAMPLE 9-14: On 1/1/X1, S Co. sold equipment to its parent P Co. for $90. P Co. owns 80% of S Co. S Co.'s original cost for the equipment was $120, and it depreciates the equipment on a straight-line basis. On the date of the sale accumulated depreciation on S Co.'s books was $40, with two years of remaining life and no salvage value.

P Co. continues to hold and use the equipment for all of 19X2. Therefore, when the combined economic entity prepares its consolidated financial statements on 12/31/X2, it must make the following entries:

1)	Equipment	30	
	Retained Earnings – P Co. (80%)	8	
	Minority Interest (20%)	2	
	Accumulated Depreciation – Equipment		40
	To restore equipment to original cost or carry value and eliminate intercompany gain on sale.		

note: The gain would have been closed to S Co. retained earnings at the end of 19X1. However, 80% of S Co. retained earnings are eliminated in the consolidation process against the "Investment in S Co." account. The remaining 20% of the gain is removed against minority interest.

2)	Accumulated Depreciation – Equipment (2 years × $5)	10	
	Depreciation expense (19X2)		5
	Retained Earnings – P Co. (19X1 depreciation of $5 × 80%)		4
	Minority Interest (19X1 depreciation of $5 × 20%)		1
	To eliminate excess depreciation recorded on the books of P Co.		

note: Excess depreciation has now been recorded by P Co. for 2 years at $5 per year.

The effect of the previous two elimination entries and the determination of the minority's interest in the subsidiary's net income as these items relate to the consolidated financial statements are depicted on the 12/31/X2 partial consolidating worksheet which follows:

P Co. & 80% Owned Subsidiary S Co.
(PARTIAL) Consolidating Worksheet
For the Year Ended 12/31/X2

Account name	P Co. Dr. (Cr.)	S Co. Dr. (Cr.)	Eliminations Dr.	Eliminations (Cr.)	CONSOLIDATED Dr. (Cr.) Income Statement	Retained Earnings	Balance Sheet
Equipment	90		30[1]				120
Accum. depr. – equip.	(90)		10[2]	(40)[1]			(120)
Retained earnings – S		*****					***** M
Retained earnings – P	*****		8[1]	(4)[2]		*****	
Minority interest			2[1]	(1)[2]			***** M
Depreciation expense	45			(5)[2]	40		
Various Accounts	*****	*****	*****	*****	*****	*****	*****
Totals	*****	*****	*****	*****			
Combined net income					(1,000)		
Minority interest*					61		(61)M
Consolidated net income					(939)	(939)	
Consolidated retained earnings						*****	*****
Total							*****

M = Minority interest

* Minority interest in S Co. net income:

20 % of S Co. net income of $300	$60
Plus: Minority interest in excess depreciation expense($5 × 20%)	1
Minority interest in S Co. net income	$61

[1] To restore equipment to original cost and carry value and eliminate intercompany gain on sale.
[2] To eliminate excess depreciation recorded on P Co.'s separate books.

If the asset is on hand and in use after it has been fully depreciated, adjustments must continue on the consolidating worksheet. The entry to eliminate the gain or loss, reinstate accumulated depreciation, and return the asset to its historical cost, remains the same. The entry to adjust the depreciation expense results in a charge or a credit to the parent's Retained Earnings account and the minority interest according to their respective ownership percentages. The entry to record previous years of excess depreciation is:

	Dr.	Cr.
Accumulated Depreciation	$X	
Retained Earnings – Parent (P%)		P% × X
Minority Interest (M%)		M% × X

The entry to record previous years of additional depreciation is:

	Dr.	Cr.
Retained Earnings – Parent (P%)	P% × X	
Minority Interest (M%)	M% × X	
Accumulated Depreciation		$X

note: no further adjustments to depreciation expense are necessary since the asset has been fully depreciated.

EXAMPLE 9-15: On 1/1/X1, S Co. sold equipment to its parent P Co. for $90. P Co. owns 80% of S Co. S Co.'s original cost for the equipment was $120, and it depreciates the equipment on a straight-line basis. On the date of the sale accumulated depreciation on S Co.'s books was $40, with two years of remaining life and no salvage value.

P Co. found that, although the equipment was fully depreciated at the end of 19X2, it was still able to be used during 19X3 and remains on hand at 12/31/X3. On 12/31/X3, therefore, the combined economic entity must make the following entries on the consolidating worksheet, to eliminate the gain on the sale, return the equipment to its original cost, and to adjust the two previous years' worth of excess depreciation:

	Dr.	Cr.
Equipment	30	
Retained Earnings – P Co. (80%)	8	
Minority Interest (20%)	2	
Accumulated Depreciation – Equipment		40

To restore equipment to original cost or carry value and eliminate intercompany gain on sale.

	Dr.	Cr.
Accumulated Depreciation – Equipment	10	
Retained Earnings – P Co. (80%)		8
Minority Interest (20%)		2

To eliminate excess depreciation recorded by P Co. during prior years (19X1 and 19X2).

note: The above two entries can simply be combined into one entry:

	Dr.	Cr.
Equipment	30	
Accumulated Depreciation – Equipment		30

This single entry shows that the end result of the entire process is to record the equipment and accumulated depreciation at $120 ($90 P Co. intercompany purchase price plus $30 worksheet adjustment), the original cost to S Co.

RAISE YOUR GRADES

Can you explain . . . ?

☑ the worksheet elimination entry (in the year of sale and in later years) to restore land to its original cost and eliminate any gain or loss on the intercompany land sales when:
- (*a*) the parent company is the seller and owner of a 100% interest in the subsidiary.
- (*b*) the parent company is the seller and owner of less than a 100% interest in the subsidiary.
- (*c*) the subsidiary company is the seller and is 100% owned by the parent company.
- (*d*) the subsidiary company is the seller and is less than 100% owned by the parent company.

☑ the special consolidation procedures required when land acquired by a parent from a subsidiary (or vice-versa) is subsequently sold to a party outside of the consolidated group.

☑ the worksheet elimination entries required (in the year of sale and in later years) to restore equipment to its original cost, eliminate any gain or loss on intercompany equipment sales, and adjust depreciaton expense and accumulated depreciation when:
- (*a*) the parent company is the seller and owner of a 100% interest in the subsidiary.
- (*b*) the parent company is the seller and owner of less than a 100% interest in the subsidiary.
- (*c*) the subsidiary company is the seller and is 100% owned by the parent company.
- (*d*) the subsidiary company is the seller and is less than 100% owned by the parent company.

☑ the effect on minority interest in combined net income when a less than 100% owned subsidiary sells land or depreciable assets to the parent company at a gain or loss.

SUMMARY

1. The worksheet elimination entries to restore land to original cost and eliminate any gain or loss on the intercompany sale when the parent is the seller and 100% owner of the subsidiary are as follows:

Year of Sale			Subsequent Years		
Gain – land sale*	x		Retained earnings – P Co.	x	
Land		x	Land		x

*If a loss is incurred on the intercompany sale, then of course the loss will be credited and the land account is charged. That is, the entries are simply reversed in this and any other case depicted here.

2. The worksheet elimination entries to restore land to its original cost and eliminate any gain or loss on the intercompany sale when the parent is the seller and owner of less than a 100% interest in the subsidiary are the same as those described in item 1 above. Since the sale is downstream (parent to subsidiary), any gain or loss is the parent's gain or loss even though a minority interest in fact exists.
3. The worksheet elimination entries to restore land to its original cost and eliminate any gain or loss on the intercompany sale when the subsidiary is the seller and is 100% owned by the parent are again the same as those described in item 1 above. Although the sale is upstream (subsidiary to parent), no minority interest exists. Therefore, any intercompany gain or loss is actually the parent's gain or loss.
4. The worksheet elimination entries to restore land to original cost and eliminate any gain or loss on the intercompany sale when the subsidiary is the seller and the subsidiary is less than 100% owned by the parent are as follows:

Year of Sale			Subsequent Years		
Gain – land sale	x		Retained earnings – P Co.	x	
Land		x	Minority interest	x	
			Land		x

5. If the buying affiliate (parent or subsidiary) eventually sells land which it purchased on an intercompany basis to a party outside of the consolidated group, the consolidated income statement must show gain or loss on sale based on the original land cost and not based on the buying affiliate's land carrying value.
6. The worksheet elimination entries to restore depreciable assets to original cost, eliminate any gain or loss on intercompany sale, and adjust depreciation and accumulated depreciation when the parent is the seller and 100% owner of the subsidiary are as follows:

Year of Sale			Subsequent Years		
Gain – asset sale	x		Retained earnings – P Co.	x	
Depreciable asset*	x		Depreciable asset	x	
Accum. depr. – asset		x	Accum. depr. – asset		x
*May also be a credit. Simply adjust to original cost.					
Accum. depr. – asset	x		Accum. depr. – asset	x	
Depreciation expense		x	Depreciation expense		x
			Retained earnings – P Co.*		x
(This entry assumes excessive depreciation charges. If depreciation is too low, this entry is reversed.)			*For excessive depreciation charges of prior years.		

7. The worksheet elimination entries to restore depreciable assets to original cost, eliminate any gain or loss on intercompany sale, and adjust depreciation and accumulated depreciation when the parent

is the seller but owns less than a 100% interest in the subsidiary are the same as those described in the previous item 6 above. Since the sale is downstream (parent to subsidiary), any gain or loss is the parent's gain or loss even though a minority interest exists.

8. The worksheet elimination entries to restore depreciable assets to original cost, eliminate any gain or loss on intercompany sale, and adjust depreciation and accumulated depreciation when a subsidiary which is 100% owned by the parent is the seller are the same as those described in item 6 above. Although the sale is upstream (subsidiary to parent), no minority interest exists. Therefore, any intercompany gain or loss is actually the parent's gain or loss.

9. The worksheet elimination entries to restore depreciable assets to original cost, eliminate any gain or loss on intercompany sale, and adjust depreciation and accumulated depreciation when a subsidiary which is less than 100% owned by the parent is the seller are as follows:

Year of Sale			Subsequent Years		
Gain–asset sale	x		Retained earnings – P Co.	x	
Depreciable asset*	x		Minority interest	x	
Accum. depr. – asset		x	Depreciable asset	x	
*May also be a credit. Simply adjust to original cost.			Accum. depr. – asset		x
Accum. depr. – asset	x		Accum. depr. – asset	x	
Depreciation expense		x	Depreciation expense		x
(This entry assumes excessive depreciation charges. If depreciation is too low, this entry is reversed.)			Retained earnings – P Co.*		x
			Minority interest*		x
			*For excessive depreciation charges of prior years.		

10. If a less than 100% owned subsidiary sells land or depreciable assets to the parent at a gain or a loss, the minority interest in combined net income will require adjustment in order that consolidated net income be properly depicted.

RAPID REVIEW

1. Berlin Co. sold a tract of land to its subsidiary Brussels Company on June 6, 19X7, for $50,000. The original cost of the land to Berlin Company was $20,000. Berlin owns 100% of Brussels. The land should appear in the December 31, 19X7, consolidated balance sheet at which of the following amounts?

(*a*) $50,000
(*b*) $30,000
(*c*) $20,000
(*d*) $0

2. Refer to the information from Question 1. The amount of intercompany gain on sale which must be eliminated from the 19X7 consolidated income statement is:

(*a*) $50,000
(*b*) $30,000
(*c*) $20,000
(*d*) $0

3. Refer to the information from Question 1. The amount of intercompany gain on sale which must be eliminated from the 19X8 consolidated income statement is:

(*a*) $50,000
(*b*) $30,000
(*c*) $20,000
(*d*) $0

4. Refer to the information from Question 1. However, assume the sale was made by the 100% owned subsidiary Brussels Co. to the parent Berlin Co. (upstream sale). The land should appear in the December 31, 19X7, consolidated balance sheet at which of the following amounts?
   (*a*) $50,000
   (*b*) $30,000
   (*c*) $20,000
   (*d*) $0

5. Refer to the information from Question 1. However, assume the sale was made by the subsidiary Brussels Co. to the parent Berlin Co. (upstream sale) and that Berlin Co. has only a 70% interest in Brussels Co. The amount of intercompany gain on sale which must be eliminated from the 19X7 consolidated income statement is:
   (*a*) $35,000
   (*b*) $21,000
   (*c*) $20,000
   (*d*) $14,000
   (*e*) $30,000

6. Big Co. sold its subsidiary Little Co. a tract of land on September 6, 19X8, for $150,000. The land originally cost Big Co. $100,000 several years earlier. On December 10, 19X9, Little Co. sold the land to Sledge Company for $140,000. The gain or loss on the land sale which should appear on the consolidated income statement for the fiscal year ending December 31, 19X9 is:
   (*a*) $40,000 gain
   (*b*) $50,000 gain
   (*c*) $10,000 loss
   (*d*) $0

Questions 7 through 14 are based on the following information:

Intercompany selling price of equipment	$200,000
Original cost to selling company	$160,000
Accumulated Depreciation as of intercompany sale date	$ 80,000
Intercompany sale date	1/3/X2
Remaining life of equipment at sale date	8 years
Estimated salvage value of equipment	$0
Depreciation method	straight-line

7. If the sale was made by a parent to its wholly owned subsidiary, the consolidated financial statements at 12/31/X2 will show the equipment and its accumulated depreciation at:
   (*a*) $200,000 and $25,000 respectively.
   (*b*) $160,000 and $90,000 respectively.
   (*c*) $160,000 and $80,000 respectively.
   (*d*) $160,000 and $10,000 respectively.

8. If the sale was made by a parent to a wholly owned subsidiary, the intercompany gain on sale which must be eliminated for the fiscal year ending December 31, 19X2, is:
   (*a*) $40,000
   (*b*) $0
   (*c*) $120,000
   (*d*) $110,000

9. If the sale was made by a parent company to a wholly owned subsidiary, the depreciation expense must be adjusted by a:
   (*a*) $15,000 worksheet increase.
   (*b*) $15,000 worksheet decrease.
   (*c*) $10,000 worksheet increase.
   (*d*) no adjustment is necessary.

10. If the sale was made by a parent company to an 80%-owned subsidiary (downstream) or by a 100%-owned subsidiary to a parent company (upstream), the answers to the previous questions 7, 8, and 9 remain the same.
(*a*) True
(*b*) False

11. If the sale was made by an 80%-owned subsidiary to a parent company (upstream), the answers to questions 7, 8, and 9 remain the same.
(*a*) True
(*b*) False

12. If the sale was made by a parent company to an 80%-owned subsidiary (downstream), the $120,000 intercompany gain on sale would not affect minority interest in combined net income.
(*a*) True
(*b*) False

13. If the sale was made by an 80%-owned subsidiary to a parent, the $120,000 intercompany gain on sale would not affect minority interest in combined net income.
(*a*) True
(*b*) False

14. If the sale was made by a parent company to an 80%-owned subsidiary (downstream), the 12/31/X3 consolidating worksheet elimination entry to remove intercompany gain on sale will result in:
(*a*) a charge of $120,000 to gain on equipment sale.
(*b*) a charge of $96,000 to gain on equipment sale.
(*c*) a charge of $120,000 to parent retained earnings.
(*d*) a charge of $96,000 to parent retained earnings and $24,000 to minority interest.

Answers:

1. (*c*) (Original cost to Berlin Co.)
2. (*b*) ($50,000 selling price less $20,000 original cost)
3. (*d*) (No intercompany gain will be removed from the 19X8 consolidated income statement. The gain would have been closed to retained earnings of Berlin Co. and would therefore be eliminated from the consolidated balance sheet retained earnings of Berlin Co.)
4. (*c*) (Original cost to Brussels Co.)
5. (*e*) (The full $30,000 gain based on the $50,000 selling price less $20,000 original cost must be eliminated. It does not matter that the sale is upstream and the parent owns only 70% of the subsidiary. However, minority interest in combined net income will be lower by $9,000 (which is 30% of the $30,000 intercompany gain) for the year-ending December 31, 19X7.)
6. (*a*) (To answer this question, intercompany sales prices must be completely ignored. The outside selling price to Sledge Co. of $140,000 less the original cost to Big Co. of $100,000 is the basis for determining a gain of $40,000. Note: In 19X8, the year of the intercompany sale, the $50,000 intercompany gain would never have appeared on the consolidated income statement.)
7. (*b*) (The equipment must be carried at the original cost of $160,000. The remaining depreciable asset value on the 1/1/X2 sale date is $80,000. If 8 years of asset life remain and straight-line depreciation is used, the depreciation expense for 19X2 is $10,000. Therefore, if 1/1/X2 accumulated depreciation was $80,000 and 19X2 depreciation is $10,000, accumulated depreciation at December 31, 19X2 is $90,000.)

8. (*c*)

Intercompany selling price	$200,000
Less: 1/1/X2 Book value)	80,000
Intercompany gain	$120,000

9. (*b*)

Depreciation expense per subsidiary's books: $200,000 divided by 8 years	$ 25,000
Depreciation expense per book value on 1/1/X2 sale date: $80,000 book value divided by 8 years	10,000
Worksheet depreciation expense decrease required for 19X2	$ 15,000

10. (*a*) True. Whether a minority interest exists or not, the intercompany sale should be fully eliminated, the equipment and accumulated depreciation should be based on original historical cost, the intercompany gain should be removed fully, and depreciation expense should be adjusted.

11. (*a*) True. (See answer to #10.)

12. (*a*) True. As long as the intercompany sale is made downstream (parent to subsidiary), none of the intercompany gain is recognized by the subsidiary. Therefore, even if a minority interest exists, it is not affected by the intercompany gain.

13. (*b*) False. Minority interest in subsidiary net income (and consequently combined net income) would be reduced by the minority interest of 20% in the $120,000 intercompany gain or $24,000.

14. (*c*) Since the parent is assumed to have made the sale, none of the gain is attributable to the subsidiary or to minority interest. The 12/31/X3 worksheet entry to eliminate the gain is therefore as follows:

	Debit	Credit
Retained earnings – P Co.	120,000	
Equipment		40,000
Accum. depr. – equipment		80,000

In addition, an entry to adjust depreciation expense and accumulated depreciation would be necessary as follows:

	Debit	Credit
Accum. depr. – equipment (2 years)	30,000	
Depreciation expense		15,000
Retained earnings – P Co.		15,000

SOLVED PROBLEMS

PROBLEM 9-1: Pepper Co. sold a parcel of land to its 80%-owned subsidiary Salt Co. on April 6, 19X6, for $85,000. The original cost of the land to Pepper Co. was $70,000.

Required:

(*a*) Prepare the December 31, 19X6, consolidating worksheet elimination entry required.

(*b*) Prepare the December 31, 19X7, consolidating worksheet elimination entry required.

(*c*) Assume that on May 10, 19X8, Salt Co. sold the land to a company not affiliated with the consolidated group for $90,000. Prepare the December 31, 19X8, consolidating worksheet elimination entry required, if any.

Answer:

(*a*)

	Debit	Credit
Gain – land sale	15,000	
Land		15,000

To restore land to its original cost and eliminate intercompany gain on sale (12/31/X6).

(*b*) The point here is that the gain on the land sale would have been closed to retained earnings of the seller (parent) in the prior year (19X6). The December 31, 19X7 worksheet entry must consider this.

Retained earnings – Pepper Co.	15,000	
Land		15,000

To restore land to its original cost and eliminate intercompany gain on sale (12/31/X7).

(*c*) The full realized gain of $20,000 ($90,000 selling price less $70,000 original cost to Pepper Co.) should be included in the consolidated income statement for the fiscal year ending December 31, 19X8. However, the seller (Salt Co.) will record gain on sale on its separate books of only $5,000 ($90,000 selling price less intercompany cost to Salt Co. of $85,000). The December 31, 19X8 worksheet adjustment must consider this so as to recognize the full gain on sale in the year in which it actually occurred through an outside sale as follows:

Retained earnings – Pepper Co.	15,000	
Gain – land sale		15,000

To record realized gain on land sale in appropriate fiscal year (12/31/X8).

note: The consolidated gain on land sale will now appropriately appear in the 19X8 consolidated income statement at the full $20,000 ($5,000 recorded by Salt Co.plus $15,000 recorded by worksheet adjustment).

PROBLEM 9-2: Assume the same facts as those described in problem 9-1 except that the19X6 sale of land was made by the 80%-owned Salt Co. to its parent Pepper Co.

Required:
(*a*) Prepare the December 31, 19X6 consolidating worksheet elimination entry required.
(*b*) Assuming Salt Co. had net income for the year ended December 31, 19X6 on its separate books of $50,000 (including the gain on land sale), determine minority interest in combined income of the consolidated group for the year ended December 31, 19X6.
(*c*) Prepare the December 31, 19X7 consolidating worksheet elimination entry required.

Answer:

(*a*)

Gain – land sale	15,000	
Land		15,000

To restore land to its original cost and eliminate intercompany gain on sale (12/31/X6). (Note that the full gain is eliminated even though a minority interest exists).

(*b*)

Minority interest in Salt Co. net income:	
20% × Salt Co. net income of $50,000	$10,000
Less: Minority interest in $15,000 gain on intercompany sale at 20%	(3,000)
Minority interest in combined net income	$ 7,000

(*c*)

Retained earnings – Pepper Co. (80%)	12,000	
Minority interest (20%)	3,000	
Land		15,000

To restore land to its original cost and eliminate intercompany gain on sale (12/31/X7).

PROBLEM 9-3: Perch Co. owns 70% of Scrod Co. and on January 5, 19X5, Perch sold Scrod a piece of equipment. The following facts are pertinent to the sale:

Selling price of the equipment	$55,000
Estimated service life remaining on the 1/1/X5 sale date	5 years
Estimated salvage value	$0
Depreciation method used	straight-line
Original cost of equipment to Perch Co.	$100,000

Accumulated depreciation on the books of Perch Co. as of the 1/1/X5 sale date	$75,000
Estimated service life of equipment on the date of original acquisition by Perch Co.	20 years

Required:

(*a*) Prepare the journal entries actually made on the separate books of Perch Co. and Scrod Company to record the equipment sale.

(*b*) Prepare the consolidating worksheet elimination entries necessary as of December 31, 19X5.

(*c*) Is minority interest in combined net income affected for the year ended December 31, 19X5 by the intercompany equipment sale?

(*d*) Prepare the consolidating worksheet elimination entries necessary as of December 31, 19X6.

Answer:

(*a*) The 19X5 entries were:

Perch Co. Books

Cash	55,000	
Accum. depr. - equip.	75,000	
Equipment		100,000
Gain – equip. sale		30,000
To record equipment sale.		

Scrod Co. Books

Equipment	55,000	
Cash		55,000
To record equipment purchase.		
Depreciation expense	11,000	
Accum. depr. – equip.		11,000
To record 19X5 depreciation.		

(*b*)

Gain – equipment sale	30,000	
Equipment	45,000	
Accum. depr. – equip.		75,000

To restore equipment to its original cost and carry value and eliminate inter-company gain on sale (12/31/X5).

Accum. depr. – equip.	6,000	
Depreciation expense		6,000

To eliminate excess depreciation recorded on Scrod Co.'s separate books (for 19X5)

Note: Scrod Co. depreciation expense ($55,000 divided by 5 years)	$11,000
Depreciation expense based on original cost to Perch Co. ($100,000 divided by 20 years)	5,000
Excess depreciation expense	$ 6,000

(*c*) No. Although minority interest exists, it is unaffected by the intercompany gain on equipment sale since the sale was downstream (from parent to subsidiary. Therefore the entire gain on sale is attributable to the parent Perch Co. only.

(*d*)

Retained earnings – Perch Co.	30,000	
Equipment	45,000	
Accum. depr. – equip.		75,000

To restore equipment to its original cost and carry value and eliminate the intercompany gain which has been closed (12/31/X6).

Accum. depr. – equip. (2 years)	12,000	
Retained earnings – Perch Co. (19X5)		6,000
Depreciation expense (19X6)		6,000

To eliminate excess depreciation recorded on Scrod Co.'s separate books (for 19X5 and 19X6)

PROBLEM 9-4: Assume the same facts as those described in problem 9-3 except that the sale was an upstream sale from Scrod Co. to Perch Co. On that basis, answer requirements a, b, c, and d of problem 9-3.

Answer:

(*a*) The 19X5 entries were:

Perch Co. Books

Equipment	55,000	
Cash		75,000
To record equipment purchase.		
Depreciation expense	11,000	
Accum. depr. equip.		11,000
To record 19X5 depreciation.		

Scrod Co. Books

Cash	55,000	
Accum. depr. equip.	75,000	
Equipment		100,000
Gain – equip. sale		30,000
To record equipment sale.		

(*b*) This answer is the same as the answer to part (*b*) of problem 9-3, except that the excess depreciation has been recorded by Perch Co.

(*c*) Yes. Minority interest in combined net income is affected for the year ended December 31, 19X5 since the intercompany sale is upstream, and Scrod Co. is less than 100% owned by Perch Co. The effect may be seen as follows:

Minority interest in Scrod Co. net income:	
30% × Scrod Co. 19X5 net income	$xxxx
Less: 30% minority interest in $30,000 intercompany gain on equipment sale	(9,000)
Plus: 30% minority interest in $6,000 excessive depreciation expense charge	1,800
Minority interest in combined ned income	$xxxx

(*d*)

Retained earnings – Perch Co. (70%)	21,000	
Minority interest (30%)	9,000	
Equipment	45,000	
Accum. depr. – equip.		75,000

To restore equipment to its original cost and carry value and eliminate the intercompany gain which has been closed (12/31/X6).

Accum. depr. – equip. (2 years)	12,000	
Retained earnings – Perch Co. (19X5)		4,200
Minority interest (19X5)		1,800
Depreciation expense (19X6)		6,000

To eliminate excess depreciation recorded on Perch Co.'s separate books (for 19X5 and 19X6).

PROBLEM 9-5: (Comprehensive. This problem includes most of the information provided in problems 6-5 and 7-5, but also includes additional information about intercompany transactions in the areas of inventory, land, and depreciable assets discussed in chapters 8 and 9.) On January 1, 19X4, Bear Co. paid $450,000 for 90% of Cub Co. common stock in a business combination appropriately accounted for as a purchase. Bear Co. carries its "Investment in Cub Co." using the equity method. On January 1, 19X4, Cub Company's net asset book values and fair values were equal except as follows:

	Book Values	Fair Values	Difference
Inventory	$ 50,000	$ 56,000*	$ 6,000
Land	200,000	210,000	10,000
Building (net)	800,000	1,000,000**	200,000
	$1,050,000	$1,266,000	$216,000

*Completely sold during 19X4.
**As of 1/1/X4, 20 year life remains, straight-line depreciation and no salvage value used.

During 19X4, the following additional intercompany transactions occurred:

(*a*) Bear Co. sold land to Cub Co. for $5,000 on June 6, 19X4. The original cost of the land to Bear Co. was $4,000. Cub Co. had not sold the land as of December 31, 19X4 and intends to build a parking lot on the site.

(*b*) Bear Co. made total sales to Cub Co. of $25,000 in inventories during 19X4. Bear Co. charges a 20% gross profit on its sales. Cub Co.'s ending inventory (at 12/31/X4) included $10,000 from these intercompany purchases. Also, Cub Co. owed Bear Co.$6,000 on account at 12/31/X4. Cub Co. made no inventory sales to Bear Co. during 19X4. No inventory purchases or sales occurred between Bear Co. and Cub Co. prior to 19X4.

(*c*) Cub Co. sold equipment to Bear Co. on January 3, 19X4 for $12,000. Cub Co.'s original equipment cost was $10,000 and accumulated depreciation on Cub Co.'s books on the intercompany sale date was $5,000. The remaining equipment life at the sale date was 5 years and the equipment is depreciated on a straight-line basis with no salvage value assumed.

Based on the information provided in this question and on the 12/31/X4 trial balance columns for Bear Co. and Cub Co. provided on Schedule I, complete the consolidating worksheet (Schedule I) which follows:

Schedule I Problem 9-5

Bear Co. & 90% Owned Subsidiary Cub Co.

Consolidating Worksheet for the Year Ended 12/31/X4

Account name	Bear Co. Dr. (Cr.)	Cub Co. Dr. (Cr.)	Eliminations Dr	Eliminations (Cr.)	CONSOLIDATED Dr.(Cr.) Income Statement	Retained Earnings	Balance Sheet
Cash	50,000	20,000					
Accounts receiv. (net)	30,000	20,000					
Inventory	50,000	30,000					
Land	50,000	20,000					
Equipment	500,000	200,000					
Accum. depr. – equip.	(250,000)	(160,000)					
Building	2,000,000	1,000,000					
Accum. depr. – bldg.	(800,000)	(240,000)					
Investment in Cub Co.	470,160						
Accounts payable	(490,000)	(330,000)					
Bonds payable	(500,000)	(300,000)					
Common stock:							
Bear Co.	(200,000)						
Cub Co.		(90,000)					
Additional paid in capital-common:							
Bear Co.	(400,000)						
Cub Co.		(60,000)					
Retained earnings:							
Bear Co.	(280,000)						
Cub Co.		(70,000)					
Dividends declared:							
Bear Co.	20,000						
Cub Co.		10,000					
Sales	(850,000)	(300,000)					
Investment inc.	(29,160)						
Cost of goods sold	400,000	160,000					
Depreciation. exp.	75,000	50,000					
Operating exp.	155,000	47,000					
Gain – land sale	(1,000)						
Gain – equip. sale		(7,000)					
Totals	0	0					
Combined net income							
Minority interest							
Consolidated net income							
Consolidated retained earnings							
Total							
Total minority interest							

Answer: Note that the 1/1/X4 original investment cost of $450,000 represents the following items:

1/1/X4 Investment cost		$450,000
Book value of underlying net assets acquired (1/1/X4 equity)	$220,000	
Ownership level	× 90%	(198,000)
Excess cost over book value		252,000
Portion of excess attributable to:		
Inventory (90% × $6,000)		(5,400)
Land (90% × $10,000)		(9,000)
Building (90% × $200,000)		(180,000)
Goodwill		$ 57,600

The equity method amortization against investment income for 19X4 on Bear's books is as follows:

Inventory (all sold during 19X4)	$ 5,400
Building ($180,000 ÷ 20 years)	9,000
Goodwill ($57,600 ÷ 40 years)	1,440
	$15,840

Investment income consists of:

90% Cub Co. net income of $50,000	$45,000
Less: 19X4 Amortization	(15,840)
Investment income	$29,160

As of 12/31/X4, the "Investment in Cub Co." consists of the following items:

1/1/X4 Investment cost	$450,000
90% of Cub Co. net income for 19X4 of $50,000	45,000
19X4 Amortization of cost in excess of book value	(15,840)
90% of Cub Co. 19X4 dividends declared and paid of $10,000	(9,000)
12/31/X4 Investment in Cub Co.	$470,160

Based on this information the first two consolidating worksheet entries are as follows:

(1)	Common stock: Cub Co. (90%)	81,000	
	Additional paid-in capital: Cub Co. (90%)	54,000	
	Retained earnings: Cub Co. (90%)	63,000	
	Investment income	29,160	
	Inventory	5,400	
	Land	9,000	
	Building	180,000	
	Goodwill	57,600	
	Investment in Cub Co.		470,160
	Dividends declared: Cub Co.		9,000
	To eliminate Investment in Cub Co. against income and 90% of Cub Co. equity and dividends declared and to adjust Cub Co. net assets to fair value.		
(2)	Goodwill amortization	1,440	
	Cost of goods sold	5,400	
	Depreciation expense	9,000	
	Goodwill		1,440
	Inventory		5,400
	Accum. depreciation – building		9,000
	To amortize adjusted S Co. asset valuations and goodwill.		

Item (*a*) of the problem results in an overvaluation of land and in an intercompany gain on land sale by virtue of the following entries made on the separate books of Bear Co. and cub Co.:

Bear Co.			Cub Co.		
Cash	5,000		Land	5,000	
Land		4,000	Cash		5,000
Gain – land sale		1,000			

As a result, the following (third) consolidating worksheet elimination entry is required:

(3) Gain – land sale	1,000	
Land		1,000

To restore land to its original cost and eliminate intercompany gain on sale. (Although minority interest exists, this entry has no effect on minority interest in combined net income since the sale was downstream, from the parent to the subsidiary.)

Item (*b*) of the problem results in the need for the following (fourth, fifth, and sixth) consolidating worksheet elimination entries:

(4) Sales	25,000	
Cost of goods sold		25,000

To eliminate intercompany inventory sales from Bear Co. to Cub Co.

(5) Cost of goods sold	2,000	
Inventory		2,000

To eliminate profit in ending inventory resulting from intercompany sales (20% gross profit on sales × $10,000 in ending inventory from intercompany sales). (Although minority interest exists, this entry has no effect on minority interest in combined net income since the sale was downstream, from the parent to the subsidiary.)

(6) Accounts payable	6,000	
Accounts receivable		6,000

To eliminate receivables and payables resulting from intercompany inventory sales.

Item (*c*) of the problem results in an overvaluation of the equipment's book or carry value, in an intercompany gain on equipment sale, and in excessive depreciation charges by virtue of the following entries made on the separate books of Bear Co. and Cub Co.:

Cub Co. (Subsidiary) Books			Bear Co. (Parent) Books		
Cash	12,000		Equipment	12,000	
Accum. depr. – equip.	5,000		Cash		12,000
Equipment		10,000			
Gain – equip. sale		7,000	Depreciation expense	2,400	
			Accum. depr. – equip.		2,400
			($12,000 divided by 5 year life remaining).		

As a result, the following (seventh and eighth) consolidating worksheet elimination entries are needed:

(7) Gain – equipment sale	7,000	
Accum. depr. – equip.		5,000
Equipment		2,000

To restore equipment to its original cost and carry value and eliminate intercompany gain on sale. (Minority interest in the combined net income exists and is affected by this elimination of intercompany gain on the equipment sale since the sale was upstream and the subsidiary Cub Co. is less than 100% owned by the parent Bear Co. See Schedule I – Problem 9-5 Answer for a description of the development of minority interest in Cub Co. net income.)

(8) Accum. depr. – equip. 1,400
    Depreciation expense 1,400
To eliminate excess depreciation recorded on Bear Co.'s separate books. ($2,400 depreciation expense per Bear Co. Books less $1,000 depreciation based on original sale date carry value. The original sale date carry value was $5,000 which, divided by 5 year remaining life, provides the depreciation for consolidation purposes of only $1,000.) Alternatively, the equipment's carry value on the sale date is overstated by $7,000 (Bear Co.'s purchase price $12,000 less original carry value $5,000). This $7,000 overvaluation divided by the remaining 5 year life also yields $1,400 excess depreciation. (Once again, minority interest in combined net income is affected by this entry as shown on Schedule I – Problem 9 Answer).

note: If the investment had been carried at cost rather than equity, consolidating worksheet elimination entries 1 and 2 would have been changed to entries 1, 2, and 3 as demonstrated in the answer to problem 7-5 of Chapter 7.

Schedule I Problem 9-5 Answer

Bear Co. & 90% Owned Subsidiary Cub Co.

Consolidating Worksheet for the Year Ended 12/31/X4

Account name	Bear Co. Dr. (Cr.)	Cub Co. Dr. (Cr.)	Eliminations Dr	Eliminations (Cr.)	CONSOLIDATED Dr.(Cr.) Income Statement	Retained Earnings	Balance Sheet
Cash	50,000	20,000					70,000
Accounts receiv. (net)	30,000	20,000		(6,000)[6]			44,000
Inventory	50,000	30,000	5,400[1]	(5,400)[2] (2,000)[5]			78,000
Land	50,000	20,000	9,000[1]	(1,000)[3]			78,000
Equipment	500,000	200,000		(2,000)[7]			698,000
Accum. depr. – equip.	(250,000)	(160,000)	1,400[8]	(5,000)[7]			(413,600)
Building	2,000,000	1,000,000	180,000[1]				3,180,000
Accum. depr. – bldg.	(800,000)	(240,000)		(9,000)[2]			(1,049,000)
Investment in Cub Co.	470,160			(470,160)[1]			0
Goodwill			57,600[1]	(1,440)[2]			56,160
Accounts payable	(490,000)	(330,000)	6,000[6]				(814,000)
Bonds payable	(500,000)	(300,000)					(800,000)
Common stock:							
Bear Co.	(200,000)						(200,000)
Cub Co.		(90,000)	81,000[1]				(9,000)[M]
Additional paid in capital-common:							
Bear Co.	(400,000)						(400,000)
Cub Co.		(60,000)	54,000[1]				(6,000)[M]
Retained earnings:							
Bear Co.	(280,000)					(280,000)	
Cub Co.		(70,000)	63,000[1]				(7,000)[M]
Dividends declared:							
Bear Co.	20,000					20,000	
Cub Co.		10,000		(9,000)[1]			1,000[M]
Sales	(850,000)	(300,000)	25,000[4]		(1,125,000)		
Investment inc.	(29,160)		29,160[1]		0		
Goodwill amortiz.			1,440[2]		1,440		
Cost of goods sold	400,000	160,000	5,400[8] 2,000[5]	(25,000)[4]	542,400		
Depreciation. exp.	75,000	50,000	9,000[2]	(1,400)[8]	132,600		
Operating exp.	155,000	47,000			202,000		
Gain – land sale	(1,000)		1,000[3]		0		
Gain – equip. sale		(7,000)	7,000[7]		0		
Totals	0	0	537,400	(537,400)			
Combined net income					(246,560)		
*Minority interest					4,440		(4,440)[M]
Consolidated net income					(242,120)	(242,120)	
Consolidated retained earnings						(502,120)	(502,120)
Total							0
Total minority interest (sum of items marked "M")							(25,440)[M]

*Minority interest (M = minority interest) in Cub Co. net income:	
10% of Cub Co. net income of $50,000	$5,000
Less: 10% minority interest in unrealized profit on intercompany equipment sale profit of $7,000 ($12,000 selling price less $5,000 Cub Co. book value)	(700)
Plus: Minority interest in excess depreciation (10% × $1,400)	140
Minority interest in Cub Co. net income	$4,440

Notes on Schedule 1:

1) To eliminate Investment in Cub Co. against investment income and 90% of Cub Co. equity and dividends declared and to adjust Cub Co. net assets to fair value.
2) To amortize adjusted S Co. asset valuations and goodwill.
3) To restore land to its original cost and eliminate intercompany gain on sale.
4) To eliminate intercompany inventory sales from Bear Co. to Cub Co.
5) To eliminate profit in ending inventory resulting from intercompany sales (20% gross profit on sales × $10,000 in ending inventory from intercompany sales).
6) To eliminate receivables and payables resulting from intercompany inventory sales.
7) To restore equipment to its original cost and carry value and eliminate intercompany gain on sale.
8) To eliminate excess depreciation recorded on Bear Co.'s separate books.

10 INTERCOMPANY LONG-TERM DEBT, SUBSIDIARY PREFERRED STOCK

THIS CHAPTER IS ABOUT

- ☑ **Elimination of Intercompany Long-Term Debt**
- ☑ **Treatment of A Subsidiary's Preferred Stock**
- ☑ **Changes in The Parent Company's Ownership Interest**
- ☑ **Effects of Subsidiary Stock Dividends and Splits**
- ☑ **Subsidiary Treasury Stock**
- ☑ **Indirect and Reciprocal Holdings**

10-1. Elimination of Intercompany Long-Term Debt.

Affiliated companies must eliminate the combined economic entity's intercompany long-term debt and related investment in bonds or notes.

Although each affiliate is a separate legal entity, any decision to loan or borrow money among affiliates merely results in intercompany transactions which must be eliminated in the consolidation process. These loans and investments held on an intercompany basis require reciprocal accounts for debt principal and investment, interest expense and interest income, and interest receivable and interest payable which must be eliminated during the consolidation process.

A. Affiliates must eliminate intercompany long-term debt and related investment.

A special problem arises when a company invests in the long-term debt of its affiliate by buying its bonds on the open market. Such a purchase effectively extinguishes the issuing company's long-term debt from the consolidated point of view, because the liability once owed to outside lenders is now completely owed within the combined economic entity.

In this case, the purchasing affiliate records on its separate books the investment in the bonds and the interest income on the investment, as it would for any investment in bonds. During the consolidation process, however, the following three items must be considered in the consolidating worksheet elimination process:

1. elimination of intercompany long-term debt.
2. elimination of intercompany interest income and expense related to the intercompany debt purchase.
3. elimination of any intercompany interest receivable or payable related to the intercompany debt purchase.

If the parent buys the bonds of its subsidiary, or if a wholly owned subsidiary buys the bonds of the parent, the most basic consolidating worksheet entry to eliminate the intercompany long-term debt related to the bond purchase is:

Bonds Payable	$X	
Investment in Affiliate Bonds		$X

The entry to eliminate intercompany interest income and expense related to the bond purchase is:

Interest Income	$X	
Interest Expense		$X

The entry to eliminate any outstanding interest receivable or payable related to the bond purchase is:

Interest Payable	$X	
Interest Receivable		$X

(***note:*** These entries are described as "most basic" since they do not contemplate bond premium or discount, which will be described in 10-1.B, 10-1.C, and 10-1.D.)

EXAMPLE 10-1: On January 1, 19X1, S Co. issued 5-year, 10 percent bonds at face value for $50,000. These bonds pay interest semiannually on July 1 and January 1.

On January 1, 19X2, P Co. purchased 70% of S Co.'s common stock, and also purchased S Co. bonds at face value for $40,000 from investors in the open market. The journal entries made on the separate books of P Co. and S Co. during 19X1 and 19X2 relative to these bonds were:

Date	P Co. Books			S Co. Books		
1/1/X1				Cash	50,000	
				Bonds payable		50,000
				To record bond issue at face value.		
7/1/X1				Interest expense	2,500	
				Cash		2,500
				To record payment of semi-annual interest (10% × $50,000 × 1/2 year)		
12/31/X1				Interest expense	2,500	
				Interest payable		2,500
				To accrue semi-annual interest.		
1/1/X2				Interest payable	2,500	
				Cash		2,500
				To pay semi-annual interest.		
1/1/X2	Investment in S Co. Bonds	40,000				
	Cash		40,000			
	To record investment in S Co. bonds.					
7/1/X2	Cash	2,000		Interest expense	2,500	
	Interest income		2,000	Cash		2,500
	To record receipt of semi-annual interest.			To record payment of semi-annual interest.		
12/31/X2	Interest receivable	2,000		Interest expense	2,500	
	Interest income		2,000	Interest payable		2,500
	To accrue semi-annual interest.			To accrue semi-annual interest.		

During 19X2, P Co. held 80% of S Co.'s outstanding bonds payable, effectively extinguishing 80% of S Co.'s long-term bonded debt. S Co. makes no entries on its separate books to acknowledge this, but on December 31, 19X2, the combined economic entity will make the following entry on the consolidating worksheet to eliminate the intercompany long-term debt:

Bonds payable	40,000	
Investment in S Co. Bonds		40,000

To eliminate intercompany investment. (Results in consolidated bonds payable of $10,000 ($50,000 less $40,000).)

This entry results in a consolidated Bonds Payable account of $10,000 ($50,000 credit and $40,000 debit), which is the face value of the bonds still held by outside investors.

The combined economic entity must also eliminate 80% of the interest income paid by S Co. during the year to its bondholders, against P Co.'s interest income:

Interest income—P Co.	4,000	
Interest expense—S Co.		4,000
To eliminate intercompany income and expense for 19X2.		

This eliminating entry results in no consolidated interest income, and a consolidated interest expense of $1,000 (20% of $5,000), which is the amount paid to outside bondholders (that is, original interest expense recorded by S Co. of $5,000 less $4,000 intercompany interest expense).

Finally, the consolidated economic entity must eliminate the intercompany interest due but not paid as of December 31, 19X2:

Interest payable	2,000	
Interest receivable		2,000
To eliminate intercompany interest payable and receivable as of 12/31/X2.		

These same eliminating entries will be needed during the consolidation process for each year until the bonds reach maturity.

B. Discount or premium on the intercompany bond purchase may exist, complicating the elimination process.

Often, discount or premium on the long-term debt or the investment in long-term debt may exist, making the elimination process more complex. In the year in which intercompany debt is first held by companies within the consolidated group, any difference between the carrying value of the investment in debt and the carrying value of the debt itself must be viewed as gain or loss on early extinguishment of debt as required by APB 26, "Early Extinguishment of Debt." If the gain or loss is material, Statement on Financial Accounting Standards 4, "Reporting Gains and Losses from Extinguishment of Debt" would require treatment of the gain or loss as an extraordinary item. Such differences may often exist since the investor's cost of the investment purchased in the open market at some date after the original issue date may not be the same as the original debt issue price of the investee. For example, the stated interest rate on the face value of the debt issued may have been above the market rate for debt issues of similar risk on the original debt issue date. This would result in a willingness on the part of investors to pay a premium on the original issue. If, however, an investor later sells the original investment to a new investor at a time when the market interest rate for similar debt is above the original debt issue stated rate, the investment in debt would be sold to the new investor at a discount.

C. Attribution of early extinguishment of debt.

When intercompany debt eliminated is (*a*) debt owed by the parent company to the subsidiary company or (*b*) debt owed by a 100% owned subsidiary company to the parent company, any gain or loss on early extinguishment of debt is attributed to the parent company. But when intercompany debt eliminated is debt owed by a less than 100% owned subsidiary company to the parent company (that is, minority interest exists), any gain or loss on early extinguishment of debt is attributed to both the parent company and to minority interest in the subsidiary company. (This is illustrated in Exhibits 10-A and 10-B of Example 10-2.)

D. Any discount or premium on the sale or purchase of the bonds is amortized over the life of the bonds.

The discount or premium paid by original outside investors on the bond issue is amortized by the issuing affiliate over the life of the bonds. Likewise, the purchasing affiliate amortizes its discount or premium paid to the outside investors over the remaining life of the bonds.

For the issuing affiliate, the amortizing of a premium on the original sale results in a decrease in the interest expense, and amortizing of a discount results in an increase in interest expense. For the purchasing affiliate, amortizing a discount on its purchase results in an increase in its interest income, and amortizing a premium results in a decrease in its interest income.

EXAMPLE 10-2: On 1/1/X1, S Co. issued five-year, 10% bonds with a face value of $50,000 for $55,000, resulting in a premium of $5,000. Interest on these bonds is payable semiannually on January 1 and July 1. The bonds mature on 1/1/X6.

On 1/1/X4, P Co., which owns 70% of S Co., bought in the open market S Co. bonds with a face value of $40,000 for $39,000, effectively retiring 80% of S Co.'s debt, and resulting in a discount on the purchase of $1,000 to P Co.

Both P Co. and S Co. amortize premiums and discounts using the straight-line method since no material difference between straight-line and effective yield amortization exists.

On 1/1/X4, the carrying value of the bonds on S Co.'s books was:

Original bond issue proceeds ($50,000 face plus $5,000 premium)	$55,000
Premium amortization to date (3 years at $1,000 per year)	3,000
Carrying value of bonds payable at 1/1/X4	$52,000
Less: Face value of bonds	50,000
Unamortized bond premium at 1/1/X4	$ 2,000

Note that 80% of the carrying value of the bonds payable (80% × $52,000 = $41,600) on S Co.'s separate books is not the same as the carrying value of P Co.'s investment in the bonds ($39,000). The difference of $2,600 ($41,600 less $39,000) represents the gain on early extinguishment of debt. That is, the combined economic entity paid only $39,000 to retire debt carried at $41,600. The relevant entries actually made on the books of P Co. and S Co. during 19X4, 19X5, and 19X6 are:

Date	P Co. Books			S Co. Books		
1/1/X4	Investment in S Co. Bonds	39,000				
	Cash		39,000			
	To record purchase of S Co. bonds.					
7/1/X4	Cash	2,000		Interest expense	2,500	
	Interest income		2,000	Cash		2,500
	To record receipt of semi-annual interest.			To record payment of semi-annual interest		
12/31/X4	Interest receivable	2,000		Interest expense	1,500	
	Investment in S Co. Bonds	500		Bond premium	1,000	
	Interest income		2,500	Interest payable		2,500
	To accrue semi-annual interest and amortize discount for year ($1,000 2 years = $500).			To accrue semi-annual interest and amortize premium for year ($5,000 5 years = $1,000).		
1/1/X5	Cash	2,000		Interest payable	2,500	
	Interest receivable		2,000	Cash		2,500
	To record receipt of semi-annual interest.			To record payment of semi-annual interest.		
7/1/X5	Cash	2,000		Interest expense	2,500	
	Interest income		2,000	Cash		2,500
	See 7/1/X4 entry explanation.			See 7/1/X4 entry explanation.		

Date	P Co. Books			S Co. Books		
12/31/X5	Interest receivable	2,000		Interest expense	1,500	
	Investment in S Co. Bonds	500		Bond premium	1,000	
	Interest income		2,500	Interest payable		2,500
	See 12/31/X4 entry explanation.			See 12/31/X4 entry explanation.		
1/1/X6	Cash	42,000		Bonds payable	50,000	
	Interest receivable		2,000	Interest payable	2,500	
	Investment in S. Co. Bonds		40,000	Cash		52,500
	To record cash receipts on investment maturity.			To record cash payments on debt maturity.		

No worksheet elimination entries will be needed for 19X6 and subsequent years since no debt or investment in debt will exist after the January 1, 19X6 payoff is made. However, based on the actual journal entries made on the books of P Co. and S Co. as just described, the following consolidating worksheet elimination entries are necessary for 19X4 and 19X5:

	Fiscal Year Ending December 31			
	19X4		19X5	
	Dr.	Cr.	Dr.	Cr.
1. Bonds payable (80% retired)	40,000		40,000	
Bond premium (80% retired)	1,600		1,600	
Investment in S Co. Bonds*		39,000		39,000
Gain on debt extinguishment		2,600		
Retained earnings—P Co. (70%)				1,820
Minority interest (30%)				780
To eliminate investment in long-term debt.				
*These are the account balances on the date the long-term debt became an intercompany holding, which was 1/1/X4.				
2. Interest payable	2,000		2,000	
Interest receivable		2,000		2,000
To eliminate intercompany interest receivable (payable).				
3. Interest income	4,500		4,500	
Retained earnings—P Co. (70%)	–		910	
Minority interest (30%)	–		390	
Interest expense		3,200		3,200
Bond premium (80%)		800		1,600
Investment in S Co. Bonds		500		1,000
To eliminate intercompany interest income ($4,500) and intercompany interest expense (80% of $4,000 = $3,200), balance remaining at year end in "Investment in S Co. Bonds," and to restore bond premium balance to 20% of unamortized premium at year end (20% × $1,000 at 12/31/X4 and 20% × $0 at 12.31/X5).				

Note that in addition to eliminating intercompany interest income and expense, consolidating worksheet entry 3 results in the appropriate bond premium balances in the consolidated balance sheets for the years ended December 31, 19X4 and 19X5:

	Dr.(Cr). 19X4	Dr.(Cr.) 19X5
12/31 Premium balance per S Co. books	($1,000)	$ 0
Worksheet entry 1	1,600	1,600
Worksheet entry 3	(800)	(1,600)
Unamortized bond premium	($ 200)*	$ 0**
	*20% of Unamortized Bond Premium of $1,000.	**20% of Unamortized Bond Premium of $0.

Entry 3 also results in the elimination of any remaining balance in the intercompany Investment in S Co. Bonds account:

	Dr.(Cr.) 19X4	Dr.(Cr.) 19X5
12/31 Investment in S Co. Bonds per P Co. books	$39,500	$40,000
Worksheet entry 1	(39,000)	(39,000)
Worksheet entry 3	(500)	(1,000)
12/31 Investment in S Co. Bonds per Consolidated Balance Sheet	$ 0	$ 0

Finally, note that worksheet elimination entry 1 results in a gain on debt extinguishment in 19X4 only. In 19X5, this gain having already been recognized in the 19X4 consolidated income statement, is now presumed to have been closed to retained earnings for worksheet adjustment purposes.

Since the bonds payable in question are carried on S Co. books and a minority interest exists, a portion of the gain (30% in this case) represents minority interest, and a portion of the gain (70% in this case) represents P Co. retained earnings, as shown in entry 1 for 19X5. The gain on early extinguishment represents nothing more than the difference between the carrying value of the bonds payable on S Co. books and the carrying value of the Investment in S Co. Bonds on P Co. books as of January 1, 19X4. Since the face value of both the debt and the investment are the same, this difference in carrying values is actually represented by the premium or discount on the books of S Co. and P Co. respectively:

1/1/X4	S Co. Unamortized bond premium on intercompany portion of debt (80% intercompany debt × $2,000 unamortized bond premium at 1/1/X4)	$1,600
1/1/X4	P Co. Unamortized discount on intercompany investment in bonds	1,000
	Gain on debt extinguishment	$2,600

The unamortized premium and discount on 1/1/X4, will be amortized over the next two years (19X4 and 19X5) actually decreasing interest expense on S Co.'s books, and increasing interest income on P Co.'s books. The consolidation process merely moves recognition of the full $2,600 in amortization ($1,000 discount on investment and $1,600 unamortized bond premium) to 1/1X4 as a gain on debt extinguishment since the debt no longer exists on 1/1/X4 from a consolidated viewpoint. The following partial consolidating worksheets, Exhibits 10A and 10B, (which assume a P Co. and S Co. combined net income of $150,000 for each of the years 19X4 and 19X5 and $50,000 in S Co. net income on its separate books for 19X4 and 19X5) show the effects of the elimination process:

Exhibit 10-A
P Co. and 70% Owned Subsidiary S Co.
(PARTIAL) Consolidating Worksheet for the Year Ended 12/31/X4

Year of Intercompany Bond Acquisition

Account Name	P Co. Dr. (Cr.)	S Co. Dr. (Cr.)	Eliminations Dr.	Eliminations (Cr.)	CONSOLIDATED Dr. (Cr.) Income Statement	Retained Earnings	Balance Sheet
Interest receivable	2,000			(2,000)[2]			0
Interest payable		(2,500)	2,000[1]				(500)
Investment in S Co. Bonds	39,500			(39,000)[1] (500)[3]			0
Bonds payable		(50,000)	40,000[1]				(10,000)
Bond premium		(1,000)	1,600[1]	(800)[3]			(200)
Interest income	(4,500)		4,500[3]		0		
Interest expense		4,000		(3,200)[3]	800		
Gain on debt extinguishment.				(2,600)[1]	(2,600)		
Various accounts.	xxxx	xxxx	xxxx	xxxx	xxxx	xxxx	xxxx
Totals	xxxx	xxxx	xxxx	xxxx			
Combined net income					(150,000)		
*Minority interest					15,390		(15,390)M
Consolidated net income					(134,610)	(134,610)	
Consolidated retained earnings						xxxx	xxxx
Total							0

M = Minority interest

* Minority interest in S Co. net income:

30% of S Co. net income of $50,000	$15,000
Plus: Minority interest in gain on debt extinguishment (30% × $2,600)	780
Less: Minority interest in discount amortization of $500 and premium amortization of 80% of$1,000 (30% × $1,300)	(390)
Minority interest in S Co. net income	$15,390

1 To eliminate Investment in S Co. Bonds and record consolidated gain on early extinguishment of debt.
2 To eliminate intercompany interest receivable and payable.
3 To eliminate intercompany interest income and expense and the balance remaining in Investment in S Co. Bonds, and to restore the bond premium balance to 20% of the unamortized bond premium at 12/31/X4 (20% of $1,000 unamortized bond premium or $200).

Exhibit A Points of Interest:

a) Minority interest in the gain on debt extinguishment exists in this case since the bonds payable which are presumed to have been retired the moment they became an intercompany holding are bonds payable on S Co.'s books. Therefore, gain on extinguishment is partially attributable to S Co. and its 30% minority shareholders. If the intercompany bonds payable were carried on P Co.'s books or if P Co. owned 100% of S Co., then minority interest in combined net income would not require adjustment, thereby simplifying the consolidation process somewhat.

b) P Co.'s Investment in S Co. Bonds, and the related interest receivable and interest income accounts are removed fully in the consolidation process.

c) S Co.'s bonds payable, bond premium, interest payable, and interest expense amounts carried to the consolidated financial statement columns represent only 20% of the original balances because 80% of the face amount of the debt ($40,000/$50,000) is now held on an intercompany basis.

Exhibit 10-B
P Co. and 70% Owned Subsidiary S Co.
(PARTIAL) Consolidating Worksheet for the Year Ended 12/31/X4

Year Subsequent to Intercompany Bond Acquisition

Account Name	P Co. Dr. (Cr.)	S Co. Dr. (Cr.)	Eliminations Dr.	Eliminations (Cr.)	CONSOLIDATED Dr. (Cr.) Income Statement	Retained Earnings	Balance Sheet
Interest receivable	2,000			(2,000)[2]			0
Interest payable		(2,500)	2,000[2]				(500)
Investment in S Co. Bonds	40,000			(39,000)[1] (1,000)[3]			0
Bonds payable		(50,000)	40,000[1]				(10,000)
Bond premium		0	1,600[1]	(1,600)[3]			0
Interest income	(4,500)		4,500[3]		0		
Interest expense		4,000		(3,200)[3]	800		
P. Co. Retained earnings	xxxx		910[3]	(1,820)[1]	0	xxxx	
Minority interest			390[3]	(780)[1]			(390)M
Various accounts.	xxxx	xxxx	xxxx	xxxx	xxxx	xxxx	xxxx
Totals	xxxx	xxxx	xxxx	xxxx			
	Combined net income				(150,000)		
	*Minority interest				14,610		(14,610)M
	Consolidated net income				(135,390)	(135,390)	
	Consolidated retained earnings					xxxx	xxxx
				Total			0

M = Minority interest

* Minority interest in S Co. net income:

30% of S Co. net income of $50,000	$15,000
Less: Minority interest in discount amortization of $500 and premium amortization of 80% of $1,000 unamortized discount on intercompany investment in bonds (30% × $1,300)	(390)
Minority interest in S Co. net income	$14,610

[1] To eliminate Investment in S Co. Bonds and record consolidated gain on early extinguishment of debt from prior year as 70% P Co. retained earnings and 30% minority interest.

[2] To eliminate intercompany interest receivable and payable.

[3] To eliminate intercompany interest income and expense and the balance remaining in Investment in S Co. Bonds, and to restore the bond premium balance to 20% of the unamortized bond premium at 12/31/X4 (20% of $1,000 unamortized bond premium or $200).

Exhibit B Points of Interest:

a) Minority interest in the gain on debt extinguishment exists in this case since the bonds payable which are presumed to have been retired the moment they became an intercompany holding are bonds payable on S Co.'s books. Therefore, gain on extinguishment is partially attributable to S Co. and its 30% minority shareholders. If the intercompany bonds payable were carried on P Co.'s books or if P Co. owned 100% of S Co., then minority interest in combined net income would not require adjustment, thereby simplifying the consolidation process somewhat.

b) P Co.'s Investment in S Co. Bonds, and the related interest receivable and interest income accounts are removed fully in the consolidation process.

c) S Co.'s bonds payable, bond premium, interest payable, and interest expense amounts carried to the consolidated financial statement columns represent only 20% of the original balances because 80% of the face amount of the debt ($40,000/$50,000) is now held on an intercompany basis.

E. Affiliates may also provide long-term loans to each other.

If the affiliates of a combined economic entity provide loans to each other, the intercompany note payable and receivable, the related interest expense and income, and any related interest payable and receivable accounts must, of course, be eliminated during the consolidation process. A special problem arises if one affiliate makes a loan to another and then sells the note receivable at a discount to an outside company. Such a sale is, in effect, borrowing the cash from an outside source, and the consolidation process must indicate such borrowing.

EXAMPLE 10-3: On December 31, 19X1, P Co. loaned $10,000 to its wholly owned subsidiary S Co. P Co. then immediately discounted the note receivable to its bank. These transactions are recorded as follows on the separate books of P Co. and S Co.:

P Co. Books			S Co. Books		
Notes receivable S Co.	10,000		Cash	10,000	
Cash		10,000	Notes payable—P Co.		10,000
To record loan to S Co.			To record loan from P Co.		
Cash	10,000				
Notes receivable discounted		10,000			
To record discounting of notes receivable by P Co. at a financial institution.					

If the note receivable had not been discounted by P Co., the December 31, 19X1 consolidating worksheet elimination entry would simply have been:

Notes payable—P Co.	10,000	
Notes receivable—S Co.		10,000
To eliminate intercompany borrowing.		

However, since P Co. and S Co. are viewed as one economic entity, and P Co. discounted the note with an outside company, the consolidated financial statements must reflect this outside borrowing. The December 31, 19X1 consolidating worksheet elimination entries are:

Notes payable—P Co.	10,000	
Notes receivable—S Co.		10,000
To eliminate intercompany borrowing.		
Notes receivable discounted	10,000	
Notes payable (outside creditor)		10,000
To reflect outside borrowing of the consolidated group.		

10-2. Treatment of a Subsidiary's Preferred Stock.

If a parent company invests in the common stock of a subsidiary that also has preferred stock issued and outstanding, the rights of the preferred stockholders to a minority interest in the subsidiary's income and equity must be considered during the consolidation process. The type of consideration needed to account for the preferred stock depends, of course, on the contractual rights attached to it.

Recall: Preferred stock may have all, none, or any combination of the following rights, as determined by the directors of the company at the time it issues the stock. The preferred stock may be:

1. **Cumulative**. Any dividends in arrears to the preferred stockholders must be paid before any dividend distribution may be made to the common stockholders.
2. **Participating**. Preferred stockholders may receive dividends in excess of the basic preferred amount, if additional amounts are paid to common shareholders.
3. **Convertible**. Preferred stock may be converted to common stock at a specified rate at the option of the preferred stockholder.
4. **Callable**. Preferred stock may be redeemed at a specified rate at the option of the issuing company.

At the very least, the subsidiary's preferred stockholders have a right in the subsidiary's equity equal to their stock's par value. If, however, the preferred stock has a liquidation value or call price above its par value, its right in the subsidiary's equity will usually be equal to the higher amount.

Further, if the stock is participating, or if it is cumulative with preferred dividends in arrears, then additional equity must be set aside to cover any dividends due the preferred stockholders.

The level of interest that the preferred stockholders have in the subsidiary's equity will, of course, reduce the level of the common stockholders' interest, and affect the consolidation process. In particular, the subsidiary's retained earnings must be correctly apportioned to the subsidiary's preferred and common stockholders during the consolidation. The result is that only the portion of retained earnings attributable to common stock held by the parent may be eliminated against the parent's Investment in Subsidiary Common Stock account. Any of the subsidiary equity attributable to preferred stock that is not owned by the parent is usually considered part of the minority interest.

A. On the acquisition date, the consolidated financial statements are affected by the rights of the preferred stock.

The particular combination of rights carried by a specific preferred stock determines how that stock is accounted for on the consolidated financial statements.

EXAMPLE 10-4: On 1/1/X1, P Co. bought 80% of the common stock of S Co. for $80,000. On that date, S Co. also had $20,000 in par value preferred stock outstanding, which was noncumulative, nonparticipating, had no call privilege, and had a liquidation value equal to its par value. The trial balances of P Co. and S Co. immediately after the purchase are shown in the first two columns of Exhibit 10-C.

This exhibit shows the single eliminating entry necessary to prepare a consolidated balance sheet on the date of the purchase. Because S Co.'s preferred stock has no rights that entitle it to additional equity above par in S Co., no additional entries are needed during the consolidation process to allocate S Co.'s retained earnings to the preferred stockholders. The $20,000 in the Preferred Stock account is attributable to the minority interest, and is clearly indicated as such on the balance sheet.

Exhibit 10-C
P Co. and 80% Owned Subsidiary S Co.
Consolidating Worksheet as of 1/1/X1

S Co. net asset fair values presumed equal to book values

Account name	P Co. Dr. (Cr.)	S Co. Dr. (Cr.)	Eliminations Dr.	Eliminations (Cr.)	CONSOLIDATED Balance Sheet
Assets (various)	430,000	200,000			630,000
Investment in S Co.	80,000			(80,000)[1]	0
Liabilities	(60,000)	(80,000)			(140,000)
Common stock: P Co.	(100,000)				(100,000)
S Co.		(40,000)	32,000[1]		(8,000)M
Additional paid-in capital: P Co.	(130,000)				(130,000)
S Co		(50,000)	40,000[1]		(10,000)M
Retained earnings: P Co.	(220,000)				(220,000)
S Co.		(10,000)	8,000[1]		(2,000)M
Preferred stock: S Co.		(20,000)			(20,000)M
Totals	0	0	80,000	(80,000)	0
Total minority interest					(40,000)

[1] To eliminate Investment in S Co. against S Co. equity.
M = Minority interest

EXAMPLE 10-5: Assume the same facts as Example 10-4, except that in this case the preferred stock is 10% cumulative, two years in arrears as of 1/1/X1, and fully participating. S Co.'s retained earnings as of 1/1/X1 are $10,000.

In this case a consolidating worksheet entry is necessary to attribute the correct amount of S Co.'s retained earnings to its preferred stockholders. First, the dividends in arrears must be attributed:

1/1/X1 S Co. Retained earnings	$10,000
Less: Dividends in arrears (2 yrs. × 10% × $20,000 par)	4,000
Subtotal	6,000

Then, because the preferred stock is fully participating, the dividends in excess of the preferred rate paid from the $6,000 are set off as well:

Subtotal	6,000
Less: Preferred stock participation of ($20,000 par/$60,000 total par) × $6,000	2,000
1/1/X1 S Co Retained earnings apportioned to S Co. Common stock	$ 4,000

Thus in this case $6,000 of S Co.'s retained earnings is attributable to the preferred stockholders. Exhibit 10-D shows a partial consolidating worksheet apportioning S Co.'s retained earnings to both preferred and common stockholders. Exhibit 10-D shows the entry to eliminate P Co.'s Investment in S Co. Common Stock account against S Co.'s equity, and the recording of goodwill.

Exhibit 10-D
P Co. and 80% Owned Subsidiary S Co.
Consolidating Worksheet as of 1/1/X1

S Co. net asset fair values presumed equal to book values

Account name	P Co. Dr. (Cr.)	S Co. Dr. (Cr.)	Eliminations Dr.	Eliminations (Cr.)	CONSOLIDATED Balance Sheet
Assets (various)	430,000	200,000			630,000
Investment in S Co.	80,000			(80,000)[2]	0
Goodwill			4,800[2]		4,800
Liabilities	(60,000)	(80,000)			(140,000)
Common stock:					
P Co.	(100,000)				(100,000)
S Co.		(40,000)	32,000[2]		(8,000)M
Additional paid-in capital: P Co.	(130,000)				(130,000)
S Co		(50,000)	40,000[2]		(10,000)M
Retained earnings:					
P Co.	(220,000)				(220,000)
S Co.		(10,000)	10,000[1]		0
Retained earnings —S Co.:					
—Common stock portion			3,200[2]	(4,000)[1]	(800)
—Pref. stock portion				(6,000)[1]	(6,000)M
Preferred stock:					
S Co.		(20,000)			(20,000)M
Totals	0	0	90,000	(90,000)	0
		Total minority interest			(44,000)

[1]To apportion S Co. retained earnings between common and preferred stock.
[2]To eliminate Investment in S Co. against S Co. equity and record goodwill.

note: The assumption in this case is that the fair and book values of S Co. net assets are equal. Therefore, the amount by which P Co.'s purchase price exceeds its interest in the underlying net assets of S Co. represents goodwill as follows:

P Co.'s purchase price			$80,000
S Co. total stockholders' equity on 1/1/X1		$120,000	
Less: S Co.'s preferred stock interest in total			
S Co. equity: Par	$20,000		
Arrears	4,000		
Participation	2,000	26,000	
S Co. equity attributable to S Co. common stock		94,000	
Multiply: P Co. interest in S Co. common stock		80%	75,200
Goodwill (per entry #2 above)			$4,800

B. In years after the acquisition, part of the subsidiary's income may be attributable to the preferred stockholders.

In the years after the acquisition, the parent company's equity in its subsidiary's net income may be affected by the rights of the preferred stockholders. If the subsidiary's preferred stock is participating or cumulative or both, the subsidiary's net income may be at least in part attributable to the preferred stockholders.

EXAMPLE 10-6: On 1/1/X1, P Co. bought 80% of S. Co.'s common stock for $80,000. On that date, S Co.'s net asset fair values and book values were equal. Among S Co.'s equity accounts was $20,000 of 10% cumulative, nonparticipating preferred stock, which was 3 years in arrears on the acquisition date. After the acquisition the trial balances of both companies were:

Account Name	1/1/X1 Trial Balance P Co. Dr. (Cr.)	1/1/X1 Trial Balance S Co. Dr. (Cr.)
Assets (various)	430,000	200,000
Investment in S Co.	80,000	
Goodwill		
Liabilities	(60,000)	(80,000)
Common Stock: P Co.	(100,000)	
S Co.		(50,000)
Additional paid-in capital: P Co.	(230,000)	
S Co.		(40,000)
Retained earnings:		
P Co.	(220,000)	
S Co.		(10,000)
Preferred stock: S Co.		(20,000)
Totals	0	0

S Co.'s net income for 19X1 was $22,000, and it declared no dividends. Goodwill of $4,800 (which will be amortized over 40 years) results from P Co.'s acquisition of S Co. as follows:

P Co.'s purchase price			$80,000
S Co. total stockholders' equity on 1/1/X1		$120,000	
Less: S Co.'s preferred stock interest in total S Co.'s equity: Par	$20,000		
Arrears (3 yrs @ $2,000 per year)	6,000	26,000	
S Co. equity attributable to S Co. common stock		94,000	
Multiply: P Co. interest in S Co. common stock		80%	75,200
Goodwill			$ 4,800

P Co. uses the equity method to carry its investment in S Co. and assigns a year life to goodwill. On 12/31/X1, P Co.'s Investment in S Co. account balance is calculated:

1/1/X1 Investment in S Co.		$80,000
S Co. 19X1 net income	$22,000	
Less: Portion of S Co. net income attributable to preferred stock (10% × $20,000 par cumulative preferred)	2,000	
S Co. 19X1 net income to common stock	20,000	
Multiply: P Co.'s interest in S Co.	80%	
P Co.'s interest in S Co. net income	$16,000	16,000
Less: Goodwill amortization ($4,800/40 years)		(120)
12/31/X1 Investment in S Co.		$95,880

When the combined economic entity of P Co. and S Co. prepares its consolidated financial statements on 12/31/X1, it must make three eliminating entries on the consolidating worksheet.

The first is to apportion S Co.'s $10,000 retained earnings to its common and preferred stock, in accordance with the rights of the preferred stock. At the acquisition date the preferred stock was $6,000 in arrears ($20,000 × 10% per year × 3 years = $6,000)

Retained Earnings—S Co.	10,000	
Retained Earnings Common Stock—S Co Portion		4,000
Retained Earnings Preferred Stock—S Co. Portion		6,000

This entry apportions $6,000 of subsidiary retained earnings to common shares and $4,000 of subsidiary retained earnings to preferred shares.

The second consolidating worksheet entry eliminates P Co.'s Investment account against its income from S Co. and 80% of S Co.'s equity, and records the goodwill:

Goodwill	4,800	
Common Stock—S Co. (80%)	40,000	
Additional Paid-In Capital—S Co. (80%)	32,000	
Retained Earnings—S Co. (80% of $4,000 remaining after entry 1)	3,200	
Investment Income	15,880	
Investment in S Co.		95,880

The third consolidating worksheet entry records the amortization of the goodwill after one year ($4,800/40 years = $120):

Expenses	120	
Goodwill		120

Exhibit 10-E is a partial consolidating worksheet for P Co. and S Co. on 12/31/X1, showing the effects of these eliminating entries.

Exhibit 10-E
P Co. and 80% Owned Subsidiary S Co.
Consolidating Worksheet for the Year Ended 12/31/X1

S Co. net asset fair values presumed equal to book values

Account Name	P Co. Dr. (Cr.)	S Co. Dr. (Cr.)	Eliminations Dr.	Eliminations (Cr.)	CONSOLIDATED Dr. (Cr.) Income Statement	Retained Earnings	Balance Sheet
Assets (various)	465,000	222,000					687,000
Investment in S Co.	95,880			(95,880)[2]			0
Goodwill			4,800[2]	(120)[3]			4,680
Liabilities	(60,000)	(80,000)					(140,000)
Common stock: P Co.	(100,000)						(100,000)
S Co.		(50,000)	40,000[2]				(10,000)M
Additional paid-in capital: P Co.	(130,000)						(130,000)
S Co.		(40,000)	32,000[2]				(8,000)M
Retained earnings: P Co.	(220,000)					(220,000)	
S Co.		(10,000)	10,000[1]				0
Retained earnings: S Co: —Common stock portion.			3,200[2]	(4,000)[1]			(800)M
—Pref. stock portion				(6,000)[1]			(6,000)M
Preferred stock S Co.:		(20,000)					(20,000)M
Revenues	(200,000)	(100,000)			(300,000)		
Expenses	165,000	78,000	120[3]		243,120		
Investment income	(15,880)		15,880[2]		0		
Totals	0	0	106,000	(106,000)			
Combined net income					(56,880)		
*Minority interest					6,000		(6,000)M
Consolidated net income					(50,880)	(50,880)	
Consolidated retained earnings						(270,880)	(270,880)
					Total		0
Total minority interest (sum of items marked "M")							(50,800)M

M = Minority interest

* Minority interest in net income:

Cumulative preferred shareholders' interest (10% × $20,000 par)	$2,000
Minority common shareholders' interest (20% × $20,000 S Co. net income available to common stock)	4,000
Total minority interest in S Co. net income for 19X1	$6,000

1 To apportion S Co. retained earnings between common and preferred stock.
2 To eliminate Investment in S Co. against investment income and 80% of S Co. equity and record goodwill.
3 To amortize goodwill.

C. A parent company may also invest in its subsidiary's preferred stock.

When a parent company acquires some or all of its subsidiary's preferred stock, the preferred stock is simply viewed as retired from a consolidated standpoint. A "gain" on this retirement (any excess of the book or carrying value of the preferred stock over its acquisition cost) is credited to additional paid-in capital. A "loss" on retirement (any excess acquisition cost over the book or carrying value of the preferred stock) is charged to additional paid-in capital to the extent that additional paid-in-capital is available, and any "loss" beyond that is charged to retained earnings. Such an investment, of course requires that any intercompany preferred stock transactions (dividend income, declaration, receivable or payable) must also be eliminated from the consolidated financial statements.

EXAMPLE 10-7: Assume all the information given in Example 10-6, with the following additional information. On 1/1/X1, P Co. also bought 40% of S Co.'s $20,000 par value preferred stock (which has a face value of 40% of $20,000 or $8,000) for $10,000 on the open market.

Recall from Example 10-6 that $6,000 of S Co.'s retained earnings must be apportioned to preferred stockholders. Because 40% of the preferred stock is effectively retired when P Co. buys it, 40% of the dividends in arrears, or $2,400 effectively does not exist from a consolidated viewpoint ($6,000 × 40% = $2,400). Thus this transaction results in a net "gain" to the combined economic entity of $400 based on the difference between the acquisition cost of P Co.'s Investment in S Co. preferred stock ($10,000) and the carrying value of S Co. preferred stock ($10,400, based on 40% of $20,000 par plus 40% of $6,000 dividends in arrears). Consequently, an additional entry is necessary on the consolidating worksheet to record the retirement of the preferred stock now owned by the combined entity, the "gain" on the purchase, and the resulting adjustment in the Additional Paid-In Capital account. This entry is shown on Exhibit 10-F as:

1) S Co. Preferred stock (40% × $20,000 par)	8,000	
S Co. Retained earnings (40% × preferred stock dividends in arrears of $6,000 at 1/1/X1)	2,400	
Investment in S Co. Preferred Stock		10,000
Additional paid-in capital		400

Exhibit 10-F shows the 12/31/X1 trial balances of P Co. and S Co. (Note that the Exhibit 10-F trial balance differs from the Exhibit 10-D trial balance in that Exhibit 10-F shows an Investment in S Co. Preferred Stock on P Co.'s books of $10,000 and $10,000 less in the account "Assets—various.") Also, Exhibit 10-F shows a different apportionment of S Co. retained earnings (entry 2) and a different calculation of minority interest in the 19X1 S Co. net income. (In future years, if S Co. declares and pays preferred stock dividends, then a reduced portion of S Co. retained earnings would be allocated to S Co. preferred stock.) Finally, Exhibit 10-F shows 12/31/X1 balances in P Co.'s Investment in S Co. and Investment income accounts based on the following:

1/1/X1 Investment in S Co. Common Stock		$80,000
19X1 S Co. net income	$22,000	
Less: Portion of S Co. net income attributable to preferred stock *outstanding* of $12,000 (10% × $12,000 par cumulative preferred outstanding)	1,200	
S Co. 19X1 net income to common stock	20,800	
Multiply: P Co.'s interest in S Co.	× 80%	
P Co.'s interest in S Co. net income	$16,640	16,640
Less: Goodwill amortization ($4,800/40 years)		(120)*
12/31/X1 Investment in S Co. Common Stock		$96,520

*Goodwill of $4,800 from the original 1/1X1 purchase has not changed and is calculated:

P Co.'s purchase price			$80,000
S Co. total stockholders' equity on 1/1/X1		$120,000	
Less: S Co.'s preferred stock deemed retired ($8,000 par plus $2,400 dividends in arrears)		10,400	
Adjusted total S Co. stockholders' equity		109,600	
Less: S Co.'s outstanding preferred stock interest in S Co.'s adjusted total stockholders' equity: Par	$12,000		
Arrears—3 yrs. @$1,200 per yr.	3,600	15,600	
S Co. equity attributable to S Co. common stock		94,000	
Multiply: P Co. interest in S Co. common stock		80%	75,200
Goodwill			$ 4,800

Exhibit 10-F
P Co. and 80% Owned Subsidiary S Co.
Consolidating Worksheet for the Year Ended 12/31/X1

S Co. net asset fair values presumed equal to book values

Account Name	P Co. Dr. (Cr.)	S Co. Dr. (Cr.)	Eliminations Dr.	Eliminations (Cr.)	CONSOLIDATED Dr. (Cr.) Income Statement	Retained Earnings	Balance Sheet
Assets (various)	455,000	222,000					677,000
Investment in S Co.							
Common stock	96,520			(96,520)[3]			0
Preferred stock	10,000			(10,000)[1]			0
Goodwill			4,800[3]	(120)[4]			4,680
Liabilities	(60,000)	(80,000)					(140,000)
Common stock: P Co.	(100,000)						(100,000)
S Co.		(50,000)	40,000[3]				(10,000)M
Additional paid-in capital: P Co.	(130,000)			(400)[1]			(130,400)
S Co.		(40,000)	32,000[3]				(8,000)M
Retained earnings:							
P Co.	(220,000)					(220,000)	
S Co.		(10,000)	2,400[1] 7,600[2]				0
Retained earnings: S Co:							
—Common stock portion.			3,200[3]	(4,000)[2]			(800)M
—Pref. stock portion				(3,600)[2]			(3,600)M
Preferred stock: S Co.		(20,000)	8,000[1]				(12,000)M
Revenues	(200,000)	(100,000)			(300,000)		
Expenses	165,000	78,000	120[4]		243,120		
Investment income	(16,520)		16,520[3]		0		
Totals	0	0	114,640	(114,640)			
Combined net income					(56,880)		
*Minority interest					5,360		(5,360)M
Consolidated net income					(51,520)	(51,520)	
Consolidated retained earnings						(271,520)	(271,520)
Total							0
Total minority interest (sum of items marked "M")							(39,760)M

M = Minority interest

* Minority interest in net income:

Cumulative preferred shareholders' interest (10% × $12,000 par outstanding)	$1,200
Minority common shareholders' interest (20% × $20,800 S Co. net income available to common stock)	4,160
Total minority interest in S Co. net income for 19X1	$5,360

1 To eliminate investment in 40% of S Co.'s preferred stock.

2 To apportion S Co. retained earnings between common and preferred stock. (At 1/1/X1, preferred stock was 3 years in arrears. S Co. preferred stock outstanding at par is $12,000 ($20,000 par less $8,000 retired). Arrears are therefore 10% of $12,000 for 3 years or $3,600 at 1/1/X1.

3 To eliminate Investment in S Co. against investment income and 80% of S Co. equity and record goodwill.

4 To amortize goodwill ($4,800/40 years = $120).

10-3. Changes in the Parent Company's Ownership Interest.

After a company acquires the controlling interest in another company through the purchase of its common stock, several types of transactions may take place that will alter the level of ownership the parent company has in its subsidiary. These changes must be accounted for in the consolidated financial statements. First, the parent may choose to acquire some or all of the remaining minority interest in its subsidiary. Second, the parent may choose to sell part or all of its interest in its subsidiary. Third, the subsidiary may issue more common stock, which may alter the ownership levels.

A. A parent may acquire some or all of the minority interest in its subsidiary.

For a number of reasons (to increase combined profits, to take advantage of favorable market conditions, etc.) a parent company may choose to reduce the minority interest and increase its controlling interest in a subsidiary by buying additional blocks of the subsidiary's common stock on the open market. APB Opinion 16, "Accounting for Business Combinations," requires that a parent company's acquisition of some or all of its subsidiary's minority interest be accounted for using the purchase method (rather than the pooling-of-interest method), so such transactions present no new accounting issues not already discussed in previous chapters which addressed the purchase method of accounting. However, the mechanics of the consolidation process become a bit more cumbersome.

The cost of each block of the subsidiary's common stock acquired by the parent must be compared with the fair and book values of the subsidiary's net assets on the date of the purchase to determine if any goodwill or adjustment to the values of the net assets (and any subsequent amortization) is necessary (see Chapter 7).

After a block of the minority's stock is acquired by the parent, the combined economic entity accounts for any remaining minority interest in the subsidiary as described in previous chapters. Note, however, that during the preparation of the consolidated financial statements the percentage of the minority's ownership level at the end of the period should be used to determine the minority's interest in the subsidiary's Common Stock, Additional Paid-In Capital, and Beginning Retained Earnings equity accounts.

EXAMPLE 10-8: On 1/1/X1, P Co. acquired a 70% interest in S. Co. for $80,000. On that date, S Co.'s book and fair values were equal, and its stockholders' equity was:

Common stock	$ 50,000
Retained earnings	50,000
Total stockholders' equity	$100,000

On 1/1/X2, P Co. purchased an additional 20% interest in S Co. for $30,000. On that date, S Co.'s book and fair values were equal except for Land, which had a fair value $10,000 above its book value. On 1/1/X2, S Co.'s stockholders' equity was:

Common stock	$ 50,000
Retained earnings	80,000
Total stockholders' equity	$130,000

S Co. had the following activity in 19X1 and 19X2:

	19X1	19X2
Net income	$30,000	$40,000
Dividends declared and paid	$ 0	$20,000

P. Co.'s two purchases can be analyzed as shown:

	Acquisition of:	
	1/1/X1	1/1/X2
Purchase price	$80,000	$30,000
S Co. stockholders' equity (book value) acquired:		
70% × $100,000	(70,000)	
20% × $130,000		(26,000)
Excess cost over book value	10,000	4,000
Excess cost over book value attributable to S co.'s net assets carried below fair value:		
Land: (20% × $10,000)		(2,000)
Goodwill	$10,000	$ 2,000

If the Investment in S Co. account is carried at equity by P Co., the 12/31/X2 balance is:

1/1/X1 Cost (Block 1)	$ 80,000
19X1 S Co. net income $30,000 × 70%	21,000
19X1 Goodwill amortization ($10,000/40 years)	(250)
1/1/X2 Cost (Block 2)	30,000
19X2 S Co. net income $40,000 × 90%	36,000
19X2 Goodwill amortization:	
Block 1: ($10,000/40 years)	(250)
Block 2: ($ 2,000/40 years)	(50)
19X2 S Co. dividends $20,000 × 90%	(18,000)
12/31/X2 Investment in S Co. (balance)	$148,450

When the combined economic entity prepares consolidated financial statements on 12/31/X2, it must make the following consolidating worksheet elimination entries.

		Debit	Credit
1.	S Co. Common stock (90% × $50,000 par)	45,000	
	S Co. Retained earnings (90% × $80,000)	72,000	
	Land	2,000	
	Goodwill	11,750*	
	Investment income	35,700**	
	S Co. dividends declared (90% × $20,000)		18,000
	Investment in S Co.		148,450

To eliminate the Investment in S Co. and the investment income against S Co. equity and dividend declarations, and to adjust S Co. net assets and record goodwill.

* $12,000 less $250 in 19X1 goodwill amortization.
**$36,000 less $300 in 19X2 goodwill amortization.

		Debit	Credit
2.	Goodwill amortization	300	
	Goodwill		300

To amortize goodwill (block 1 amortization of $250 plus block 2 amortization of $50).

B. A parent company may sell all or part of its interest in a subsidiary.

For a number of reasons (to raise cash, to take advantage of favorable market conditions, to get rid of a poorly performing operation), a parent may choose to reduce its controlling interest and increase the minority interest in a subsidiary by selling its shares of the subsidiary's stock on the open market. Such a sale is accounted for the same way as the sale of any noncurrent assets. Any difference between the parent's carrying value of the portion of investment sold and the selling price received is recorded by the parent as a gain or loss on sale. No major change in the consolidating worksheet eliminating entries will be needed, except that the minority interest in the subsidiary's equity and net income will increase accordingly, and the parent's Investment in Subsidiary account will decrease to reflect both its reduced investment level and its decreased ownership percentage.

C. A subsidiary may issue additional shares of stock.

In order to increase its capital and expand its operations a subsidiary may (with the consent of its parent, of course) offer additional shares of its common stock to the public.

If the parent company buys a greater percentage of the new stock than its percentage of ownership in the subsidiary, its level of ownership in the subsidiary will naturally increase. Any difference between the parent's cost for its additional shares and the increase in the parent's interest in the subsidiary's net assets resulting from the purchase, results in either goodwill or an adjustment to the fair values of specific subsidiary assets. Any goodwill or adjustment to the subsidiary's net assets are amortized in future years during the consolidation process. The consolidation process after a subsidiary issues additional shares of stock is essentially the same, except that the parent company and minority interest levels will change accordingly, and any adjustment to the Investment in Subsidiary account will be amortized. The procedures to account for these transactions were described in previous chapters.

If the parent company buys a smaller percentage of the new stock than its percentage of ownership in the subsidiary, its level of ownership in the subsidiary will naturally decrease, and the minority interest will increase. Further, any decrease in the parent's level of ownership is treated as a sale. The dollar value of the change in the parent's ownership level in its subsidiary as a result of new stock being issued by the subsidiary should be computed. The parent company records this change on its books as an adjustment to its Investment in Subsidiary account, and as a Gain (if its investment increases) or a Loss (if its investment decreases).

If the parent company buys a percentage of the new stock that is equal to its percentage of ownership in the subsidiary, its ownership interest remains the same. Because the parent buys the stock directly from its subsidiary (rather than on the open market), there is no difference between the parent's cost of its investment and its interest in the increase in the subsidiary's increase in its Common Stock or Additional Paid-In Capital accounts. Therefore no goodwill or need to revalue the subsidiary's assets will result from such a sale.

10-4. Effects of Subsidiary Splits and Stock Dividends.

A. Subsidiary stock splits have no effect on the consolidation process.

When a subsidiary declares a stock split, only the total number of outstanding shares changes; the parent's Investment in Subsidiary account balance, and the subsidiary's net asset and equity accounts, remain exactly the same. Therefore a stock split by the subsidiary has no effect on the consolidation process.

B. Subsidiary stock dividends have little effect on the consolidation process.

When a subsidiary issues shares of common stock as a dividend, all shareholders of the subsidiary's common stock retain the same percentage of ownership as they did before the dividend was declared. Only the total number of shares, and the number of shares held by each shareholder, increases. Thus there is no change in the parent's Investment in Subsidiary account balance, or in its ownership percentage.

The only complication regarding a subsidiary stock dividend may arise from the fact that the subsidiary must "capitalize" its stock dividend. That is, it records the conversion of its retained earnings (the dividends paid out) to capital (stock) by decreasing its Retained Earnings account and increasing its Common Stock account (and possibly its Additional Paid-In Capital account). Once these adjustments are made on the subsidiary's separate books, the consolidation process proceeds as usual, and the parent's Investment account is eliminated against the appropriate percentage of the subsidiary's revalued equity accounts.

Note that although the consolidated retained earnings would not be changed by such a revaluation of the subsidiary's equity accounts, the true change in the subsidiary's retained earnings, from the date of the parent's original investment in the subsidiary to the end of the current accounting period, may be concealed. (This unadjusted change would have to be increased by stock dividend charges to retained earnings to determine the true charge.) If the parent company carries its Investment in Subsidiary on a cost basis, the Investment account balance must be adjusted to a beginning-of-the-year position (as if the investment had been carried at equity) before the consolidation process continues (see Chapter 7).

10-5. Subsidiary Treasury Stock

A. A subsidiary's treasury stock is considered retired by the combined economic entity.

A parent company calculates its ownership percentage in its subsidiary based on the outstanding shares of subsidiary stock. Any treasury stock held by the subsidiary is considered by the combined economic entity to be retired. During the consolidation process an entry must be made on the consolidating worksheet to eliminate the subsidiary's treasury stock against its equity accounts.

EXAMPLE 10-9: On 12/31/X1, P Co. acquired all 99,000 outstanding shares of S Co. for $200,000. On that date S Co. held 1,000 shares of treasury stock, for which it had paid $1,500. S Co.'s net asset fair values and book values were equal, and its stockholders' equity was:

Common stock, $1 par	$100,000
Additional paid-in capital (100,000 shares ÷ 20,000 shares = $0.20/share)	20,000
Retained earnings	51,500
Subtotal	171,500
Less: 1,000 shares of treasury stock, at cost	1,500
Total stockholders' equity	$170,000

When the combined economic entity of P Co. and S Co. prepares consolidated financial statements after the purchase on 12/31/X1, it must make a worksheet elimination entry to retire S Co.'s treasury stock against S Co.'s equity accounts:

S Co. Common stock (1,000 shares @ $1 par)	1,000	
S Co. Additional paid-in capital (1,000 shares @ $.20)	200	
S Co. Retained earnings	300	
S Co. Treasury stock		1,500
To treat S Co. treasury stock as retired.		

Because P Co. bought all the outstanding shares of S Co., its ownership interest is 100% (not 99%). Therefore, goodwill resulting from the purchase is determined as:

P Co. purchase price of investment		$200,000
S Co. net assets	$170,000	
P Co. interest acquired	100%	170,000
Goodwill (assuming S Co. net asset fair and book values are equal)		$ 30,000

The entry on the consolidating worksheet to eliminate P Co.'s Investment in S Co. account is:

S Co. Common stock	99,000	
S Co. Additional paid-in capital	19,800	
S Co. Retained earnings	51,200	
Goodwill	30,000	
Investment in S Co.		200,000
To eliminate Investment in S Co. against S Co. equity and record goodwill.		

B. Purchase by a subsidiary of treasury stock at a price above or below book value changes the subsidiary's book value.

When a subsidiary buys shares of treasury stock from minority stockholders, it reduces the total number of shares outstanding, and therefore increases the percentage of its parent's ownership. But the subsidiary may pay a price for its treasury stock that differs from that stock's book value. If it pays more than the stock's book value, then the subsidiary's overall book value will decrease. If it pays less, then its overall book value will increase. In either case, the increase in the parent's ownership interest in the subsidiary will be the same, because the same number of subsidiary shares is retired. However, if the value of the parent's Investment in Subsidiary account changes as a result of the price the subsidiary paid for treasury shares, then the parent must make an entry on its separate books to adjust its Investment account, and to increase or decrease its Additional Paid-In Capital account, by the amount of the change in the subsidiary's book value. If, for example, the parent owns

85% of the subsidiary after the acquisition of treasury stock, and the subsidiary spent $2,000 morethan book value to acquire those shares, the subsidiary's book value decreases by $2,000, and the parent must decrease its Investment in Subsidiary and Additional Paid-In Capital accounts by $1,700 (2,000 × 85% = 1,700):

Additional Paid-In Capital	1,700	
Investment in Subsidiary		1,700

Likewise, if the subsidiary spent $2,000 less than book value to acquire the shares, its book value increases by $2,000, and the parent increases its accounts by $1,700:

Investment in Subsidiary	1,700	
Additional Paid-In Capital		1,700

S Co. Balance Sheet (before treasury stock acquisition)

Cash	$ 22,000	Common stock, 50,000 shares, $1 par*	$50,000
Other assets	103,000	Retained earnings	75,000
	$125,000		$125,000

*P Co. owns 39,100 shares or 78.2% of S Co. stock outstanding.
Therefore, P Co. owns 78.2% of $125,000 or $97,750
note: Book value per share = $125,000/50,000 shares = $2.50

If S Co. buys 4,000 shares of treasury stock at $3.00 per share then S. Co. will record the acquisition as:

Treasury stock	$12,000	
Cash		$12,000

Note that this is a payment of $2,000 above book value:

Paid: $3.00 × 4,000 shares =	$12,000
Book value: $2.50 × 4,000 shares	10,000
Amount paid above book value	$ 2,000

But S Co.'s balance sheet is now:

S Co. Balance Sheet (after treasury stock acquisition)

Cash	$ 10,000	Common stock, 50,000 shares, $1 par*	$50,000
Other assets	103,000	Retained earnings	75,000
		Treasury stock (at cost)	(12,000)
	$113,000		$113,000

*P Co. still owns 39,100 shares but this now represents 85% of S. Co stock outstanding (39,100/46,000 shares).
Therefore, P Co. owns 85% of $113,000 or $96,050.

Note adjustment needed:

Before S Co. purchased treasury stock, P Co. owned 78.2% of $125,000 or	$97,750
After S Co. purchased treasury stock, P Co. owned 85% of $113,000 or	$96,050
Difference	$ 1,700

This difference results in an adjusting entry on P. Co.'s separate books:

Additional paid-in capital	$1,700	
Investment in S Co.		$1,700

To reduce investment as a result of S Co. purchase of treasury stock at $2,000 above book value (based on P Co. 85% interest × $2,000).

10-6. Indirect and Reciprocal Holdings

A. There are a number of ways a parent company can exercise indirect control over its subsidiaries.

In all the examples used so far, the parent company's interest in the subsidiary company (or companies) was a direct controlling interest. However, a parent-subsidiary relationship may exist by virtue of an indirect controlling interest as shown in the following two cases.

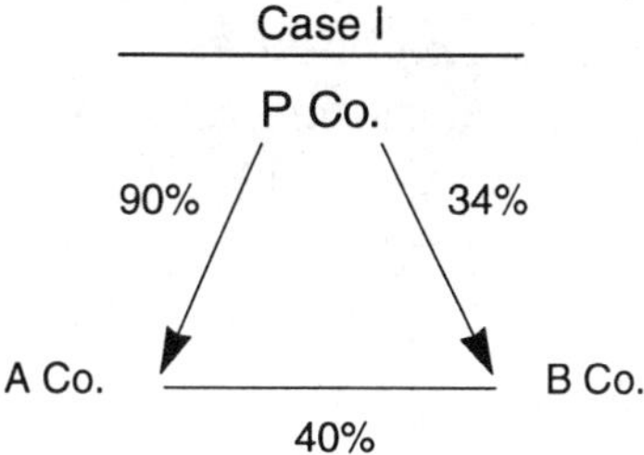

In case I, P Co. owns a direct controlling (90%) interest in A Co. and an indirect controlling (34% plus 36% or 70%) interest in B Co. Therefore, consolidated financial statements are generally necessary for P Co., A Co., and B Co.

Case II

P Co. —80%→ A Co. —75%→ B Co.

In case II, P Co. owns a direct controlling interest (80%) in A Co. and an indirect controlling interest (80% × 75% = 60%) in B Co. Again, consolidated financial statements for P Co., A Co., and B Co. would generally be necessary.

B. When indirect control exists, eliminate all intercompany investment during the consolidation process.

When an indirect interest exists between a parent and one of its subsidiaries, the consolidated financial statements should include the indirect holding as part of the combined economic entity. All intercompany investments must be eliminated, following the procedures shown in this chapter and in Chapters 4 through 9. That is, the first subsidiary's investment in the second is eliminated, then the parent's investment in the first subsidiary (and possibly the second, depending on the exact configuration) is also eliminated.

EXAMPLE 10-10: On 1/1/X1, P Co. bought an 80 percent interest in A Co. for $100,000. On that date, A Co.'s net asset fair values and book values were equal, and its stockholder equity was:

A Co. Common stock (no par)	$ 50,000
A Co. Retained earnings	50,000
A Co. Total stockholders' equity	$100,000

This transaction resulted in goodwill of $20,000 to A Co. ($100,000 purchase price – $80,000 assets acquired = $20,000 goodwill).

Also on 1/1/X1, A Co. bought a 75% interest in B Co. for $41,500. On that date, B Co.'s net asset fair values and book values were equal, and its stockholder equity was:

B Co. Common stock	$15,000
A Co. Retained earnings	35,000
A Co. Total stockholders' equity	$50,000

This transaction resulted in goodwill to B Co. of $4,000 ($41,500 purchase price – $37,500 assets acquired = $4,000 goodwill).

When the newly combined economic entity of P Co., A Co., and B Co. prepares consolidated financial statements on 1/1/X1, it must make two entries on the consolidating worksheet. The first is to eliminate A Co.'s investment in B Co., and to record the goodwill. The second is to eliminate P Co.'s investment in A Co., and to record that goodwill.

Exhibit 10-G shows the consolidating worksheet for P Co. and its subsidiaries (both directly and indirectly held) on 1/1/X1. Note that if A Co. or B Co. fair values and book values were not equal, then their net assets would need to be appropriately revalued, and subsequently amortized.

Exhibit 10-G
P Co. and Subsidiaries A Co. and B Co.
Consolidating Worksheet as of 1/1/X1

A and B Co. net asset fair values presumed equal to book values

Account name	P Co. Dr. (Cr.)	A Co. Dr. (Cr.)	B Co. Dr. (Cr.)	Eliminations Dr.	Eliminations (Cr.)	Consolidated Balance Sheet Dr. (Cr.)
Assets (various)	600,000	68,500	65,000			733,500
Investment in A Co.	100,000				(100,000)[2]	0
Investment in B Co.		41,500			(41,500)[1]	0
Goodwill*				20,000[2]		20,000
Goodwill**				4,000[1]		4,000
Liabilities (various)	(100,000)	(10,000)	(15,000)			(125,000)
Common stock:						
P Co.	(350,000)					(350,000)M
A Co.		(50,000)		40,000[2]		(10,000)M
B Co.			(15,000)	11,250[1]		(3,750)M
Retained earnings:						
P Co.	(250,000)					(250,000)M
A Co.		(50,000)		40,000[2]		(10,000)M
B Co.			(35,000)	26,250[1]		(8,750)M
Totals	0	0	0	141,500	(141,500)	0

M = Minority interest
*P Co. paid $100,000 for 80% of A Co.'s net assets totalling $100,000 fair and book value, resulting in goodwill of $20,000 ($100,000 - (80% × 100,000)).
**A Co. paid $41,500 for 75% of B Co.'s net assets totalling $50,000 fair and book value, resulting in goodwill of $4,000 ($41,500 - (75% × $50,000)).
[1]To eliminate A Co.'s 75% interest in B Co. and record goodwill.
[2]To eliminate P Co.'s 80% interest in A Co. and record goodwill.
note: If A Co. or B Co. fair values and book values were not equal, then net asset revaluations and subsequent amortization would be necessary as already demonstrated in Chapters 4, 5, 6, and 7.

C. In subsequent years, continue to eliminate all intercompany investment.

When a combined entity prepares consolidated financial statements after the date of the acquisition, it continues to eliminate all intercompany investment.

EXAMPLE 10-11: Refer to the information given in Example 10-10. The combined economic entity of P Co. and its subsidiaries A Co. and B Co. carries its investments using the equity method.

On 12/31/X1, the combined group prepares consolidated financial statements. The trial balances on that date for all three companies are given in the first three columns of Exhibit 10-H.

A Co.'s Investment in B Co. account balance at 12/31/X1 shown on Exhibit 10-H is calculated as:

1/1/X1	Investment in B Co.	$41,500
Plus:	75% × B Co. 19X1 income of $15,000	11,250
Less:	Goodwill amortization ($4,000/40 years)	(100)
Less	75% × B Co. 19X1 dividends of $10,000	(7,500)
12/31/X1	Investment in B Co.	$45,150

The first two entries on the 12/31/X1 consolidating worksheet are to eliminate this investment, and to record the amortization of goodwill:

		Debit	Credit
1.	B Co. Common stock (75%)	11,250	
	B Co. Retained earnings (75%)	26,250	
	Goodwill	4,000	
	Investment income ($11,250 less 100)	11,150	
	Dividends declared (75%)		7,500
	Investment in B Co.		45,150
	To eliminate Investment in B Co. and investment income against B Co. equity and dividend declarations and record goodwill.		
2.	Goodwill amortization (expense)	100	
	Goodwill		100
	To amortize goodwill ($4,000/40 years).		

A Co.'s total income for the year ended 12/31/X1, including income from its investment in B Co., is $15,000:

A Co. Revenues	$75,000
Less: A Co. Expenses	71,150
Subtotal	3,850
Plus: Investment income	11,150
A Co. 19X1 Net Income	$15,000

P Co.'s Investment in A Co. account balance at 12/31/X1 as shown on Exhibit 10-H is calculated as:

1/1/X1	Investment in A Co.	$100,000
Plus:	80% × A Co. 19X1 income of $15,000	12,000
Less:	Goodwill amortization ($20,000/40 years)	(500)
Less	80% × A Co. 19X1 dividends of $0	0
12/31/X1	Investment in A Co.	$111,500

The next two entries on the 12/31/X1 consolidating worksheet are to eliminate this investment, and to record the amortization of goodwill:

		Debit	Credit
3.	A Co. Common stock (80%)	40,000	
	A Co. Retained earnings (80%)	40,000	
	Investment Income	11,500	
	Goodwill	20,000	
	Investment in A Co.		111,500
	To eliminate Investment in A Co. and investment income against A Co. equity and record goodwill.		
4.	Goodwill amortization (expense)	500	
	Goodwill		500
	To amortize goodwill ($20,000/40 years).		

Exhibit 10-H shows the partial consolidating worksheet for these transactions.

Exhibit 10-H
P Co. and Subsidiaries A Co. and B Co.
Consolidating Worksheet for the Year Ended 12/31/X1

A and B Co. net asset fair values presumed equal to book values

Account Name	P Co. Dr. (Cr.)	A Co. Dr. (Cr.)	B Co. Dr. (Cr)	Eliminations Dr.	Eliminations (Cr.)	CONSOLIDATED Dr. (Cr.) Income Statement	Retained Earnings	Balance Sheet
Assets (various)	640,000	75,000	60,000					775,000
Investment in A Co.	111,500				(111,500)[3]			0
Investment in B Co.		45,150			(45,150)[1]			0
Goodwill				20,000[3]	(500)[4]			19.500
Goodwill				4,000[1]	(100)[2]			3,900
Liabilities (various)	(120,000)	(5,150)	(5,000)					(130,150)
Common stock:								
P Co.	(350,000)							(350,000)
A Co.		(50,000)		40,000[3]				(10,000)[M]
B Co.			(15,000)	11,250[1]				(3,750)[M]
Retained earnings:								
P Co.	(250,000)						(250,000)	
A Co.		(50,000)		40,000[3]				(10,000)[M]
B Co.			(35,000)	26,250[1]				(8,750)[M]
Dividends declared:								
P Co.	30,000						30,000	
A Co.		0						0[M]
B Co.			10,000		(7,500)[1]			2,500[M]
Investment income:								
From A Co.	(11,500)			11,500[2]		0		
From B Co.		(11,150)		11,150[1]		0		
Revenues	(100,000)	(75,000)	(50,000)			(225,000)		
Expenses	50,000	71,150	35,000	100[2] 500[4]		156,750		
Totals	0	0	0	164,750	(164,750)			
Combined net income						(68,250)		
*Minority interest						6,750		(6,750)[M]
Consolidated net income						(61,500)	(61,500)	
Consolidated retained earnings							(281,500)	(281,500)
Total								0
Total minority interest (sum of items marked "M")								(36,750)[M]

M = Minority interest

* Minority interest in combined net income:

Minority interest in B Co. net income: 25% of B Co. net income of $15,000	$3,750
Minority interest in A Co. net income: 20% of A Co. net income of $15,000	3,000
Minority interest in combined net income	$6,750

[1] To eliminate investment in B Co. and investment income against B Co. equity and declarations and record goodwill.

[2] To amortize goodwill ($4,000/40 years).

[3] To eliminate investment in A Co. and investment income against A Co. equity and record goodwill.

[4] To amortize goodwill ($20,000/40 years).

D. A reciprocal relationship exists when a subsidiary holds stock in its parent.

A subsidiary may hold the stock of, and therefore own a minority interest in the parent. Such a situation is called a **reciprocal relationship**. From the consolidated point of view, shares of the parent company held by the subsidiary which are not intended for resale are considered retired. In such a case, the subsidiary's investment is eliminated against the parent's equity. If the subsidiary intends to resell the stock, such stock should be considered temporary treasury stock.

EXAMPLE 10-12: S Co. acquired 1,000 shares of its parent P Co.'s stock on the open market at $15 per share for $15,000. The par value per share on P Co.'s books is $10 and additional paid-in capital $4 per share.

If S Co. has no intention to resell the stock, then it is considered retired, and an entry is made on the consolidating worksheet to eliminate the Investment in P Co. account, and to decrease P Co.'s equity:

P Co. Common stock ($10 par × 1,000 shares)	10,000	
P Co. Additional paid in capital ($4 × 1,000 shares	4,000	
P Co. Retained earnings	1,000	
Investment in P Co.		15,000
To eliminate S Co. Investment in P Co.		

If S Co. plans to resell the P Co. stock, its acquisition is considered a treasury purchase, and the consolidating worksheet records it as such:

Treasury stock (at cost)	15,000	
Investment in P Co.		15,000
To eliminate S Co. Investment in P Co.		

RAISE YOUR GRADES

Can you explain . . . ?

- ☑ why affiliated companies must eliminate intercompany long-term debt
- ☑ the three types of eliminating entries that may be necessary after an intercompany bond purchase
- ☑ how to treat any premium or discount that may result from an intercompany bond purchase
- ☑ how to amortize a premium or discount that results from an intercompany bond purchase
- ☑ how to treat the sale of an intercompany note receivable at a discount to an outside company
- ☑ how the rights of a subsidiary's preferred stock may affect the preparation of consolidated financial statements
- ☑ how to allocate a subsidiary's retained earnings or net income to its preferred stock and common stock
- ☑ how to account for a company's investment in its affiliate's preferred stock
- ☑ how to account for a change in ownership interest between affiliates when the parent acquires some or all of the subsidiary's minority interest
- ☑ how to account for a change in ownership interest between affiliates when the parent sells part or all of its interest in the subsidiary
- ☑ how to account for a change in ownership interest between affiliates when the subsidiary issues more common stock

- ☑ how to account for stock splits and stock dividends by the subsidiary
- ☑ how to account for a subsidiary's treasury stock
- ☑ how a purchase of treasury stock above or below book value may change the value of the parent's investment in its subsidiary
- ☑ how a parent may indirectly (as well as directly) obtain control over a subsidiary
- ☑ how to account for indirect ownership in the consolidated financial statements
- ☑ a reciprocal relationship between affiliates
- ☑ how to account for a reciprocal relationship when the subsidiary does not plan to resell the stock
- ☑ how to account for a reciprocal relationship when the subsidiary plans to resell the stock

SUMMARY

1. If a parent company invests in bonds payable (or other long-term debt) of the subsidiary company (or the subsidiary invests in bonds payable of the parent company), the debt is viewed as retired from a consolidated perspective.
2. Intercompany long-term debt should be eliminated with consolidated gain or loss in the year the debt is first held on an intercompany basis for the difference between the carrying values of the long-term debt and the investment (if any):

Bonds payable	x	
Unamortized premium on debt (if any)	x	
Unamortized discount on debt (if any)		x
Investment in Debt Securities (carrying value)		x
Gain on debt extinguishment		x*

*Alternatively, debit loss on debt extinguishment if applicable.

3. In years subsequent to the year in which long-term debt is first held on an intercompany basis, the gain (or loss) for any difference between the carrying values of the long-term debt and the investment is credited (or charged) to parent retained earnings (or to both parent retained earnings and minority interest if the debt was originally held by a subsidiary in which a minority interest exists).
4. Minority interest in combined net income is affected by its share of gain (loss) on extinguishment, and by its share of premium or discount amortization (see Exhibits 10-A and 10-B).
5. All intercompany bond (long-term debt) interest receivable, payable, expense, and income must be eliminated in the consolidation process.
6. If a subsidiary company's equity includes issued and outstanding preferred stock, the preferred stock is viewed as additional minority interest.
7. Preferred stock rights (liquidation value, cumulative rights and related arrearages, participation rights) must be considered in the consolidation process as a portion of subsidiary retained earnings unavailable to (not owned by) the subsidiary company's common shareholders. This situation results in a need to apportion retained earnings between the subsidiary company's common and preferred stock. Such rights also may affect minority interest in the combined net income of the consolidated group.
8. If an intercompany investment in preferred stock exists (parent invests in subsidiary preferred stock or vice-versa), the preferred stock investment is viewed as retired and must be eliminated against the portion of stockholders' equity to which it relates. Any excess preferred stock book value over investment cost results in a credit to additional paid in capital. Any excess investment cost over preferred stock book value results in a charge first to additional paid in capital on a pro-rata basis, and then, if necessary, in a charge to retained earnings.

9. If a parent company acquires some or all of the minority interest of a subsidiary (block acquisition), minority interest decreases and controlling interest increases. Such a block acquisition is viewed as a purchase. Therefore, if the purchase price exceeds the fair value of the portion of subsidiary net assets acquired, goodwill results. If differences between subsidiary net asset fair and book values exist on the block acquisition date, they will also be recorded and amortized in the consolidation process. The end of the period minority interest percentage remaining is used to determine minority interest in subsidiary common stock, additional paid in capital, and retained earnings.
10. Sale by a parent company of any portion of its interest in a subsidiary is treated as a sale of a noncurrent asset with gain or loss recorded for any difference between book value and selling price of the investment. Such sales result in an increased minority interest and a decreased controlling interest.
11. If a subsidiary company issues additional shares of stock, controlling interest may:
    - increase if the parent buys more than its proportionate share of the additional issue.
    - remain the same if the parent buys a proportionate share of the additional issue.
    - decrease if the parent buys less than its proportionate share of the additional issue.

    These factors, of course, may affect the development of minority interest in the consolidation process.
12. Subsidiary stock dividends and splits do not change the level of parent company interest in the subsidiary company.
13. Subsidiary treasury stock is generally viewed as retired stock from a consolidated perspective, and a worksheet elimination entry retiring treasury stock against related subsidiary equity should be made. The parent company's percentage interest in the subsidiary company is computed on the basis of parent company shares owned divided by subsidiary company shares issued *and outstanding*. Treasury stock is not outstanding stock.
14. Subsidiary treasury stock purchased a a price above or below book value will change the overall value of the subsidiary, and therefore the parent's Investment account balance.
15. A parent company may have an indirect interest in a company which gives the parent control over that company. When this occurs, a parent-subsidiary relationship exists, and consequently, there is a need for consolidation of that subsidiary.
16. A subsidiary may invest in its parent's stock. When such a reciprocal relationship exists, the subsidiary's investment in the parent is generally eliminated by charging the related parent equity (retirement method) or by charging treasury stock (treasury stock method).

RAPID REVIEW

1. If one affiliate of a consolidated group invests in another affiliate's long-term debt, and in the year the intercompany holding first develops a difference exists between the balance in the "Investment in Debt" asset account and the long-term debt carrying value, in the consolidation process this difference should be
   (*a*) charged to additional paid in capital or to retained earnings (if a "loss" exists) or credited to additional paid-in capital (if a "gain" exists).
   (*b*) charged to loss on extinguishment of debt or credited to gain on extinguishment of debt.
   (*c*) a deferred charge or a deferred credit from consolidation.
   (*d*) ignored since the bonds are not viewed as constructively retired.
   (*e*) none of the above.
2. Gain or loss resulting from intercompany long-term debt holdings is recorded in the consolidated process, and both the debt-issuing company and the purchasing company record their respective portions of the gain or loss.
   (*a*) True
   (*b*) False
3. In all periods during which bonds are held on an intercompany basis, interest income, interest expense, interest receivable, and interest payable relative to these intercompany holdings must also be eliminated.
   (*a*) True
   (*b*) False

4. From a consolidated perspective, the existence of subsidiary preferred stock is generally viewed as
(*a*) additional consolidated equity (additional paid in capital or preferred stock).
(*b*) treasury stock.
(*c*) retired stock.
(*d*) minority interest.

5. If preferred stock rights (cumulative, participating) exist, these rights
(*a*) have no special impact on the consolidation process since preferred stock must still simply be treated as additional minority interest.
(*b*) will never affect minority interest in the combined net income of the consolidated group.
(*c*) have no effect on either the percentage or dollar amount of controlling interest in combined net income of the consolidated group.
(*d*) may result in both a need to apportion subsidiary retained earnings between common and preferred shareholders, and in an adjustment to minority interest in combined net income of the consolidated group.

6. If an intercompany investment in preferred stock exists, from a consolidated perspective, this investment is viewed as
(*a*) treasury stock.
(*b*) additional minority interest.
(*c*) a retirement of preferred stock.
(*d*) an item not affecting the consolidation process.

7. An intercompany investment in preferred stock is eliminated in the consolidation process against the portion of stockholders' equity (preferred stock at par, related additional paid-in capital, and related retained earnings) to which it relates. Any difference between the investment in preferred stock balance and the related equity is charged (or credited) to
(*a*) loss (or gain) on retirement.
(*b*) additional paid-in capital and retained earnings (or additional paid-in capital).
(*c*) treasury stock (or deferred credit from preferred stock retirement).
(*d*) deferred loss (or deferred gain) on retirement.

8. When a parent company acquires some or all of the minority interest in a block acquisition, the transaction is
(*a*) accounted for as a pooling of interests.
(*b*) accounted for as purchase.

9. If a parent company sells any portion of its interest in a subsidiary company, any difference between the selling price and investment carrying value is viewed from a consolidated perspective as a
(*a*) credit to additional paid-in capital (if "gain" on sale) or debit to additional paid-in capital or retained earnings (if "loss" on sale).
(*b*) deferred credit from consolidations (if "gain" on sale) or deferred charge from consolidation (if "loss" on sale). (These deferrals should be amortized against consolidated net income of future periods.)
(*c*) gain or loss on sale on the parent company's books in the same manner as such gains or losses are determined in the sale of any noncurrent asset.
(*d*) none of the above.

10. If a subsidiary issues additional shares of stock, the implications of such stock issues must be considered in the consolidation process as they relate to
(*a*) the controlling and minority interests.
(*b*) the subsidiary's product line(s).
(*c*) the parent's product line(s).
(*d*) none of the above.

11. Subsidiary stock dividends will change the percentage of parent and minority interest, and must therefore be considered in the consolidation process.
(*a*) True
(*b*) False

12. Subsidiary treasury stock is generally viewed from a consolidated perspective as
   (*a*) an asset.
   (*b*) a contra-equity account.
   (*c*) a consolidated loss on retirement.
   (*d*) a retirement of stock.

13. Prichard Co. owns 90% of Stanley Co. and 30% of Silver Co. Also, Stanley owns 50% of Silver Co. The companies which should be included in the development of consolidated financial statements are
   (*a*) Prichard and Stanley.
   (*b*) Prichard and Silver.
   (*c*) Stanley and Silver.
   (*d*) Prichard, Stanley, and Silver.

14. A subsidiary's investment in parent company stock is termed a reciprocal relationship, and in such a relationship, the investment in the parent's stock, from a consolidated perspective, is
   (*a*) eliminated by charging related parent company equity, or by charging treasury stock.
   (*b*) not eliminated.
   (*c*) eliminated by charging loss on investment retirement.
   (*d*) eliminated by charging goodwill from consolidation.

Answers

1. (*b*)
2. (*b*) The consolidated gain or loss is not recorded on any affiliate's books. It is a worksheet elimination. The bonds payable and the investment in bonds accounts continue to be carried on the books of the separate companies.
3. (*a*)
4. (*d*)
5. (*d*)
6. (*c*)
7. (*b*)
8. (*b*)
9. (*c*)
10. (*a*)
11. (*b*)
12. (*d*)
13. (*d*) ***note:*** Prichard Co. directly owns a controlling interest in Stanley Co., but also owns an indirect controlling interest in Silver Co. totalling 75% (30% + (90% × 50%)).
14. (*a*)

SOLVED PROBLEMS

PROBLEM 10-1: Pringle Co. owns 90% of Salem Co. On January 1, 1989, Pringle Co. purchased Salem Co. bonds on the open market at 100 for $100,000. The bonds are 10 year, 10% stated rate bonds, and were originally issued on January 1, 1981 by Salem Co. at face value. The bonds reach maturity on January 1, 1991, and pay interest semiannually on July 1 and January 1 each year.

(*a*) Prepare the December 31, 1988 consolidating worksheet elimination entries.
(*b*) Prepare the December 31, 1989 consolidating worksheet elimination entries.
(*c*) Prepare the December 31, 1990 consolidating worksheet elimination entries.

Answer:

(*a*) No entries required. Bonds were not yet held on an intercompany basis at 12/31/88.

(*b*)

	Dr.	Cr.
Bonds payable	100,000	
Investment in S Co. Bonds		100,000
To eliminate intercompany bond holdings.		
Interest income	10,000	
Interest expense		10,000
To eliminate intercompany interest income and expense. ($100,000 × 10% × full year.)		
Interest payable	5,000	
Interest receivable		5,000
To eliminate intercompany interest payable and receivable. ($100,000 × 10% × one-half year.)		

(*c*) Same entries as shown in answer to part *b*, because debt is still outstanding at 12/31/90. On 1/1/91, the debt will be paid and the investment account removed. Therefore, no eliminations will be needed for the year ending 12/31/91.

PROBLEM 10-2: Prepare the date of intercompany acquisition worksheet elimination entries required for each of the five situations listed below involving a parent company's acquisition of a subsidiary company's bonds on the open market.

	Parent Company's Books @ Acquisition Date		Subsidiary Company's Books @ Acquisition Date	
Situation	Investment Cost	Face Value of Debt Acquired	Bonds Payable (Face Value)	Unamortized Premium (Discount)
1	$104,000	$100,000	$500,000	$ 25,000
2	$105,000	$100,000	$500,000	$ 10,000
3	$101,000	$100,000	$500,000	$ (25,000)
4	$ 96,000	$100,000	$500,000	$ (10,000)
5	$ 95,000	$100,000	$500,000	$ (25,000)

Answer:

		Dr.	Cr.
1.	Bonds payable	100,000	
	Unamortized bond premium	5,000*	
	Investment in S Co. Bonds		104,000
	Gain on debt extinguishment		1,000
	*Retired 1/5 of the bonds. Therefore, retire 1/5 of any related unamortized discount or premium.		
2.	Bonds payable	100,000	
	Unamortized bond premium	2,000	
	Loss on debt extinguishment	3,000	
	Investment in S Co. Bonds		105,000
3.	Bonds payable	100,000	
	Loss on debt extinguishment	6,000	
	Unamortized bond discount		5,000
	Investment in S Co. Bonds		101,000
4.	Bonds payable	100,000	
	Unamortized bond discount		2,000
	Investment in S Co. Bonds		96,000
	Gain on debt extinguishment		2,000
5.	Bonds payable	100,000	
	Unamortized bond discount		5,000
	Investment in S Co. Bonds		95,000

PROBLEM 10-3: Pen Co. purchased for $52,000 bonds of its subsidiary Sun Co. with a face value of $50,000 on January 1, 19X7. These bonds mature in 2 tears on January 1, 19X9. The bonds pay interest at a 10% stated rate. Sun Co.'s trial balance of January 1, 19X7 shows bonds payable at face value of $100,000 and an unamortized bond discount of $2,000. Both Sun Co. and Pen Co. amortize discounts and premiums on a straight-line basis. Sun Co. pays interest on bonds semiannually on July 1 and January 1 each year. Pen Co. owns 90% of Sun Co.'s issued and outstanding common stock. Prepare the January 1, 19X7 intercompany bond acquisition date consolidating worksheet elimination entry required relative to this intercompany bond holding.

Answer:

	Dr.	Cr.
Bonds payable	50,000	
Loss on debt extinguishment	3,000	
Unamortized bond discount		1,000*
Investment in Sun Co. Bonds		52,000

To eliminate intercompany investment in long-term debt as of the 1/1/X7 acquisition date.

*1/1/X7 Unamortized bond discount of $2,000 presumed one-half retired because one-half of the bonds ($50,000 of $100,000) are now held on an intercompany basis.

PROBLEM 10-4: Refer to the facts of Problem 10-3 and prepare a consolidating worksheet elimination entries required relative to the intercompany bond holding on 12/31/X7, one year after the original acquisition date.

Answer:

At 12/31/X7, the bonds would be carried on Sun Co.'s books:

Bonds payable (face		$100,000
1/1/X7 Unamortized discount	$2,000	
Less: 19X7 Amortization	1,000	
12/31/X7 Unamortized discount		1,000
12/31/X7 Carrying value		$ 99,000

Since only one-half of the bonds are still held by parties outside of the consolidated group, only one-half of the bonds payable and related unamortized discount should appear on the 12/31/X7 consolidated balance sheet. The Investment in Sun Co. Bonds account on Pen Co.'s books must be fully eliminated at 12/31/X7, and its balance on that date is $51,000 (original cost $52,000 less $1,000 premium amortization for 19X7). The 12/31/X7 consolidating worksheet entries to accomplish this are:

		Dr.	Cr.
1.	Bonds payable	50,000	
	Loss on debt extinguishment	3,000	
	Unamortized bond discount		1,000
	Investment in Sun Co. Bonds		52,000

To eliminate intercompany investment in long-term debt as of the 1/1/X7 date the intercompany debt was first held on an intercompany basis.

		Dr.	Cr.
2.	Interest payable	2,500	
	Interest receivable		2,500

To eliminate intercompany interest payable and receivable ($50,000 × 10% × 1/2 year).

		Dr.	Cr.
3.	Interest income	4,000*	
	Investment in Sun Co. Bonds	1,000	
	Unamortized bond discount	500*	
	Interest expense		5,500**

To eliminate intercompany interest income and expense and the balance remaining in In vestment in Sun Co. Bonds, and to restore the bond discount balance to 50% of the unamortized bond discount at year end 12/31/X7 of $1,000.

*10% × $50,000 bond face value	$ 5,000
Less: Premium amortization for 19X7	1,000
Interest income (on Pen Co.'s books)	$ 4,000

**Intercompany interest expense on Sun Co.'s books for 19X7 is:

10% × $100,000 bond face value	$10,000
19X7 Discount amortization	1,000
Total interest expense	$11,000
Portion of debt held on intercompany basis	× 50%
Intercompany interest expense	$ 5,500

Note that after these entries are made, appropriate 12/31/X7 consolidated balances appear as shown on the following partial consolidating worksheet:

Pen Co. and 80% Owned Subsidiary Sun Co.
(PARTIAL) Consolidating Worksheet for the Year Ended 12/31/X7

					CONSOLIDATED Dr. (Cr.)		
	Pen Co.	Sun Co.	Eliminations		Income	Retained	Balance
Account Name	Dr. (Cr.)	Dr. (Cr.)	Dr.	(Cr.)	Statement	Earnings	Sheet
Interest payable		(5,000)	2,500[2]			(2,500)	
Invest.—Sun Co. Bonds	51,000		1,000[3]	(52,000)[1]			0
Bonds payable		(100,000)	50,000[1]			(50,000)	
Bond discount		1,000	500[3]	(1,000)[1]			500
Interest income	(4,000)		4,000[3]		0		
Interest expense		11,000		(5,500)[3]	5,500		
Loss on debt extinguishment			3,000[1]		3,000		
Various accounts	xxxx	xxxx	xxxx	xxxx	xxxx	xxxx	xxxx
Totals	xxxx	xxxx	xxxx	xxxx	xxxx	xxxx	xxxx

[1] To eliminate Investment in Sun Co. Bonds and record consolidated loss on early extinguishment of debt.
[2] To eliminate intercompany interest receivable and payable.
[3] To eliminate intercompany interest income and expense and the balance remaining in Investment in Sun Co Bonds, and to restore the bond discount balance to 50% of the unamortized bond discount at year-end 12/31/X7 of $1,000.

PROBLEM 10-5: On December 31, 19X8, Parnell Co. gave a loan of $400,000 to its 90% owned subsidiary, Seaver Co., for which a note payable was prepared by Seaver Co.

(*a*) Prepare the required 12/31/X8 consolidating worksheet elimination entry.

(*b*) Prepare the required 12/31/X8 consolidating worksheet elimination entries assuming Parnell Co. discounted the note on 12/31/X8, making the following entry on its separate books.

Cash	400,000	
Notes receivable—S Co. (discounted)		400,000

Answer:

(*a*)	Notes payable—P Co.	400,000	
	Notes receivable—S Co.		400,000
	To eliminate intercompany borrowing.		
(*b*)	Notes payable—P Co.	400,000	
	Notes receivable—S Co.		400,000
	To eliminate intercompany borrowing.		
	Notes receivable—S Co. (discounted)	400,000	
	Notes payable (outside creditor)		400,000
	To reflect outside borrowing of the consolidated group.		

PROBLEM 10-6: On 1/1/X1, P Co. purchased 90% of S Co. common stock for $400,000 and purchased 20% of S Co. preferred stock for $25,000. Immediately after this acquisition, the trial balances of P Co. and S Co. were:

Account name	1/1/X1 Trial Balance P Co. Dr. (Cr.)	S Co. Dr. (Cr.)*
Assets (various)	600,000	500,000
Investments in S Co.:		
Common stock	400,000	
Preferred stock	25,000	
Liabilities	(200,000)	(100,000)
Common stock: P Co.	(300,000)	
S Co.		(100,000)
Additional paid-in capital:		
P Co.	(250,000)	
S Co.		(50,000)
Retained earnings:		
P Co.	(275,000)	
S Co.		(150,000)
Preferred stock:		
S Co.**		(100,000)
Totals	0	0

*S Co. net asset fair and book values are presumed equal on the 1/1/X1 acquisition date.
**S Co. preferred stock is 10% cumulative, nonparticipating preferred. On the 1/1/X1 acquisition date, the preferred stock was 5 years in arrears.

Based on the information provided, determine if goodwill on the original acquisition exists. (Assume that the $100,000 amount for preferred stock on S Co.'s books represents both total par and liquidation value of the preferred stock.)

Answer:

P Co.'s purchase price			$400,000
S Co.'s total stockholders' equity on 1/1/X1		$400,000	
Less: S Co.'s preferred stock deemed retired ($20,000 par plus $10,000 dividends in arrears)		30,000	
Adjusted total S Co. stockholders' equity		370,000	
Less: S Co.'s preferred stock interest in total S Co. equity: Par (outstanding)	$80,000		
Arrears (5 yrs. @ $8,000 per year)	40,000	120,000	
S Co. equity attributable to S Co. common stock		250,000	
Multiply: P Co. interest in S Co. common stock		90%	225,000
Goodwill			$175,000

PROBLEM 10-7: Refer to the facts of Problem 10-6, and also assume that during 19X1, S Co. generated net income of $90,000 and paid no dividends. Determine the balance in the Investment in S Co. Common Stock account on P Co.'s books at 12/31/X1 assuming the investment is carried at equity.

Answer:

1/1/X1 Investment in S Co. Common Stock (cost)		$400,000
19X1 S Co. net income	$90,000	
Less: Portion of S Co. net income attributable to preferred stock *outstanding* of $80,000 (10% × $80,000 cumulative par preferred outstanding)	8,000	
S Co. 19X1 net income to common stock	$82,000	
Multiply: P Co.'s interest in S Co.	× 90%	
P Co.'s interest in S Co.'s net income	$73,800	73,800
Less: Goodwill amortization ($175,000/40 years)		(4,375)
12/31/X1 Investment in S Co. Common Stock		$469,425

PROBLEM 10-8: Based on the information and solutions provided for Problems 10-6 and 10-7, complete the consolidating worksheet (Schedule I) which follows. (***hint:*** Note that rows are available in Schedule I to apportion S Co.'s retained earnings after elimination of P Co.'s Investment in S Co. Preferred Stock.)

Schedule I
P Co. and 90% Owned Subsidiary S Co.
Consolidating Worksheet for the Year Ended 12/31/X1

Account Name	P Co. Dr. (Cr.)	S Co. Dr. (Cr.)	Eliminations Dr.	Eliminations (Cr.)	CONSOLIDATED Dr. (Cr.) Income Statement	Retained Earnings	Balance Sheet
Assets (various)	750,000	600,000					
Investment in S Co.:							
Common stock	469,425						
Preferred stock	25,000						
Goodwill (if any)							
Liabilities	(220,000)	(110,000)					
Common stock:							
P Co.	(300,000)						
S Co.		(100,000)					
Additional paid-in capital: P Co.	(250,000)						
S Co.		(50,000)					
Retained earnings:							
P Co.	(275,000)						
S Co.		(150,000)					
Retained earnings: S Co.							
—Common stock portion.							
—Pref. stock portion							
Preferred stock:							
S Co.		(100,000)					
Revenues	(1,000,000)	(500,000)					
Expenses	870,000	410,000					
Investment income	(69,425)						
Totals	0	0					
	Combined net income						
	*Minority interest						
	Consolidated net income						
	Consolidated retained earnings						
					Total		
	Total minority interest						

Answer:

Worksheet (Schedule I) elimination entries are as follows:

	Dr.	Cr.
1. S Co. Preferred stock (par) 20%	20,000	
S Co. Retained earnings (20% × preferred stock dividends in arrears of $50,000 at 1/1/X1)	10,000	
Investment in S Co. Preferred stock		25,000
Additional paid-in capital		5,000
To eliminate investment in 20% of S Co.'s preferred stock.		
2. S Co. Retained earnings ($150,000 - $10,000)	140,000	
S Co. Retained earnings (common)		100,000
S Co. Retained earnings (preferred)		40,000

To apportion S Co. retained earnings between common and preferred stock. (At 1/1/X1, preferred stock was 5 years in arrears. S Co. preferred stock outstanding at par is $80,000 ($100,000 par less $20,000 retired.) Arrears are therefore 10% of $80,000 for 5 years or $40,000 at 1/1/X1.

		Dr.	Cr.
3.	S Co. Common stock (90%)	90,000	
	S Co. Additional paid-in capital (90%)	45,000	
	S Co. Retained earnings (common) (90%)	90,000	
	Investment income	69,425	
	Goodwill	175,000	
	Investment in S Co. Common Stock		469,425
	To eliminate investment in S Co. against investment income and 90% of S Co. equity and record goodwill.		
4.	Goodwill amortization (expense)	4,375	
	Goodwill		4,375
	To amortize goodwill ($175,000/40 years = $4,375).		

Note also that the minority interest in net income calculation shown on the worksheet considers the rights of outstanding cumulative preferred shares.

Schedule I
P Co. and 90% Owned Subsidiary S Co.
Consolidating Worksheet for the Year Ended 12/31/X1

Account Name	P Co. Dr. (Cr.)	S Co. Dr. (Cr.)	Eliminations Dr.	Eliminations (Cr.)	CONSOLIDATED Dr. (Cr.) Income Statement	CONSOLIDATED Dr. (Cr.) Retained Earnings	CONSOLIDATED Dr. (Cr.) Balance Sheet
Assets (various)	750,000	600,000					1,350,000
Investment in S Co.:							
Common stock	469,425			(469,425)3			0
Preferred stock	25,000			(25,000)1			0
Goodwill (if any)			175,0003	(4,375)4			170,625
Liabilities	(220,000)	(110,000)					(330,000)
Common stock:							
P Co.	(300,000)						(300,000)
S Co.		(100,000)	90,0003				(10,000)M
Additional paid-in capital: P Co.	(250,000)			(5,000)1			(255,000)
S Co.		(50,000)	45,0003				(5,000)M
Retained earnings:							
P Co.	(275,000)					(275,000)	
S Co.		(150,000)	10,0001 140,0002				0
Retained earnings: S Co.							
—Common stock portion.			90,0003	(100,000)2			(10,000)M
—Pref. stock portion				(40,000)2			(40,000)M
Preferred stock:							
S Co.		(100,000)	20,0001				(80,000)M
Revenues	(1,000,000)	(500,000)			(1,500,000)		
Expenses	870,000	410,000	4,3754		1,284,375		
Investment income	(69,425)		69,4253		0		
Totals	0	0	643,800	(643,800)			
Combined net income					(215,625)		
*Minority interest					16,200		(16,200)M
Consolidated net income					(199,425)	(199,425)	
Consolidated retained earnings						(474,425)	(474,425)
Total							0
Total minority interest (sum of items marked "M")							(161,200)M

M = Minority interest

* Minority interest in net income:

Cumulative preferred shareholders' interest: 10% × $80,000 par outstanding	$ 8,000
Minority common shareholders' interest (10% × $82,000 S Co. net income available to common stock)	8,200
Total minority interest in S Co. net income for 19X1	$16,200

1 To eliminate investment in 20% of S Co.'s preferred stock.
2 To apportion S Co. retained earnings between common and preferred stock. (At 1/1/X1, preferred stock was 5 years in arrears. S Co. preferred stock outstanding at par is $80,000 ($100,000 par less $20,000 retired). Arrears are therefore 10% of $80,000 for 5 years or $40,000 at 1/1/X1.
3 To eliminate Investment in S Co. against investment income and 90% of S Co. equity and record goodwill.
4 To amortize goodwill ($175,000/40 years = $4,375).

PROBLEM 10-9: On 1/1/X5, Prime Co. purchased a 60% controlling interest in Simple Co. for $200,000. On 1/1/X5, Simple Co.'s stockholders' equity was:

Common stock	$100,000
Retained earnings	200,000
Total stockholders' equity	$300,000

Simple Co.'s net asset book and fair values were equal on 1/1/X5 except for land which had a fair value of $20,000 above book value. On 1/1/X6, Prime Co. purchased an additional 20% interest in Simple Co. for $88,000. On 1/1/X6, Prime Co.'s net asset book and fair values were equal except for land which still had a fair value of $20,000 above book value and inventory which had a fair value of $10,000 above book value. (This inventory was completely sold during 19X6.) On 1/1/X6, Simple Co.'s stockholders' equity was:

Common stock	$100,000
Retained earnings	260,000
Total stockholders' equity	$360,000

Simple Co. had the following 19X5 and 19X6 activity:

	19X5	19X6
Net income	$60,000	$90,000
Dividends declared and paid	0	$50,000

(*a*) Determine the balance in Prime Co.'s Investment in Simple Co. account on 12/31/X6.
(*b*) Prepare the 12/31/X6 consolidating worksheet elimination entries necessary in the circumstances.

Answer:

(*a*) The block acquisitions are analyzed as:

	Acquisition of:	
	1/1/X5	1/1/X6
Purchase price	$200,000	$ 88,000
Simple Co. stockholders' equity (book value) acquired:		
60% × $300,000	(180,000)	
20% × $360,000		(72,000)
Excess cost over book value	20,000	16,000
Excess attributable to:		
Land (60% × $20,000)	(12,000)	
Land (20% × $20,000)		(4,000)
Inventory (20% × $10,000)		(2,000)
Goodwill	$ 8,000	$ 10,000

Carried at equity, the 12/31/X6 investment balance is:

1/1/X5 Cost (Block 1)	$200,000
19X5 Simple Co. net income of $60,000 × 60%	36,000
19X5 Goodwill amortization ($8,000/40 years)	(200)
1/1/X6 Cost (Block 2)	88,000
19X6 Simple Co. net income of $90,000 × 80%	72,000
19X6 Goodwill amortization:	
Block 1: ($8,000/40 years)	(200)
Block 2: ($10,000/40 years)	(250)
19X6 Inventory (to cost of goods sold)	(2,000)
19X6 Simple dividends of $50,000 × 80%	(40,000)
12/31/X6 Investment in Simple Co. (balance)	$353,350

(*b*) The 12/31/X6 consolidating worksheet elimination entries are:

1. Simple Co. Common stock (80% × $100,000)	80,000	
Simple Co. Retained earnings (80% × $260,000)	208,000	
Goodwill	17,800*	
Inventory	2,000	
Land ($12,000 plus $4,000)	16,000	
Investment income	69,550**	
Simple Co. dividends declared (80% × $50,000)		40,000
Investment in Simple Co.		353,350

To eliminate Investment in Simple Co. and the investment income against Simple Co. equity and dividend declarations, and to adjust Simple Co. net assets and record goodwill.

*$18,000 total less 19X5 amortization of $200.

**$72,000 less goodwill amortization of $450 and inventory amortization of $2,000.

2. Goodwill amortization	450	
Cost of goods sold	2,000	
Goodwill		450
Inventory		2,000

To record 19X6 goodwill amortization and to adjust inventory.

PROBLEM 10-10: Bear Co. acquired 3,600 shares of Cub Co. stock on 1/1/X8 for $197,500. Cub Co.'s stockholders' equity on this date was:

Common stock, $10 par, 5,000 shares	$ 50,000
Additional paid-in capital	50,000
Retained earnings	154,400
Subtotal	$254,400
Less: 200 shares of treasury stock (at cost)	4,400
Total stockholders' equity	$250,000

(*a*) Determine the percentage of interest Bear Co. has purchased in Cub Co.

(*b*) Assuming that on the 1/1/X8 acquisition date Cub Co.'s net asset fair and book values were equal except for equipment which had a fair value of $10,000 in excess of book value, prepare the acquisition date consolidating worksheet elimination entries necessary.

Answer:

(*a*) Bear Co. owns a 75% interest. This level of interest is determined based on the number of shares issued and outstanding:

$$\frac{\text{3,600 shares acquired}}{\text{4,800 shares issued and outstanding}} = 75\%$$

Note that treasury stock must be excluded in determining Bear Co.'s level of interest.

(*b*)

Cub Co. Common Stock (200 shares at $10 par)	2,000	
Cub Co. Additional paid-in capital (200 shares at $10)	2,000	
Cub Co. Retained earnings	400	
Cub Co. Treasury stock		4,400

To treat Cub Co. Treasury stock as retired.

Cub Co. Common stock (75% × $48,000)	36,000	
Cub Co. Additional paid-in capital (75% × $48,000)	36,000	
Cub Co. Retained earnings (75% × $154,000)	115,500	
Equipment (75% × $10,000)	7,500	
Goodwill	2,500*	
Investment in Cub Co.		197,500

To eliminate investment in Cub Co. against Cub Co. equity, adjust Cub Co. net assets to fair value, and record goodwill.

*Purchase price	$197,500
Bear Co. interest (75% × $250,000) in Cub Co.	(187,500)
Excess cost over book value	10,000
Portion attributable to equipment (75% × $10,000)	(7,500)
Goodwill	$ 2,500

PROBLEM 10-11: Several years ago, Plack Co. purchased a 90% interest in Ahren Co. Plack Co. has no direct interest in Baker Co. However, Ahren Co. owns a 70% interest in Baker Co. Although Plack Co. has no direct interest in Baker Co,the interest of Ahren Co. in Baker Co. provides Plack Co. with a 63% (90% × 70%) indirect controlling interest in Baker Co. The consolidation process should include all three companies. Both Plack Co. and Ahren Co. carry their investments in subsidiaries using the equity method. When Plack Co. and Ahren Co. made their original investments, differences arose between their purchase prices and their underlying interests in the net subsidiary assets acquired. These differences were attributed to goodwill. At January 1, 19X8, any remaining goodwill from the original purchase of the investment in Baker Co. by Ahren Co. had a 9-year life remaining, and any remaining goodwill from the original purchase of the investment in Ahren Co. by Plack Co. had a 30-year life remaining.

Based on this information and on the trial balances provided for the three companies on Schedule II, complete the Schedule II December 31, 19X8 consolidating worksheet. (Note that although Baker Co.'s separate books show a net income of $5,000 for 19X8, Ahren Co.'s 19X8 investment income account does not show 70% of $5,000 or $3,500. Rather, the investment income appears at only $3,000 due to $500 in goodwill amortization for one year. If, on January 1, 19X8, goodwill from the original acquisition by Ahren Co. of its interest in Baker Co. had a 9-year life remaining, then remaining goodwill at January 1, 19X8 must total 9 × $500 or $4,500. Similarly, Plack Co.'s books show investment income from Ahren Co. of only $19,000 for 19X8, while Plack Co.'s 90% interest in Ahren Co. net income of $22,000 results in $19,800. The $800 difference is also attributable to goodwill amortization for 19X8.)

Schedule II
Plack Co. and Subsidiaries Ahren Co. and Baker Co.
Consolidating Worksheet for the Year Ended 12/31/X8

Account Name	Plack Co. Dr. (Cr.)	Ahren Co. Dr. (Cr.)	Baker Co. Dr. (Cr)	Eliminations Dr.	Eliminations (Cr.)	CONSOLIDATED Dr. (Cr.) Income Statement	Retained Earnings	Balance Sheet
Assets (various)	700,000	100,000	70,000					
Investment in A Co.	132,100							
Investment in B Co.		39,000						
Goodwill*								
Goodwill**								
Liabilities (various)	(130,000)	(15,000)	(20,000)					
Common stock:								
Plack Co.	(410,000)							
Ahren Co.		(60,000)						
Baker Co			(20,000)					
Retained earnings:								
Plack Co.	(222,100)							
Ahren Co.		(40,000)						
Baker Co.			(30,000)					
Dividends declared:								
Plack Co.	70,000							
Ahren Co.		1,000						
Baker Co.			5,000					
Investment income:								
From Ahren Co.	(19,000)							
From Baker Co.		(3,000)						
Revenues	(200,000)	(80,000)	(70,000)					
Expenses	79,000	58,000	65,000					
Totals	0	0	0					
Combined net income								
Minority interest								
Consolidated net income								
Consolidated retained earnings								
						Total		
Total minority interest								

* Space provided for remaining goodwill, if any, on investment of Plack Co. in Ahren Co.
** Space provided for remaining goodwill, if any, on investment of Ahren Co. in Baker Co.

Answer:

Schedule II
Plack Co. and Subsidiaries Ahren Co. and Baker Co.
Consolidating Worksheet for the Year Ended 12/31/X8

Account Name	Plack Co. Dr. (Cr.)	Ahren Co. Dr. (Cr.)	Baker Co. Dr. (Cr)	Eliminations Dr.	Eliminations (Cr.)	CONSOLIDATED Dr. (Cr.) Income Statement	CONSOLIDATED Dr. (Cr.) Retained Earnings	CONSOLIDATED Dr. (Cr.) Balance Sheet
Assets (various)	700,000	100,000	70,000					870,000
Investment in Ahren Co.	132,100				(132,100)[3]			0
Investment in Baker Co.		39,000			(39,000)[1]			0
Goodwill —Plack's purchase				24,000[3]	(800)[4]			23,200
Goodwill —Ahren's purchase				4,500[1]	(500)[2]			4,000
Liabilities (various)	(130,000)	(15,000)	(20,000)					(165,000)
Common stock:								
Plack Co.	(410,000)							(410,000)
Ahren Co.		(60,000)		54,000[3]				(6,000)M
Baker Co			(20,000)	14,000[1]				(6,000)M
Retained earnings:								
Plack Co.	(222,100)						(222,100)	
Ahren Co.		(40,000)		36,000[3]				(4,000)M
Baker Co.			(30,000)	21,000[1]				(9,000)M
Dividends declared:								
Plack Co.	70,000						70,000	
Ahren Co.		1,000			(900)[3]			100M
Baker Co.			5,000		(3,500)[1]			1,500M
Investment income:								
From Ahren Co.	(19,000)			19,000[3]		0		
From Baker Co.		(3,000)		3,000[1]		0		
Revenues	(200,000)	(80,000)	(70,000)			(350,000)		
Expenses	79,000	58,000	65,000	500[2] 800[4]		203,300		
Totals	0	0	0	176,800	(176,800)			
Combined net income						(146,700)		
*Minority interest						4,000		(4,000)M
Consolidated net income						(142,700)	(142,700)	
Consolidated retained earnings							(294,800)	(294,800)
						Total		0
Total minority interest (sum of items marked "M")								(27,400)

M = Minority interest

Minority interest in Baker Co. net income: 30% of Baker Co. net income of $5,000	$1,500
Minority interest in Ahren Co. net income: 10% of Ahren Co. net income of $25,000	2,500
Minority interest in combined net income	$4,000

1 To eliminate Investment in Baker Co. and investment income against Baker Co. equity and dividend declarations and record goodwill.

2 To amortize goodwill ($4,500/9 years remaining life at 1/1/X8).

3 To eliminate Investment in Ahren Co. and investment income against Ahren Co. equity and dividend declarations and record goodwill.

4 To amortize goodwill ($24,000/30 years remaining life at 1/1/X8).

PROBLEM 10-12: Landmark Co., a subsidiary of Jenkins Inc., purchased 10,000 shares of Jenkins Inc. common stock at $9.50 per share on 6/30/X7. On that date, stockholders' equity on Jenkins Inc.'s books was:

Common Stock, 250,000 shares authorized, 200,000 issued, $5 par	$1,000,000
Additional paid-in capital—common stock	800,000
Preferred stock, 50,000 shares authorized, issued, and outstanding, $3 par	150,000
Additional paid-in capital—preferred stock	75,000
Retained earnings	675,000
Total stockholders' equity	$2,700,000

Prepare the consolidating worksheet elimination entry necessary to appropriately reflect the 6/30/X7 consolidated balance sheet amounts relative to Landmark Co.'s acquisition of Jenkins Inc. stock assuming:
(*a*) the intercompany acquisition is viewed as a retirement of stock.
(*b*) the intercompany acquisition is viewed as treasury stock since an intent to reissue the stock exists.

Answer:

(*a*)	Common Stock ($5 par × 10,000 shares)	50,000	
	Additional paid-in capital ($4 × 10,000 shares)	40,000	
	Retained earnings	5,000	
	Investment in Jenkins Inc. ($9.50 × 10,000 shares)		95,000
	To eliminate portion of Jenkins Inc. stockholders' equity viewed as retired against Landmark Co.'s Investment in Jenkins Inc. account.		
(*b*)	Treasury stock (at cost)	95,000	
	Investment in Jenkins Inc. ($9.50 × 10,000 shares)		95,000
	To eliminate Landmark Co.'s Investment in Jenkins Inc. and record treasury stock.		

11 THE POOLING-OF-INTERESTS BUSINESS COMBINATION

THIS CHAPTER IS ABOUT

- ☑ Theoretical Differences (Purchases vs. Pooling-of-Interest)
- ☑ Accounting Differences (Purchases vs. Pooling-of-Interest)
- ☑ One Company Continues As Legal Entity in a Pooling-of-Interest
- ☑ Two or More Companies Continue as Legal Entities in a Pooling-of-Interest

11-1. The Theoretical Differences between Purchase and Pooling-of-Interest Business Combinations

A. Pooling-of-interest business combinations are considered mergers rather than sales.

The fundamental difference between the two methods used to account for business combinations is that, under the purchase method, the ownership rights in an acquired company pass to the acquiring company; a sale and a purchase of assets takes place. In contrast, under the pooling-of-interest method, the owners of the combining companies merge their ownership interests in the equities of those companies to form a newly combined economic entity. Under the pooling-of-interest method there is continuity of ownership; the owners of the acquired company (before the combination) own a proportional amount of the combined entity. There is no transfer of ownership rights, and no sale or purchase takes place.

The mechanism by which a pooling of interests is effected is for the "acquiring" company to issue its common stock, with all the rights and privileges of any of its previously issued common stock, in exchange for "substantially all" (defined as 90 percent or more) of the voting common stock of the "acquired" company. (The terms *acquiring* and *acquired* are used in this chapter largely for convenience, because under the pooling-of-interest method no sale, i.e., no acquiring, actually takes place. In this chapter, the term *acquiring company* simply refers to the company that issues the stock, and the term acquired company refers to the other combining firm.) Thus, in a pooling-of-interest combination, the common stockholders of both combining companies do not give up their ownership interest; they continue as common stockholders of the combined entity.

B. A business combination must meet strict conditions before it may be considered a pooling of interests.

A business combination accounted for as a pooling of interests may result in higher net income, and lower depreciation and amortization expenses, for the combined economic entity than it would if accounted for as a purchase. Therefore, management or owners of companies may frequently prefer the pooling-of-interest method to account for a business combination. However, the accounting method that may be used during a combination is not a matter of choice or preference. APB Opinion 16, "Business Combinations,"* specifies 12 conditions that must be met in order for a business combination to be accounted for as a pooling of interests. Failure to meet any one of these 12 conditions means that the business combination must be accounted for as a purchase. Conversely, if all 12 conditions of the APB Opinion are met, the combination must be accounted for as a pooling of interests. The use of one approach or another is not a matter of choice.

As summarized from APB Opinion 16, the 12 conditions for a pooling-of-interest combination are:

Combining Companies (Autonomy and Independence)

1. Each of the combining companies is autonomous and has not been a subsidiary or division of another corporation within two years before the plan of combination is initiated.
2. Each of the combining companies is independent of other combining companies.

Combining of Interests (Manner of Exchange of Stock)

3. The combination is effected in a single transaction or is completed in accordance with a specific plan within one year after the plan is initiated.
4. A corporation issues only common stock with rights identical to those of the majority of its outstanding voting common stock in exchange for substantially all (90% or more) of the voting common stock interest of another company.
5. None of the combining companies changes the equity interest of the voting common stock in contemplation of effecting the combination either within two years before the plan of combination is initiated, or between the dates the combination is initiated and consummated.
6. Each of the combining companies reacquires shares of voting common stock only for purposes other than business combinations, and no company reacquires more than a normal number of shares between the dates the plan of combination is initiated and consummated.
7. The ratio of interest of an individual common stockholder to those of other common stockholders in a combining company remains the same as a result of the exchange of stock to effect the combination.
8. The common stockholders' voting rights in the resulting combined corporation are exercisable without restrictions.
9. The combination is resolved at the date the plan is consummated, and no provisions of the plan relating to securities issuance or other consideration are pending.

Absence of Planned Transaction

10. The combined corporation does not agree directly or indirectly to retire or reacquire all or part of the common stock issued to effect the combination.
11. The combined corporation does not enter into other financial arrangements benefiting former stockholders of a combining company, which, in effect, negates the exchange of equity securities.
12. The combined corporation does not intend or plan to dispose of a significant part of the assets of the combining companies within two years after the combination other than disposals in the ordinary course of business of the formerly separate companies, and to eliminate duplicate facilities or excess capacity.

*Accounting Principles Board Opinion 16, Business Combinations, American Institute of CPAs, paragraphs 45-48, New York, August 1970.

11-2. The Accounting Differences between Purchase and Pooling-of-Interest Business Combinations

A. A pooling-of-interest business combination is based on book values.

Because no sale of the acquired company's assets takes place in a pooling-of-interest combination, the fair market values of the acquired company's net assets on the date of the combination are not considered. All the accounting procedures that take place in a pooling of interests are based on the book values (that is, the historical or carrying costs) of the assets and liabilities involved.

Because fair market values of the acquired company are not relevant to a business combination accounted for as a pooling of interests, no goodwill results from the combination, and none of the acquired company's asset accounts need be revalued on the date of the combination. Therefore, there is no amortization of goodwill or depreciation of net asset revaluations in future periods. (This is one of the reasons net income tends to be higher for an entity combined under the pooling-of-interest method.) Any other amortization or depreciation that is recorded subsequent to the combination as a result of normal operations is based on historical costs for the acquired company's assets.

B. Under the pooling-of-interest method, consolidated financial statements are prepared by adding asset and liability book values as shown in the the separate statements of the affiliated companies.

In order to prepare consolidated financial statements for the combined economic entity, the asset and liability book value amounts on the various financial statements of the separate affiliates are simply added together, at historical costs (or carrying costs), both on the date of the combination and for subsequent periods of combined operation. (Some minor adjustments to the equity account balances may be needed before they can be combined. See Sections 11-3B and 11-3C.)

C. After a pooling-of-interests combination, the affiliated companies are treated as if they had been operating as a single company.

Under the pooling-of-interest method, the consolidated financial statements are the same as if the new affiliates had been operating as a single entity throughout their histories.

For this reason, the consolidated financial statements of newly combined companies should reflect combined operations (that is, combined net income) for the full period in which the combination occurs, even if the combination did not occur until nearly the end of the period. (This is unlike the purchase method which reflects net income from operations from the date of purchase only.)

Furthermore, when consolidated financial statements are prepared for a group affiliated under the pooling-of-interest method in order to compare current performance with previous performance, the pooling-of-interest combination is retroactive and requires restatement of prior period financial statements to reflect operations as if the acquired and acquiring entities had always represented one economic entity. (This is, again, unlike the purchase method which reflects net income from operations from the date of purchase only.)

EXAMPLE 11-1: P Co. and S Co. merged on 7/1/X6, when P Co. acquired 100 percent of S Co.'s common stock. On that date, the investment cost for S Co., and its fair values and book values, were equal.

After the merger, the separate net incomes of P Co. and S Co., for the 6-month and 12-month periods ending 12/31/X6, are:

	P Co.	S Co.
Net income for 12 months ended 12/31/X6	$110,000*	$60,000
Net income for 6 months ended 12/31/X6	$ 50,000*	$35,000

*Excludes any portion of S Co. net income.

If P Co. and S Co. combined under the purchase method, their consolidated financial statements should reflect combined net income from the acquisition date only:

Purchase method	$145,000 ($110,000 + $35,000)

However, if P Co. and S Co. combined under the pooling-of-interest method, their consolidated financial statements should reflect combined net income for the entire 12-month period ended 12/31/X6, as if the two companies had functioned as a single entity during that time:

Pooling-of-Interest Method	$170,000 ($110,000 + $60,000)

D. Under the pooling-of-interest method, costs associated with the combination are treated as expenses.

All costs incurred during a pooling-of-interest business combination are considered expenses of the combined economic entity. They should be recorded in a Business Combination Expenses account, or other appropriate expense account. These expenses will, therefore, affect the net income of the combined entity for the period in which they are incurred. (See Chapter 4, Section 4-1.C for treatment of business combination costs under the purchase method, which differs from treatment required under the pooling of interests methods.)

EXAMPLE 11-2: P Co. issued 100,000 shares of its common stock (par value $2.00) in exchange for all the outstanding common stock of S Co. On the acquisition date the fair value of S Co.'s common stock was $7.00 per share.

P Co. incurred the following costs during its combination with S Co.:

SEC registration costs	$ 8,000
Finder's fees and other direct costs of acquisition or merger	27,000
Indirect and general expenses related to acquisition or merger	3,000

If P Co. and S Co. combined under the pooling-of-interest method, the expenses associated with the combination would be $38,000 ($8,000 + $27,000 + $3,000), and these expenses would be reflected in income for the period in which they are incurred.

If P Co. and S Co. combined under the purchase method, the expenses associated with the combination would only be $3,000. The finder's fees and any other direct cost of an acquisition or merger ($27,000 in this case) are treated as part of P Co.'s investment cost. The registration costs are treated as a reduction of the fair market value of the stock P Co. issued to effect the combination, and are recorded as a reduction of P Co.'s Additional Paid-in Capital account. (See Chapter 4.)

11-3. Pooling-of-Interest Combinations in which Only One Company Continues as a Legal Entity

A pooling-of-interests merger may be accomplished in such a way that only one of the two or more companies originally involved survives as a legal entity. If this is the case there is no reason to prepare consolidated financial statements, of course, because only one company exists after the merger. Problems may arise when reporting the value of the merged companies, however, if the par value of the stock issued by the surviving company differs from the par value of the stock surrendered by the combining companies. If there is a difference in par values, apply the following rules:

1. If the par value of the capital stock issued to effect the combination exceeds the par value of the stock surrendered by the combining company (or companies), charge the difference first to combined Additional Paid-In Capital, and then to combined Retained Earnings.
2. If the par value of the stock surrendered by the combining company (or companies) exceeds the par value of the capital stock issued to effect the combination, credit the difference to combined Additional Paid-In Capital.

No matter what the par values of the stock of the issuing and combining companies, the net assets (assets less liabilities) of the combining company (or companies) are always recorded by the issuing company at book value during a pooling-of-interest merger. Therefore, the grand total equity of the issuing company will always increase after the merger by the book value of these net assets, although the changes in the specific equity account balances will vary according to the par values of the issuing and combining companies.

Examples 11-3, 11-4, and 11-5 are based on the following balance sheets for A Co. and B Co., just before their pooling-of-interest merger occurs:

	A Co.	B Co.	Combined totals
Assets	$100,000	$10,000*	$110,000
Liabilities	$ 30,000	$ 5,000*	$ 35,000
Common stock, $10 par	50,000	2,000	52,000
Additional paid in capital	3,000	1,000	4,000
Retained earnings	17,000	2,000	19,000
Total liabilities and equity	$100,000	$10,000	$110,000

*The fair value of B Co.'s assets is $12,000 and the fair value of B. Co.'s liabilities is $5,000.

A. If the par values of the issuing and combining companies are equal, the balance sheets of the companies are simply combined.

If the par value of the stock issued by one company is equal to the par value of the stock of another company (or companies), for which it is being traded in order to effect a pooling-of-interest merger, and if only the issuing company is to continue after the merger, then the balances of the combining company's (or companies') assets, liabilities, and equity accounts are simply added to the corresponding accounts on the books of the issuing company.

EXAMPLE 11-3: A Co. and B Co. merge operations in a business combination that may be appropriately accounted for as a pooling of interests. A Co. issues 200 shares of its common stock to B Co.'s shareholders for 100 percent of B Co.'s common stock. After the merger, B Co. ceases to exist as a legal entity.

The par value of the issuing company's stock (A Co. issues to the stockholders of B Co. $10 par × 200 shares = $2,000) equals the par value of the combining company's stock (B Co. stock total par = $2,000). Therefore, the entry on A Co.'s books to record the combination is:

Assets (book value)	10,000	
Liabilities (book value)		5,000
A Co. Common stock (200 @ $10 par)		2,000
A Co. Additional paid-in capital		1,000
A Co. Retained earnings		2,000
To record merger of B Co. on A Co.'s books as a *pooling*.		

A Co.'s balance sheet will now simply appear as shown in the "Combined Totals" column of the balance sheet information given above.

Note that if the combination of A Co. and B Co. were accounted for as a purchase instead of a pooling of interests, the entry on A Co.'s books to record the purchase of B Co.'s stock would be radically different:

Assets (fair value of purchase)	12,000	
Liabilities (fair value of purchase)		5,000
A Co. Common stock (200 @ $10 par)		2,000
A Co. Additional paid-in capital		5,000
To record *purchase* of B. Co.'s net assets on A Co.'s books.		

Under the purchase method, B Co.'s net assets are recorded at their fair value of $7,000 ($12,000 – $5,000), whereas under the pooling-of-interest method they are recorded at their book value of $5,000 ($10,000 – $5,000).

B. If the par value of the shares issued exceeds that of the shares surrendered, adjust the combined equity accounts to reflect the difference (reducing additional paid-in-capital and, possibly, retained earnings).

When the par value of the shares issued exceeds the par value of the shares of the combining company (or companies) in a merger, the issuing company must adjust the combined equity accounts to record the difference between the par values.

First, it must *increase* the combined Common Stock account by the amount of the difference, because this account must reflect the par value of the surviving company's common stock before the merger, plus the par value of all the additional shares it issued to effect the merger.

Next, to offset this increase, the issuing company must *decrease* the combined Additional Paid-In Capital account by the amount of the difference. If the amount of this difference exceeds the Additional Paid-In Capital account balance, the remaining portion of the difference is charged to combined Retained Earnings.

The journal entry that the issuing company makes on its books to record the merger is based on these adjusted equity account amounts.

EXAMPLE 11-4: A Co. and B Co. merge operations in a business combination that may be appropriately accounted for as a pooling of interests. A Co. issues 700 shares of its common stock to B Co.'s shareholders for 100 percent of B Co.'s common stock. After the merger, B Co. ceases to exist as a legal entity.

The par value of the stock A Co. issues to the stockholders of B Co. ($10 par × 700 shares = $7,000) exceeds the par value of the combining B Co. stock (100% of $2,000) by $5,000. Therefore, the combined Common Stock account must be increased by $5,000, and the combined Additional Paid-In Capital account decreased as much of the $5,000 as possible (in this case, by $4,000). The remaining $1,000 of the adjustment is made by decreasing the combined Retained Earnings account:

	Combined Totals	Adjustments	Adjusted Combined Totals*
Assets	$110,000		$110,000
Liabilities	$ 35,000		$ 35,000
Common stock, $10 par	52,000	$5,000	57,000
Additional paid-in capital	4,000	(4,000)	-0-
Retained earnings	19,000	(1,000)	18,000
Total liabilities and equity	$110,000		$110,000

*This column represents the carrying values of assets, liabilities, and equity which should appear on A Co.'s books after A Co.'s journal entry is made to accomplish a pooling of interests with B Co. Note that net asset book value of $75,000 ($110,000 – $35,000) is not adjusted. A Co.'s common stock at par must total $57,000 (A Co.'s $50,000 par before issuance of 700 shares plus $7,000 on issuance). The combined total par is only $52,000, and therefore combined additional paid-in capital is first reduced by $4,000, and then retained earnings is reduced by $1,000.

The journal entry that A Co. makes on its books to record the merger changes its pre-merger balances to these adjusted combined totals:

	Pre-merger A Co. Balance Sheet	Adjusted Combined Totals	Basis for A Co. Journal Entry —Difference
Assets	$110,000	$110,000	$ 10,000
Liabilities	$ 30,000	$ 35,000	$ 5,000
Common stock, $10 par	50,000	57,000	7,000
Additional paid-in capital	3,000	-0-	(3,000)
Retained earnings	17,000	18,000	1,000
Total liabilities and equity	$110,000	$110,000	$ 10,000

Therefore, the journal entry on A Co.'s books to record the merger is:

Assets (book value)	10,000	
A Co. Additional paid-in capital	3,000	
Liabilities (book value)		5,000
A Co. Common stock (700 @ $10 par)		7,000
A Co. Retained earnings		1,000
To record merger of B Co. on A Co.'s books as a pooling.		

C. If the par value of the shares issued is less than that of the shares surrendered, adjust the combined equity accounts to reflect the difference (by increasing additional paid-in capital).

When the par value of the shares issued is less than the par value of the shares of the combining company (or companies) in a merger, the issuing company must adjust the combined equity accounts to record the difference between the par values.

First, it must *decrease* the combined Common Stock account by the amount of the difference, because this account must reflect the par value of the surviving company's common stock before the merger, plus the par value of all the additional shares it issued to effect the merger.

Next, to offset this decrease, the issuing company must *increase* the combined Additional Paid-In Capital account by the amount of the difference.

The journal entry that the issuing company makes on its books to record the merger is based on these adjusted equity account amounts.

EXAMPLE 11-5: A Co. and B Co. merge operations in a business combination that may be appropriately accounted for as a pooling of interests. A Co. issues 100 shares of its common stock to B Co.'s shareholders for 100 percent of B Co.'s common stock. After the merger, B Co. ceases to exist as a legal entity.

The par value of the stock A Co. issues to the stockholders of B Co. ($10 par × 100 shares = $1,000) is $1,000 less than the par value of the combining B Co. stock (100% of $2,000). Therefore, the combined Common Stock account must be decreased by $1,000, and the combined Additional Paid-In Capital account increased by $1,000:

	Combined Totals	Adjustments	Adjusted Combined Totals*
Assets	$110,000		$110,000
Liabilities	$ 35,000		$ 35,000
Common stock, $10 par	52,000	$(1,000)	51,000
Additional paid-in capital	4,000	1,000	5,000
Retained earnings	19,000		19,000
Total liabilities and equity	$110,000		$110,000

The journal entry that A Co. makes on its books to record the merger changes its pre-merger balances to these adjusted combined totals:

	Pre-merger A Co. Balance Sheet	Adjusted Combined Totals	Basis for A Co. Journal Entry —Difference
Assets	$100,000	$110,000	$10,000
Liabilities	$30,000	$ 35,000	$ 5,000
Common stock, $10 par	50,000	51,000	1,000
Additional paid-in capital	3,000	5,000	2,000
Retained earnings	17,000	19,000	2,000
Total liabilities and equity	$100,000	$110,000	$10,000

Therefore, the journal entry on A Co.'s books to record the merger is:

Assets (book value)	10,000	
Liabilities (book value)		5,000
A Co. Common stock (100 @ $10 par)		1,000
A Co. Additional paid-in capital		2,000
A Co. Retained earnings		2,000
To record merger of B Co. on A Co.'s books as a pooling.		

Note that in Examples 11-3 through 11-5 the grand total equity of A Co. after the merger increased in each case by the amount of B Co.'s net assets, or $5,000, although the balances of the specific combined equity accounts were changed to account for the differences in par values of the issuing and combining companies.

11-4. Pooling-of-Interest Combinations in which All Companies Continue as a Legal Entities

A. If more than one company continues after a pooling-of-interests merger, consolidated financial statements will be necessary.

In the examples given in Section 11-3, only one company continued as a legal entity after the pooling-of-interest merger took place, and therefore there was no need for consolidated financial statements. However, there is no requirement that this be the case in a pooling; as long as all 12 conditions of APB Opinion 16 are met, a pooling of interests may take place in which a parent-subsidiary relationship is established, and one of the combining companies becomes the subsidiary of the other. In this situation, the need arises for the preparation of consolidated financial statements that will view the legally separate companies as a single economic entity.

The consolidation process for a pooling-of-interest combination is simpler than it might be for a purchase combination. The parent company generally records an investment in the subsidiary at book value of the subsidiary's net assets. Because only book values are used during a pooling of interests, no goodwill, or differences between the book values and fair values of the subsidiary's net assets, need be recorded. Consequently, no amortization of goodwill or asset revaluation will result either.

Once the pooling-of-interest combination is completed, however, the standard consolidating worksheet entries will be necessary to eliminate the parent's intercompany investment account against the subsidiary's equity. Also, any intercompany transactions made over the course of the accounting period (such as sales and purchases of inventory or services, profits in beginning or ending inventories, sales of fixed assets and any related gains or losses, intercompany long-term debt, intercompany preferred stock holdings, and any intercompany receivables, payables, income, or expenses) must be eliminated. The methods used to make these eliminating entries are discussed in Chapters 4 through 10.

B. If more than one company continues after a pooling-of-interests merger, the parent company creates an Investment in Subsidiary account.

If more than one company is to continue after a pooling-of-interest combination, the issuing, or parent, company records the combination on its separate books in a different manner than it would if it were the only company to continue after a merger. It does not simply combine its asset, liability, and equity accounts with the book values of the subsidiary's asset, liability, and equity accounts, as it would in the former case. Rather, it creates an Investment in Subsidiary account, and records its investment at the book value of the subsidiary's net assets, adjusting its own equity accounts to account for any differences in par values between parent and subsidiary company stock involved.

No matter what the par value of the stock the parent company issues to effect the combination, the parent generally records on its own books its investment in the subsidiary at the book value of the subsidiary's net assets. Therefore, the consolidating worksheet entry to eliminate the Investment in Subsidiary account against subsidiary's equity on the date of the combination is always the same, regardless of the par values of the stock involved.

EXAMPLE 11-6: Refer to the journal entries made by A Co. in Examples 11-3, 11-4, and 11-5.

If both A Co. and B Co. continue as legal entities after the combination, A Co. must set up an Investment in B Co. account in which it records B Co.'s net assets at book value. A Co. then adjusts its equity accounts to account for any differences in par values. The following journal entries show how A Co. would record on its separate books the combination with B Co. under both conditions:

Entries if only A Co. Survives the Pooling			Entries if both A Co. and B Co. Survive the Pooling		
Example 11-3					
Assets (book value	10,000		Investment in B Co.	5,000	
Liabilities (book value)		5,000			
A Co. Common stock		2,000	A Co. Common stock		2,000
A Co. Additional paid-in capital		1,000	A Co. Additional paid-in capital		1,000
A Co. Retained earnings		2,000	A Co. Retained earnings		2,000
Example 11-4					
Assets (book value)	10,000		Investment in B Co.	5,000	
A Co. Additional paid-in capital	3,000		A Co. Additional paid-in capital	3,000	
Liabilities (book value)		5,000			
A Co. Common stock		7,000	A Co. Common stock		7,000
A Co. Retained earnings		1,000	A Co. Retained earnings		1,000
Example 11-5					
Assets (book value)	10,000		Investment in B Co.	5,000	
Liabilities (book value)		5,000			
A Co. Common stock		1,000	A Co. Common stock		1,000
A Co. Additional paid-in capital		2,000	A Co. Additional paid-in capital		2,000
A Co. Retained earnings		2,000	A Co. Retained earnings		2,000

No matter what the par value of the stock A Co. issues to effect the combination, A Co. generally records its investment in B Co. at the book value of B Co.'s net assets ($10,000 - $5,000 = $5,000). Therefore, the consolidating worksheet entry to eliminate the Investment in B Co. account against B Co.'s equity on the date of the combination in all cases is:

B Co. Common stock	2,000	
B Co. Additional paid-in capital	1,000	
B Co. Retained earnings	2,000	
Investment in B Co.		5,000
To eliminate Investment in B Co. against B Co. equity.		

C. A minority interest may exist after a pooling-of-interest combination.

According to APB Opinion 16, a small minority interest (10 percent or less) may remain in the subsidiary after a pooling-of-interest combination. In such a case, the minority interest in the subsidiary's equity accounts and net income must be determined and indicated on the consolidated financial statements. (The methods for accounting for such a minority interest during the preparation of consolidated financial statements, both on the date of the combination and after, are demonstrated in Chapters 4 through 10.)

EXAMPLE 11-7: The trial balances of P Co. and S Co. on 1/1/X1, just prior to a pooling-of-interests combination, are:

	P Co. Dr. (Cr.)	S Co. Dr. (Cr.)
Cash	250,000	50,000
Accounts receivable	350,000	200,000
Inventory	400,000	100,000
Fixed Assets	1,100,000	350,000
Accum. depreciation	(400,000)	(150,000)
Liabilities	(300,000)	(100,000)
Common stock, $10 par	(600,000)	(200,000)
Additional paid-in capital	(500,000)	(100,000)
Retained earnings	(300,000)	(150,000)
Totals	0	0

On 1/1/X1, P Co. issued 30,000 shares of its stock in return for 95 percent of the common stock of S Co. in a business combination appropriately accounted for as a pooling of interests. On that date, P Co. made the following journal entry on its separate books to record its investment in S Co.:

Investment in S Co. (book value of $450,000 × 95% interest)	427,500	
P Co. Additional paid-in capital	15,000	
P Co. Common stock (30,000 @ $10 par)		300,000
P Co. Retained earnings (95% interest × $150,000)		142,500

To record the Investment in S Co. on P Co.'s separate books in a pooling of interests.

The par value of the stock issued by P Co. is $300,000 (30,000 share × $10 par value). The par value of the stock surrendered by the S Co. stockholders is $190,000 ($200,000 × 95% = $190,000). The difference is $110,000, and is charged first to the combined Additional Paid-In Capital. This decrease of $110,000, in combination with the increase of $95,000 (S Co.'s Additional Paid-In Capital of $100,000 × 95%), results in a net decrease of $15,000, as recorded by P Co. above. The $15,000 charge to Additional Paid-In Capital may be further analyzed as follows:

	P Co. Equity (Pre-merger)	95% S Co. Equity (Pre-merger	Combined Totals*
Common stock	$ 600,000	$190,000	$ 790,000
Additional paid-in capital	500,000	95,000	595,000
Retained earnings	300,000	142,500	442,500
Total liabilities and equity	$1,400,000	$427,500	$1,827,500

	Combined Totals	Adjustments	Adjusted Combined Totals*
Common Stock	$ 790,000	110,000	$ 900,000*
Additional paid-in capital	595,000	(110,000)	485,000
Retained earnings	442,500		442,500
Total liabilities and equity	$1,827,500		$1,827,500

*600,000 original par plus $300,000 on stock issue.

The adjusted combined totals shown above give the equity account balances that should appear on P Co.'s books after recording the combination with S Co. Note that P Co.'s. Common Stock account increased by $300,000 (from $600,000 to $900,000), its Additional Paid-in Capital account decreased by $15,000 (from $500,000 to $485,000), and its Retained Earnings account increased by $142,500 (from $300,000 to $442,500). Exhibit 11-A shows the trial balances of P Co. and S Co. on 1/1/X1 immediately after their pooling of interests, as well as the eliminating entries necessary on the consolidating worksheet to develop the consolidated balance sheet for that date. Note that the five-percent minority interest in S Co. is clearly indicated on the balance sheet.

Exhibit 11-A
P Co. and 95% Owned Subsidiary S Co.
Consolidating Worksheet as of 1/1/X1

Pooling of interests on date of merger—with minority interest

Account name	P Co. Dr. (Cr.)	S Co. Dr. (Cr.)	Eliminations Dr.	Eliminations (Cr.)	CONSOLIDATED Balance Sheet
Cash	250,000	50,000			300,000
Accounts receivable	350,000	200,000			550,000
Inventory	400,000	100,000			500,000
Fixed assets	1,100,000	350,000			1,450,000
Accum depr.	(400,000)	(150,000)			(550,000)
Investment in S Co.	427,500			(427,500)[1]	0
Liabilities	(300,000)	(100,000)			(400,000)
Common stock: P Co.	(900,000)				(900,000)
S Co.		(200,000)	190,000[1]		(10,000)M
Additional paid-in capital: P Co.	(485,000)				(485,000)
S Co.		(100,000)	95,000[1]		(5,000)M
Retained earnings: P Co.	(442,500)				(442,500)
S Co		(150,000)	142,500[1]		(7,500)M
Totals	0	0	427,500	(427,500)	0
Total minority interest (sum of items marked "M")					(22,500)

[1]To eliminate Investment in S Co. against S Co. equity.

D. At the end of a period of combined operations after a pooling of interests, standard consolidating worksheet eliminating entries are necessary.

When both companies continue as legal entities after a pooling-of-interest merger, consolidated financial statements are required. Naturally, during the course of preparation of those statements the standard eliminating entries (including those to eliminate the parent's investment against the subsidiary's equity, to eliminate any intercompany transactions, and to set off the minority interest) must be made on the consolidating worksheet.

EXAMPLE 11-8: Refer to the information given in Example 11-7, and assume that P Co. carries its investment in S Co. using the equity method.

During 19X1, P Co. sold inventory to S Co. totalling $40,000, at a gross profit of 20 percent of the selling price. One-half of this inventory ($20,000) remained in S Co.'s ending inventory on 12/31/X1. The trial balances on 12/31/X1 for both P Co. and S Co. are given in the first two columns of Exhibit 11-B.

P Co.'s Investment in S Co. account balance on that date is determined as follows:

1/1/X1 Investment in S Co. balance	$427,500
Plus: 95% × S Co. 19X1 net income $100,000	95,000
Less: 95% × S Co. 19X1 dividends of $80,000	(76,000)
12/31/X1 Investment in S Co. balance	$446,500

When the combined entity prepares consolidated financial statements on 12/31/X1, it must make entries to eliminate P Co.'s Investment in S Co. account and P Co.'s income from S Co.'s operations against S Co.'s equity accounts and its dividends declared. It must also eliminate the intercompany sale of inventory from P Co. to S Co. Finally, it must eliminate the profit remaining in S Co.'s ending inventory ($20,000 remaining intercompany inventory × 20% gross profit rate = $4,000 remaining profit). With these eliminating entries completed, the final step is to indicate the minority's interest in S Co.'s equity and net income for 19X1.

Exhibit 11-B shows the consolidating worksheet and consolidated financial statements for the combined entity of P Co. and S Co. one year after their pooling-of-interest merger.

Exhibit 11-B
P Co. and 95% Owned Subsidiary S Co.
Consolidating Worksheet for the Year Ended 12/31/X1

Pooling of interests one year after merger—with minority interest

Account Name	P Co. Dr. (Cr.)	S Co. Dr. (Cr.)	Eliminations Dr.	Eliminations (Cr.)	CONSOLIDATED Dr. (Cr.) Income Statement	Retained Earnings	Balance Sheet
Cash	300,000	140,000					440,000
Accounts receivable	400,000	150,000					550,000
Inventory	500,000	150,000		(4,000)[3]			646,000
Fixed assets	1,100,000	350,000					1,450,000
Accum. depr.	(450,000)	(170,000)					(620,000)
Investment in S Co.	446,500			(446,500)[1]			0
Liabilities	(369,000)	(150,000)					(519,000)
Common stock:							
P Co.	(900,000)						(900,000)
S Co.		(200,000)	190,000[1]				(10,000)M
Additional paid-in capital: P Co.	(485,000)						(485,000)
S Co.		(100,000)	95,000[1]				(5,000)M
Retained earnings:							
P Co.	(442,500)					(442,500)	
S Co.		(150,000)	142,500[1]				(7,500)M
Dividends declared:							
P Co.	200,000					200,000	
S Co.		80,000		(76,000)[1]			4,000M
Investment income	(95,000)		95,000[1]		0		
Sales revenues	(2,800,000)	(900,000)	40,000[2]		(3,660,000)		
Cost of goods sold	1,400,000	500,000	4,000[3]	(40,000)[2]	1,864,000		
Other expenses	1,195,000	300,000			1,495,000		
Totals	0	0	566,500	(566,500)			
	Consolidated net income				(301,000)		
	*Minority interest				5,000		(5,000)M
	Consolidated net income				(296,000)	(296,000)	
	Consolidated retained earnings					(538,500)	(538,500)
					Total		0
	Total minority interest (sum of items marked "M")						(23,500)

M = Minority interest

*Minority interest in net income: 5% × S Co. net income of $100,000 = %5,000

[1]To eliminate Investment in S Co. and investment income against S Co. equity and dividend declarations.

[2]To eliminate intercompany sales of $40,000 from P Co. to S Co.

[3]To eliminate profit in ending inventory on sales from P Co. to S Co. (Ending inventory on S Co.'s books purchased from P Co. of $20,000 × 20% gross profit rate = $4,000).

RAISE YOUR GRADES

Can you explain . . . ?

- ☑ the fundamental difference between a pooling-of-interest and a purchase business combination
- ☑ the mechanism by which two companies may pool their interests
- ☑ the definition of "substantially all" of a company's stock
- ☑ the consequence of failing to meet any of the 12 points of APB Opinion 16
- ☑ why net income tends to be higher for a business combined under the pooling-of-interest method

- ☑ why consolidated financial statements for companies combined under the pooling-of-interest method reflect operations for the full accounting period, and may even be retroactive to periods well before the combination
- ☑ how to treat any costs incurred during a pooling-of-interest combination
- ☑ how a difference in the par values of the stock issued and the stock surrendered during a pooling-of-interest combination will affect the equity accounts of the newly combined economic entity
- ☑ the effects of a minority interest on a pooling-of-interest combination on the date of the combination
- ☑ the effects of a minority interest on a pooling-of-interest combination after a period of combined operation

SUMMARY

1. Under a pooling of interest business combination there is a continuity of ownership before and after the combination; the owners equity interests are merged.
2. Original ownership rights remain essentially intact, and no sale or purchase is presumed in a pooling of interests.
3. To effect a pooling-of-interest combination, the "acquiring" company issues common stock, with all the rights and privileges of its previously issued common stock, in exchange for "substantially all" (defined as 90 percent or more) of the common stock of the "acquired" company.
4. In order for a business combination to be accounted for as a pooling of interests, it must meet the 12 conditions described in APB Opinion 16.
5. Failure to meet any of these 12 conditions means that the combination *must* be accounted for as a purchase.
6. If the combination meets all 12 conditions set out in APB Opinion 16, it *must* be accounted for as a pooling of interests. The method used to account for the combination is not a matter of choice.
7. Because a pooling of interests is considered a merger of equity interests rather than a purchase, all accounting procedures in the combination are based on historical costs, or book values, rather than fair market values.
8. Because all accounting procedures in a pooling of interests are based on book values, no goodwill can result from the combination, and none of the acquired company's assets need be revalued.
9. There is no amortization of goodwill or depreciation of net asset revaluation as a result of a pooling-of-interest combination.
10. Consolidated financial statements for companies combined under the pooling-of-interest method are prepared by adding the statements of the individual companies together (after elimination of inter-company transactions and balances).
11. The consolidated financial statements for companies combined under the pooling-of-interest method should show results of operations for the full accounting period, even if the combination did not occur until nearly the end of the period.
12. All costs incurred during a pooling-of-interest combination should be considered expenses of the period in which the combination occurred. (This treatment is different from that which is required in a purchase. See Chapter 4, Section 4-1.C.)
13. If the par value of the capital stock issued to effect the combination exceeds the par value of the stock surrendered by the combining companies, charge the difference first to combined Additional Paid-In Capital, and then to combined Retained Earnings.
14. If the par value of the stock surrendered by the combining companies exceeds the par value of the capital stock issued to effect the combination, credit the difference to combined Additional Paid-In Capital.
15. If more than one company continues as a legal entity after a pooling-of-interest combination, the parent company creates an Investment in Subsidiary account rather than combining its asset and liability accounts with the subsidiary's.

16. A minority interest (not to exceed 10%) may exist in a pooling-of-interest combination, and must be treated as it would be treated under a purchase combination.
17. Intercompany eliminations in years after the pooling of interests (for items such as intercompany sales, purchases, receivables, payables, and so on) must continue as described in previous chapters.

RAPID REVIEW

1. In a pooling of interests, a sale is deemed to have occurred by one of the combining companies while no such presumption exists in a purchase.
   (*a*) True
   (*b*) False
2. Which of the following is not required within the 12 specific conditions that must be met in order for a business combination to be viewed as a pooling of interests?
   (*a*) Autonomy of combining companies.
   (*b*) Common voting rights exercisable without restrictions.
   (*c*) Independence of combining companies.
   (*d*) Absence of planned sale of excess capacity after merger.
   (*e*) Absence of planned transactions;
3. If all 12 conditions required for a pooling-of-interest combination are met,
   (*a*) the merging companies are in the advantageous position of choosing between a purchase and a pooling.
   (*b*) the merging companies are required to use the pooling-of-interests approach.
   (*c*) the merging companies may treat the business combination as part pooling and part purchase provided the pooling of interests is fairly reflected.
   (*d*) although the combining companies may select one approach or the other under generally accepted accounting principles, the pooling-of-interests approach is probably superior.
4. In which of the following situations must a business combination be accounted for as a purchase?
   (*a*) As a part of the combination, the combined company agrees to retire some of the common stock issued to effect the combination.
   (*b*) The issuing company in the combination issues only its common stock for substantially all (94%) of the combining company's common stock.
   (*c*) Each of the combining companies is independent of the other combining companies.
   (*d*) The combined company will dispose of property, plant and equipment representing duplicate facilities resulting from the merger.
5. A fundamental accounting difference between the purchase and pooling of interests methods is that
   (*a*) net asset fair values are used in a pooling but not in a purchase.
   (*b*) goodwill may develop as a result of a pooling but not as a result of a purchase.
   (*c*) net assets of the combining (acquired) company may be adjusted to fair value in a purchase but these adjustments are never amortized.
   (*d*) net asset books values are used in a pooling but not in a purchase.

Numbers 6, 7, 8, and 9 are based on the following data:

Parrot Corporation issued 100,000 additional shares of its $20 par value common stock for 100% of the common stock of Sparrow Inc. on July 1, 19X4. Net income for the fiscal year ended December 31, 19X4 for Sparrow Inc. was $1,000,000 and for Parrot Corporation was $3,000,000 exclusive of any consideration of Sparrow Inc. Net income of Sparrow Inc. for the six months ended December 31, 19X4 was $550,000. The fair value per share of Parrot Corporation's stock was $50 on July 1, 19X4. The book and fair value of Sparrow Inc.'s net assets on July 1, 19X4 was $4,000,000.

6. Consolidated net income for the fiscal year ended December 31, 19X4 assuming the business combination is appropriately accounted for as a pooling of interests is $________.
7. Goodwill implicit in the purchase price paid by Parrot Corporation if the transaction is appropriately accounted for as a pooling of interests is $________.

8. Goodwill implicit in the purchase price paid by Parrot Corporation if the transaction is appropriately accounted for as a purchase is$________.
9. Consolidated net income for the fiscal year ended December 31, 19X4 assuming the business combination is appropriately accounted for as a purchase is $________.

Items 10 and 11 are based on the following information:

On August 1, 19X2, Prairie Co. issued 50,000 shares of its $10 par value common stock for all of the common stock of Seedling Co. The fair value per share of this stock on August 1, 19X2 was $40. Business combination costs incurred by Prairie Co. included $30,000 in finder's fees and other direct costs, $10,000 in SEC registration fees, and $6,000 in indirect general corporate overhead charges.

10. Assuming the business combination is appropriately viewed as a pooling of interests, business combination expenses for 19X2 are $________.
11. Assuming the business combination is appropriately viewed as a purchase, business combination expenses for 19X2 are $________.
12. Planet Co. issued 10,000 shares of its $10 par value common stock for all of the common stock of Star Co. on May 1, 19X5. On this date, stockholders' equity was:

	Planet Co.	Star Co.
Common stock, $10 par	$1,000,000	$200,000
Additional paid-in capital	100,000	50,000
Retained earnings	400,000	100,000
Total stockholders' equity	$1,500,000	$350,000

Assuming the business combination is appropriately accounted for as pooling of interests, the consolidated common stock par value, additional paid-in capital, and retained earnings immediately after the combination are $________, $________, and $________, respectively.

13. Assuming the same facts as those shown in Question 12 except that Planet Co. issues 30,000 shares to effect the merger, consolidated common stock par value, additional paid-in capital, and retained earnings immediately after the combination are $________, $________, and $________, respectively.
14. If a pooling-of-interests situation exists, consolidating workpapers must be prepared at year-end, because by definition, a situation of control exists wherein the issuing company obtains substantially all (90% or more) of the company's stock. True or False? ________
15. Intercompany transactions (inventory sales, fixed asset sales, intercompany preferred stock or debt holdings, intercompany receivables, payables, revenues or expenses) which occur after a pooling of interests are eliminated the same way as they are eliminated in a purchase-type business combination. True or False? ________

Answers:

1. (*b*) False. The reverse is true.
2. (*d*) See condition 12 in APB Opinion 16, as described in Chapter 11.
3. (*b*) The use of one approach or the other is not a matter of choice.
4. (*a*) See condition 10 in APB Opinion 16, which prohibits agreement to retire common stock issued to effect the combination if the combination represents a pooling of interests.
5. (*d*) See Section 11-2.
6. $4,000,000. Note that in a pooling of interests, Parrot Corporation's income of $3,000,000 is added to Sparrow Inc.'s income of $1,000,000 for the full year in the year of the merger even though the merger did not occur until July 1, 19X4.
7. $0. Goodwill cannot result from a pooling. Book values are used.
8. $1,000,000.

Price paid by Parrot Corporation (100,000 shares × $50 fair value per share)	$5,000,000
Fair and book value of net assets acquired	(4,000,000)
Goodwill	$1,000,000

9. $3,537,500.

Parrot Corporation's net income (full year)	$3,000,000
Plus: Sparrow Inc.'s net income from July 1, 19X4 (purchase date) to December 31, 19X4	550,000
Less: Goodwill amortization ($1,000,000 divided by 40 years times one-half year)	(12,500)
19X4 Consolidated net income	$3,537,500

10. $46,000. All costs to effect a business combination as a pooling are expensed as incurred. (See Chapter 4, Section 4-1.C.)

11. $6,000. In a purchase, only the indirect and general expenses are recorded as expenses. Finder's fees and direct costs are viewed as a part of the investment's purchase price, and registration fees are viewed as a reduction of additional paid-in capital on the securities issued. (See Chapter 4, Section 4-1.C.)

12. $1,100,000, $250,000, $500,000. The journal entry on Planet Co.'s books to effect the merger in this case would be:

Investment in Star Co. (book value)	350,000	
Planet Co. Common stock (10,000 shares @ $10 par)		100,000
Planet Co. Additional paid-in capital		250,000
Planet Co. Retained earnings		100,000

Since the combining Star Co.'s stock par value of $200,000 was greater than the issuing Planet Co.'s stock par value of only $100,000, the difference is credited to additional paid-in capital. (The consolidated totals are Planet Co.'s totals for common stock, additional paid-in capital and retained earnings after the above entry. In consolidation, Star Co.'s equity will be eliminated against the Investment in Star Co. account.)

13. $1,300,000, $50,000, $500,000. The journal entry on Planet Co.'s books to effect the merger would now be:

Investment in Star Co.	350,000	
Planet Co. Additional paid-in capital	50,000	
Planet Co. Common stock (30,000 shares @ $10 par)		300,000
Planet Co. Retained earnings		100,000

Note that in this case, the issuing Planet Co.'s par stock value of $300,000 exceeds the combining Star Co.'s par stock value of $200,000. The $100,000 is first charged to combined additional paid-in capital and then, if necessary, to retained earnings.

14. False. If only one company survives the pooling of interests as a separate legal entity, there will be no consolidating workpapers.

15. True.

SOLVED PROBLEMS

PROBLEM 11-1: Immediately before the business combination of Plastics Corp. and Shimmer Co., the January 1, 19X6 stockholders' equity of the two companies was:

	Plastics Corp.	Shimmer Co.
Common stock, $10 par value	$2,000,000	$400,000
Additional paid-in capital	1,500,000	250,000
Retained earnings	2,000,000	50,000
Total stockholders' equity	$5,500,000	$700,000

The following additional information regarding the two companies is also available as of January 1, 19X6:

	Plastics Corp.	Shimmer Co.
Fair value per share of common stock	$ 30	$ 20
Fair value of net assets	$5,800,000	$750,000

Plastic Corp. issues 30,000 shares of its $10 par value common stock for 100% of the outstanding stock of Shimmer Co. Assume the merger qualifies as a pooling of interests.

Requirements:

(*a*) Prepare the journal entry on Plastics Corp.'s books to record the merger assuming only Plastics Corp. survives the merger as a separate legal entity.

(*b*) Prepare both the journal entry on Plastics Corp.'s books to record the merger and the consolidating worksheet elimination entry necessary to eliminate Plastics Corp.'s Investment in Shimmer Co. account assuming both companies survive the merger as separate legal entities.

Answer:

(*a*) Entry on Plastics Corp.'s Books

	Debit	Credit
Net assets (book value)	700,000	
Plastics Corp. Common stock (30,000 shares @ $10 par)		300,000
Plastics Corp. Additional paid-in capital		350,000
Plastics Corp. Retained earnings		50,000

To record merger of Plastics Corp. and Shimmer Co. as a pooling of interests. (Note that fair values are ignored. Also note that the combining Shimmer Co.'s par value of $400,000 exceeded the par value of the issuing Plastic Corp. stock of $300,000 by $100,000. This $100,000 excess increases the additional paid-in capital from $250,000 to $350,000 as shown in the journal entry.)

(*b*) Entry on Plastics Corp.'s Books

	Debit	Credit
Investment in Shimmer Co.	700,000	
Plastics Corp. Common stock (30,000 shares @ $10 par)		300,000
Plastics Corp. Additional paid-in capital		350,000
Plastics Corp. Retained earnings		50,000

To record merger of Plastics Corp. and Shimmer Co. as a pooling of interests. (Note that this entry is the same as the entry in answer to part *a*, except that the debit is to the Investment in Shimmer Co. account rather than to specific assets and liabilities (net assets). This investment account must be eliminated in the consolidation process.)

Consolidating Worksheet Elimination Entry

	Debit	Credit
Shimmer Co. Common stock	400,000	
Shimmer Co. Additional paid-in capital	250,000	
Shimmer Co. Retained earnings	50,000	
Investment in Shimmer Co.		700,000

To eliminate Investment in Shimmer Co. against Shimmer Co. equity.

PROBLEM 11-2: Assume the same facts as those described in Problem 11-1 except that the merger does not meet pooling of interests criteria and must therefore be accounted for as a purchase. Based on this new assumption, respond once again to requirements *a* and *b* of Problem 11-1.

Answer:

(*a*) Entry on Plastics Corp.'s Books

	Debit	Credit
Net assets (fair value)	750,000	
Goodwill	150,000	
Plastics Corp. Common stock (30,000 shares @ $10 par)		300,000
Plastics Corp. Additional paid-in capital (30,000 shares @ $20)		600,000

To record purchase by Plastics Corp. of Shimmer Co.'s net assets.

(*b*) Entry on Plastics Corp.'s Books

	Debit	Credit
Investment in Shimmer Co.	900,000	
Plastics Corp. Common stock (30,000 shares @ $10 par)		300,000
Plastics Corp. Additional paid-in capital (30,000 shares @ $20)		600,000

To record investment of Plastics Corp. in Shimmer Co. as a purchase.

Consolidating Worksheet Elimination Entry

	Debit	Credit
Shimmer Co. Common stock	400,000	
Shimmer Co. Additional paid-in capital	250,000	
Shimmer Co. Retained earnings	50,000	
Net assets ($750,000 fair value—$700,000 book value)	50,000	
Goodwill	150,000	
Investment in Shimmer Co.		900,000

To eliminate Investment in Shimmer Co. against Shimmer Co. equity, adjust Shimmer Co. net assets to fair value, and record goodwill.

PROBLEM 11-3: On January 1, 19X1, Premium Co. issued common stock to acquire 100% of the outstanding common stock, of Singleton Co. The business combination met all the conditions for treatment as a pooling of interests. Immediately before the merger, stockholders' equity of the two companies was:

	Premium Co.	Singleton Co.
Common stock, $20 par	$200,000	
Common stock, $10 par		$100,000
Additional paid-in capital	50,000	10,000
Retained earnings	40,000	20,000
Total stockholders' equity	$290,000	$130,000

Both companies continue to exist as separate legal entities after the merger.

(*a*) Prepare the journal entry required on the books of Premium Co. to record the merger in each of the following three different cases:

Case I: Premium issues 5,000 shares.
Case II: Premium issues 6,000 shares.
Case III: Premium issues 4,000 shares.

(*b*) Prepare the consolidating worksheet elimination entry required on the January 1, 19X1 merger date for each of the three cases.

Answer:

(*a*) Entry on Premium Co.'s Books—Case I

	Debit	Credit
Investment in Singleton Co. (book value)	130,000	
Premium Co. Common stock (5,000 shares @ $20 par)		100,000
Premium Co. Additional paid-in capital		10,000
Premium Co. Retained earnings		20,000

(In Case I, par value of issuing Premium Co. equals par value of combining Singleton Co. and therefore no adjustments to equity book values were necessary.)

Entry on Premium Co.'s Books—Case II

	Debit	Credit
Investment in Singleton Co. (book value)	130,000	
Premium Co. Additional paid-in capital	10,000	
Premium Co. Common stock (6,000 shares @ $20 par)		120,000
Premium Co. Retained earnings		20,000

(In Case II, the par value of the issuing Premium Co. exceeds the par value of combining Singleton Co. and the difference is first charged to combined additional paid-in capital, and then, if necessary, to combined retained earnings. In Case II, sufficient additional paid-in capital exists, and therefore no reduction in retained earnings was necessary.)

Entry on Premium Co.'s Books—Case III

Investment in Singleton Co. (book value)	130,000	
Premium Co. Common stock (4,000 shares @ $20 par)		80,000
Premium Co. Additional paid-in capital		30,000
Premium Co. Retained earnings		20,000

(In Case III, the combining Singleton Co.'s par exceeded the issuing Premium Co.'s par, and the difference increases additional paid-in capital.)

(*b*) The consolidating worksheet elimination entry required on the January 1, 19X1 merger date is the same in all three cases:

Singleton Co. Common stock	100,000	
Singleton Co. Additional paid-in capital	10,000	
Singleton Co. Retained earnings	20,000	
Investment in Singleton Co.		130,000

PROBLEM 11-4: Assume all of the same facts as those described in Problem 11-3 except that Premium Co. acquired only a 90% interest in Singleton Co. by virtue of Premium Co.'s stock issue. Based on this new assumption, again answer requirements *a* and *b* of Problem 11-3.

Answer:

(*a*) Entry on Premium Co.'s Books—Case I

Investment in Singleton Co. (90% book value)	117,000	
Premium Co. Additional paid-in capital	1,000	
Premium Co. Common stock (5,000 shares @ $20 par)		100,000
Premium Co. Retained earnings (90%)		18,000

Entry on Premium Co.'s Books—Case II

Investment in Singleton Co. (90% book value)	117,000	
Premium Co. Additional paid-in capital	21,000	
Premium Co. Common stock (6,000 shares @ $20 par)		120,000
Premium Co. Retained earnings (90%)		18,000

Entry on Premium Co.'s Books—Case III

Investment in Singleton Co. (90% book value)	117,000	
Premium Co. Common stock (4,000 shares @ $20 par)		80,000
Premium Co. Additional paid-in capital		19,000
Premium Co. Retained earnings (90%)		18,000

(*b*) The consolidating worksheet elimination entry required on the January 1, 19X1 merger date is the same in all cases:

Singleton Co. Common stock (90%)	90,000	
Singleton Co. Additional paid-in capital (90%)	9,000	
Singleton Co. Retained earnings	18,000	
Investment in Singleton Co.		117,000

PROBLEM 11-5: (AICPA Adapted) Spellman Co. will acquire 90% of Moore Co. in a business combination. The total consideration has been agreed upon. The nature of Spellman's payment has not been fully agreed upon. Therefore, it is possible that this business combination might be accounted for as either a purchase or a pooling of interests. It is expected that at the date the business combination is to be consummated, the fair value will exceed the book value of Moore's assets minus liabilities. Spellman desires to prepare consolidated financial statements which will include the financial statements of Moore.

(*a*) 1. Would the method of accounting for the business combination (purchase vs. pooling of interests) affect whether or not goodwill is reported?

2. If goodwill is reported, explain how the amount of goodwill is determined.

3. Would the method of accounting for the business combination (purchase vs. pooling of interests) affect whether or not minority interest is reported? If the amount reported differs, explain why.

(*b*) 1. From a theoretical standpoint, why should consolidated financial statements be prepared?

2. From a theoretical standpoint, what is the usual first necessary condition to be met before consolidated financial statements can be prepared?

3. From a theoretical standpoint, does the method of accounting for the business combination (purchase vs. pooling of interests) affect the decision to prepare consolidated financial statements? Why?

Answer:

(*a*) 1. Goodwill does not arise and, therefore, should not be reported if the business combination is accounted for as a pooling of interests. The recorded assets and liabilities of the separate companies generally become the recorded assets and liabilities of the combined corporation.However, goodwill should be reported if the business combination is accounted for as a purchase.

2. All identifiable assets acquired, either individually or by type, and liabilities assumed in a business combination, whether or not shown in the financial statements of Moore, should be assigned a portion of the cost of Moore, normally equal to their fair values at date of acquisition. Then the excess of the cost of Moore over the sum of the amounts assigned to identifiable assets acquired less liabilities assumed should be recorded as goodwill.

3. Minority interest should be reported whether the business combination is accounted for as a purchase or a pooling of interests. The amount of minority interest reported would be the same whether the business combination is accounted for as a purchase or a pooling of interests.

(*b*) 1. Consolidated financial statements should be prepared in order to present financial position and operating results in a manner more meaningful than in separate state-ments.

2. The usual first necessary condition for consolidation is control as evidenced by ownership of a majority voting interest. Therefore, as a general rule, ownership by one company, directly or indirectly, of over 50% of the outstanding voting shares of another company is a condition necessary for consolidation.

3. Consolidated financial statements should be prepared whether a businesscombination is accounted for as a purchase or a pooling of interests. Control exists and is independent of the method of accounting used.

PROBLEM 11-6: Plum Co. and Seed Co. agreed on terms of a merger on January 1, 19X5. The merger meets all of the conditions required to be deemed a pooling of interests. Immediately before the merger, the January 1, 19X5 trial balances of Plum Co. and Seed Co. were:

	1/1/X5 Pre-merger Trial Balances	
Account name	Plum Co. Dr. (Cr.)	Seed Co. Dr. (Cr.)
Cash	400,000	100,000
Accounts receivable	500,000	200,000
Inventory	350,000	200,000
Fixed assets	3,700,000	1,700,000
Accumulated depreciation	(1,700,000)	(800,000)
Liabilities	(750,000)	(500,000)
Common stock: Plum Co.	(1,800,000)*	
Seed Co.		(600,000)*
Additional paid-in capital:		
Plum Co.	(200,000)	
Seed Co.		(100,000)
Retained earnings:		
Plum Co.	(500,000)	
Seed Co.		(200,000)
Totals	0	0

*Common stock par value per share = $30.

Plum Co. issued 25,000 shares of its stock in exchange for 90% of Seed Co.'s stock, and both companies continued as separate legal entities after this issuance.

(*a*) Prepare the journal entry necessary on Plum Co.'s books to record the issuance of the 25,000 shares.
(*b*) Complete the following Schedule I consolidating worksheet as of the January 1, 19X5 merger date.

Schedule I
Plum Co. and 90% Owned Subsidiary Seed Co.
Consolidating Worksheet as of 1/1/X5

Account name	Plum Co. Dr. (Cr.)	Seed Co. Dr. (Cr.)	Eliminations Dr.	Eliminations (Cr.)	CONSOLIDATED Balance Sheet
Cash	400,000	100,000			
Accounts receivable	500,000	200,000			
Inventory	350,000	200,000			
Fixed assets	3,700,000	1,700,000			
Accum depr.	(1,700,000)	(800,000)			
Investment in Seed Co.	*				
Liabilities	(750,000)	(500,000)			
Common stock:					
Plum Co.	*				
Seed Co.		(600,000)			
Additional paid-in capital: Plum Co.	*				
Seed Co.		(100,000)			
Retained earnings:					
Plum Co.	*				
Seed Co		(200,000)			
Totals		0			
Total minority interest					

*Determination of these balances on Plum Co.'s books subsequent to the merger is based on Plum Co.'s premerger trial balance plus the effects of your answer to part (*a*) of this question.

Answer:

(*a*)

	Dr.	Cr.
Investment in Seed Co. (book value of \$900,000 × 90% interest)	810,000	
Plum Co. Additional paid-in capital	120,000	
Plum Co. Common stock (25,000 shares @ \$30 par)		750,000
Plum Co. Retained earnings (\$200,000 × 90%)		180,000

To record Investment in Seed Co. on Plum Co.'s separate books in a pooling of interests.
(***note:*** charge is first made to additional paid-in capital and then, only if necessary, to retained earnings when issuing company's par exceeds combining company's par.)

(*b*) See Schedule I, Problem 11-6 Answer.

Schedule I
Plum Co. and 90% Owned Subsidiary Seed Co.
Consolidating Worksheet as of 1/1/X5

Account name	Plum Co. Dr. (Cr.)	Seed Co. Dr. (Cr.)	Eliminations Dr.	Eliminations (Cr.)	CONSOLIDATED Balance Sheet
Cash	400,000	100,000			500,000
Accounts receivable	500,000	200,000			700,000
Inventory	350,000	200,000			550,000
Fixed assets	3,700,000	1,700,000			5,400,000
Accum depr.	(1,700,000)	(800,000)			(2,500,000)
Investment in Seed Co.	810,000			(810,000)[1]	0
Liabilities	(750,000)	(500,000)			(1,250,000)
Common stock:					
Plum Co.	(2,550,000)				(2,550,000)
Seed Co.		(600,000)	540,000[1]		(60,000)M
Additional paid-in capital: Plum Co.	(80,000)				(80,000)
Seed Co.		(100,000)	90,000[1]		(10,000)M
Retained earnings:					
Plum Co.	(680,000)				(680,000)
Seed Co		(200,000)	180,000[1]		(20,000)M
Totals	0	0	810,000	(810,000)	0
Total minority interest (sum of items marked "M")					(90,000)

[1]To eliminate Investment in Seed Co. against Seed Co. equity.

PROBLEM 11-7: This problem is a continuation of Problem 11-6 and requires preparation of a consolidating worksheet for Plum Co. and its subsidiary Seed Co. on December 31, 19X5, one year after the merger. The following information is available for the fiscal year ended December 31, 19X5.

- Seed Co. sold inventory to Plum Co. for \$100,000. Seed Co.'s markup on cost is 20%. On December 31, 19X5, \$24,000 from these intercompany purchases remained in Plum Co.'s ending inventory. Plum Co. made these purchases on account and still owed Seed Co. \$30,000 as of December 31, 19X5.
- Pre-closing trial balances for Plum Co. and Seed Co. for the year-ended December 31, 19X5 follow on Schedule II. Additional intercompany transactions are evident on this trial balance.

Requirement:
Complete the Schedule II consolidating worksheet provided.

Schedule II
Plum Co. and 90% Owned Subsidiary Seed Co.
Consolidating Worksheet for the Year Ended 12/31/X5

Account Name	Plum Co. Dr. (Cr.)	Seed Co. Dr. (Cr.)	Eliminations Dr.	Eliminations (Cr.)	CONSOLIDATED Dr. (Cr.) Income Statement	Retained Earnings	Balance Sheet
Cash	450,000	110,000					
Accounts receivable	650,000	250,000					
Dividends receivable	27,000						
Inventory	450,000	180,000					
Fixed assets	3,700,000	1,855,000					
Accum. depr.	(1,800,000)	(850,000)					
Investment in Seed Co.	868,500						
Dividends payable	(20,000)	(30,000)					
Liabilities (all other)	(780,000)	(550,000)					
Common stock:							
Plum Co.	(2,550,000)						
Seed Co.		(600,000)					
Additional paid-in capital: Plum Co.	(80,000)						
Seed Co.		(100,000)					
Retained earnings:							
Plum Co.	(680,000)						
Seed Co.		(200,000)					
Dividends declared:							
Plum Co.	264,500						
Seed Co.		85,000					
Investment income	(135,000)						
Sales revenues	(3,000,000)	(1,150,000)					
Cost of goods sold	1,220,000	650,000					
Other expenses	1,415,000	350,000					
Totals	0	0					
	Combined net income						
	Minority interest						
	Consolidated net income						
	Consolidated retained earnings						
					Total		
	Total minority interest						

Answer:

Note that the Investment in Seed Co. must be carried at equity since the December 31, 19X5 account balance is supportable on that basis:

1/1/X5 Investment in Seed Co. (from Problem 11-6)		$810,000
Plus:	90% × Seed Co.'s net income of $150,000	135,000
Less:	90% × Seed Co.'s dividend declarations of $85,000	(76,500)
12/31/X5 Investment in Seed Co.		$868,500

This information becomes the basis for the first worksheet elimination entry. The second worksheet elimination entry eliminates the intercompany dividend receivable and payable remaining on the separate books of the two companies. Consolidating worksheet elimination entries 3, 4, and 5 eliminate intercompany sales, intercompany profit in ending inventory, and intercompany accounts receivable and payable respectively. Note that the profit in ending inventory carried on Plum Co.'s books which resulted from intercompany sales is computed as follows:

Selling price	=	120% × Cost
$24,000	=	120% × Cost
$24,000/120%	=	Cost
$20,000	=	Cost
$24,000 selling price – $20,000 cost	=	$4,000 profit.

Finally, a minority interest of 10% in Seed Co.'s net income must be determined as shown in the answer on Schedule II.

Schedule II
Plum Co. and 90% Owned Subsidiary Seed Co.
Consolidating Worksheet for the Year Ended 12/31/X5

					CONSOLIDATED Dr. (Cr.)		
Account Name	Plum Co. Dr. (Cr.)	Seed Co. Dr. (Cr.)	Eliminations Dr.	Eliminations (Cr.)	Income Statement	Retained Earnings	Balance Sheet
Cash	450,000	110,000					560,000
Accounts receivable	650,000	250,000		(30,000)[5]			870,000
Dividends receivable	27,000			(27,000)[2]			0
Inventory	450,000	180,000		(4,000)[4]			626,000
Fixed assets	3,700,000	1,855,000					5,555,000
Accum. depr.	(1,800,000)	(850,000)					(2,650,000)
Investment in Seed Co..	868,500			(868,500)[1]			0
Dividends payable	(20,000)	(30,000)	27,000[2]				(23,000)
Liabilities (all other)	(780,000)	(550,000)	30,000[5]				(1,300,000)
Common stock:							
Plum Co.	(2,550,000)						(2,550,000)
Seed Co.		(600,000)	540,000[1]				(60,000)M
Additional paid-in capital: Plum Co.	(80,000)						(80,000)
Seed Co.		(100,000)	90,000[1]				(10,000)M
Retained earnings:							
Plum Co.	(680,000)					(680,000)	
Seed Co.		(200,000)	180,000[1]				(20,000)M
Dividends declared:							
Plum Co.	264,500					264,500	
Seed Co.		85,000		(76,500)[1]			8,500M
Investment income	(135,000)		135,000[1]		0		
Sales revenues	(3,000,000)	(1,150,000)	100,000[3]		(4,050,000)		
Cost of goods sold	1,220,000	650,000	4,000[4]	(100,000)[3]	1,774,000		
Other expenses	1,415,000	350,000			1,765,000		
Totals	0	0	1,106,000	(1,106,000)			
	Combined net income				(511,000)		
	*Minority interest				14,600		(14,600)M
	Consolidated net income				(496,400)	(496,400)	
	Consolidated retained earnings					(911,900)	(911,900)
					Total		0
	Total minority interest (sum of items marked "M")						(96,100)

M = Minority interest

*Minority interest in net income: 10% × Seed Co. net income of $150,000 =	$15,000
Less minority interest in unrealized profit in ending inventory from Seed Co. sales to Plum Co. (10% minority interest × $4,000 profit)	(400)
	$14,600

[1]To eliminate 90% Investment in Seed Co. and investment income against 90% of Seed Co. equity and dividend declarations.
[2]To eliminate intercompany dividends receivable and payable at year end.
[3]To eliminate intercompany sales of $100,000 from Seed Co. to Plum Co.
[4]To eliminate profit of $4,000 in ending inventory on sales from Seed Co. to Plum Co.
[5]To eliminate intercompany accounts receivable and payable at year end.

PROBLEM 11-8: (AICPA Adapted) Case, Inc. acquired all of the outstanding $25 par common stock of Frey, Inc., on June 30,19X4, in exchange for 40,000 shares of its $25 par common stock. The business combination meets all conditions for a pooling of interests. On June 30, 19X4, Case's common stock closed at $65 per share on a national stock exchange. Both corporations continued to operate as separate businesses maintaining separate accounting records with years ending December 31.

On December 31, 19X4, after year-end adjustments and closing nominal accounts, the companies had condensed balance sheet accounts as follows:

	Case, Inc.	Frey, Inc.
Assets:		
Cash	$ 825,000	$ 330,000
Accounts and other receivables	2,140,000	835,000
Inventories	2,310,000	1,045,000
Land	650,000	300,000
Depreciable assets, net	4,575,000	1,980,000
Investment in Frey, Inc.	2,430,000	
Long-term investments and other assets	865,000	385,000
	$13,795,000	$4,875,000
Liabilities and Stockholders' Equity:		
Accounts payable and other current liabilities	$ 2,465,000	$1,145,000
Long-term debt	1,900,000	1,300,000
Common stock, $25 par value	3,200,000	1,000,000
Additional paid-in capital	1,850,000	190,000
Retained earnings	4,380,000	1,240,000
	$13,795,000	$4,875,000

In addition:

- Case uses the equity method of accounting for its investment in Frey. The investment in Frey has not been adjusted for any intercompany transactions.
- On June 30, 19X4, Frey's assets and liabilities had fair values equal to the book balances with the exception of Land, which had a fair value of $550,000.
- On June 15, 19X4, Frey paid a cash dividend of $4 per share on its common stock.
- On December 10, 19X4, Case paid a cash dividend totaling $256,000 on its common stock.
- On June 30, 19X4, immediately before the combination, the stockholders' equities were:

	Case, Inc.	Frey, Inc.
Common stock	$2,200,000	$1,000,000
Additional paid-in capital	1,660,000	190,000
Retained earnings	3,036,000	980,000
	$6,896,000	$2,170,000

- Frey's long-term debt consisted of 10% ten-year bonds issued at face value on March 31,19X8 (81 months prior to fiscal year ended 12.31/X4). Interest is payable semi-annually on March 31 and September 30. Case had purchased Frey's bonds at face value of $320,000 in 19X8, and there was no change in ownership though December 31, 19X4.
- During October 19X4 Case sold merchandise to Frey at an aggregate invoice price of $720,000, which included a profit of $180,000. At December 31, 19X4, one-half of the merchandise remained in Frey's inventory, and Frey had not paid Case for the merchandise purchased.

- The 19X4 net income amounts per the separate books of Case and Frey were $890,000 (exclusive of equity in Frey's earnings) and $580,000, respectively.
- The balances in retained earnings at December 31, 19X3, were $2,506,000 and $820,000 for Case and Frey, respectively.

(*a*) Complete the Schedule III consolidating worksheet which follows to prepare a consolidated balance sheet of Case, Inc., and its subsidiary, Frey, Inc. at December 31, 19X4. A formal consolidated balance sheet and journal entries are not required.

(*b*) Prepare a formal consolidated statement of retained earnings for the year ended December 31, 19X4.

Schedule III
Case, Inc. and Subsidiary
Consolidated Balance Sheet Worksheet, December 31, 19X4

	Case, Inc.	Frey, Inc.	Adjustments and Eliminations Debit	Adjustments and Eliminations Credit	Consolidated
Assets:					
Cash	$ 825,000	$ 330,000			
Accts & other receivables	2,140,000	835,000			
Inventories	2,310,000	1,045,000			
Land	650,000	300,000			
Depreciable assets, net	4,575,000	1,980,000			
Investment in Frey, Inc.	2,430,000				
Long-term investments & other assets	865,000	385,000			
	$13,795,000	$4,875,000			
Liabilities and Stockholders' Equity:					
Accounts payable & other current liabilities	$ 2,465,000	$1,145,000			
Long-term debt	1,900,000	1,300,000			
Common stock, $25 par	3,200,000	1,000,000			
Additional paid-in capital	1,850,000	190,000			
Retained earnings	4,380,000	1,240,000			
	$13,795,000	$4,875,000			

Answer:

(*a*)

Schedule III
Case, Inc. and Subsidiary
Consolidated Balance Sheet Worksheet, December 31, 19X4

	Case, Inc.	Frey, Inc.	Adjustments and Eliminations Debit	Adjustments and Eliminations Credit	Consolidated
Assets:					
Cash	$ 825,000	$ 330,000			$ 1,155,000
Accts & other receivables	2,140,000	835,000		$ 8,000[3] 720,000[4]	2,247,000
Inventories	2,310,000	1,045,000		90,000[5]	3,265,000
Land	650,000	300,000			950,000
Depreciable assets, net	4,575,000	1,980,000			6,555,000
Investment in Frey, Inc.	2,430,000			2,430,000[1]	
Long-term investments & other assets	865,000	385,000		320,000[2]	930,000
	$13,795,000	$4,875,000			$15,102,000
Liabilities and Stockholders' Equity:					
Accounts payable & other current liabilities	$ 2,465,000	$1,145,000	$ 8,000[3] 720,000[4]		$ 2,882,000
Long-term debt	1,900,000	1,300,000	320,000[2]		2,880,000
Common stock, $25 par	3,200,000	1,000,000	1,000,000[1]		3,200,000
Additional paid-in capital	1,850,000	190,000	190,000[1]		1,850,000
Retained earnings	4,380,000	1,240,000	1,240,000[1] 90,000[5]		4,290,000
	$13,795,000	$4,875,000	$3,568,000	$3,568,000	$15,102,000

(*b*)

Case, Inc. and Subsidiary
Consolidated Statement of Retained Earnings
For the Year Ended December 31,19X4

Balance, December 31, 19X3:	
As originally reported	$2,506,000
Adjustment for pooling of interests with Frey, Inc.	820,000
As restated	3,326,000
Net income	1,380,000[6]
	4,706,000
Deduct cash dividends paid:	
By Frey, Inc., prior to combination	160,000[7]
By Case Inc., after the combination	256,000
	416,000
Balance, December 31, 19X4	$4,290,000

Explanations of Worksheet Entries & Other Amounts

[1]To eliminate the reciprocal elements in investment and equity accounts.

[2]To eliminate Case's investment in Frey's bonds.

[3]To eliminate Case's intercompany accrued interest receivable on its investment in Frey's bonds for the period 10/1—12/31/X4. ($320,000 × 10% × 1/4 = $8,000).

[4]To eliminate Case's intercompany balance for merchandise owed by Frey.

[5]To eliminate intercompany profit in ending inventory of Frey ($180,000 × 1/2 = $90,000)

[6]Consolidated net income for 19X4

Case, Inc.	$ 890,000
Frey, Inc.	580,000
	$1,470,000
Deduct intercompany profit in inventory	90,000
	$1,380,000

[7]Dividend paid 6/15/X4 [40,000 shares × $4] $ 160,000

(AICPA adapted)

EXAMINATION II (CHAPTERS 4 THROUGH 11)

Problem 1: Problem 1 consists of the following multiple choice and fill in the blank questions.

1. Under the equity method of accounting, dividends received by a parent company from its subsidiary should be accounted for as

(*a*) a deferred credit.
(*b*) a reduction in the parent's investment carrying value.
(*c*) dividend (or investment) income.
(*d*) dividend (or investment) income provided the dividend represents post-acquisition earnings of the subsidiary.

2. Brighton Corporation purchased a controlling interest in Henley, Inc. at a price which indicates that Henley's depreciable assets have a fair value in excess of book value. Brighton Corporation carries its investment using the equity method. On Brighton's separate books, the difference between fair and book value of the depreciable assets acquired should be

(*a*) used to reduce Brighton's investment income in the year of acquisition.
(*b*) a part of the Investment in Henley, Inc. carrying value as long as the investment is held by Brighton Corporation.
(*c*) charged against investment income over the depreciable assets' remaining useful life.
(*d*) charged as additional depreciation expense over the depreciable assets' remaining useful life on Brighton's separate books.

Questions 3 and 4 are based on the following information:

On January 1, 19X4, Parrot Co. sold equipment to its 90% owned subsidiary Sparrow Inc. for $990,000. On this date, the equipment appeared on the books of Parrot Co. at an historical cost of $1,500,000 with $600,000 in accumulated depreciation. Parrot Co. had been depreciating the asset over a 15 year, straight-line, no salvage value assumption, which Sparrow Inc. continued.

3. The 12/31/X4 consolidating worksheet elimination process should include

(*a*) an entry to eliminate an intercompany gain of $90,000.
(*b*) an entry to eliminate an intercompany gain of $81,000 (90% × $90,000).
(*c*) no entry to eliminate the intercompany gain since a sale has legally occurred.
(*d*) an entry to eliminate an intercompany loss of $510,000.

4. The 12/31/X4 consolidated balance sheet will show equipment cost and accumulated depreciation respectively of

(*a*) $990,000 and $110,000.
(*b*) $990,000 and $600,000.
(*c*) $1,500,000 and $110,000.
(*d*) $1,500,000 and $700,000.

Questions 5, 6, and 7 are based on the following information:

Smith Co. was created to merge the resources of Jones Co. and King Co. in a pooling of interests. Immediately before the pooling occurred, the equity positions of Jones Co. and King Co. were as follows:

	Jones Co.	King Co.	Total
Common stock, par	$200,000	$100,000	$300,000
Additional paid-in capital	30,000	20,000	50,000
Retained earnings	100,000	80,000	80,000
Total Assets	$330,000	$200,000	$530,000

Smith Co. issued 70,000 shares of its $4 par value stock in exchange for all of the outstanding stock of Jones and King.

5. The combined additional paid-in capital after the merger is $ __________.

6. Assuming the same information as that provided in question 5 except that Smith Co. par is $5 per share, the combined additional paid-in capital after the merger is $ __________.

7. Assuming the same information as that provided in question 5 except that Smith Co. par is $6 per share, the combined retained earnings after the merger is $ __________.

Questions 8 through 12 (AICPA Adapted) are based on the following data:

The separate condensed balance sheets and income statements of Par Corp. and its wholly-owned subsidiary, Sub Corp., are as follows:

BALANCE SHEETS
December 31, 19X6

	Par	Sub
Assets		
Current		
Cash	$ 150,000	$ 50,000
Accounts Receivable (net)	190,000	60,000
Inventories	90,000	40,000
Total current assets	430,000	150,000
Property, plant, and equipment (net)	365,000	200,000
Investment in Sub (equity method)	315,000	—
Total Assets	$1,110,000	$350,000
Liabilities and Stockholders' Equity		
Current liabilities		
Accounts payable	$ 100,000	$ 60,000
Accrued liabilities	30,000	20,000
Total current liabilities	130,000	80,000
Stockholders' equity		
Common stock ($10 par)	220,000	30,000
Additional paid-in capital	140,000	100,000
Retained earnings	620,000	140,000
Total stockholders' equity	980,000	270,000
Total liabilities and stockholders' equity	$1,110,000	$350,000

INCOME STATEMENTS
For the Year Ended December 31, 19X6

	Par	Sub
Sales	$1,000,000	$300,000
Cost of goods sold	770,000	200,000
Gross margin	230,000	100,000
Other operating expenses	130,000	50,000
Operating income	100,000	50,000
Equity in earnings of Sub	25,000	—
Income before income taxes	125,000	50,000
Provision for income taxes	40,000	20,000
Net income	$ 85,000	$ 30,000

Additional information:

- On January 1, 19X6, Par purchased for $300,000 all of Sub's $10 par, voting common stock. On January 1, 19X6, the fair value of Sub's assets and liabilities equaled their carrying amount of $330,000 and $80,000, respectively. Par's policy is to amortize intangible assets over a 10-year period, unless a definite life is ascertainable.
- During 19X6, Par and Sub paid cash dividends of $50,000 and $10,000, respectively. For tax purposes, Par receives the 100% exclusion for dividends received from Sub.
- There were no intercompany transactions except for Par's receipt of dividends from Sub, and Par's recording of its share of Sub's earnings.
- On June 30, 19X6, Par issued 2,000 shares of common stock for $17 per share. There were no other changes in either Par's or Sub's common stock during 19X6.
- Both Par and Sub paid income taxes at the rate of 40%.

8. In the 19X6 consolidated income statement of Par and its subsidiary, Sub, what amount should be reported as consolidated net income?
(*a*) $60,000
(*b*) $85,000
(*c*) $90,000
(*d*) $115,000

9. The consolidated balance sheet of Par and its subsidiary, Sub, should report total consolidated assets of
(*a*) $1,110,000
(*b*) $1,145,000
(*c*) $1,190,000
(*d*) $1,460,000

10. The consolidated balance sheet of Par and its subsidiary, Sub, should report total retained earnings of
(*a*) $620,000
(*b*) $640,000
(*c*) $650,000
(*d*) $760,000

11. In the consolidated income statement of Par and its subsidiary, Sub, how much expense should be reported for amortization of goodwill?
(*a*) $0
(*b*) $3,000
(*c*) $5,000
(*d*) $10,000

12. In the December 31, 19X6 consolidated balance sheet of Par and its subsidiary, Sub, how much should be reported as total current assets?
(*a*) $150,000
(*b*) $280,000
(*c*) $430,000
(*d*) $580,000

13. Grant, Inc., has current receivables from affiliated companies at December 31, 19X2 as follows:

- A $50,000 cash advance to Adams Corporation. Grant owns 30% of the voting stock of Adams and accounts for the investment by the equity method.
- A receivable of $160,000 from Bullard Corporation for administrative and selling services. Bullard is 100% owned by Grant and is included in Grant's consolidated statements.
- A receivable of $100,000 from Carpenter Corporation for merchandise sales on open account. Carpenter is a 90% owned, unconsolidated subsidiary of Grant.

In the current assets section of its December 31, 19X2, consolidated balance sheet, Grant should report accounts receivable from investees in the total amount of
(*a*) \$90,000
(*b*) \$140,000
(*c*) \$150,000
(*d*) \$310,000

14. On July 1, 19X2, Diamond, Inc., paid \$1,000,000 for 100,000 shares (40%) of the outstanding common stock of Ashley Corporation. At that date the net assets of Ashley totaled \$2,500,000 and the fair values of all of Ashley's identifiable assets and liabilities were equal to their book values. Ashley reported net income of \$500,000 for the year ended December 31, 19X2, of which \$300,000 was for the six months ended December 31, 19X2. Ashley paid cash dividends of \$250,000 on September 30, 19X2. In its income statement for the year ended December 31, 19X2, what amount of income should Diamond report from its investment in Ashley?
(*a*) \$80,000
(*b*) \$100,000
(*c*) \$120,000
(*d*) \$200,000

15. Cash dividends declared out of current earnings are distributed to an investor. How will the investor's investment account be affected by those dividends under each of the following accounting methods?

	Cost method	Equity method
(*a*)	Decrease	No effect
(*b*)	Decrease	Decrease
(*c*)	No effect	Decrease
(*d*)	No effect	No effect

16. When an investor uses the equity method to account for investments in common stock, the equity in the earnings of the investee reported in the investor's income statement will be affected by which of the following?

	Cash dividends from investee	Goodwill amortization related to purchase
(*a*)	No	Yes
(*b*)	No	No
(*c*)	Yes	No
(*d*)	Yes	Yes

17. On November 1, 19X2, Company X acquired all of the outstanding common stock of Company Y in a business combination accounted for as a pooling of interests. Both companies have a December 31 year end and have been in business for many years. Consolidated net income for the year ended December 31, 19X2 should include net income for 12 months of

	Company X	Company Y
(*a*)	Yes	Yes
(*b*)	Yes	No
(*c*)	No	No
(*d*)	No	Yes

18. In order to report a business combination as a pooling of interests, the minimum amount of an investee's common stock which must be acquired during the combination period in exchange for the investor's common stock is
(*a*) 100 percent
(*b*) 51 percent
(*c*) 80 percent
(*d*) 90 percent

Questions 19, 20, and 21 are based on the following information:

Silver Co. sold a tract of land to its parent, Gold Co. on February 9, 19X8 for $60,000. Silver Co.'s original cost of the land was $40,000. Gold Co. owns 80% of Silver Co.

19. The consolidated balance sheet at December 31, 19X8 should reflect this land at which of the following amounts?
(*a*) $60,000
(*b*) $40,000
(*c*) $20,000
(*d*) $0

20. The amount of intercompany gain on sale which must be eliminated is
(*a*) $4,000
(*b*) $20,000
(*c*) $16,000
(*d*) $0

21. Assuming the separate books of Silver Co. show a net income of $50,000 (including the intercompany gain on land sale), minority interest in combined net income will be
(*a*) $50,000
(*b*) $40,000
(*c*) $10,000
(*d*) $6,000
(*e*) $4,000

Questions 22 and 23 are based on the following information:

Pepper Co. acquired $100,000 in face value bonds from its 90% owned subsidiary, Salt Co., on December 31, 19X4 for $106,000. These bonds mature in 12 years and Salt Co. carried the entire bond issue on its books at December 31, 19X4 as follows:

Bonds payable (face value)	$1,000,000
Unamortized bond premium	100,000

22. The bonds payable (face value) should appear on the December 31, 19X4 consolidated balance sheet at $__________.

23. As a result of the intercompany bond holding, a gain (loss) on retirement will appear in the consolidated income statement for the year ended December 31, 19X4 of $__________ __________ (indicate gain or loss).

24. The existence of subsidiary preferred stock is generally viewed as
(*a*) additional consolidated equity (additional paid-in capital or preferred stock).
(*b*) treasury stock.
(*c*) retired stock.
(*d*) minority interest.

25. If an intercompany investment in preferred stock exists, from a consolidated perspective this investment is viewed as
(*a*) treasury stock.
(*b*) retired stock.
(*c*) an item not affecting the consolidation process.
(*d*) an intercompany investment which must be removed in the consolidation process with consolidated gain or loss recorded for any difference between the investment's carrying value and the preferred stock's carrying value.

26. Bordon Co. owns 90% of Bremer Corp. Bordon Co. owns 40% of Crimson, Inc. Bremer Corp. owns 50% of Crimson, Inc. The companies which should be included in the development of consolidated financial statements are
   (*a*) Bordon Co. and Bremer Corp.
   (*b*) Bordon Co. and Crimson, Inc.
   (*c*) Bremer Co. and Crimson, Inc.
   (*d*) Bordon Co., Bremer Corp., and Crimson, Inc.

27. Registration costs associated with business combinations accounted for as either a purchase or a pooling of interests are expensed. __________ (True or False).

28. Indirect and general expenses associated with business combinations accounted for as either a purchase or a pooing of interests are expensed. __________ (True or False).

29. Finders' fees and direct costs associated with business combinations accounted for as either a purchase or pooling of interests are expensed. __________ (True or False).

30. A fundamental difference between a purchase and a pooling of interests is that in a purchase, a sale is presumed to have occurred, whereas no such presumption of sale exists in a pooling of interests. (True or False).

Problem 2: (AICPA Adapted)

Madison, Inc., acquired all of the outstanding $10 par voting common stock of Adams Corporation on December 31, 19X9, in exchange for 90,000 shares of its $10 par voting common stock in a business combination which meets all of the conditions for a pooling of interests. On the acquisition date, Madison's common stock had a closing market price of $26 per share on a national stock exchange. Both corporations continued to operate as separate businesses maintaining separate accounting records with years ending December 31.

On December 31, 19X9, after the nominal accounts were closed and immediately after acquisition, the condensed balance sheets for both corporations were as follows:

	Madison	Adams
Assets		
Cash	$ 750,000	$ 300,000
Accounts receivable, net	1,950,000	750,000
Inventories	2,100,000	950,000
Land	500,000	200,000
Depreciable assets, net	4,160,000	1,800,000
Investment in Adams Corporation	2,205,000	
Long-term investments and other assets	785,000	350,000
Total assets	$12,450,000	$4,350,000
Liabilities and Stockholders' Equity		
Accounts payable and other current liabilities	$1,750,000	$945,000
Long-term debt	1,500,000	1,200,000
Common stock, par value $10 per share	3,000,000	900,000
Additional paid-in capital	1,370,000	175,000
Retained earnings	4,830,000	1,130,000
Total liabilities and stockholders' equity	$12,450,000	$4,350,000

Additional information:

- Madison recorded its investment in Adams at the underlying equity in the net assets of Adams of $2,205,000.
- On December 31, 19X9, Adams' assets and liabilities had fair values equal to the book balances with the exception of Land, which had a fair value of $400,000.
- Madison's accounting policy is to amortize excess cost over fair market value of net assets acquired over a 40-year period.

- On December 15, 19X9, Adams paid a cash dividend of $3 per share on its common stock.
- Adams' Long-Term Debt consisted of 9% ten-year bonds, issued at face value on June 30, 19X5, and due 10 years from the issue date. Interest is paid semiannually on June 30 and December 31. Madison had purchased Adams' bonds at face value of $250,000. There was no change in Madison's ownership of Adams bonds through December 31, 19X9.
- During the three-month period ended December 31, 19X9, Madison purchased merchandise from Adams at an aggregate invoice price of $600,000. Madison had not paid for the merchandise as of December 31, 19X9. The amount of profit realized by Adams on these transactions was $120,000. At December 31, 19X9, one-half of the merchandise remained in Madison's inventory. There were no intercompany merchandise transactions prior to October 1, 19X9.
- The 19X9 net income amounts per the separate books of Madison and Adams were $2,100,000 and $1,125,000, respectively.
- The balances in Retained earnings at December 31, 19X8 were $1,600,000 and $275,000 for Madison and Adams, respectively.

Required:

1. Complete the worksheet to prepare a consolidated balance sheet of Madison, Inc., and its subsidiary, Adams Corporation, as of December 31, 19X9. A formal consolidated balance sheet and journal entries are not required. Supporting computations should be in good form.
2. Prepare a formal consolidated statement of retained earnings for the year ended December 31, 19X9. Show supporting computations in good form.

Madison, Inc. and Subsidiary
Consolidated Balance Sheet Worksheet
December 31, 19X9

	Madison Inc.	Adams Corporation	Adjustments and Eliminations		Consolidated
			Debit	Credit	
Assets:					
Cash	$ 750,000	$ 300,000			
Accounts receivable, net	1,950,000	750,000			
Inventories	2,100,000	950,000			
Land	500,000	200,000			
Depreciable assets, net	4,160,000	1,800,000			
Investment in Adams Corp.	2,205,000				
Long-term investments and other assets	785,000	350,000			
	$12,450,000	$4,350,000			
Liabilities and Stockholders' equity:					
Accounts payable and other current liabilities	$ 1,750,000	$ 945,000			
Long-term debt	1,500,000	1,200,000			
Common stock, $10 par value	3,000,000	900,000			
Additional paid-in capital	1,370,000	175,000			
Retained earnings	4,830,000	1,130,000			
	$12,450,000	$4,350,000			

Problem 3: (AICPA Adapted)

On April 1, 19X3, Jared, Inc., purchased 100% of the common stock of Munson Manufacturing Company for $5,850,000 and 20% of its preferred stock for $150,000. At the date of purchase the book and fair values of Munson's assets and liabilities were as follows:

	Book Value	Fair Value
Cash	$ 200,000	$ 200,000
Notes receivable	85,000	85,000
Accounts receivable, net	980,000	980,000
Inventories	828,000	700,000
Land	1,560,000	2,100,000
Machinery and equipment	7,850,000	10,600,000
Accumulated depreciation	(3,250,000)	(4,000,000)
Other assets	140,000	50,000
	$ 8,393,000	$10,715,000
Notes payable	$ 115,000	$ 115,000
Accounts payable	400,000	400,000
Subordinated debentures – 7%	5,000,000	5,000,000
Preferred stock; noncumulative, non participating, par value $5 per share; authorized, issued and outstanding 150,000 shares	750,000	—
Common stock, par value $10 per share; authorized, issued, and outstanding 100,000 shares	1,000,000	—
Additional paid-in capital (common stock)	122,000	—
Retained earnings	1,006,000	—
	$8,393,000	—

Additional information:

By the year end, December 31, 19X3, the following transactions had occurred:

- The balance of Munson's net accounts receivable at April 1, 19X3, had been collected.
- The inventory on hand at April 1, 19X3, had been charged to cost of sales. Munson used a perpetual inventory system in accounting for inventories.
- Prior to 19X3, Jared had purchased at face value $1,500,000 of Munson's 7% subordinated debentures. These debentures mature on October 31, 19X9, with interest payable annually on October 31.
- As of April 1, 19X3, the machinery and equipment had an estimated remaining life of six years. Munson uses the straight-line method of depreciation. Munson's depreciation expense calculation for the nine months ended December 31, 19X3, was based upon the old depreciation rates.
- The other assets consist entirely of long-term investments made by Munson and do not include any investment in Jared.
- During the last nine months of 19X3, the following intercompany transactions occurred between Jared and Munson.

  Intercompany sales:

	Jared to Munson	Munson to Jared
Net sales	$158,000	$230,000
Included in purchaser's inventory at December 31, 19X3	36,000	12,000
Balance unpaid at December 31, 19X3	16,800	22,000

Jared sells merchandise to Munson at cost. Munson sells merchandise to Jared at regular selling price including a normal gross profit margin of 35 percent. There were no intercompany sales between the two companies prior to April 1, 19X3.

Accrued interest on intercompany debt is recorded by both companies in their respective accounts receivable and accounts payable accounts.

- The account, "Investment in Munson Manufacturing Company," includes Jared's investment in munson's debentures and its investment in the common and preferred stock of Munson.
- Jared's policy is to amortize intangible assets over a twenty-year period.

Required:
Complete the worksheet to prepare the consolidated trial balance for Jared, Inc., and its subsidiary, Munson Manufacturing Company, at December 31, 19X3. Show computations in good form where appropriate to support worksheet entries.

Jared's revenue and expense figures are for the twelve-month period while Munson's are for the last nine months of 19X3. You may assume that both companies made all the adjusting entries required for separate financial statements unless stated to the contrary. Round all computations to the nearest dollar. Ignore income taxes.

(AICPA Adapted)

Problem 3 worksheet:

Jared, Inc. and 100% Owned Subsidiary Munson Manufacturing Co.
Consolidating Worksheet
For the Year Ended 12/31/X3

Account name	Jared Dr. (Cr.)	Munson Dr. (Cr.)	Eliminations Dr.	Eliminations (Cr.)	CONSOLIDATED Dr. (Cr.) Income Statement	Retained Earnings	Balance Sheet
Cash	822,000	530,000					
Accounts receiv. (net) and interest receiv.	2,758,000	1,453,400					
Inventories	3,204,000	1,182,000					
Land	4,000,000	1,560,000					
Machinery and equip.	15,875,000	7,850,000					
Accum. depr. – mach. and equip.	(6,301,000)	(3,838,750)					
Buildings	1,286,000						
Accum. depr. – bldgs.	(372,000)						
Other Assets	263,000	140,000					
Investment in Munson	7,500,000						
Accounts payable and interest payable	(1,364,000)	(319,000)					
Long-term debt	(10,000,000)						
7% Subordinated debentures		(5,000,000)					
Preferred stock		(750,000)					
Common stock: Jared	(2,400,000)						
Munson		(1,000,000)					
Additional paid-in capital: Jared	(240,000)						
Munson		(122,000)					
Retained earnings: Jared	(12,683,500)						
Munson		(1,006,000)					
Sales	(18,200,000)	(5,760,000)					
Cost of goods sold	10,600,000	3,160,000					
General and administrative expenses	3,448,500	1,063,900					
Depr. exp. – mach. and equip.	976,000	588,750					
Depr. exp. – bldgs.	127,000						
Interest revenue	(105,000)	(1,700)					
Interest expense	806,000	269,400					
Totals	0	0					
Consolidated net income							
Consolidated retained earnings							
Total							

Problem 4:

This problem is based on the information provided in problem 3. Assume, however, that a minority interest in Munson's common stock exists and that Jared's payment of $5,850,000 resulted in a purchase of 80% of Munson's common stock outstanding.

Required:

(*a*) Prepare revised worksheet elimination entries.

(*b*) Complete the problem 4 worksheet provided.

Problem 4 worksheet:

Jared, Inc. and 80% Owned Subsidiary Munson Manufacturing Co.
Consolidating Worksheet
For the Year Ended 12/31/X3

Account name	Jared Dr. (Cr.)	Munson Dr. (Cr.)	Eliminations Dr.	Eliminations (Cr.)	CONSOLIDATED Dr. (Cr.) Income Statement	Retained Earnings	Balance Sheet
Cash	822,000	530,000					
Accounts receiv. (net) and interest receiv.	2,758,000	1,453,400					
Inventories	3,204,000	1,182,000					
Land	4,000,000	1,560,000					
Machinery and equip.	15,875,000	7,850,000					
Accum. depr. – mach and equip.	(6,301,000)	(3,838,750)					
Buildings	1,286,000						
Accum. depr. – bldgs.	(372,000)						
Other Assets	263,000	140,000					
Investment in Munson	7,500,000						
Accounts payable and interest payable	(1,364,000)	(319,000)					
Long-term debt	(10,000,000)						
7% Subordinated debentures		(5,000,000)					
Preferred stock		(750,000)					
Common stock: Jared	(2,400,000)						
Munson		(1,000,000)					
Additional paid-in capital: Jared	(240,000)						
Munson		(122,000)					
Retained earnings: Jared	(12,683,500)						
Munson		(1,006,000)					
Sales	(18,200,000)	(5,760,000)					
Cost of goods sold	10,600,000	3,160,000					
General and administrative expenses	3,448,500	1,063,900					
Depr. exp. – mach. and equip.	976,000	588,750					
Depr. exp. – bldgs.	127,000						
Interest revenue	(105,000)	(1,700)					
Interest expense	806,000	269,400					
Totals	0	0					
	Combined net income						
	Minority interest						
	Consolidated net income						
	Consolidated retained earnings						
				Total			
	Total minority interest						

Problem 5:

Refer to the information of problem 3 once again. Suppose, however, that Jared, Inc. had carried its Investment in Munson common stock at equity.

Requirements:

(*a*) Determine the December 31, 19X3 balance in the "Investment in Munson" account assuming the investment is carried at equity.

(*b*) Assuming the investment had been carried at equity, prepare 12/31/X3 consolidating worksheet elimination entries to eliminate Jared, Inc.'s investments in Munson Manufacturing Company's common stock, preferred stock, and bonds.

Problem 6: (AICPA Adapted)

Flaherty Company entered into a business combination with Steeley Company in the middle of the year. The combination was accounted for as a pooling of interests. Both companies use the same methods of accounting. Registration fees for the equity securities involved in the combination were incurred. There were no intercompany transactions before or after the combination.

Flaherty Company acquired all of the voting common stock of Rubin Company in the middle of the year. This combination was accounted for as a purchase and resulted in goodwill. Both companies use the same methods of acounting. Registration fees for the equity securities involved in the combination were incurred. There were no intercompany transactions before or after the combination.

Required:

(*a*) 1. In the business combination accounted for as a pooling of interests, how should the recorded assets and liabilities of the separate companies be accounted for? What is the rationale for accounting for a business combination as a pooling of interests?

2. In the business combination accounted for as a pooling of interests, how should the registration fees and direct costs related to effecting the business combination be accounted for?

3. In the business combination accounted for as a pooling of interests, how should the results of operations for the year in which the business combination occurred be reported?

(*b*) 1. In the business combination accounted for as a purchase, how should the assets acquired and liabilities assumed be reported? What is the rationale for accounting for a business combination as a purchase?

2. In the business combination accounted for as a purchase, how should the registration fees and direct costs related to effecting the business combination be accounted for?

3. In the business combination accounted for as a purchase, how should the results of operations of the acquired company for the year in which the business combination occurred be reported?

ANSWERS

Problem 1:

1. (*b*) (See Chapter 5, equity method.)

2. (*c*) (See Chapter 5, equity method.)

3. (*a*) The required worksheet elimination entries are as follows:

Equipment	510,000	
Gain – equipment sale	90,000	
Accum. depr. – equipment		600,000

To eliminate intercompany gain on equipment sale and restore equipment to original carrying value.

Accum. depr. – equipment	10,000	
Depreciation expense		10,000

To adjust depreciation expense as follows:

Depreciation expense per separate books of Sparrow, Inc. ($990,000/9 year life remaining)	$110,000
Depreciation expense based on original cost ($1,500,000/15 year life)	100,000
Excess depreciation expense	$ 10,000

4. (*d*) The asset should be carried at original cost $1,500,000 less accumulated depreciation of $700,000 ($600,000 + $100,000 depreciation expense for 19X4), as if no sale ever occurred.

5. $70,000. The combining companies' par ($300,000) exceeds the issuing company's par ($280,000) by $20,000. This difference increases additional paid-in capital from $50,000 to $70,000.

6. $ 0 . The issuing company's par ($350,000) exceeds the combining companies' par ($300,000) by $50,000. This difference reduces additional paid-in capital from $50,000 to $0.

7. $110,000. The issuing company's par ($420,000) exceeds the combining companies' par ($300,000) by $120,000. This difference reduces additional paid-in capital from $50,000 to $0 and retained earnings from $180,000 to $110,000.

8. (*b*) $85,000. In this case, Par Corp.'s separate books which carry the investment at equity reflect the consolidated net income. The consolidated net income may alternatively be computed as follows:

Net income on separate books of:	
Par Corp. ($85,000 – $25,000 investment income)	$ 60,000
Sub Corp.	30,000
Subtotal	90,000
Less: Goodwill amortization ($50,000/10 years)	(5,000)*
Consolidated net income	$ 85,000

*Goodwill is based on the following:	
Purchase price of investment	$300,000
Fair and book value of net assets acquired ($330,000 – $80,000)	(250,000)
Goodwill	$ 50,000

9. (*c*) $1,190,000. Note that the consolidating worksheet elimination entries in this case would result in the elimination of the $315,000 Investment in Sub account and in the creation of $45,000 in goodwill ($50,000 less $5,000 first year amortization). Therefore, the consolidated balance will show the following assets:

Current assets ($430,000 plus $150,000)	$ 580,000
Property, plant, and equipment (net) ($365,000 plus $200,000)	565,000
Goodwill	45,000
Total consolidated balance sheet assets	$1,190,000

10. (*a*) $620,000. This business combination is a purchase (not a pooling of interests) and the parent, Par Corp., will not record the retained earnings of Sub Corp. The consolidating worksheet elimination entry to eliminate the investment account balance will also completely eliminate Sub Corp.'s equity.

11. (*c*) $5,000. (See answer to question #8.)

12. (*d*) $580,000. (See answer to question #9.)

13. (*c*) $150,000. The $160,000 receivable from Bullard Corporation which will be included in Grant, Inc.'s consolidated financial statements would be eliminated in the consolidation process (not included on the consolidated balance sheet). The receivables from the unconsolidated subsidiary of $100,000 and from the 30% owned company of $50,000 will appear on the consolidated balance sheet.

14. (*c*) $120,000. 40% × $300,000 income for last 6 months of 19X2 = $120,000. One point of this question is that the investor's share of investee net income is recognized from the purchase date forward. Also, under the equity method, cash dividends are not part of investor income, but rather they represent a reduction of the investment account balance.

15. (*c*) (See Chapter 5.)

16. (*a*) (See Chapter 5.)

17. (*a*) (See Chapter 11.)

18. (*d*) (See Chapter 11, Condition 4 of requirements for treatment as a pooling of interests.)

19. (*b*) $40,000. The land should be shown at its original (historical) cost to the consolidated group.

20. (*b*) $20,000. The full $20,000 intercompany gain on sale must be eliminated despite the fact that minority interest exists. Minority interest in combined net income is, however, reduced by its share of the intercompany gain.

21. (*d*) $6,000.

Subsidiary net income	$50,000
Minority interest	× 20%
Subtotal	$10,000
Less: Minority interest in unrealized profit on intercompany land sale ($20,000 × 20%)	(4,000)
Minority interest in combined net income	$ 6,000

22. $900,000. $1,000,000 less $100,000 viewed as retired.

23. $4,000 gain. The consolidating worksheet elimination entry which follows shows how the gain is developed:

Bonds payable	100,000	
Unamortized bond premium	10,000*	
Investment in Salt Co. Bonds		106,000
Gain – debt extinguishment		4,000

To eliminate intercompany bond holding.
*10% retired × $100,000 unamortized premium on entire issue.

24. (*d*) (See Chapter 10.)

25. (*b*) (See Chapter 10.)

26. (*d*) Bordon has a direct controlling interest in Bremer of 90%. Also, Bordon has an indirect controlling interest in Crimson, Inc. of 85% (40% plus (90% of 50%)). Therefore, all three companies should be included in the consolidation process.

27. False. Registration costs are expensed in a pooling but no in a purchase. In a purchase, these costs reduce additional paid-in capital on securities issued as part of the merger. (See Exhibit A, Chapter 4.)

28. True. (See Exhibit A, Chapter 4.)

29. False. These costs are expensed in a pooling but not in a purchase. In a purchase, finders' fees and direct costs are viewed as a part of the purchase price of the investment. (See Exhibit A, Chapter 4.)

30. True. (See Chapter 11.)

Problem 2:

Note that because the pooling of interests approach to this business combination is appropriate, the fair value of the stock ($26 per share) and the fair value of the land ($400,000) are ignored in the consolidation process. Only net asset book values are used. Note also that the December 15, 19X9 cash dividend paid by Adams does not result in a worksheet elimination entry since it occurred before the December 31, 19X9 merger. However, this dividend is included in answer to requirement 2 in the preparation of a consolidated statement of retained earnings.

Requirement 1:
The consolidating elimination entries which are shown on the worksheet which follows are explained as follows:

(1) To eliminate Investment in Adams Corp. against Adam's equity.
(2) To eliminate intercompany investment in 9 year, 10% bonds. (Note that no elimination of intercompany interest receivable or payable is necessary in this case since the last payment date was December 31, 19X9, the date of the consolidation. Also, elimination of intercompany interest expense and income is unnecessary since only a consolidated balance sheet is required in this case.)
(3) To eliminate intercompany receivable and payable from inventory purchase.
(4) To eliminate profit in ending inventory (based on total profit of $120,000 times one-half of the merchandise remaining in Madison's ending inventory). (Note that the $60,000 charge on the worksheet is against retained earnings rather than against cost of goods sold for the profit in ending inventory. This is simply because only a consolidated balance sheet is required which includes no income statement accounts such as cost of goods sold.)

Problem 2:

Madison, Inc. and Subsidiary
Consolidated Balance Sheet Worksheet
December 31, 19X9

	Madison Inc.	Adams Corporation	Adjustments and Eliminations Debit	Adjustments and Eliminations Credit	Consolidated
Assets:					
Cash	$ 750,000	$ 300,000			$ 1,050,000
Accounts receivable, net	1,950,000	750,000		$ 600,000[3]	2,100,000
Inventories	2,100,000	950,000		60,000[4]	2,990,000
Land	500,000	200,000			700,000
Depreciable assets, net	4,160,000	1,800,000			5,960,000
Investment in Adams Corp.	2,205,000			2,205,000[1]	–0–
Long-term investments and other assets	785,000	350,000		250,000[2]	885,000
	$12,450,000	$4,350,000			$13,685,000
Liabilities and Stockholders' equity:					
Accounts payable and other current liabilities	$ 1,750,000	$ 945,000	$ 600,000[3]		$ 2,095,000
Long-term debt	1,500,000	1,200,000	250,000[2]		2,450,000
Common stock, $10 par value	3,000,000	900,000	900,000[1]		3,000,000
Additional paid-in capital	1,370,000	175,000	175,000[1]		1,370,000
Retained earnings	4,830,000	1,130,000	1,130,000[1]		4,770,000
			60,000[4]		
	$12,450,000	$4,350,000	$3,115,000	$3,115,000	$13,685,000

Requirement 2:

Madison Inc., and Subsidiary
Consolidated Statement of Retained Earnings
For the Year Ended December 31, 19X9

Balance, December 31, 19X8	
As originally reported	$1,600,000
Adjustment for pooling of interests with Adams Corporation	275,000
As restated	$1,875,000
Plus: Consolidated net income*	3,165,000
Less: Cash dividend paid by pooled company prior to combination ($3 × 90,000 shares)	(270,000)
Balance, December 31, 19X9	$4,770,000

*Consolidated net income is determined as follows:	
Madison, Inc. net income	$2,100,000
Adams Corp. net income (full year in a pooling)	1,125,000
Intercompany profit in ending inventory ($120,000 × one-half)	(60,000)
Consolidated net income	$3,165,000

(AICPA Adapted)

Problem 3:

Special Points of Interest:

Note that the Investment in Munson Manufacturing Company is carried at cost. This is evidenced by the fact that the original investment costs (for common stock, preferred stock, and bonds) represent the year-end "Investment in Munson" account balance as follows:

April 1, 19X3 cost of common stock	$5,850,000
April 1, 19X3 cost of preferred stock	150,000
Prior year purchase of 7% bonds at face value	1,500,000
December 31, 19X3 "Investment in Munson" account balance per worksheet	$7,500,000

A first step to be considered when an investment is carried at cost is to bring the investment account balance to a beginning of the period (or to the April 1, 19X3 purchase date) position as if it were carried at equity. This step is unnecessary in this case. Since the problem represents the first year of the investment, the beginning balance would be the same at cost or equity and can be matched against the beginning (April 1, 19X3) retained earnings balance on Munson's books in the investment elimination process. Also, preferred stock exists in this case and normally subsidiary retained earnings must be allocated between preferred and common stock before proceeding with the consolidation process. However, since the problem states that the preferred stock is noncumulative and nonparticipating, preferred stock has no rights in retained earnings and the entry to split retained earnings is therefore not required. Both net asset adjustments to fair value and goodwill result in this case as described below.

Price paid by Jared Inc. for 100% of Munson Manufacturing Company's common stock		$5,850,000
Fair value of net assets ($10,715,000 total assets less $5,515,000 total debts)	$5,200,000	
Portion of net assets owned by preferred shareholders (par)	750,000	
Portion of net assets owned by common shareholders	4,450,000	
Percentage interest of Jared, Inc. in Munson Company	× 100%	
Fair value of net assets acquired by Jared, Inc.		4,450,000
Goodwill		$1,400,000

Goodwill of $1,400,000 will therefore be recorded on the consolidating worksheet in the investment elimination process and will subsequently be amortized against consolidated net income over a 20-year period (problem specifies amortization of intangible assets should be over a 20-year period). Also, certain assets had book and fair values which differed and must therefore be adjusted as follows:

	Per problem		
	Book Value	Fair Value	Dr. (Cr.) Worksheet Adjustment
Inventories	$ 828,000	$ 700,000	$ (128,000)
Land	1,560,000	2,100,000	540,000
Machinery and equipment	7,850,000	10,600,000	2,750,000
Accumulated depreciation	(3,250,000)	(4,000,000)	(750,000)
Other assets	140,000	50,000	(90,000)
Total adjustment to fair value			$2,322,000

The $5,850,000 purchase price is therefore supported as follows:

Book value of net assets ($8,393,000 – $5,515,000)	$2,878,000
Adjustment of net assets to fair value	2,322,000
Goodwill included in purchase price	1,400,000
SUBTOTAL	$6,600,000
Less: Preferred stock ownership	(750,000)
Purchase price of 100% of common stock	$5,850,000

Consolidating Worksheet Elimination Entries

		Dr.	Cr.
(1)	Munson Common stock	1,000,000	
	Munson Additional paid-in capital	122,000	
	Munson Retained earnings	1,006,000	
	Land	540,000	
	Machinery and equipment	2,750,000*	
	Goodwill	1,400,000*	
	Inventories		128,000*
	Accum. depr. – mach. and equipment		750,000*
	Other assets		90,000
	Investment in Munson (common)		5,850,000

To eliminate Investment in Munson's common stock against Munson's equity, adjust net assets to fair value and record goodwill.

*Worksheet amortization of these amounts will be required and performed as information is provided in the question.

		Dr.	Cr.
(2)	Munson Preferred stock	150,000	
	Investment in Munson (preferred)		150,000

To eliminate intercompany preferred stock holding.

		Dr.	Cr.
(3)	Inventories	128,000	
	Cost of goods sold		128,000

To amortize reduction in inventory cost (entry #1 above) against cost of goods sold. (Problem states that all inventory which Munson Co. had on hand on the purchase date was sold and that a perpetual inventory system is used. This means Munson Co., on its separate books, charged cost of goods sold for $828,000 in April 1, 19X3 inventory. But the cost to the consolidated group of this inventory is only $700,000.)

(4) Subordinated debentures – 7% 1,500,000
Investment in Munson (bonds) 1,500,000
To eliminate intercompany investment in bonds. (Note that the Investment in Munson is now eliminated fully.)

(5) Interest payable 17,500
Interest receivable 17,500
To eliminate intercompany bond interest payable and receivable. (Problem states interest is payable annually on October 31. Therefore, intercompany interest for the last 2 months of 19X3 would have been accrued as follows: $1,500,000 × 7% × 2 mos./12 mos. = $17,500)

(6) Interest revenue 78,750
Interest expense 78,750
To eliminate intercompany interest revenue and expense. (From the 4/1/X3 date of Jared, Inc.'s acquisition of Munson Manufacturing Co., 9 months of intercompany interest revenue and expense had been recorded as follows: $1,500,000 × 7% × 9 mos./12 mos. = $78,750)

(7) Depr. expense – mach. and equipment 236,250
Accum. depr. – mach. and equipment 236,250
To amortize machinery and equipment fair value in excess of book value from original purchase. (Problem states that a 6-year life remains at April 1, 19X3. The depreciation adjustment is therefore determined as follows:

Equipment fair value (net)	$6,600,000
Divide: Useful life remaining at 4/1/X3	6 yrs.
Annual depreciation expense	$1,100,000
Multiply: 9 mos./12 mos.	75%
Consolidated machinery and equipment depreciation expense should be	$ 825,000
Machinery and equipment depreciation expense recorded on separate books of Munson Co. per trial balance	588,750
Worksheet adjustment required (entry 7)	$ 236,250

(8) Sales 388,000
Cost of goods sold 388,000
To eliminate intercompany sales. ($158,000 plus $230,000)

(9) Cost of goods sold 4,200
Inventories 4,200
To eliminate intercompany profit in ending inventory on sales from Munson to Jared. (35% × $12,000 = $4,200)

(10) Accounts payable 38,800
Accounts receivable 38,800
To eliminate intercompany accounts receivable and payable. ($16,800 + $22,000)

(11) General and administrative expenses (goodwill amortization) 52,500
Goodwill 52,500
To amortize goodwill. ($1,400,000 divided by 20 years times 9 mos./12 mos. = $52,500)

Problem 3:

Jared, Inc. and 100% Owned Subsidiary Munson Manufacturing Co.
Consolidating Worksheet
For the Year Ended 12/31/X3

					CONSOLIDATED Dr. (Cr.)		
	Jared	Munson	Eliminations		Income	Retained	Balance
Account name	Dr. (Cr.)	Dr. (Cr.)	Dr.	(Cr.)	Statement	Earnings	Sheet
Cash	822,000	530,000					1,352,000
Accounts receiv. (net) and interest receiv.	2,758,000	1,453,400		(17,500)[5]			4,155,100
				(38,800)[10]			
Inventories	3,204,000	1,182,000	128,000[3]	(128,000)[1]			4,381,800
				(4,200)[9]			
Land	4,000,000	1,560,000	540,000[1]				6,100,000
Machinery and equip.	15,875,000	7,850,000	2,750,000[1]				26,475,000
Accum. depr. – mach. and equip.	(6,301,000)	(3,838,750)		(750,000)[1]			(11,126,000)
				(236,250)[7]			
Buildings	1,286,000						1,286,000
Accum. depr. – bldgs.	(372,000)						(372,000)
Other Assets	263,000	140,000		(90,000)[1]			313,000
Investment in Munson	7,500,000			(5,850,000)[1]			0
				(150,000)[2]			
				(1,500,000)[4]			
Goodwill			1,400,000[1]	(52,500)[11]			1,347,500
Accounts payable and interest payable	(1,364,000)	(319,000)	17,500[5]				(1,626,700)
			38,800[10]				
Long-term debt	(10,000,000)						(10,000,000)
7% Subordinated debentures		(5,000,000)	1,500,000[4]				(3,500,000)
Preferred stock		(750,000)	150,000[2]				(600,000)[M]
Common stock: Jared	(2,400,000)						(2,400,000)
Munson		(1,000,000)	1,000,000[1]				0
Additional paid-in capital:							
Jared	(240,000)						(240,000)
Munson		(122,000)	122,000[1]				0
Retained earnings:							
Jared	(12,683,500)					(12,683,500)	
Munson		(1,006,000)	1,006,000[1]				0
Sales	(18,200,000)	(5,760,000)	388,000[8]		(23,572,000)		
Cost of goods sold	10,600,000	3,160,000	4,200[9]	(128,000)[3]	13,248,200		
				(388,000)[8]			
General and administrative expenses	3,448,500	1,063,900	52,500[11]		4,564,900		
Depr. exp. – mach. and equip.	976,000	588,750	236,250[7]		1,801,000		
Depr. exp. – bldgs.	127,000				127,000		
Interest revenue	(105,000)	(1,700)	78,750[6]		(27,950)		
Interest expense	806,000	269,400		(78,750)[6]	996,650		
Totals	0	0	9,412,000	(9,412,000)			
Consolidated net income					(2,862,200)	(2,862,200)	
Consolidated retained earnings						(15,545,700)	(15,545,700)
Total							0

M = Minority interest

See explanations for consolidating worksheet elimination entries (#1 through #11 above) on preceding pages.

Problem 4: Worksheet elimination entries are now as follows:

		Debit	Credit
(1)	Munson Common stock (80%)	800,000	
	Munson Additional paid-in capital (80%)	97,600	
	Munson Retained earnings (80%)	804,800	
	Land (80%)	432,000	
	Machinery and equipment (80%)	2,200,000	
	Goodwill	2,290,000	
	Inventories (80%)		102,400
	Accum. depr. – mach. and equipment (80%)		600,000
	Other assets (80%)		72,000
	Investment in Munson (common).		5,850,000

To eliminate Investment in Munson's common stock against 80% of Munson's equity, adjust net assets to fair value and record goodwill.

(2) Entry 2 to eliminate Investment in Munson's preferred stock is unchanged (see entry 2, problem 3 answer).

		Debit	Credit
(3)	Inventories	102,400	
	Cost of goods sold		102,400

To amortize reduction in inventory cost (entry 1 above) against cost of goods sold.

(4, 5, 6) Entries 4, 5, and 6 to eliminate the intercompany bond investment and debt, interest receivable and payable, and interest revenue and expense are unchanged (see entries 4, 5, and 6, problem 3 answer).

		Debit	Credit
(7)	Depr. expense – mach. and equipment	189,000	
	Accum. depr. – mach. and equipment		189,000

To amortize machinery and equipment fair value in excess of book value from original purchase. (The adjustment when the parent owned 100% of the subsidiary in problem 3 was $236,250. The parent is now assumed to own only 80% of the subsidiary, so the adjustment is 80% × $236,250 or $189,000.)

(8, 9, 10) Entries 8, 9, and 10 to eliminate intercompany inventory sales and purchases, receivables and payables, and ending inventory profit are unchanged (see entries 8, 9, and 10, problem 3 answer). (However, minority interest in combined net income will be reduced by 20% to $4,200 profit on the upstream sale from Munson to Jared.)

		Debit	Credit
(11)	General and administrative expenses (goodwill amortization)	85,875	
	Goodwill		85,875

To amortize goodwill. ($2,290,000 divided by 20 years times 9 mos./12 mos. = $85,875.)

Finally, minority interest in combined net income as shown on the worksheet is determined as follows:

Munson Manufacturing Company's trial balance:		
Sales	$5,760,000	
Interest revenue	1,700	
Total revenues		$5,761,700
Cost of goods sold	3,160,000	
General and administrative expense	1,063,900	
Depreciation expense	588,750	
Interest expense	269,400	
Total expenses		5,082,050
Subsidiary net income		$ 679,650
Minority interest		× 20%
Subtotal		135,930
Less: Minority share of unrealized profit in ending inventory on upstream sales (20% × $4,200)		(840)
Minority interest in combined net income		$ 135,090

Problem 4: **Jared, Inc. and 80% Owned Subsidiary Munson Manufacturing Co.**
Consolidating Worksheet
For the Year Ended 12/31/X3

					CONSOLIDATED Dr. (Cr.)		
Account name	Jared Dr. (Cr.)	Munson Dr. (Cr.)	Eliminations Dr.	Eliminations (Cr.)	Income Statement	Retained Earnings	Balance Sheet
Cash	822,000	530,000					1,352,000
Accounts receiv. (net) and interest receiv.	2,758,000	1,453,400		(17,500)[5]			4,155,100
				(38,800)[10]			
Inventories	3,204,000	1,182,000	102,400[3]	(102,400)[1]			4,381,800
				(4,200)[9]			
Land	4,000,000	1,560,000	432,000[1]				5,992,000
Machinery and equip.	15,875,000	7,850,000	2,200,000[1]				25,925,000
Accum. depr. – mach and equip.	(6,301,000)	(3,838,750)		(600,000)[1]			(10,928,750)
				(189,000)[7]			
Buildings	1,286,000						1,286,000
Accum. depr. – bldgs.	(372,000)						(372,000)
Other Assets	263,000	140,000		(72,000)[1]			331,000
Investment in Munson	7,500,000			(5,850,000)[1]			0
				(150,000)[2]			
				(1,500,000)[4]			
Goodwill			2,290,000[1]	(85,875)[11]			2,204,125
Accounts payable and interest payable	(1,364,000)	(319,000)	17,500[5]				(1,626,700)
			38,800[10]				
Long-term debt	(10,000,000)						(10,000,000)
7% Subordinated debentures		(5,000,000)	1,500,000[4]				(3,500,000)
Preferred stock		(750,000)	150,000[2]				(600,000)[M]
Common stock: Jared	(2,400,000)						(2,400,000)
Munson		(1,000,000)	800,000[1]				(200,000)[M]
Additional paid-in capital:							
Jared	(240,000)						(240,000)
Munson		(122,000)	97,600[1]				(24,400)[M]
Retained earnings:							
Jared	(12,683,500)					(12,683,500)	
Munson		(1,006,000)	804,800[1]				(201,200)[M]
Sales	(18,200,000)	(5,760,000)	388,000[8]		(23,572,000)		
Cost of goods sold	10,600,000	3,160,000	4,200[9]	(102,400)[3]	13,273,800		
				(388,000)[8]			
General and administrative expenses	3,448,500	1,063,900	85,875[11]		4,598,275		
Depr. exp. – mach. and equip.	976,000	588,750	189,000[7]		1,753,750		
Depr. exp. – bldgs.	127,000				127,000		
Interest revenue	(105,000)	(1,700)	(78,750)[6]		(27,950)		
Interest expense	806,000	269,400		78,750[6]	996,650		
Totals	0	0	9,178,925	(9,178,925)			
		Combined net income			(2,850,475)		
		*Minority interest			135,090		(135,090)[M]
		Consolidated net income			(2,715,385)	(2,715,385)	
		Consolidated retained earnings				(15,398,885)	(15,398,885)
				Total			0
		Total minority interest (sum of items marked "M")					(1,160,690)

*Minority interest in combined net income and eliminating entries are explained on the preceding pages.
M = Minority interest

Problem 5:

(*a*)

Investment in Munson Common stock at 4/1/X3	$5,850,000
Add: Investment income*	518,900
Deduct: Dividends declared (if any)	0
Investment in Munson Common stock at 12/31/X3 (equity method)	6,368,900
Investment in Munson Preferred stock	150,000
Investment in Munson 7% Subordinated debentures	1,500,000
Total Investment in Munson account balance at 12/31/X3	$8,018,900

*Investment income is determined as follows:

Munson's separate net income per trial balance (revenues less expenses)	$679,650
Goodwill amortization (per problem 3)	(52,500)
Machinery and equipment depreciation expense (per problem 3)	(236,250)
Cost of goods sold adjustment for reduced inventory cost (per problem 3)	128,000
19X3 Investment income	$518,900

(*b*) Consolidating worksheet elimination entries, assuming the investment is carried at equity, to eliminate the 12/31/X3 "Investment in Munson" account are as follows:

		Debit	Credit
(1)	Munson Common stock	1,000,000	
	Munson Additional paid-in capital	122,000	
	Munson Retained earnings	1,006,000	
	Land	540,000	
	Machinery and equipment	2,750,000*	
	Goodwill	1,400,000*	
	Investment income	518,900	
	Inventory		128,000
	Accum. depr. – mach. and equipment		750,000
	Other assets		90,000
	Investment in Munson (common)		6,368,900

To eliminate Investment in Munson (common) and investment income against Munson's equity, adjust net assets to fair value, and record goodwill.

*Worksheet amortization entries will, of course, be necessary for these items as shown in the answer to problem 3 (entries 3, 7, and 11).

		Debit	Credit
(2)	Munson Preferred stock	150,000	
	Investment in Munson (preferred)		150,000

To eliminate intercompany preferred stock holding.

		Debit	Credit
(3)	7% Subordinated debentures	1,500,000	
	Investment in Munson (bonds)		1,500,000

To eliminate intercompany investment in bonds.

Note that the "Investment in Munson" is now eliminated fully. Although the problem merely requires consolidating worksheet elimination entries to eliminate the investment account, worksheet elimination for other intercompany transactions as shown in the answer to problem 3 would, of course, be necessary.

Problem 6:

(*a*) 1. In a pooling of interests, the recorded amounts of the assets and liabilities of the separate companies generally become the recorded amounts of the assets and liabilities of the combined corporation. The existing basis of accounting continues. A pooling of interests transaction is regarded as an arrangement among stockholder groups.

2. In a pooling of interests, the registration fees and direct costs related to effecting the business combination should be deducted in determining the net income of the resulting combined corporation for the period in which the expenses are incurred.

3. In a pooling of interests, the results of operations for the year in which the business combination occurred should be reported as though the companies had been combined as of the beginning of the year.

(*b*) 1. In a purchase, the acquiring corporation should allocate the cost of the acquired company to the assets acquired and liabilities assumed. All identifiable assets acquired and liabilities assumed in the business combination should be recorded at their fair values at date of acquisition. The excess of the cost of the acquired company over the sum of the amounts assigned to identifiable assets acquired less liabilities assumed should be recorded as goodwill. A purchase transaction is regarded as a bargained transaction (i.e., a significant economic event which results from bargaining between independent parties) which establishes a new basis of accounting.

2. In a purchase, the registration fees related to effecting the business combination are a reduction of the otherwise determinable fair value of the securities, (usually as a reduction of paid of capital). The direct costs related to effecting the business combination are included as part of the acquisition cost of the acquired company.

3. In a purchase, the results of operations for the year in which the business combination occurred should include income of the acquired company after the date of acquisition by including the revenues and expenses of the acquired company based on the cost to the acquiring corporation.

(AICPA Adapted)

12 TRANSLATING FOREIGN CURRENCY TRANSACTIONS

THIS CHAPTER IS ABOUT

☑ **Accounting Problems Encountered in International Business**
☑ **Terminology Used in Transactions Involving Foreign Currency**
☑ **General Accounting Techniques for Foreign Currency Transactions**
☑ **Forward Exchange Contract in Foreign Currency Transactions**

12-1. Accounting Problems Encountered in International Business

Two types of accounting problems may arise when a company has business transactions with companies in foreign countries. Both problems involve translation of foreign currency into dollars.

First, if the domestic company buys (or sells) goods or services to a foreign company, and agrees to make payments (or accept receipts) in the foreign currency (that is, if the transaction is **denominated** in the foreign currency), then the foreign currency must be translated into the domestic company's currency.

Second, if a domestic company has a foreign investment that it carries under the equity method or for which it prepares consolidated parent and foreign subsidiary financial statements, it must translate the foreign company's financial statements into U.S. dollars.

This chapter addresses the problem of translation of foreign currency transactions. Chapter 13 address the problem of translating a foreign subsidiary's financial statements. The primary authoritative pronouncement regarding both types of translation problems is Statement on Financial Accounting Standards No. 52, "Foreign Currency Translation."

12-2. Terminology Used in Transactions Involving Foreign Currency

The terms listed below have specific meaning when used in business transactions that involve foreign currency and will be useful in the first phase of the study of foreign currency transactions.

current exchange rate. the exchange rate on the date of a balance sheet.

denominated currency. the currency specified in a contract to be used to settle an international transaction (foreign versus domestic).

direct exchange rate. an exchange rate that indicates the number of domestic currency units required to obtain one unit of foreign currency.

exchange rate. the number of units of one currency that must be used to obtain one unit of another currency.

foreign currency transaction. an international transaction denominated in a currency other than a business entity's domestic currency.

foreign transaction. an international transaction denominated in a business entity's domestic currency.

forward exchange contract. an agreement between a business entity and a foreign currency dealer to exchange dollars for foreign currency at a specified rate at a specified date in the future.

forward exchange rate. the rate of exchange agreed upon in a forward exchange contract for delivery of foreign currency for dollars on a specific date.
functional currency. the currency of the primary economic environment in which an entity operates (generates and expends cash).
intervening balance sheet date. a balance sheet date which falls between a transaction date and a settlement date.
hedging. avoiding loss on a foreign currency transaction through the use of forward exchange contracts.
historic exchange rate. the rate that existed when a specific transaction occurred.
indirect exchange rate. an exchange rate that indicates the number of foreign currency units required to obtain one unit of domestic currency.
settlement date. the date on which a payment is received or a debt is paid.
spot rate. the current exchange rate, assuming an immediate exchange of currencies.
transaction date. the date on which a transaction is recorded under generally accepted accounting principles.

12-3. General Accounting Techniques for Foreign Currency Transactions

A. The appropriate exchange rate must be used in foreign currency transactions.

The exchange rate, as defined in the previous section, is the rate at which a unit of one currency may be exchanged for a unit of another currency. These rates are established in open markets, such as those in New York, London, and Tokyo. Exchange rates are very volatile and may change significantly from day to day. Business transactions involving the translation of one currency to another should be recorded at the "*transaction date exchange rate*" (the date on which the transaction is recorded under generally accepted accounting principles).

If no credit is extended by the selling party in the course of the transaction, and the necessary currency conversions are made on the transaction date, no special accounting problems arise from a foreign currency transaction. Each company records the transaction as it normally would on its books in its own domestic currency.

EXAMPLE 12-1: On 11/30/X1, Jamestown Co. purchased inventory from Frankfurt Co. of Germany for 50,000 German marks (or deutsche marks, abbreviated DM). On that date the exchange rate or spot rate for marks was $.40.

Jamestown Co. immediately purchased DM 50,000 for $20,000 (50,000 × $.40 = $20,000), paid Frankfurt Co., and recorded the purchase as follows:

Merchandise inventory	20,000	
Cash		20,000
To record purchase of inventory.		

EXAMPLE 12-2: On 11/30/X1, Jamestown Co. sold inventory to Frankfurt Co. of Germany for DM 50,000. On that date the exchange rate or spot rate for marks was $.40.

Jamestown Co. received immediate payment of DM 50,000 on the sale, exchanged the marks for $20,000 (50,000 × $.40 = $20,000), and recorded the sale as follows:

Cash	20,000	
Sales		20,000
To record sale of inventory.		

B. Extending credit during foreign currency transactions makes accounting for them more complicated.

A problem resulting from fluctuation in the exchange rates may arise when one party to a foreign currency transaction extends credit to another. The problem is how to account for a change in the exchange rate between the transaction date and any intervening balance sheet date, or a change in the exchange rate between the balance sheet date and the settlement date.

Under current generally accepted accounting principles, the purchase (or sale) of goods from any source is viewed as a separate transaction from the commitment to pay (or receive) foreign currency. Therefore, any difference between the original transaction date exchange rate and the intervening balance sheet date exchange rate will result in a gain or loss on the transaction. The gain or loss should be recorded in the payable or receivable accounts relating to the transactions. No adjustment is made to the original transaction date recording of cost of goods sold or sales. Likewise, any difference between the intervening balance sheet date and settlement date exchange rates results in further loss or gain on the transaction, and these too will be recorded in the related payable or receivable accounts.

EXAMPLE 12-3: A Co., a domestic (U.S.) company, ends its fiscal year on 6/30/X4. On 6/15/X4, it purchases inventory from B Co. (a foreign company) for 50,000 local currency units (LCUs) of B Co. (That is, the purchase transaction is denominated in LCUs, not dollars, and is therefore a foreign currency transaction, as well as a purchase for A Co.)

Payment from A Co. to B Co. is due on 7/12/X4.

Spot rates of exchange for the time period involved are:

6/15/X4	$.75
6/26/X4	$.76
6/30/X4	$.78
7/12/X4	$.79
7/15/X4	$.80

A Co.'s journal entry to record the purchase on the transaction date (6/15/X4) is:

Inventory	37,500	
Accounts payable ($.75 × 50,000 LCUs)		37,500
To record purchase (at transaction date exchange rate).		

A Co. prepares a financial statement on 6/30/X4. For the year ended 7/30/X4, A Co. must record a loss on the foreign currency transaction, totaling $1,500, as a result of changes in the exchange rate from the transaction date (6/15/X4) to the balance sheet date (6/30/X4). The amount of the loss is calculated by finding the difference in the amount payable, in dollars, on the two dates. An increase in the debt results in a loss on the transaction, and decrease in the debt results in a gain on the transaction:

Debt due in foreign currency	50,000 LCUs
Intervening balance-sheet date exchange rate (6/30/X4)	× 78
Debt in U.S. dollars on 6/30/X4	$39,000
Debt recorded on 6/15/X4 transaction date	37,500
Increase in debt in U.S. dollars	$ 1,500

A Co.'s journal entry to record the loss on the intervening balance sheet date is:

Foreign currency transaction loss	1,500	
Accounts payable		1,500
To record foreign currency transaction loss based on the change in the exchange rate from the transaction date to the intervening balance sheet date.		

An alternate method for determining the loss on the transaction is to multiply the increase in the cost per unit of foreign currency by the number of foreign currency units due:

Transaction date exchange rate	$ .75
Intervening balance-sheet date exchange rate	.78
Increase in value of one foreign currency unit	.03
Number of foreign currency units due at settlement	× 50,000 LCUs
Foreign currency transaction loss	$1,500.00

On 7/12/X4, A Co. pays B Co. On that date A Co. must make three entries on its books: (1) to record further loss on the foreign currency transaction, based on continued changes in the exchange rates, (2) to record its acquisition of the foreign currency, and (3) to record its payment of the debt using the foreign currency.

The amount of the additional loss on the foreign currency transaction since the balance sheet date is determined by finding the difference between the rates on 6/30/X4 and 7/12/X4 and multiplying this difference by the number of LCUs due:

Intervening balance-sheet date exchange rate	$ .78
Settlement date exchange rate	.79
Increase in value of one foreign currency unit	.01
Number of foreign currency units due at settlement	× 50,000 LCUs
Foreign currency transaction loss	$ 500.00

The journal entry to record this additional loss is:

Foreign currency transaction loss	500	
Accounts payable		500

To record foreign currency transaction loss based on the change in the exchange rate from the intervening balance sheet date to the settlement date.

A Co.'s Accounts Payable balance is now $39,500 ($37,500 + $1,500 + $500).

A Co. then purchases 50,000 LCUs at the rate current on the 7/12/X4 settlement date, and records that transaction on its books:

Foreign currency	39,500	
Cash		39,500

To record purchase of 50,000 LCUs for $39,500 (50,000 LCUs × $.79).

A Co. then pays B Co. 50,000 LCUs, and records that transaction:

Accounts payable	39,500	
Foreign currency		39,500

To record payment of $39,500 debt using 50,000 LCUs.

An alternate method for recording settlement of foreign currency transactions is to to combine all three entries shown above into a single entry:

Foreign currency transaction loss	500	
Accounts payable (as booked as of 6/30/X4)	39,000	
Cash (50,000 LCUs × $.79)		39,500

To record foreign currency transaction loss and purchase of foreign currency in settlement of debt.

EXAMPLE 12-4: A Co., a domestic (U.S.) company, ends its fiscal year on 6/30/X4. On 6/26/X4, it sells inventory to C Co. (a foreign company) for 100,000 LCUs of C Co. (That is, the sale transaction is denominated in LCUs, not dollars, and is therefore a foreign currency transaction, as well as a sale, for A Co.)

Payment from C Co. to A Co. is due on 7/15/X4.

Spot rates of exchange for the time period involved are:

6/15/X4	$.75
6/26/X4	$.76
6/30/X4	$.78
7/12/X4	$.79
7/15/X4	$.80

A Co.'s journal entry to record the sale on the transaction date (6/26/X4) was:

Accounts receivable ($.75 × 100,000 LCUs)	76,000	
Sales		76,000
To record sale (at transaction date exchange rate).		

A Co. prepares financial statements on 6/30/X4. For the year ended 6/30/X4, A Co. must record a gain on the foreign currency transaction, totaling $2,000, as a result of changes in the exchange rate from the transaction date (6/26/X4) to the balance sheet date (6/30/X4). The amount of the gain is calculated by finding the difference in the amount receivable, in dollars, on the two dates. An increase in the receivable results in a gain on the transaction, and decrease in the receivable results in a loss on the transaction:

Receivable due in foreign currency	100,000 LCUs
Intervening balance sheet date exchange rate (6/30/X4)	× $.78
Receivable in U.S. dollars on 6/30/X4	$78,000
Receivable recorded on 6/26/X4 transaction date	76,000
Increase in receivable in U.S. dollars	$ 2,000

A Co.'s journal entry to record the gain on the intervening balance sheet date is:

Accounts receivable	2,000	
Foreign currency transaction gain		2,000
To record foreign currency transaction gain based on the change in the exchange rate from the transaction date to the intervening balance sheet date.		

An alternate method for determining the gain on the transaction is to multiply the increase in the cost per unit of foreign currency by the number of foreign currency units due:

Transaction date exchange rate	$.76
Intervening balance sheet date exchange rate	.78
Increase in value of one foreign currency unit	.02
Number of foreign currency units receivable at settlement	× 100,000 LCUs
Foreign currency transaction gain	$2,000.00

On 7/15/X4, A Co. receives payment from C Co. On that date A Co. must make three entries on its books: (1) to record further gain on the foreign currency transaction, based on continued changes in the exchange rates, (2) to record its receipt of the foreign currency, and (3) to record its conversion of the foreign currency into dollars.

The amount of the additional gain on the foreign currency transaction since the balance sheet date is determined by finding the difference between the rates on 6/30/X4 and 7/15/X4 and multiplying the difference by the number of LCUs receivable:

Intervening balance sheet date exchange rate	$.78
Settlement date exchange rate	.80
Increase in value of one foreign currency unit	.02
Number of foreign currency units receivable at settlement	× 100,000 LCUs
Foreign currency transaction gain	$2,000

The journal entry to record this additional gain is:

Accounts receivable ($.75 × 100,000 LCUs)	2,000	
Foreign currency transaction gain		2,000
To record foreign currency transaction gain based on the change in the exchange rate from the intervening balance sheet date to the settlement date.		

A Co.'s Accounts Receivable balance is now $80,000 ($76,000 + $2,000 + $2,000).

A Co. then records receipt of C Co.'s LCUs (in dollars at the 7/15/X4 settlement date spot rate):

Foreign currency	80,000	
Accounts receivable		80,000
To record receipt of 100,000 LCUs at $80,000 (100,00 LCUs × $.80).		

A Co. then converts the LCUs to dollars and records the transaction:

Cash	80,000	
Foreign currency		80,000
To record conversion of foreign currency into dollars.		

An alternate method for recording settlement of foreign currency transactions is to to combine all three entries shown above into a single entry:

Cash	80,000	
Accounts receivable		78,000
Foreign currency transaction gain		2,000
To record foreign currency transaction gain and receipt of foreign currency in settlement of receivable.		

12-4. Forward Exchange Contracts in Foreign Currency Transactions

A forward exchange contract is an agreement between a participant in a foreign currency transaction and a foreign currency broker to exchange foreign currency for dollars on a specified date at a rate specified in the contract. The forward exchange rate could differ from the spot rate on the settlement date and represents a method of protection against loss (due to fluctuations in currency value) called hedging.

EXAMPLE 12-5: On May 1, 19X1, U.S. company agrees to buy 100,000 foreign currency units (LCUs) on August 1, 19X1 for $1.80 each. At the May 1, 19X1 forward exchange contract date, the exchange rate is $1.79 for 1 LCU. On August 1, 19X1, the exchange rate is $1.82 for 1 LCU. The U.S. company will purchase 100,000 LCUs for $180,000 (100,000 LCUs × $1.80) on August 1, 19X1 even though these securities are selling at a higher price of $182,000 (100,000 LCUs × $1.82) on that date as a result of the existence of the forward exchange contract with an international securities broker.

A. There are a number of reasons to enter into a forward exchange contract.

Companies may avoid losses, and even realize gains, in a number of different ways through the use of forward exchange contracts. Among the reasons for entering into forward exchange contracts are:

- to hedge against (that is, to offset) losses on foreign currency transactions that have been recorded but not settled.
- to hedge against losses on foreign currency transactions that have not been recorded, such as purchase orders for foreign goods.
- to speculate in foreign currency.
- to hedge against the decline in value of an investment in foreign operations.

Each of these involves slightly different accounting techniques.

B. A forward exchange contract may be a hedge against losses on recorded but unsettled purchase transactions.

In order to avoid loss from unfavorable changes in the exchange rate that may result from market fluctuations in the period of time from the transaction date to the settlement date, the company that makes a purchase and has an obligation payable in a foreign currency may simultaneously enter into a forward exchange contract with a foreign currency dealer to buy the currency it will need to pay its debt on the settlement date at a specified exchange rate, the forward exchange rate.

Any difference between the forward rate and the spot rate on the date that the forward exchange contract is signed is considered either a "deferred premium" or a "deferred discount" on the exchange contract.

If the forward rate exceeds the spot rate, the liability due to the foreign currency dealer exceeds the foreign currency receivable at the exchange contract date. This difference is charged to a Deferred Premium on Exchange Contract account.

Conversely, if the spot rate exceeds the forward rate, the foreign currency receivable exceeds the liability due to the foreign currency dealer on the exchange contract date. This difference is credited to a Deferred Discount on Exchange Contract account.

Any premium or discount that results from a forward exchange contract is amortized to income or expenses over the life of the contract. The foreign currency that the buyer has agreed to purchase from the currency dealer will eventually be used to settle the buyer's debt which is denominated in the foreign currency.

EXAMPLE 12-6: Refer to the information given in Example 12-3. Assume additionally that on 6/15/X4, A Co. also entered into a forward exchange contract to purchase 50,000 LCUs to pay B Co. The contract provides for a forward rate of $.77 per LCU, which is to be paid to the currency dealer on the 7/12/X4 settlement date.

In addition to its journal entry to record the purchase, A Co. must now make another entry on 6/15/X4, to record its forward exchange contract. The liability due the currency dealer on 7/12/X4 is $38,500 (50,000 LCUs × the $.77 forward rate). The foreign currency receivable, according to the spot rate on 6/15/X4, is $37,500 (50,000 LCUs × $.75). The difference between the foreign currency receivable and liability due to the dealer is $1,000, and is considered a deferred premium on the exchange contract. The journal entry to record the forward exchange contract is therefore:

Foreign currency receivable	37,500	
Deferred premium on exchange contract	1,000	
Due to currency dealer		38,500

When A Co. prepares its financial statements on 6/30/X4, it records the loss on the foreign currency transaction as shown in Example 12-3. But because of the forward exchange contract, it must also make two additional entries.

The first is to record the gain that results from the use of the forward exchange contract. Because of the increase in the spot rate, the market value of the foreign currency receivable by A Co. on 6/30/X4 is $39,000 (50,000 LCUs × the $.78 spot rate), a $1,500 gain credit and charge to the Foreign Currency Receivable account ($39,000 – $37,500). This gain is recorded as follows:

Foreign currency receivable	1,500	
Foreign currency transaction gain		1,500

This $1,500 gain may alternatively be determined by multiplying the $.03 increase in the cost of an LCU by the 50,000 LCUs receivable. The $.03 increase occurred from the 6/15/X4 transaction date ($.75) to the 6/30/X4 intervening balance sheet date ($.78).

The second extra entry on the balance sheet date is to amortize the deferred premium on the forward exchange contract recorded on the transaction date. The life of the contract, from 6/15/X4 to 7/12X4, is

27 days. The period from 6/15/X4 through 6/30/X4 represents 15/27 of the contract period. The deferred premium is therefore amortized as follows: 15/27 × $1,000 = $556. The entry to record the amortization through 6/30/X4 is:

Premium amortization expense	556	
Deferred premium on exchange contract		556

On the 7/12/X4 settlement date A Co. will make four entries on its books to account for the forward exchange contract, in addition to the entries shown in Example 12-3 to record its loss on the foreign currency transaction and its payment to B Co.

The first entry is to record the additional gain that results from the forward exchange contract. The spot rate on 7/12/X4 is $.79 per LCU. Therefore the value of the LCUs A Co. will receive from the currency dealer is $39,500 (50,000 × $.79), an increase of $500 over the Foreign Currency Receivable account balance of $39,000 recorded on 6/30/X4. The entry to record the gain is:

Foreign currency receivable	500	
Foreign currency transaction gain		500

This $500 gain may alternatively be determined by multiplying the $.01 increase in the cost of an LCU by the 50,000 LCUs receivable. The $.01 increase occurred from the 6/30/X4 intervening balance sheet date ($.78) to the 7/12/X4 settlement date ($.79).

The second entry is to record the remaining amortization of the premium paid on the contract (12/27 × $1,000 = $444). The entry to record the amortization is:

Premium amortization expense	444	
Deferred premium on exchange contract		444

The third entry is to record the purchase of the LCUs from the foreign currency dealer at the forward exchange rate in accordance with the terms of the forward exchange contract (50,000 at $.77 each = $38,500):

Due to currency dealer	38,500	
Cash		38,500

The final entry is to record the receipt of the LCUs from the foreign currency dealer based on the spot rate upon their receipt on 7/12/X4 ($.79 × 50,000 LCUs = $39,500):

Foreign currency	39,500	
Foreign currency receivable		39,500

Note that the losses incurred by A Co. on the foreign currency transaction in Example 12-3 ($1,500 and $500) are exactly offset by the gains it makes on the forward exchange contract. For a clear depiction of these relationships see Exhibit 12-A which shows the entries A Co. makes to record both its purchase from B Co. (the same as those in Example 12-3) and the results of the forward exchange contract.

Exhibit 12-A

A Co. Purchase (from Example 12-3)			Forward Exchange Contract		
Transaction date — 6/15/X4					
Inventory	37,500		Foreign currency receivable	37,500*	
Accounts payable		37,500	Deferred premium on exchange contract	1,000	
($.0051282 × 50,000 yen)			Due to currency dealer		38,500**
			To record forward exchange contract. *50,000,000 LCUs × $.75 spot rate = $37,500 **50,000,000 LCUs × $.77 forward rate = $38,500.		
Intervening balance sheet date — 6/30/X4					
Foreign currency transaction loss	1,500		Foreign currency receivable	1,500	
Accounts payable		675	Foreign currency transaction gain		1,500
To record transaction loss on exchange rate change of $.03 increase per LCU times 50,000 LCUs to be paid.			To record foreign currency transaction gain of $.03 per LCU times 50,000 LCUs to be received.		

(Note that the foreign currency transaction loss of $1,500 is exactly offset by the foreign currency transaction gain of $1,500 through the use of the forward exchange contract.)

			Premium amortization expense	556	
			Deferred premium on exchange contract		556
			To amortize deferred premium on forward exchange contract over contract life. (15 days./27 days. × $1,000 premium = $556. Note that the contract life is the 27-day period from 6/15/X4 to 7/12/X4. The period 6/15/X4 through 6/30/X4 represents 15 days of the contract period.)		
Settlement date — 7/12/X4					
Foreign currency transaction loss	500		Foreign currency receivable	500	
Accounts payable		500	Foreign currency transaction gain		500
To record transaction loss on exchange rate change of $.01 increase per LCU times 50,000 LCUs to be paid.			To record foreign currency transaction gain of $.01 per LCU times 50,000 LCUs to be received.		

(Note again that the foreign currency transaction loss of $500 is exactly offset by the foreign currency transaction gain of $500 through the use of the forward exchange contract.)

			Premium amortization expense	444	
			Deferred premium on exchange contract		444
			To amortize deferred premium on forward exchange contract over contract life. (12 days/27 day × $1,000 premium = $444. Or, $1,000 total deferred premium less 6/30/X4 amortization of $556 also yields $444.)		
			Due to currency dealer	38,500	
			Cash		38,500
			To record purchase of 50,000 LCUs at forward rate of $.77 each. (50,000 LCUs × $.77 = $38,500.)		
Accounts payable	39,500		Foreign currency	39,500	
Foreign currency		39,500	Foreign currency receivable		39,500
To record payment of 50,000 LCUs to B Co. (foreign company). (50,000 LCUs × $.79 = $39,500.)			To record receipt of 50,000 LCUs from foreign currency dealer worth $.79 each. (50,000 LCUs × $.79 = 39,500.)		

(Note that the 50,000 LCUs purchased from the foreign currency dealer are used to pay the foreign vendor, B Co., for goods purchased.)

C. A forward exchange contract may be a hedge against losses on recorded but unsettled sales transactions.

A company that makes a sale to a foreign company, and has an amount receivable in a foreign currency, may enter into a forward exchange contract, just as with a purchase transaction, in order to avoid loss from unfavorable changes in the exchange rate between the transaction date and the settlement date. In a sales transaction, the company contracts to sell the foreign currency it will receive on the settlement date to the foreign currency dealer at a specified rate (the forward rate).

Again, any difference between the spot rate on the date of the contract and the forward rate agreed upon is considered a premium or discount, and is amortized over the life of the contract. Eventually, the seller will receive payment from the buyer (in foreign currency) on the original sales transaction. The seller will then exchange this foreign currency with the foreign currency dealer for local currency (dollars) at the agreed upon forward rate.

EXAMPLE 12-7: Refer to the information given in Example 12-4. Assume additionally that on 6/26/X4, A Co. also entered into a forward exchange contract to sell 100,000 LCUs it will receive from C Co on the settlement date. The contract provides for a forward rate of $.77 per LCU, which is to be received from the currency dealer on the 7/15/X4 date.

In addition to its journal entry to record the sale of inventory, A Co. must now make another entry on 6/26/X4, to record its forward exchange contract. The amount due from the currency dealer on 7/15/X4 is $77,000 (100,000 LCUs × the $.77 forward rate). The foreign currency payable, according to the spot rate on 6/26/X4, is $76,000 (100,000 LCUs × $.76). The difference between the amount due from the foreign currency dealer and foreign currency payable is $1,000, and is considered a discount on the contract. The entry to record the forward exchange contract is therefore:

Due from currency dealer	77,000	
Deferred discount on exchange contract		1,000
Foreign Currency Payable		76,000

When A Co. prepares its financial statements on 6/30/X4, its records the gain on the foreign currency transaction as shown in Example 12-4. But because of the forward exchange contract, it must also make two additional entries.

The first is to record the loss that results from the use of the forward exchange contract. Because of the increase in the spot rate, the market value of the foreign currency payable by A Co. on 6/30/X4 is $78,000 (100,000 LCUs × the $.78 spot rate), a $2,000 increase to the Foreign Currency Payable account ($78,000 – $76,000). This loss is recorded as follows:

Foreign Currency Transaction Loss	2,000	
Foreign Currency Payable		2,000

This $2,000 loss may alternatively be determined by multiplying the $.02 increase in the cost of an LCU by the 100,000 LCUs to be paid to the dealer. The $.02 increase occurred from the 6/26/X4 transaction date ($.76) to the 6/30/X4 intervening balance sheet date ($.78).

The second entry on the balance sheet date is to amortize the deferred discount on the forward exchange contract recorded on the transaction date. The life of the contract, from 6/26/X4 to 7/15/X4, is 19 days. The period from 6/26/X4 through 6/30/X4 represents 4/19 of the contract period. The deferred discount is therefore amortized as follows: 4/19 × $1,000 = $210. The entry to record the amortization through 6/30/X4 is:

Deferred discount on exchange contract	210	
Discount amortization revenue		210

On the 7/15/X4 settlement date, A Co. will make four entries on its books to account for the forward exchange contract, in addition to those shown in Example 12-4 to record its gain on the foreign currency transaction and the payment received from C Co.

The first entry is to record the additional loss that results from the forward exchange contract. The spot rate on 7/15/X4 is $.80 per LCU. Therefore the value of the LCUs A Co. will receive from C Co. is $80,000 (100,000 × $.80), an increase of an additional $2,000 in the Foreign Currency Payable account balance of $78,000 recorded on 6/30/X4. The entry to record the loss is:

Foreign currency transaction loss	2,000	
Foreign currency payable		2,000

This $2,000 loss may alternatively be determined by multiplying the $.02 increase in the cost of an LCU by the 100,000 LCUs payable. The $.02 increase occurred from the 6/30X4 intervening balance sheet date ($.78) to the 7/15/X4 settlement date ($.80).

The second entry is to record the remaining amortization of the discount on the contract (15/19 × $1,000 = $790). The entry to record the amortization is:

Deferred discount on exchange contract	790	
Discount amortization revenue		790

After A Co. receives its LCUs from C Co., it makes a third entry to record the payment of these LCUs, which have a value according to the spot rate of $80,000 (100,000 at $.80 each) to the foreign currency dealer based on the terms of the forward exchange contract:

Foreign currency payable	80,000	
Foreign currency		80,000

The final entry is to record the receipt of cash from the foreign currency dealer based on the $.77 forward exchange rate (100,000 LCUs × $.77) is:

Cash	77,000	
Due from currency dealer		77,000

Note that the gains recorded by A Co. on the foreign currency transaction in Example 12-4 ($4,000) are exactly offset by the losses it takes on the forward exchange contract. For a clear depiction of these relationships see Exhibit 12-B which shows the entries A Co. makes to record both its sale to C Co. (the same as those in Example 12-4) and the results of the forward exchange contract.

Exhibit 12-B

A Co. Sales to C Co. (from Example 12-4) | **Forward Exchange Contract**

Transaction date — 6/26/X4

A Co. Sales to C Co.

Account	Debit	Credit
Accounts receivable	76,000	
Sales		37,500
($.76 × 100,000 LCUs)		

Forward Exchange Contract

Account	Debit	Credit
Due from currency dealer	77,000*	
Deferred premium on exchange contract	1,000	
Foreign currency payable		76,000**

To record forward exchange contract.
*100,000 LCUs × $.77 forward rate = $77,000
**100,000 LCUs × $.76 spot rate = $76,000.

Intervening balance sheet date — 6/30/X4

A Co. Sales to C Co.

Account	Debit	Credit
Accounts receivable	2,000	
Foreign currency transaction gain		2,000

To record transaction gain on exchange rate change of $.02 increase per LCU times 100,000 LCUs to be received.

Forward Exchange Contract

Account	Debit	Credit
Foreign currency transaction loss	2,000	
Foreign currency payable		2,000

To record foreign currency transaction loss of $.02 per LCU times 100,000 LCUs to be paid to dealer.

(Note that the foreign currency transaction gain of $2,000 is exactly offset by the foreign currency transaction loss of $2,000 through the use of the forward exchange contract.)

Account	Debit	Credit
Deferred discount on exchange contract	210	
Discount amortization revenue		210

To amortize deferred discount on forward exchange contract over contract life. (4 days/19 days × $1,000 discount = $210. Note that the contract life is the 19-day period from 6/26/X4 to 7/15/X4. The period 6/26/X4 through 6/30/X4 represents 4 days of the contract period.)

Settlement date — 3/1/X4

A Co. Sales to C Co.

Account	Debit	Credit
Accounts receivable	2,000	
Foreign currency transaction gain		2,000

To record transaction gain on exchange rate change of $.02 increase per LCU times 100,000 LCUs to be received.

Forward Exchange Contract

Account	Debit	Credit
Foreign currency transaction loss	2,000	
Foreign currency payable		2,000

To record foreign currency transaction loss of $.02 per LCU times 100,000 LCUs to be paid to dealer.

(Note again that the foreign currency transaction gain of $2,000 is exactly offset by the foreign currency transaction loss of $2,000 through the use of the forward exchange contract.)

Account	Debit	Credit
Deferred discount on exchange contract	790	
Discount amortization expense		790

To amortize deferred discount on forward exchange contract over contract life. (15 days/19 days × $1,000 discount = $790. Or, $1,000 total deferred discount less 6/30/X4 amortization of $210 also yields $790.)

A Co. Sales to C Co.

Account	Debit	Credit
Foreign currency	80,000	
Accounts receivable		80,000

To record receipt of 100,000 LCUs at $80,000. ($.80 × 100,000 LCUs.)

Forward Exchange Contract

Account	Debit	Credit
Foreign currency payable	80,000	
Foreign currency		80,000

To record payment of 100,000 LCUs to dealer worth $.80 each.

Account	Debit	Credit
Cash	77,000	
Due from currency dealer		77,000

To record receipt of $.77 forward rate for each of 100,000 LCUs paid to the currency dealer.

(Note that the receipt of 100,000 LCUs from the sale to C Co. at settlement is used to pay the foreign currency dealer.)

D. A forward exchange contract may be a hedge against losses on unrecorded transactions.

A company may place or receive a purchase order, or make some other type of legal commitment, for goods or services. Under generally accepted accounting principles, however, until the goods or services change hands, and an invoice is transmitted, no legal liability is incurred, and no entries are recorded on the books of the companies involved. But if the unrecorded transaction involves a commitment to make payment in a foreign currency, a hedge may be considered to avoid loss from fluctuation in the foreign currency's cost. Therefore, a forward exchange contract may be entered into.

On the date that the contract is signed, a Foreign Currency Receivable account is charged at the day's spot rate, and a Due to Currency Dealer account is credited at the forward rate specified in the contract.

Any difference between the receivable and payable is treated as either a deferred discount or a deferred premium on the exchange contract, and is amortized to income over the life of the contract (as described in section 12-4B and 12-4C). (An alternate method that may be used to account for the deferred discount or premium is to treat it as an adjustment to the acquired asset's cost. This method is discussed following Example 12-8.)

An additional consideration arises when a forward exchange contract is entered. If the foreign currency exchange rate changes between the date of the forward exchange contract and the date of the settlement, a foreign currency transaction gain or loss results (as described in section 12-4B and 12-4C). However, unlike situations involving recorded but unsettled transactions, any gain or loss that results from the forward exchange contract is not simultaneously offset by a gain or loss on a recorded transaction since no transaction would yet have been recorded for an order or commitment under generally accepted accounting principles. Therefore, the gain or loss on the foreign currency transaction will generally be deferred and treated as part of the cost of the asset acquired. (Losses on foreign currency transactions should not be deferred if the deferral will lead to recognition of the loss in a later accounting period.) As a result, the asset acquired will generally be recorded at the spot rate on the date of the commitment to buy foreign currency from the dealer.

(Alternatively, as described earlier, the asset will be recorded at the forward rate of exchange if discount or premium is not amortized but treated as an adjustment to the asset's cost.) In Example 12-8, the difference between the spot rate and the forward rate is not viewed as an adjustment to the asset's cost but rather as an expense generated in eliminating exposure to exchange rate fluctuations. In Example 12-9, the alternate treatment of premium or discount as an adjustment to the asset's cost is demonstrated.

EXAMPLE 12-8: On 11/1/X8, A Co. (a U.S. company) places a purchase order for inventory with B Co. (a foreign company) and agrees to pay 100,000 LCUs when the inventory is delivered. B Co. has scheduled delivery of the inventory for four months in the future, on 3/1/X9.

Under generally accepted accounting principles, A Co. makes no formal accounting entry on its books to record the purchase order. On 11/1/X8, however, A Co. also obtains a forward exchange contract with a foreign currency dealer to hedge against currency fluctuations before its inventory arrives. It agrees to pay \$.90 per LCU for 100,000 LCUs. The following spot rates are available:

November 1, 19X8	\$.88
December 31, 19X8	\$.91
March 1, 19X9	\$.89

On 11/1/X8, A Co. does make an entry on its books to record the forward exchange contract. The Foreign Currency Receivable account is valued at the day's spot rate of \$.88 per LCU (100,000 LCUs × \$.88 = \$88,000). The Due to Currency Dealer account is valued at the forward rate of \$.90 per LCU (100,000 × \$.90 = \$90,000). The difference between the two accounts is entered as a deferred premium A Co. pays on the contract:

11/1/X8	Foreign currency receivable	88,000	
	Deferred premium on exchange contract	2,000	
	Due to currency dealer		90,000
	To record forward exchange contract.		

On 12/31/X8, before A Co. prepares financial statements, it must make two entries regarding the forward exchange contract. The first is to record a gain that results from changes in the currency exchange rate since the date of the contract. The increase in the spot rate from \$.88 to \$.91 from 11/1/X8 to 12/31/X8 means that the Foreign Currency Receivable account has increased by \$3,000 (100,000 LCUs × \$.03 = \$3,000).

12/31/X8	Foreign currency receivable	3,000	
	Deferred foreign currency transaction gain		3,000
	To record deferred gain.		

The second entry is to record amortization of the \$2,000 deferred premium on the contract. The life of the contract is four months, from 11/1/X8 to 3/1/X9. On 12/31/X8, two months, or one half of the contract life, have lapsed. Therefore the entry based on one half of \$2,000 is:

12/31/X8	Premium amortization expense	1,000	
	Deferred premium on exchange contract		1,000
	To amortize deferred premium on hedging contract.		

When the inventory arrives from B Co. on 3/1/X9, A Co. makes four entries on its books relative to its forward exchange contract. The first is to record the deferred loss incurred since the balance sheet date as a result of the spot rate dropping from \$.91 on 12/31/X8 to \$.89 on 3/1/X9 (100,000 LCUs to be received × \$.02 = \$2,000).

3/1/X9	Deferred foreign currency transaction loss	2,000	
	Foreign currency receivable		2,000
	To record deferred loss.		

The second entry is to complete the amortization of the premium:

3/1/X9	Premium amortization expense	1,000	
	Deferred premium on exchange contract		1,000
	To amortize deferred premium on hedging contract (2 months/4 months × \$2,000 = \$1,000).		

The third entry is record payment to the foreign currency dealer at the rate specified in the forward exchange contract; that is, \$90,000 (100,000 LCUs at \$.90 each):

3/1/X9	Due to foreign currency dealer	90,000	
	Cash		90,000
	To record acquisition of 100,000 LCUs at \$.90 forward rate.		

The Foreign Currency Receivable account has already been adjusted to \$89,000 (\$88,000 on 11/1/X8 plus \$3,000 on 12/31/X8 less \$2,000 on 3/1/X9). The fourth entry records the receipt of the LCUs from the foreign currency dealer, valued at the day's spot rate (\$.89). This entry removes the balance in the Foreign Currency Receivable account:

3/1/X9	Foreign currency	89,000	
	Foreign currency receivable		89,000
	To record receipt from currency dealer of 100,000 LCUs at the spot rate of \$.89 per LCU. (Note that this entry removes the balance in the foreign currency receivable account.)		

At this point A Co. records the purchase of its inventory, valued at the spot rate in effect on 11/1/X8, or \$88,000 (100,000 LCUs × \$.88). It used the LCUs it acquired (\$89,000) to pay for the inventory. It is also at this point that the deferred gain and loss are removed from the books, and treated as part of the cost of the inventory acquired. The final entry to record the purchase of the inventory from B Co. is:

3/1/X9	Inventory	88,000	
	Deferred foreign currency transaction gain	3,000	
	Foreign currency		89,000
	Deferred foreign currency transaction loss		2,000
	To record inventory purchase from B Co. using foreign currency received from dealer. (***note:*** The deferred gain/loss is removed and inventory is recorded at the spot rate on the 11/1/X8 commitment date of \$.88 × 100,000 LCUs.)		

As mentioned above, an alternate method exists regarding the accounting of deferred discounts or premiums on forward exchange contracts. Under this method, the discounts or premiums are also treated as adjustments to the cost of the acquired assets on the date the purchase of those assets is recorded, rather than amortized to income or expenses over the life of the contract. If the alternate method is used, the asset is recorded by the purchasing company at the forward rate of exchange, rather than at the spot rate on the date of the contract as it was in Example 12-8.

Observation: It appears reasonable to argue that the asset's cost should be determined based on management's intent. For example, if management intends to use the LCUs it has contracted to purchase at a forward rate from the currency dealer to pay for the asset, then it would appear reasonable to record the asset at the forward rate. If this is the case, then all premium, discount, gain, or loss should be deferred and viewed as part of the asset's cost (as shown in Example 12-9). On the other hand, if management is simply speculating in foreign currency which it may or may not use to buy the asset, then the asset should be recorded at the spot rate on the date of acquisition. Furthermore, the speculation in foreign currency should be accounted for as described in Section 12-E.

EXAMPLE 12-9: Refer to the information given in Example 12-8. Assume, however, that A Co. prefers to view deferred premiums or discounts on forward exchange contracts as an adjustment to an asset's cost, rather than as an item to be amortized to income.

In this case, all the entries shown in Example 12-8 to account for the forward exchange contract remain the same, except that the two entries (on 12/31/X9 and 3/1/X9) recording premium amortization expense are not made. A Co.'s balance sheet on 12/31/X9 shows the Deferred Premium on Exchange Contract account balance at the full (unamortized) \$2,000.

Because A Co. uses the alternate method, the entry on 3/1/X9 to record the purchase of inventory from B Co. differs from the one shown in Example 12-8 in two ways: (1) the inventory is recorded at the forward rate (100,000 LCUs × \$.90 each = \$90,000), and (2) the deferred premium (\$2,000) is recorded as a part of the cost of the inventory.

3/1/X9	Inventory	90,000	
	Deferred foreign currency transaction gain	3,000	
	Foreign currency		89,000
	Deferred foreign currency transaction loss		2,000
	Deferred premium on exchange contract		2,000

E. A forward exchange contract may be a means of speculating in foreign currency.

A company may use a forward exchange contract strictly as a means of speculation, without applying it to any specific recorded or unrecorded foreign currency transaction. The entries to account for the contract are relatively simple. However, important additional are points raised by Statement on Financial Accounting Standards No. 52, "Foreign Currency Translation," paragraph 19 as follows:

> "A gain or loss on a speculative forward contract . . . shall be computed by multiplying the foreign currency amount of the forward contract by the difference between the forward rate available for the remaining maturity of the contract and the contracted forward rate (or the rate last used to measure a gain or loss on that contract for an earlier period). No separate accounting recognition is given to the discount or premium on a speculative forward contract."

That is, gain or loss would not for example be measured based on the intervening balance sheet date spot rate but rather gain or loss would be measured based on the forward rate available at an intervening balance sheet date.

EXAMPLE 12-10: A Co.'s management is of the opinion that a certain foreign currency (the LCU) is going to strengthen over the next three months. Consequently, on 12/1/X1, A Co. contracts with a foreign currency dealer to buy 100,000 LCUs, at a forward rate of $.50 per LCU, on 3/1/X2.

On 12/1/X1, A Co. records its contract, based on the forward rate. No separate accounting recognition is given to any premium or discount.

12/1/X1	Foreign currency receivable	50,000	
	Due to foreign currency dealer		50,000
	To record forward exchange contract. ($.50 forward rate × 100,000 LCUs). Note that no separate accounting recognition is given to premium or discount as described in the earlier reference to SFAS No. 52.		

On 12/31/X1, A Co. prepares its financial statements. On that date, as a result of fluctuations in the market, the forward rate available from the currency dealer for LCUs to be purchased on 3/1/X2 has increased to $.51 each, a gain of $.01 over the 12/1/X1 rate. A Co. therefore records a gain of $1,000 (100,000 LCUs × $.01).

12/31/X1	Foreign currency receivable	1,000	
	Foreign currency transaction gain		1,000
	To record foreign currency transaction gain based on 100,000 LCUs × $.01 increase in forward rate.		

On 3/1/X2, the spot rate for LCUs is $.54 each. This is a gain of $.03 over the forward rate available on 12/31/X1. A Co. records this gain.

3/1/X2	Foreign currency receivable	3,000	
	Foreign currency transaction gain		3,000
	To record purchase of 100,000 LCUs × $.03 increase in the exchange rate from the 12/31/X1 forward rate available of $.51 to the contract expiration date spot rate of $.54.		

A Co. then records the purchase of the LCUs from the foreign currency dealer at the forward rate agreed upon on 12/1/X1, and the receipt of the LCUs valued at the 3/1/X2 spot rate.

3/1/X2	Due to foreign currency dealer	50,000	
	Cash		50,000
	To record purchase of 100,000 LCUs at $.50 forward rate from currency dealer.		
3/1/X2	Foreign currency	54,000	
	Foreign currency receivable		54,000
	To record receipt of 100,000 LCUs received from currency dealer at spot rate on 3/1/X2 of $.54 per LCU.		

A Co. then converts the LCUs to dollars at the 3/1/X2 spot rate, and records the conversion.

3/1/X2	Cash	54,000	
	Foreign currency		54,000
	To record exchange of foreign currency for dollars (100,000 LCUs × $.54).		

F. A forward exchange contract may be a hedge against the decline in value of a foreign investment.

The value of a domestic company's investment in a foreign subsidiary or foreign stock will first be determined in the LCU of the foreign company, then converted to dollars for the purposes of financial reporting by the domestic company. Although the foreign subsidiary or investment may be financially healthy, and may even be increasing in value in the country of origin, fluctuations in the international currency markets may result in unfavorable rates of exchange, and a loss for the domestic company. The domestic company may therefore hedge against a decline in the value of its foreign investment by entering into a forward exchange contract.

Any difference between the forward rate and the spot rate on the date of the contract will result in a deferred premium or discount. Further, gains or losses on the foreign currency transactions may develop on any intervening balance sheet date, and the settlement date.

Amortization of any premium or discount, and any gain or loss on the foreign currency transaction, are reported in the domestic company's income statement only when the dollar is the functional currency of the foreign subsidiary or investment. If the foreign currency is the functional currency, then amortization, gains, and losses are instead shown as a separate component of the domestic company's stockholders' equity entitled "Cumulative Translation Adjustment."

The concept of functional currency, including the determination of which currency is the functional currency, is considered in Chapter 13.

RAISE YOUR GRADES

Can you explain . . . ?

- ☑ the two types of accounting problems that may arise from international business transactions
- ☑ the meaning of the various terms used in transactions involving foreign currency
- ☑ why extending credit during a foreign currency transaction (purchase or sale) may make accounting for the transaction more complicated
- ☑ how gains or losses on foreign currency transactions are generally recognized at intervening balance sheet dates and on settlement dates, rather than as adjustments to purchases or sales recorded on the original transaction date
- ☑ how a forward exchange contract acts as a hedge against loss on foreign currency transactions
- ☑ the two methods of accounting for deferred premiums or discounts on forward exchange contracts
- ☑ how using a forward exchange contract exclusively for speculation differs from other uses

SUMMARY

1. When a domestic company agrees to buy or sell goods in a foreign currency, the transaction is said to be denominated in the foreign currency.

2. If a foreign currency's exchange rate changes from the date of an original (purchase or sale) transaction to the intervening balance sheet date, a foreign currency transaction gain or loss occurs (if the transaction is denominated in the foreign currency).
3. If a foreign currency's exchange rate changes from the intervening balance sheet date to a transaction's settlement date, a foreign currency transaction gain or loss occurs (if the transaction is denominated in the foreign currency).
4. Foreign currency transaction gains and losses may be hedged (offset) through the use of forward exchange contracts.
5. Forward exchange contracts permit a company to buy or sell foreign currency to a foreign currency dealer at a specified time for a specified rate of exchange called the forward rate of exchange.
6. Any foreign currency exchange gains or losses from purchase or sale transactions are offset by gains or losses resulting from the forward exchange contract.
7. When hedging a purchase transaction through the use of a forward exchange contract, any difference between the foreign currency receivable (recorded at the spot rate when the contract is prepared) and the amount due to the foreign currency dealer (recorded at the forward rate) represents deferred premium or discount on the exchange contract. This deferred premium or discount is amortized to income over the life of the exchange contract. (See Exhibit 12-A.)
8. When hedging a sales transaction through the use of a forward exchange contract, any difference between the amount due from the foreign currency dealer (recorded at the forward rate) and the foreign currency payable (recorded at the spot rate when the contract is prepared) represents deferred premium or discount on the exchange contract. This deferred premium or discount is amortized to income over the life of the exchange contract. (See Exhibit 12-B.)
9. Forward exchange contracts may be used to avoid foreign currency transaction losses on unrecorded transactions such as purchase orders. Foreign currency transaction gain or loss from a forward exchange contract used to hedge against losses on unrecorded transactions are deferred and eventually treated as part of the asset cost.
10. If a forward exchange contract is used to hedge against foreign currency purchase order transaction loss on unrecorded transactions, any difference which develops between the foreign currency receivable from a currency dealer (recorded at the contract date spot rate) and the amount due to the currency dealer (recorded at the forward rate) represents deferred premium or discount on the exchange contract. This deferred premium or discount may either be amortized against income or treated as part of the asset's cost. Treatment depends on management intent.
11. Forward exchange contracts may be entered into simply to speculate in a foreign currency. If this is the case, foreign currency transaction gain or loss is computed at interim dates by comparing the original forward rate (or the forward rate last used to measure gain or loss) with the forward rate currently available. At settlement of the forward exchange contract, gain or loss is computed by comparing the settlement date spot rate with the last forward rate used to compute gain or loss in a previous period.
12. At the time a forward exchange contract is entered into to purchase foreign currency for speculative purposes, both the foreign currency receivable and the amount due to the foreign currency dealer are recorded at the forward rate. That is, no premium or discount on the exchange contract develops. (Similarly, if the forward exchange contract involved an agreement to sell foreign currency, the amount due from the currency dealer and the foreign currency payable would be recorded at the forward rate with no recognition of discount or premium.)

RAPID REVIEW

1. The currency specified to be used to settle an international purchase or sales transaction is known as the
   (*a*) local currency
   (*b*) foreign currency
   (*c*) denominated currency
   (*d*) functional currency

2. The currency of the primary economic environment in which an entity operates (expends cash) is known as the
   (*a*) local currency
   (*b*) foreign currency
   (*c*) denominated currency
   (*d*) functional currency
3. The number of units of one currency that must be used to obtain one unit of another currency is the
   (*a*) exchange rate
   (*b*) indirect exchange rate
   (*c*) direct exchange rate
   (*d*) functional rate
4. An exchange rate that indicates the number of domestic units needed to buy one unit of foreign currency is known as the
   (*a*) exchange rate
   (*b*) indirect exchange rate
   (*c*) direct exchange rate
   (*d*) functional rate
5. Forward exchange contracts are entered into to
   (*a*) avoid losses on recorded but unsettled foreign currency transactions
   (*b*) avoid losses on unrecorded foreign currency transactions
   (*c*) speculate in a foreign currency
   (*d*) none of the above
   (*e*) all of the above
6. If a purchase of sale transaction occurs that is denominated in a foreign currency, any difference between the spot rate on the transaction date and the spot rate on an intervening balance sheet date results in
   (*a*) adjustment to the cost of the item purchased or the selling price of the item sold
   (*b*) a deferred charge or credit treated as an asset or liability which is subsequently amortized
   (*c*) both of the above
   (*d*) neither of the above
7. If a purchase or sales transaction occurs that is denominated in the foreign currency, any difference between the spot rate on the last intervening balance sheet date and the transaction's settlement date results in
   (*a*) adjustment to the cost of the item purchased or the selling price of the item sold
   (*b*) a foreign currency transaction gain or loss
   (*c*) both of the above
   (*d*) neither of the above
8. When hedging to avoid foreign currency fluctuation losses on a purchase transaction denominated in a foreign currency, any difference between the foreign currency receivable from a currency dealer and the amount due to the currency dealer represents
   (*a*) foreign currency transaction gain or loss
   (*b*) an adjustment to the cost of the asset being purchased
   (*c*) an adjustment to the amount payable to the foreign vendor from whom the purchase is made
   (*d*) a deferred premium or discount on the exchange contract that is amortized to income
9. When hedging to avoid foreign currency fluctuation losses on a sales transaction denominated in a foreign currency, any difference between the foreign currency payable to the currency dealer and the amount due from the currency dealer represents
   (*a*) foreign currency transaction gain or loss
   (*b*) an adjustment to selling price of the asset being sold
   (*c*) an adjustment to the amount receivable from the foreign customer to whom the sale was made
   (*d*) a deferred premium or discount on the exchange contract that is amortized to income

10. When hedging to avoid foreign currency fluctuation losses on unrecorded purchase order transactions, foreign currency exchange rates may change between the date of origination of the forward exchange contract and the date of the contract settlement. These exchange rate differences generally are
(*a*) deferred and subsequently treated as a part of the asset's cost
(*b*) foreign currency transaction gains or losses
(*c*) adjustments to revenue or expense in the year in which exchange rates change
(*d*) none of the above

11. When hedging to avoid foreign currency fluctuation losses on unrecorded purchase order transactions, any difference that results from recording of foreign currency receivable from the currency dealer (recorded at the spot rate on the contract date) and the amount due to the currency dealer (recorded at the forward rate) represents
(*a*) an adjustment to the cost of the asset that is ultimately acquired
(*b*) a deferred premium or discount on the exchange contract that must be amortized to income over the contract life
(*c*) either of the above
(*d*) neither of the above

12. If a forward exchange contract is entered into purely for speculative reasons,
(*a*) deferred premium or discount on the exchange contract cannot develop
(*b*) deferred premium or discount on the contract which develops must be amortized to income over the contract life
(*c*) foreign currency transaction gains and losses are always deferred
(*d*) none of the above

Answers:

1. (*c*)
2. (*d*)
3. (*a*)
4. (*c*)
5. (*e*)
6. (*d*)
7. (*b*)
8. (*d*) (See Exhibit 12-A.)
9. (*d*) (See Exhibit 12-B.)
10. (*a*)
11. (*c*) (See Examples 12-8 and 12-9.)
12. (*a*) (See Example 12-10.)

SOLVED PROBLEMS

PROBLEM 12-1: Darin Company, a U.S. corporation, buys merchandise from a Japanese supplier. On December 1, 19X3, Darin Company purchased 100,000 units of merchandise. The merchandise contract is denominated in yen, and is due on February 1, 19X4. Exchange rates between the dollar and the yen are:

Date	Yen to dollar
Dec. 1, 19X3	Y195 = $1.00
Dec. 31, 19X3	Y190 = $1.00
Feb. 1, 29X4	Y180 = $1.00

Each unit of merchandise costs Y50.

Darin Company's annual financial statements are prepared as of December 31.

Determine the amount of gain or loss, if any, that should be recognized in 19X3 and 19X4 as a result of fluctuations in the exchange rate.

***Answer*:**

Dollars required to settle contract on Feb. 1, 19X4 (Y5,000,000/$180)	$27,778*
Dollars that would have been required to settle contract on Dec. 31, 19X3 (Y5,000,000/$190)	26,316**
Foreign currency transaction loss—19X4	$ 1,462
Dollars that would have been required to settle contract on Dec. 31, 19X3 (Y5,000,000/$190)	26,316
Dollars that would have been required to settle contract on Dec. 1, 19X3 (Y5,000,000/$195)	25,641+
Foreign currency transaction loss—19X3	$ 675

Note that in this problem an indirect exchange rate was provided (number of foreign currency units needed to buy one unit of domestic currency). These indirect exchange rates may simply be viewed as direct rates as follows:

Date	Yen for dollar		Dollar for yen
Dec. 1, 19X3	Y195 = $1	1/195	$.0051282 = Y1
Dec. 31, 19X3	Y190 = $1	1/190	$.0052631 = Y1
Feb. 1, 19X4	Y180 = $1	1/180	$.0055555 = Y1

*Also, Y5,000,000 × $.0055555 = $27,778.
**Also, Y5,000,000 × $.0052631 = $26,316.
+Also, Y5,000,000 × $.0051282 = $25,641.

PROBLEM 12-2: Refer to the information in Problem 12-1. Prepare journal entries that should be made by Darin Co. on the following dates:

* December 1, 19X3
* December 31, 19X3
* February 1, 19X4

***Answer*:** Supporting computations for the following entries are provided in the solution to Problem 12-1.

	Debit	Credit
December 1, 19X3 (Transaction Date)		
Inventory	$25,641	
Accounts payable		$25,641
To record purchase of merchandise denominated in yen.		
December 31, 19X3 (Intervening Balance-Sheet Date)		
Foreign currency transaction loss	$ 675	
Accounts payable		$ 675
To record foreign exchange fluctuation at year end.		
February 1, 19X4 (Settlement Date)		
Foreign currency transaction loss	$ 1,462	
Accounts payable		$ 1,462
To record foreign exchange fluctuation at settlement.		
Foreign currency	$27,778	
Cash		$27,778
To record purchase of Japanese foreign currency.		
Accounts payable	$27,778	
Foreign currency		$27,778
To record payment to Japanese supplier.		

Alternatively some authors replace the last three entries at settlement with one entry:

	Debit	Credit
Accounts payable	$16,316	
Foreign currency transaction loss	1,462	
Cash		$27,778

PROBLEM 12-3: Refer to the information provided in Problem 12-2. However, assume that on December 1, 19X3, Darin Co. signed a forward exchange contract with a foreign currency dealer and agreed to purchase the 5,000,000 yen needed to pay the Japanese supplier on February 1, 19X4 for $.0053 each. Prepare the necessary journal entries for both the purchase from the Japanese supplier and the forward exchange contract on the transaction, intervening balance sheet, and settlement dates.

Answer:

Darin Co. Purchase from Japanese Supplier			Forward Exchange Contract		
Transaction date — 12/1/X3					
Inventory	25,641		Foreign currency receivable	25,641*	
Accounts payable		25,641	Deferred premium on exchange contract	859	
($.0051282 × 50,000 yen)			Due to currency dealer		26,500**
			To record forward exchange contract. * 5,000,000 yen × $.0051282 spot rate = $25,641 ** 5,000,000 yen × $.0053 forward rate = $26,500.		
Intervening balance sheet date — 12/31/X3					
Foreign currency transaction loss	675		Foreign currency receivable	675	
Accounts payable		675	Foreign currency transaction gain		675
To record transaction loss on exchange rate change of $.0001349 increase per yen times 5,000,000 yen to be paid.			To record foreign currency transaction gain of $.0001349 per yen times 5,000,000 yen to be received.		
(Note that the foreign currency transaction loss of $675 is exactly offset by the foreign currency transaction gain of $675 through the use of the forward exchange contract.)					
			Premium amortization expense	430	
			Deferred premium on exchange contract		430
			To amortize deferred premium on forward exchange contract over contract life. (1 mo./2 mos. × $859 premium = $430. Note that the contract life is the 2-month period from 12/1/X3 to 2/1/X4. The period 12/1/X3 through 12/31/X3 represents 1 month of the contract period.)		
Settlement date — 2/1/X4					
Foreign currency transaction loss	1,462		Foreign currency receivable	1,462	
Accounts payable		1,462	Foreign currency transaction gain		1,462
To record transaction loss on exchange rate change of $.0002924 increase per yen times 5,000,000 yen to be paid.			To record foreign currency transaction gain of $.0002924 per yen times 5,000,000 yen to be received.		
(Note again that the foreign currency transaction loss of $1,462 is exactly offset by the foreign currency transaction gain of $1,462 through the use of the forward exchange contract.)					
			Premium amortization expense	429	
			Deferred premium on exchange contract		429
			To amortize deferred premium on forward exchange contract over contract life. (1 mo./2 mos. × $859 premium = $429. Or, $859 total deferred premium less 12/31/X3 amortization of $430 also yields $429.)		
			Due to currency dealer	26,500	
			Cash		26,500
			To record purchase of 5,000,000 yen at forward rate of $.0053 each. (5,000,000 yen × $.0053 = $26,500.)		
Accounts payable	27,778		Foreign currency	27,778	
Foreign currency		27,778	Foreign currency receivable		27,778
To record payment of 5,000,000 yen to Japanese supplier. (5,000,000 yen × $.0055555 = $27,778.)			To record receipt of 5,000,000 yen from foreign currency dealer worth $.0055555 each. (5,000,000 yen × $.0055555 = 27,778.)		

(Note that the 5,000,000 yen purchased from the foreign currency dealer are used to pay the Japanese supplier for goods purchased.)

PROBLEM 12-4: Denver Co., a U.S. company, sold merchandise to Rheims Co., a French company, for 200,000 francs on November 1, 19X3 (that is, the sale is denominated in francs). Denver Co.'s fiscal year ends on December 31, 19X3. Receipt, in francs, occurs on March 1, 19X4. Exchange rates are as follows:

Date	Francs	Dollars
11/01/X3	1F	$.13
12/31/X3	1F	$.12
03/01/X4	1F	$.11

Determine the amount of exchange gain or loss, if any, that should be recognized in 19X3 and 19X4 as a result of fluctuations in the exchange rate.

***Answer*:**

Dollars received at settlement on 3/1/X4 (200,000F × $.11)	$22,000
Dollars that would have been received if settlement occurred 12/31/X3 (200,000F × $.12)	24,000
Foreign currency transaction loss—19X4	$ 2,000
Dollars that would have been received if settlement occurred 12/31/X3 (200,000F × $.12)	$24,000
Dollars that would have been received if settlement occurred 11/1/X3 (200,000F × $.13)	26,000
Foreign currency transaction loss—19X3	$ 2,000

PROBLEM 12-5: Refer to the information in Problem 12-4. Prepare journal entries that should be made by Denver Co. on the following dates:

* November 1, 19X3
* December 31, 19X3
* March 1, 19X4

***Answer*:** Supporting computations for the following entries are provided in the solution to Problem 12-4.

November 1, 19X3 (Transaction Date)		
Accounts receivable	26,000	
Sales		26,000
To record sale of merchandise denominated in francs.		
December 31, 19X3 (Intervening Balance Sheet Date)		
Foreign currency transaction loss	2,000	
Accounts receivable		2,000
To record foreign exchange fluctuation at year end.		
March 1, 19X4 (Settlement Date)		
Foreign currency transaction loss	2,000	
Accounts receivable		2,000
To record foreign exchange fluctuation at settlement.		
Foreign currency	22,000	
Accounts receivable		22,000
To record receipt of 200,000 francs (200,000 francs × $.11).		
Cash	22,000	
Foreign currency		22,000
To record exchange of 200,000 francs for dollars.		

Alternatively, some authors replace the last three entries with one entry as follows:

Cash	22,000	
Foreign currency transaction loss	2,000	
Accounts receivable		24,000

PROBLEM 12-6: Refer to the information provided in Problem 12-5. However, assume that on November 1, 19X3, Denver Co. signed a forward exchange contract with a foreign currency dealer and agreed to sell the 200,000 francs it will receive on March 1, 19X4 for $.122 each. Prepare the necessary journal entries for both the sale to Rheims Co. and the forward exchange contract on the transaction, intervening balance sheet, and settlement dates.

Answer:

Transaction date — 11/1/X3

Denver Co. Sales to Rheims Co.			Forward Exchange Contract		
Acccounts receivable	26,000		Due from currency dealer	24,400*	
Sales		26,000	Deferred premium on exchange contract	1,600	
($.13 × 200,000 francs)			Foreign currency payable		26,000**
			To record forward exchange contract.		
			* 200,000 francs × $.122 forward rate = $24,400		
			** 200,000 francs × $.13 spot rate = $26,000.		

Intervening balance sheet date — 12/31/X3

Denver Co. Sales to Rheims Co.			Forward Exchange Contract		
Foreign currency transaction loss	2,000		Foreign currency payable	2,000	
Accounts receivable		2,000	Foreign currency transaction gain		2,000
To record transaction loss on exchange rate change of $.01 increase per franc times 200,000 francs to be received.			To record foreign currency transaction gain of $.01 per franc times 200,000 francs to be paid to dealer.		

(Note that the foreign currency transaction loss of $2,000 is exactly offset by the foreign currency transaction gain of $2,000 through the use of the forward exchange contract.)

Forward Exchange Contract		
Premium amortization expense	800	
Deferred premium on exchange contract		800
To amortize deferred premium on forward exchange contract over contract life. (2 mos./4 mos. × $1,600 premium = $800. Note that the contract life is the 4-month period from 11/1/X3 to 3/1/X4. The period 11/1/X3 through 12/31/X3 represents 2 months of the contract period.)		

Settlement date — 3/1/X4

Denver Co. Sales to Rheims Co.			Forward Exchange Contract		
Foreign currency transaction loss	2,000		Foreign currency payable	2,000	
Accounts receivable		2,000	Foreign currency transaction gain		2,000
To record transaction loss on exchange rate change of $.01 increase per franc times 200,000 francs to be received.			To record foreign currency transaction gain of $.01 per franc times 200,000 francs to be paid to dealer.		

(Note again that the foreign currency transaction loss of $2,000 is exactly offset by the foreign currency transaction gain of $2,000 through the use of the forward exchange contract.)

Denver Co. Sales to Rheims Co.			Forward Exchange Contract		
			Premium amortization expense	800	
			Deferred premium on exchange contract		800
			To amortize deferred premium on forward exchange contract over contract life. (2 mos./4 mos. × $1,600 premium = $800. Or, $1,600 total deferred premium less 12/31/X3 amortization of $800 also yields $800.)		
Foreign currency	22,000		Foreign currency payable	22,000	
Accounts receivable		22,000	Foreign currency		22,000
To record receipt of 200,000 francs at $22,000. ($.11 × 200,000 francs.)			To record payment of 200,000 francs to dealer worth $.11 each.		
			Cash	24,400	
			Due from currency dealer		24,400
			To record receipt of $.122 forward rate for each of 200,000 francs paid to the currency dealer.		

(Note that the receipt of 200,000 francs from the sale to Rheims Co. at settlement is used to pay the foreign currency dealer.)

PROBLEM 12-7: Lantern Co. (a U.S. company) ordered inventory from Berlin Co. (a German company) and will pay 500,000 marks for the merchandise in 90 days if the order is accepted by Berlin Co. The order was placed on June 1, 19X5. One June 1, 19X5, Lantern Co. obtains a forward exchange contract with a foreign currency dealer to avoid currency fluctuation loss and agrees to pay $.43 per mark for 500,000 marks. The following currency spot rates are available:

June 1, 19X5	$.418
June 30, 19X5*	$.440
August 29, 19X5 (90 days)	$.410
*Lantern Co.'s fiscal year end	

Prepare journal entries to record the forward exchange contract and the purchase of the inventory from Berlin Co. on August 29, 19X5. (Assume that deferred discount or premium if any, on the forward exchange contract is amortized to income over the contract life.

Answer:

Date	Account	Debit	Credit
6/1/X5	Foreign currency receivable	209,000*	
	Deferred premium on exchange contract	6,000	
	Due to currency dealer		215,000**
	To record forward exchange contract.		
	*Spot rate $.418 × 500,000 marks = $209,000		
	**Forward rate $.43 × 500,000 marks = $215,000		
6/30/X5	Foreign currency receivable	11,000	
	Deferred foreign currency transaction gain		11,000
	To record deferred gain based on increase in value of $.022 per mark ($.44 – $.418) from 6/1/X5 to 6/30/X5 times 500,000 marks to be received from currency dealer.		
6/30/X5	Premium amortization expense	2,000	
	Deferred premium on exchange contract		2,000
	To amortize deferred premium on forward exchange contract. (30 days/90 days times $6,000 = $2,000. Note that the contract life is 90 days from 6/1/X5 to 8/29/X5 and that 30 days of the contract period have passed as of 6/30/X5.)		
8/29/X5	Deferred foreign currency transaction loss	15,000	
	Foreign currency receivable		15,000
	To record deferred loss based on decrease in value of $.03 ($.44 – $.41) from 6/30/X5 to 8/29/X5 times 500,000 marks to be received from foreign currency dealer.		
8/29/X5	Premium amortization expense	4,000	
	Deferred premium on exchange contract		4,000
	To amortize deferred premium on forward exchange contract. (60 days/90 days times $6,000 = $4,000.)		
8/29/X5	Due to currency dealer	215,000	
	Cash		215,000
	To record payment for purchase of 500,000 marks at forward rate of $.43 per mark.		
8/29/X5	Foreign currency	205,000	
	Foreign currency receivable		205,000
	To record receipt of 500,000 marks from the foreign currency dealer at the spot rate of $.41 per mark.		

8/29/X5	Deferred foreign currency transaction gain	11,000	
	Inventory	209,000	
	Deferred foreign currency transaction loss		15,000
	Foreign currency		205,000
	To record inventory purchase from Berlin Co. using foreign currency received from dealer. (The inventory is recorded at the spot rate of $.418 on the order date times 500,000 marks since deferred gain/loss is treated as part of the cost.)		

note: Alternatively, the inventory may be recorded at the forward rate at the exchange contract date if deferred premium is not amortized as an expense of reducing exposure to rate fluctuations but is instead viewed as part of the asset cost. In this case, no premium amortization would occur and the entry to record the purchase of inventory would be as follows:

Deferred foreign currency transaction gain	11,000	
Inventory ($.43 forward rate × 500,000 marks)	215,000	
Deferred foreign currency transaction loss		15,000
Deferred premium on exchange contract		6,000
Foreign currency		205,000

PROBLEM 12-8: Barton Corp. believes that pesos are going up in value over the next two months. On December 1, 19X6, Barton Corp. contracts with a foreign currency dealer to buy 10,000,000 pesos at the forward rate of $.006 on February 1, 19X7. The following exchange rate information is available:

December 1, 19X6	$.0060	(2/1/X7 forward rate)
December 31, 19X6	$.0059	(2/1/X7 forward rate)
February 1, 19X7	$.0064	(2/1/X7 spot rate)

Prepare the journal entries Barton Corp. would record on this speculation and assume that foreign currency eventually received from the currency dealer is immediately exchanged by Barton Corp. for dollars.

Answer:

12/1/X6	Foreign currency receivable	60,000	
	Due to foreign currency dealer		60,000
	To record forward exchange contract. ($.006 forward rate × 10,000,000 pesos.)		
12/31/X6	Foreign currency transaction loss	1,000	
	Foreign currency receivable		1,000
	To record foreign currency transaction loss based on 10,000,000 pesos times $.0001 decrease in forward rate (from $.0060 on 12/1/X6 to $.0059 on 12/31/X6).		
2/1/X7	Foreign currency receivable	5,000	
	Foreign currency transaction gain		5,000
	To record foreign currency transaction gain based on 10,000,000 pesos times $.0005 increase as follows:		

12/31/X6 forward rate	$.0059
2/1/X7 spot rate	$.0064
Increase in exchange rate	$.0005

2/1/X7	Due to foreign currency dealer	60,000	
	Cash		60,000
	To record purchase from dealer of 10,000,000 pesos at $.006 forward rate each.		

2/1/X7	Foreign currency	64,000	
	Foreign currency receivable		64,000
	To record receipt of 10,000,000 pesos from dealer at $.0064 spot rate.		
2/1/X7	Cash	64,000	
	Foreign currency		64,000
	To record exchange of foreign currency for dollars. (10,000,000 pesos × $.0064.)		

13 CONVERSION OF FOREIGN FINANCIAL STATEMENTS

THIS CHAPTER IS ABOUT

- ☑ The Basic Translation Process
- ☑ Identification of the Functional Currency
- ☑ The Translation Method
- ☑ The Remeasurement Method
- ☑ Converting Inventory
- ☑ Converting Property, Plant, and Equipment
- ☑ Conversions in Highly Inflationary Economies
- ☑ Changes in Functional Currency

13-1. The Basic Translation Process

A. Statement on Financial Accounting Standards 52 establishes the standards for the conversion of foreign financial statements.

The authority to establish accounting procedures is given by Congress to the Securities and Exchange Commission (SEC), and the SEC currently delegates that authority to the independent Financial Accounting Standards Board (FASB). The FASB periodically issues statements that create or modify accounting practice. Prior to the issuance of Financial Accounting Standards Board Statement 52, "Foreign Currency Translation," the generally accepted accounting principles (GAAP) governing the translation of financial statements denominated in a foreign currency received sharp criticism. For example, before FASB-52 domestic companies were required to report on their income statements any gains or losses resulting from foreign currency conversions of the value of their long-term investments in foreign subsidiaries. But because future fluctuations of the exchange rates might reverse such gains or losses, they might never actually be realized by the parent (or investor) company. Therefore, recognition of these gains or losses failed to make the consolidated financial statements any more useful, and may, in fact, have misled the users of the statements. FASB-52 revised the GAAP and partially (although not entirely) eliminated this problem by requiring that in certain situations such gains or losses not be recognized as a part of periodic net income, but rather as a separate component of stockholders' equity entitled "Cumulative Translation Adjustment."

FASB-52 also addressed controversy regarding the foreign currency exchange rates that should be used to convert the account balances of foreign financial statements into U.S. dollars. It established two distinct methods to accomplish this conversion (the translation method and the remeasurement method), each discussed below, determined when each method should be used, and indicated which exchange rates should be used under each method.

B. The basic process of financial statement conversion involves three broad steps.

The three basic steps involved in the process of converting foreign financial statements are:

1. Determine the functional currency of the foreign company.
2. If necessary, restate the foreign company's financial statements in terms of the generally accepted accounting principles of the domestic company.
3. Convert the foreign financial statements into the currency of the domestic company.

Steps 1 and 3 are discussed in detail in the sections that follow. Regarding the second step, it is quite possible that a foreign company's financial statements are not prepared in accordance with the GAAP of the domestic company. For example, in Australia, Brazil, Italy, and Mexico the annual revaluation of fixed assets, based on indexes or appraisals, is either sanctioned or required. In the United States, these assets are reported at their historic costs. When a U.S. parent company prepares consolidated financial statements with a subsidiary in any of these countries, it must first adjust the fixed assets accounts of its subsidiary to their historical costs. Only then may it proceed to Step 3 and convert the foreign financial statements into U.S. dollars. In this chapter we will assume that, unless otherwise stated, all information regarding foreign financial statements is already prepared in accordance with U.S. GAAP.

13-2. Identification of the Functional Currency

Paragraph 5 of FASB-52 defines an economic entity's *functional currency* as

> ". . . the currency of the primary economic environment in which the entity operates; normally, that is the currency of the environment in which an entity primarily generates and expends cash."

The establishment of the functional currency of a foreign operation is critical to the determination of the method of conversion of foreign financial statements into U.S. dollars. As stated above, FASB-52 describes two methods that may be used to carry out the conversions. The use of one method or the other is not optional, however, but is determined by the functional currency of the foreign entity.

Generally, the foreign currency is the functional currency if the foreign entity's operations are self-contained and largely separate from the parent company's operations. Appendix A of FASB-52 gives six indicators to be considered when determining the functional currency of a foreign operation. These indicators are summarized in Table 13-1.

Table 13-1. Functional Currency Indicators.

Indicators	Foreign Currency Functional	Domestic Currency Functional
1. Cash Flow	Cash flow occurs primarily in the foreign currency. No direct impact on parent company.	Cash flow directly affects the parent company. Cash flow is readily available to the parent.
2. Sales Price	The foreign entity's sales prices are not responsive to short-term exchange rate fluctuation but rather to local competition.	The foreign entity's sale prices are responsive to exchange rate fluctuation.
3. Sales Market	An active local market exists for the foreign entity's products.	The sales market is primarily in the parent's country or currency.
4. Expense	The foreign entity's operational costs are mostly local costs. purchases from the parent's country.	The foreign entity's operational costs are largely the result of

5. Financing	The foreign entity's operations are sufficient to service debt denominated primarily in the foreign currency.	The foreign entity's financing is done by the parent or in dollars. The foreign operations are insufficient to service debt.
6. Intercompany Transactions and Arrangements	A low volume of parent-subsidiary transactions exist.	A high volume of parent-subsidiary transactions exist.

If a foreign entity exhibits substantially all of the indicators in one column or the other of Table 13–1, its functional currency is considered to be the one at top of the column, and the method that must be used to convert its financial statements is then established.

If consideration of the six points of FASB-52 indicates that the foreign currency is the functional currency of a foreign operation, the translation method must be used to convert the foreign financial statements into the domestic currency (see section 13–7 for exception to this rule).

If consideration of the six points of FASB-52 indicates that the domestic currency is the functional currency of a foreign operation, the remeasurement method must be used to convert the foreign financial statements into the domestic currency.

13-3. The Translation Method

A. The translation method does not recognize conversion gains or losses as part of income.

After considering the six points in FASB-52, and determining that the foreign currency is the functional currency, an implication is that the foreign entity's operations are largely self-contained and separate from the parent's. This means that the parent company is not likely to sustain losses or realize gains from its foreign operations due to fluctuations in the exchange rates, at least not in the short term. Therefore, the translation method of converting foreign financial statements does not result in recognition of any exchange gains or losses in the parent company's income statement. If any such "gain" or "loss" develops as a result of the translation process, it is recorded as an adjustment to the stockholders' equity portion of the balance sheet in an account entitled "cumulative translation adjustment."

B. Specific exchange rates must be used to convert the foreign entity's account balances.

The translation method of converting foreign financial statements requires that specific exchange rates be used when the foreign subsidiary's account balances are converted from its local currency units (LCUs) into the domestic currency. The specific rates to be used with the various types of accounts are summarized in Table 13-2.

Table 13-2. Exchange Rates to Be Used under the Translation Method.

Account	Appropriate Exchange Rate
All assets and liabilities.	Current rate at balance-sheet date.
Paid-in capital (stock and related accounts)	Historical rate at date of issuance
Revenues, expenses, gains, losses	Exchange rate at date on which recognized*
Retained earnings	No single rate**

*For practical reasons, FASB-52 permits the use of a weighted average exchange rate when converting the revenue, expenses, gains, and losses to determine income. Such an average exchange rate is determined by (1) multiplying each historic exchange rate by the number of months (or days, if necessary) that it is in effect, (2) adding these products together, and (3) dividing that total by the total number of months (or days):

$$
\begin{aligned}
&x \text{ months at Rate } 1 = \$X\\
&y \text{ months at Rate } 2 = \$Y\\
&z \text{ months at Rate } 3 = \$Z\\
&\$(X + Y + Z) \div (x + y + z) = \text{weighted average exchange rate}
\end{aligned}
$$

**No single rate is used when converting the Retained Earnings account balance. The Retained Earnings account balance, in the domestic currency (in this case, U.S. dollars), is determined as follows:

	Beginning Retained Earnings in dollars, determined from the end of the preceding period:	$X
Add:	**Periodic Net Income** in dollars, determined by converting the revenue, expense, gain, and loss accounts at the rates in effect on the date they were recognized (or by using the weighted average exchange rate):	$X
Deduct:	**Periodic Net Loss** in dollars (determined in the same manner as the net income):	($X)
	Periodic Dividends Declared in dollars, determined at the historic rate on the declaration date:	($X)
	Ending Retained Earnings in dollars:	$X

Any difference between total assets and the sum of liabilities and stockholders' equity resulting from the conversion of specific account balances according to the exchange rates outlined in Table 13–2 is treated as an adjustment to the stocksholders' equity. As mentioned above, the difference is not considered a loss or gain, does not affect the income statement, and is shown in the stockholders' equity section of the balance sheet in the account entitled "Cumulative Translation Adjustment.."

EXAMPLE 13-1: On 1/1/X7, Planet Co. (a U.S. company) created a foreign subsidiary named Belem Co. All of Belem's stock was issued on that date. During 19X7, Belem's first year of operations, the direct exchange rates for the LCU were:

January 1 to March 31:	$.50
April 1 to September 30:	$.47
October 1 to December 31:	$.42

On 12/15/X7, Belem declared and paid a 200,000 LCU dividend.

Belem Co.'s local currency unit (the LCU) is its functional currency (that is, the foreign currency is the functional currency). Therefore, Planet Co. will use the translation method to convert Belem's financial statements into dollars.

The financial statements for Belem Co. as of and for the year ended 12/31/X7, in both LCUs and U.S. dollars, are shown in Exhibit 13-A. The LCUs were converted to dollars as shown below.

Planet Co. converted Belem's net income by using a weighted average exchange rate, which was calculated in the following manner:

3 months at $.50	=	$1.500
6 months at $.47	=	2.820
3 months at $.42	=	1.260
		5.580
Divide # months		12
Weighted average exchange rate		$0.465

This rate was applied to all Belem's revenue and expense account balances in LCUs. The results of these conversions are shown in the Income Statement portion of Exhibit 13-A.

Once the income statement was converted, Planet calculated Belem's retained earnings. Because 19X7 is Belem's first year of operations, it has no opening balance in its Retained Earnings account. Its closing Retained Earnings balance is calculated simply by deducting the dividends declared from the net income. The dividends declared are converted to dollars at the historical exchange rate effective on the date of declaration, which on 12/15/X7 was $.42.

Having converted the income statement and statement of retained earnings, Planet then converts Belem's balance sheet. Under the translation method, Planet converts all Belem's asset and liability accounts to dollars at the current exchange rate on the balance-sheet date (which at 12/31/X7 was $.42), and its Common Stock account at the historical exchange rate effective on the date of issuance (which on 1/1/X7 was $.50).

After converting all of Belem's account balances from LCUs to dollars, Planet finds that total assets on the balance sheet equal $378,000, while the sum of liabilities and stockholders' equity equals $417,250. This difference of $39,250 is a result of the change in the exchange rate during 19X7, and represents a decrease in stockholders' equity in terms of U.S. dollars. But recall that under the translation method no gain or loss resulting from changes in the foreign currency exchange rate may be recognized as part of income. Therefore, in order to make the total assets equal to the sum of liabilities and stockholders' equity, Planet creates an account entitled "Cumulative Translation Adjustment" to decrease equity by $39,250.

Exhibit 13-A. Foreign Currency = Functional Currency
Belem Co. Financial Statement
At and for the Year Ended December 31, 19X7

Income Statement	LCUs	Exchange Rate	Dollars
Sales	900,000	$0.465*	$418,500
Cost of goods sold	450,000	$0.465	209,250
Gross profit	450,000		209,250
Operating expenses:			
Depreciation expense	50,000	$0.465	23,250
Other operating expenses	150,000	$0.465	69,750
Total operating expenses	200,000		93,000
Net income	250,000		$116,250
Statement of Retained Earnings			
1/1/X7 Retained earnings	0	First year	$ 0
Add: 19X7 Net income	250,000	See above	116,250
Deduct: 19X7 Dividend declarations	(200,000)	$0.420	(84,000)
12/31/X7 Retained earnings	50,000		$ 32,250
Balance Sheet			
Assets			
Cash	100,000	$0.420	$ 42,000
Accounts receivable	200,000	$0.420	84,000
Inventory	50,000	$0.420	21,000
Plant and equipment	600,000	$0.420	252,000
Accumulated depreciation	(50,000)	$0.420	(21,000)
Total Assets	900,000		$378,000
Liabilities and Stockholders' Equity			
Accounts payable	200,000	$0.420	$ 84,000
Long-term note payable	300,000	$0.420	126,000
Common stock	350,000	$0.500	175,000
Retained earnings	50,000	See above	32,250
Cumulative translation adjustment		To balance	(39,250)
Total Liabilities and Stockholders' Equity	900,000		$378,000

*Weighted average exchange rate.

EXAMPLE 13-2: Refer to the information given in Example 13-1. Belem Co. continued its operations throughout 19X8. On 12/21/X8 it declared and paid dividends of 150,000 LCUs.

During 19X8 the direct exchange rates for the LCU were:

January 1 to April 30:	$.42
May 1 to August 31:	$.46
September 1 to December 31:	$.48

Once again, because the LCU is the functional currency of Belem Co., Planet Co. will use the translation method to convert Belem's financial statements into dollars when it prepares consolidated financial statements on 12/31/X8.

The financial statements for Belem Co. as of and for the year ended 12/31/X8, in both LCUs and U.S. dollars, are shown in Exhibit 13-B. Planet converted the LCUs to dollars as shown below.

Planet Co. converted Belem's net income by using a weighted average exchange rate, which was calculated in the following manner:

4 months at $.42 =	$1.680
4 months at $.46 =	1.840
4 months at $.48 =	1.920
	5.440
Divide # months	12
Weighted average exchange rate	$0.453

This rate was applied to all Belem's revenue and expense account balances in LCUs. The results of these conversions are shown in the income statement portion of Exhibit 13-B.

Once the Income Statement was converted, Planet calculated Belem's retained earnings. The closing Retained Earnings account balance of $32,250 from 19X7 in both LCUs and dollars (see Exhibit 13-A) is simply carried forward as the opening balance for 19X8. Belem's net income for 19X8 is then added to the balance and the dividends declared in 19X8 are deducted from the balance. The dividends declared are converted to dollars at the historical exchange rate effective on the date of declaration, which on 12/21/X8 was $.48.

Having converted Belem's income statement and statement of retained earnings, Planet then converts the balance sheet. Under the translation method, Planet Co. converts all Belem's asset and liability accounts to dollars at the current exchange rate on the balance-sheet date (which at 12/31/X8 was $.48), and its Common Stock account at the historical exchange rate effective on the date of issuance (which on 1/1/X7 was $.50).

After converting all of Belem's account balances from LCUs to dollars, Parent discovers that total assets on the balance sheet equal $465,600, while the sum of liabilities and stockholders' equity equals $473,560. Note that as a result of the increase in the exchange rate in 19X8, the cumulative translation adjustment has decreased from a debit of $39,250 on 12/31/X7 to debit of $7,960 on 12/31/X8. Still, this difference of $7,960 represents a decrease in stockholders' equity, in terms of U.S. dollars. But under the translation method no gain or loss resulting from changes in the foreign currency exchange rate may be recognized as part of income. Therefore, in order to make the total assets equal to the sum of liabilities and stockholders' equity, Parent creates an account entitled "Cumulative Translation Adjustment" to decrease equity by $7,960.

Exhibit 13-B. Foreign Currency = Functional Currency
Belem Co. Financial Statement
At and for the Year Ended December 31, 19X8

Income Statement	LCUs	Exchange Rate	Dollars
Sales	990,000	$0.453*	$448,470
Cost of goods sold	480,000	$0.453	217,440
Gross profit	510,000		231,030
Operating expenses:			
Depreciation expense	50,000	$0.453	22,650
Other operating expenses	190,000	$0.453	86,070
Total operating expenses	240,000		108,720
Net income	270,000		$122,310
Statement of Retained Earnings			
1/1/X8 Retained earnings	50,000	First year	$ 32,250
Add: 19X8 Net income	270,000	See above	122,310
Deduct: 19X8 Dividend declarations	(150,000)	$0.480	(72,000)
12/31/X8 Retained earnings	170,000		$ 82,560
Balance Sheet			
Assets			
Cash	180,000	$0.480	$ 86,400
Accounts receivable	220,000	$0.480	105,600
Inventory	70,000	$0.480	33,600
Plant and equipment	600,000	$0.480	288,000
Accumulated depreciation	(100,000)	$0.480	(48,000)
Total Assets	970,000		$465,600
Liabilities and Stockholders' Equity			
Accounts payable	150,000	$0.480	$ 72,000
Long-term note payable	300,000	$0.480	144,000
Common stock	350,000	$0.500	175,000
Retained earnings	170,000	See above	82,560
Cumulative translation adjustment		To balance	(7,960)
Total Liabilities and Stockholders' Equity	970,000		$465,600

*Weighted average exchange rate.

13-4. The Remeasurement Method

A. The remeasurement method does recognize any conversion gains or losses as part of income.

After considering the six points in FASB-52, and determining that the domestic currency is the functional currency, an implication is that the foreign entity's operations are not self-contained or separate from the parent's. Rather, the foreign subsidiary's operations are considered reliant on the domestic parent's. This means that the parent company is far more likely to sustain losses or realize gains from its foreign operations due to fluctuations in the exchange rates over the course of the year. For example, if the parent company finances any of the foreign operation's debt, gains or losses from currency conversion may occur on a regular basis. Therefore, the remeasurement method of converting foreign financial statements does recognize any gain or loss resulting from changes in the foreign currency exchange rates as part of the foreign subsidiary's income. If such a gain or loss develops, it is recorded on the foreign company's income statement in an account entitled Remeasurement Loss or Remeasurement Gain.

B. When remeasuring foreign financial statements a distinction must be made between monetary and nonmonetary items.

Monetary assets represent money, or claims to receive fixed amounts of money that do not change as the price of goods and services changes. **Monetary liabilities** represent obligations to pay fixed amounts of money that do not change as the price of goods and services change. Other balance-sheet items, including paid in capital (common stock, preferred stock and related accounts), are generally considered nonmonetary items. Table 13-3 provides a guide to determining which balance sheet items are considered monetary and which are considered nonmonetary.

Table 13-3. Monetary and Nonmonetary Balance Sheet Items.

Item	Monetary	Nonmonetary
Assets		
Cash on hand and demand bank deposits (U.S. dollars)	X	
Time deposits (U.S. dollars)	X	
Foreign currency on hand and claims to foreign currency	X	
Securities:		
Common stocks (not accounted for on the equity method)		X
Common stocks represent residual interests in the underlying net assets and earnings of the issuer.		
Preferred stock (convertible or participating)		
Circumstances may indicate that such a stock is either monetary or nonmonetary. See convertible bonds.		
Preferred stock (nonconvertible, non-participating)		
Future cash receipts are likely to be substantially unaffected by changes in specific prices.	X	
Convertible bonds.		
If the market values the security primarily as a bond, it is monetary; if it values the security primarily as a stock, it is nonmonetary.		
Bonds (other than convertible)	X	
Accounts and notes receivable	X	
Allowance for doubtful accounts and notes receivable	X	
Variable rate mortgage loans	X	
The terms of such loans do not link them directly to the rate of inflation. Also, there are practical rasons for classifying all loans as monetary.		
Inventories used on contracts		
They are, in substance, rights to receive sums of money if the future cash receipts on the contracts will not vary due to future changes in specific prices. (Goods used on contracts to be priced at market upon delivery are nonmonetary.)		
Inventories (other than inventories used on contracts)		X
Loans to employees	X	
Prepaid insurance, advertising, rent, and other prepayments		
Claims to future services are nonmonetary. Prepayments that are deposits, advance payments or receivables are monetary because the prepayment does not obtain a given quantity of future services, but rather is a fixed money offset.		
Long-term receivables	X	
Refundable deposits	X	
Advances to unconsolidated subsidiaries	X	
Equity investment in unconsolidated subsidiaries or other investees.		X

Item	Monetary	Nonmonetary
Pension, sinking, and other funds under an enterprise's control		
The specific assets in the fund should be classified as monetary or nonmonetary. (See listings under securities above.)		
Property, plant, and equipment		X
Accumulated depreciation of property, plant and equipment		X
Cash surrender value of life insurance	X	
Purchase commitments—portion paid on fixed price contracts		X
An advance on a fixed price contract is the portion of the purchaser's claim to nonmonetary goods or services that is recognized in the accounts; it is not a right to receive money.		
Advances to supplier—not on a fixed price contract	X	
A right to receive credit for a sum of money; not a claim to a specified quantity of goods or services.		
Deferred income tax charges	X	
Offsets to prospective monetary liabilities		
Patents, trademarks, licenses and formulas		X
Goodwill		X
Deferred life insurance policy acquisition costs	X	
The portion of future cash receipts for premiums that is recognized in the accounts. Alternatively, viewed as an offset to the policy reserve.		
Deferred property and casualty insurance policy acquisition costs		X
Related to unearned premiums		
Other intangible assets and deferred charges		X
Liabilities		
Accounts and notes payable	X	
Accrued expenses payable (wages, etc.)	X	
Accrued vacation pay		
Nonmonetary if it is paid at the wage rates as of the vacation dates and if those rates may vary.		
Cash dividends payable	X	
Obligations payable in foreign currency	X	
Sales commitments—portion collected on fixed price contracts		X
An advance received on a fixed price contract is the portion of the seller's obligation to deliver goods or services that is recognized in the accounts; it is not an obligation to pay money.		
Advance from customers—not on a fixed price contract.	X	
Equivalent of a loan from the customer; not an obligation to furnish a specified quantity of goods or services.		
Accrued losses on firm purchase commitments.	X	
In essence, these are accounts payable.		
Deferred revenue		
Nonmonetary if an obligation to furnish goods or services is involved. Certain "deferred income" items of savings and loan associations are nonmonetary.		
Refundable deposits	X	
Bonds payable and other long-term debt	X	
Unamortized premium or discount and prepaid interest on bonds or notes payable	X	
Inseparable from the debt to which it relates—a monetary item.		

Item	Monetary	Nonmonetary
Convertible bonds payable Until converted these are obligations to pay sums of money.	X	
Accrued pension obligations Fixed amounts payable to a fund are monetary; all other amounts are nonmonetary.		
Obligations under warranties These are nonmonetary because they oblige the enterprise to furnish goods or services or their future price.		X
Deferred income tax credits Cash requirements will not vary materially due to changes in specific prices.	X	
Deferred investment tax credits Not to be settled by payment of cash; associated with nonmonetary assets.		X
Life insurance policy reserves Portions of policies face values that are now deemed liabilities.	X	
Property and casualty insurance loss reserves	X	
Unearned property and casualty insurance premiums These are nonmonetary because they are principally obligations to furnish insurance coverage. The dollar amount of payments to be made under that coverage might vary materially due to changes in specific prices.		X
Deposit liabilities of financial institutions	X	

Adapted from: FASB-33, "Financial Reporting and Changing Prices," Appendix D. In addition, FASB-8, "Accounting for the Translation of Foreign Currency Transactions and Foreign Currency Financial Statements, Appendix A," which has been superseded by FASB-52, provides a similar listing of accounts, and shows items classified as monetary translated at the current exchange rate and items classified as nonmonetary translated at the historical exchange rate. FASB-89, paragraphs 96–108, "Financial Reporting and Changing Prices," which supersedes FASB-33 also provides a table of monetary/nonmonetary items which is essentially the same as the list provided in FASB-33 except for the addition of items not relevant to this presentation such as trading account investments in fixed income securities, commodity inventories, and assets and liabilities peculiar to leasing arrangements. FASB-89 did, however, indicate that minority interests in consolidated subsidiaries is a nonmonetary item and that capital stock subject to redemption is a monetary item.

C. Certain exchange rates must be used to convert the foreign entity's account balances.

The remeasurement method of converting foreign financial statements also requires that certain exchange rates be used when the foreign subsidiary's account balances are converted from local currency units (LCUs) into the domestic currency. All monetary items are converted using the exchange rate in effect on the balance-sheet date. All nonmonetary items are converted using the historical exchange rate in effect on the transaction date. Revenues, expenses, gains, and losses that relate to monetary items are converted using the weighted average exchange rate (as shown in Section 13-3B). Revenues and expenses that relate to nonmonetary items, such as depreciation expenses, amortization of intangible assets, deferred charges or credits, and cost of goods sold are converted at the historical exchange rate in effect on the transaction date. The specific rates to be used with the various types of accounts are summarized in Table 13-4.

Table 13-4. Exchange Rates to Be Used under the Remeasurement Method.

Account	Appropriate Exchange Rate
Monetary items	Current rate at balance-sheet date.
Nonmonetary items	Historical rate at transaction date
Revenues, expenses, gains, and losses	Weighted averate rate—except for expenses and revenues which relate to nonmonetary items which use a historical rate (such as cost of goods sold, depreciation, and amortization).
Retained earnings	No single rate*

*End of period retained earnings is determined as follows:

Remeasured assets	$X
Less: Remeasured debts	(X)
End of period total stockholders' equity	$X
Less: Remeasured paid-in capital (stock and related accounts)	(X)
End-of-period total retained earnings	$X

Under the remeasurement method, retained earnings are calculated differently than they are under the translation method. To find retained earnings under the remeasurement method, subtract the remeasured liabilities from the remeasured assets. This gives the end-of-period total stockholders' equity. From this amount subtract the remeasured paid-in capital (the stock and related accounts). The remainder is the end-of-period total retained earnings.

The end-of-period retained earnings are compared with the beginning-of-period retained earnings yielding the change in retained earnings for the period. To the extent this change in retained earnings is not supported by the remeasured net income or loss and current dividend declarations, a remeasurement gain or loss develops as follows:

End-of-period retained earnings	$X
Less: Beginning-of -period retained earnings	(X)
Change in retained earnings	$X
Plus: Dividends declared	X
Net income (loss) for period	$X
Less: Remeasured net income (loss)	(X)
Remeasurement gain (loss)	$X

Any remeasurement gain or loss is included in the income statement.

EXAMPLE 13-3: On 1/1/X7, Planet Co. (a U.S. company) created a foreign subsidiary named Belem Co. All of Belem's stock was issued on that date. All of its plant and equipment was acquired on 3/10/X7. Belem's operating expenses, purchases, and revenues occurred evenly during 19X7. All of Belem's ending inventory (which it carries on a first-in, first-out basis) was purchased on 12/12/X7. On 12/15/X7, Belem declared and paid a 200,000 LCU dividend.

During 19X7, Belem's first year of operations, the direct exchange rates for the LCU were:

January 1 to March 31	$.50
April 1 to September 30	$.47
October 1 to December 31	$.42
Weighted average	$.465

Because Belem's operations are not self-contained, the dollar rather than the LCU is its functional currency. Therefore, Planet Co. will use the remeasurement method to convert Belem's financial statements into dollars.

The financial statements for Belem Co. as of and for the year ended 12/31/X7, in both LCUs and U.S. dollars, are shown in Exhibit 13-C. Planet Co. converted the LCUs to dollars as shown below.

Planet Co. begins the remeasurement process by converting each of Belem Co.'s balance sheet accounts to dollars by applying the exchange rate appropriate for each account, based on whether it is considered a monetary or nonmonetary item. Then, Belem's end-of-period retained earnings in dollars is computed by subtracting liabilities and common stock from assets: $422,000 in assets – ($210,000 in liabilities + $175,000 in common stock) = $37,000 in retained earnings.

Planet then converts the amounts on Belem's income statement, using a weighted average rate of exchange for the monetary revenues and expenses, and the historical rate of exchange for the nonmonetary items such as depreciation expenses and, in part, cost of goods sold. This combination of exchange rates produces a remeasured net income for Belem Co. for 19X7 of $112,250.

Planet can then determine the loss or gain that results from the remeasurement. In this case, the $37,000 increase in retained earnings from 1/1/X7 to 12/31/X7, plus the $84,000 in dividends (200,000 LCUs × $.42 per LCU on the declaration date) gives a net income for 19X7 of $121,000. This net income, less the remeasured net income from the income statement ($112,250), shows a remeasurement gain for Belem Co. of $8,750 ($121,000 – $112,250). This gain is included on the final income statement, as shown in Exhibit 13-C.

Exhibit 13-C. Dollar = Functional Currency
Belem Co. Financial Statements
At and for the Year Ended December 31, 19X7

Balance Sheet	LCUs	Exchange Rate	Dollars
Assets			
Cash	100,000	$0.420 M	$ 42,000
Accounts receivable	200,000	$0.420 M	84,000
Inventory	50,000	$0.420 NM	21,000
Plant and equipment	600,000	$0.500 NM	300,000
Accumulated depreciation	(50,000)	$0.500 NM	(25,000)
Total Assets	900,000		$422,000
Liabilities and Stockholders' Equity			
Accounts payable	200,000	$0.420 M	$ 84,000
Long-term note payable	300,000	$0.420 M	126,000
Common stock	350,000	$0.500 NM	175,000
Retained earnings	50,000	To balance	37,000
Total Liabilities and Stockholders' Equity	900,000		$422,000

Determination of net income for the period:	
12/31/X7 Retained earnings (per above balance sheet	$ 37,000
Less: 1/1/X7 Retained earnings (first year of operations)	0
Change in retained earnings	$ 37,000
Plus: Dividends declared	
(200,000 LCUs × $.42 declaration date exchange rate)	84,000
Net income for the year ended 12/31/X7	$121,000
Less: Remeasured net income (per income statement below)	112,250
Remeasurement gain (loss)	$ 8,750

Income Statement			
Sales	900,000	$0.465*	$418,500
Cost of goods sold:			
1/1/X7 Inventory	0		0
Plus: Purchases	500,000	$0.465*	232,500
Available for sale	500,000		232,500
Less: 12/31/X7 Inventory	(50,000)	$0.420 NM	(21,000)
Cost of goods sold	450,000		211,500
Gross profit	450,000		207,000
Operating expenses:			
Depreciation expense	50,000	$0.500 NM	25,000
Other operating expenses	150,000	$0.465*	69,750
Total operating expenses	200,000		94,750
Remeasured net income	250,000		$112,250
Remeasurement gain (loss) ($121,000 less $112,250)			8,750
		Net income	$121,000

* Weighted average rate of exchange
M = Monetary item (balance sheet date exchange rate used)
NM = Nonmonetary item (historical transaction date exchange rate used)

EXAMPLE 13-4: Refer to the information given in Example 13-3. Belem Co. continued its operations through 19X8. During the year Belem bought no additional property, plant, or equipment. Its beginning inventory (which it carries on a first-in, first-out basis) was all bought on 12/12/X7 (see Example 13-3), and all of its ending inventory for 19X8 was purchased on 12/15/X8. Finally, on 12/21/X8 Belem declared and paid a 150,000 LCU dividend.

During 19X8 the direct exchange rates for the LCU were:

January 1 to April 30	$.42
May 1 to August 31	$.46
September 1 to December 31	$.48
Weighted average	$.453

Because Belem's operations are not self-contained, the dollar rather than the LCU is its functional currency. Therefore, Planet Co. will use the remeasurement method to convert Belem's financial statements into dollars.

The financial statements for Belem Co. as of and for the year ended 12/31/X8, in both LCUs and U.S. dollars, are shown in Exhibit 13-D. Planet Co. converts the LCUs to dollars as shown below.

Planet Co. begins the remeasurement process by converting each of Belem Co.'s balance sheet accounts to dollars by applying the exchange rate appropriate for each account, based on whether it is considered a monetary or nonmonetary item. Then, Belem's end-of-period retained earnings in dollars is computed by subtracting liabilities and common stock from assets: $475,600 in assets – ($216,000 in liabilities + $175,000 in common stock) = $84,600 in retained earnings.

Planet then converts the amounts on Belem's income statement, using a weighted average rate of exchange for the monetary revenues and expenses, and the historical rate of exchange for the nonmonetary items such as depreciation expenses, and, in part, cost of goods sold. This combination of exchange rates produces a remeasured net income for Belem Co. for 19X8 of $123,500.

Planet can then determine the loss or gain that results from the remeasurement. In this case, the $47,600 increase in retained earnings ($84,600 in retained earnings on 12/31/X8 less the $37,000 in retained earnings on 1/1/X8), plus the $72,000 in dividends (150,000 LCUs × $.48 per LCU on the declaration date) gives a net income for 19X8 of $119,600. This net income, less the remeasured net income from the income statement ($123,500), results in a remeasurement loss for Belem Co. of $3,900 ($119,600 – $123,500). This loss is included on the final income statement, as shown in Exhibit 13-D.

Exhibit 13-D. Dollar = Functional Currency
Belem Co. Financial Statements
At and for the Year Ended December 31, 19X8

Balance Sheet	LCUs	Exchange Rate	Dollars
Assets			
Cash	180,000	$0.480 M	$ 86,400
Accounts receivable	220,000	$0.480 M	105,600
Inventory	70,000	$0.480 NM	33,600
Plant and equipment	600,000	$0.500 NM	300,000
Accumulated depreciation	(100,000)	$0.500 NM	(50,000)
Total Assets	970,000		$475,600
Liabilities and Stockholders' Equity			
Accounts payable	150,000	$0.480 M	$ 72,000
Long-term note payable	300,000	$0.480 M	144,000
Common stock	350,000	$0.500 NM	175,000
Retained earnings	170,000	To balance	84,600
Total Liabilities and Stockholders' Equity	970,000		$475,600

Determination of net income for the period:	
12/31/X8 Retained earnings (per above balance sheet)	$ 84,600
Less: 1/1/X8 Retained earnings (see Exhibit C)	(37,000)
Change in retained earnings	$ 47,600
Plus: Dividends declared (150,000 LCUs X $.48 declaration date exchange rate)	72,000
Net income for the year ended 12/31/X8	$119,600
Less: Remeasured net income (per income statement below)	123,500
Remeasurement gain (loss)	$ (3,900)

Income Statement			
Sales	990,000	$0.453*	$448,470
Cost of goods sold:			
1/1/X8 Inventory	50,000	$0.420 NM	21,000
Plus: Purchases	500,000	$0.453*	226,500
Available for sale	550,000		247,500
Less: 12/31/X8 Inventory	(70,000)	$0.480 NM	(33,600)
Cost of goods sold	480,000		213,900
Gross profit	510,000		234,570
Operating expenses:			
Depreciation expense	50,000	$0.500 NM	25,000
Other operating expenses	190,000	$0.453*	86,070
Total operating expenses	240,000		111,070
Remeasured net income	270,000		$123,500
Remeasurement gain (loss) ($119,600 less $123,500)			(3,900)
		Net income	$119,600

* Weighted average rate of exchange
M = Monetary item (balance sheet date exchange rate used)
NM = Nonmonetary item (historical transaction date exchange rate used)

13-5. Converting Inventory

If the foreign currency is determined to be the functional currency of foreign operations, then the translation method is used to convert inventory held by a foreign subsidiary to the domestic currency on the balance-sheet date. Under the translation method, asset accounts such as inventory are simply converted using the current exchange rate effective on the balance-sheet date (see Table 13-2).

If, however, the domestic currency is determined to be the functional currency of foreign operations, then the remeasurement method is used. Under the remeasurement method, inventories are considered nonmonetary items, and all nonmonetary items are converted using the historical exchange rate effective on the date of purchase (see Tables 13-3 and 13-4). A problem arises when the ending inventory was acquired on different dates with different historical exchange rates. If this is the case, the remeasurement method of conversion requires that each "layer" of inventory be converted at its appropriate historical exchange rate.

EXAMPLE 13-5: A U.S. company's foreign subsidiary made the following inventory purchases in LCUs during 19X1, the first year of the subsidiary's operations:

	LCUs
January 10, 19X1	200,000
April 5, 19X1	300,000
July 16, 19X1	700,000
November 29, 19X1	200,000

Direct exchange rates for the LCU for 19X1 were:

January 1 through February 28	$.60
March 1 through July 31	$.56
August 1 through December 31	$.54

The foreign company uses the last-in, first-out (LIFO) method of inventory cost flow assumption, and its functional currency is the U.S. dollar.

The foreign company's ending inventory on 12/31/X1 is shown on its books at 300,000 LCUs. Of that amount, 200,000 LCUs represent purchases of 1/10/X1, and 100,000 LCUs represent purchases of 4/5/X1.

Because the foreign company's functional currency is the dollar, its U.S. parent will use the remeasurement method to convert the ending inventory to dollars. The U.S. company must therefore convert each remaining "layer" of the foreign company's ending inventory at the historical exchange rate when the "layer" was acquired as follows:

(1) Acquisition Date	(2) Cost in LCU's	(3) Historical Exchange Rate	(2) × (3) Cost in Dollars
1/10/X1	200,000	$.60	$120,000
4/5/X1	100,000	$.56	56,000
12/31/X1	300,000		$176,000

EXAMPLE 13-6: Refer to the information given in Example 13-5, but assume that the functional currency is the foreign currency. In that case, the U.S. company uses the translation method to convert the ending inventory to dollars.

Under the translation method, the ending inventory in LCUs is converted at the rate of exchange effective on the balance-sheet date, or $.54 per LCU at 12/31/X1. This results in an ending inventory of $162,000 (300,000 LCUs × $.54).

13-6. Converting Property, Plant, and Equipment

If the foreign currency is determined to be the functional currency of foreign operations, then the translation method is used to convert property, plant, and equipment of the foreign subsidiary to domestic currency on the balance-sheet date. Under the translation method, these asset accounts are simply converted using the current exchange rate effective on the balance-sheet date (see Table 13-2).

If, however, the domestic currency is determined to be the functional currency of foreign operations, then the remeasurement method is used. Under the remeasurement method, property, plant, and equipment assets are considered nonmonetary items, and all nonmonetary items are converted using the historical exchange rate effective on the date of purchase (see Tables 13-3 and 13-4). In addition, all accumulated depreciation accounts and depreciation expense accounts related to the property, plant, or equipment must also be converted at their historical rates of exchange.

EXAMPLE 13-7: The foreign subsidiary of a U.S. company made the following equipment purchases:

Acquisition Date	Cost in LCU's	Acquisition Date Exchange Rate
6/30/X1	100,000	$.70
3/15/X2	100,000	$.65

Assuming the equipment the foreign subsidiary acquired has a 10-year life with no salvage value, and that a full year's depreciation is taken in the year of acquisition as a matter of company policy, the accumulated depreciation relating to the equipment in LCUs on 12/31/X2 would be:

6/30/X1	Acquisition:	100,000/10 yrs.	=	10,000 × 2 yrs.	=	20,000
3/15/X2	Acquisition:	100,000/10 yrs.	=	10,000 × 1 yr.	=	10,000
12/31/X2	Accumulated depreciation					30,000

The annual depreciation expense for 19X2 on the acquired equipment would be $20,000 ($10,000 per year for each of the two pieces of equipment). Therefore, the financial statements for the foreign subsidiary as of and for the year ended 12/31/X2 would show the following amounts in LCUs relating to the two equipment purchases:

Balance Sheet	LCUs
Property, plant, and equipment	200,000
Less: Accumulated depreciation	30,000
Property, plant, and equipment (net)	170,000

Income Statement	LCUs
Depreciation expense	20,000*

*10,000 Depreciation expense on year x1 acquisition plus 10,000 depreciation expense on year x2 acquisition.

If the U.S. dollar is the functional currency of the foreign company, the U.S. parent converts the foreign company's financial statements to dollars on 12/31/X2 using the remeasurement method. Under the remeasurement method, the amounts on the balance sheet and income statement relating to the two equipment purchases, as of and for the year ended 12/31/X2, must be converted at the exchange rates in effect on the dates of purchase:

	LCUs	Appropriate Historical Exchange Rate	Dollars
Property, plant, and equip.:			
19X1 Acquisition	100,000	$.70	$70,000
19X2 Acquisition	100,000	$.65	65,000
Cost	200,000		135,000
Accumulated depreciation:			
6/30/X1 Acquisition	20,000	$.70	14,000
3/15/X2 Acquisition	10,000	$.65	6,500
Accumulated depreciation	30,000		20,500
Property, plant, and equip. (net):	170,000		$114,500
Depreciation expense:			
19X1 Acquisition	10,000	$.70	7,000
19X2 Acquisition	10,000	$.65	6,500
Depreciation expense	20,000		$13,500

Therefore, the balance sheet on 12/31/X2 will show a Property, Plant, and Equipment account balance, net of accumulated depreciation, of $114,500. The income statement will show a depreciation expense related to the equipment of $13,500.

13-7. Conversions in Highly Inflationary Economies

A highly inflationary economy is one that has a cumulative inflation rate over a three-year period of 100 percent or more. If a foreign operation is conducted in a highly inflationary economy, generally accepted accounting principles require that all conversions of financial statements from the foreign currency to the domestic currency be made using the remeasurement method, even if indicators point to the foreign currency as the functional currency of the foreign operation.

13-8. Changes in Functional Currency

It is possible that the functional currency of a foreign operation may change. In such a case, no changes or adjustments are made to previous periods.

Specifically, if the change is from the foreign currency to the domestic currency (such as the dollar), then Paragraph 46 of FASB-52 states that:

- the cumulative translation adjustment resulting from conversions in prior periods should not be removed from the stockholders' equity, and
- the translated amounts of the nonmonetary asset accounts at the end of the prior period should become the basis for those accounts in subsequent periods.

Further, if the change is from the domestic currency to the foreign currency, FASB-52 states that:

- any adjustment resulting from conversion of nonmonetary asset accounts at the current rate on the date of the change should become part of the cumulative translation adjustment in stockholders' equity.

RAISE YOUR GRADES

Can you explain . . . ?

☑ how FASB-52 changed the process of converting foreign financial statements

- ☑ the meaning of the term *functional currency*
- ☑ the six indicators of functional currency
- ☑ why the translation method does not recognize conversion gains or losses as a part of income
- ☑ why the remeasurement method does recognize conversion gains or losses as a part of income
- ☑ how to calculate a weighted-average exchange rate
- ☑ the distinction between monetary and nonmonetary assets and liabilities
- ☑ the special considerations that must be used when converting inventory under the remeasurement method
- ☑ the special considerations that must be used when converting property, plant, and equipment, and related depreciation, under the remeasurement method
- ☑ the meaning of the term *highly inflationary economy*
- ☑ the effects of a change in functional currency

SUMMARY

1. The basic process of financial statement conversion involves three broad steps: a) determination of the functional currency, b) restatement of foreign financial statements into GAAP of the reporting entity, c) conversion of foreign statements into currency of the reporting entity..
2. In order to properly convert foreign financial statements, the reporting company must first determine the functional currency of the foreign company.
3. If necessary, the reporting company must restate the foreign company's financial statements in terms of its own generally accepted accounting principles.
4. The functional currency is the currency of the primary economic environment in which an entity operates.
5. If the foreign currency is the functional currency of a foreign operation, the the translation method must be used to convert the foreign financial statements into the domestic currency (unless the foreign economy is highly inflationary).
6. If the domestic currency is the functional currency of a foreign operation, the remeasurement method must be used to convert the foreign financial statements into the domestic currency.
7. The translation method does not recognize any gains or losses in the income statement resulting from currency translations
8. The remeasurement method does recognize gains or losses in the income statement resulting from currency conversions.
9. Specific exchange rates must be used to convert foreign financial statements when using both the translation method and the remeasurement method.
10. Depending on the method of conversion used, and the type of account being converted, either the historical exchange rate, the current exchange rate, or a weighted-average exchange rate should be used.
11. When using the translation method, any gain or loss on the conversion of foreign financial statements is shown as an adjustment to stockholders' equity.
12. When using the remeasurement method, any gain or loss on the conversion of foreign financial statements is shown on the income statement.
13. When using the remeasurement method, a distinction must be made between monetary and nonmonetary assets and liabilities.
14. When using the translation method, inventory is converted using the current exchange rate.
15. When using the remeasurement method, each "layer" of inventory must be converted at the appropriate historical exchange rate.
16. When using the translation method, property, plant, and equipment accounts are converted using the current exchange rate.

17. When using the remeasurement method, property, plant, and equipment are considered nonmonetary assets and are converted at their historical rates of exchange.

18. When using the remeasurement method, all accumulated depreciation accounts and depreciation expense accounts related to property, plant, and equipment must also be converted at their historical rates of exchange.

19. If a foreign operation is conducted in a highly inflationary economy, all conversions of financial statements must be made using the remeasurement method, even if indications are that the foreign currency is the functional currency of the foreign operation.

20. If the functional currency of a foreign operation changes, no modifications or adjustments are made to the financial statements from previous periods.

RAPID REVIEW

1. The appropriate method of conversion of financial statements of a foreign subsidiary into U.S. dollars depends on
   (*a*) the effect of the method chosen on periodic net income.
   (*b*) the functional currency of the foreign subsidiary.
   (*c*) the effect of the method chosen on year-end financial position.
   (*d*) whether or not management wishes to disclose gain or loss in the income statement or as a component of stockholders's equity.

2. If the U.S. dollar is the functional currency of the foreign operation, then generally
   (*a*) income statement remeasurement gain or loss is not possible.
   (*b*) income statement remeasurement gain or loss is possible.
   (*c*) translation gain or loss is viewed as a component of stockholders' equity.
   (*d*) both *a* and *c* are true.

3. If the foreign currency is the functional currency of the foreign operation, then generally
   (*a*) income statement remeasurement gain or loss is not possible.
   (*b*) income statement remeasurement gain or loss is possible.
   (*c*) translation gain or loss is viewed as a component of stockholders' equity.
   (*d*) both *a* and *c* are true.

4. If the foreign currency is the functional currency of the foreign operation, and the foreign operation exists in a highly inflationary economy, then
   (*a*) income statement remeasurement gain or loss is not possible.
   (*b*) income statement remeasurement gain or loss is possible.
   (*c*) translation gain or loss is viewed as a component of stockholders' equity.
   (*d*) both *a* and *c* are true.

5. Which of the following provides an indication that the foreign currency is the functional currency of a foreign subsidiary?
   (*a*) the foreign entity's sales prices are responsive to exchange rate fluctuations.
   (*b*) the foreign entity's operational costs are largely the result of purchases from the parent's country.
   (*c*) cash flows occur primarily in the foreign currency with no direct parent company impact.
   (*d*) a high volume of intercompany transactions exists between the parent and subsidiary.

6. Which of the following provides an indication that the U.S. dollar of a U.S. parent company is the functional currency of a foreign subsidiary?
   (*a*) the sales market for the foreign subsidiary's products is primarily in the parent's country or currency.
   (*b*) the foreign entity's operations are sufficient to service its debt which is denominated primarily in the foreign currency.
   (*c*) a low volume of intercompany transactions exists between the parent and subsidiary.
   (*d*) an active local sales market exists for the foreign entity's products.

7. A highly inflationary economy exists if
(*a*) the inflation rate in the foreign environment is 100% or more for each of 3 consecutive years.
(*b*) the inflation rate in the foreign environment is 33 1/3% or more for each of 3 consecutive years.
(*c*) both *a* and *b*.

8. Monetary items are
(*a*) items fixed in amount regardless of the changes in the prices of goods and services .
(*b*) items fixed in amount, fluctuating in value as the prices of goods and services fluctuate.

9. Which of the following items is nonmonetary?
(*a*) bonds payable
(*b*) premium on bonds payable
(*c*) cash
(*d*) equipment

10. Which of the following items is monetary?
(*a*) common stock
(*b*) inventory
(*c*) equipment
(*d*) accounts payable

11. A change in the functional currency (from the dollar to the foreign currency or vice-versa) is treated as
(*a*) a change in reporting entity.
(*b*) a change in accounting estimate.
(*c*) an accounting reclassification.
(*d*) a change in accounting principle.

Questions 12 and 13 are based on the following information:

A U.S. company's foreign subsidiary had balance sheet accounts at December 31, 19X6, which included the following:

	Translated at	
	Current Rate	Historical Rate
Inventory	$600,000	$650,000
Accounts receivable	$ 50,000	$ 55,000
Bonds payable	$100,000	$107,000
Common stock	$200,000	$216,000

12. If the U.S. dollar is the functional currency, the inventory, accounts receivable, bonds payable, and common stock are carried at
(*a*) $600,000, $50,000, $100,000, and $200,000, respectively.
(*b*) $650,000, $55,000, $107,000, and $216,000, respectively.
(*c*) $650,000, $50,000, $100,000, and $216,000, respectively.
(*d*) $600,000, $50,000, $100,000, and $216,000, respectively.

13. If the foreign currency is the functional currency, the inventory, accounts receivable, bonds payable, and common stock are carried at
(*a*) $600,000, $50,000, $100,000, and $200,000, respectively.
(*b*) $650,000, $55,000, $107,000, and $216,000, respectively.
(*c*) $650,000, $50,000, $100,000, and $216,000, respectively.
(*d*) $600,000, $50,000, $100,000, and $216,000, respectively.

14. Gains or losses from translation of a foreign subsidiary's financial statements into U.S. dollars, when the foreign currency is the functional currency, should be
(*a*) recorded as an extraordinary item.
(*b*) recorded as deferred credits or charges.
(*c*) treated as a component of stockholders' equity.
(*d*) treated as a part of income from operations.

15. Standard Co., a U.S. company, owns a foreign subsidiary which has equipment that originally cost 500,000 LCUs and was purchased in 19X8 when the direct exchange rate was $.60 for 1 LCU. The weighted average exchange rate for the year ended December 31, 19X8 was $.59 for 1 LCU. Equipment is depreciated on a straight-line basis and has a 10-year life and no salvage value. If the U.S. dollar is the functional currency, 19X8 depreciation expense is

(*a*) $30,000.
(*b*) $50,000.
(*c*) $29,500.
(*d*) $25,000.

16. Assume the facts provided in the previous question except that the foreign currency is the functional currency. In this case, 19X8 depreciation expense is

(*a*) $30,000.
(*b*) $50,000.
(*c*) $29,500.
(*d*) $25,000.

Answers:

1. (*b*)
2. (*b*) The remeasurement method is appropriate.
3. (*d*) The translation method is appropriate.
4. (*b*) In a highly inflationary economy, the remeasurement method is appropriate.
5. (*c*) (See Table 13-1.)
6. (*a*) (See Table 13-1.)
7. (*c*) The economy is highly inflationary if the *cumulative* inflation is 100% or more over a three-year period. This is the situation in both answer choices *a* and *b*.
8. (*a*)
9. (*d*) (See Table 13-3.)
10. (*d*) (See Table 13-3.)
11. (*b*)
12. (*c*) If the U.S. dollar is the functional currency, monetary items (accounts receivable and bonds payable) must be carried at the current rate and nonmonetary items (inventory and common stock) must be carried at historical rates.
13. (*d*) If the foreign currency is the functional currency, all assets and liabilities (inventory, accounts receivable, and bonds payable) are carried at the current rate and common stock is carried at historical rates.
14. (*c*) (See translation method examples.)
15. (*a*) Equipment and related depreciation expense is remeasured at the historical rates of exchange when purchased as follows:

	19X8 purchase
	500,000 LCUs
Historical rate	× $.60
	$300,000
# of years	÷ 10
Depreciation expense	$ 30,000

Total depreciation expense is $30,000.

16. (*c*) Depreciation expense is translated at the weighted average rate of exchange as follows:

Original cost	500,000. LCUs (total)
# of years	÷ 10
19X8 Depreciation expense	50,000. LCUs
Weighted average rate	× $.59
Depreciation expense	$ 29,500

SOLVED PROBLEMS

PROBLEM 13-1: The following accounts appear on the trial balance of the Klarn Company for the year ended December 31, 19X3:

Cash	Y1,200*
Inventories	Y4,800

*Y = Yen

The Klarn Company is located in Japan but is wholly owned by Davis Company, which is a U.S. corporation.

Required: Explain how the two accounts would be translated in order to appear on the Davis company's consolidated balance sheet (*a*) if Klarn Company's functional currency is the yen and (*b*) if Klarn company's functional currency is the dollar.

Answer:
(*a*) When the yen is the functional currency, all asset accounts are translated at the current exchange rate (December 31, 19X3).
(*b*) When the dollar is the functional currency, monetary items are translated at the current exchange rate and nonmonetary items are translated at the historical exchange rate. Thus, cash would be translated at the current exchange rate (December 31, 19X3) and inventory would be translated at the exchange rate that existed when the inventory was purchased.

PROBLEM 13-2: Pacific Company is a foreign subsidiary which is owned by a U.S. corporation. A summarized income statement for Pacific Company, translated into dollars, appears below:

Sales	$400,000
Cost of goods sold	100,000
Gross margin	$300,000
Operating expenses	250,000
Income from operations	$ 50,000
Translation adjustment	20,000
Net income	$ 30,000

Required: When the U.S. Corporation prepares its consolidated financial statements, will the determination of whether Pacific Company exists in a highly inflationary economy have an effect on the consolidated financial statements? Explain fully.

Answer: Yes. If the foreign company does not exist in a highly inflationary economy, translation adjustments resulting from the process of translating from the functional currency to the reporting currency are reported as a separate component of equity and do not appear on the consolidated income statement. If the foreign company does exist in a highly inflationary economy, translation adjustments are reported on the consolidated income statement.

PROBLEM 13-3: A U.S. corporation owns Far East Corporation. Far East Corporation has the following account on its balance sheet at December 31, 19X3:

Inventory	Y900,000*

*Y = Yen

The functional currency for Far East Corporation is the deutsche mark (DM). The inventory was acquired on November 1, 19X3. Foreign currency exchange rates are presented below:

Date	Dollar to Yen	Dollar to Mark	Mark to Yen
12/31/X3	\$.00526 = 1Y	\$.54054 = 1DM	1DM = .00952Y
11/01/X3	\$.00541 = 1Y	\$.52632 = 1DM	1DM = .01064Y
19X3 Average	\$.00588 = 1Y	\$.50000 = 1DM	1DM = .01111Y

Required: At what amount should the inventory be reported in the U.S. corporation's consolidated balance sheet?

Answer: Inventory would be reported at \$5,176 which requires two computations:

(1) Y900,000 × .01064 = DM9,576
(2) DM9,576 × .54054 = \$5,176

The first computation is required to convert to the *functional currency* (DM), and since inventory is a nonmonetary asset, the historical exchange rate must be used. The second computation is required to convert to the *reporting currency* (\$), and the current exchange rate must be used.

PROBLEM 13-4: Bluefield Company owns a foreign subsidiary that operates in West Germany. A trial balance for the foreign subsidiary is summarized below for the year ended December 31, 19X3:

	Debit	Credit
Nonmonetary assets*	DM100,000**	
Monetary assets	150,000	
Monetary liabilities		DM 50,000
Common stock		160,000
Retained earnings, Jan. 1, 19X3		0
Sales		400,000
Operating expenses	360,000	
Total	DM610,000	DM610,000

*Nonmonetary assets were purchased on January 4, 19X3.
**DM = deutsche mark.

Foreign exchange rates are presented below:

Date	Dollar to Deutsche mark
Dec. 31, 19X3	\$.40 = 1DM
Average—19X3	\$.46 = 1DM
Jan.4, 19X3	\$.49 = 1DM
Jan. 1, 19X3	\$.54 = 1DM

The foreign subsidiary was organized early in January of 19X3.

Required: Prepare the translated balance sheet and income statement for the foreign subsidiary, assuming the deutsche mark is the functional currency and the dollar is the reporting currency.

Answer: Work Sheet for Translating to Dollars

	Deutsche marks Dr. (Cr.)	Rate		Dollars Dr. (Cr.)
Nonmonetary assets	100,000 DM	\$0.40	(a)	\$40,000
Monetary assets	150,000	\$0.40		60,000
Monetary liabilities	(50,000)	\$0.40		(20,000)
Common stock	(160,000)	\$0.54	(b)	(86,400)
Retained earnings	—	—		—
Sales	(400,000)	\$0.46	(c)	(184,000)
Operating expenses	360,000	\$0.46		165,600
	0 DM			(24,800)
	Translation adjustment			24,800
	Total			0

(a) current rate at 12/31/X3
(b) historical rate (January 19X3)
(c) 19X3 average rate

Translated Balance Sheet

Nonmonetary assets	$ 40,000
Monetary assets	60,000
Total assets	$100,000
Monetary liabilities	$ 20,000
Common stock	86,400
Retained earnings (first year net income)	18,400
Translation adjustment	(24,800)
Total stockholders' equity	80,000
Total liabilities and stockholders' equity	$100,000

Translated Income Statement

Sales	$184,000
Operating expenses	165,600
Net income	$ 18,400

PROBLEM 13-5: Refer to the bacts of problem 13-4. However, assume that the dollar is the functional currency rather than the deutsche mark. Prepare the translated balance sheet and income statement for the foreign subsidiary assuming the nonmonetary assets were acquired on January 4, 19X3:

Answer:

Work Sheet for Translating to Dollars

	Deutsche marks Dr. (Cr.)	Rate		Dollars Dr. (Cr.)
Nonmonetary assets*	100,000 DM	$0.49	(a)	$49,000
Monetary assets	150,000	$0.40	(b)	60,000
Monetary liabilities	(50,000)	$0.40		(20,000)
Common stock	(160,000)	$0.54	(c)	(86,400)
Retained earnings	—	—		—
Sales	(400,000)	$0.46	(d)	(184,000)
Operating expenses	360,000	$0.46		165,600
	0 DM			(15,800)
	Remeasurement loss			15,800
	Total			0

(a) historical rate on January 4, 19X3
(b) current rate at 12/31/X3
(c) historical rate (January 19X3)
(d) 19X3 average rate

Translated Balance Sheet

Nonmonetary assets	$ 49,000
Monetary assets	60,000
Total assets	$109,000

Monetary liabilities	$ 20,000
Common stock	86,400
Retained earnings (to balance)	2,600
Total stockholders' equity	89,000
Total liabilities and stockholders' equity	$109,000

Retained Earnings Statement

12/31/X3 Retained earnings	$2,600
1/1/X3 Retained earnings	0
Change in retained earnings	2,600
Add: Dividends declared	0
19X3 Net income	$2,600

Translated Income Statement

Sales	$184,000
Operating expenses	165,600
	18,400
Remeasurement loss (see worksheet)	15,800
Net income	$ 2,600

PROBLEM 13-6: Bute Co., a U.S. company, formed a foreign Japanese subsidiary, the Soni Co., on January 1, 19X1. Soni Co.'s financial statements at December 31, 19X1 were as follows:

Balance Sheet	Yen
Assets	
Cash	Y 1,000,000
Accounts receivable	4,000,000
Inventory	3,000,000
Plant and equipment	20,000,000
Accumulated depreciation	(1,000,000)
Total Assets	Y 27,000,000
Liabilities and Stockholders' Equity	
Accounts payable	Y 5,000,000
Long-term note payable	9,400,000
Common stock	10,000,000
Retained earnings	2,600,000
Total Liabilities and Stockholders' Equity	Y 27,000,000

Income Statement	Yen
Sales	Y 28,000,000
Cost of goods sold	21,000,000
Gross profit	7,000,000
Operating expenses:	
Depreciation expense	1,000,000
Other operating expenses	3,300,000
Total operating expenses	4,300,000
Net income	Y 2,700,000

Statement of Retained Earnings	
1/1/X1 Retained earnings	Y 0
Add: 19X1 Net income	2,700,000
Deduct: 19X1 Dividend declarations	(100,000)
12/31/X1 Retained earnings	Y 2,600,000

Exchange rates during 19X1 were as follows:

Date	Dollar to Yen
Dec. 31, 19X3	$0.00530 = 1 Yen
Average—19X1	$0.00560 = 1 Yen
Jan. 20, 19X1	$0.00580 = 1 Yen
Jan. 1, 19X1	$0.00590 = 1 Yen
Dec. 20, 19X1	$0.00540 = 1 Yen

Additional information regarding Soni Co. is as follows:
—All plant and equipment was acquired on Jan. 20, 19X1.
—Dividends were declared and paid on Dec. 20, 19X1
—The first-in first-out inventory cost flow assumption is used.
The entire ending inventory was purchased on Dec. 20, 19X1.

Required: Assuming the yen is the functional currency, complete the worksheet provided below.

Problem 13–6: Yen = Functional Currency
Worksheet for Soni Co. Financial Statements
At and for the Year Ended December 31, 19X1

Income Statement	Yen	Exchange Rate	Dollars
Sales	28,000,000		
Cost of goods sold	21,000,000		
Gross profit	7,000,000		
Operating expenses:			
Depreciation expense	1,000,000		
Other operating expenses	3,300,000		
Total operating expenses	4,300,000		
Net income	2,700,000		
Statement of Retained Earnings			
1/1/X1 Retained earnings	0		
Add: 19X1 Net income	2,700,000		
Deduct: 19X1 Dividend declarations	(100,000)		
12/31/X1 Retained earnings	2,600,000		
Balance Sheet			
Assets			
Cash	Y 1,000,000		
Accounts receivable	4,000,000		
Inventory	3,000,000		
Plant and equipment	20,000,000		
Accumulated depreciation	(1,000,000)		
Total Assets	Y 27,000,000		

Liabilities and Stockholders' Equity		
Accounts payable	Y 5,000,000	
Long-term note payable	9,400,000	
Common stock	10,000,000	
Retained earnings	2,600,000	
Total Liabilities and Stockholders' Equity	Y 27,000,000	

Answer:

Problem 13–6: Yen = Functional Currency
Worksheet for Soni Co. Financial Statements
At and for the Year Ended December 31, 19X1

Income Statement	Yen	Exchange Rate		Dollars
Sales	28,000,000	$0.00560	(a)	$156,800
Cost of goods sold	21,000,000	$0.00560		117,600
Gross profit	7,000,000			39,200
Operating expenses:				
Depreciation expense	1,000,000	$0.00560		5,600
Other operating expenses	3,300,000	$0.00560		18,480
Total operating expenses	4,300,000			24,080
Net income	2,700,000			$ 15,120
Statement of Retained Earnings				
1/1/X1 Retained earnings	0	First year		$0
Add: 19X1 Net income	2,700,000	See above		15,120
Deduct: 19X1 Dividend declarations	(100,000)	$0.00540	(b)	(540)
12/31/X1 Retained earnings	2,600,000			$ 14,580
Balance Sheet				
Assets				
Cash	Y 1,000,000	$0.00530	(c)	$ 5,300
Accounts receivable	4,000,000	$0.00530		21,200
Inventory	3,000,000	$0.00530		15,900
Plant and equipment	20,000,000	$0.00530		106,000
Accumulated depreciation	(1,000,000)	$0.00530		(5,300)
Total Assets	Y 27,000,000			$143,100
Liabilities and Stockholders' Equity				
Accounts payable	Y 5,000,000	$0.00530		$ 26,500
Long-term note payable	9,400,000	$0.00530		49,820
Common stock	10,000,000	$0.00590	(d)	59,000
Retained earnings	2,600,000	See above		14,580
Cumulative translation adjustment		To balance		(6,800)
Total Liabilities and Stockholders' Equity	Y 27,000,000			$143,100

(a) Weighted average exchange rate for 19X1
(b) Dividend declaration date exchange rate at 12/20/X1
(c) Current exchange rate at 12/31/X1
(d) Historical exchange rate at stock issue date of Jan. 1, 19X1

PROBLEM 13-7: Refer to the information provided in the previous question. However, assume that the dollar is the functional currency rather than the yen. On this basis, complete the worksheet provided below.

Problem 13–7: Dollar = Functional Currency
Worksheet for Soni Co. Financial Statements
At and for the Year Ended December 31, 19X1

Balance Sheet	Yen	Exchange Rate	Dollars
Assets			
Cash	Y 1,000,000		
Accounts receivable	4,000,000		
Inventory	3,000,000		
Plant and equipment	20,000,000		
Accumulated depreciation	(1,000,000)		
Total Assets	Y 27,000,000		
Liabilities and Stockholders' Equity			
Accounts payable	Y 5,000,000		
Long-term note payable	9,400,000		
Common stock	10,000,000		
Retained earnings	2,600,000		
Total Liabilities and Stockholders' Equity	Y 27,000,000		

Determination of net income for the period:

	Dollars
12/31/X1 Retained earnings	
Less: 1/1/X1 Retained earnings	
Change in retained earnings	
Plus: Dividends declared	
Net income for the year ended 12/31/X1	
Less: Remeasured net income	
Remeasurement gain (loss)	

Income Statement	Yen	Exchange Rate	Dollars
Sales	Y 28,000,000		
Cost of goods sold:			
1/1/X1 Inventory	0		
Plus: Purchases	24,000,000		
Available for sale	24,000,000		
Less: 12/31/X1 Inventory	(3,000,000)		
Cost of goods sold	21,000,000		
Gross profit	7,000,000		
Operating expenses:			
Depreciation expense	1,000,000		
Other operating expenses	3,300,000		
Total operating expenses	4,300,000		
Remeasured net income	Y 2,700,000		
Remeasurement gain (loss)			
Net income			

Answer:

Problem 13–7: Dollar = Functional Currency
Worksheet for Soni Co. Financial Statements
At and for the Year Ended December 31, 19X1

Balance Sheet	Yen	Exchange Rate	Dollars
Assets			
Cash	Y 1,000,000	$0.00530 M	$ 5,300
Accounts receivable	4,000,000	$0.00530 M	21,200
Inventory	3,000,000	$0.00540 NM	16,200
Plant and equipment	20,000,000	$0.00580 NM	116,000
Accumulated depreciation	(1,000,000)	$0.00580 NM	(5,800)
Total Assets	27,000,000		$152,900
Liabilities and Stockholders' Equity			
Accounts payable	Y 5,000,000	$0.00530 M	$ 26,500
Long-term note payable	9,400,000	$0.00530 M	49,820
Common stock	10,000,000	$0.00590 NM	59,000
Retained earnings	2,600,000	To balance	17,580
Total Liabilities and Stockholders' Equity	Y 27,000,000		$152,900

Determination of net income for the period:	
12/31/X1 Retained earnings (per above balance sheet)	$ 17,580
Less: 1/1/X1 Retained earnings (first year of operations)	0
Change in retained earnings	$ 17,580
Plus: Dividends declared (100,000 yen X $.0054 declaration date exchange rate)	540
Net income for the year ended 12/31/X1	$ 18,120
Less: Remeasured net income (per income statement below)	14,320
Remeasurement gain (loss)	$ 3,800

Income Statement	Yen	Exchange Rate	Dollars
Sales	Y 28,000,000	$0.00560*	$156,800
Cost of goods sold:			
1/1/X1 Inventory	0		0
Plus: Purchases	24,000,000	$0.00560*	134,400
Available for sale	24,000,000		134,400
Less: 12/31/X1 Inventory	(3,000,000)	$0.00540 NM	(16,200)
Cost of goods sold	21,000,000		118,200
Gross profit	7,000,000		38,600
Operating expenses:			
Depreciation expense	1,000,000	$0.00580 NM	5,800
Other operating expenses	3,300,000	$0.00560*	18,480
Total operating expenses	4,300,000		24,280
Remeasured net income	Y 2,700,000		$ 14,320
Remeasurement gain (loss) ($18,120 less $14,320)			3,800
		Net income	$ 18,120

* Weighted average rate of exchange
M = Monetary item (balance sheet date exchange rate used)
NM = Nonmonetary item (historical transaction date exchange rate used)

PROBLEM 13-8: Refer again to the information provided in problem 13-6. Assume the following:

19X2 net income in yen was 3,000,000
19X2 dividends declared and paid on 12/22/X2 in yen were 150,000
the 19X2 average exchange rate was $.0050
the 12/31/X2 exchange rate was $.0049
the 1/1/X2 exchange rate was $.0053
the 12/22/X2 exchange rate was $.00495

Required:
Determine the 12/31/X2 retained earnings in dollars assuming the yen is the functional currency.

Answer:

Statement of Retained Earnings			
1/1/X1 Retained earnings	Y 2,600,000	(a)	$ 14,580
Add: 19X2 Net income	Y 3,000,000	(b)	15,000
Deduct: 19X2 Dividend declarations	Y (150,000)	(c)	(743)
12/31/X2 Retained earnings	Y 5,450,000		$ 28,837

(a) From ending balance (12/31/X1) in answer to problem 13-6
(b) All income statement items are translated at the 19X2 average rate of exchange of $.0050
(c) Translated at dividend declaration date exchange rate on 12/22/X2 of $.00495

PROBLEM 13-9 (AICPA Adapted)**:** On January 1 19X5, the Franklin Company formed a foreign subsidiary which issued all of its currently outstanding common stock on that date. Selected captions from the balance sheets, all of which are shown in local currency units (LCU), are as follows:

	December 31,	
	19X6	19X5
Accounts receivable (net of allowance for uncollectible accounts of 2,200 LCU at December 31,19X6 and 2,000 LCU at December 31, 19X5)	40,000 LCU	35,000 LCU
Inventories, at cost	80,000	75,000
Property,plant and equipment (net allowance for accumulated depreciation of 31,000 LCU at December 31, 19X6 and 14,000 LCU at December 31, 19X5)	163,000	150,000
Long-term debt	100,000	120,000
Common stock, authorized 10,000 shares par value 10 LCU per share, issued and outstanding 5,000 shares at December 31, 19X6 and December 31, 19X5	50,000	50,000

Additional information is as follows:

*Exchange rates are as follows:

January 1, 19X5 – July 31, 19X5	2 LCU to $1
August 1, 19X5 – October 31, 19X5	1.8 LCU to $1
November 1, 19X5 – June 30, 19X6	1.7 LCU to $1
July 1, 19X6 –December 31, 19X6	1.5 LCU to $1
Average monthly rate for 19X5	1.9 LCU to $1
Average monthly rate for 19X6	1.6 LCU to $1

*An analysis of the accounts receivable balance is as follows:

Accounts receivable:	19X6	19X5
Balance at beginning of year	37,000 LCU	- - - LCU
Sales (36,000 LCU per month in 19X6 and 31,000 LCU per month in 19X5)	432,000	372,000
Collections	(423,600)	(334,000)
Write-offs (May 19X6 and December 19X5)	(3,200)	(1,000)
Balance at end of year	42,200 LCU	37,000 LCU

Allowance for uncollectible accounts:	19X6	19X5
Balance at beginning of year	2,000 LCU	- - - LCU
Provision for uncollectible accounts	3,400	3,000
Write-offs (May 19X6 and December 19X5)	(3,200)	(1,000)
Balance at end of year	2,200 LCU	2,000 LCU

*An analysis of inventories, for which the first-in, first-out (FIFO) inventory method is used, is as follows:

	19X6	19X5
Inventory at beginning of year	75,000 LCU	- - - LCU
Purchases (June 19X6 and June19X5)	335,000	375,000
Goods available for sale	410,000	375,000
Inventory at end of year	80,000	75,000
Cost of goods sold	330,000 LCU	300,000 LCU

*On January 1, 19X5, Franklin's foreign subsidiary purchased land for 24,000 LCU and plant and equipment for 140,000 LCU. On July 4, 19X6, additional equipment was purchased for 30,000 LCU. Plant and equipment is being depreciated on a straight-line basis over a ten-year period with no salvage value. A full year's depreciation is taken in the year of purchase.

*On January 15, 7% bonds with a face value of 120,000 LCU were sold. Interest is paid semiannually on July 15 and January 15.

Required:
Prepare a schedule translating the selected captions above into United States dollars at December 31, 19X6, and December 31, 19X5, respectively. Show supporting computations in good form and assume that the U.S. dollar is the functional currency.

Answer:

Franklin Company's Foreign Subsidiary
TRANSLATION OF SELECTED CAPTIONS INTO UNITED STATES DOLLARS
December 31, 19X6 and December 31, 19X5

	LCU	Translation Rate	U.S. Dollars
December 31, 19X6			
Accounts receivable (net)	40,000 LCU	1.5 LCU to $1	$ 26,667
Inventories, at cost	80,000	1.7 LCU to $1	47,059
Property, plant and equipment (net)	163,000	Schedule 1	86,000
Long-term debt	100,000	1.5 LCU to $1	66,667
Common stock	50,000	2 LCU to $1	25,000

December 31, 19X5			
Accounts receivable (net)	35,000	1.7 LCU to $1	$ 20,588
Inventories, at cost	75,000	2 LCU to $1	37,500
Property, plant and equipment (net)	150,000	2 LCU to $1	75,000
Long-term debt	120,000	1.7 LCU to $1	70,588
Common stock	50,000	2 LCU to $1	25,000

Schedule 1 Computation of Translation of Property, Plant, and Equipment (Net) into United States Dollars at December 31, 19X6

	LCU	Translation Rate	U.S. Dollars
Land purchased on January 1, 19X5	24,000 LCU	2 LCU to $1	$ 12,000
Plant and equipment purchased on January 1, 19X5			
Original cost	140,000	2 LCU to $1	70,000
Depreciation for 19X5	(14,000)	2 LCU to $1	(7,000)
Depreciation for 19X6	(14,000)	2 LCU to $1	(7,000)
	112,000 LCU	2 LCU to $1	56,000
Plant and equipment purchased on July 4, 19X6			
Original cost	30,000	1.5 LCU to $1	20,000
Depreciation for 19X6	(3,000)	1.5 LCU to $1	(2,000)
	27,000 LCU	1.5 LCU to $1	$ 18,000
	163.000 LCU		$ 86,000

(AICPA Adapted)

EXAMINATION III (CHAPTERS 12 AND 13)

Problem 1: Hamilton Co., a U.S. company, purchased inventory from Windsor Co., a British company. The purchase occurred on December 19, 19X3. Hamilton Co. agreed to pay 70,000 pounds for the purchase. Payment to Windsor Co. for the purchase is due on January 16, 19X4. Hamilton Co.'s fiscal year ends on December 31 each year. Direct (spot) rates of exchange were as follows:

12/19/X3	$0.560
12/31/X3	$0.555
1/16/X4	$0.549

Required:
Prepare the journal entries which would be made on the books of Hamilton Co. on the transaction date, intervening balance sheet date, and settlement date.

Problem 2: Refer to the facts of problem 1. However, assume that Hamilton Co., the U.S. company, entered into a forward exchange contract on December 19, 19X3 to purchase the 70,000 pounds needed to pay Windsor Co., the British company. The forward exchange contract provides for a forward rate of $.565 per pound which is to be paid to the foreign currency dealer on the January 16, 19X4 settlement date.

Required:
Prepare the journal entries which would be made on the books of Hamilton Co. on the transaction date, intervening balance sheet date, and settlement date to account for the foreign currency hedge.

Problem 3: Washington Co., a U.S. company, ordered inventory from Recife Co., a Brazilian company, and will pay 400,000 cruzados for the goods in 3 months if the order is accepted by Recife Co. The order was placed on December 1, 19X1 and on the same date Washington Co. also signed a forward exchange contract with a foreign currency dealer and agreed to pay $.12 per cruzado for 400,000 cruzados in three months. Washington Co. is concerned about fluctuating exchange rates and sees hedging through the currency dealer as an attractive option. Direct exchange rates for the cruzado are as follows:

December 1, 19X1	$0.117
December 31, 19X1*	$0.125
February 29, 19X2 (3 months)	$0.112
*Washington Co.'s fiscal year end	

Required:
(*a*) Prepare journal entries for the forward exchange contract and the purchase of inventory from Recife Co. on February 28, 19X2 assuming that deferred discount or premium on the forward exchange contract, if any, is amortized to income over the contract life.
(*b*) Prepare journal entries for the forward exchange contract and the purchase of inventory from Recife Co. on February 28, 19X2 assuming that deferred discount or premium, if any, is not amortized to income but treated as an adjustment to the asset's cost.

Problem 4: The financial statements of Belem Co., a foreign subsidiary of Planet Co. (a U.S. company), are shown in Schedule 1 which follows at and for the year ended December 31, 19X9. Schedule 1 shows the financial statements in the local currency units (LCUs) in one column and also includes blank columns for the exchange rates and for the U.S. dollars. The foreign currency is the functional currency. Planet Co. created the subsidiary on January 1, 19X7. Direct exchange rates for the LCU in the past were as follows:

19X7	19X8	19X9	
$0.500	$0.420	$0.490	January 1 to March 31
$0.470	$0.460	$0.530	April 1 to September 30
$0.420	$0.480	$0.520	October 1 to December 31
$0.465	$0.453	$0.513	Weighted average exchange rate

Berlin Co. declared and paid a 100,000 LCU dividend on December 15, 19X9. All Belem Co.'s common stock was issued on January 1, 19X7.

Required:
Complete Schedule 1 by placing the appropriate exchange rate in the exchange rate column and translating LCUs to dollars.

Schedule 1: Foreign Currency = Functional Currency
Belem Co. Financial Statements
At and for the Year Ended December 31, 19X9

Income Statement	LCUs	Exchange Rate	Dollars
Sales	995,000		
Cost of goods sold	460,000		
Gross profit	535,000		
Operating expenses:			
Depreciation expense	50,000		
Other operating expenses	240,000		
Total operating expenses	290,000		
Net income	245,000		

Statement of Retained Earnings	LCUs	Exchange Rate	Dollars
1/1/X9 Retained earnings	170,000	Prior year end	$ 82,560*
Add: 19X9 Net income	245,000		
Deduct: 19X9 Dividend declarations	(100,000)		
12/31/X9 Retained earnings	315,000		

Balance Sheet	LCUs	Exchange Rate	Dollars
Assets			
Cash	215,000		
Accounts receivable	240,000		
Inventory	90,000		
Plant and equipment	600,000		
Accumulated depreciation	(150,000)		
Total Assets	995,000		
Liabilities and Stockholders' Equity			
Accounts payable	130,000		
Long-term note payable	200,000		
Common stock	350,000		
Retained earnings	315,000		
Cumulative translation adjustment			
Total Liabilities and Stockholders' Equity	995,000		

*Note that the $82,560 in retained earnings simply represents the dollar amount of translated retained earnings at year end 12/31/X8 which have been carried forward from the prior period's financial statements.

Problem 5: The financial statements of Belem Co., a foreign subsidiary of Planet Co. (a U.S. company), are shown in Schedule 2 which follows at and for the year ended December 31, 19X9. Schedule 2 shows the financial statements in the local currency units (LCUs) in one column and also includes blank columns for the exchange rates and for the U.S. dollars. The U.S. dollar is the functional currency. Planet Co. created the subsidiary on January 1, 19X7. Direct exchange rates for the LCU in the past were as follows:

19X7	19X8	19X9	
$0.500	$0.420	$0.490	January 1 to March 31
$0.470	$0.460	$0.530	April 1 to September 30
$0.420	$0.480	$0.520	October 1 to December 31
$0.465	$0.453	$0.513	Weighted average exchange rate

The following additional information is available:

- Berlin Co. declared and paid a 100,000 LCU dividend on December 15, 19X9.
- All Belem Co.'s common stock was issued on January 1, 19X7.
- The retained earnings stated in dollars at 12/31/X8 were $84,600.
- All plant and equipment was acquired on 3/10/X7.
- Operating expenses, purchases, and sales occurred evenly during 19X9.
- Inventory is carried on a FIFO basis. The beginning inventory on 1/1/X9 of 70,000 LCUs was all purchased on December 9, 19X8. The ending inventory on 12/31/X9 of 90,000 LCUs was purchased as follows:

	LCUs Paid
August 31, 19X9	20,000
December 14, 19X9	70,000
	90,000

Required:
Complete Schedule 2 by placing the appropriate exchange rate in the exchange rate column and converting LCUs to dollars.

Schedule 2: Dollar = Functional Currency
Belem Co. Financial Statements
At and for the Year Ended December 31, 19X9

Balance Sheet	LCUs	Exchange Rate	Dollars
Assets			
Cash	215,000		
Accounts receivable	240,000		
Inventory	90,000		
Plant and equipment	600,000		
Accumulated depreciation	(150,000)		
Total Assets	995,000		
Liabilities and Stockholders' Equity			
Accounts payable	130,000		
Long-term note payable	200,000		
Common stock	350,000		
Retained earnings	315,000		
Total Liabilities and Stockholders' Equity	995,000		

Determination of net income for the period:

12/31/X9 Retained earnings			
Less: 1/1/X9 Retained earnings (given in question)			$ 84,600
Change in retained earnings			
Plus: Dividends declared			
Net income for the year ended 12/31/X9			
Less: Remeasured net income			
Remeasurement gain (loss)			

Income Statement	LCUs	Exchange Rate	Dollars
Sales	995,000		
Cost of goods sold:			
1/1/X9 Inventory	70,000		
Plus: Purchases	480,000		
Available for sale	550,000		
Less: 12/31/X9 Inventory	(90,000)		
Cost of goods sold	460,000		
Gross profit	535,000		
Operating expenses:			
Depreciation expense	50,000		
Other operating expenses	240,000		
Total operating expenses	290,000		
Remeasured net income	245,000		
Remeasurement gain (loss)			
Net income			

Problem 6: (AICPA Adapted)
Jay Co.'s 1990 consolidated financial statements include two wholly owned subsidiaries, Jay Co. of Australia (Jay A) and Jay Co. of France (Jay F). Functional currencies are the U.S. dollar for Jay A and the franc for Jay F.

Required:

(*a*) What are the objectives of translating a foreign subsidiary's financial statements?

(*b*) How are gains and losses arising from translating or remeasuring of each subsidiary's financial statements measured and reported in Jay's consolidated financial statements?

(*c*) FASB Statement No. 52 identifies several economic indicators that are to be considered both individually and collectively in determining the functional currency for a consolidated subsidiary. List three of those indicators.

(*d*) What exchange rate is used to incorporate each subsidiary's equipment cost, accumulated depreciation, and depreciation expense in Jay's consolidated financial statements?

ANSWERS

Problem 1:

Transaction date – 12/19/X3

Inventory	39,200	
Accounts payable (70,000 pounds × $.56)		39,200

To record purchase (at transaction date exchange rate).

Intervening balance sheet date – 12/31/X3

Accounts payable	350	
Foreign currency transaction gain		350

To record foreign currency transaction gain based on the change in the exchange rate as follows:

Debt due in foreign currency	70,000 pounds
Intervening balance sheet date exchange rate (12/31/X3)	× .555
Debt in U.S. dollars at 12/31/X3	$38,850
Debt recorded on 12/19/X3 transaction date	39,200
Decrease in debt in U.S. dollars	$350

Alternatively, the gain may be computed simply by multiplying the decrease in the cost of one foreign currency unit of $.005 from 12/19/X3 to 12/31/X3 by the debt of 70,000 pounds. (70,000 × $.005 = $350.)

Settlement date – 1/16/X4

Accounts payable	420	
Foreign currency transaction gain		420

To record foreign currency transaction gain based on the change in the exchange rate as follows:

Debt due in foreign currency	70,000 pounds
Settlement date exchange rate (1/16/X4)	× .549
Debt in U.S. dollars at 1/16/X4	$38,430
Debt recorded on 12/31/X3 balance sheet date ($39,200 – $350)	38,850
Decrease in debt in U.S. dollars	$420

Alternatively, the gain may be computed simply by multiplying the decrease in the cost of one foreign currency unit of $.006 from 12/31/X3 to 1/16/X4 by the debt of 70,000 pounds. (70,000 × $.006 = $420.)

note: The accounts payable balance is now $38,430 based on the original $39,200 balance less recorded gains of $350 and $420.

Foreign currency	38,430	
Cash		38,430

To record purchase of 70,000 pounds for $38,430 (70,000 pounds × $.549).

Accounts payable	38,430	
Foreign currency		38,430

To record payment of debt using the foreign currency acquired.

Note that three settlement date entries were made to (1) record the foreign currency gain, (2) record the foreign currency acquisition, and (3) record payment of debt using the foreign currency. Some authors simply combine these three entries into one entry as follows:

Accounts payable (12/31/X3 balance)	38,850	
Foreign currency transaction gain		420
Cash ($.549 × 70,000 pounds)		38,430

To record foreign currency transaction gain and purchase of foreign currency in settlement of debt.

Problem 2:

Transaction date – 12/19/X3

Foreign currency receivable*	39,200	
Deferred premium on exchange contract	350	
Due to currency dealer**		39,550

To record forward exchange contract.

*70,000 pounds × $.56 spot rate on 12/19/X3 = $39,200.
**70,000 pounds × $.565 forward rate = $39,550.

Intervening balance sheet date – 12/31/X3

Foreign currency transaction loss	350	
Foreign currency receivable		350

To record foreign currency transaction loss as follows:

12/19/X3 direct exchange rate	$0.560
Less 12/19/X3 direct exchange rate	0.555
Reduction in foreign currency exchange rate	$0.005
Times number of pounds receivable from currency dealer	× 70,000
Foreign currency transaction loss	$350

note: The $350 loss recorded here exactly offsets the gain which was recorded on the 12/31/X3 intervening balance sheet date in answer to problem 1.

Premium amortization expense	150	
Deferred premium on exchange contract		150

To amortize deferred premium on forward exchange contract over the contract life as follows:

12 days/28 days × $350 premium on forward exchange contract = $150.

(Note that the contract life is the 28-day period from 12/19/X3 through the 1/16/X4 settlement date. The period 12/19/X3 through 12/31/X3 represents 12 days of the contract period.)

Settlement date – 1/16/X4

Foreign currency transaction loss	420	
Foreign currency receivable		420

To record foreign currency transaction loss as follows:

12/31/X3 direct exchange rate	$0.555
Less 1/16/X4 direct exchange rate	0.549
Reduction in foreign currency exchange rate	$0.006
Times number of pounds receivable from currency dealer	× 70,000
Foreign currency transaction loss	$420

note: The $420 loss recorded here exactly offsets the gain which was recorded on the 1/16/X4 settlement date in answer to problem 1.

Premium amortization expense	200	
Deferred premium on exchange contract		200

To amortize deferred premium on forward exchange contract over the contract life as follows:

16 days/28 days × $350 premium on forward exchange contract = $200.

(Note that the contract life is the 28-day period from 12/19/X3 through the 1/16/X4 settlement date. The period 1/1/X4 through 1/16/X4 represents 16 days of the contract period.)

Due to currency dealer	39,550	
Cash		39,550

To record purchase of 70,000 pounds at the forward rate of $.565 each (70,000 pounds × $.565 = $39,550).

Foreign currency	38,430	
Foreign currency receivable		38,430

To record the receipt of 70,000 pounds from the currency dealer worth $.549 each on 1/16/X4. (70,000 pounds × $.549 = $38,430).

note: The foreign currency purchased is now used to pay the $38,430 debt incurred in the purchase of inventory as described in problem 1 as follows:

Accounts payable	38,430	
Foreign currency		38,430

Problem 3:

Requirement (*a*):

12/1/X1	Foreign currency receivable*	46,800	
	Deferred premium on exchange contract	1,200	
	Due to currency dealer**		48,000

To record forward exchange contract.
*Spot rate $.117 × 400,000 cruzados = $46,800.
**Forward rate $.12 × 400,000 cruzados = $48,000.

12/31/X1	Foreign currency receivable	3,200	
	Deferred foreign currency transaction gain		3,200

To record deferred gain based on an $.008 increase in the value of the cruzado ($.117 – $.125) from 12/1/X3 to 12/31/X3 times 400,000 cruzados to be received from the foreign currency dealer. (See Chapter 12, section E, if further information is desired.)

12/31/X1	Premium amortization expense	400	
	Deferred premium on exchange contract		400

To amortize deferred premium on exchange contract.
(1 mo./3 mos. × $1,200 = $400. Note that the contract life is 3 months from 12/1/X1 to 2/28/X2 and that 1 month of the contract period has passed as of 12/31/X1.)

2/28/X2	Deferred foreign currency transaction loss	5,200	
	Foreign currency receivable		5,200

To record deferred loss based on decrease in value of $.013 ($.125 – $.112) from 12/31/X1 to 2/28/X2 times 400,000 cruzados to be received from the foreign currency dealer.

2/28/X2	Premium amortization expense	800	
	Deferred premium on exchange contract		800

To amortize remainder of deferred premium on exchange contract. ($1,200 – $400 = $800)

2/28/X2	Due to currency dealer	48,000	
	Cash		48,000

To record payment for 400,000 cruzados at the forward rate of $.12 per cruzado. ($.12 × 400,000 cruzados = $48,000).

2/28/X2	Foreign currency	44,800	
	Foreign currency receivable		44,800

To record receipt of 400,000 cruzados from the foreign currency dealer at the spot rate on 2/28/X2 of $.112 per cruzado.

2/28/X2	Deferred foreign currency transaction gain	3,200	
	Inventory	46,800	
	Deferred foreign currency transaction loss		5,200
	Foreign currency		44,800
	To record inventory purchase from Recife Co. using the foreign currency received from the dealer. (The inventory is recorded at the spot rate of $.117 on the order date times 400,000 cruzados since the deferred gain/loss is treated as part of the cost.)		

Requirement (*b*):
Note that the entries are the same except that the premium is not amortized but is instead treated as part of the asset cost as evidenced by the last journal entry.

12/1/X1	Foreign currency receivable*	46,800	
	Deferred premium on exchange contract	1,200	
	Due to currency dealer**		48,000
	To record forward exchange contract. *Spot rate $.117 × 400,000 cruzados = $46,800. **Forward rate $.12 × 400,000 cruzados = $48,000.		
12/31/X1	Foreign currency receivable	3,200	
	Deferred foreign currency transaction gain		3,200
	To record deferred gain based on an $.008 increase in the value of the cruzado ($.117 – $.125) from 12/1/X3 to 12/31/X3 times 400,000 cruzados to be received from the foreign currency dealer.		
2/28/X2	Deferred foreign currency transaction loss	5,200	
	Foreign currency receivable		5,200
	To record deferred loss based on decrease in value of $.013 ($.125 – $.112) from 12/31/X1 to 2/28/X2 times 400,000 cruzados to be received from the foreign currency dealer.		
2/28/X2	Due to currency dealer	48,000	
	Cash		48,000
	To record payment for 400,000 cruzados at the forward rate of $.12 per cruzado. ($.12 × 400,000 cruzados = $48,000).		
2/28/X2	Foreign currency	44,800	
	Foreign currency receivable		44,800
	To record receipt of 400,000 cruzados from the foreign currency dealer at the spot rate on 2/28/X2 of $.112 per cruzado.		
2/28/X2	Deferred foreign currency transaction gain	3,200	
	Inventory	48,000	
	Deferred premium on exchange contract		1,200
	Deferred foreign currency transaction loss		5,200
	Foreign currency		44,800
	To record inventory purchase from Recife Co. using the foreign currency received from the dealer. (The inventory is recorded at the forward rate of $.12 times 400,000 cruzados since, in addition to treating the deferred foreign currency transaction gains (or losses) as part of the asset cost, the deferred premium is not amortized but also treated as part of the asset cost.)		

Problem 4:

Since the foreign currency is the functional currency, the "translation method" must be used (see Chapter 13, section 13-3 for the support for the exchange rates which were used in this answer). Revenues and expenses were translated at the 19X9 weighted average rate of exchange of $.513. Dividend declarations were translated at the declaration date exchange rate of $.52. Assets and liabilities were translated at the December 31, 19X9 balance sheet date exchange rate of $.52. Common stock was translated at the original issuance date exchange rate of $.50 on January 1, 19X7. When the income statement translation was finished, the statement of retained earnings was prepared. The retained earnings developed were then shown in the balance sheet. Finally, as a part of stockholders equity, a "cumulative translation adjustment" account balance was developed as follows:

Total Assets		$517,400
Less total liabilities and equity:		
Accounts payable	$ 67,600	
Long-term note payable	104,000	
Common stock	175,000	
Retained earnings	156,245	502,845
Cumulative translation adjustment		$ 14,555

Schedule 1: Foreign Currency = Functional Currency
Belem Co. Financial Statements
At and for the Year Ended December 31, 19X9

Income Statement	LCUs	Exchange Rate	Dollars
Sales	995,000	$0.513 W	$510.435
Cost of goods sold	460,000	$0.513 W	235,980
Gross profit	535,000		274,455
Operating expenses:			
Depreciation expense	50,000	$0.513 W	25,650
Other operating expenses	240,000	$0.513 W	123,120
Total operating expenses	290,000		148,770
Net income	245,000		$125,685
Statement of Retained Earnings			
1/1/X9 Retained earnings	170,000	Prior year end	$ 82,560
Add: 19X9 Net income	245,000	See above	125,685
Deduct: 19X9 Dividend declarations	(100,000)	$0.520 H	(52,000)
12/31/X9 Retained earnings	315,000		$156,245
Balance Sheet			
Assets			
Cash	215,000	$0.520 C	$111,800
Accounts receivable	240,000	$0.520 C	124,800
Inventory	90,000	$0.520 C	46,800
Plant and equipment	600,000	$0.520 C	312,000
Accumulated depreciation	(150,000)	$0.520 C	(78,000)
Total Assets	995,000		$517,400
Liabilities and Stockholders' Equity			
Accounts payable	130,000	$0.520 C	$ 67,600
Long-term note payable	200,000	$0.520 C	104,000
Common stock	350,000	$0.500 H	175,000
Retained earnings	315,000	See above	156,245
Cumulative translation adjustment		To balance	14,555
Total Liabilities and Stockholders' Equity	995,000		$517,400

W = Weighted average rate of exchange for 19X9.
H = Historical rate of exchange at the transaction date.
C = Current rate of exchange at the 12/31/X9 balance sheet date.

Problem 5:

Since the U.S. dollar is the functional currency, the "remeasurement method" must be used (see Chapter 13, section 13-4 for the support for the exchange rates which were used in this answer). Monetary items are converted at the current exchange rate at the balance sheet date. Nonmonetary items are converted at the historical exchange rate at the transaction date. Revenues, expenses, gains, and losses are converted at the weighted average rate except for expenses and revenues which relate to nonmonetary items such as depreciation expense and cost of goods sold. Note in particular that the ending inventory of 12/31/X9, which is shown in Schedule 2 which follows, is carried by Belem Co. on a FIFO basis. Therefore, this ending inventory must be converted to dollars as follows:

12/31/X9 Layered FIFO Inventory	LCUs paid	Exchange Rate	Dollars
August 31, 19X9	20,000	$0.530	$10,600
December 14, 19X9	70,000	$0.520	36,400
Net income	90,000		$47,000

No single rate is used to convert end of period retained earnings to dollars. Rather, end of period retained earnings as shown on Schedule 2, are computed as follows:

Remeasured Assets (see Schedule 2 which follows)		$508,600
Less: Remeasured debts (see Schedule 2 which follows)		
Accounts payable	$ 67,600	
Long-term note payable	104,000	(171,600)
Total stockholders' equity at 12/31/X9		337,000
Less: Remeasured common stock (see Schedule 2 which follows)		(175,000)
12/31/X9 Retained earnings (end of period)		$162,000

Finally, as shown on Schedule 2, net income for the period and remeasurement gain (or loss) are computed as follows:

End of period retained earnings at 12/31/X9	$162,000
Less:Beginning of period retained earnings at 1/1/X9	($84,600)
Change in retained earnings for the year	77,400
Plus: Dividends declared (100,000 LCUs × $.52 declaration date exchange rate)	52,000
Net income for the year ended 12/31/X9	$129,400
Less: Remeasured net income (per Schedule 2 income statement)	129,475
Remeasurement gain (loss)	($75)

Schedule 2: Dollar = Functional Currency
Belem Co. Financial Statements
At and for the Year Ended December 31, 19X9

Balance Sheet	LCUs	Exchange Rate	Dollars
Assets			
Cash	215,000	$0.520 M	$111,800
Accounts receivable	240,000	$0.520 M	124,800
Inventory	90,000	Layered NM	47,000
Plant and equipment	600,000	$0.500 NM	300,000
Accumulated depreciation	(150,000)	$0.500 NM	(75,000)
Total Assets	995,000		$508,600
Liabilities and Stockholders' Equity			
Accounts payable	130,000	$0.520 M	$ 67,600
Long-term note payable	200,000	$0.520 M	104,000
Common stock	350,000	$0.500 NM	175,000
Retained earnings	315,000	To balance	162,000
Total Liabilities and Stockholders' Equity	995,000		$508,600

Determination of net income for the period:	
12/31/X9 Retained earnings (per above balance sheet)	$162,000
Less: 1/1/X9 Retained earnings	(84,600)
Change in retained earnings	$ 77,400
Plus: Dividends declared (100,000 LCUs × $.52 declaration date exchange rate)	52,000
Net income for the year ended 12/31/X9	$129,400
Less: Remeasured net income (per income statement below)	129,475
Remeasurement gain (loss)	($75)

Income Statement	LCUs	Exchange Rate	Dollars
Sales	995,000	$0.513 W	$510,435
Cost of goods sold:			
1/1/X9 Inventory	70,000	$0.480 NM	33,600
Plus: Purchases	480,000	$0.513 W	246,240
Available for sale	550,000		279,840
Less: 12/31/X9 Inventory	(90,000)	Layered NM	(47,000)
Cost of goods sold	460,000		232,840
Gross profit	535,000		277,595
Operating expenses:			
Depreciation expense	50,000	$0.500 NM	25,000
Other operating expenses	240,000	$0.513 W	123,120
Total operating expenses	290,000		148,120
Remeasured net income	245,000		$129,475
Remeasurement gain (loss) ($129,400 less $129,475)			(75)
		Net income	$129,400

W = Weighted average rate of exchange
M = Monetary item (balance sheet date exchange rate used)
NM = Nonmonetary item (historical transaction date exchange rate used)

Problem 6: (AICPA Adapted)

(*a*) The objectives of translating a foreign subsidiary's financial statements are to:

- Provide information that is generally compatible with the expected economic effects of a rate change on a subsidiary's cash flows and equity.
- Reflect the subsidiary's financial results and relationships in single currency consolidated financial statements, as measured in its functional currency and in conformity with GAAP.

(*b*) Applying different exchange rates to the various financial statement accounts causes the restated statements to be unbalanced. The amount required to bring the restated statements into balance is termed the gain or loss from the translation or remeasurement. The gain or loss arising from remeasuring Jay A's financial statements is reported in the consolidated income statement. The gain or loss arising from translating Jay F's financial statements is reported separately under stockholders' equity in the balance sheet.

(*c*) The functional currency is the foreign currency or parent's currency that most closely correlates with the following economic indicators:

- Cash flow indicators
- Sales price indicators
- Sales market indicators
- Expense indicators
- Financing indicators
- Intercompany transactions and arrangement indicators

(*d*) All accounts relating to Jay A's equipment are remeasured by the exchange rate prevailing between the U.S. and Australian dollars at the time equipment was purchased.

All accounts relating to Jay F's equipment are translated by the current exchange rates prevailing between the U.S. dollar and French franc. For the equipment cost and accumulated depreciation this is the current exchange rate at December 31, 1990. Depreciation expense is translated at the rate prevailing on the date the depreciation expense was recognized or an appropriate weighted average exchange rate for 1990.

INDEX